MILITARY MARKINGS 2011

REVISED 32nd EDITION

Howard J. Curtis

An imprint of
Ian Allan Publishing

www.ianallanpublishing.co.uk

Contents

This 32nd edition published 2011

ISBN 978 1 85780 347 1

Published by Ian Allan Publishing

an imprint of Ian Allan Publishing Ltd, Hersham, Surrey KT12 4RG.
Printed in England by Ian Allan Printing Ltd, Hersham, Surrey KT12 4RG.

Visit the Ian Allan Publishing website at

www.ianallanpublishing.com

Distributed in the United States of America and Canada by BookMasters Distribution Services

Photographs by Howard J Curtis (HJC) unless otherwise credited.

Front cover: Harrier GR9s from Nos 1 and 4 Squadron and 800NAS formate on 13 December 2010 just two days before the Harriers were retired from service. *Jamie Hunter*

FLYING TIGERS
CALL US ON 01706 522112
www.flying-tigers.co.uk
BRITAIN'S DIE-CAST AVIATION SPECIALISTS
ALL NEW 1/32nd SCALE DIE-CAST 'WOODEN WONDER'
THE AVIATION ARCHIVE
1:32nd Scale LIMITED EDITION
MOSQUITO FB.VI
Grp. Capt PICKARD
'AMIENS RAIDER'
HUGE
1/32nd SCALE
RELEASE!
THIS FANTASTIC MODEL
MUST BE PRE-ORDERED
OUR PRICE £125.99
Inc. FREE UK POSTAGE
(Mainland Address)
DUE MARCH 2011
MODIFIED TOOLING!
LATEST 1/72nd SCALE RELEASE
HOBBYMASTER
MAGNIFICENT NEW HOBBYMASTER ANNOUNCEMENT
RAF UPPER HEYFORD EF-111A 'ELECTRIC FOX'
OUR PRICE £59.99 (Inc FREE UK Mainland Postage)
1/48th SCALE
SALE OFFER!
P-51D MUSTANG
GLENN EAGLESTON
18.5 VICTORIES
WAS £37.99 NOW £24.99
(Whilst stocks last!)
EXPERIENCE THESE FANTASTIC MODELS!
CALL FLYING TIGERS ON 01706 522112

Introduction

This 32nd annual edition of abc *Military Aircraft Markings* follows the pattern of previous years and lists in alphabetical and numerical order the aircraft that carry a United Kingdom military serial and which are normally based, or might be seen, in the UK. It also includes airworthy and current RAF/RN/Army aircraft that are based permanently or temporarily overseas. The term 'aircraft' used here covers powered, manned aeroplanes, helicopters, airships and gliders as well as target drones. Included are all the current Royal Air Force, Royal Navy, Army Air Corps, Ministry of Defence, QinetiQ - operated, manufacturers' test aircraft and civilian-owned aircraft with military markings or operated for the Ministry of Defence.

Aircraft withdrawn from operational use but which are retained in the UK for ground training purposes or otherwise preserved by the Services and in the numerous museums or collections are listed. The serials of some incomplete aircraft have been included, such as the cockpit sections of machines displayed by the RAF, aircraft used by airfield fire sections and for service battle damage repair training (BDRT), together with significant parts of aircraft held by preservation groups and societies. Where only part of the aircraft fuselage remains, the abbreviation <ff> for front fuselage/cockpit section or <rf> for rear fuselage, is shown after the type. Many of these aircraft are allocated, and sometimes wear, a secondary identity, such as an RAF 'M' maintenance number; these numbers are listed against those aircraft to which they have been allocated.

A serial 'missing' from a sequence is either because it was never issued as it formed part of a 'black-out block' or because the aircraft has been written off, scrapped, sold abroad or allocated an alternative marking. Aircraft used as targets on MoD ranges to which access is restricted, and UK military aircraft that have been permanently grounded overseas and unlikely to return to Britain have generally been omitted. With the appearance of some military-registered UAVs, drones and small target aircraft at public events, these have now been included if they are likely to be seen.

In the main, the serials listed are those markings presently displayed on the aircraft. Where an aircraft carries a false serial it is quoted in italic type. Very often these serials are carried by replicas, that are denoted by <R> after the type. The manufacturer and aircraft type are given, together with recent alternative, previous, secondary or civil identity shown in round brackets. Complete records of multiple previous identities are only included where space permits. The operating unit and its based location, along with any known unit and code markings, in square brackets, are given as accurately as possible. Where aircraft carry special or commemorative markings, a $ indicates this. Unit markings are normally carried boldly on the sides of the fuselage or on the aircraft's tail. In the case of RAF and AAC machines currently in service, they are usually one or two letters or numbers, while the RN continues to use a well-established system of three-figure codes between 000 and 999 often with a two-letter code on the tail, denoting the aircraft's operational base. RN squadrons, units and bases are allocated blocks of numbers from which individual aircraft codes are issued. To help identification of RN bases and landing platforms on ships, a list of tail-letter codes with their appropriate name, helicopter code number, ship pennant number and type of vessel, is included; as is a helicopter code number/ships' tail-letter code grid cross-reference.

Code changes, for example when aircraft move between units and therefore the markings currently painted on a particular aircraft, might not be those shown in this edition because of subsequent events. Aircraft still under manufacture or not yet delivered to the Service, such as Eurofighter Typhoons and Airbus A400Ms are listed under their allocated serial numbers. Likewise there are a number of newly built aircraft for overseas air arms that carry British serials for their UK test and delivery flights. The airframes which will not appear in the next edition because of sale, accident, etc., have their fates, where known, shown in italic type in the *locations* column.

The Irish Army Air Corps fleet is listed, together with the serials of other overseas air arms whose aircraft might be seen visiting the UK from time to time. The serial numbers are as usually presented on the individual machine or as they are normally identified. Where possible, the aircraft's base and operating unit have been shown.

USAF, US Army and US Navy aircraft based in the UK and in Western Europe, and types that regularly visit the UK from the USA, are each listed in separate sections by aircraft type. The serial number actually displayed on the aircraft is shown in full, with additional Fiscal Year (FY) or full serial information also provided. Where appropriate, details of the operating wing, squadron allocation and base are added. The USAF is, like the RAF, in a continuing period of change, resulting in the adoption of new unit titles, squadron and equipment changes and the closure of bases. Only details that concern changes effected by January 2011 are shown.

Veteran and vintage aircraft which carry overseas military markings but which are based in the UK or regularly visit from mainland Europe, have been separately listed, showing their principal means of identification. The growing list of aircraft in government or military service, often under contract to private operating companies, which carry civil registrations has again been included at the end of the respective country.

With the use of the Internet now very well established as a rich source of information, the section listing a selection of military aviation 'world wide web' sites, has again been updated this year. Although only a few of these provide details of aircraft serials and markings, they do give interesting insights into air arms and their operating units, aircraft, museums and a broad range of associated topics.

Information shown is believed to be correct at 31 January 2011.

Acknowledgements

The compiler wishes to thank the many people who have taken the trouble to send comments, additions, deletions and other useful information since the publication of the previous edition of Military Aircraft Markings. In particular the following individuals: Peter Alcock, Gordon Avery, Chris Barkby, Allan Barley, Peter Budden, Cheryl Baumgärtner, Mick Boulanger, David Cenciotti, John Clarke, Glyn Coney, Neil Damsell, Patrick Dirksen, Ben Dunnell, Hugh Gibson, Mark Green, Jerry Gunner, Howard Heeley/Newark Air Museum,James Lawson, Peter R March, Doug McDonald, Dave Morgan, Norman Roberson, Paul Rushton, Mike Screech, Mark Shepherd, Kev Slade, Dave Taylor, David Thompson, Andy Thomson, Mike Tighe, Dave Turner, Howard Walker & Dave Webb.

The 2011 edition has also relied upon the printed publications and/or associated internet web-sites as follows: Aerodata Quantum+, 'Aircraft' magazine, Airfields e-mail group, 'Air Forces Monthly' magazine, 'Aviation News' magazine, BAEG e-mail group, Andy Carney/British Military Aviation Lists, CAA G-INFO Web Site, 'Combat Aircraft' magazine, Delta Reflex, Graham Gaff/East London Aviation Society, Fighter Control, 'FlyPast' magazine, Joe Baugher's Home Page, Roger Smith/Lowestoft Aviation Society, Brian Pickering/'Military Aviation Review', Mil Spotters' Forum, NAMAR e-mail group, Howard Heeley/Newark Air Museum, Pacific Database (DatAir), RAF Leeming e-mail group, RAF Shawbury e-mail group, 'Scramble' magazine, Souairport e-mail group, Tom McGhee/UK Serials Resource Centre, Vintage British Military Jets e-mail group, Mark Ray/Wolverhampton Aviation Group and 'Wrecks & Relics'.

HJC **January 2011**

ZZ401 was the second Wildcat to fly, taking to the air in October 2010.

Abbreviations

$	Aircraft in special markings
AAC	Army Air Corps
ACC	Air Combat Command
ACCGS	Air Cadets Central Gliding School
ACS	Air Control Squadron
ACTS	Air Control Training Squadron
ACW	Air Control Wing
AD&StA	Aberdeen, Dundee & St Andrews
AEF	Air Experience Flight
AESS	Air Engineering & Survival School
AEW	Airborne Early Warning
AF	Arméflyget (Army Air Battalion)
AFB	Air Force Base
AFD	Air Fleet Department
AFRC	Air Force Reserve Command
AFSC	Air Force Systems Command
AFSK	Armeflygskolan (Army Flying School)
AFWF	Advanced Fixed Wing Flight
AG	Airlift Group
AGA	Academia General del Aire (General Air Academy)
AkG	Aufklärüngsgeschwader (Reconnaissance Wing)
AMC	Air Mobility Command
AMD-BA	Avions Marcel Dassault-Breguet Aviation
AMF	Aircraft Maintenance Flight
AMG	Aircraft Maintenance Group
AMIF	Aircraft Maintenance Instruction Flight
AMW	Air Mobility Wing
ANG	Air National Guard
APS	Aircraft Preservation Society
ARF	Aircraft Repair Flight
ARS	Air Refueling Squadron
ARW	Air Refueling Wing
ARWS	Advanced Rotary Wing Squadron
AS	Airlift Squadron/Air Squadron
ASF	Aircraft Servicing Flight
AS&RU	Aircraft Salvage and Repair Unit
ATC	Air Training Corps
ATCC	Air Traffic Control Centre
AVDEF	Aviation Defence Service
Avn	Aviation
AW	AgustaWestland/Airlift Wing/Armstrong Whitworth Aircraft
AWC	Air Warfare Centre
BAC	British Aircraft Corporation
BAe	British Aerospace PLC
BAPC	British Aviation Preservation Council
BATUS	British Army Training Unit Suffield
BBMF	Battle of Britain Memorial Flight
BDRF	Battle Damage Repair Flight
BDRT	Battle Damage Repair Training
Be	Beech
Bf	Bayerische Flugzeugwerke
BG	Bomber Group
BGA	British Gliding & Soaring Association
bk	black (squadron colours and markings)
bl	blue (squadron colours and markings)
BNFL	British Nuclear Fuels Ltd
BP	Boulton & Paul
br	brown (squadron colours and markings)
BS	Bomber Squadron
B-V	Boeing-Vertol
BW	Bomber Wing
CAARP	Co-operative des Ateliers Air de la Région Parisienne
CAC	Commonwealth Aircraft Corporation
CARG	Cotswold Aircraft Restoration Group
CASA	Construcciones Aeronautics SA
Cav	Cavalry
CC	County Council
CCF	Combined Cadet Force/Canadian Car & Foundry Company
CDE	Chemical Defence Establishment
CEAM	Centre d'Expérimentation Aériennes Militaires (Military Air Experimental Centre)
CEPA	Centre d'Expérimentation Pratique de l'Aéronautique Navale
CEV	Centre d'Essais en Vol (Flight Test Centre)
CFS	Central Flying School
CGMF	Central Glider Maintenance Flight
CHFMU	Commando Helicopter Force Maintenance Unit
CIFAS	Centre d'Instruction des Forces Aériennes Stratégiques (Air Strategic Training Centre)
CinC	Commander in Chief
CinCLANT	Commander in Chief Atlantic
CITac	Centre d'Instruction Tactique (Tactical Training Centre)
CLV	Centrum Leteckeho Vycviku (Air Training Centre)
Co	Company
COMALAT	Commandement de l'Aviation Légère de l'Armée de Terre
Comp	Composite with
CT	College of Technology
CTE	Central Training Establishment
CV	Chance-Vought
D-BA	Daimler-Benz Aerospace
D-BD	Dassault-Breguet Dornier
D&G	Dumfries and Galloway
DCAE	Defence College of Aeronautical Engineering
DE&S	Defence Equipment & Support
DEFTS	Defence Elementary Flying Training School
DEODS	Defence Explosives Ordnance Disposal School
Det	Detachment
DFTDC	Defence Fire Training and Development Centre
DH	de Havilland
DHC	de Havilland Canada
DHFS	Defence Helicopter Flying School
DLMW	Dywizjon Lotniczy Marynarki Wojennej
DMS	Defence Movements School
DSDA	Defence Storage & Distribution Agency
DS&TL	Defence Science & Technology Laboratory
DSG	Defence Support Group
DTI	Department of Trade and Industry
EA	Escadron Aérien (Air Squadron)
EAAT	Escadrille Avions de l'Armée de Terre
EAC	Ecole de l'Aviation de Chasse (Fighter Aviation School)
EALAT	Ecole de l'Aviation Légère de l'Armée de Terre
EAP	European Aircraft Project
EAT	Ecole de l'Aviation de Transport (Transport Aviation School)
EC	Escadre de Chasse (Fighter Wing)
ECATS	EADS Cognac Aviarion Training Services
ECG	Electronic Combat Group
ECM	Electronic Counter Measures
ECS	Electronic Countermeasures Squadron
EDA	Escadre de Detection Aéroportée (Air Detection Wing)
EdC	Escadron de Convoyage
EDCA	Escadron de Détection et de Control Aéroportée (Airborne Detection & Control Sqn)
EE	English Electric/Escadrille Electronique
EEA	Escadron Electronique Aéroporté

EFA Ecole Franco Allemande
EFTS Elementary Flying Training School
EH Escadron d'Helicoptères (Helicopter Flight)
EHADT Escadrille Helicoptères de l'Armée de Terre
EHI European Helicopter Industries
EKW Eidgenössiches Konstruktionswerkstätte
EL Escadre de Liaison (Liaison Wing)
EL Eskadra Lotnicza (Air Sqn)
ELT Eskadra Lotnictwa Taktycznego (Tactical Air Squadron)
ELTR Eskadra Lotnictwa Transportowego (Air Transport Squadron)
EMA East Midlands Airport
EMVO Elementaire Militaire Vlieg Opleiding (Elementary Flying Training)
ENOSA Ecole des Navigateurs Operationales Systemes d'Armees (Navigation School)
EoN Elliot's of Newbury
EPAA Ecole de Pilotage Elementaire de l'Armée de l'Air (Air Force Elementary Flying School)
EPE Ecole de Pilotage Elementaire (Elementary Flying School)
EPNER Ecole du Personnel Navigant d'Essais et de Reception
ER Escadre de Reconnaissance (Reconnaissance Wing)
ERS Escadron de Reconnaissance Stratégique (Strategic Reconnaissance Squadron)
ES Escadrille de Servitude
ESAM Ecole Supérieur d'Application du Matériel
Esc Escuadron (Squadron)
Esk Eskadrille (Squadron)
Eslla Escuadrilla (Squadron)
Esq Esquadra (Squadron)
ET Escadre de Transport (Transport Squadron)
ETD Escadron de Transformation des Equipages Mirage 2000D
ETE Escadron de Transport et Entrainement (Transport Training Squadron)
ETEC Escadron de Transport d'Entrainement et de Calibration (Transport Training & Calibration Sqn)
ETL Escadron de Transport Légère (Light Transport Squadron)
ETO Escadron de Transition Operationnelle
ETOM Escadron de Transport Outre Mer (Overseas Transport Squadron)
ETPS Empire Test Pilots' School
ETR Escadron de Tranformation Rafale
ETS Engineering Training School
EVAA Ecole de Voltige de l'Armée de l'Air (French Air Force Aerobatics School)
FAA Fleet Air Arm/Federal Aviation Administration
FBS Flugbereitschaftstaffel
FBW Fly-by-wire
FC Forskokcentralen (Flight Centre)
FE Further Education
FETC Fire and Emergency Training Centre
ff Front fuselage
FG Fighter Group
FH Fairchild-Hiller
FI Falkland Islands
FJWOEU Fast Jet & Guided Weapon Operational Evaluation Unit
FLO Forsvarets Logistikk Organisasjon (Defence Logistics Organisation)
FISt Flieger Staffel (Flight Squadron)
Flt Flight
FMA Fabrica Militar de Aviones
FMT Flotila Militara de Transport (Transport Regiment)
FMV Forsvarets Materielwerk
FONA Flag Officer Naval Aviation
FRADU Fleet Requirements and Air Direction Unit
FRA FR Aviation
FS Fighter Squadron
FSAIU Flight Safety & Accident Investigation Unit
FSCTE Fire Services Central Training Establishment
FTS Flying Training School
FTW Flying Training Wing
Fw Focke Wulf
FW Fighter Wing/Foster Wickner
FWTS Fixed Wing Test Squadron
FY Fiscal Year
F3 OCU Tornado F3 Operational Conversion Unit
GAF Government Aircraft Factory
GAFFTC German Air Force Flight Training Centre
GAL General Aircraft Ltd
GAM Groupe Aerien Mixte (Composite Air Group)
GAM/STAT Groupement Aéromobile/Section Technique de l'Armée de Terre
gd gold (squadron colours and markings)
GD General Dynamics
GDSH Gazelle Depth Support Hub
GHL Groupe d'Helicopteres Legeres (Light Helicopter Group)
GI Ground Instruction/Groupement d'Instruction (Instructional Group)
gn green (squadron colours and markings)
GRD Gruppe fur Rustunggdienste (Group for Service Preparation)
GRV Groupe de Ravitaillement en Vol (Air Refuelling Group)
GT Grupo de Transporte (Transport Wing)
GTT Grupo de Transporte de Tropos (Troop Carrier Wing)
gy grey (squadron colours and markings)
H&W Hereford and Worcester
HAF Historic Aircraft Flight
HAT&ES Heavy Aircraft Test & Evaluation Squadron
HC Helicopter Combat Support Squadron
HCS Hunting Contract Services
HF Historic Flying Ltd
HFUS Heeresfliegerunterstützungsstaffel
HFVAS Heeresfliegerverbindungs/Aufklärungsstaffel
HFVS Heeresfliegerversuchstaffel
HFWS Heeresflieger Waffenschule (Army Air Weapons School)
Hkp.Bat Helikopter Bataljon (Helicopter Battalion)
HMA Helicopter Maritime Attack
HMF Harrier Maintenance Flight/Helicopter Maintenance Flight
HMS Her Majesty's Ship
HOCU Harrier OCU
HP Handley-Page
HQ Headquarters
HS Hawker Siddeley
HSG Hubschraubergeschwader
IAF Israeli Air Force
IAP International Airport
INTA Instituto Nacional de Tecnica Aerospacial
IOW Isle Of Wight
IWM Imperial War Museum
JARTS Joint Aircraft Recovery & Transportation Sqn
JATE Joint Air Transport Establishment
JbG Jagdbombergeschwader (Fighter Bomber Wing)
JFACTSU Joint Forward Air Control Training & Standards Unit
JG Jagdgeschwader (Fighter Wing)

JHC	Joint Helicopter Command
JHF	Joint Helicopter Force
KHR	Kampfhubschrauberregiment
Kridlo	Wing
lbvr	letka Bitevnich Vrtulník (Attack Helicopter Squadron)
Letka	Squadron
LTG	Lufttransportgeschwader (Air Transport Wing)
LTO	Transportna en Letalska Transportni Oddelek
LTSF	Long Term Storage Flight
LTV	Ling-Temco-Vought
LVG	Luftwaffen Versorgungs Geschwader (Air Force Maintenance Wing)/Luft Verkehrs Gesellschaft
LZO	Letecky Zkušební Odbor (Aviation Test Department)
m	multi-coloured (squadron colours and markings)
MAPK	Mira Anachestisis Pantos Kerou (All Weather Interception Sqn)
MASD	Marine Air Support Detachment
MASU	Mobile Aircraft Support Unit
MBB	Messerschmitt Bolkow-Blohm
MCAS	Marine Corps Air Station
McD	McDonnell Douglas
MDMF	Merlin Depth Maintenance Facilities
Med	Medical
MFG	Marine Flieger Geschwader (Naval Air Wing)
MH	Max Holste
MIB	Military Intelligence Battalion
MiG	Mikoyan-Gurevich
Mod	Modified
MoD	Ministry of Defence
MR	Maritime Reconnaissance
MRH	Multi-role Helikopters
M&RU	Marketing & Recruitment Unit
MS	Morane-Saulnier
MTHR	Mittlerer Transporthubschrauber Regiment (Medium Transport Helicopter Regiment)
MTM	Mira Taktikis Metaforon (Tactical Transport Sqn)
MTSF	Medium Term Storage Flight
NA	North American
NACDS	Naval Air Command Driving School
NAEW&CF	NATO Airborne Early Warning & Control Force
NAF	Naval Air Facility
NAS	Naval Air Squadron (UK)/Naval Air Station (US)
NASU	Naval Air Support Unit
NATO	North Atlantic Treaty Organisation
NAWC	Naval Air Warfare Center
NAWC-AD	Naval Air Warfare Center Aircraft Division
NBC	Nuclear, Biological and Chemical
NE	North-East
NFATS	Naval Force Aircraft Test Squadron
NI	Northern Ireland
NMSU	Nimrod Major Servicing Unit
NOCU	Nimrod Operational Conversion Unit
NSW	Naval Strike Wing
NTOCU	National Tornado Operational Conversion Unit
NYARC	North Yorks Aircraft Restoration Centre
OCU	Operational Conversion Unit
OEU	Operation Evaluation Unit
OFMC	Old Flying Machine Company
OGMA	Oficinas Gerais de Material Aeronautico
or	orange (squadron colours and markings)
OSAC	Operational Support Airlift Command
OSBL	Oddelek Sholskih Bojni Letal (Training &

	Combat School)
OVH Kmp	Observations-Helicopter Kompagni
PAT	Priority Air Transport Detachment
PBN	Pilatus Britten-Norman
PDSH	Puma Depth Support Hub
PLM	Pulk Lotnictwa Mysliwskiego (Fighter Regiment)
pr	purple (squadron colours and markings)
PRU	Photographic Reconnaissance Unit
PVH Kmp	Panservaerns-Helicopter Kompagni
r	red (squadron colours and markings)
R	Replica
RAeS	Royal Aeronautical Society
RAF	Royal Aircraft Factory/Royal Air Force
RAFC	Royal Air Force College
RAFM	Royal Air Force Museum
RAFGSA	Royal Air Force Gliding and Soaring Association
RE	Royal Engineers
Regt	Regiment
REME	Royal Electrical & Mechanical Engineers
rf	Rear fuselage
RFA	Royal Fleet Auxiliary
RHC	Régiment d'Helicoptères de Combat
RHFS	Régiment d'Helicoptères des Forces Spéciales
RJAF	Royal Jordanian Air Force
RM	Royal Marines
RMB	Royal Marines Base
RMC of S	Royal Military College of Science
RN	Royal Navy
RNAS	Royal Naval Air Station
RNGSA	Royal Navy Gliding and Soaring Association
ROF	Royal Ordnance Factory
RQS	Rescue Squadron
R-R	Rolls-Royce
RS	Reid & Sigrist/Reconnaissance Squadron
RSV	Reparto Sperimentale Volo (Experimental Flight School)
RW	Reconnaissance Wing
SA	Scottish Aviation
SAAB	Svenska Aeroplan Aktieboleg
SAH	School of Air Handling
SAL	Scottish Aviation Limited
SAR	Search and Rescue
Saro	Saunders-Roe
SARTU	Search and Rescue Training Unit
SCW	Strategic Communications Wing
SEAE	School of Electrical & Aeronautical Engineering
SEPECAT	Société Européenne de Production de l'avion Ecole de Combat et d'Appui Tactique
SFDO	School of Flight Deck Operations
SHAPE	Supreme Headquarters Allied Forces Europe
SHOPS	Sea Harrier Operational Support Unit
si	silver (squadron colours and markings)
SIET	Section d'Instruction et d'Etude du Tir
SKAMG	Sea King Aircraft Maintenance Group
SKTU	Sea King Training Unit
Skv	Skvadron (Squadron)
SLK	Stíhacie Letecké Kridlo (Fighter Air Wing)
slt	stíhací letka (Fighter Squadron)
SLV	School Licht Vliegwezen (Flying School)
Sm	Smaldeel (Squadron)
smdl	Smisena Dopravní Letka
SNCAN	Société Nationale de Constructions Aéronautiques du Nord
SOF	Special Operations Flight
SOG	Special Operations Group
SOS	Special Operations Squadron
SoTT	School of Technical Training
SOW	Special Operations Wing
SPAD	Société Pour les Appareils Deperdussin
SPP	Strojirny Prvni Petilesky
Sqn	Squadron
Sz.D.REB	'Szentgyörgyi Deszö' Harcászati Repülö Bázis
TA	Territorial Army
TAP	Transporten Avio Polk (Air Transport Regiment)
TCF	Training Consolidation Flight
TFC	The Fighter Collection
TGp	Test Groep
TIARA	Tornado Integrated Avionics Research Aircraft
TL	Taktická Letka (Tactical Squadron)
TMF	Tornado Maintenance Flight
TMTS	Trade Management Training School
TOCU	Typhoon Operational Conversion Unit
tpzlt	taktická a prùzkumná letka (Tactical & Reconnaissance Squadron)
TS	Test Squadron
TsAGI	Tsentral'ny Aerogidrodinamicheski Instut (Central Aero & Hydrodynamics Institute)
TsLw	Technische Schule der Luftwaffe (Luftwaffe Technical School)
TW	Test Wing
UAS	University Air Squadron
UAV	Unmanned Air Vehicle
Uberwg	Uberwachunggeschwader (Surveillance Wing)
UK	United Kingdom
UKAEA	United Kingdom Atomic Energy Authority
UNFICYP	United Nations' Forces in Cyprus
US	United States
USAF	United States Air Force
USAFE	United States Air Forces in Europe
USAREUR	US Army Europe
USCGS	US Coast Guard Station
USEUCOM	United States European Command
USMC	United States Marine Corps
USN	United States Navy
NWTSPM	United States Navy Test Pilots School
VAAC	Vectored thrust Advanced Aircraft flight Control
VFW	Vereinigte Flugtechnische Werke
VGS	Volunteer Gliding Squadron
VISSAGE	VC10 Integrated Systems & Structures Ageing Exploration
VLA	Vojenska Letecka Akademia
vlt	vycviková letka (Training Squadron)
VMGR	Marine Aerial Refuelling/Transport Squadron
VMGRT	Marine Aerial Refuelling/Transport Training Squadron
VQ	Fleet Air Reconnaissance Squadron
VR	Fleet Logistic Support Squadron
VrK	Vrtulnikové Letecké Kridlo
VS	Vickers-Supermarine
VSD	Vegyes Szàllitorepülö Dandàr (Aircraft Transport Brigade)
w	white (squadron colours and markings)
Wg	Wing
WHL	Westland Helicopters Ltd
WLT	Weapons Loading Training
WRS	Weather Reconnaissance Squadron
WS	Westland
WSK	Wytwornia Sprzetu Kominikacyjnego
WTD	Wehrtechnische Dienstelle (Technical Support Unit)
WW2	World War II
y	yellow (squadron colours and markings)
zDL	základna Dopravního Letectva (Air Transport Base)
zL	základna Letectva
zSL	základna Speciálního Letectva (Training Air Base)
zTL	základna Taktického Letectva (Tactical Air Base)
zVrL	základna Vrtulníkového Letectva (Helicopter Air Base)

A Guide to the Location of Operational Military Bases in the UK

This section is to assist the reader to locate the places in the United Kingdom where operational military aircraft (including helicopters and gliders) are based.

The alphabetical order listing gives each location in relation to its county and to its nearest classified road(s) (by means adjoining; of means proximate to), together with its approximate direction and mileage from the centre of a nearby major town or city. Some civil airports are included where active military units are also based, but **excluded** are MoD sites with non-operational aircraft (eg gate guardians), the bases of privately-owned civil aircraft that wear military markings and museums.

User	*Base name*	*County/Region*	*Location*	*Distance/direction from (town)*
Army	Abingdon	Oxfordshire	W by B4017, W of A34	5m SSW of Oxford
Army	Aldergrove/ Belfast Airport	Co Antrim	W by A26	13m W of Belfast
RM	Arbroath	Angus	E of A933	2m NW of Arbroath
RAF	Barkston Heath	Lincolnshire	W by B6404, S of A153	5m NNE of Grantham
RAF	Benson	Oxfordshire	E by A423	1m NE of Wallingford
QinetiQ/ RAF	Boscombe Down	Wiltshire	S by A303, W of A338	6m N of Salisbury
RAF	Boulmer	Northumberland	E of B1339	4m E of Alnwick
RAF	Brize Norton	Oxfordshire	W of A4095	5m SW of Witney
Marshall	Cambridge Airport/ Teversham	Cambridgeshire	S by A1303	2m E of Cambridge
RM/RAF	Chivenor	Devon	S of A361	4m WNW of Barnstaple
RAF	Church Fenton	Yorkshire North	S of B1223	7m WNW of Selby
Army	Colerne	Wiltshire	S of A420, E of Fosse Way	5m NE of Bath
RAF	Coningsby	Lincolnshire	S of A153, W by B1192	10m NW of Boston
DCAE	Cosford	Shropshire	W of A41, N of A464	9m WNW of Wolverhampton
RAF	Cottesmore	Rutland	W of A1, N of B668	9m NW of Stamford
RAF	Cranwell	Lincolnshire	N by A17, S by B1429	5m WNW of Sleaford
RN	Culdrose	Cornwall	E by A3083	1m SE of Helston
Army	Dishforth	Yorkshire North	E by A1	4m E of Ripon
USAF	Fairford	Gloucestershire	S of A417	9m ESE of Cirencester
RN	Fleetlands	Hampshire	E by A32	2m SE of Fareham
RAF	Halton	Buckinghamshire	N of A4011, S of B4544	4m ESE of Aylesbury
RAF	Henlow	Bedfordshire	E of A600, W of A6001	1m SW of Henlow
Army	Hullavington	Wiltshire	W of A429	1m N of M4 jn 17
RAF	Kenley	Greater London	W of A22	1m W of Warlingham
RAF	Kinloss	Grampian	E of B9011, N of B9089	3m NE of Forres
RAF	Kirknewton	Lothian	E by B7031, N by A70	8m SW of Edinburgh
USAF	Lakenheath	Suffolk	W by A1065	8m W of Thetford
RAF	Leeming	Yorkshire North	E by A1	5m SW of Northallerton
RAF	Leuchars	Fife	E of A919	7m SE of Dundee
RAF	Linton-on-Ouse	Yorkshire North	E of B6265	10m NW of York
RAF	Lossiemouth	Grampian	W of B9135, S of B9040	4m N of Elgin
RAF	Lyneham	Wiltshire	W of A3102, S of A420	10m WSW of Swindon
RAF	Marham	Norfolk	N by A1122	6m W of Swaffham
Army	Middle Wallop	Hampshire	S by A343	6m SW of Andover
USAF	Mildenhall	Suffolk	S by A1101	9m NNE of Newmarket
RAF	Northolt	Greater London	N by A40	3m E of M40 jn 1
RAF	Odiham	Hampshire	E of A32	2m S of M3 jn 5
RN	Predannack	Cornwall	W by A3083	7m S of Helston
MoD	St Athan	South Glamorgan	N of B4265	13m WSW of Cardiff
RAF	Scampton	Lincolnshire	W by A15	6m N of Lincoln
RAF	Shawbury	Shropshire	W of B5063	7m NNE of Shrewsbury
RAF	Syerston	Nottinghamshire	W by A46	5m SW of Newark
RAF	Ternhill	Shropshire	SW by A41	3m SW of Market Drayton
RAF/Army	Topcliffe	Yorkshire North	E of A167, W of A168	3m SW of Thirsk
RAF	Valley	Gwynedd	S of A5 on Anglesey	5m SE of Holyhead
RAF	Waddington	Lincolnshire	E by A607, W by A15	5m S of Lincoln
Army/RAF	Wattisham	Suffolk	N of B1078	5m SSW of Stowmarket

User	Base name	County/Region	Location	Distance/direction from (town)
RAF	Weston-on-the-Green	Oxfordshire	E by A43	9m N of Oxford
RAF	Wittering	Cambridgeshire	W by A1, N of A47	3m S of Stamford
RAF	Woodvale	Merseyside	W by A565	5m SSW of Southport
RAF	Wyton	Cambridgeshire	E of A141, N of B1090	3m NE of Huntingdon
RN	Yeovilton	Somerset	S by B3151, S of A303	5m N of Yeovil

BE505 is a beautiful Hawker Hurricane IIB with civil registration G-HHII, operated by the Hangar 11 Collection at North Weald.

RAF Typhoon FGR4 ZJ920 is operated by 3 Sqn at Coningsby. Unusually, it wore the non-standard code Q-OA until laye 2010 when it was changed to QO-A.

British Military Aircraft Serials

The Committee of Imperial Defence through its Air Committee introduced a standardised system of numbering aircraft in November 1912. The Air Department of the Admiralty was allocated the first batch 1-200 and used these to cover aircraft already in use and those on order. The Army was issued with the next block from 201-800, which included the number 304 which was given to the Cody Biplane now preserved in the Science Museum. By the outbreak of World War I, the Royal Navy was on its second batch of serials 801-1600 and this system continued with alternating allocations between the Army and Navy until 1916 when number 10000, a Royal Flying Corps BE2C, was reached.

It was decided not to continue with five digit numbers but instead to start again from 1, prefixing RFC aircraft with the letter A and RNAS aircraft with the prefix N. The RFC allocations commenced with A1 an FE2D and before the end of the year had reached A9999 an Armstrong Whitworth FK8. The next group commenced with B1 and continued in logical sequence through the C, D, E and F prefixes. G was used on a limited basis to identify captured German aircraft, while H was the last block of wartime-ordered aircraft. To avoid confusion I was not used, so the new post-war machines were allocated serials in the J range. A further minor change was made in the serial numbering system in August 1929 when it was decided to maintain four numerals after the prefix letter, thus omitting numbers 1 to 999. The new K series therefore commenced at K1000, which was allocated to an AW Atlas.

The Naval N prefix was not used in such a logical way. Blocks of numbers were allocated for specific types of aircraft such as seaplanes or flying-boats. By the late 1920s the sequence had largely been used up and a new series using the prefix S was commenced. In 1930 separate naval allocations were stopped and subsequent serials were issued in the 'military' range which had by this time reached the K series. A further change in the pattern of allocations came in the L range. Commencing with L7272 numbers were issued in blocks with smaller blocks of serials between not used. These were known as 'black-out blocks'. As M had already been used as a suffix for Maintenance Command instructional airframes it was not used as a prefix. Although N had previously been used for naval aircraft it was used again for serials allocated from 1937.

With the build-up to World War II, the rate of allocations quickly accelerated and the prefix R was being used when war was declared. The letters O and Q were not allotted, nor was S, which had been used up to S1865 for naval aircraft before integration into the RAF series. By 1940 the serial Z9999 had been reached, as part of a black-out block, with the letters U and Y not used to avoid confusion.

The option to recommence serial allocation at A1000 was not taken up; instead it was decided to use an alphabetical two-letter prefix with three numerals running from 100 to 999. Thus, AA100 was allocated to a Blenheim IV and this two-letter, three-numeral serial system which started in 1940 continues today. The letters C, I, O, Q, U and Y were, with the exception of NC, not used. For various reasons the following letter combinations were not issued: DA, DB, DH, EA, GA to GZ, HA, HT, JE, JH, JJ, KR to KT, MR, NW, NZ, SA to SK, SV, TN, TR and VE. The first post-war serials issued were in the VP range while the end of the WZs had been reached by the Korean War.

In January 1952 a civil servant at the then Air Ministry penned a memo to his superiors alerting them to the fact that a new military aircraft serial system would soon have to be devised. With allocations accelerating to accommodate a NATO response to the Korean War and a perceived Soviet threat building, he estimated that the end of the ZZs would quickly be reached. However, over five decades later the allocations are only at the start of the ZKs and at the present rate are unlikely to reach ZZ999 until the end of this century!

Military aircraft serials are allocated by Defence Equipment & Support, where the Military Aircraft Register is maintained. A change in policy in 2003 resulted in the use of the first 99 digits in the ZK sequence (ZK001 to ZK099), following on from ZJ999. The first of these, ZK001 to ZK004, were allocated to AgustaWestland Merlins. There is also a growing trend for 'out-of-sequence' serial numbers to be issued. At first this was to a manufacturer's prototype or development aircraft. However, following the Boeing C-17 Globemasters leased and subsequently purchased from Boeing (ZZ171-ZZ177), more allocations have been noted, including ZM400 to ZM424 for the RAF's prospective Airbus A400Ms and ZR321 to ZR323 for a trio of Agusta A.109Es for No 32 (The Royal) Squadron. In a strange twist, serials ZZ190 and ZZ191 were allocated to a pair of former Swiss Air Force Hawker Hunter F58s operated under a military contract.

Since 2002 there has also been a new official policy concerning the use of military serial numbers on some types of UAV. 'Where a UAV is of modular construction the nationality and registration mark shall be applied to the fuselage of the vehicle or on the assembly forming the main part of the fuselage. To prevent the high usage of numbers for target drones which are eventually destroyed, a single registration mark (prefix) should be issued relating to the UAV type. The agency or service operating the target drone will be responsible for the identification of each individual UAV covered by that registration mark by adding a suffix.' This has resulted in the use of the same serial on a number of UAVs with a letter following it. Hence the appearance of ZK201A, ZK201B, ZK201C et seq on Army Meggitt Banshee drones. UAVs using this system are denoted in the text by an asterisk (*).

Note: The compiler will be pleased to receive comments, corrections and further information for inclusion in subsequent editions of *Military Aircraft Markings* and the monthly up-date of additions and amendments. Please send your information to Military Aircraft Markings, Ian Allan Publishing Ltd, Riverdene Business Park, Molesey Road, Hersham, Surrey, KT12 4RG or e-mail to HJCurtis@aol.com.

British Military Aircraft Markings

A serial in *italics* denotes that it is not the genuine marking for that airframe.

Serial	*Type (code/other identity)*	*Owner/operator, location or fate*	*Notes*
46	VS361 Spitfire LF IX <R> (*MH486*/BAPC 206) [FT-E]	RAF Museum, Hendon	
168	Sopwith Tabloid Scout <R> (G-BFDE)	RAF Museum, Hendon	
304	Cody Biplane (BAPC 62)	Science Museum, South Kensington	
687	RAF BE2b <R> (BAPC 181)	RAF Museum, Hendon	
2345	Vickers FB5 Gunbus <R> (G-ATVP)	RAF Museum, Hendon	
2699	RAF BE2c	Imperial War Museum, Lambeth	
2783	RAF BE2b <R>	Privately owned, stored Old Sarum	
3066	Caudron GIII (G-AETA/9203M)	RAF Museum, Hendon	
5964	DH2 <R> (BAPC 112)	Privately owned, Stretton on Dunsmore	
5964	DH2 <R> (G-BFVH)	Privately owned, Wickenby	
6232	RAF BE2c <R> (BAPC 41)	Yorkshire Air Museum, stored Elvington	
8359	Short 184 <ff>	FAA Museum, RNAS Yeovilton	
9917	Sopwith Pup (G-EBKY/N5180)	The Shuttleworth Collection, Old Warden	
A301	Morane BB (frame)	RAF Museum Reserve Collection, Stafford	
A1452	Vickers FB5 Gunbus <R>	Privately owned, Sywell	
A1742	Bristol Scout D <R> (BAPC 38)	Privately owned, Old Warden	
A6526	RAF FE2b <R>	RAF Museum, Hendon	
A7288	Bristol F2b Fighter <R>	Bristol Aero Collection, Filton	
A7317	Sopwith Pup <R> (BAPC 179)	Privately owned, Sywell	
A8226	Sopwith 1½ Strutter <R> (G-BIDW)	RAF Museum, Hendon	
B595	RAF SE5a <R> (G-BUOD) [W]	Privately owned, Kemble	
B2458	Sopwith 1F.1 Camel <R> (G-BPOB/*F542*) [R]	Privately owned, Booker	
B5539	Sopwith 1F.1 Camel <R>	Privately owned, Booker	
B5577	Sopwith 1F.1 Camel <R> (*D3419*/BAPC 59) [W]	Montrose Air Station Heritage Centre	
B6401	Sopwith 1F.1 Camel <R> (G-AWYY/C1701)	FAA Museum, stored RNAS Yeovilton	
B7270	Sopwith 1F.1 Camel <R> (G-BFCZ)	Brooklands Museum, Weybridge	
C1904	RAF SE5a <R> (G-PFAP) [Z]	Privately owned, Castle Bytham, Lincs	
C3009	Currie Wot (G-BFWD)	Privately owned, Dunkeswell	
C3011	Phoenix Currie Super Wot (G-SWOT) [S]	Privately owned, Temple Bruer, Lincs	
C3988	Sopwith 5F.1 Dolphin	RAF Museum Restoration Centre, Cosford	
C4451	Avro 504J <R> (BAPC 210)	Solent Sky, Southampton	
C4918	Bristol M1C <R> (G-BWJM)	The Shuttleworth Collection, Old Warden	
C4994	Bristol M1C <R> (G-BLWM)	RAF Museum, Hendon	
C5430	RAF SE5a <R> (G-CCXG) [V]	Privately owned, Wrexham	
C6468	RAF SE5a <R> (G-CEKL) [A]	Privately owned, RAF Halton	
C8996	RAF SE5a (G-ECAE/A2-25)	Privately owned, Milden	
C9533	RAF SE5a <R> (G-BUWE) [M]	Privately owned, Boscombe Down	
D276	RAF SE5a <R> (BAPC 208) [A]	Prince's Mead Shopping Centre, Farnborough	
D5649	Airco DH9	Imperial War Museum, Duxford	
D7560	Avro 504K	Science Museum, South Kensington	
D8096	Bristol F2b Fighter (G-AEPH) [D]	The Shuttleworth Collection, Old Warden	
E449	Avro 504K (G-EBJE/9205M)	RAF Museum, Hendon	
E2466	Bristol F2b Fighter (BAPC 165) [I]	RAF Museum, Hendon	
E2581	Bristol F2b Fighter [13]	Imperial War Museum, Duxford	
E8894	Airco DH9 (G-CDLI)	Aero Vintage, Westfield, Sussex	
F141	RAF SE5a <R> (G-SEVA) [G]	Privately owned, Boscombe Down	
F235	RAF SE5a <R> (G-BMDB) [B]	Privately owned, Boscombe Down	
F904	RAF SE5a (G-EBIA)	The Shuttleworth Collection, Old Warden	
F904	RAF SE5a <R>	Aeroventure, Doncaster	
F938	RAF SE5a (G-EBIC/9208M)	RAF Museum, Hendon	
F943	RAF SE5a <R> (G-BIHF) [S]	Privately owned, White Waltham	
F943	RAF SE5a <R> (G-BKDT)	Yorkshire Air Museum, Elvington	
F1010	Airco DH9A [C]	RAF Museum, Hendon	
F3556	RAF RE8	Imperial War Museum, Duxford	

Notes	Serial	Type (code/other identity)	Owner/operator, location or fate
	F5447	RAF SE5a <R> (G-BKER) [N]	Privately owned, Bridge of Weir
	F5459	RAF SE5a <R> (G-INNY) [Y]	Privately owned, North Coates
	F5475	RAF SE5a <R> (BAPC 250)	Brooklands Museum, Weybridge
	F6314	Sopwith 1F.1 Camel (9206M) [B]	RAF Museum, Hendon
	F8010	RAF SE5a <R> (G-BDWJ) [Z]	Privately owned, Langport, Somerset
	F8614	Vickers FB27A Vimy IV <R> (G-AWAU)	RAF Museum, Hendon
	H1968	Avro 504K <R> (BAPC 42)	Yorkshire Air Museum, stored Elvington
	H3426	Hawker Hurricane <R> (BAPC 68)	*Repainted as P2725*
	H5199	Avro 504K (BK892/3118M/ G-ACNB/G-ADEV)	The Shuttleworth Collection, Old Warden
	J7326	DH53 Humming Bird (G-EBQP)	Mosquito Aircraft Museum, London Colney
	J8067	Westland Pterodactyl 1a	Science Museum, South Kensington
	J9941	Hawker Hart 2 (G-ABMR)	RAF Museum, Hendon
	K1786	Hawker Tomtit (G-AFTA)	The Shuttleworth Collection, Old Warden
	K1930	Hawker Fury <R> (G-BKBB/ OO-HFU)	*Sold to the USA, September 2009*
	K2046	Isaacs Fury II (G-AYJY)	Privately owned, Little Rissington
	K2048	Isaacs Fury II (G-BZNW)	Privately owned, Linton-on-Ouse
	K2050	Isaacs Fury II (G-ASCM)	Privately owned, Little Rissington
	K2059	Isaacs Fury II (G-PFAR)	Privately owned, Netherthorpe
	K2060	Isaacs Fury II (G-BKZM)	Privately owned stored, Limetree, Ireland
	K2075	Isaacs Fury II (G-BEER)	Privately owned, Combrook, Warks
	K2227	Bristol 105 Bulldog IIA (G-ABBB)	RAF Museum, Hendon
	K2567	DH82A Tiger Moth (DE306/ 7035M/G-MOTH)	Privately owned, Tadlow
	K2572	DH82A Tiger Moth (NM129/ G- AOZH)	Privately owned, Wanborough, Wilts
	K2585	DH82A Tiger Moth II (T6818/ G-ANKT)	The Shuttleworth Collection, Old Warden
	K2587	DH82A Tiger Moth <R> (G-BJAP)	Privately owned, Shobdon
	K3241	Avro 621 Tutor (K3215/G-AHSA)	The Shuttleworth Collection, Old Warden
	K3661	Hawker Nimrod II (G-BURZ) [362]	Aero Vintage, Duxford
	K3731	Isaacs Fury <R> (G-RODI)	Privately owned, Hailsham
	K4232	Avro 671 Rota I (SE-AZB)	RAF Museum, Hendon
	K4259	DH82A Tiger Moth (G-ANMO) [71]	Privately owned, Sywell
	K4972	Hawker Hart Trainer IIA (1764M)	RAF Museum, Hendon
	K5054	Supermarine Spitfire <R> (BAPC 190/*EN398*)	Privately owned, Hawkinge
	K5054	Supermarine Spitfire <R> (BAPC 214)	Tangmere Military Aviation Museum
	K5054	Supermarine Spitfire <R> (G-BRDV)	Solent Sky, stored Romsey
	K5054	Supermarine Spitfire <R>	Kent Battle of Britain Museum, Hawkinge
	K5054	Supermarine Spitfire <R>	Southampton Airport, on display
	K5409	Hawker Hind	Privately owned, Hastings
	K5414	Hawker Hind (G-AENP/BAPC 78) [XV]	The Shuttleworth Collection, Old Warden
	K5462	Hawker Hind	Privately owned, Hastings
	K5554	Hawker Hind	Privately owned, Hastings
	K5600	Hawker Audax I (2015M/G-BVVI)	Aero Vintage, Westfield, Sussex
	K5673	Isaacs Fury II (G-BZAS)	Privately owned, Morpeth
	K5673	Hawker Fury I <R> (BAPC 249)	Brooklands Museum, Weybridge
	K5674	Hawker Fury I (G-CBZP)	Aero Vintage, Westfield, Sussex
	K6035	Westland Wallace II (2361M)	RAF Museum, Hendon
	K6618	Hawker Hind	Privately owned, Hastings
	K6833	Hawker Hind	Privately owned, Hastings
	K7271	Hawker Fury II <R> (BAPC 148)	Shropshire Wartime Aircraft Recovery Grp Mus, Sleap
	K7271	Isaacs Fury II <R> (G-CCKV)	Privately owned, Roche, Cornwall
	K7985	Gloster Gladiator I (L8032/ G-AMRK)	The Shuttleworth Collection, Old Warden
	K8042	Gloster Gladiator II (8372M)	RAF Museum, Hendon
	K8203	Hawker Demon I (G-BTVE/2292M)	Demon Displays, Hatch
	K8303	Isaacs Fury II (G-BWWN) [D]	Privately owned, RAF Henlow
	K9926	VS300 Spitfire I <R> (BAPC 217) [JH-C]	RAF Bentley Priory, on display
	K9942	VS300 Spitfire I (8383M) [SD-D]	RAF Museum, Cosford
	K9998	VS300 Spitfire I <R> [QJ-K]	RAF Biggin Hill, on display

Serial	Type (code/other identity)	Owner/operator, location or fate	Notes
L1067	VS300 Spitfire I <R> (BAPC 227) [XT-D]	Edinburgh Airport, on display	
L1592	Hawker Hurricane I [KW-Z]	Science Museum, South Kensington	
L1639	Hawker Hurricane I	Cambridge Fighter & Bomber Society, Little Gransden	
L1679	Hawker Hurricane I <R> (BAPC 241) [JX-G]	Tangmere Military Aviation Museum	
L1710	Hawker Hurricane I <R> (BAPC 219) [AL-D]	RAF Northolt, for display	
L2301	VS Walrus I (G-AIZG)	FAA Museum, RNAS Yeovilton	
L2940	Blackburn Skua I	FAA Museum, RNAS Yeovilton	
L5343	Fairey Battle I	RAF Museum, Hendon	
L6906	Miles M14A Magister I (G-AKKY/T9841/BAPC 44)	Museum of Berkshire Aviation, Woodley	
L7005	Boulton Paul P82 Defiant I <R> [PS-B]	Boulton Paul Association, Wolverhampton	
L7181	Hawker Hind (G-CBLK)	Aero Vintage, Duxford	
L7191	Hawker Hind	Privately owned, Hastings	
L7775	Vickers Wellington B IC <ff>	Lincolnshire Avn Heritage Centre, E Kirkby	
L8756	Bristol 149 Bolingbroke IVT (RCAF 10001) [XD-E]	RAF Museum, Hendon	
N248	Supermarine S6A (*S1596*)	Solent Sky, Southampton	
N500	Sopwith LC-1T Triplane <R> (G-PENY/G-BWRA)	Privately owned, Yarcombe, Devon/RNAS Yeovilton	
N546	Wright Quadruplane 1 <R> (BAPC 164)	Solent Sky, Southampton	
N1671	Boulton Paul P82 Defiant I (8370M) [EW-D]	Medway Aircraft Preservation Society, Rochester	
N1854	Fairey Fulmar II (G-AIBE)	FAA Museum, RNAS Yeovilton	
N2078	Sopwith Baby (8214/8215)	FAA Museum, stored RNAS Yeovilton	
N2532	Hawker Hurricane I <R> (BAPC 272) [GZ-H]	Kent Battle of Britain Museum, Hawkinge	
N2980	Vickers Wellington IA [R]	Brooklands Museum, Weybridge	
N3194	VS300 Spitfire I <R> (BAPC 220) [GR-Z]	Privately owned	
N3200	VS300 Spitfire IA (G-CFGJ) (fuselage)	Airframe Assemblies Ltd, Sandown	
N3289	VS300 Spitfire I <R> (BAPC 65) [DW-K]	Kent Battle of Britain Museum, Hawkinge	
N3290	VS300 Spitfire I <R> [AI-H]	Privately owned, St Mawgan	
N3310	VS361 Spitfire IX [A] <R>	Privately owned, Wellesbourne Mountford	
N3313	VS300 Spitfire I <R> (*MH314*/ BAPC 69) [KL-B]	Kent Battle of Britain Museum, Hawkinge	
N3378	Boulton Paul P82 Defiant I	Boulton Paul Association, Wolverhampton	
N3788	Miles M14A Magister I (V1075/G-AKPF)	Privately owned, Old Warden	
N4389	Fairey Albacore (N4172) [4M]	FAA Museum, stored RNAS Yeovilton	
N4877	Avro 652A Anson I (G-AMDA) [MK-V]	Imperial War Museum, Duxford	
N5137	DH82A Tiger Moth (N6638/G-BNDW)	Caernarfon Air World	
N5177	Sopwith 1½ Strutter <R>	Privately owned, Sedgensworth, Hants	
N5182	Sopwith Pup <R> (G-APUP/9213M)	RAF Museum, Hendon	
N5195	Sopwith Pup (G-ABOX)	Museum of Army Flying, Middle Wallop	
N5199	Sopwith Pup <R> (G-BZND)	Privately owned, Yarcombe, Devon	
N5459	Sopwith Triplane <R> (BAPC 111)	FAA Museum, stored RNAS Yeovilton	
N5518	Gloster Sea Gladiator	FAA Museum, RNAS Yeovilton	
N5628	Gloster Gladiator II	RAF Museum, Hendon	
N5719	Gloster Gladiator II (G-CBHO)	Privately owned, Dursley, Glos	
N5903	Gloster Gladiator II (*N2276*/G-GLAD)	The Fighter Collection, Duxford	
N5912	Sopwith Triplane (8385M)	RAF Museum, Hendon	
N6290	Sopwith Triplane <R> (G-BOCK)	The Shuttleworth Collection, Old Warden	
N6452	Sopwith Pup <R> (G-BIAU)	FAA Museum, RNAS Yeovilton	
N6466	DH82A Tiger Moth (G-ANKZ)	Privately owned, Winchester	
N6473	DH82A Tiger Moth (G-AOBO)	Privately owned, Orbigny, France	
N6537	DH82A Tiger Moth (G-AOHY)	Privately owned, Wickenby	
N6635	DH82A Tiger Moth (comp G-APAO & G-APAP) [25]	Imperial War Museum, Duxford	
N6720	DH82A Tiger Moth (G-BYTN/7014M) [VX]	Privately owned, Wickenby	

Notes	*Serial*	*Type (code/other identity)*	*Owner/operator, location or fate*
	N6797	DH82A Tiger Moth (G-ANEH)	Privately owned, Swyncombe
	N6812	Sopwith 2F.1 Camel	Imperial War Museum, Lambeth
	N6847	DH82A Tiger Moth (G-APAL)	Privately owned, Leicester
	N6965	DH82A Tiger Moth (G-AJTW) [FL-J]	Privately owned, Tibenham
	N7033	Noorduyn AT-16 Harvard IIB (FX442)	Kent Battle of Britain Museum, Hawkinge
	N9191	DH82A Tiger Moth (G-ALND)	Privately owned, Pontypool
	N9192	DH82A Tiger Moth (G-DHZF) [RCO-N]	Privately owned, Sywell
	N9389	DH82A Tiger Moth (G-ANJA)	Privately owned, Thruxton
	N9899	Supermarine Southampton I (fuselage)	RAF Museum, Hendon
	P1344	HP52 Hampden I (9175M) [PL-K]	RAF Museum Restoration Centre, Cosford
	P2617	Hawker Hurricane I (8373M) [AF-F]	RAF Museum, Hendon
	P2725	Hawker Hurricane I (wreck)	Imperial War Museum, Lambeth
	P2725	Hawker Hurricane I <R> (BAPC 68) [TM-B]	Privately owned, Delabole, Cornwall
	P2793	Hawker Hurricane I <R> (BAPC 236) [SD-M]	Eden Camp Theme Park, Malton, North Yorkshire
	P2902	Hawker Hurricane I (G-ROBT)	Privately owned, Milden
	P2921	Hawker Hurricane I <R> (BAPC 273) [GZ-L]	Kent Battle of Britain Museum, Hawkinge
	P2921	Hawker Hurricane I <R> [GZ-L]	RAF Biggin Hill, on display
	P2954	Hawker Hurricane I <R> (BAPC 267) [WX-E]	Imperial War Museum, Duxford
	P2970	Hawker Hurricane I <R> (BAPC 291) [US-X]	Battle of Britain Memorial, Capel le Ferne, Kent
	P3059	Hawker Hurricane I <R> (BAPC 64) [SD-N]	Kent Battle of Britain Museum, Hawkinge
	P3144	Hawker Hurricane I <R> [CZ-B]	Privately owned
	P3175	Hawker Hurricane I (wreck)	RAF Museum, Hendon
	P3179	Hawker Hurricane I <ff>	Tangmere Military Aviation Museum
	P3208	Hawker Hurricane I <R> (BAPC 63/*L1592*) [SD-T]	Kent Battle of Britain Museum, Hawkinge
	P3386	Hawker Hurricane I <R> (BAPC 218) [FT-A]	RAF Bentley Priory, on display
	P3395	Hawker Hurricane IV (KX829) [JX-B]	Thinktank, Birmingham
	P3398	Supermarine Aircraft Spitfire 26 (G-CEPL)	Privately owned, Thurrock
	P3554	Hawker Hurricane I (composite)	The Air Defence Collection, Salisbury
	P3679	Hawker Hurricane I <R> (BAPC 278) [GZ-K]	Kent Battle of Britain Museum, Hawkinge
	P3717	Hawker Hurricane I (composite) (DR348/G-HITT)	Privately owned, Milden
	P3873	Hawker Hurricane I <R> (BAPC 265) [YO-H]	Yorkshire Air Museum, Elvington
	P4139	Fairey Swordfish II (HS618) [5H]	FAA Museum, RNAS Yeovilton
	P6382	Miles M14A Hawk Trainer 3 (G-AJRS) [C]	The Shuttleworth Collection, Old Warden
	P7350	VS329 Spitfire IIA (G-AWIJ) [QJ-K]	RAF BBMF, Coningsby
	P7540	VS329 Spitfire IIA [DU-W]	Dumfries & Galloway Avn Mus, Ripon (on rebuild)
	P7666	VS329 Spitfire II <R> [EB-Z]	RAF High Wycombe, on display
	P7966	VS329 Spitfire II <R> [D-B]	Manx Aviation & Military Museum, Ronaldsway
	P8140	VS329 Spitfire II <R> (*P9390*/BAPC 71) [ZF-K]	Norfolk & Suffolk Avn Museum, Flixton
	P8208	VS329 Spitfire IIB (G-RRFF)	Privately owned, Oxon
	P8448	VS329 Spitfire II <R> (BAPC 225) [UM-D]	RAF Cranwell, on display
	P9373	VS300 Spitfire IA (G-CFGN) (wreck)	Privately owned, Duxford
	P9374	VS300 Spitfire IA (G-MKIA) [J]	Privately owned, Duxford
	P9444	VS300 Spitfire IA [RN-D]	Science Museum, South Kensington
	P9637	Supermarine Aircraft Spitfire 26 (G-RORB) [GR-B]	Privately owned, Perth
	R1914	Miles M14A Magister (G-AHUJ)	Privately owned, Strathallan

Serial	Type (code/other identity)	Owner/operator, location or fate	Notes
R3821	Bristol 149 Bolingbroke IVT (G-BPIV/*Z5722*) [UX-N]	Blenheim(Duxford) Ltd, Duxford (on rebuild)	
R4118	Hawker Hurricane I (G-HUPW) [UP-W]	Privately owned, Didcot, Oxon	
R4922	DH82A Tiger Moth II (G-APAO)	Privately owned, Henlow	
R4959	DH82A Tiger Moth II (G-ARAZ) [59]	Privately owned, Temple Bruer, Lincs	
R5136	DH82A Tiger Moth II (G-APAP)	Privately owned, Henlow	
R5172	DH82A Tiger Moth II (G-AOIS) [FIJ-E]	Privately owned, Breighton	
R5868	Avro 683 Lancaster I (7325M) [PO-S]	RAF Museum, Hendon	
R6690	VS300 Spitfire I <R> (BAPC 254) [PR-A]	Yorkshire Air Museum, Elvington	
R6775	VS300 Spitfire I <R> (BAPC 299) [YT-J]	Battle of Britain Memorial, Capel le Ferne, Kent	
R6904	VS300 Spitfire I <R> [BT-K]	Privately owned, Cornwall	
R6915	VS300 Spitfire I	Imperial War Museum, Lambeth	
R9125	Westland Lysander III (8377M) [LX-L]	RAF Museum, Hendon	
S1287	Fairey Flycatcher <R> (G-BEYB)	FAA Museum, stored RNAS Yeovilton	
S1579	Hawker Nimrod I <R> (G-BBVO) [571]	Privately owned, stored Felixkirk	
S1581	Hawker Nimrod I (G-BWWK) [573]	The Fighter Collection, Duxford	
S1595	Supermarine S6B [1]	Science Museum, South Kensington	
S1615	Isaacs Fury II (G-BSMU)	Privately owned, stored Netherthorpe	
T5298	Bristol 156 Beaufighter I (4552M) <ff>	Midland Air Museum, Coventry	
T5424	DH82A Tiger Moth II (G-AJOA)	Privately owned, Swindon	
T5854	DH82A Tiger Moth II (G-ANKK)	Privately owned, Baxterley	
T5879	DH82A Tiger Moth II (G-AXBW) [RUC-W]	Privately owned, Frensham	
T6296	DH82A Tiger Moth II (8387M)	RAF Museum, Hendon	
T6562	DH82A Tiger Moth II (G-ANTE)	Privately owned, Sywell	
T6953	DH82A Tiger Moth II (G-ANNI)	Privately owned, Compton Abbas	
T6991	DH82A Tiger Moth II (DE694/HB-UPY)	Privately owned, Lausanne, Switzerland	
T7281	DH82A Tiger Moth II (G-ARTL)	Privately owned, Egton, nr Whitby	
T7793	DH82A Tiger Moth II (G-ANKV)	Privately owned, Booker	
T7842	DH82A Tiger Moth II (G-AMTF)	Privately owned, Headcorn	
T7909	DH82A Tiger Moth II (G-ANON)	Privately owned, Sherburn-in-Elmet	
T7997	DH82A Tiger Moth II (NL750/G-AHUF)	Privately owned, Wickenby	
T8191	DH82A Tiger Moth II (G-BWMK)	Privately owned, Welshpool	
T9707	Miles M14A Magister I (G-AKKR/8378M/T9708)	Museum of Army Flying, Middle Wallop	
T9738	Miles M14A Magister I (G-AKAT)	Privately owned, Breighton	
V3388	Airspeed AS10 Oxford I (G-AHTW)	Imperial War Museum, Duxford	
V6028	Bristol 149 Bolingbroke IVT (G-MKIV) [GB-D] <rf>	The Aircraft Restoration Co, stored Duxford	
V6799	Hawker Hurricane I <R> (BAPC 72/*V7767*) [SD-X]	Gloucestershire Avn Coll, stored Gloucester	
V7313	Hawker Hurricane I <R> [US-F]	Privately owned, North Weald, on display	
V7350	Hawker Hurricane I (fuselage)	Brenzett Aeronautical Museum	
V7467	Hawker Hurricane I <R> (BAPC 223) [LE-D]	RAF High Wycombe, on display	
V7467	Hawker Hurricane I <R> (BAPC 288) [LE-D]	Wonderland Pleasure Park, Farnsfield, Notts	
V7497	Hawker Hurricane I (G-HRLI)	Hawker Restorations, Milden	
V9367	Westland Lysander IIIA (G-AZWT) [MA-B]	The Shuttleworth Collection, Old Warden	
V9673	Westland Lysander IIIA (V9300/G-LIZY) [MA-J]	Imperial War Museum, Duxford	
V9723	Westland Lysander IIIA (V9546/OO-SOT) [MA-D]	SABENA Old Timers, Brussels, Belgium	
V9312	Westland Lysander IIIA (G-CCOM)	The Aircraft Restoration Co, Duxford	
W1048	HP59 Halifax II (8465M) [TL-S]	RAF Museum, Hendon	

Notes	Serial	Type (code/other identity)	Owner/operator, location or fate
	W2068	Avro 652A Anson I (9261M/VH-ASM) [68]	RAF Museum, Hendon
	W2718	VS Walrus I (G-RNLI)	Privately owned, Audley End
	W3850	VS349 Spitfire V <R> [PR-A]	Privately owned, Cheshire
	W4041	Gloster E28/39	Science Museum, South Kensington
	W4050	DH98 Mosquito	Mosquito Aircraft Museum, London Colney
	W5856	Fairey Swordfish II (G-BMGC) [A2A]	RN Historic Flight, Yeovilton
	W9385	DH87B Hornet Moth (G-ADND) [YG-L,3]	Privately owned, Hullavington
	X4276	VS300 Spitfire I (G-CDGU)	Privately owned, Sandown
	X4474	VS509 Spitfire T9 (PV202/*H-98*/G-CCCA) [QV-I]	Historic Flying Ltd, Duxford
	X4590	VS300 Spitfire I (8384M) [PR-F]	RAF Museum, Hendon
	X4650	VS300 Spitfire I	Privately owned, Bentwaters
	X4683	Jurca MJ10 Spitfire (G-CDPM) [EB-N]	Privately owned, Fishburn
	X7688	Bristol 156 Beaufighter I (3858M/G-DINT)	Privately owned, Hatch
	Z1206	Vickers Wellington IV (fuselage)	Privately owned, Kenilworth
	Z2033	Fairey Firefly I (G-ASTL) [275/N]	FAA Museum, RNAS Yeovilton
	Z2315	Hawker Hurricane IIA [JU-E]	Imperial War Museum, Duxford
	Z2389	Hawker Hurricane IIA [XR-T]	Brooklands Museum, Weybridge
	Z3427	Hawker Hurricane IIC <R> (BAPC 205) [AV-R]	RAF Museum, Hendon
	Z5140	Hawker Hurricane XIIA (*Z7381*/G-HURI) [HA-C]	Historic Aircraft Collection, Duxford
	Z5207	Hawker Hurricane IIB (G-BYDL)	Privately owned, Dursley, Glos
	Z5252	Hawker Hurricane IIB (G-BWHA/Z5053) [GO-B]	Privately owned, Milden
	Z7015	Hawker Sea Hurricane IB (G-BKTH) [7-L]	The Shuttleworth Collection, Old Warden
	Z7197	Percival P30 Proctor III (G-AKZN/8380M)	RAF Museum Reserve Collection, Stafford
	Z7258	DH89A Dragon Rapide (NR786/G-AHGD)	Privately owned, Membury (wreck)
	AB196	Supermarine Aircraft Spitfire 26 (G-CCGH)	Privately owned, Horsham
	AB550	VS349 Spitfire VB <R> (BAPC 230/*AA908*) [GE-P]	Eden Camp Theme Park, Malton, North Yorkshire
	AB910	VS349 Spitfire VB (G-AISU) [RF-D]	RAF BBMF, Coningsby
	AD540	VS349 Spitfire VB (wreck)	Kennet Aviation, Tollerton (on rebuild)
	AE436	HP52 Hampden I [PL-J] (parts)	Lincolnshire Avn Heritage Centre, E Kirkby
	AL246	Grumman Martlet I	FAA Museum, RNAS Yeovilton
	AP506	Cierva C30A (G-ACWM)	The Helicopter Museum, Weston-super-Mare
	AP507	Cierva C30A (G-ACWP) [KX-P]	Science Museum, South Kensington
	AR213	VS300 Spitfire IA (*K9853*/G-AIST) [JZ-E]	Privately owned, Kemble
	AR501	VS349 Spitfire LF VC (G-AWII/*AR4474*) [NN-A]	The Shuttleworth Collection, Old Warden
	BB697	DH82A Tiger Moth (G-ADGT)	Privately owned, Headcorn
	BB807	DH82A Tiger Moth (G-ADWO)	Solent Sky, Southampton
	BD713	Hawker Hurricane IIB	Privately owned, Taunton
	BE505	Hawker Hurricane IIB (RCAF 5403/G-HHII) [XP-L]	Hangar 11 Collection, North Weald
	BL614	VS349 Spitfire VB (4354M) [ZD-F]	RAF Museum, Hendon
	BL655	VS349 Spitfire VB (wreck)	Lincolnshire Avn Heritage Centre, East Kirkby
	BL924	VS349 Spitfire VB <R> (BAPC 242) [AZ-G]	Tangmere Military Aviation Museum
	BM361	VS349 Spitfire VB <R> [XR-C]	RAF Lakenheath, on display
	BM481	VS349 Spitfire VB <R> [YO-T] (also wears *PK651*/RAO-B)	Thornaby Aerodrome Memorial
	BM539	VS349 Spitfire LF VB (G-CGBI)	Privately owned, Hastings
	BM597	VS349 Spitfire LF VB (5718M/G-MKVB) [JH-C]	Historic Aircraft Collection, Duxford

Serial	Type (code/other identity)	Owner/operator, location or fate	Notes
BN230	Hawker Hurricane IIC (LF751/5466M) [FT-A]	RAF Manston, Memorial Pavilion	
BP926	VS353 Spitfire PR IV (G-PRIV)	Privately owned, Newport Pagnell	
BR600	VS361 Spitfire IX <R> (BAPC 222) [SH-V]	RAF Uxbridge, on display	
BS410	VS361 Spitfire IXC (G-TCHI)	Airframe Assemblies Ltd, Sandown	
BS435	VS361 Spitfire IX <R> [FY-F]	Privately owned, Lytham St Annes	
BS853	Hawker Hurricane XIIA (G-BRKE) (fuselage)	Privately owned, Kemble	
DD931	Bristol 152 Beaufort VIII (9131M) [L]	RAF Museum, Hendon	
DE208	DH82A Tiger Moth II (G-AGYU)	Privately owned, Treswell, Notts	
DE470	DH82A Tiger Moth II (G-ANMY) [16]	Privately owned, RAF Cosford	
DE623	DH82A Tiger Moth II (G-ANFI)	Privately owned, Withybush	
DE673	DH82A Tiger Moth II (6948M/G-ADNZ)	Privately owned, Tibenham	
DE992	DH82A Tiger Moth II (G-AXXV)	Privately owned, Upavon	
DF112	DH82A Tiger Moth II (G-ANRM)	Privately owned, Clacton/Duxford	
DF128	DH82A Tiger Moth II (G-AOJJ) [RCO-U]	Privately owned, White Waltham	
DF155	DH82A Tiger Moth II (G-ANFV)	Privately owned, Shempston Farm, Lossiemouth	
DF198	DH82A Tiger Moth II (G-BBRB)	Privately owned, Biggin Hill	
DG202	Gloster F9/40 (5758M)	RAF Museum, Cosford	
DG590	Miles M2H Hawk Major (8379M/G-ADMW)	RAF Museum Reserve Collection, Stafford	
DP872	Fairey Barracuda II <ff>	FAA Museum, RNAS Yeovilton	
DV372	Avro 683 Lancaster I <ff>	Imperial War Museum, Lambeth	
DZ313	DH98 Mosquito B IV <R>	Privately owned, Little Rissington	
EB518	Airspeed AS10 Oxford V	Privately owned, Kenilworth	
EE416	Gloster Meteor F3 <ff>	Martin Baker Aircraft, Chalgrove, fire section	
EE425	Gloster Meteor F3 <ff>	Gloucestershire Avn Coll, stored Gloucester	
EE531	Gloster Meteor F4 (7090M)	Midland Air Museum, Coventry	
EE549	Gloster Meteor F4 (7008M) [A]	Tangmere Military Aviation Museum	
EF545	VS349 Spitfire LF VC (G-CDGY)	Aero Vintage, Rye	
EJ693	Hawker Tempest V (N7027E) [SA-J]	Privately owned, Booker	
EJ922	Hawker Typhoon IB <ff>	Privately owned, Hawkinge	
EM720	DH82A Tiger Moth II (G-AXAN)	Privately owned, Sandtoft	
EM840	DH82A Tiger Moth II (G-ANBY)	Assault Glider Trust, Shawbury	
EN179	VS361 Spitfire F IX (G-TCHO)	Privately owned, Exeter	
EN224	VS366 Spitfire F XII (G-FXII)	Privately owned, Newport Pagnell	
EN343	VS365 Spitfire PR XI <R> (BAPC 226)	RAF Benson, on display	
EN398	VS361 Spitfire F IX <R> (BAPC 184) [JE-J]	Rolls-Royce, Derby	
EN398	VS361 Spitfire F IX <R> [JE-J]	Shropshire Wartime Aircraft Recovery Grp Mus, Sleap	
EN526	VS361 Spitfire IX <R> (*MH777*/BAPC 221) [SZ-G]	RAF Northolt, on display	
EN961	Isaacs Spitfire <R> (G-CGIK) [SD-X]	Privately owned,	
EP120	VS349 Spitfire LF VB (5377M/8070M/G-LFVB) [AE-A]	The Fighter Collection, Duxford	
EX976	NA AT-6D Harvard III (FAP 1657)	FAA Museum, RNAS Yeovilton	
FB226	Bonsall Mustang <R> (G-BDWM) [MT-A]	Privately owned, Gamston	
FE695	Noorduyn AT-16 Harvard IIB (G-BTXI) [94]	The Fighter Collection, Duxford	
FE788	CCF Harvard IV (MM54137/G-CTKL)	Privately owned, Rochester	
FE905	Noorduyn AT-16 Harvard IIB (LN-BNM)	RAF Museum, Hendon	
FJ992	Boeing-Stearman PT-17 Kaydet (OO-JEH) [44]	Privately owned, Wevelgem, Belgium	
FK338	Fairchild 24W-41 Argus I (G-AJOZ)	Yorkshire Air Museum, Elvington	
FL586	Douglas C-47B Dakota (OO-SMA) [AI-N] (fuselage)	WWII Remembrance Museum, Handcross, W Sussex	
FR886	Piper L-4J Cub (G-BDMS)	Privately owned, Old Sarum	
FS628	Fairchild Argus 2 (43-14601/ G-AIZE)	RAF Museum, Cosford	

Notes	Serial	Type (code/other identity)	Owner/operator, location or fate
	FS728	Noorduyn AT-16 Harvard IIB (D-FRCP)	Privately owned, Gelnhausen, Germany
	FT118	Noorduyn AT-16 Harvard IIB (G-BZHL)	Privately owned, Wickenby
	FT323	NA AT-6D Harvard III (FAP 1513)	Air Engineering Services, Swansea
	FT391	Noorduyn AT-16 Harvard IIB (G-AZBN)	Privately owned, Shoreham
	FX301	NA AT-6D Harvard III (EX915/ G-TXAN) [FD-NQ]	Privately owned, Bryngwyn Bach, Clwyd
	FX322	Noorduyn AT-16 Harvard IIB <ff>	Privately owned, Doncaster
	FX760	Curtiss P-40N Kittyhawk IV (A29-556/9150M) [GA-?]	RAF Museum, Hendon
	FZ626	Douglas Dakota III (KN566/ G-AMPO) [YS-DH]	RAF Lyneham, on display
	HB275	Beech C-45 Expeditor II (RCAF 2324/G-BKGM)	Privately owned, Exeter
	HB751	Fairchild Argus III (G-BCBL)	Privately owned, Woolsery, Devon
	HG691	DH89A Dragon Rapide (G-AIYR)	Privately owned, Clacton/Duxford
	HH268	GAL48 Hotspur II (HH379/BAPC 261) [H]	Museum of Army Flying, Middle Wallop
	HJ711	DH98 Mosquito NF II [VI-C]	Night-Fighter Preservation Tm, Elvington
	HM580	Cierva C-30A (G-ACUU) [KX-K]	Imperial War Museum, Duxford
	HS503	Fairey Swordfish IV (BAPC 108)	RAF Museum Reserve Collection, Stafford
	IR206	Eurofighter Typhoon F2 <R> [IR]	RAF M&RU, Bottesford
	IR808	B-V Chinook HC2 <R>	RAF M&RU, Bottesford
	JF343	Supermarine Aircraft Spitfire 26 (G-CCZP) [JW-P]	Privately owned, Panshanger
	JG668	VS359 Spitfire LF VIIIC (A58-441/G-CFGA)	Privately owned, Haverfordwest
	JP843	Hawker Typhoon IB [Y]	Privately owned, Shrewsbury
	JR505	Hawker Typhoon IB <ff>	Midland Air Museum, Coventry
	JV482	Grumman Wildcat V	Ulster Aviation Society, Long Kesh
	JV579	Grumman FM-2 Wildcat (N4845V/G-RUMW) [F]	The Fighter Collection, Duxford
	JV928	Consolidated PBY-5A Catalina (N423RS) [Y]	Super Catalina Restoration, North Weald
	KB889	Avro 683 Lancaster B X (G-LANC) [NA-I]	Imperial War Museum, Duxford
	KB976	Avro 683 Lancaster B X <ff>	Brooklands Museum, Weybridge
	KB976	Avro 683 Lancaster B X (G-BCOH) <rf>	Aeroventure, Doncaster
	KB994	Avro 683 Lancaster B X (G-BVBP) <ff>	Privately owned
	KD345	Goodyear FG-1D Corsair (88297/G-FGID) [130-A]	The Fighter Collection, Duxford
	KD431	CV Corsair IV [E2-M]	FAA Museum, RNAS Yeovilton
	KE209	Grumman Hellcat II	FAA Museum, RNAS Yeovilton
	KE418	Hawker Tempest <rf>	*Currently not known*
	KF183	Noorduyn AT-16 Harvard IIB [3]	MoD/AFD/QinetiQ, Boscombe Down
	KF435	Noorduyn AT-16 Harvard IIB <ff>	Privately owned, Swindon
	KF488	Noorduyn AT-16 Harvard IIB (comp KF388)	Bournemouth Aviation Museum
	KF532	Noorduyn AT-16 Harvard IIB <ff>	Newark Air Museum, Winthorpe
	KF584	CCF T-6J Texan (FT239/ G-BIWX/G-RAIX) [RAI-X]	Privately owned, Lee-on-Solent
	KF729	CCF T-6J Texan (G-BJST)	Privately owned, Thruxton
	KF741	Noorduyn AT-16 Harvard IIB <ff>	Privately owned, Kenilworth
	KG374	Douglas Dakota IV (KP208) [YS-DM]	Merville Barracks, Colchester, on display
	KG427	Douglas Dakota IV (KN353/ G-AMYJ)	Yorkshire Air Museum, Elvington
	KG651	Douglas Dakota III (G-AMHJ)	Assault Glider Trust, Shawbury
	KJ351	Airspeed AS58 Horsa II (TL659/BAPC 80) [23]	Museum of Army Flying, Middle Wallop
	KJ994	Douglas Dakota III (F-AZTE)	Dakota et Cie, La Ferté Alais, France
	KK116	Douglas Dakota IV (G-AMPY)	Air Atlantique Classic Flight, Coventry
	KK995	Sikorsky Hoverfly I [E]	RAF Museum, Hendon
	KL216	Republic P-47D Thunderbolt (45-49295/9212M) [RS-L]	RAF Museum, Hendon

Serial	*Type (code/other identity)*	*Owner/operator, location or fate*	*Notes*
KN645	Douglas Dakota IV (*KG374*/8355M)	RAF Museum, Cosford	
KN751	Consolidated Liberator C VI (IAF HE807) [F]	RAF Museum, Hendon	
KP208	Douglas Dakota IV [YS]	*Repainted as KG374, 2010*	
KZ191	Hawker Hurricane IV (frame only)	Privately owned, East Garston, Bucks	
LA198	VS356 Spitfire F21 (7118M) [RAI-G]	Kelvingrove Art Gallery & Museum, Glasgow	
LA226	VS356 Spitfire F21 (7119M)	RAF Museum Reserve Collection, Stafford	
LA255	VS356 Spitfire F21 (6490M) [JX-U]	RAF No 1 Sqn, Cottesmore (preserved)	
LA543	VS474 Seafire F46 <ff>	The Air Defence Collection, Salisbury	
LA546	VS474 Seafire F46 (G-CFZJ)	Privately owned, Colchester	
LA564	VS474 Seafire F46 (G-FRSX)	Kennet Aviation, North Weald	
LB264	Taylorcraft Plus D (G-AIXA)	RAF Museum, Hendon	
LB294	Taylorcraft Plus D (G-AHWJ)	Museum of Army Flying, Whitchurch, Hants	
LB312	Taylorcraft Plus D (*HH982*/G-AHXE)	Privately owned, Netheravon	
LB323	Taylorcraft Plus D (G-AHSD)	Privately owned, Old Buckenham	
LB367	Taylorcraft Plus D (G-AHGZ)	Privately owned, Henstridge	
LB375	Taylorcraft Plus D (G-AHGW)	Privately owned, Coventry	
LF363	Hawker Hurricane IIC [YB-W]	RAF BBMF, Coningsby	
LF738	Hawker Hurricane IIC (5405M) [UH-A]	RAF Museum, Cosford	
LF789	DH82 Queen Bee (K3584/BAPC 186) [R2-K]	Mosquito Aircraft Museum, London Colney	
LF858	DH82 Queen Bee (G-BLUZ)	Privately owned, Henlow	
LH291	Airspeed AS51 Horsa I <R> (BAPC 279)	Assault Glider Trust, RAF Shawbury	
LS326	Fairey Swordfish II (G-AJVH) [L2]	RN Historic Flight, Yeovilton	
LV907	HP59 Halifax III (HR792) [NP-F]	Yorkshire Air Museum, Elvington	
LZ551	DH100 Vampire	FAA Museum, RNAS Yeovilton	
LZ766	Percival P34 Proctor III (G-ALCK)	Imperial War Museum, Duxford	
LZ842	VS361 Spitfire F IX [EF-D]	Privately owned, Sandown	
MA764	VS361 Spitfire F IX (G-MCDB)	Privately owned, Bentwaters	
MB293	VS357 Seafire IIC (G-CFGI) (wreck)	Privately owned, Duxford	
MD338	VS359 Spitfire LF VIII	Privately owned, Sandown	
MF628	Vickers Wellington T10 (9210M)	RAF Museum Restoration Centre, Cosford	
MH434	VS361 Spitfire LF IXB (G-ASJV) [ZD-B]	The Old Flying Machine Company, Duxford	
MH486	VS361 Spitfire LF IX <R> (BAPC 206) [EF-T]	*Repainted as 46*	
MH415	VS361 Spitfire IX <R> (*MJ751*/BAPC 209) [DU-V]	The Aircraft Restoration Co, Duxford	
MJ627	VS509 Spitfire T9 (G-BMSB) [9G-P]	Privately owned, RAF Waddington	
MJ832	VS361 Spitfire IX <R> (*L1096*/BAPC 229) [DN-Y]	RAF Digby, on display	
MK356	VS361 Spitfire LF IXC (5690M) [UF-Q]	RAF BBMF, Coningsby	
MK356	VS361 Spitfire LF IXC <R> [2I-V]	Kent Battle of Britain Museum, Hawkinge	
MK356	VS361 Spitfire LF IXC (BAPC 289) <R>	RAF Cosford, on display	
ML407	VS509 Spitfire T9 (G-LFIX) [OU-V]	Privately owned, Bentwaters	
ML411	VS361 Spitfire LF IXE (G-CBNU)	Privately owned, Ashford, Kent	
ML427	VS361 Spitfire IX (6457M) [HK-A]	Thinktank, Birmingham	
ML796	Short S25 Sunderland V [NS-F]	Imperial War Museum, Duxford	
ML824	Short S25 Sunderland V [NS-Z]	RAF Museum, Hendon	
MN235	Hawker Typhoon IB	RAF Museum, Hendon	
MP425	Airspeed AS10 Oxford I (G-AITB) [G]	RAF Museum, Hendon	
MS902	Miles M25 Martinet TT1 (TF-SHC)	Museum of Berkshire Aviation, Woodley	
MT197	Auster IV (G-ANHS)	Privately owned, Spanhoe	
MT438	Auster III (G-AREI)	Privately owned, Eggesford	
MT818	VS502 Spitfire T8 (G-AIDN)	Privately owned, Booker	
MT847	VS379 Spitfire FR XIVE (6960M) [AX-H]	Museum of Science & Industry, Manchester	
MT928	VS359 Spitfire HF VIIIC (D-FEUR/MV154/*AR654*)[ZX-M]	Privately owned, Bremgarten, Germany	
MV262	VS379 Spitfire FR XIV (G-CCVV)	*Sold as N808U, January 2009*	
MV268	VS379 Spitfire FR XIVE (MV293/G-SPIT) [JE-J]	The Fighter Collection, Duxford	
MW401	Hawker Tempest II (IAF HA604/G-PEST)	Privately owned, Wickenby	

Notes	*Serial*	*Type (code/other identity)*	*Owner/operator, location or fate*
	MW404	Hawker Tempest II (IAF HA557)	Privately owned, stored Wickenby
	MW763	Hawker Tempest II (IAF HA586/G-TEMT) [HF-A]	Privately owned, Wickenby
	MW810	Hawker Tempest II (IAF HA591) <ff>	Privately owned, Bentwaters
	NF370	Fairey Swordfish III [NH-L]	Imperial War Museum, Duxford
	NF389	Fairey Swordfish III [D]	RN Historic Flight, Yeovilton
	NH238	VS361 Spitfire LF IXE (G-MKIX) [D-A]	Privately owned, stored Greenham Common
	NJ633	Auster 5D (G-AKXP)	Privately owned, English Bicknor
	NJ673	Auster 5D (G-AOCR)	Privately owned, Shenington, Oxon
	NJ695	Auster 4 (G-AJXV)	Privately owned, Newark
	NJ703	Auster 5 (G-AKPI)	Privately owned, Ellerton
	NJ719	Auster 5 (TW385/G-ANFU)	Newcastle Motor Museum
	NJ889	Auster 3 (G-AHLK)	Privately owned, Leicester East
	NL750	DH82A Tiger Moth II (T7997/G-AOBH)	Privately owned, Eaglescott
	NL985	DH82A Tiger Moth I (7015M/G-BWIK)	Privately owned, Sywell
	NM181	DH82A Tiger Moth I (G-AZGZ)	Privately owned, Rush Green
	NP294	Percival P31 Proctor IV [TB-M]	Lincolnshire Avn Heritage Centre, E Kirkby
	NV778	Hawker Tempest TT5 (8386M)	RAF Museum, Hendon
	NX534	Auster III (G-BUDL)	Privately owned, Spanhoe
	NX611	Avro 683 Lancaster B VII (8375M/G-ASXX) [DX-C,LE-C]	Lincolnshire Avn Heritage Centre, E Kirkby
	PA474	Avro 683 Lancaster B I [BQ-B,HW-R]	RAF BBMF, Coningsby
	PD685	Slingsby T7 Cadet TX1	Boulton Paul Association, Wolverhampton
	PF179	HS Gnat T1 (XR541/8602M)	Privately owned, Bruntingthorpe
	PK624	VS356 Spitfire F22 (8072M)	The Fighter Collection, Duxford
	PK664	VS356 Spitfire F22 (7759M) [V6-B]	RAF Museum Reserve Collection, Stafford
	PK683	VS356 Spitfire F24 (7150M)	Solent Sky, Southampton
	PK724	VS356 Spitfire F24 (7288M)	RAF Museum, Hendon
	PL256	VS361 Spitfire IX <R> [TM-L]	East Midlands Airport Aeropark
	PL279	VS361 Spitfire IX <R> (*N3317*/BAPC 268) [ZF-Z]	Privately owned, St Mawgan
	PL344	VS361 Spitfire LF IXE (G-IXCC) [TL-B]	*Sold to the USA, September 2010*
	PL965	VS365 Spitfire PR XI (G-MKXI) [R]	Hangar 11 Collection, North Weald
	PL983	VS365 Spitfire PR XI (G-PRXI)	Privately owned, Duxford (on rebuild)
	PM631	VS390 Spitfire PR XIX	RAF BBMF, Coningsby
	PM651	VS390 Spitfire PR XIX (7758M) [X]	RAF Museum Restoration Centre, Cosford
	PN323	HP Halifax VII <ff>	Imperial War Museum, Lambeth
	PP566	Fairey Firefly I <rf>	Privately owned, Newton Abbott, Devon
	PP972	VS358 Seafire LF IIIC (G-BUAR)	Privately owned, stored Greenham Common
	PR536	Hawker Tempest II (IAF HA457) [OQ-H]	RAF Museum, Hendon
	PS853	VS390 Spitfire PR XIX (G-RRGN) [C]	Rolls-Royce, East Midlands
	PS890	VS390 Spitfire PR XIX (F-AZJS) [UM-E]	Privately owned, Dijon, France
	PS915	VS390 Spitfire PR XIX (7548M/7711M)	RAF BBMF, Coningsby
	PT462	VS509 Spitfire T9 (G-CTIX/N462JC) [SW-A]	Privately owned, Caernarfon/Duxford
	PV303	Supermarine Aircraft Spitfire 26 (G-CCJL) [ON-B]	Privately owned, Perranporth
	PZ865	Hawker Hurricane IIC (G-AMAU) [JX-E]	RAF BBMF, Duxford (on overhaul)
	QQ100	Agusta A109E Power Elite	MoD/AFD/QinetiQ, Boscombe Down
	RA848	Slingsby T7 Cadet TX1	Privately owned, Leeds
	RA854	Slingsby T7 Cadet TX1	Yorkshire Air Museum, Elvington
	RA897	Slingsby T7 Cadet TX1	Newark Air Museum, Winthorpe
	RA905	Slingsby T7 Cadet TX1 (BGA1143)	Trenchard Museum, RAF Halton
	RB142	Supermarine Aircraft Spitfire 26 (G-CEFC) [DW-B]	Privately owned, Basingstoke, Hants
	RB159	VS379 Spitfire F XIV <R> [DW-D]	Privately owned, Delabole, Cornwall
	RD220	Bristol 156 Beaufighter TF X	Royal Scottish Mus'm of Flight, stored E Fortune

Serial	*Type (code/other identity)*	*Owner/operator, location or fate*	*Notes*
RD253	Bristol 156 Beaufighter TF X (7931M)	RAF Museum, Hendon	
RF398	Avro 694 Lincoln B II (8376M)	RAF Museum, Cosford	
RG333	Miles M38 Messenger IIA (G-AIEK)	Privately owned, Felton, Bristol	
RG904	VS Spitfire <R> [BT-K]	RAF Museum, Cosford	
RH746	Bristol 164 Brigand TF1 (fuselage)	RAF Museum Restoration Centre, Cosford	
RL962	DH89A Dominie II (G-AHED)	RAF Museum Reserve Collection, Stafford	
RM169	Percival P31 Proctor IV (SE-CEA) [4-47]	Privately owned, Great Oakley, Essex	
RM221	Percival P31 Proctor IV (G-ANXR)	Privately owned, Biggin Hill	
RM689	VS379 Spitfire F XIV (G-ALGT)	Rolls-Royce, Filton (on rebuild)	
RM694	VS379 Spitfire F XIV (G-DBKL/6640M)	Privately owned, Booker	
RM927	VS379 Spitfire F XIV (G-JNMA)	Privately owned, Sandown	
RN218	Isaacs Spitfire <R> (G-BBJI) [N]	Privately owned, Builth Wells	
RR232	VS361 Spitfire HF IXC (G-BRSF)	Privately owned, Langford, Devon	
RT486	Auster 5 (G-AJGJ)	Privately owned, Lee-on-Solent	
RT520	Auster 5 (G-ALYB)	Aeroventure, Doncaster	
RT610	Auster 5A-160 (G-AKWS)	Privately owned, Crowfield	
RW382	VS361 Spitfire LF XVIE (7245M/8075M/G-PBIX)	Privately owned, Sandown (on rebuild)	
RW386	VS361 Spitfire LF XVIE (6944M/SE-BIR) [NG-D]	Privately owned, Angelholm, Sweden	
RW388	VS361 Spitfire LF XVIE (6946M) [U4-U]	Stoke-on-Trent City Museum, Hanley	
RX168	VS358 Seafire L IIIC (IAC 157/G-BWEM)	Privately owned, Exeter	
SL611	VS361 Spitfire LF XVIE	Supermarine Aero Engineering, Stoke-on-Trent	
SL674	VS361 Spitfire LF IX (8392M) [RAS-H]	RAF Museum Reserve Collection, Stafford	
SM520	VS509 Spitfire T9 (*H-99*/G-ILDA) [KJ-I]	Privately owned, Kemble	
SM845	VS394 Spitfire FR XVIII (SE-BIN) [GZ-J]	*Crashed 21 August 2010, Tynset, Norway*	
SX137	VS384 Seafire F XVII	FAA Museum, RNAS Yeovilton	
SX300	VS384 Seafire F XVII (G-RIPH)	Kennet Aviation, North Weald	
SX336	VS384 Seafire F XVII (G-KASX) [105/VL]	Kennet Aviation, Yeovilton	
TA122	DH98 Mosquito FB VI [UP-G]	Mosquito Aircraft Museum, London Colney	
TA634	DH98 Mosquito TT35 (G-AWJV) [8K-K]	Mosquito Aircraft Museum, London Colney	
TA639	DH98 Mosquito TT35 (7806M) [AZ-E]	RAF Museum, Cosford	
TA719	DH98 Mosquito TT35 (G-ASKC)	Imperial War Museum, Duxford	
TA805	VS361 Spitfire HF IX (G-PMNF) [FX-M]	Privately owned, Biggin Hill	
TB382	VS361 Spitfire LF XVIE (*X4277/MK673*)	RAF BBMF, stored Coningsby	
TB675	VS361 Spitfire LF XVIE (RW393/7293M) [4D-V]	RAF Museum Reserve Collection, Stafford	
TB752	VS361 Spitfire LF XVIE (8086M) [KH-Z]	RAF Manston, Memorial Pavilion	
TD248	VS361 Spitfire LF XVIE (7246M/G-OXVI) [CR-S]	Spitfire Limited, Duxford	
TD248	VS361 Spitfire LF XVIE [8Q-T] (fuselage)	Norfolk & Suffolk Avn Mus'm, Flixton	
TD314	VS361 Spitfire LF IX (*N601DA*)	Privately owned, Bentwaters	
TE184	VS361 Spitfire LF XVIE (6850M/G-MXVI) [EJC]	Privately owned, Booker	
TE311	VS361 Spitfire LF XVIE (*MK178*/7241M) [4D-V]	RAF BBMF, Coningsby (on rebuild)	
TE462	VS361 Spitfire LF XVIE (7243M)	Royal Scottish Mus'm of Flight, E Fortune	
TE517	VS361 Spitfire LF IXE (G-JGCA) [HL-K]	Privately owned, Sussex	
TG263	Saro SR A1 (G-12-1)	Solent Sky, Southampton	
TG511	HP67 Hastings T5 (8554M)	RAF Museum, Cosford	
TG517	HP67 Hastings T5	Newark Air Museum, Winthorpe	
TG528	HP67 Hastings C1A	Imperial War Museum, Duxford	
TJ118	DH98 Mosquito TT35 <ff>	Mosquito Aircraft Museum, stored London Colney	

Notes	*Serial*	*Type (code/other identity)*	*Owner/operator, location or fate*
	TJ138	DH98 Mosquito B35 (7607M) [VO-L]	RAF Museum, Hendon
	TJ343	Auster 5 (G-AJXC)	Privately owned, Hook
	TJ398	Auster AOP6 (BAPC 70)	North-East Aircraft Museum, Usworth
	TJ534	Auster 5 (G-AKSY)	Privately owned, Breighton
	TJ569	Auster 5 (G-AKOW)	Museum of Army Flying, Middle Wallop
	TJ652	Auster 5 (TJ565/G-AMVD)	Privately owned, Hardwick, Norfolk
	TJ672	Auster 5D (G-ANIJ) [TS-D]	Privately owned, Netheravon
	TK718	GAL59 Hamilcar I	The Tank Museum, Bovington
	TK777	GAL59 Hamilcar I (fuselage)	Museum of Army Flying, Middle Wallop
	TP298	VS394 Spitfire FR XVIII [UM-T]	Privately owned, Sandown
	TS291	Slingsby T7 Cadet TX1 (BGA852)	Royal Scottish Mus'm of Flight, stored Granton
	TS798	Avro 685 York C1 (G-AGNV/*MW100*)	RAF Museum, Cosford
	TV959	DH98 Mosquito T III [AF-V]	Privately owned,
	TW439	Auster 5 (G-ANRP)	Privately owned, Lavenham, Suffolk
	TW467	Auster 5 (G-ANIE)	Privately owned, Spanhoe
	TW477	Auster 5 (OY-EFI)	Privately owned, Ringsted, Denmark
	TW511	Auster 5 (G-APAF)	Privately owned, Chisledon, Wilts
	TW536	Auster AOP6 (7704M/G-BNGE) [TS-V]	Privately owned, Netheravon
	TW591	Auster 6A (G-ARIH) [6]	Privately owned, Eaglescott
	TW641	Beagle A61 Terrier 2 (G-ATDN)	Privately owned, Biggin Hill
	TX213	Avro 652A Anson C19 (G-AWRS)	North-East Aircraft Museum, Usworth
	TX214	Avro 652A Anson C19 (7817M)	RAF Museum, Cosford
	TX226	Avro 652A Anson C19 (7865M)	Air Atlantique Classic Flight, stored Compton Verney
	TX235	Avro 652A Anson C19	Air Atlantique Classic Flight, stored Compton Verney
	TX310	DH89A Dragon Rapide 6 (G-AIDL)	Air Atlantique Classic Flight, Coventry
	VF301	DH100 Vampire F1 (7060M) [RAL-G]	Midland Air Museum, Coventry
	VF512	Auster 6A (G-ARRX) [PF-M]	Privately owned, Popham
	VF516	Beagle A61 Terrier 2 (G-ASMZ)	Privately owned, Eggesford
	VF519	Auster AOP6 (G-ASYN)	Privately owned, Doncaster
	VF526	Auster 6A (G-ARXU) [T]	Privately owned, Netheravon
	VF557	Auster 6A (G-ARHM) [H]	Privately owned, Spanhoe
	VF560	Auster 6A (frame)	Aeroventure, Doncaster
	VF581	Beagle A61 Terrier 1 (G-ARSL) [G]	Privately owned, Eggesford
	VH127	Fairey Firefly TT4 [200/R]	FAA Museum, RNAS Yeovilton
	VL348	Avro 652A Anson C19 (G-AVVO)	Newark Air Museum, Winthorpe
	VL349	Avro 652A Anson C19 (G-AWSA) [V7-Q]	Norfolk & Suffolk Avn Mus'm, Flixton
	VM325	Avro 652A Anson C19	Privately owned, Carew Cheriton, Pembrokeshire
	VM360	Avro 652A Anson C19 (G-APHV)	Royal Scottish Mus'm of Flight, E Fortune
	VM684	Slingsby Cadet T2 (BGA791)	*Currently not known*
	VM687	Slingsby T8 Tutor (BGA794)	Privately owned, Lee-on-Solent
	VM791	Slingsby Cadet TX3 (XA312/8876M)	RAF Manston History Museum
	VN485	VS356 Spitfire F24 (7326M)	Imperial War Museum, Duxford
	VN799	EE Canberra T4 (WJ874/G-CDSX)	Air Atlantique Classic Flight, Coventry
	VP293	Avro 696 Shackleton T4 [X] <ff>	Shackleton Preservation Trust, Coventry
	VP519	Avro 652A Anson C19 (G-AVVR) <ff>	Privately owned, Wolverhampton
	VP952	DH104 Devon C2 (8820M)	RAF Museum, Cosford
	VP955	DH104 Devon C2 (G-DVON)	Privately owned, Little Rissington
	VP957	DH104 Devon C2 (8822M) <ff>	No 1137 Sqn ATC, Belfast
	VP967	DH104 Devon C2 (G-KOOL)	Yorkshire Air Museum, Elvington
	VP975	DH104 Devon C2 [M]	Science Museum, Wroughton
	VP981	DH104 Devon C2 (G-DHDV)	Air Atlantique Classic Flight, Coventry
	VR137	Westland Wyvern TF1	FAA Museum, stored RNAS Yeovilton
	VR192	Percival P40 Prentice T1 (G-APIT)	Privately owned, Cambs
	VR249	Percival P40 Prentice T1 (G-APIY) [FA-EL]	Newark Air Museum, Winthorpe
	VR259	Percival P40 Prentice T1 (G-APJB) [M]	Air Atlantique Classic Flight, Coventry
	VR930	Hawker Sea Fury FB11 (8382M) [110/Q]	RN Historic Flight, Yeovilton
	VS356	Percival P40 Prentice T1 (G-AOLU)	Privately owned, Montrose

Serial	*Type (code/other identity)*	*Owner/operator, location or fate*	*Notes*
VS562	Avro 652A Anson T21 (8012M)	Privately owned, Market Drayton	
VS610	Percival P40 Prentice T1 (G-AOKL) [K-L]	The Shuttleworth Collection, Old Warden	
VS618	Percival P40 Prentice T1 (G-AOLK)	RAF Museum, Hendon	
VS623	Percival P40 Prentice T1 (G-AOKZ) [KQ-F]	Midland Air Museum, Coventry	
VT812	DH100 Vampire F3 (7200M) [N]	RAF Museum, Hendon	
VT935	Boulton Paul P111A (VT769)	Midland Air Museum, Coventry	
VT987	Auster AOP6 (G-BKXP)	Privately owned, Thruxton	
VV106	Supermarine 510 (7175M)	FAA Museum, stored RNAS Yeovilton	
VV217	DH100 Vampire FB5 (7323M)	Mosquito Aircraft Museum, stored London Colney	
VV612	DH112 Venom FB50 (J-1523/*WE402*/G-VENI)	Privately owned, Bournemouth	
VV901	Avro 652A Anson T21	Yorkshire Air Museum, Elvington	
VW453	Gloster Meteor T7 (8703M) [Z]	RAF Innsworth, on display	
VW957	DH103 Sea Hornet NF21 <rf>	Privately owned, Chelmsford	
VW993	Beagle A61 Terrier 2 (G-ASCD)	Yorkshire Air Museum, Elvington	
VX113	Auster AOP6 (G-ARNO) [36]	Privately owned, Eggesford	
VX147	Alon A2 Aircoupe (G-AVIL)	Privately owned, Eaglescott	
VX185	EE Canberra B(I)8 (7631M) <ff>	Royal Scottish Mus'm of Flight, E Fortune	
VX250	DH103 Sea Hornet NF21 [48] <rf>	Mosquito Aircraft Museum, London Colney	
VX272	Hawker P.1052 (7174M)	FAA Museum, stored RNAS Yeovilton	
VX275	Slingsby T21B Sedbergh TX1 (8884M/BGA572)	RAF Museum Reserve Collection, Stafford	
VX281	Hawker Sea Fury T20S (G-RNHF) [120/VL]	RN Historic Flight, North Weald	
VX573	Vickers Valetta C2 (8389M)	RAF Museum, stored Cosford	
VX580	Vickers Valetta C2	Norfolk & Suffolk Avn Museum, Flixton	
VX595	WS51 Dragonfly HR1	FAA Museum, RNAS Yeovilton	
VX665	Hawker Sea Fury FB11 <rf>	RN Historic Flight, at BAE Systems Brough	
VX926	Auster T7 (G-ASKJ)	Privately owned, Gamlingay, Cambs	
VX927	Auster T7 (G-ASYG)	Privately owned, Wickenby	
VZ193	DH100 Vampire FB5 <ff>	Privately owned, Hooton Park	
VZ345	Hawker Sea Fury T20S	The Fighter Collection, Duxford	
VZ440	Gloster Meteor F8 (WA984) [X]	Tangmere Military Aviation Museum	
VZ477	Gloster Meteor F8 (7741M) <ff>	Midland Air Museum, Coventry	
VZ608	Gloster Meteor FR9	Newark Air Museum, Winthorpe	
VZ634	Gloster Meteor T7 (8657M)	Newark Air Museum, Winthorpe	
VZ638	Gloster Meteor T7 (G-JETM) [HF]	Gatwick Aviation Museum, Charlwood, Surrey	
VZ728	RS4 Desford Trainer (G-AGOS)	Snibston Discovery Park, stored Coalville	
VZ962	WS51 Dragonfly HR1 [904]	The Helicopter Museum, Weston-super-Mare	
WA346	DH100 Vampire FB5	RAF Museum, stored Cosford	
WA473	VS Attacker F1 [102/J]	FAA Museum, RNAS Yeovilton	
WA576	Bristol 171 Sycamore 3 (7900M/G-ALSS)	Dumfries & Galloway Avn Mus, Dumfries	
WA577	Bristol 171 Sycamore 3 (7718M/G-ALST)	North-East Aircraft Museum, Usworth	
WA591	Gloster Meteor T7 (7917M/G-BWMF) [W]	Meteor Flight, Kemble	
WA630	Gloster Meteor T7 [69] <ff>	Robertsbridge Aviation Society, Newhaven	
WA634	Gloster Meteor T7/8	RAF Museum, Cosford	
WA638	Gloster Meteor T7(mod)	Martin Baker Aircraft, Chalgrove	
WA662	Gloster Meteor T7	Aeroventure, Doncaster	
WA984	Gloster Meteor F8 [X]	*Repainted as VZ440, 2010*	
WB188	Hawker Hunter F3 (7154M)	Tangmere Military Aviation Museum	
WB188	Hawker Hunter GA11 (WV256/G-BZPB)	Privately owned, Coventry (duck egg green)	
WB188	Hawker Hunter GA11 (XF300/G-BZPC)	Privately owned, Kemble (red)	
WB440	Fairey Firefly AS6 <ff>	Privately owned, Newton Abbott, Devon	
WB491	Avro 706 Ashton 2 (TS897/G-AJJW) <ff>	Newark Air Museum, Winthorpe	
WB555	DHC1 Chipmunk T10 <ff>	Privately owned, Ellerton	
WB556	DHC1 Chipmunk T10 (fuselage)	Privately owned, Coleford, Somerset	
WB560	DHC1 Chipmunk T10 (comp WG403)	Privately owned, South Molton, Devon	
WB565	DHC1 Chipmunk T10 (G-PVET) [X]	Privately owned, Rendcomb	

Notes	Serial	Type (code/other identity)	Owner/operator, location or fate
	WB569	DHC1 Chipmunk T10 (G-BYSJ) [R]	Privately owned, Kemble
	WB571	DHC1 Chipmunk T10 (G-AOSF) [34]	Privately owned, Trier, Germany
	WB584	DHC1 Chipmunk T10 (7706M) <ff>	Royal Scottish Mus'm of Flight, stored E Fortune
	WB585	DHC1 Chipmunk T10 (G-AOSY) [M]	Privately owned, Seething
	WB588	DHC1 Chipmunk T10 (G-AOTD) [D]	Privately owned, Old Sarum
	WB615	DHC1 Chipmunk T10 (G-BXIA) [E]	Privately owned, Blackpool
	WB624	DHC1 Chipmunk T10	Newark Air Museum, Winthorpe
	WB626	DHC1 Chipmunk T10 <ff>	No 1365 Sqn ATC, Aylesbury
	WB627	DHC1 Chipmunk T10 (9248M) (fuselage) [N]	Dulwich College CCF
	WB654	DHC1 Chipmunk T10 (G-BXGO) [U]	Privately owned, Booker
	WB657	DHC1 Chipmunk T10 [908]	RN Historic Flight, Yeovilton
	WB670	DHC1 Chipmunk T10 (comp WG303)(8361M)	Privately owned, East Fortune
	WB671	DHC1 Chipmunk T10 (G-BWTG) [910]	Privately owned, Teuge, The Netherlands
	WB685	DHC1 Chipmunk T10 (comp WP969/G-ATHC)	Mosquito Aircraft Museum, London Colney
	WB685	DHC1 Chipmunk T10 <rf>	North-East Aircraft Museum, stored Usworth
	WB697	DHC1 Chipmunk T10 (G-BXCT) [95]	Privately owned, Wickenby
	WB702	DHC1 Chipmunk T10 (G-AOFE)	Privately owned, Kindford
	WB703	DHC1 Chipmunk T10 (G-ARMC)	Privately owned, Compton Abbas
	WB711	DHC1 Chipmunk T10 (G-APPM)	Privately owned, Sywell
	WB726	DHC1 Chipmunk T10 (G-AOSK) [E]	Privately owned, RAF Halton
	WB733	DHC1 Chipmunk T10 (comp WG422)	Aeroventure, Doncaster
	WB763	DHC1 Chipmunk T10 (G-BBMR) [14]	Privately owned, Bodmin
	WB922	Slingsby T21B Sedbergh TX1 (BGA4366)	Privately owned, Hullavington
	WB924	Slingsby T21B Sedbergh TX1 (BGA3901)	Privately owned, Dunstable
	WB943	Slingsby T21B Sedbergh TX1 (BGA2941)	Privately owned, Rufforth
	WB944	Slingsby T21B Sedbergh TX1 (BGA3160)	Privately owned, Bicester
	WB945	Slingsby T21B Sedbergh TX1 (BGA1254)	Privately owned, Lasham
	WB971	Slingsby T21B Sedbergh TX1 (BGA3324)	Privately owned, Tibenham
	WB975	Slingsby T21B Sedbergh TX1 (BGA3288) [FJB]	Privately owned, Shipdham
	WB980	Slingsby T21B Sedbergh TX1 (BGA3290)	Privately owned, Husbands Bosworth
	WB981	Slingsby T21B Sedbergh TX1 (BGA3238)	Privately owned, Keevil
	WD286	DHC1 Chipmunk T10 (G-BBND)	Privately owned, Little Gransden
	WD292	DHC1 Chipmunk T10 (G-BCRX)	Privately owned, White Waltham
	WD293	DHC1 Chipmunk T10 (7645M) <ff>	Privately owned, St Athan
	WD305	DHC1 Chipmunk T10 (G-ARGG)	Privately owned, Prestwick
	WD310	DHC1 Chipmunk T10 (G-BWUN) [B]	Privately owned, Deanland
	WD319	DHC1 Chipmunk T10 (OY-ATF)	Privately owned, Stauning, Denmark
	WD325	DHC1 Chipmunk T10 [N]	AAC Historic Aircraft Flight, Middle Wallop
	WD331	DHC1 Chipmunk T10 (G-BXDH) [J]	Privately owned, Enstone
	WD347	DHC1 Chipmunk T10 (G-BBRV)	*Sold as HB-TUT, June 2010*
	WD355	DHC1 Chipmunk T10 (WD335/G-CBAJ)	Privately owned, Eastleigh
	WD363	DHC1 Chipmunk T10 (G-BCIH) [5]	Privately owned, Audley End
	WD370	DHC1 Chipmunk T10 <ff>	No 225 Sqn ATC, Brighton
	WD373	DHC1 Chipmunk T10 (G-BXDI) [12]	Privately owned, Booker
	WD377	DHC1 Chipmunk T10 <ff>	Privately owned, Millom
	WD386	DHC1 Chipmunk T10 (comp WD377)	Privately owned, Lisburn, Northern Ireland

Serial	*Type (code/other identity)*	*Owner/operator, location or fate*	*Notes*
WD388	DHC1 Chipmunk T10 (D-EPAK) [68]	Quax Flieger, Hamm, Germany	
WD390	DHC1 Chipmunk T10 (G-BWNK) [68]	Privately owned, Wickenby	
WD413	Avro 652A Anson T21 (7881M/G-VROE)	Air Atlantique Classic Flight, Coventry	
WD615	Gloster Meteor TT20 (WD646/8189M) [R]	RAF Manston History Museum	
WD686	Gloster Meteor NF11 [S]	Muckleburgh Collection, Weybourne	
WD790	Gloster Meteor NF11 (8743M)<ff>	North-East Aircraft Museum, Usworth	
WD889	Fairey Firefly AS5 (comp VT809)	Privately owned, Haverigg	
WD931	EE Canberra B2 <ff>	RAF Museum, stored Cosford	
WD935	EE Canberra B2 (8440M) <ff>	Aeroventure, Doncaster	
WD954	EE Canberra B2 <ff>	Privately owned, St Mawgan	
WE113	EE Canberra B2 <ff>	Privately owned, Woodhurst, Cambridgeshire	
WE122	EE Canberra TT18 [845] <ff>	Blyth Valley Aviation Collection, Walpole, Suffolk	
WE139	EE Canberra PR3 (8369M)	RAF Museum, Hendon	
WE168	EE Canberra PR3 (8049M) <ff>	Norfolk & Suffolk Avn Museum, Flixton	
WE173	EE Canberra PR3 (8740M) <ff>	Robertsbridge Aviation Society, Mayfield	
WE188	EE Canberra T4	Solway Aviation Society, Carlisle	
WE192	EE Canberra T4 <ff>	Blyth Valley Aviation Collection, Walpole, Suffolk	
WE275	DH112 Venom FB50 (J-1601/G-VIDI)	BAE Systems Hawarden, Fire Section	
WE569	Auster T7 (G-ASAJ)	Privately owned, Coventry	
WE570	Auster T7 (G-ASBU)	Privately owned, Stonehaven	
WE591	Auster T7 (F-AZTJ)	Privately owned, Toussus-le-Noble, France	
WE600	Auster T7 Antarctic (7602M)	RAF Museum, Cosford	
WE724	Hawker Sea Fury FB11 (VX653/G-BUCM) [062]	The Fighter Collection, Duxford	
WE982	Slingsby T30B Prefect TX1 (8781M)	RAF Museum, stored Cosford	
WE987	Slingsby T30B Prefect TX1 (BGA2517)	Aeroventure, Doncaster	
WE990	Slingsby T30B Prefect TX1 (BGA2583)	Privately owned, stored Beds	
WE992	Slingsby T30B Prefect TX1 (BGA2692)	Privately owned, Hullavington	
WF118	Percival P57 Sea Prince T1 (G-DACA)	Gatwick Aviation Museum, Charlwood, Surrey	
WF122	Percival P57 Sea Prince T1 [575/CU]	Aeroventure, Doncaster	
WF128	Percival P57 Sea Prince T1 (8611M)	Norfolk & Suffolk Avn Museum, Flixton	
WF137	Percival P57 Sea Prince C1	Privately owned, Booker	
WF145	Hawker Sea Hawk F1 <ff>	Privately owned, Newton Abbott, Devon	
WF219	Hawker Sea Hawk F1 <rf>	FAA Museum, stored RNAS Yeovilton	
WF225	Hawker Sea Hawk F1 [CU]	RNAS Culdrose, at main gate	
WF259	Hawker Sea Hawk F2 [171/A]	Royal Scottish Mus'm of Flight, E Fortune	
WF369	Vickers Varsity T1 [F]	Newark Air Museum, Winthorpe	
WF372	Vickers Varsity T1 [A]	Brooklands Museum, Weybridge	
WF408	Vickers Varsity T1 (8395M) <ff>	Privately owned, Ashford, Kent	
WF643	Gloster Meteor F8 [P]	Norfolk & Suffolk Avn Museum, Flixton	
WF714	Gloster Meteor F8 (WK914)	Hooton Park Trust	
WF784	Gloster Meteor T7 (7895M)	Gloucestershire Avn Coll, stored Gloucester	
WF825	Gloster Meteor T7 (8359M) [A]	Montrose Air Station Heritage Centre	
WF911	EE Canberra B2 [CO] <ff>	Gloster Aviation Club, Gloucester	
WF922	EE Canberra PR3	Midland Air Museum, Coventry	
WG303	DHC1 Chipmunk T10 (8208M) <ff>	Privately owned, Partridge Green, W Sussex	
WG308	DHC1 Chipmunk T10 (G-BYHL) [8]	Privately owned, Syerston	
WG316	DHC1 Chipmunk T10 (G-BCAH)	Privately owned, Church Fenton	
WG321	DHC1 Chipmunk T10 (G-DHCC)	Privately owned, Wevelgem, Belgium	
WG348	DHC1 Chipmunk T10 (G-BBMV)	Privately owned, Biggin Hill	
WG350	DHC1 Chipmunk T10 (G-BPAL)	Privately owned, Cascais, Portugal	
WG362	DHC1 Chipmunk T10 (8437M/8630M/*WX643*) <ff>	No 1094 Sqn ATC, Ely	
WG407	DHC1 Chipmunk T10 (G-BWMX) [67]	Privately owned, Croydon, Cambs	

Notes	*Serial*	*Type (code/other identity)*	*Owner/operator, location or fate*
	WG418	DHC1 Chipmunk T10 (8209M/G-ATDY) <ff>	No 1940 Sqn ATC, Levenshulme, Gr Manchester
	WG419	DHC1 Chipmunk T10 (8206M) <ff>	Sywell Aviation Museum
	WG422	DHC1 Chipmunk T10 (8394M/G-BFAX) [16]	Privately owned, Eggesford
	WG432	DHC1 Chipmunk T10 [L]	Museum of Army Flying, Middle Wallop
	WG458	DHC1 Chipmunk T10 (N458BG) [2]	Privately owned, Breighton
	WG465	DHC1 Chipmunk T10 (G-BCEY)	Privately owned, White Waltham
	WG469	DHC1 Chipmunk T10 (G-BWJY) [72]	Privately owned, Sligo, Eire
	WG471	DHC1 Chipmunk T10 (8210M) <ff>	Thameside Aviation Museum, East Tilbury
	WG472	DHC1 Chipmunk T10 (G-AOTY)	Privately owned, Bryngwyn Bach, Clwyd
	WG477	DHC1 Chipmunk T10 (8362M/G-ATDP) <ff>	No 281 Sqn ATC, Birkdale, Merseyside
	WG486	DHC1 Chipmunk T10 [G]	RAF BBMF, Coningsby
	WG498	Slingsby T21B Sedbergh TX1 (BGA3245)	Privately owned, Aston Down
	WG511	Avro 696 Shackleton T4 (fuselage)	Flambards Village Theme Park, Helston
	WG655	Hawker Sea Fury T20 (NX20MD) [910/GN]	The Fighter Collection, Duxford
	WG719	WS51 Dragonfly HR5 (G-BRMA)	The Helicopter Museum, Weston-super-Mare
	WG724	WS51 Dragonfly HR5 [932]	North-East Aircraft Museum, Usworth
	WG751	WS51 Dragonfly HR5 [710/GJ]	World Naval Base, Chatham
	WG760	EE P1A (7755M)	RAF Museum, Cosford
	WG763	EE P1A (7816M)	Museum of Science & Industry, Manchester
	WG768	Short SB5 (8005M)	RAF Museum, Cosford
	WG774	BAC 221	Science Museum, at FAA Museum, RNAS Yeovilton
	WG777	Fairey FD2 (7986M)	RAF Museum, Cosford
	WG789	EE Canberra B2/6 <ff>	Norfolk & Suffolk Avn Museum, Flixton
	WH132	Gloster Meteor T7 (7906M) [J]	RAF Leconfield, for display
	WH166	Gloster Meteor T7 (8052M) [A]	Privately owned, Birlingham, Worcs
	WH291	Gloster Meteor F8	Privately owned, Booker
	WH301	Gloster Meteor F8 (7930M) [T]	RAF Museum, Hendon
	WH364	Gloster Meteor F8 (8169M)	Gloucestershire Avn Coll, stored Gloucester
	WH453	Gloster Meteor D16 [L]	Bentwaters Cold War Air Museum
	WH646	EE Canberra T17A <ff>	Midland Air Museum, Coventry
	WH657	EE Canberra B2	Brenzett Aeronautical Museum
	WH725	EE Canberra B2	Imperial War Museum, Duxford
	WH734	EE Canberra B2(mod) <ff>	Privately owned, Pershore
	WH739	EE Canberra B2 <ff>	No 2475 Sqn ATC, Ammanford, Dyfed
	WH740	EE Canberra T17 (8762M) [K]	East Midlands Airport Aeropark
	WH773	EE Canberra PR7 (8696M)	Gatwick Aviation Museum, Charlwood, Surrey
	WH775	EE Canberra PR7 (8128M/8868M) <ff>	Privately owned, Welshpool
	WH779	EE Canberra PR7 <ff>	Newark Air Museum, Winthorpe
	WH779	EE Canberra PR7 [BP] <rf>	RAF, stored Shawbury
	WH792	EE Canberra PR7 (WH791/ 8165M/8176M/8187M)	Newark Air Museum, Winthorpe
	WH798	EE Canberra PR7 (8130M) <ff>	Privately owned, Kesgrave, Suffolk
	WH840	EE Canberra T4 (8350M)	Privately owned, Flixton
	WH846	EE Canberra T4	Yorkshire Air Museum, Elvington
	WH850	EE Canberra T4 <ff>	Privately owned, Narborough
	WH863	EE Canberra T17 (8693M) <ff>	Newark Air Museum, Winthorpe
	WH876	EE Canberra B2(mod) <ff>	Boscombe Down Aviation Collection
	WH887	EE Canberra TT18 [847] <ff>	Privately owned, Upwood, Cambs
	WH903	EE Canberra B2 <ff>	Yorkshire Air Museum, Elvington
	WH904	EE Canberra T19	Newark Air Museum, Winthorpe
	WH953	EE Canberra B6(mod) <ff>	Blyth Valley Aviation Collection, Walpole, Suffolk
	WH957	EE Canberra E15 (8869M) <ff>	Lincolnshire Avn Heritage Centre, East Kirkby
	WH960	EE Canberra B15 (8344M) <ff>	Rolls-Royce Heritage Trust, Derby
	WH964	EE Canberra E15 (8870M) <ff>	Privately owned, Lewes
	WH984	EE Canberra B15 (8101M) <ff>	City of Norwich Aviation Museum
	WH991	WS51 Dragonfly HR3	Yorkshire Helicopter Preservation Group, Elvington

Serial	Type (code/other identity)	Owner/operator, location or fate	Notes
WJ231	Hawker Sea Fury FB11 (*WE726*) [115/O]	FAA Museum, RNAS Yeovilton	
WJ306	Slingsby T21B Sedbergh TX1 (BGA3240)	Privately owned, Weston-on-the-Green	
WJ306	Slingsby T21B Sedbergh TX1 (WB957/BGA2720)	Privately owned, Parham Park, Sussex	
WJ358	Auster AOP6 (G-ARYD)	Museum of Army Flying, Middle Wallop	
WJ368	Auster AOP6 (G-ASZX)	Privately owned, Eggesford	
WJ404	Auster AOP6 (G-ASOI)	Privately owned, Wickenby	
WJ476	Vickers Valetta T3 <ff>	North-East Aircraft Museum, Usworth	
WJ565	EE Canberra T17 (8871M) <ff>	Aeroventure, Doncaster	
WJ567	EE Canberra B2 <ff>	Privately owned, Houghton, Cambs	
WJ576	EE Canberra T17 <ff>	Boulton Paul Association, Wolverhampton	
WJ633	EE Canberra T17 <ff>	City of Norwich Aviation Museum	
WJ639	EE Canberra TT18 [39]	North-East Aircraft Museum, Usworth	
WJ676	EE Canberra B2 (7796M) <ff>	Privately owned, South Shields	
WJ677	EE Canberra B2 <ff>	Privately owned, Redruth	
WJ717	EE Canberra TT18 (9052M) <ff>	RAF St Athan, Fire Section	
WJ721	EE Canberra TT18 [21] <ff>	No 2405 Det Flt ATC, Gairloch	
WJ731	EE Canberra B2T [BK] <ff>	Privately owned, Golders Green	
WJ775	EE Canberra B6 (8581M) <ff>	Privately owned, Upwood, Cambs	
WJ821	EE Canberra PR7 (8668M)	Army, Bassingbourn, on display	
WJ865	EE Canberra T4	Boscombe Down Aviation Collection	
WJ866	EE Canberra T4	MoD, Bicester	
WJ880	EE Canberra T4 (8491M) <ff>	Dumfries & Galloway Avn Mus, Dumfries	
WJ903	Vickers Varsity T1 <ff>	Aeroventure, Doncaster	
WJ945	Vickers Varsity T1 (G-BEDV) [21]	Imperial War Museum, Duxford	
WJ975	EE Canberra T19 <ff>	Aeroventure, Doncaster	
WJ992	EE Canberra T4	Bournemouth Airport Fire Section	
WK001	Thales Watchkeeper 450 UAV (4X-USC)	Thales, for Army	
WK002	Thales Watchkeeper 450 UAV	Thales, for Army	
WK003	Thales Watchkeeper 450 UAV	Thales, for Army	
WK004	Thales Watchkeeper 450 UAV	Thales, for Army	
WK005	Thales Watchkeeper 450 UAV	Thales, for Army	
WK006	Thales Watchkeeper 450 UAV	Thales, for Army	
WK007	Thales Watchkeeper 450 UAV	Thales, for Army	
WK008	Thales Watchkeeper 450 UAV	Thales, for Army	
WK009	Thales Watchkeeper 450 UAV	Thales, for Army	
WK010	Thales Watchkeeper 450 UAV	Thales, for Army	
WK011	Thales Watchkeeper 450 UAV	Thales, for Army	
WK012	Thales Watchkeeper 450 UAV	Thales, for Army	
WK013	Thales Watchkeeper 450 UAV	Thales, for Army	
WK014	Thales Watchkeeper 450 UAV	Thales, for Army	
WK015	Thales Watchkeeper 450 UAV	Thales, for Army	
WK016	Thales Watchkeeper 450 UAV	Thales, for Army	
WK017	Thales Watchkeeper 450 UAV	Thales, for Army	
WK018	Thales Watchkeeper 450 UAV	Thales, for Army	
WK019	Thales Watchkeeper 450 UAV	Thales, for Army	
WK020	Thales Watchkeeper 450 UAV	Thales, for Army	
WK021	Thales Watchkeeper 450 UAV	Thales, for Army	
WK022	Thales Watchkeeper 450 UAV	Thales, for Army	
WK023	Thales Watchkeeper 450 UAV	Thales, for Army	
WK024	Thales Watchkeeper 450 UAV	Thales, for Army	
WK025	Thales Watchkeeper 450 UAV	Thales, for Army	
WK026	Thales Watchkeeper 450 UAV	Thales, for Army	
WK027	Thales Watchkeeper 450 UAV	Thales, for Army	
WK028	Thales Watchkeeper 450 UAV	Thales, for Army	
WK029	Thales Watchkeeper 450 UAV	Thales, for Army	
WK030	Thales Watchkeeper 450 UAV	Thales, for Army	
WK031	Thales Watchkeeper 450 UAV	Thales, for Army	
WK032	Thales Watchkeeper 450 UAV	Thales, for Army	
WK033	Thales Watchkeeper 450 UAV	Thales, for Army	
WK034	Thales Watchkeeper 450 UAV	Thales, for Army	
WK035	Thales Watchkeeper 450 UAV	Thales, for Army	
WK036	Thales Watchkeeper 450 UAV	Thales, for Army	
WK037	Thales Watchkeeper 450 UAV	Thales, for Army	
WK038	Thales Watchkeeper 450 UAV	Thales, for Army	
WK039	Thales Watchkeeper 450 UAV	Thales, for Army	
WK040	Thales Watchkeeper 450 UAV	Thales, for Army	
WK060	Thales Watchkeeper 450 UAV	Thales, for Army	

Notes	Serial	Type (code/other identity)	Owner/operator, location or fate
	WK102	EE Canberra T17 (8780M) <ff>	Privately owned, Welshpool
	WK118	EE Canberra TT18 <ff>	Hawker Hunter Aviation Ltd, Scampton
	WK122	EE Canberra TT18 <ff>	Privately owned, Chipperfield, Herts
	WK124	EE Canberra TT18 (9093M) [CR]	MoD DFTDC, Manston
	WK126	EE Canberra TT18 (N2138J) [843]	Gloucestershire Avn Coll, stored Gloucester
	WK127	EE Canberra TT18 (8985M) <ff>	Privately owned, Peterborough
	WK146	EE Canberra B2 <ff>	Gatwick Aviation Museum, Charlwood, Surrey
	WK163	EE Canberra B2/6 (G-BVWC)	Air Atlantique Classic Flight, Coventry
	WK198	VS Swift F4 (7428M) (fuselage)	Privately owned, Haverigg
	WK275	VS Swift F4	Privately owned, Upper Hill, nr Leominster
	WK277	VS Swift FR5 (7719M) [N]	Newark Air Museum, Winthorpe
	WK281	VS Swift FR5 (7712M) [S]	Tangmere Military Aviation Museum
	WK393	DH112 Venom FB1 <ff>	Aeroventure, Doncaster
	WK436	DH112 Venom FB50 (J-1614/G-VENM)	Air Atlantique Classic Flight, Coventry
	WK512	DHC1 Chipmunk T10 (G-BXIM) [A]	Privately owned, Brize Norton
	WK514	DHC1 Chipmunk T10 (G-BBMO)	Privately owned, Wellesbourne Mountford
	WK517	DHC1 Chipmunk T10 (G-ULAS)	Privately owned, Denham
	WK518	DHC1 Chipmunk T10 [K]	RAF BBMF, Coningsby
	WK522	DHC1 Chipmunk T10 (G-BCOU)	Privately owned, Duxford
	WK549	DHC1 Chipmunk T10 (G-BTWF)	Privately owned, Breighton
	WK570	DHC1 Chipmunk T10 (8211M) <ff>	No 424 Sqn ATC, Solent Sky, Southampton
	WK576	DHC1 Chipmunk T10 (8357M) <ff>	No 1206 Sqn ATC, Lichfield
	WK577	DHC1 Chipmunk T10 (G-BCYM)	Privately owned, Oaksey Park
	WK584	DHC1 Chipmunk T10 (7556M) <ff>	No 511 Sqn ATC, Ramsey, Cambs
	WK585	DHC1 Chipmunk T10 (9265M/ G-BZGA)	Privately owned, Duxford
	WK586	DHC1 Chipmunk T10 (G-BXGX) [V]	Privately owned, Slinfold
	WK590	DHC1 Chipmunk T10 (G-BWVZ) [69]	Privately owned, Spanhoe
	WK608	DHC1 Chipmunk T10 [906]	RN Historic Flight, Yeovilton
	WK609	DHC1 Chipmunk T10 (G-BXDN) [93]	Privately owned, Booker
	WK611	DHC1 Chipmunk T10 (G-ARWB)	Privately owned, Thruxton
	WK620	DHC1 Chipmunk T10 [T] (fuselage)	Privately owned, Twyford, Bucks
	WK622	DHC1 Chipmunk T10 (G-BCZH)	Privately owned, Horsford
	WK624	DHC1 Chipmunk T10 (G-BWHI)	Privately owned, Woodvale
	WK626	DHC1 Chipmunk T10 (8213M) <ff>	Aeroventure, stored Doncaster
	WK628	DHC1 Chipmunk T10 (G-BBMW)	Privately owned, Goodwood
	WK630	DHC1 Chipmunk T10 (G-BXDG)	Privately owned, Felthorpe
	WK633	DHC1 Chipmunk T10 (G-BXEC) [A]	Privately owned, Redhill
	WK635	DHC1 Chipmunk T10 (G-HFRH)	Privately owned, Henley-on-Thames
	WK638	DHC1 Chipmunk T10 (G-BWJZ) (fuselage)	Privately owned, South Molton, Devon
	WK640	DHC1 Chipmunk T10 (G-BWUV) [C]	Privately owned, Bagby
	WK642	DHC1 Chipmunk T10 (G-BXDP) [94]	Privately owned, Kilrush, Eire
	WK654	Gloster Meteor F8 (8092M) [B]	City of Norwich Aviation Museum
	WK800	Gloster Meteor D16 [Z]	Boscombe Down Aviation Collection
	WK864	Gloster Meteor F8 (WL168/7750M) [C]	Yorkshire Air Museum, Elvington
	WK935	Gloster Meteor Prone Pilot (7869M)	RAF Museum, Cosford
	WK991	Gloster Meteor F8 (7825M)	Imperial War Museum, Duxford
	WL131	Gloster Meteor F8 (7751M) <ff>	Aeroventure, Doncaster
	WL181	Gloster Meteor F8 [X]	North-East Aircraft Museum, Usworth
	WL332	Gloster Meteor T7 [888]	Privately owned, Long Marston
	WL345	Gloster Meteor T7	St Leonard's Motors, Hollington, E Sussex
	WL349	Gloster Meteor T7	Gloucestershire Airport, Staverton, on display
	WL375	Gloster Meteor T7(mod)	Dumfries & Galloway Avn Mus, Dumfries
	WL405	Gloster Meteor T7	Hooton Park Trust
	WL419	Gloster Meteor T7(mod)	Martin Baker Aircraft, Chalgrove
	WL505	DH100 Vampire FB9 (7705M/ G-FBIX)	Privately owned, Bournemouth
	WL626	Vickers Varsity T1 (G-BHDD) [P]	East Midlands Airport Aeropark

Serial	Type (code/other identity)	Owner/operator, location or fate	Notes
WL627	Vickers Varsity T1 (8488M) [D] <ff>	Privately owned, Preston, E Yorkshire	
WL679	Vickers Varsity T1 (9155M)	RAF Museum, Cosford	
WL732	BP P108 Sea Balliol T21	RAF Museum, stored Cosford	
WL795	Avro 696 Shackleton MR2C (8753M) [T]	RAF St Mawgan, on display	
WL798	Avro 696 Shackleton MR2C (8114M) <ff>	Privately owned, Elgin	
WM145	AW Meteor NF11 <ff>	Privately owned, Gatenby, N Yorks	
WM167	AW Meteor NF11 (G-LOSM)	Air Atlantique Classic Flight, Kemble	
WM224	AW Meteor TT20 (*WM311*/8177M)	East Midlands Airport Aeropark	
WM267	AW Meteor NF11 <ff>	City of Norwich Aviation Museum	
WM292	AW Meteor TT20 [841]	FAA Museum, stored RNAS Yeovilton	
WM366	AW Meteor NF13 (4X-FNA) (comp VZ462)	Privately owned, Enstone	
WM367	AW Meteor NF13 <ff>	East Midlands Airport Aeropark	
WM571	DH112 Sea Venom FAW21 [VL]	Solent Sky, stored Romsey	
WM729	DH113 Vampire NF10 <ff>	Mosquito Aircraft Museum, stored London Colney	
WM913	Hawker Sea Hawk FB5 (8162M) [456/J]	Newark Air Museum, Winthorpe	
WM961	Hawker Sea Hawk FB5 [J]	Caernarfon Air World	
WM969	Hawker Sea Hawk FB5 [10/Z]	Imperial War Museum, Duxford	
WN105	Hawker Sea Hawk FB3 (WF299/8164M)	Privately owned, Birlingham, Worcs	
WN108	Hawker Sea Hawk FB5 [033]	Ulster Aviation Society, Long Kesh	
WN149	BP P108 Balliol T2 [AT]	Boulton Paul Association, Wolverhampton	
WN411	Fairey Gannet AS1 (fuselage)	Privately owned, Sholing, Hants	
WN493	WS51 Dragonfly HR5	FAA Museum, RNAS Yeovilton	
WN499	WS51 Dragonfly HR5	Aeroventure, Doncaster	
WN516	BP P108 Balliol T2 <ff>	Privately owned, Haverigg	
WN534	BP P108 Balliol T2 <ff>	Boulton Paul Association, Wolverhampton	
WN890	Hawker Hunter F2 <ff>	Air Defence Collection, Boscombe Down	
WN904	Hawker Hunter F2 (7544M) [3]	RE 39 Regt, Waterbeach, on display	
WN907	Hawker Hunter F2 (7416M) <ff>	Robertsbridge Aviation Society, Newhaven	
WN957	Hawker Hunter F5 <ff>	Privately owned, Stockport	
WP185	Hawker Hunter F5 (7583M)	Privately owned, Great Dunmow, Essex	
WP190	Hawker Hunter F5 (7582M/8473M/ *WP180*) [K]	Tangmere Military Aviation Museum	
WP255	DH113 Vampire NF10 <ff>	Aeroventure, Doncaster	
WP269	EoN Eton TX1 (BGA3214)	Privately owned, stored Keevil	
WP270	EoN Eton TX1 (8598M)	RAF Museum Reserve Collection, Stafford	
WP308	Percival P57 Sea Prince T1 (G-GACA) [572/CU]	Gatwick Aviation Museum, Charlwood, Surrey	
WP313	Percival P57 Sea Prince T1 [568/CU]	FAA Museum, stored RNAS Yeovilton	
WP314	Percival P57 Sea Prince T1 (8634M) [573/CU]	Privately owned, Carlisle Airport	
WP321	Percival P57 Sea Prince T1 (G-BRFC) [750/CU]	Privately owned, Bournemouth	
WP772	DHC1 Chipmunk T10 [Q] (wreck)	RAF Manston History Museum	
WP784	DHC1 Chipmunk T10 <ff>	East Midlands Airport Aeropark	
WP788	DHC1 Chipmunk T10 (G-BCHL)	Privately owned, Sleap	
WP790	DHC1 Chipmunk T10 (G-BBNC) [T]	Mosquito Aircraft Museum, London Colney	
WP795	DHC1 Chipmunk T10 (G-BVZZ) [901]	Privately owned, Lee-on-Solent	
WP800	DHC1 Chipmunk T10 (G-BCXN) [2]	Privately owned, Halton	
WP803	DHC1 Chipmunk T10 (G-HAPY) [G]	Privately owned, Booker	
WP805	DHC1 Chipmunk T10 (G-MAJR) [D]	Privately owned, Lee-on-Solent	
WP808	DHC1 Chipmunk T10 (G-BDEU)	Privately owned, Prestwick	
WP809	DHC1 Chipmunk T10 (G-BVTX) [78]	Privately owned, Husbands Bosworth	
WP833	DHC1 Chipmunk T10 (G-BZDU) [H]	*Sold to the USA, May 2010*	
WP835	DHC1 Chipmunk T10 (D-ERTY)	Privately owned, Teuge, The Netherlands	
WP840	DHC1 Chipmunk T10 (G-BXDM) [9]	Privately owned, Reims, France	
WP844	DHC1 Chipmunk T10 (G-BWOX) [85]	Privately owned, Shobdon	
WP857	DHC1 Chipmunk T10 (G-BDRJ) [24]	Privately owned, Prestwick	
WP859	DHC1 Chipmunk T10 (G-BXCP) [E]	Privately owned, Spanhoe	
WP860	DHC1 Chipmunk T10 (G-BXDA) [6]	Privately owned, Kirknewton	
WP863	DHC1 Chipmunk T10 (8360M/G-ATJI) <ff>	No 1011 Sqn ATC, Boscombe Down	

Notes	*Serial*	*Type (code/other identity)*	*Owner/operator, location or fate*
	WP869	DHC1 Chipmunk T10 (8215M) <ff>	Mosquito Aircraft Museum, London Colney
	WP870	DHC1 Chipmunk T10 (G-BCOI) [12]	Privately owned, Rayne Hall Farm, Essex
	WP896	DHC1 Chipmunk T10 (G-BWVY)	Privately owned, RAF Halton
	WP901	DHC1 Chipmunk T10 (G-BWNT) [B]	Privately owned, East Midlands Airport
	WP903	DHC1 Chipmunk T10 (G-BCGC)	Privately owned, Henlow
	WP912	DHC1 Chipmunk T10 (8467M)	RAF Museum, Cosford
	WP921	DHC1 Chipmunk T10 (G-ATJJ) <ff>	Privately owned, Brooklands
	WP925	DHC1 Chipmunk T10 (G-BXHA) [C]	Privately owned, Seppe, The Netherlands
	WP927	DHC1 Chipmunk T10 (8216M/G-ATJK) <ff>	Privately owned, St Neots, Cambs
	WP928	DHC1 Chipmunk T10 (G-BXGM) [D]	Privately owned, Shoreham
	WP929	DHC1 Chipmunk T10 (G-BXCV) [F]	Privately owned, Duxford
	WP930	DHC1 Chipmunk T10 (G-BXHF) [J]	Privately owned, Redhill
	WP962	DHC1 Chipmunk T10 (9287M) [C]	RAF Museum, Hendon
	WP971	DHC1 Chipmunk T10 (G-ATHD)	Privately owned, Denham
	WP977	DHC1 Chipmunk T10 (G-BHRD) <ff>	Privately owned, Yateley, Hants
	WP983	DHC1 Chipmunk T10 (G-BXNN) [B]	Privately owned, Eggesford
	WP984	DHC1 Chipmunk T10 (G-BWTO) [H]	Privately owned, Little Gransden
	WR360	DH112 Venom FB50 (J-1626/G-DHSS) [K]	Privately owned, Bournemouth
	WR410	DH112 Venom FB50 (J-1539/G-DHUU/*WE410*)	Privately owned, Bournemouth
	WR410	DH112 Venom FB54 (J-1790/ G-BLKA) [N]	Mosquito Aircraft Museum, London Colney
	WR421	DH112 Venom FB50 (J-1611/ G-DHTT)	Privately owned, Bournemouth
	WR470	DH112 Venom FB50 (J-1542/ G-DHVM)	Air Atlantique Classic Flight, Coventry
	WR539	DH112 Venom FB4 (8399M) <ff>	Mosquito Aircraft Museum, stored London Colney
	WR960	Avro 696 Shackleton AEW2 (8772M)	Museum of Science & Industry, Manchester
	WR963	Avro 696 Shackleton AEW2 [X]	Air Atlantique Classic Flight, Coventry
	WR971	Avro 696 Shackleton MR3 (8119M) [Q]	Fenland & W Norfolk Aviation Museum, Wisbech
	WR974	Avro 696 Shackleton MR3 (8117M) [K]	Gatwick Aviation Museum, Charlwood, Surrey
	WR977	Avro 696 Shackleton MR3 (8186M) [B]	Newark Air Museum, Winthorpe
	WR982	Avro 696 Shackleton MR3 (8106M) [J]	Gatwick Aviation Museum, Charlwood, Surrey
	WR985	Avro 696 Shackleton MR3 (8103M) [H]	Privately owned, Long Marston
	WS103	Gloster Meteor T7 [709]	FAA Museum, stored RNAS Yeovilton
	WS692	Gloster Meteor NF12 (7605M) [C]	Newark Air Museum, Winthorpe
	WS726	Gloster Meteor NF14 (7960M) [H]	No 1855 Sqn ATC, Royton, Gr Manchester
	WS739	Gloster Meteor NF14 (7961M)	Newark Air Museum, Winthorpe
	WS760	Gloster Meteor NF14 (7964M)	East Midlands Airport Aeropark
	WS776	Gloster Meteor NF14 (7716M) [K]	Bournemouth Aviation Museum
	WS788	Gloster Meteor NF14 (7967M) [Z]	Yorkshire Air Museum, Elvington
	WS792	Gloster Meteor NF14 (7965M) [K]	Brighouse Bay Caravan Park, Borgue, D&G
	WS807	Gloster Meteor NF14 (7973M) [N]	Gloucestershire Avn Coll, stored Gloucester
	WS832	Gloster Meteor NF14	Solway Aviation Society, Carlisle
	WS838	Gloster Meteor NF14 [D]	Midland Air Museum, Coventry
	WS843	Gloster Meteor NF14 (7937M) [J]	RAF Museum, Cosford
	WT121	Douglas Skyraider AEW1 [415/CU]	FAA Museum, stored RNAS Yeovilton
	WT205	EE Canberra B15 <ff>	RAF Manston History Museum
	WT308	EE Canberra B(I)6	RN, Predannack Fire School
	WT309	EE Canberra B(I)6 <ff>	Farnborough Air Sciences Trust, Farnborough

Serial	*Type (code/other identity)*	*Owner/operator, location or fate*	*Notes*
WT319	EE Canberra B(I)6 <ff>	Aeroventure, Doncaster	
WT333	EE Canberra B6(mod) (G-BVXC)	Privately owned, Bruntingthorpe	
WT339	EE Canberra B(I)8 (8198M)	RAF Barkston Heath Fire Section	
WT483	EE Canberra T4 [83]	*Sold to Malta, 2010*	
WT486	EE Canberra T4 (8102M) <ff>	Privately owned, Newtownards	
WT507	EE Canberra PR7 (8131M/8548M) [44] <ff>	No 384 Sqn ATC, Mansfield	
WT520	EE Canberra PR7 (8094M/8184M) <ff>	No 967 Sqn ATC, Warton	
WT525	EE Canberra T22 [855] <ff>	Privately owned, St Mawgan	
WT532	EE Canberra PR7 (8728M/8890M) <ff>	Bournemouth Aviation Museum	
WT534	EE Canberra PR7 (8549M) [43] <ff>	Privately owned, Upwood	
WT536	EE Canberra PR7 (8063M) <ff>	Privately owned, Shirrell Heath, Hants	
WT537	EE Canberra PR7	Privately owned, Millom	
WT555	Hawker Hunter F1 (7499M)	Vanguard Haulage, Greenford, London	
WT569	Hawker Hunter F1 (7491M)	No 2117 Sqn ATC, Kenfig Hill, Mid-Glamorgan	
WT612	Hawker Hunter F1 (7496M)	RAF Henlow, on display	
WT619	Hawker Hunter F1 (7525M)	RAF Museum, stored Cosford	
WT648	Hawker Hunter F1 (7530M) <ff>	Air Defence Collection, Boscombe Down	
WT651	Hawker Hunter F1 (7532M) [C]	Newark Air Museum, Winthorpe	
WT660	Hawker Hunter F1 (7421M) [C]	Highland Aviation Museum, Inverness	
WT680	Hawker Hunter F1 (7533M) [J]	Privately owned, Holbeach, Lincs	
WT684	Hawker Hunter F1 (7422M) <ff>	Privately owned, Olney, Bucks	
WT694	Hawker Hunter F1 (7510M)	Caernarfon Air World	
WT711	Hawker Hunter GA11 [833/DD]	Privately owned, Spark Bridge, Cumbria	
WT720	Hawker Hunter F51 (RDAF E-408/ 8565M) [B]	Privately owned, North Scarle, Lincs	
WT722	Hawker Hunter T8C (G-BWGN) [878/VL]	Privately owned, Coventry	
WT741	Hawker Hunter GA11 [791] <ff>	Privately owned, Doncaster	
WT744	Hawker Hunter GA11 [868/VL]	Privately owned, Ilfracombe	
WT804	Hawker Hunter GA11 [831/DD]	FETC, Moreton-in-Marsh, Glos	
WT806	Hawker Hunter GA11	Privately owned, Bruntingthorpe	
WT859	Supermarine 544 <ff>	Boscombe Down Aviation Collection	
WT867	Slingsby T31B Cadet TX3	Privately owned, Eaglescott	
WT877	Slingsby T31B Cadet TX3	Air Training Heritage Collection, Wolverhampton	
WT899	Slingsby T31B Cadet TX3	*Sold to the Netherlands*	
WT900	Slingsby T31B Cadet TX3 (BGA33372)	Privately owned, Lee-on-Solent	
WT905	Slingsby T31B Cadet TX3	Privately owned, Keevil	
WT908	Slingsby T31B Cadet TX3 (BGA3487)	Privately owned, Dunstable	
WT910	Slingsby T31B Cadet TX3 (BGA3953)	Privately owned, Llantisilio	
WT914	Slingsby T31B Cadet TX3 (BGA3194) (fuselage)	Privately owned, Tibenham	
WT933	Bristol 171 Sycamore 3 (G-ALSW/7709M)	Newark Air Museum, Winthorpe	
WV106	Douglas Skyraider AEW1 [427/C]	FAA Museum, stored RNAS Yeovilton	
WV198	Sikorsky S55 Whirlwind HAR21 (G-BJWY) [K]	Solway Aviation Society, Carlisle	
WV318	Hawker Hunter T7B (9236M/ G-FFOX)	Delta Jets, Kemble	
WV322	Hawker Hunter T8C (G-BZSE/ 9096M) [Y]	Hunter Flying Ltd, Exeter	
WV332	Hawker Hunter F4 (7673M) <ff>	Tangmere Military Aircraft Museum	
WV372	Hawker Hunter T7 (G-BXFI) [R]	Privately owned, Exeter	
WV381	Hawker Hunter GA11 [732] <ff>	Privately owned, Chiltern Park, Wallingford	
WV382	Hawker Hunter GA11 [830/VL]	East Midlands Airport Aeropark	
WV383	Hawker Hunter T7	Farnborough Air Sciences Trust, Farnborough	
WV396	Hawker Hunter T8C (9249M) [91]	RAF Valley, at main gate	
WV486	Percival P56 Provost T1 (7694M) [N-D]	Privately owned, Thatcham, Berks	
WV493	Percival P56 Provost T1 (G-BDYG/ 7696M) [29]	Royal Scottish Mus'm of Flight, stored E Fortune	
WV499	Percival P56 Provost T1 (G-BZRF/ 7698M) [P-G]	Privately owned, Westonzoyland, Somerset	

Notes	*Serial*	*Type (code/other identity)*	*Owner/operator, location or fate*
	WV514	Percival P56 Provost T51 (G-BLIW) [N-C]	Privately owned, Shoreham
	WV562	Percival P56 Provost T1 (7606M) [P-C]	RAF Museum, Cosford
	WV605	Percival P56 Provost T1 [T-B]	Norfolk & Suffolk Avn Museum, Flixton
	WV606	Percival P56 Provost T1 (7622M)[P-B]	Newark Air Museum, Winthorpe
	WV679	Percival P56 Provost T1 (7615M) [O-J]	Wellesbourne Wartime Museum
	WV705	Percival P66 Pembroke C1 <ff>	Privately owned, Awbridge, Hants
	WV740	Percival P66 Pembroke C1 (G-BNPH)	Privately owned, Bournemouth
	WV746	Percival P66 Pembroke C1 (8938M)	RAF Museum, Cosford
	WV781	Bristol 171 Sycamore HR12 (G-ALTD/7839M) <ff>	Caernarfon Air World
	WV783	Bristol 171 Sycamore HR12 (G-ALSP/7841M)	RAF Museum, Hendon
	WV787	EE Canberra B2/8 (8799M)	Newark Air Museum, Winthorpe
	WV795	Hawker Sea Hawk FGA6 (8151M)	Privately owned, Dunsfold
	WV797	Hawker Sea Hawk FGA6 (8155M) [491/J]	Midland Air Museum, Coventry
	WV798	Hawker Sea Hawk FGA6 [026/CU]	Privately owned, Booker
	WV838	Hawker Sea Hawk FGA4 [182] <ff>	Privately owned, Liverpool
	WV856	Hawker Sea Hawk FGA6 [163]	FAA Museum, RNAS Yeovilton
	WV903	Hawker Sea Hawk FGA4 (8153M) [128] <ff>	Privately owned, Mold, Flintshire
	WV903	Hawker Sea Hawk FGA4 (8153M) [C] <rf>	The Griffin Trust, Hooton Park
	WV908	Hawker Sea Hawk FGA6 (8154M) [188/A]	RN Historic Flight, Yeovilton
	WV910	Hawker Sea Hawk FGA6 <ff>	Boscombe Down Aviation Collection
	WV911	Hawker Sea Hawk FGA4 [115/C]	RN Historic Flight, stored Yeovilton
	WW138	DH112 Sea Venom FAW22 [227/Z]	FAA Museum, stored RNAS Yeovilton
	WW145	DH112 Sea Venom FAW22 [680/LM]	Royal Scottish Mus'm of Flight, E Fortune
	WW217	DH112 Sea Venom FAW22 [351]	Newark Air Museum, Winthorpe
	WW388	Percival P56 Provost T1 (7616M) [O-F]	Privately owned, stored Hinstock, Shrops
	WW421	Percival P56 Provost T1 (WW450/G-BZRE/7689M) [P-B]	Bournemouth Aviation Museum
	WW442	Percival P56 Provost T1 (7618M) [N]	Gatwick Aviation Museum, Charlwood, Surrey
	WW444	Percival P56 Provost T1 [D]	Privately owned, Brownhills, Staffs
	WW447	Percival P56 Provost T1	Privately owned, Grazeley, Berks
	WW453	Percival P56 Provost T1 (G-TMKI) [W-S]	Privately owned, Westonzoyland, Somerset
	WW654	Hawker Hunter GA11 [834/DD]	Privately owned, Ford, W Sussex
	WW664	Hawker Hunter F4 <ff>	Privately owned, Spanhoe
	WX788	DH112 Venom NF3	Aeroventure, Doncaster
	WX853	DH112 Venom NF3 (7443M)	Mosquito Aircraft Museum, stored London Colney
	WX905	DH112 Venom NF3 (7458M)	Newark Air Museum, Winthorpe
	WZ425	DH115 Vampire T11	Privately owned, Birlingham, Worcs
	WZ450	DH115 Vampire T11 <ff>	Privately owned, Corscombe, Dorset
	WZ507	DH115 Vampire T11 (G-VTII) [74]	Vampire Preservation Group, North Weald
	WZ515	DH115 Vampire T11 [60]	Solway Aviation Society, Carlisle
	WZ518	DH115 Vampire T11 [B]	North-East Aircraft Museum, Usworth
	WZ549	DH115 Vampire T11 (8118M) [F]	Ulster Aviation Society, Long Kesh
	WZ553	DH115 Vampire T11 (G-DHYY) <ff>	Privately owned, Stockton, Warks
	WZ557	DH115 Vampire T11	Privately owned, Leeming
	WZ572	DH115 Vampire T11 (8124M) [65] <ff>	Privately owned, Sholing, Hants
	WZ581	DH115 Vampire T11 <ff>	The Vampire Collection, Hemel Hempstead
	WZ584	DH115 Vampire T11 (G-BZRC) [K]	Privately owned, Cantley, Norfolk
	WZ589	DH115 Vampire T11 [19]	Privately owned, Rochester
	WZ589	DH115 Vampire T55 (U-1230/LN-DHZ)	Privately owned, Norway
	WZ590	DH115 Vampire T11 [19]	Imperial War Museum, Duxford

Serial	Type (code/other identity)	Owner/operator, location or fate	Notes
WZ662	Auster AOP9 (G-BKVK)	Privately owned, Eggesford	
WZ706	Auster AOP9 (7851M/G-BURR)	Privately owned, Carlisle	
WZ711	Auster AOP9/Beagle E3 (G-AVHT)	Privately owned, Spanhoe	
WZ721	Auster AOP9	Museum of Army Flying, Middle Wallop	
WZ724	Auster AOP9 (7432M)	AAC Middle Wallop, at main gate	
WZ729	Auster AOP9 (G-BXON)	Privately owned, Newark-on-Trent	
WZ736	Avro 707A (7868M)	Museum of Science & Industry, Manchester	
WZ744	Avro 707C (7932M)	RAF Museum, Cosford	
WZ753	Slingsby T38 Grasshopper TX1	Solent Sky, Southampton	
WZ755	Slingsby T38 Grasshopper TX1 (BGA3481)	Boulton Paul Association, Wolverhampton	
WZ757	Slingsby T38 Grasshopper TX1 (comp XK820)	Privately owned, Kirton-in-Lindsey, Lincs	
WZ767	Slingsby T38 Grasshopper TX1	North-East Aircraft Museum, stored Usworth	
WZ772	Slingsby T38 Grasshopper TX1	Trenchard Museum, RAF Halton	
WZ773	Slingsby T38 Grasshopper TX1	Edinburgh Academy	
WZ784	Slingsby T38 Grasshopper TX1	Privately owned, stored Southend	
WZ791	Slingsby T38 Grasshopper TX1 (8944M)	RAF Museum, Hendon	
WZ792	Slingsby T38 Grasshopper TX1	*Destroyed by fire, July 2010*	
WZ793	Slingsby T38 Grasshopper TX1	Privately owned, Keevil	
WZ796	Slingsby T38 Grasshopper TX1	Privately owned, stored Nympsfield	
WZ798	Slingsby T38 Grasshopper TX1	Bournemouth Aviation Museum, stored	
WZ816	Slingsby T38 Grasshopper TX1 (BGA3979)	Privately owned, Redhill	
WZ818	Slingsby T38 Grasshopper TX1 (BGA4361)	Privately owned, Nympsfield	
WZ819	Slingsby T38 Grasshopper TX1 (BGA3498)	Privately owned, Halton	
WZ820	Slingsby T38 Grasshopper TX1	Sywell Aviation Museum	
WZ822	Slingsby T38 Grasshopper TX1	Aeroventure, stored Doncaster	
WZ824	Slingsby T38 Grasshopper TX1	Solway Aviation Society, Carlisle	
WZ826	Vickers Valiant B(K)1 (XD826/7872M) <ff>	Privately owned, Rayleigh, Essex	
WZ828	Slingsby T38 Grasshopper TX1 (BGA4421)	Privately owned, Hullavington	
WZ831	Slingsby T38 Grasshopper TX1	Privately owned, stored Nympsfield, Glos	
WZ846	DHC1 Chipmunk T10 (G-BCSC/8439M)	No 2427 Sqn ATC, Biggin Hill	
WZ847	DHC1 Chipmunk T10 (G-CPMK) [F]	Privately owned, Sleap	
WZ869	DHC1 Chipmunk T10 (8019M) <ff>	Privately owned, Leicester	
WZ872	DHC1 Chipmunk T10 (G-BZGB) [E]	Privately owned, Blackpool	
WZ876	DHC1 Chipmunk T10 (G-BBWN) <ff>	Privately owned, Yateley, Hants	
WZ879	DHC1 Chipmunk T10 (G-BWUT) [X]	Privately owned, Duxford	
WZ882	DHC1 Chipmunk T10 (G-BXGP) [K]	Privately owned, Eaglescott	
XA109	DH115 Sea Vampire T22	Royal Scottish Mus'm of Flight, Leuchars	
XA127	DH115 Sea Vampire T22 <ff>	FAA Museum, RNAS Yeovilton	
XA129	DH115 Sea Vampire T22	FAA Museum, stored RNAS Yeovilton	
XA225	Slingsby T38 Grasshopper TX1	Privately owned, Keevil	
XA226	Slingsby T38 Grasshopper TX1	Norfolk & Suffolk Avn Museum, Flixton	
XA228	Slingsby T38 Grasshopper TX1	Royal Scottish Mus'm of Flight, stored Granton	
XA230	Slingsby T38 Grasshopper TX1 (BGA4098)	Privately owned, Henlow	
XA231	Slingsby T38 Grasshopper TX1 (8888M)	RAF Manston History Museum	
XA240	Slingsby T38 Grasshopper TX1 (BGA4556)	Privately owned, Portmoak, Perth & Kinross	
XA241	Slingsby T38 Grasshopper TX1	Shuttleworth Collection, Old Warden	
XA243	Slingsby T38 Grasshopper TX1 (8886M)	Privately owned, Gransden Lodge, Cambs	
XA244	Slingsby T38 Grasshopper TX1	Privately owned, Keevil	
XA282	Slingsby T31B Cadet TX3	Caernarfon Air World	
XA289	Slingsby T31B Cadet TX3	Privately owned, Eaglescott	
XA290	Slingsby T31B Cadet TX3	Privately owned, Portmoak, Perth & Kinross	
XA293	Slingsby T31B Cadet TX3 <ff>	Privately owned, Breighton	
XA295	Slingsby T31B Cadet TX3 (BGA3336)	Privately owned, Aston Down	
XA302	Slingsby T31B Cadet TX3 (BGA3786)	RAF Museum, Hendon	

Notes	Serial	Type (code/other identity)	Owner/operator, location or fate
	XA310	Slingsby T31B Cadet TX3 (BGA4963)	Privately owned, Hullavington
	XA459	Fairey Gannet ECM6 [E]	Privately owned, White Waltham
	XA460	Fairey Gannet ECM6 [768/BY]	Aeroventure, Doncaster
	XA466	Fairey Gannet COD4 [777/LM]	FAA Museum, stored RNAS Yeovilton
	XA508	Fairey Gannet T2 [627/GN]	FAA Museum, at Midland Air Museum, Coventry
	XA564	Gloster Javelin FAW1 (7464M)	RAF Museum, Cosford
	XA634	Gloster Javelin FAW4 (7641M)	RAF Leeming, on display
	XA699	Gloster Javelin FAW5 (7809M)	Midland Air Museum, Coventry
	XA847	EE P1B (8371M)	Privately owned, Stowmarket, Suffolk
	XA862	WS55 Whirlwind HAR1 (G-AMJT) <ff>	Yorkshire Helicopter Preservation Group, Elvington
	XA864	WS55 Whirlwind HAR1	FAA Museum, stored RNAS Yeovilton
	XA870	WS55 Whirlwind HAR1 [911]	Aeroventure, Doncaster
	XA880	DH104 Devon C2 (G-BVXR)	Privately owned, Little Rissington
	XA893	Avro 698 Vulcan B1 (8591M) <ff>	RAF Museum, Cosford
	XA903	Avro 698 Vulcan B1 <ff>	Privately owned, Wellesbourne Mountford
	XA917	HP80 Victor B1 (7827M) <ff>	Privately owned, Cupar, Fife
	XB259	Blackburn B101 Beverley C1 (G-AOAI)	Fort Paull Armoury
	XB261	Blackburn B101 Beverley C1 <ff>	Newark Air Museum, Winthorpe
	XB446	Grumman TBM-3 Avenger ECM6B	FAA Museum, Yeovilton
	XB480	Hiller HT1 [537]	FAA Museum, stored RNAS Yeovilton
	XB812	Canadair CL-13 Sabre F4 (9227M) [U]	RAF Museum, Cosford
	XD145	Saro SR53	RAF Museum, Cosford
	XD163	WS55 Whirlwind HAR10 (8645M) [X]	The Helicopter Museum, Weston-super-Mare
	XD165	WS55 Whirlwind HAR10 (8673M)	Caernarfon Airfield Fire Section
	XD215	VS Scimitar F1 <ff>	Privately owned, Cheltenham
	XD235	VS Scimitar F1 <ff>	Privately owned, Olney, Bucks
	XD317	VS Scimitar F1 [112/R]	FAA Museum, RNAS Yeovilton
	XD332	VS Scimitar F1 [194/C]	Solent Sky, stored Romsey
	XD375	DH115 Vampire T11 (7887M)	Privately owned, Elland, W Yorks
	XD377	DH115 Vampire T11 (8203M) <ff>	Aeroventure, stored Doncaster
	XD425	DH115 Vampire T11 <ff>	Privately owned, Haverigg
	XD434	DH115 Vampire T11 [25]	Fenland & W Norfolk Aviation Museum, Wisbech
	XD445	DH115 Vampire T11 [51]	Privately owned, Abbots Bromley
	XD447	DH115 Vampire T11 [50]	East Midlands Airport Aeropark
	XD452	DH115 Vampire T11 (7990M) [66] <ff>	Privately owned, Dursley, Glos
	XD459	DH115 Vampire T11 [63] <ff>	Aeroventure, stored Doncaster
	XD506	DH115 Vampire T11 (7983M)	Gloucestershire Avn Coll, stored Gloucester
	XD515	DH115 Vampire T11 (7998M/*XM515*)	RAF Museum Restoration Centre, Cosford
	XD534	DH115 Vampire T11 [41]	East Midlands Airport Aeropark
	XD542	DH115 Vampire T11 (7604M) [N]	Montrose Air Station Heritage Centre
	XD547	DH115 Vampire T11 [Z] (composite)	Dumfries & Galloway Avn Mus, Dumfries
	XD593	DH115 Vampire T11	Newark Air Museum, Winthorpe
	XD595	DH115 Vampire T11 <ff>	Privately owned, Glentham, Lincs
	XD596	DH115 Vampire T11 (7939M)	Solent Sky, Southampton
	XD599	DH115 Vampire T11 [A] <ff>	Sywell Aviation Museum
	XD602	DH115 Vampire T11 (7737M) <ff>	Privately owned, Ripon
	XD616	DH115 Vampire T11 [56]	Mosquito Aircraft Museum, stored Gloucester
	XD622	DH115 Vampire T11 (8160M)	No 2214 Sqn ATC, Usworth
	XD624	DH115 Vampire T11	Privately owned, Millom
	XD626	DH115 Vampire T11 [Q]	Midland Air Museum, stored Coventry
	XD674	Hunting Jet Provost T1 (7570M)	RAF Museum, Cosford
	XD693	Hunting Jet Provost T1 (XM129/G-AOBU) [Z-Q]	Kennet Aviation, North Weald
	XD816	Vickers Valiant B(K)1 <ff>	Brooklands Museum, Weybridge
	XD818	Vickers Valiant B(K)1 (7894M)	RAF Museum, Cosford
	XD857	Vickers Valiant B(K)1 <ff>	Norfolk & Suffolk Aviation Museum, Flixton
	XD875	Vickers Valiant B(K)1 <ff>	Highland Aviation Museum, Inverness

Serial	Type (code/other identity)	Owner/operator, location or fate	Notes
XE317	Bristol 171 Sycamore HR14 (G-AMWO) [S-N]	Aeroventure, stored Doncaster	
XE339	Hawker Sea Hawk FGA6 (8156M) [149] <ff>	Privately owned, Glos	
XE339	Hawker Sea Hawk FGA6 (8156M) [E] <rf>	Privately owned, Hooton Park	
XE340	Hawker Sea Hawk FGA6 [131/Z]	FAA Museum, stored RNAS Yeovilton	
XE364	Hawker Sea Hawk FGA6 (G-JETH) (comp WM983) [485/J]	Gatwick Aviation Museum, Charlwood, Surrey	
XE368	Hawker Sea Hawk FGA6 [200/J]	Privately owned, Barrow-in-Furness	
XE521	Fairey Rotodyne Y (parts)	The Helicopter Museum, Weston-super-Mare	
XE584	Hawker Hunter FGA9 <ff>	Privately owned, Hooton Park	
XE597	Hawker Hunter FGA9 (8874M) <ff>	Privately owned, Halfpenny Green	
XE601	Hawker Hunter FGA9 (G-ETPS)	Skyblue Aviation Ltd, Exeter	
XE606	Hawker Hunter F6A (*XJ673*/8841M)	RAF Cottesmore, preserved	
XE624	Hawker Hunter FGA9 (8875M) [G]	Privately owned, Metheringham	
XE627	Hawker Hunter F6A [T]	Imperial War Museum, Duxford	
XE643	Hawker Hunter FGA9 (8586M) <ff>	RAF M&RU, Aldergrove	
XE650	Hawker Hunter FGA9 (G-9-449) <ff>	Farnborough Air Sciences Trust, Farnborough	
XE664	Hawker Hunter F4 <ff>	Gloucestershire Avn Coll, stored Gloucester	
XE665	Hawker Hunter T8C (G-BWGM) [876/VL]	Air Atlantique Classic Flight, Kemble	
XE668	Hawker Hunter GA11 [832/DD]	Hamburger Hill Paintball, Marksbury, Somerset	
XE670	Hawker Hunter F4 (7762M/8585M) <ff>	RAF Museum, Cosford	
XE683	Hawker Hunter F51 (RDAF E-409) [G]	City of Norwich Aviation Museum	
XE685	Hawker Hunter GA11 (G-GAII) [861/VL]	Privately owned, Exeter	
XE689	Hawker Hunter GA11 (G-BWGK) [864/VL]	Privately owned, Kemble	
XE707	Hawker Hunter GA11 (N707XE) [863]	Bentwaters Cold War Museum	
XE786	Slingsby T31B Cadet TX3 (BGA4033)	Privately owned, Arbroath	
XE793	Slingsby T31B Cadet TX3 (8666M)	Privately owned, Tamworth	
XE796	Slingsby T31B Cadet TX3	*Scrapped*	
XE799	Slingsby T31B Cadet TX3 (8943M) [R]	Privately owned, Abbots Bromley	
XE802	Slingsby T31B Cadet TX3 (BGA5283)	Privately owned, Shipdham	
XE849	DH115 Vampire T11 (7928M) [V3]	Privately owned, Barton	
XE852	DH115 Vampire T11 [H]	No 2247 Sqn ATC, Hawarden	
XE855	DH115 Vampire T11	Midland Air Museum, stored Coventry	
XE856	DH115 Vampire T11 (G-DUSK)	Bournemouth Aviation Museum	
XE864	DH115 Vampire T11(comp XD435) <ff>	Privately owned, Ingatestone, Essex	
XE872	DH115 Vampire T11 [62]	Midland Air Museum, Coventry	
XE874	DH115 Vampire T11 (8582M)	Paintball Commando, Sandel, W Yorks	
XE897	DH115 Vampire T11 (XD403)	Privately owned, Errol, Tayside	
XE921	DH115 Vampire T11 [64] <ff>	Privately owned, Yarmouth, IoW	
XE935	DH115 Vampire T11	Aeroventure, Doncaster	
XE946	DH115 Vampire T11 (7473M) <ff>	RAF Cranwell Aviation Heritage Centre	
XE956	DH115 Vampire T11 (G-OBLN)	De Havilland Aviation, stored Rochester	
XE979	DH115 Vampire T11 [54]	Privately owned, Birlingham, Worcs	
XE982	DH115 Vampire T11 (7564M) [01]	Privately owned, Weston, Eire	
XE985	DH115 Vampire T11 (*WZ476*)	Hunter Flying Ltd, Exeter	
XE993	DH115 Vampire T11 (8161M) <ff>	Privately owned, Staffs	
XE998	DH115 Vampire T11 (*U-1215*)	Solent Sky, Southampton	
XF113	VS Swift F7 [19] <ff>	Boscombe Down Aviation Collection	
XF114	VS Swift F7 (G-SWIF)	Solent Sky, stored Romsey	
XF314	Hawker Hunter F51 (RDAF E-412) [N]	Brooklands Museum, Weybridge	
XF321	Hawker Hunter T7 <ff>	Privately owned, Crediton, Devon	
XF321	Hawker Hunter T7 <rf>	Phoenix Aviation, Bruntingthorpe	
XF375	Hawker Hunter F6A (8736M/G-BUEZ) [05]	Boscombe Down Aviation Collection	
XF382	Hawker Hunter F6A [15]	Midland Air Museum, Coventry	
XF383	Hawker Hunter F6 (8706M) <ff>	Gloucester Aviation Club, Gloucester	

Notes	Serial	Type (code/other identity)	Owner/operator, location or fate
	XF418	Hawker Hunter F51 (RDAF E-430)	Gatwick Aviation Museum, Charlwood, Surrey
	XF506	Hawker Hunter F4 (WT746/7770M) [A]	Dumfries & Galloway Avn Mus, Dumfries
	XF509	Hawker Hunter F6 (8708M)	Fort Paull Armoury
	XF522	Hawker Hunter F6 <ff>	No 2366 Sqn ATC, Bletchley Park
	XF526	Hawker Hunter F6 (8679M) [78/E]	Privately owned, Birlingham, Worcs
	XF527	Hawker Hunter F6 (8680M)	RAF Halton, on display
	XF545	Percival P56 Provost T1 (7957M) [O-K]	Privately owned, Thatcham
	XF597	Percival P56 Provost T1 (G-BKFW) [AH]	Privately owned, Brimpton, Berks
	XF603	Percival P56 Provost T1 (G-KAPW)	Shuttleworth Collection, Old Warden
	XF690	Percival P56 Provost T1 (8041M/G-MOOS)	Kennet Aviation, Yeovilton
	XF708	Avro 716 Shackleton MR3 [C]	Imperial War Museum, Duxford
	XF785	Bristol 173 (7648M/G-ALBN)	Bristol Aero Collection, Kemble
	XF836	Percival P56 Provost T1 (8043M/G-AWRY) [JG]	Privately owned, Thatcham
	XF926	Bristol 188 (8368M)	RAF Museum, Cosford
	XF940	Hawker Hunter F4 <ff>	Privately owned, Kew Stoke, Somerset
	XF994	Hawker Hunter T8C (G-CGHU) [873/VL]	Hawker Hunter Aviation, Scampton
	XF995	Hawker Hunter T8B (G-BZSF/9237M) [K]	Hawker Hunter Aviation, Scampton
	XG154	Hawker Hunter FGA9 (8863M) [54]	RAF Museum, Hendon
	XG160	Hawker Hunter F6A (8831M/G-BWAF) [U]	Bournemouth Aviation Museum
	XG164	Hawker Hunter F6 (8681M)	Privately owned, Wellington, Somerset
	XG168	Hawker Hunter F6A (XG172/8832M) [10]	City of Norwich Aviation Museum
	XG190	Hawker Hunter F51 (RDAF E-425) [C]	Solway Aviation Society, Carlisle
	XG193	Hawker Hunter FGA9 (XG297) (comp with WT741) <ff>	Aeroventure, Doncaster
	XG194	Hawker Hunter PR11 (WT723/G-PRII) [N]	Hunter Flying Ltd, Exeter
	XG195	Hawker Hunter FGA9 <ff>	Privately owned, Lewes
	XG196	Hawker Hunter F6A (8702M) [31]	Army, Mytchett, Surrey, on display
	XG209	Hawker Hunter F6 (8709M) <ff>	Privately owned, Kingston-on-Thames
	XG210	Hawker Hunter F6	Privately owned, Beck Row, Suffolk
	XG225	Hawker Hunter F6A (8713M)	DCAE Cosford, at main gate
	XG226	Hawker Hunter F6A (8800M) <ff>	RAF Manston History Museum
	XG252	Hawker Hunter FGA9 (8840M) [U]	Privately owned, Bosbury, Hereford
	XG254	Hawker Hunter FGA9 (8881M)	Norfolk & Suffolk Avn Museum, Flixton
	XG274	Hawker Hunter F6 (8710M) [71]	Privately owned, Newmarket
	XG290	Hawker Hunter F6 (8711M) <ff>	Air Defence Collection, Boscombe Down
	XG290	Hawker Hunter T7 (comp XL578 & XL586)	Privately owned, Kirkstead, Lincs
	XG297	Hawker Hunter FGA9 <ff>	Aeroventure, Doncaster
	XG325	EE Lightning F1 <ff>	No 1476 Sqn ATC, Southend
	XG329	EE Lightning F1 (8050M)	Privately owned, Flixton
	XG331	EE Lightning F1 <ff>	Privately owned, Glos
	XG337	EE Lightning F1 (8056M) [M]	RAF Museum, Cosford
	XG452	Bristol 192 Belvedere HC1 (7997M/G-BRMB)	The Helicopter Museum, Weston-super-Mare
	XG454	Bristol 192 Belvedere HC1 (8366M)	Museum of Science & Industry, Manchester
	XG462	Bristol 192 Belvedere HC1 <ff>	The Helicopter Museum, stored Weston-super-Mare
	XG474	Bristol 192 Belvedere HC1 (8367M) [O]	RAF Museum, Hendon
	XG502	Bristol 171 Sycamore HR14	Museum of Army Flying, Middle Wallop
	XG518	Bristol 171 Sycamore HR14 (8009M) [S-E]	Norfolk & Suffolk Avn Museum, Flixton
	XG523	Bristol 171 Sycamore HR14 <ff> [V]	Norfolk & Suffolk Avn Museum, Flixton
	XG574	WS55 Whirlwind HAR3 [752/PO]	FAA Museum, stored RNAS Yeovilton
	XG588	WS55 Whirlwind HAR3 (G-BAMH/VR-BEP)	East Midlands Airport Aeropark

Serial	Type (code/other identity)	Owner/operator, location or fate	Notes
XG592	WS55 Whirlwind HAS7	Task Force Adventure Park, Cowbridge, S Glam	
XG594	WS55 Whirlwind HAS7 [517]	FAA Museum, stored Yeovilton	
XG596	WS55 Whirlwind HAS7 [66]	The Helicopter Museum, Weston-super-Mare	
XG613	DH112 Sea Venom FAW21	Imperial War Museum, Duxford	
XG629	DH112 Sea Venom FAW22	Privately owned, Stone, Staffs	
XG680	DH112 Sea Venom FAW22 [438]	North-East Aircraft Museum, Usworth	
XG692	DH112 Sea Venom FAW22 [668/LM]	Privately owned, Stockport	
XG730	DH112 Sea Venom FAW22 [499/A]	Mosquito Aircraft Museum, London Colney	
XG736	DH112 Sea Venom FAW22	Privately owned, East Midlands	
XG737	DH112 Sea Venom FAW22 [220/Z]	East Midlands Airport Aeropark	
XG743	DH115 Sea Vampire T22 [597/LM]	Imperial War Museum, Duxford	
XG797	Fairey Gannet ECM6 [277]	Imperial War Museum, Duxford	
XG831	Fairey Gannet ECM6 [396]	Davidstow Airfield & Cornwall At War Museum	
XG882	Fairey Gannet T5 (8754M) [771/LM]	Privately owned, Errol, Tayside	
XG883	Fairey Gannet T5 [773/BY]	FAA Museum, at Museum of Berkshire Aviation, Woodley	
XG900	Short SC1	Science Museum, South Kensington	
XG905	Short SC1	Ulster Folk & Transpt Mus, Holywood, Co Down	
XH131	EE Canberra PR9	Ulster Aviation Society, Long Kesh	
XH134	EE Canberra PR9 (G-OMHD)	Privately owned, Kemble	
XH135	EE Canberra PR9	Privately owned, Kemble	
XH136	EE Canberra PR9 (8782M) [W] <ff>	Privately owned, Spanhoe	
XH165	EE Canberra PR9 <ff>	Blyth Valley Aviation Collection, Walpole	
XH168	EE Canberra PR9	RAF Marham Fire Section	
XH169	EE Canberra PR9	RAF Marham, on display	
XH170	EE Canberra PR9 (8739M)	RAF Wyton, on display	
XH171	EE Canberra PR9 (8746M) [U]	RAF Museum, Cosford	
XH174	EE Canberra PR9 <ff>	Privately owned, Staffs	
XH175	EE Canberra PR9 <ff>	Privately owned, Bewdley, Worcs	
XH177	EE Canberra PR9 <ff>	Newark Air Museum, Winthorpe	
XH278	DH115 Vampire T11 (8595M/7866M) [42]	Yorkshire Air Museum, Elvington	
XH313	DH115 Vampire T11 (G-BZRD) [E]	Tangmere Military Aviation Museum	
XH318	DH115 Vampire T11 (7761M) [64]	Privately owned, Sholing, Hants	
XH328	DH115 Vampire T11 <ff>	Privately owned, Norfolk	
XH330	DH115 Vampire T11 [73]	Privately owned, Camberley, Surrey	
XH537	Avro 698 Vulcan B2MRR (8749M) <ff>	Privately owned, Bournemouth	
XH558	Avro 698 Vulcan B2 (G-VLCN)	Vulcan To The Sky Trust, Lyneham	
XH560	Avro 698 Vulcan K2 <ff>	Privately owned, Foulness	
XH563	Avro 698 Vulcan B2MRR <ff>	Privately owned, Over Dinsdale, N Yorks	
XH584	EE Canberra T4 (G-27-374) <ff>	Aeroventure, Doncaster	
XH592	HP80 Victor B1A (8429M) <ff>	Phoenix Aviation, Bruntingthorpe	
XH648	HP80 Victor K1A	Imperial War Museum, Duxford	
XH669	HP80 Victor K2 (9092M) <ff>	Privately owned, Foulness	
XH670	HP80 Victor SR2 <ff>	Privately owned, Foulness	
XH672	HP80 Victor K2 (9242M)	RAF Museum, Cosford	
XH673	HP80 Victor K2 (8911M)	RAF Marham, on display	
XH767	Gloster Javelin FAW9 (7955M) [L]	Yorkshire Air Museum, Elvington	
XH783	Gloster Javelin FAW7 (7798M) <ff>	Privately owned, Catford	
XH837	Gloster Javelin FAW7 (8032M) <ff>	Caernarfon Air World	
XH892	Gloster Javelin FAW9R (7982M) [J]	Norfolk & Suffolk Avn Museum, Flixton	
XH897	Gloster Javelin FAW9	Imperial War Museum, Duxford	
XH903	Gloster Javelin FAW9 (7938M)	Gloucester Airport, on display	
XH992	Gloster Javelin FAW8 (7829M) [P]	Newark Air Museum, Winthorpe	
XJ314	RR Thrust Measuring Rig	Science Museum, South Kensington	
XJ380	Bristol 171 Sycamore HR14 (8628M)	Boscombe Down Aviation Collection	
XJ389	Fairey Jet Gyrodyne (XD759/G-AJJP)	Museum of Berkshire Aviation, Woodley	
XJ398	WS55 Whirlwind HAR10 (XD768/G-BDBZ)	Aeroventure, Doncaster	
XJ409	WS55 Whirlwind HAR10 (XD779)	*Scrapped at Llanbedr*	
XJ435	WS55 Whirlwind HAR10 (XD804/8671M) [V]	RAF Manston History Museum, spares use	
XJ476	DH110 Sea Vixen FAW1 <ff>	Boscombe Down Aviation Collection	
XJ481	DH110 Sea Vixen FAW1 [VL]	FAA Museum, stored RNAS Yeovilton	

Notes	Serial	Type (code/other identity)	Owner/operator, location or fate
	XJ482	DH110 Sea Vixen FAW1 [713/VL]	Norfolk & Suffolk Avn Museum, Flixton
	XJ488	DH110 Sea Vixen FAW1 <ff>	Robertsbridge Aviation Society, Mayfield
	XJ494	DH110 Sea Vixen FAW2 [121/E]	Privately owned, Bruntingthorpe
	XJ560	DH110 Sea Vixen FAW2 (8142M) [243/H]	Newark Air Museum, Winthorpe
	XJ565	DH110 Sea Vixen FAW2 [127/E]	Mosquito Aircraft Museum, London Colney
	XJ571	DH110 Sea Vixen FAW2 (8140M) [242/R]	Solent Sky, Southampton
	XJ575	DH110 Sea Vixen FAW2 <ff> [SAH-13]	Wellesbourne Wartime Museum
	XJ579	DH110 Sea Vixen FAW2 <ff>	Midland Air Museum, Coventry
	XJ580	DH110 Sea Vixen FAW2 [131/E]	Tangmere Military Aviation Museum
	XJ714	Hawker Hunter FR10 (comp XG226)	East Midlands Airport Aeropark
	XJ723	WS55 Whirlwind HAR10	Privately owned, Newcastle upon Tyne
	XJ726	WS55 Whirlwind HAR10	Caernarfon Air World
	XJ727	WS55 Whirlwind HAR10 (8661M) [L]	Privately owned, Ramsgate
	XJ758	WS55 Whirlwind HAR10 (8464M) <ff>	Privately owned, Welshpool
	XJ771	DH115 Vampire T55 (U-1215/G-HELV)	Air Atlantique Classic Flight, Coventry
	XJ772	DH115 Vampire T11 [H]	Mosquito Aircraft Museum, London Colney
	XJ823	Avro 698 Vulcan B2A	Solway Aviation Society, Carlisle
	XJ824	Avro 698 Vulcan B2A	Imperial War Museum, Duxford
	XJ917	Bristol 171 Sycamore HR14 [H-S]	Bristol Sycamore Group, stored Kemble
	XJ918	Bristol 171 Sycamore HR14 (8190M)	RAF Museum, Cosford
	XK416	Auster AOP9 (7855M/G-AYUA)	Privately owned, Widmerpool
	XK417	Auster AOP9 (G-AVXY)	Privately owned, Messingham, Lincs
	XK418	Auster AOP9 (7976M)	Privately owned, South Molton, Devon
	XK421	Auster AOP9 (8365M) (frame)	Privately owned, South Molton, Devon
	XK488	Blackburn NA39 Buccaneer S1	FAA Museum, stored RNAS Yeovilton
	XK526	Blackburn NA39 Buccaneer S2 (8648M)	RAF Honington, at main gate
	XK527	Blackburn NA39 Buccaneer S2D (8818M) <ff>	Privately owned, North Wales
	XK532	Blackburn NA39 Buccaneer S1 (8867M) [632/LM]	Highland Aviation Museum, Inverness
	XK533	Blackburn NA39 Buccaneer S1 <ff>	Royal Scottish Mus'm of Flight, stored Granton
	XK590	DH115 Vampire T11 [V]	Wellesbourne Wartime Museum
	XK623	DH115 Vampire T11 (*G-VAMP*) [56]	Caernarfon Air World
	XK624	DH115 Vampire T11 [32]	Norfolk & Suffolk Avn Museum, Flixton
	XK625	DH115 Vampire T11 [14]	Brenzett Aeronautical Museum
	XK627	DH115 Vampire T11 <ff>	Privately owned,
	XK632	DH115 Vampire T11 <ff>	Privately owned, Greenford, London
	XK637	DH115 Vampire T11 [56]	Privately owned, Millom
	XK695	DH106 Comet C2(RC) (G-AMXH/9164M) <ff>	Mosquito Aircraft Museum, London Colney
	XK699	DH106 Comet C2 (7971M)	RAF Lyneham on display
	XK724	Folland Gnat F1 (7715M)	RAF Museum, Cosford
	XK740	Folland Gnat F1 (8396M)	Solent Sky, Southampton
	XK776	ML Utility 1	Museum of Army Flying, Middle Wallop
	XK788	Slingsby T38 Grasshopper TX1	*Destroyed by fire, July 2010*
	XK789	Slingsby T38 Grasshopper TX1	Midland Air Museum, stored Coventry
	XK790	Slingsby T38 Grasshopper TX1	Privately owned, stored Husbands Bosworth
	XK819	Slingsby T38 Grasshopper TX1	Privately owned, Breighton
	XK822	Slingsby T38 Grasshopper TX1	Privately owned, Partridge Green, W Sussex
	XK885	Percival P66 Pembroke C1 (8452M/N46EA)	Gatwick Aviation Museum, Charlwood, Surrey
	XK895	DH104 Sea Devon C20 (G-SDEV) [19/CU]	Air Atlantique Classic Flight, Coventry
	XK907	WS55 Whirlwind HAS7	Midland Air Museum, stored Coventry
	XK911	WS55 Whirlwind HAS7 [519/PO]	Privately owned, Shepherds Bush
	XK936	WS55 Whirlwind HAS7 [62]	Imperial War Museum, Duxford
	XK940	WS55 Whirlwind HAS7 (G-AYXT) [911]	The Helicopter Museum, Weston-super-Mare
	XK970	WS55 Whirlwind HAR10 (8789M)	Army, Bramley, Hants

Serial	Type (code/other identity)	Owner/operator, location or fate	Notes
XL149	Blackburn B101 Beverley C1 (7988M) <ff>	Aeroventure, Doncaster	
XL160	HP80 Victor K2 (8910M) <ff>	Norfolk & Suffolk Avn Museum, Flixton	
XL164	HP80 Victor K2 (9215M) <ff>	Gatwick Aviation Museum, Charlwood, Surrey	
XL190	HP80 Victor K2 (9216M) <ff>	RAF Manston History Museum	
XL231	HP80 Victor K2	Yorkshire Air Museum, Elvington	
XL318	Avro 698 Vulcan B2 (8733M)	RAF Museum, Hendon	
XL319	Avro 698 Vulcan B2	North-East Aircraft Museum, Usworth	
XL360	Avro 698 Vulcan B2A	Midland Air Museum, Coventry	
XL388	Avro 698 Vulcan B2 <ff>	Aeroventure, Doncaster	
XL426	Avro 698 Vulcan B2 (G-VJET)	Vulcan Restoration Trust, Southend	
XL445	Avro 698 Vulcan K2 (8811M) <ff>	Norfolk & Suffolk Avn Museum, Flixton	
XL449	Fairey Gannet AEW3 <ff>	Privately owned, Camberley, Surrey	
XL472	Fairey Gannet AEW3 [044/R]	Gatwick Aviation Museum, Charlwood, Surrey	
XL497	Fairey Gannet AEW3 [041/R]	Dumfries & Galloway Avn Mus, Dumfries	
XL500	Fairey Gannet AEW3 (G-KAEW) [CU]	Hunter Flying Ltd, Exeter	
XL502	Fairey Gannet AEW3 (8610M/G-BMYP)	Yorkshire Air Museum, Elvington	
XL503	Fairey Gannet AEW3 [070/E]	FAA Museum, RNAS Yeovilton	
XL563	Hawker Hunter T7 (9218M)	Privately owned, Southmoor, Oxon	
XL565	Hawker Hunter T7 (parts of WT745) [Y]	Privately owned, Bruntingthorpe	
XL568	Hawker Hunter T7A (9224M) [X]	RAF Museum, Cosford	
XL569	Hawker Hunter T7 (8833M)	East Midlands Airport Aeropark	
XL571	Hawker Hunter T7 (XL572/8834M/G-HNTR) [V]	Yorkshire Air Museum, Elvington	
XL573	Hawker Hunter T7 (G-BVGH)	Hunter Flying Ltd, Exeter	
XL577	Hawker Hunter T7 (G-BXKF/8676M)	Privately owned, Kemble	
XL578	Hawker Hunter T7 (comp XL586)	*Rebuilt as XG290, 2010*	
XL580	Hawker Hunter T8M [723]	FAA Museum, RNAS Yeovilton	
XL586	Hawker Hunter T7 (comp XL578)	Delta Jets, Kemble	
XL587	Hawker Hunter T7 (8807M/G-HPUX) [Z]	Hawker Hunter Aviation, stored Scampton	
XL591	Hawker Hunter T7	Gatwick Aviation Museum, Charlwood, Surrey	
XL592	Hawker Hunter T7 (8836M) [Y]	Hunter Flying Club, Kemble	
XL601	Hawker Hunter T7 (G-BZSR) [874/VL]	Classic Fighters, Brustem, Belgium	
XL602	Hawker Hunter T8M (G-BWFT)	Hunter Flying Ltd, Exeter	
XL609	Hawker Hunter T7 <ff>	Privately owned, Yarmouth, IoW	
XL612	Hawker Hunter T7 [2]	Hunter Flying Ltd, Exeter	
XL618	Hawker Hunter T7 (8892M)	Caernarfon Air World	
XL621	Hawker Hunter T7 (G-BNCX)	Privately owned, Dunsfold	
XL623	Hawker Hunter T7 (8770M)	The Planets Leisure Centre, Woking	
XL629	EE Lightning T4	MoD/QinetiQ Boscombe Down, at main gate	
XL703	SAL Pioneer CC1 (8034M)	RAF Museum, Cosford	
XL714	DH82A Tiger Moth II (T6099/G-AOGR)	Privately owned, Boughton, Lincs	
XL716	DH82A Tiger Moth II (T7363/G-AOIL)	Privately owned, Compton Abbas	
XL738	Saro Skeeter AOP12 (7860M)	Privately owned, Aeroventure, Doncaster	
XL739	Saro Skeeter AOP12	AAC, stored Wattisham	
XL762	Saro Skeeter AOP12 (8017M)	Royal Scottish Mus'm of Flight, E Fortune	
XL763	Saro Skeeter AOP12	Privately owned, Aeroventure, Doncaster	
XL764	Saro Skeeter AOP12 (7940M) [J]	Newark Air Museum, Winthorpe	
XL765	Saro Skeeter AOP12	Privately owned, Melksham, Wilts	
XL770	Saro Skeeter AOP12 (8046M)	Solent Sky, Southampton	
XL809	Saro Skeeter AOP12 (G-BLIX)	Privately owned, Wilden, Beds	
XL811	Saro Skeeter AOP12	The Helicopter Museum, Weston-super-Mare	
XL812	Saro Skeeter AOP12 (G-SARO)	AAC Historic Aircraft Flight, stored Middle Wallop	
XL813	Saro Skeeter AOP12	Museum of Army Flying, Middle Wallop	
XL814	Saro Skeeter AOP12	AAC Historic Aircraft Flight, Middle Wallop	
XL824	Bristol 171 Sycamore HR14 (8021M)	RAF Museum Reserve Collection, Stafford	
XL829	Bristol 171 Sycamore HR14	The Helicopter Museum, Weston-super-Mare	
XL840	WS55 Whirlwind HAS7	Privately owned, Bawtry	
XL853	WS55 Whirlwind HAS7 [PO]	FAA Museum, stored RNAS Yeovilton	
XL875	WS55 Whirlwind HAR9	Perth Technical College	

Notes	*Serial*	*Type (code/other identity)*	*Owner/operator, location or fate*
	XL929	Percival P66 Pembroke C1 (G-BNPU)	Air Atlantique Classic Flight, stored Compton Verney
	XL954	Percival P66 Pembroke C1 (9042M/N4234C/G-BXES)	Air Atlantique Classic Flight, Coventry
	XL993	SAL Twin Pioneer CC1 (8388M)	RAF Museum, Cosford
	XM135	BAC Lightning F1 [B]	Imperial War Museum, Duxford
	XM144	BAC Lightning F1 (8417M) <ff>	Privately owned, Spark Bridge, Cumbria
	XM169	BAC Lightning F1A (8422M) <ff>	Highland Aviation Museum, Inverness
	XM172	BAC Lightning F1A (8427M)	Privately owned, Spark Bridge, Cumbria
	XM173	BAC Lightning F1A (8414M) [A]	Privately owned, Newton-with¬-Scales, Lancs
	XM191	BAC Lightning F1A (7854M/8590M) <ff>	RAF M&RU, Bottesford
	XM192	BAC Lightning F1A (8413M) [K]	Thorpe Camp Preservation Group, Lincs
	XM223	DH104 Devon C2 (G-BWWC) [J]	Air Atlantique Classic Flight, stored Compton Verney
	XM279	EE Canberra B(I)8 <ff>	Privately owned, Flixton
	XM300	WS58 Wessex HAS1	Privately owned, Nantgarw, Rhondda
	XM328	WS58 Wessex HAS3 [653/PO]	The Helicopter Museum, Weston-super-Mare
	XM330	WS58 Wessex HAS1	The Helicopter Museum, Weston-super-Mare
	XM349	Hunting Jet Provost T3A (9046M) [T]	*Sold to the USA*
	XM350	Hunting Jet Provost T3A (9036M) [89]	Aeroventure, Doncaster
	XM351	Hunting Jet Provost T3 (8078M) [Y]	RAF Museum, Cosford
	XM355	Hunting Jet Provost T3 (8229M) [D]	Privately owned, Newcastle
	XM358	Hunting Jet Provost T3A (8987M) [53]	Privately owned, Newbridge, Powys
	XM362	Hunting Jet Provost T3 (8230M)	DCAE, No 1 SoTT, Cosford
	XM365	Hunting Jet Provost T3A (G-BXBH) [37]	Privately owned, Bruntingthorpe
	XM369	Hunting Jet Provost T3 (8084M) [C]	Privately owned, Lumb, Lancs
	XM370	Hunting Jet Provost T3A (G-BVSP) [10]	Privately owned, Long Marston
	XM373	Hunting Jet Provost T3 (7726M) [Z] <ff>	Yorkshire Air Museum, Elvington
	XM383	Hunting Jet Provost T3A [90]	Newark Air Museum, Winthorpe
	XM402	Hunting Jet Provost T3 (8055AM) [18]	Fenland & W Norfolk Aviation Museum, Wisbech
	XM404	Hunting Jet Provost T3 (8055BM)	FETC, Moreton-in-Marsh, Glos
	XM409	Hunting Jet Provost T3 (8082M) <ff>	Air Scouts, Guernsey Airport
	XM410	Hunting Jet Provost T3 (8054AM) [B]	Privately owned, Gillingham, Kent
	XM411	Hunting Jet Provost T3 (8434M) <ff>	Aeroventure, Doncaster
	XM412	Hunting Jet Provost T3A (9011M) [41]	Privately owned, Balado Bridge, Scotland
	XM414	Hunting Jet Provost T3A (8996M)	Ulster Aviation Society, Long Kesh
	XM417	Hunting Jet Provost T3 (8054BM) [D] <ff>	Privately owned, Cannock
	XM419	Hunting Jet Provost T3A (8990M) [102]	Privately owned, Newcastle
	XM425	Hunting Jet Provost T3A (8995M) [88]	Privately owned, Longton, Staffs
	XM463	Hunting Jet Provost T3A [38] (fuselage)	RAF Museum, Hendon
	XM468	Hunting Jet Provost T3 (8081M) <ff>	Privately owned, Terrington St Clement, Norfolk
	XM473	Hunting Jet Provost T3A (8974M/*G-TINY*)	Bedford College, instructional use
	XM474	Hunting Jet Provost T3 (8121M) <ff>	No 2517 Sqn ATC, Levenshulme
	XM479	Hunting Jet Provost T3A (G-BVEZ) [54]	Privately owned, Newcastle
	XM480	Hunting Jet Provost T3 (8080M)	4x4 Car Centre, Chesterfield

Serial	*Type (code/other identity)*	*Owner/operator, location or fate*	*Notes*
XM496	Bristol 253 Britannia C1 (EL-WXA)	Britannia Preservation Society, Kemble	
XM497	Bristol 175 Britannia 312F (G-AOVF)	RAF Museum, Cosford	
XM529	Saro Skeeter AOP12 (7979M/G-BDNS)	Privately owned, Handforth	
XM553	Saro Skeeter AOP12 (G-AWSV)	Yorkshire Air Museum, Elvington	
XM555	Saro Skeeter AOP12 (8027M)	RAF Museum, Hendon	
XM569	Avro 698 Vulcan B2 <ff>	Gloucestershire Avn Coll, stored Gloucester	
XM575	Avro 698 Vulcan B2A (G-BLMC)	East Midlands Airport Aeropark	
XM594	Avro 698 Vulcan B2	Newark Air Museum, Winthorpe	
XM597	Avro 698 Vulcan B2	Royal Scottish Mus'm of Flight, E Fortune	
XM598	Avro 698 Vulcan B2 (8778M)	RAF Museum, Cosford	
XM602	Avro 698 Vulcan B2 (8771M) <ff>	Manchester Museum of Science & Industry, stored	
XM603	Avro 698 Vulcan B2	Avro Aircraft Heritage Society, Woodford	
XM607	Avro 698 Vulcan B2 (8779M)	RAF Waddington, on display	
XM612	Avro 698 Vulcan B2	City of Norwich Aviation Museum	
XM651	Saro Skeeter AOP12 (XM561/7980M)	Aeroventure, Doncaster	
XM652	Avro 698 Vulcan B2 <ff>	Privately owned, Welshpool	
XM655	Avro 698 Vulcan B2 (G-VULC)	Privately owned, Wellesbourne Mountford	
XM660	WS55 Whirlwind HAS7	*Scrapped January 2011*	
XM685	WS55 Whirlwind HAS7 (G-AYZJ) [513/PO]	Newark Air Museum, Winthorpe	
XM692	HS Gnat T1 <ff>	Privately owned, Welshpool	
XM693	HS Gnat T1 (7891M)	BAE Systems Hamble, on display	
XM697	HS Gnat T1 (G-NAAT)	Reynard Garden Centre, Carluke, S Lanarkshire	
XM708	HS Gnat T1 (8573M)	Privately owned, Lytham St Annes	
XM715	HP80 Victor K2	Cold War Jets Collection, Bruntingthorpe	
XM717	HP80 Victor K2 <ff>	RAF Museum, Hendon	
XM819	Lancashire EP9 Prospector (G-APXW)	Museum of Army Flying, Middle Wallop	
XM833	WS58 Wessex HAS3	North-East Aircraft Museum, Usworth	
XN126	WS55 Whirlwind HAR10 (8655M) [S]	Pinewood Studios, Elstree	
XN137	Hunting Jet Provost T3 <ff>	Privately owned, South Molton, Devon	
XN156	Slingsby T21B Sedbergh TX1 (BGA3250)	Privately owned, Portmoak	
XN157	Slingsby T21B Sedbergh TX1 (BGA3255)	Privately owned, stored Long Mynd	
XN185	Slingsby T21B Sedbergh TX1 (8942M/BGA4077)	RAF Museum Reserve Collection, Stafford	
XN186	Slingsby T21B Sedbergh TX1 (BGA3905) [HFG]	Privately owned, Watton	
XN187	Slingsby T21B Sedbergh TX1 (BGA3903)	Privately owned, Halton	
XN198	Slingsby T31B Cadet TX3	Privately owned, Bodmin	
XN238	Slingsby T31B Cadet TX3 <ff>	Aeroventure, Doncaster	
XN239	Slingsby T31B Cadet TX3 (8889M) [G]	Imperial War Museum, Duxford	
XN246	Slingsby T31B Cadet TX3	Solent Sky, Southampton	
XN258	WS55 Whirlwind HAR9 [589/CU]	North-East Aircraft Museum, Usworth	
XN297	WS55 Whirlwind HAR9 (XN311) [12]	Privately owned, Hull	
XN298	WS55 Whirlwind HAR9 [810/LS]	Privately owned, Haverigg	
XN299	WS55 Whirlwind HAS7 [758]	Tangmere Military Aviation Museum	
XN304	WS55 Whirlwind HAS7 [WW/B]	Norfolk & Suffolk Avn Museum, Flixton	
XN332	Saro P531 (G-APNV) [759]	FAA Museum, stored RNAS Yeovilton	
XN334	Saro P531	FAA Museum, stored RNAS Yeovilton	
XN341	Saro Skeeter AOP12 (8022M)	Stondon Transport Mus & Garden Centre, Beds	
XN344	Saro Skeeter AOP12 (8018M)	Science Museum, South Kensington	
XN351	Saro Skeeter AOP12 (G-BKSC)	Privately owned, Ipswich	
XN380	WS55 Whirlwind HAS7	RAF Manston History Museum	
XN385	WS55 Whirlwind HAS7	Battleground Paintball, Yarm, Cleveland	
XN386	WS55 Whirlwind HAR9 [435/ED]	Aeroventure, Doncaster	
XN412	Auster AOP9	Auster 9 Group, Melton Mowbray	
XN437	Auster AOP9 (G-AXWA)	Privately owned, North Weald	
XN441	Auster AOP9 (G-BGKT)	Privately owned, Eggesford	
XN458	Hunting Jet Provost T3 (8234M/*XN594*)	Privately owned, Northallerton	

Notes	Serial	Type (code/other identity)	Owner/operator, location or fate
	XN459	Hunting Jet Provost T3A (G-BWOT)	Transair(UK) Ltd, North Weald
	XN462	Hunting Jet Provost T3A [17]	FAA Museum, stored RNAS Yeovilton
	XN466	Hunting Jet Provost T3A [29] <ff>	No 1005 Sqn ATC, Radcliffe, Gr Manchester
	XN492	Hunting Jet Provost T3 (8079M) <ff>	No 2434 Sqn ATC, Church Fenton
	XN493	Hunting Jet Provost T3 (XN137) <ff>	Privately owned, Camberley
	XN494	Hunting Jet Provost T3A (9012M) [43]	Gatwick Aviation Museum, Charlwood, Surrey
	XN500	Hunting Jet Provost T3A	Norfolk & Suffolk Avn Museum, Flixton
	XN503	Hunting Jet Provost T3 <ff>	Boscombe Down Aviation Collection
	XN508	Hunting Jet Provost T3A <ff>	MoD/DSG, St Athan
	XN511	Hunting Jet Provost T3 [64] <ff>	Aeroventure, Doncaster
	XN549	Hunting Jet Provost T3 (8235M) <ff>	Privately owned, Warrington
	XN551	Hunting Jet Provost T3A (8984M)	Privately owned, Felton Common, Bristol
	XN554	Hunting Jet Provost T3 (8436M) [K]	Gunsmoke Paintball, Hadleigh, Suffolk
	XN573	Hunting Jet Provost T3 [E] <ff>	Newark Air Museum, Winthorpe
	XN579	Hunting Jet Provost T3A (9137M) [14]	Gunsmoke Paintball, Hadleigh, Suffolk
	XN582	Hunting Jet Provost T3A (8957M) [95,H]	Privately owned, Bruntingthorpe
	XN584	Hunting Jet Provost T3A (9014M) [E]	Phoenix Aviation, Bruntingthorpe
	XN586	Hunting Jet Provost T3A (9039M) [91,S]	Brooklands Technical College
	XN589	Hunting Jet Provost T3A (9143M) [46]	RAF Linton-on-Ouse, on display
	XN597	Hunting Jet Provost T3 (7984M) <ff>	Privately owned, Haverigg
	XN607	Hunting Jet Provost T3 <ff>	Highland Aviation Museum, Inverness
	XN623	Hunting Jet Provost T3 (XN632/8352M)	Privately owned, Birlingham, Worcs
	XN629	Hunting Jet Provost T3A (G-BVEG/G-KNOT) [49]	Bentwaters Cold War Museum
	XN634	Hunting Jet Provost T3A <ff>	Privately owned, Preston, Lancs
	XN634	Hunting Jet Provost T3A [53] <rf>	BAE Systems Warton Fire Section
	XN637	Hunting Jet Provost T3 (G-BKOU) [03]	Privately owned, North Weald
	XN647	DH110 Sea Vixen FAW2 <ff>	Privately owned, Bicester
	XN650	DH110 Sea Vixen FAW2 [456] <ff>	Privately owned, Spanhoe
	XN651	DH110 Sea Vixen FAW2 <ff>	Privately owned, Olney, Bucks
	XN685	DH110 Sea Vixen FAW2 (8173M) [703/VL]	Midland Air Museum, Coventry
	XN696	DH110 Sea Vixen FAW2 [751] <ff>	Norfolk & Suffolk Avn Museum, Flixton
	XN714	Hunting H126	RAF Museum, Cosford
	XN726	EE Lightning F2A (8545M) <ff>	Boscombe Down Aviation Collection
	XN728	EE Lightning F2A (8546M) [V]	Privately owned, Balderton, Notts
	XN774	EE Lightning F2A (8551M) <ff>	Privately owned, Boston
	XN776	EE Lightning F2A (8535M) [C]	Royal Scottish Mus'm of Flight, E Fortune
	XN795	EE Lightning F2A <ff>	Privately owned, Foulness
	XN817	AW660 Argosy C1	QinetiQ West Freugh Fire Section
	XN819	AW660 Argosy C1 (8205M) <ff>	Newark Air Museum, Winthorpe
	XN923	HS Buccaneer S1 [13]	Gatwick Aviation Museum, Charlwood, Surrey
	XN928	HS Buccaneer S1 (8179M) <ff>	Privately owned, Gravesend
	XN957	HS Buccaneer S1 [630/LM]	FAA Museum, RNAS Yeovilton
	XN964	HS Buccaneer S1 [118/V]	Newark Air Museum, Winthorpe
	XN967	HS Buccaneer S1 [233] <ff>	City of Norwich Aviation Museum
	XN972	HS Buccaneer S1 (8183M/XN962) <ff>	RAF Museum, Cosford
	XN974	HS Buccaneer S2A	Yorkshire Air Museum, Elvington
	XN979	HS Buccaneer S2 <ff>	*Currently not known*
	XN981	HS Buccaneer S2B (fuselage)	Privately owned, Errol
	XN983	HS Buccaneer S2B <ff>	Fenland & W Norfolk Aviation Museum, Wisbech
	XP110	WS58 Wessex HAS3 (A2636)	DCAE AESS, *HMS Sultan*, Gosport
	XP137	WS58 Wessex HAS3 [711/DD]	RN, Predannack Fire School
	XP142	WS58 Wessex HAS3	FAA Museum, stored RNAS Yeovilton
	XP150	WS58 Wessex HAS3 [LS]	FETC, Moreton-in-Marsh, Glos
	XP165	WS Scout AH1	The Helicopter Museum, Weston-super-Mare

Serial	Type (code/other identity)	Owner/operator, location or fate	Notes
XP190	WS Scout AH1	Aeroventure, Doncaster	
XP191	WS Scout AH1	Privately owned, Prenton, The Wirral	
XP226	Fairey Gannet AEW3	Newark Air Museum, Winthorpe	
XP241	Auster AOP9 (G-CEHR)	Privately owned, Eggesford	
XP242	Auster AOP9 (G-BUCI)	AAC Historic Aircraft Flight, Middle Wallop	
XP244	Auster AOP9 (7864M/*M7922*)	Privately owned, Stretton on Dunsmore	
XP248	Auster AOP9 (7863M/WZ679)	Privately owned, Coventry	
XP254	Auster AOP11 (G-ASCC)	Privately owned, Widmerpool	
XP279	Auster AOP9 (G-BWKK)	Privately owned, Popham	
XP280	Auster AOP9	Snibston Discovery Park, Coalville	
XP281	Auster AOP9	Imperial War Museum, Duxford	
XP286	Auster AOP9	Privately owned, Eggesford	
XP299	WS55 Whirlwind HAR10 (8726M)	RAF Museum, Hendon	
XP330	WS55 Whirlwind HAR10	CAA Fire School, Durham/Tees Valley	
XP344	WS55 Whirlwind HAR10 (8764M) [H723]	RAF North Luffenham Training Area	
XP345	WS55 Whirlwind HAR10 (8792M) [N]	Yorkshire Helicopter Preservation Group, Doncaster	
XP346	WS55 Whirlwind HAR10 (8793M)	Privately owned, Long Marston	
XP350	WS55 Whirlwind HAR10	Privately owned, Bassetts Pole, Staffs	
XP351	WS55 Whirlwind HAR10 (8672M) [Z]	Gatwick Aviation Museum, Charlwood, Surrey	
XP355	WS55 Whirlwind HAR10 (8463M/G-BEBC)	City of Norwich Aviation Museum	
XP360	WS55 Whirlwind HAR10 [V]	Privately owned, Bicton, nr Leominster	
XP398	WS55 Whirlwind HAR10 (8794M)	Gatwick Aviation Museum, Charlwood, Surrey	
XP404	WS55 Whirlwind HAR10 (8682M)	The Helicopter Museum, Weston-super-Mare	
XP411	AW660 Argosy C1 (8442M) [C]	RAF Museum, Cosford	
XP454	Slingsby T38 Grasshopper TX1	Privately owned, Sywell	
XP459	Slingsby T38 Grasshopper TX1	Privately owned, stored Nayland, Suffolk	
XP463	Slingsby T38 Grasshopper TX1 (BGA4372)	Privately owned, Lasham	
XP488	Slingsby T38 Grasshopper TX1	Privately owned, Keevil	
XP490	Slingsby T38 Grasshopper TX1 (BGA4552)	Privately owned, stored Watton	
XP492	Slingsby T38 Grasshopper TX1 (BGA3480)	Privately owned, Gallows Hill, Dorset	
XP493	Slingsby T38 Grasshopper TX1	Privately owned, stored Aston Down	
XP494	Slingsby T38 Grasshopper TX1	Privately owned, Wolverhampton	
XP502	HS Gnat T1 (8576M)	Privately owned, Kemble	
XP505	HS Gnat T1	Science Museum, Wroughton	
XP516	HS Gnat T1 (8580M) [16]	Farnborough Air Sciences Trust, Farnborough	
XP540	HS Gnat T1 (8608M) [62]	Privately owned, North Weald	
XP542	HS Gnat T1 (8575M)	Solent Sky, Southampton	
XP556	Hunting Jet Provost T4 (9027M) [B]	RAF Cranwell Aviation Heritage Centre	
XP557	Hunting Jet Provost T4 (8494M) [72]	Dumfries & Galloway Avn Mus, Dumfries	
XP558	Hunting Jet Provost T4 (8627M) <ff>	Privately owned, Sheffield	
XP558	Hunting Jet Provost T4 (8627M) [20] <rf>	Privately owned, Sproughton	
XP563	Hunting Jet Provost T4 (9028M) [C]	Privately owned, Sproughton	
XP568	Hunting Jet Provost T4	East Midlands Airport Aeropark	
XP573	Hunting Jet Provost T4 (8236M) [19]	Jersey Airport Fire Section	
XP585	Hunting Jet Provost T4 (8407M) [24]	NE Wales Institute, Wrexham	
XP627	Hunting Jet Provost T4	North-East Aircraft Museum, stored Usworth	
XP629	Hunting Jet Provost T4 (9026M) [P]	Gunsmoke Paintball, Hadleigh, Suffolk	
XP640	Hunting Jet Provost T4 (8501M) [M]	Yorkshire Air Museum, Elvington	
XP642	Hunting Jet Provost T4 <ff>	Privately owned, Lavendon, Bucks	
XP672	Hunting Jet Provost T4 (8458M/G-RAFI) [03]	Privately owned, Gamston	
XP680	Hunting Jet Provost T4 (8460M)	FETC, Moreton-in-Marsh, Glos	
XP686	Hunting Jet Provost T4 (8401M/8502M) [G]	Gunsmoke Paintball, Hadleigh, Suffolk	
XP701	BAC Lightning F3 (8924M) <ff>	Robertsbridge Aviation Society, Mayfield	
XP703	BAC Lightning F3 <ff>	Lightning Preservation Group, Bruntingthorpe	
XP706	BAC Lightning F3 (8925M)	Aeroventure, Doncaster	
XP743	BAC Lightning F3 <ff>	Wattisham Airfield Museum	
XP745	BAC Lightning F3 (8453M) <ff>	Vanguard Haulage, Greenford, London	

Notes	Serial	Type (code/other identity)	Owner/operator, location or fate
	XP820	DHC2 Beaver AL1	AAC Historic Aircraft Flight, Middle Wallop
	XP821	DHC2 Beaver AL1 [MCO]	Museum of Army Flying, Middle Wallop
	XP822	DHC2 Beaver AL1	Museum of Army Flying, Middle Wallop
	XP831	Hawker P.1127 (8406M)	Science Museum, South Kensington
	XP841	Handley-Page HP115	FAA Museum, RNAS Yeovilton
	XP847	WS Scout AH1	Museum of Army Flying, Middle Wallop
	XP848	WS Scout AH1	DCAE Arborfield, on display
	XP853	WS Scout AH1	Privately owned, Sutton, Surrey
	XP854	WS Scout AH1 (7898M/TAD 043)	Mayhem Paintball, Abridge, Essex
	XP855	WS Scout AH1	DCAE SEAE, Arborfield
	XP856	WS Scout AH1	Privately owned, Gloucester
	XP883	WS Scout AH1	Privately owned, Bruntingthorpe
	XP884	WS Scout AH1	AAC, stored Middle Wallop
	XP885	WS Scout AH1	AAC Wattisham, instructional use
	XP886	WS Scout AH1	The Helicopter Museum, Weston-super-Mare
	XP888	WS Scout AH1	Privately owned, Sproughton
	XP890	WS Scout AH1 [G] (fuselage)	Privately owned, Ipswich
	XP893	WS Scout AH1	AAC Middle Wallop, BDRT
	XP895	WS Scout AH1	Privately owned, Woodley, Berks
	XP899	WS Scout AH1 [D]	DCAE SEAE, Arborfield
	XP900	WS Scout AH1	AAC Wattisham, instructional use
	XP902	WS Scout AH1 <ff>	Aeroventure, Doncaster
	XP905	WS Scout AH1	Privately owned, stored Sproughton
	XP907	WS Scout AH1 (G-SROE)	Privately owned, Wattisham
	XP910	WS Scout AH1	Museum of Army Flying, Middle Wallop
	XP924	DH110 Sea Vixen D3 (G-CVIX) [134/E]	Privately owned, Bournemouth
	XP925	DH110 Sea Vixen FAW2 [752] <ff>	No 1268 Sqn ATC, Haslemere, Surrey
	XP980	Hawker P.1127	FAA Museum, RNAS Yeovilton
	XP984	Hawker P.1127	Brooklands Museum, Weybridge
	XR220	BAC TSR2 (7933M)	RAF Museum, Cosford
	XR222	BAC TSR2	Imperial War Museum, Duxford
	XR232	Sud Alouette AH2 (F-WEIP)	Museum of Army Flying, Middle Wallop
	XR239	Auster AOP9	Privately owned, Stretton on Dunsmore
	XR240	Auster AOP9 (G-BDFH)	Privately owned, Yeovilton
	XR241	Auster AOP9 (G-AXRR)	Privately owned, Eggesford
	XR244	Auster AOP9	AAC Historic Aircraft Flight, Middle Wallop
	XR246	Auster AOP9 (7862M/G-AZBU)	Privately owned, Melton Mowbray
	XR267	Auster AOP9 (G-BJXR)	Privately owned, Hucknall
	XR271	Auster AOP9	Royal Artillery Experience, Woolwich
	XR346	Northrop Shelduck D1 (comp XW578)	Bournemouth Aviation Museum
	XR371	SC5 Belfast C1	RAF Museum, Cosford
	XR379	Sud Alouette AH2	AAC Historic Aircraft Flight, Middle Wallop
	XR453	WS55 Whirlwind HAR10 (8873M) [A]	RAF Odiham, on gate
	XR458	WS55 Whirlwind HAR10 (8662M) [H]	Privately owned, Kettering
	XR485	WS55 Whirlwind HAR10 [Q]	Norfolk & Suffolk Avn Museum, Flixton
	XR486	WS55 Whirlwind HCC12 (8727M/G-RWWW)	The Helicopter Museum, Weston-super-Mare
	XR498	WS58 Wessex HC2 (9342M) [X]	DCAE, No 1 SoTT, Cosford
	XR501	WS58 Wessex HC2	Army, Keogh Barracks, Aldershot, instructional use
	XR502	WS58 Wessex HC2 (G-CCUP) [Z]	Privately owned, Westerham, Kent
	XR503	WS58 Wessex HC2	MoD DFTDC, Manston
	XR506	WS58 Wessex HC2 (9343M) [V]	Army, Longmoor Camp, Hants, instructional use
	XR516	WS58 Wessex HC2 (9319M) [V]	RAF Shawbury, on display
	XR517	WS58 Wessex HC2 [N]	Ulster Aviation Society, Long Kesh
	XR518	WS58 Wessex HC2	DCAE AESS, *HMS Sultan*, Gosport
	XR523	WS58 Wessex HC2 [M]	RN *HMS Raleigh*, Torpoint, instructional use
	XR525	WS58 Wessex HC2 [G]	RAF Museum, Cosford
	XR526	WS58 Wessex HC2 (8147M)	The Helicopter Museum, Weston-super-Mare
	XR528	WS58 Wessex HC2	RAF Lyneham, fire section
	XR529	WS58 Wessex HC2 (9268M) [E]	RAF Aldergrove, on display
	XR534	HS Gnat T1 (8578M) [65]	Newark Air Museum, Winthorpe
	XR537	HS Gnat T1 (8642M/G-NATY)	Privately owned, Bournemouth
	XR538	HS Gnat T1 (8621M/G-RORI) [01]	Heritage Aircraft Trust, North Weald

Serial	Type (code/other identity)	Owner/operator, location or fate	Notes
XR571	HS Gnat T1 (8493M)	RAF Red Arrows, Scampton, on display	
XR574	HS Gnat T1 (8631M) [72]	Trenchard Museum, Halton	
XR595	WS Scout AH1 (G-BWHU) [M]	Privately owned, Staddon Heights, Devon	
XR601	WS Scout AH1	Army Whittington Barracks, Lichfield, on display	
XR627	WS Scout AH1 [X]	Privately owned, Townhill, Fife	
XR628	WS Scout AH1	Privately owned, Ipswich	
XR629	WS Scout AH1 (fuselage)	Privately owned, Ipswich	
XR635	WS Scout AH1	Coventry University, instructional use	
XR650	Hunting Jet Provost T4 (8459M) [28]	Boscombe Down Aviation Collection	
XR654	Hunting Jet Provost T4 <ff>	Privately owned, Chester	
XR658	Hunting Jet Provost T4 (8192M)	Deeside College, Connah's Quay, Clwyd	
XR662	Hunting Jet Provost T4 (8410M) [25]	Boulton Paul Association, Wolverhampton	
XR673	Hunting Jet Provost T4 (G-BXLO/9032M) [L]	Privately owned, Church Fenton	
XR681	Hunting Jet Provost T4 (8588M) <ff>	Robertsbridge Aviation Society, Mayfield	
XR700	Hunting Jet Provost T4 (8589M) <ff>	RAF Aldergrove	
XR713	BAC Lightning F3 (8935M) [C]	RAF Leuchars, on display	
XR718	BAC Lightning F6 (8932M) [DA]	Privately owned, Over Dinsdale, N Yorks	
XR724	BAC Lightning F6 (G-BTSY)	The Lightning Association, Binbrook	
XR725	BAC Lightning F6	Privately owned, Binbrook	
XR726	BAC Lightning F6 <ff>	Privately owned, Harrogate	
XR728	BAC Lightning F6 [JS]	Lightning Preservation Grp, Bruntingthorpe	
XR747	BAC Lightning F6 <ff>	Privately owned, Cubert, Cornwall	
XR749	BAC Lightning F3 (8934M) [DA]	Privately owned, Peterhead	
XR751	BAC Lightning F3 <ff>	Privately owned, Queensbury, W Yorks	
XR753	BAC Lightning F6 (8969M) [XI]	RAF Coningsby on display	
XR753	BAC Lightning F53 (ZF578) [A]	Tangmere Military Aviation Museum	
XR754	BAC Lightning F6 (8972M) <ff>	Aeroventure, Doncaster	
XR755	BAC Lightning F6	Privately owned, Callington, Cornwall	
XR757	BAC Lightning F6 <ff>	RAF Scampton Historical Museum	
XR759	BAC Lightning F6 <ff>	Privately owned, Haxey, Lincs	
XR770	BAC Lightning F6 [AA]	RAF Waddington, for display	
XR771	BAC Lightning F6 [BF]	Midland Air Museum, Coventry	
XR806	BAC VC10 C1K (9285M) <ff>	RAF Brize Norton, BDRT	
XR807	BAC VC10 C1K [Q]	*Scrapped at Bruntingthorpe, July 2010*	
XR808	BAC VC10 C1K [R]	RAF No 101 Sqn, Brize Norton	
XR810	BAC VC10 C1K <ff>	Privately owned, Crondall, Hants	
XR944	Wallis WA116 (G-ATTB)	Privately owned, Reymerston Hall, Norfolk	
XR977	HS Gnat T1 (8640M) [3]	RAF Museum, Cosford	
XR991	HS Gnat T1 (8624M/XS102/G-MOUR)	Heritage Aircraft Trust, North Weald	
XR993	HS Gnat T1 (8620M/XP534/G-BVPP)	Privately owned, Bruntingthorpe	
XS100	HS Gnat T1 (8561M) <ff>	Privately owned, London SW3	
XS100	HS Gnat T1 (8561M) <rf>	Privately owned, Fyfield, Essex	
XS104	HS Gnat T1 (8604M/G-FRCE)	Privately owned, North Weald	
XS111	HS Gnat T1 (8618M/XP504/G-TIMM)	Heritage Aircraft Trust, North Weald	
XS149	WS58 Wessex HAS3 [661/GL]	The Helicopter Museum, Weston-super-Mare	
XS176	Hunting Jet Provost T4 (8514M) <ff>	Highland Aviation Museum, Inverness	
XS177	Hunting Jet Provost T4 (9044M) [N]	Metheringham Airfield Visitors Centre	
XS179	Hunting Jet Provost T4 (8237M) [20]	Museum of Science & Industry, stored Manchester	
XS180	Hunting Jet Provost T4 (8238M) [21]	RAF JARTS, St Athan	
XS181	Hunting Jet Provost T4 (9033M) <ff>	Privately owned, Spanhoe	
XS183	Hunting Jet Provost T4 <ff>	Privately owned, Plymouth	
XS186	Hunting Jet Provost T4 (8408M) [M]	Metheringham Airfield Visitors Centre	
XS209	Hunting Jet Provost T4 (8409M)	Solway Aviation Society, Carlisle	
XS216	Hunting Jet Provost T4 <ff>	Aeroventure, Doncaster	
XS218	Hunting Jet Provost T4 (8508M) <ff>	No 447 Sqn ATC, Henley-on-Thames, Berks	
XS231	BAC Jet Provost T5 (G-ATAJ)	Boscombe Down Aviation Collection	
XS235	DH106 Comet 4C (G-CPDA)	Cold War Jets Collection, Bruntingthorpe	
XS238	Auster AOP9 (TAD 200)	Newark Air Museum, stored Winthorpe	
XS416	BAC Lightning T5	Privately owned, New York, Lincs	
XS417	BAC Lightning T5 [DZ]	Newark Air Museum, Winthorpe	
XS420	BAC Lightning T5	Privately owned, Farnborough	
XS421	BAC Lightning T5 <ff>	Privately owned, Foulness	
XS456	BAC Lightning T5 [DX]	Skegness Water Leisure Park	
XS457	BAC Lightning T5 <ff>	Privately owned, Binbrook	
XS458	BAC Lightning T5 [T]	T5 Projects, Cranfield	

Notes	Serial	Type (code/other identity)	Owner/operator, location or fate
	XS459	BAC Lightning T5 [AW]	Fenland & W Norfolk Aviation Museum, Wisbech
	XS463	WS Wasp HAS1 (comp XT431)	Gatwick Aviation Museum, Charlwood, Surrey
	XS481	WS58 Wessex HU5	Aeroventure, Doncaster
	XS482	WS58 Wessex HU5	RAF Manston History Museum
	XS486	WS58 Wessex HU5 (9272M) [524/CU,F]	The Helicopter Museum, Weston-super-Mare
	XS488	WS58 Wessex HU5 (9056M) [F]	DCAE AESS, *HMS Sultan*, Gosport
	XS489	WS58 Wessex HU5 [R]	Privately owned, Westerham, Kent
	XS493	WS58 Wessex HU5	Vector Aerospace, stored Fleetlands
	XS496	WS58 Wessex HU5 [625/PO]	DCAE AESS, *HMS Sultan*, Gosport
	XS507	WS58 Wessex HU5	RAF Benson, for display
	XS508	WS58 Wessex HU5	FAA Museum, stored RNAS Yeovilton
	XS510	WS58 Wessex HU5 [626/PO]	No 1414 Sqn ATC, Crowborough, Sussex
	XS511	WS58 Wessex HU5 [M]	Tangmere Military Aircraft Museum
	XS513	WS58 Wessex HU5	RNAS Yeovilton Fire Section
	XS514	WS58 Wessex HU5 (A2740) [L/PO]	DCAE AESS, *HMS Sultan*, Gosport
	XS515	WS58 Wessex HU5 [N]	Army, Keogh Barracks, Aldershot, instructional use
	XS516	WS58 Wessex HU5 [Q]	Privately owned, Redruth, Cornwall
	XS520	WS58 Wessex HU5 [F]	RN, Predannack Fire School
	XS522	WS58 Wessex HU5 [ZL]	Blackball Paintball, Truro, Cornwall
	XS527	WS Wasp HAS1	FAA Museum, stored RNAS Yeovilton
	XS529	WS Wasp HAS1	Privately owned, Redruth, Cornwall
	XS539	WS Wasp HAS1 [435]	Vector Aerospace Fleetlands Apprentice School
	XS567	WS Wasp HAS1 [434/E]	Imperial War Museum, Duxford
	XS568	WS Wasp HAS1 (A2715) [441]	DCAE AESS, *HMS Sultan*, Gosport
	XS570	WS Wasp HAS1 [445/P]	Warship Preservation Trust, Birkenhead
	XS574	Northrop Shelduck D1 <R>	FAA Museum, stored RNAS Yeovilton
	XS576	DH110 Sea Vixen FAW2 [125/E]	Imperial War Museum, Duxford
	XS587	DH110 Sea Vixen FAW(TT)2 (8828M/G-VIXN)	Gatwick Aviation Museum, Charlwood, Surrey
	XS590	DH110 Sea Vixen FAW2 [131/E]	FAA Museum, RNAS Yeovilton
	XS596	HS Andover C1(PR)	MoD, Boscombe Down (wfu)
	XS598	HS Andover C1 (fuselage)	FETC, Moreton-in-Marsh, Glos
	XS606	HS Andover C1	MoD/ETPS, Boscombe Down
	XS639	HS Andover E3A (9241M)	RAF Museum, Cosford
	XS643	HS Andover E3A (9278M) <ff>	Privately owned, Stock, Essex
	XS646	HS Andover C1(mod)	RAF/AWC/No 206(R) Sqn, Boscombe Down
	XS652	Slingsby T45 Swallow TX1 (BGA1107)	Privately owned, North Wales
	XS674	WS58 Wessex HC2 [R]	Privately owned, Biggin Hill
	XS695	HS Kestrel FGA1	RAF Museum Restoration Centre, Cosford
	XS709	HS125 Dominie T1 [M]	RAF Cranwell (wfu)
	XS710	HS125 Dominie T1 (9259M) [O]	RAF Cranwell Fire Section
	XS711	HS125 Dominie T1 (fuselage)	MoD, Boscombe Down
	XS712	HS125 Dominie T1 [A]	RAF Cranwell (wfu)
	XS713	HS125 Dominie T1 [C]	RAF Cranwell (wfu)
	XS714	HS125 Dominie T1 (9246M) [P]	MoD DFTDC, Manston
	XS726	HS125 Dominie T1 (9273M) [T]	Privately owned, Sproughton
	XS727	HS125 Dominie T1 [D]	RAF Cranwell (wfu)
	XS728	HS125 Dominie T1 [E]	RAF Cranwell (wfu)
	XS729	HS125 Dominie T1 (9275M) [G]	Sold to Spain, November 2009
	XS730	HS125 Dominie T1 [H]	RAF Cranwell (wfu)
	XS731	HS125 Dominie T1 [J]	RAF Cranwell (wfu)
	XS733	HS125 Dominie T1 (9276M) [Q]	Privately owned, Sproughton
	XS734	HS125 Dominie T1 (9260M) [N]	Privately owned, Sproughton
	XS735	HS125 Dominie T1 (9264M) [R]	Penwyllt Adventure Training Centre, Powys
	XS736	HS125 Dominie T1 [S]	Privately owned, Winterbourne Gunner, Wilts
	XS737	HS125 Dominie T1 [K]	RAF Cranwell (wfu)
	XS738	HS125 Dominie T1 (9274M) [U]	RN, Predannack Fire School
	XS739	HS125 Dominie T1 [F]	RAF Cranwell (wfu)
	XS743	Beagle B206Z	MoD/ETPS, Boscombe Down
	XS765	Beagle B206 Basset CC1 (G-BSET)	MoD, QinetiQ, Boscombe Down (spares use)
	XS770	Beagle B206 Basset CC1 (G-HRHI)	MoD, QinetiQ, Boscombe Down (spares use)
	XS790	HS748 Andover CC2 <ff>	Boscombe Down Aviation Collection
	XS791	HS748 Andover CC2 (fuselage)	Privately owned, Stock, Essex

Serial	Type (code/other identity)	Owner/operator, location or fate	Notes
XS863	WS58 Wessex HAS1 [304]	Imperial War Museum, Duxford	
XS876	WS58 Wessex HAS1 [523/PO]	East Midlands Airport Aeropark	
XS885	WS58 Wessex HAS1 [512/DD]	RN, Predannack Fire School	
XS886	WS58 Wessex HAS1 [527/CU]	Privately owned, Sproughton	
XS887	WS58 Wessex HAS1 [403/FI]	Aeroventure, Doncaster	
XS888	WS58 Wessex HAS1 [521]	Guernsey Airport Fire Section	
XS897	BAC Lightning F6	Privately owned, RAF Coningsby	
XS898	BAC Lightning F6 <ff>	Privately owned, Lavendon, Bucks	
XS899	BAC Lightning F6 <ff>	Privately owned, Binbrook	
XS903	BAC Lightning F6 [BA]	Yorkshire Air Museum, Elvington	
XS904	BAC Lightning F6 [BQ]	Lightning Preservation Grp, Bruntingthorpe	
XS919	BAC Lightning F6	Wonderland Pleasure Park, Farnsfield, Notts	
XS922	BAC Lightning F6 (8973M) <ff>	Privately owned, Spark Bridge, Cumbria	
XS923	BAC Lightning F6 <ff>	Privately owned, Welshpool	
XS925	BAC Lightning F6 (8961M) [BA]	RAF Museum, Hendon	
XS928	BAC Lightning F6 [AD]	BAE Systems Warton, on display	
XS932	BAC Lightning F6 <ff>	Privately owned, Walcott, Lincs	
XS933	BAC Lightning F6 <ff>	Privately owned, Farnham	
XS933	BAC Lightning F53 (ZF594) [BF]	North-East Aircraft Museum, Usworth	
XS936	BAC Lightning F6	Castle Motors, Liskeard, Cornwall	
XT108	Agusta-Bell 47G-3 Sioux AH1 [U]	Museum of Army Flying, Middle Wallop	
XT123	WS Sioux AH1 (XT827) [D]	AAC Middle Wallop, at main gate	
XT131	Agusta-Bell 47G-3 Sioux AH1 [B]	AAC Historic Aircraft Flight, Middle Wallop	
XT140	Agusta-Bell 47G-3 Sioux AH1	Perth Technical College	
XT141	Agusta-Bell 47G-3 Sioux AH1	Privately owned, Newcastle	
XT150	Agusta-Bell 47G-3 Sioux AH1 (7883M) [R]	Privately owned, Aeroventure, Doncaster	
XT151	WS Sioux AH1	Museum of Army Flying, stored Middle Wallop	
XT176	WS Sioux AH1 [U]	FAA Museum, stored RNAS Yeovilton	
XT190	WS Sioux AH1	The Helicopter Museum, Weston-super-Mare	
XT200	WS Sioux AH1 [F]	Newark Air Museum, Winthorpe	
XT208	WS Sioux AH1 (wreck)	Blessingbourne Museum, Fivemiletown, Co Tyrone, NI	
XT223	WS Sioux AH1 (G-XTUN)	Privately owned, Sherburn-in-Elmet	
XT236	WS Sioux AH1 (frame only)	Aeroventure, Doncaster	
XT242	WS Sioux AH1 (composite) [12]	Aeroventure, Doncaster	
XT257	WS58 Wessex HAS3 (8719M)	Bournemouth Aviation Museum	
XT277	HS Buccaneer S2A (8853M) <ff>	Privately owned, Welshpool	
XT280	HS Buccaneer S2A <ff>	Dumfries & Galloway Avn Mus, Dumfries	
XT284	HS Buccaneer S2A (8855M) <ff>	Privately owned, Felixstowe	
XT288	HS Buccaneer S2B (9134M)	Royal Scottish Museum of Flight, stored E Fortune	
XT420	WS Wasp HAS1 (G-CBUI) [606]	Privately owned, Thruxton	
XT427	WS Wasp HAS1 [606]	FAA Museum, stored RNAS Yeovilton	
XT434	WS Wasp HAS1 (G-CGGK) [455]	Privately owned, Breighton	
XT435	WS Wasp HAS1 (NZ3907/G-RIMM) [430]	Privately owned, Badwell Green, Suffolk	
XT437	WS Wasp HAS1 [423]	Boscombe Down Aviation Collection	
XT439	WS Wasp HAS1 [605]	Privately owned, Hemel Hempstead	
XT443	WS Wasp HAS1 [422/AU]	The Helicopter Museum, Weston-super-Mare	
XT453	WS58 Wessex HU5 (A2756) [A/B]	DCAE AESS, *HMS Sultan*, Gosport	
XT455	WS58 Wessex HU5 (A2654) [U]	DCAE AESS, *HMS Sultan*, Gosport	
XT456	WS58 Wessex HU5 (8941M) [XZ]	RAF Aldergrove, BDRT	
XT458	WS58 Wessex HU5 (A2768)	DCAE AESS, HMS Sultan, Gosport	
XT466	WS58 Wessex HU5 (A2617/8921M) [XV]	Army Whittington Barracks, Lichfield, on display	
XT467	WS58 Wessex HU5 (8922M) [BF]	Gunsmoke Paintball, Hadleigh, Suffolk	
XT469	WS58 Wessex HU5 (8920M)	Privately owned, Newton-with-Scales, Lancs	
XT472	WS58 Wessex HU5 [XC]	The Helicopter Museum, Weston-super-Mare	
XT480	WS58 Wessex HU5 [468/RG]	East Midlands Airport Aeropark	
XT482	WS58 Wessex HU5 [ZM/VL]	FAA Museum, RNAS Yeovilton	
XT484	WS58 Wessex HU5 (A2742) [H]	DCAE AESS, *HMS Sultan*, Gosport	
XT485	WS58 Wessex HU5 (A2680)	DCAE AESS, *HMS Sultan*, Gosport	
XT486	WS58 Wessex HU5 (8919M)	Dumfries & Galloway Avn Mus, Dumfries	
XT550	WS Sioux AH1 [D]	AAC, stored Middle Wallop	
XT575	Vickers Viscount 837 <ff>	Brooklands Museum, Weybridge	

Notes	Serial	Type (code/other identity)	Owner/operator, location or fate
	XT581	Northrop Shelduck D1	Imperial War Museum, Duxford
	XT583	Northrop Shelduck D1	Royal Artillery Experience, Woolwich
	XT596	McD F-4K Phantom FG1	FAA Museum, RNAS Yeovilton
	XT597	McD F-4K Phantom FG1	Boscombe Down Aviation Collection
	XT601	WS58 Wessex HC2 (9277M) (composite)	RAF Odiham, BDRT
	XT604	WS58 Wessex HC2	East Midlands Airport Aeropark
	XT617	WS Scout AH1	AAC Wattisham, on display
	XT621	WS Scout AH1	Defence Academy of the UK, Shrivenham
	XT623	WS Scout AH1	DCAE SEAE, Arborfield
	XT626	WS Scout AH1 [Q]	AAC Historic Aircraft Flt, Middle Wallop
	XT630	WS Scout AH1 (G-BXRL) [X]	Privately owned, Bruntingthorpe
	XT631	WS Scout AH1 [D]	Privately owned, Ipswich
	XT633	WS Scout AH1	DCAE SEAE, Arborfield
	XT634	WS Scout AH1 (G-BYRX) [T]	Privately owned, Tollerton
	XT638	WS Scout AH1 [N]	AAC Middle Wallop, at gate
	XT640	WS Scout AH1	Privately owned, Sproughton
	XT643	WS Scout AH1 [Z]	Army, Thorpe Camp, East Wretham
	XT672	WS58 Wessex HC2 [WE]	RAF Stafford, on display
	XT681	WS58 Wessex HC2 (9279M) [U] <ff>	Privately owned, Wallingford, Oxon
	XT761	WS58 Wessex HU5	DCAE AESS, *HMS Sultan*, Gosport
	XT762	WS58 Wessex HU5	Hamburger Hill Paintball, Marksbury, Somerset
	XT765	WS58 Wessex HU5 [J]	RNAS Yeovilton, on display
	XT769	WS58 Wessex HU5 [823]	FAA Museum, RNAS Yeovilton
	XT771	WS58 Wessex HU5 [620/PO]	DCAE AESS, HMS Sultan, Gosport
	XT773	WS58 Wessex HU5 (9123M)	RAF Shawbury Fire Section
	XT778	WS Wasp HAS1 [430]	FAA Museum, stored RNAS Yeovilton
	XT780	WS Wasp HAS1 [636]	Fareham Tertiary College, Hants
	XT787	WS Wasp HAS1 (NZ3905/G-KAXT)	Kennet Aviation, Old Warden
	XT788	WS Wasp HAS1 (G-BMIR) [474]	Privately owned, Dunkeswell
	XT793	WS Wasp HAS1 (G-BZPP) [456]	Privately owned, Yeovilton
	XT852	McD YF-4M Phantom FGR2	QinetiQ West Freugh Fire Section
	XT863	McD F-4K Phantom FG1 <ff>	Privately owned, Cowes, IOW
	XT864	McD F-4K Phantom FG1 (8998M/*XT684*) [BJ]	RAF Leuchars on display
	XT891	McD F-4M Phantom FGR2 (9136M) [P]	RAF Coningsby, at main gate
	XT903	McD F-4M Phantom FGR2 <ff>	RAF Museum Restoration Centre, Cosford
	XT905	McD F-4M Phantom FGR2 (9286M) [P]	RAF North Luffenham Training Area
	XT907	McD F-4M Phantom FGR2 (9151M) [W]	DEODS, Chattenden, Kent
	XT914	McD F-4M Phantom FGR2 (9269M) [Z]	RAF Brampton, Cambs, on display
	XV101	BAC VC10 K1 [S]	MoD/DSG, St Athan
	XV102	BAC VC10 C1K [T]	RAF No 101 Sqn, Brize Norton
	XV104	BAC VC10 C1K [U]	RAF No 101 Sqn, Brize Norton
	XV105	BAC VC10 C1K [V]	RAF No 101 Sqn, Brize Norton
	XV106	BAC VC10 C1K [W]	RAF No 101 Sqn, Brize Norton
	XV107	BAC VC10 C1K [X]	RAF No 101 Sqn, Brize Norton
	XV108	BAC VC10 C1K [Y]	MoD/DSG, St Athan
	XV109	BAC VC10 C1K <ff>	Privately owned, Bruntingthorpe
	XV118	WS Scout AH1 (9141M)	Kennet Aviation, North Weald
	XV122	WS Scout AH1 [D]	Defence Academy of the UK, Shrivenham
	XV123	WS Scout AH1	RAF Shawbury, on display
	XV124	WS Scout AH1 [W]	Privately owned, Bentwaters
	XV127	WS Scout AH1	Museum of Army Flying, Middle Wallop
	XV130	WS Scout AH1 (G-BWJW) [R]	Privately owned, Tollerton
	XV131	WS Scout AH1 [Y]	AAC 70 Aircraft Workshops, Middle Wallop, BDRT
	XV134	WS Scout AH1 (G-BWLX) [P]	*Sold to the USA, August 2010*
	XV136	WS Scout AH1 [X]	AAC Netheravon, on display
	XV137	WS Scout AH1 (G-CRUM)	Privately owned, Chiseldon, Wilts
	XV137	WS Scout AH1 (XV139)	Aeroventure, stored Doncaster
	XV138	WS Scout AH1 (G-SASM)	Privately owned, Thruxton
	XV141	WS Scout AH1	REME Museum, Arborfield
	XV148	HS Nimrod MR1(mod) <ff>	Privately owned, Malmesbury
	XV161	HS Buccaneer S2B (9117M) <ff>	Dundonald Aviation Centre

Serial	Type (code/other identity)	Owner/operator, location or fate	Notes
XV165	HS Buccaneer S2B <ff>	Privately owned, Spanhoe	
XV168	HS Buccaneer S2B [AF]	BAE Systems Brough, on display	
XV177	Lockheed C-130K Hercules C3A	RAF No 47 Sqn, Lyneham	
XV188	Lockheed C-130K Hercules C3A	RAF No 47 Sqn, Lyneham	
XV196	Lockheed C-130K Hercules C1	RAF No 47 Sqn, Lyneham	
XV197	Lockheed C-130K Hercules C3	Privately owned, Hixon, Staffs	
XV200	Lockheed C-130K Hercules C1	RAF No 47 Sqn, Lyneham	
XV201	Lockheed C-130K Hercules C1K <ff>	Marshalls, Cambridge	
XV202	Lockheed C-130K Hercules C3	RAF No 47 Sqn, Lyneham	
XV208	Lockheed C-130K Hercules W2	Marshalls, Cambridge (wfu)	
XV209	Lockheed C-130K Hercules C3A	RAF No 47 Sqn, Lyneham	
XV212	Lockheed C-130K Hercules C3	MoD/Marshalls, stored Cambridge	
XV214	Lockheed C-130K Hercules C3A	RAF No 47 Sqn, Lyneham	
XV217	Lockheed C-130K Hercules C3	Privately owned, Hixon, Staffs	
XV220	Lockheed C-130K Hercules C3	Privately owned, Hixon, Staffs	
XV221	Lockheed C-130K Hercules C3	RAF No 47 Sqn, Lyneham	
XV226	HS Nimrod MR2 $	Cold War Jets Collection, Bruntingthorpe	
XV229	HS Nimrod MR2	MoD DFTDC, Manston	
XV231	HS Nimrod MR2	Aviation Viewing Park, Manchester	
XV232	HS Nimrod MR2	Airbase, Coventry	
XV235	HS Nimrod MR2	MoD/AFD/QinetiQ, Boscombe Down	
XV240	HS Nimrod MR2	RAF Kinloss, on display	
XV241	HS Nimrod MR2	*Scrapped at Kinloss, January 2011*	
XV244	HS Nimrod MR2	RAF Kinloss (wfu)	
XV246	HS Nimrod MR2	MoD/BAE Systems, Woodford	
XV248	HS Nimrod MR2	*Scrapped at Kinloss, July 2010*	
XV249	HS Nimrod R1 $	RAF No 51 Sqn, Waddington	
XV250	HS Nimrod MR2	Yorkshire Air Museum, Elvington	
XV252	HS Nimrod MR2	*Scrapped at Kinloss, January 2011*	
XV253	HS Nimrod MR2 (9118M)	MoD/BAE Systems, Woodford	
XV254	HS Nimrod MR2 <ff>	Highland Aviation Museum, Inverness	
XV255	HS Nimrod MR2	City of Norwich Aviation Museum	
XV259	BAe Nimrod AEW3 <ff>	Privately owned, Carlisle	
XV260	HS Nimrod MR2	*Scrapped at Kinloss, November 2010*	
XV263	BAe Nimrod AEW3P (8967M) <ff>	BAE Systems, Brough	
XV263	BAe Nimrod AEW3P (8967M) <rf>	MoD/BAE Systems, Woodford	
XV268	DHC2 Beaver AL1 (G-BVER)	Privately owned, Cumbernauld	
XV277	HS P.1127(RAF)	Royal Scottish Mus'm of Flight, E Fortune	
XV279	HS P.1127(RAF) (8566M)	RAF Cottesmore, preserved	
XV280	HS P.1127(RAF) <ff>	RNAS Yeovilton Fire Section	
XV290	Lockheed C-130K Hercules C3	Privately owned, Hixon, Staffs	
XV294	Lockheed C-130K Hercules C3	MoD/Marshalls, stored Cambridge	
XV295	Lockheed C-130K Hercules C1	RAF No 47 Sqn, Lyneham	
XV299	Lockheed C-130K Hercules C3	MoD/Marshalls, stored Cambridge	
XV301	Lockheed C-130K Hercules C3	RAF No 47 Sqn, Lyneham	
XV302	Lockheed C-130K Hercules C3	Marshalls, Cambridge, fatigue test airframe	
XV303	Lockheed C-130K Hercules C3A	RAF No 47 Sqn, Lyneham	
XV304	Lockheed C-130K Hercules C3A	RAF Brize Norton, instructional use	
XV305	Lockheed C-130K Hercules C3 $	Privately owned, Hixon, Staffs	
XV307	Lockheed C-130K Hercules C3 (G-52-40)	MoD/Marshalls, stored Cambridge	
XV328	BAC Lightning T5 <ff>	Phoenix Aviation, Bruntingthorpe	
XV333	HS Buccaneer S2B [234/H]	FAA Museum, RNAS Yeovilton	
XV344	HS Buccaneer S2C	QinetiQ Farnborough, on display	
XV350	HS Buccaneer S2B	East Midlands Airport Aeropark	
XV352	HS Buccaneer S2B <ff>	RAF Manston History Museum	
XV359	HS Buccaneer S2B [035/R]	Privately owned, Topsham, Devon	
XV361	HS Buccaneer S2B	Ulster Aviation Society, Long Kesh	
XV370	Sikorsky SH-3D (A2682) [260]	DCAE AESS, *HMS Sultan*, Gosport	
XV371	WS61 Sea King HAS1(DB) [61/DD]	SFDO, RNAS Culdrose	
XV372	WS61 Sea King HAS1	RAF, St Mawgan, instructional use	
XV383	Northrop Shelduck D1 (fuselage)	Privately owned, Wimborne, Dorset	
XV401	McD F-4M Phantom FGR2 [I]	Boscombe Down Aviation Collection	
XV402	McD F-4M Phantom FGR2 <ff>	*Currently not known*	
XV406	McD F-4M Phantom FGR2 (9098M) [CK]	Solway Aviation Society, Carlisle	
XV408	McD F-4M Phantom FGR2 (9165M) [Z]	Tangmere Military Aviation Museum	
XV411	McD F-4M Phantom FGR2 (9103M) [L]	MoD DFTDC, Manston	
XV415	McD F-4M Phantom FGR2] (9163M) [E	RAF Boulmer, on display	

Notes	Serial	Type (code/other identity)	Owner/operator, location or fate
	XV424	McD F-4M Phantom FGR2 (9152M) [I]	RAF Museum, Hendon
	XV426	McD F-4M Phantom FGR2 <ff>	City of Norwich Aviation Museum
	XV426	McD F-4M Phantom FGR2 [P] <rf>	RAF Coningsby, BDRT
	XV460	McD F-4M Phantom FGR2 <ff>	No 2214 Sqn ATC, Usworth
	XV474	McD F-4M Phantom FGR2 [T]	The Old Flying Machine Company, Duxford
	XV490	McD F-4M Phantom FGR2 <ff>	Privately owned, Nantwich
	XV497	McD F-4M Phantom FGR2 (9295M) [D]	RAF Waddington, (preserved)
	XV499	McD F-4M Phantom FGR2	RAF Leeming, WLT
	XV581	McD F-4K Phantom FG1 (9070M) <ff>	No 2481 Sqn ATC, Bridge of Don
	XV582	McD F-4K Phantom FG1 (9066M) [M]	RAF Leuchars, on display
	XV586	McD F-4K Phantom FG1 (9067M) [AJ]	RAF Leuchars, on display
	XV591	McD F-4K Phantom FG1 [013] <ff>	RAF Museum, Cosford
	XV625	WS Wasp HAS1 (A2649) [471]	DCAE AESS, *HMS Sultan*, Gosport
	XV631	WS Wasp HAS1 (fuselage)	Farnborough Air Sciences Trust, Farnborough
	XV642	WS61 Sea King HAS2A (A2614) [259]	DCAE AESS, *HMS Sultan*, Gosport
	XV643	WS61 Sea King HAS6 [262]	DCAE, No 1 SoTT, Cosford
	XV647	WS61 Sea King HU5 [28]	RN No 771 NAS, Culdrose
	XV648	WS61 Sea King HU5 [818/CU] $	MoD/Vector Aerospace, Fleetlands
	XV649	WS61 Sea King ASaC7 [180]	MoD/Vector Aerospace, Fleetlands
	XV651	WS61 Sea King HU5	MoD/AFD/QinetiQ, Boscombe Down
	XV653	WS61 Sea King HAS6 (9326M) [63/CU]	DCAE, No 1 SoTT, Cosford
	XV654	WS61 Sea King HAS6 [05/DD] (wreck)	SFDO, RNAS Culdrose
	XV655	WS61 Sea King HAS6 [270/N]	DCAE AESS, *HMS Sultan*, Gosport
	XV656	WS61 Sea King ASaC7 [185]	RN No 857 NAS, Culdrose
	XV657	WS61 Sea King HAS5 *(ZA135)* [32/DD]	SFDO, RNAS Culdrose
	XV659	WS61 Sea King HAS6 (9324M) [62/CU]	DCAE, No 1 SoTT, Cosford
	XV660	WS61 Sea King HAS6 [69/N]	DCAE AESS, *HMS Sultan*, Gosport
	XV661	WS61 Sea King HU5 [26]	MoD/Vector Aerospace, stored Fleetlands
	XV663	WS61 Sea King HAS6	DCAE, stored HMS Sultan, Gosport
	XV664	WS61 Sea King ASaC7 [190]	RN No 857 NAS, Culdrose
	XV665	WS61 Sea King HAS6 [507/CU]	DCAE AESS, HMS Sultan, Gosport
	XV666	WS61 Sea King HU5 [21]	RN No 771 NAS, Culdrose
	XV670	WS61 Sea King HU5	RN No 771 NAS, Culdrose
	XV671	WS61 Sea King ASaC7 [183]	RN No 854 NAS, Culdrose
	XV672	WS61 Sea King ASaC7 [187]	MoD/AFD/QinetiQ, Boscombe Down
	XV673	WS61 Sea King HU5 [27/CU]	RN No 771 NAS, Culdrose
	XV675	WS61 Sea King HAS6 [701/PW]	DCAE AESS, *HMS Sultan*, Gosport
	XV676	WS61 Sea King HC6 [ZE]	DCAE, stored *HMS Sultan*, Gosport
	XV677	WS61 Sea King HAS6 [269]	Aeroventure, Doncaster
	XV696	WS61 Sea King HAS6 [267/L]	DCAE AESS, *HMS Sultan*, Gosport
	XV697	WS61 Sea King ASaC7 [181]	RN No 849 NAS, Culdrose
	XV699	WS61 Sea King HU5 [823/PW]	RN No 771 NAS, Prestwick
	XV700	WS61 Sea King HC6 [ZC]	DCAE, stored *HMS Sultan*, Gosport
	XV701	WS61 Sea King HAS6 [268/N,64]	DCAE, No 1 SoTT, Cosford
	XV703	WS61 Sea King HC6 [ZD]	DCAE, stored *HMS Sultan*, Gosport
	XV705	WS61 Sea King HAR5 [29]	RN No 771 NAS, Culdrose
	XV706	WS61 Sea King HAS6 (9344M) [017/L]	RN ETS, Culdrose
	XV707	WS61 Sea King ASaC7 [184]	RN No 849 NAS, Culdrose
	XV708	WS61 Sea King HAS6 [501/CU]	DCAE AESS, *HMS Sultan*, Gosport
	XV709	WS61 Sea King HAS6 (9303M) [263]	RAF Valley, instructional use
	XV711	WS61 Sea King HAS6 [15/CW]	DCAE AESS, *HMS Sultan*, Gosport
	XV712	WS61 Sea King HAS6 [66]	Imperial War Museum, Duxford
	XV713	WS61 Sea King HAS6 (A2646) [018/L]	DCAE AESS, HMS Sultan, Gosport
	XV714	WS61 Sea King ASaC7 [188]	MoD/Vector Aerospace, Fleetlands
	XV720	WS58 Wessex HC2 (A2701)	DCAE AESS, *HMS Sultan*, Gosport
	XV724	WS58 Wessex HC2	DCAE AESS, *HMS Sultan*, Gosport
	XV725	WS58 Wessex HC2 [C]	MoD DFTDC, Manston

Serial	Type (code/other identity)	Owner/operator, location or fate	Notes
XV726	WS58 Wessex HC2 [J]	Privately owned, Biggin Hill	
XV728	WS58 Wessex HC2 [A]	Newark Air Museum, Winthorpe	
XV731	WS58 Wessex HC2 [Y]	Privately owned, stored Redhill	
XV732	WS58 Wessex HCC4	RAF Museum, Hendon	
XV733	WS58 Wessex HCC4	The Helicopter Museum, Weston-super-Mare	
XV741	HS Harrier GR3 (A2608) [41/DD]	DCAE AESS, *HMS Sultan*, Gosport	
XV744	HS Harrier GR3 (9167M) [3K]	Defence Academy of the UK, Shrivenham	
XV748	HS Harrier GR3 [3D]	Yorkshire Air Museum, Elvington	
XV751	HS Harrier GR3	Gatwick Aviation Museum, Charlwood	
XV752	HS Harrier GR3 (9075M) [B]	Bletchley Park Museum, Bucks	
XV753	HS Harrier GR3 (9078M) [53]	RN, Predannack Fire School	
XV755	HS Harrier GR3 [M]	RNAS Yeovilton Fire Section	
XV759	HS Harrier GR3 [O] <ff>	Privately owned, Hitchin, Herts	
XV760	HS Harrier GR3 <ff>	Solent Sky, Southampton	
XV779	HS Harrier GR3 (8931M)	RAF Wittering on display	
XV783	HS Harrier GR3 [83]	RN, Predannack Fire School	
XV784	HS Harrier GR3 (8909M) <ff>	Boscombe Down Aviation Collection	
XV786	HS Harrier GR3 <ff>	RNAS Culdrose	
XV786	HS Harrier GR3 [S] <rf>	RN, Predannack Fire School	
XV798	HS Harrier GR1(mod)	Bristol Aero Collection, stored Kemble	
XV804	HS Harrier GR3 (9280M) [O]	RAF North Luffenham Training Area	
XV806	HS Harrier GR3 <ff>	Privately owned, South Molton, Devon	
XV808	HS Harrier GR3 (9076M/A2687) [08/DD]	DCAE AESS, *HMS Sultan*, Gosport	
XV810	HS Harrier GR3 (9038M) [K]	Privately owned, Bruntingthorpe	
XV814	DH106 Comet 4 (G-APDF) <ff>	Privately owned, Chipping Campden	
XV863	HS Buccaneer S2B (9115M/9139M/9145M) [S]	Privately owned, Weston, Eire	
XV864	HS Buccaneer S2B (9234M)	MoD DFTDC, Manston	
XV865	HS Buccaneer S2B (9226M)	Imperial War Museum, Duxford	
XV867	HS Buccaneer S2B <ff>	Highland Aviation Museum, Inverness	
XW175	HS Harrier T4(VAAC)	MoD, Boscombe Down (wfu)	
XW198	WS Puma HC1	RAF No 33 Sqn/No 230 Sqn, Benson	
XW199	WS Puma HC1	RAF No 33 Sqn/No 230 Sqn, Benson	
XW200	WS Puma HC1 (wreck)	RAF, stored Shawbury	
XW201	WS Puma HC1	RAF Benson, BDRT	
XW202	WS Puma HC1	RAF, stored Shawbury	
XW204	WS Puma HC1	RAF No 33 Sqn/No 230 Sqn, Benson	
XW206	WS Puma HC1	AgustaWestland, Yeovil	
XW207	WS Puma HC1	RAF No 33 Sqn/No 230 Sqn, Benson	
XW208	WS Puma HC2	MoD/Eurocopter, Marseilles, France (on rebuild)	
XW209	WS Puma HC1	RAF No 33 Sqn/No 230 Sqn, Benson	
XW210	WS Puma HC1 (comp XW215)	RAF No 33 Sqn/No 230 Sqn, Benson	
XW211	WS Puma HC1	RAF No 33 Sqn/No 230 Sqn, Benson	
XW212	WS Puma HC1	RAF No 33 Sqn/No 230 Sqn, Benson	
XW213	WS Puma HC1	RAF No 33 Sqn/No 230 Sqn, Benson	
XW214	WS Puma HC1	RAF No 33 Sqn/No 230 Sqn, Benson	
XW216	WS Puma HC2	MoD/Eurocopter, Oxford (conversion)	
XW217	WS Puma HC1	RAF No 33 Sqn/No 230 Sqn, Benson	
XW218	WS Puma HC1 (wreck)	RAF, stored Shawbury	
XW219	WS Puma HC1	RAF No 33 Sqn/No 230 Sqn, Benson	
XW220	WS Puma HC1	AgustaWestland, Yeovil	
XW222	WS Puma HC1	RAF No 33 Sqn/No 230 Sqn, Benson	
XW223	WS Puma HC1	RAF No 33 Sqn/No 230 Sqn, Benson	
XW224	WS Puma HC1	RAF No 33 Sqn/No 230 Sqn, Benson	
XW226	WS Puma HC1	RAF No 33 Sqn/No 230 Sqn, Benson	
XW227	WS Puma HC1	Privately owned, Colsterworth, Leics	
XW229	WS Puma HC1	RAF No 33 Sqn/No 230 Sqn, Benson	
XW231	WS Puma HC1	RAF No 33 Sqn/No 230 Sqn, Benson	
XW232	WS Puma HC2	MoD/Eurocopter, Oxford (conversion)	
XW235	WS Puma HC2	MoD/Eurocopter, Oxford (conversion)	
XW236	WS Puma HC1	RAF No 33 Sqn/No 230 Sqn, Benson	
XW237	WS Puma HC1	RAF No 33 Sqn/No 230 Sqn, Benson	
XW241	Sud SA330E Puma	Farnborough Air Sciences Trust, Farnborough	
XW264	HS Harrier T2 <ff>	Gloucestershire Avn Coll, stored Gloucester	
XW265	HS Harrier T4A (9258M) <ff>	No 2345 Sqn ATC, RAF Leuchars	
XW265	HS Harrier T4A (9258M) <rf>	DSG, St Athan	
XW267	HS Harrier T4 (9263M) [SA]	Territorial Army, Toton, Notts	

Notes	Serial	Type (code/other identity)	Owner/operator, location or fate
	XW268	HS Harrier T4N	City of Norwich Aviation Museum
	XW269	HS Harrier T4	Privately owned, Queensbury, W Yorks
	XW270	HS Harrier T4 (fuselage)	Coventry University, instructional use
	XW271	HS Harrier T4 [71]	RN, Predannack Fire School
	XW272	HS Harrier T4 (8783M) (fuselage) (comp XV281)	Marsh Lane Technical School, Preston
	XW276	Aérospatiale SA341 Gazelle (F-ZWRI)	Newark Air Museum, Winthorpe
	XW281	WS Scout AH1 (G-BYNZ) [T]	Privately owned, Wembury, Devon
	XW283	WS Scout AH1 [U]	RM, stored Yeovilton
	XW289	BAC Jet Provost T5A (G-BVXT/G-JPVA) [73]	Kennet Aviation, Yeovilton
	XW290	BAC Jet Provost T5A (9199M) [41,MA]	DCAE, No 1 SoTT, Cosford
	XW293	BAC Jet Provost T5 (G-BWCS) [Z]	Privately owned, Bournemouth
	XW299	BAC Jet Provost T5A (9146M) [60,MB]	DCAE, No 1 SoTT, Cosford
	XW301	BAC Jet Provost T5A (9147M) [63,MC]	DCAE, No 1 SoTT, Cosford
	XW303	BAC Jet Provost T5A (9119M) [127]	RAF Halton
	XW304	BAC Jet Provost T5 (9172M) [MD]	Privately owned, Eye, Suffolk
	XW309	BAC Jet Provost T5 (9179M) [V,ME]	Hartlepool College of Further Education
	XW311	BAC Jet Provost T5 (9180M) [W,MF]	Privately owned, North Weald
	XW315	BAC Jet Provost T5A <ff>	Privately owned, Wolverhampton
	XW318	BAC Jet Provost T5A (9190M) [78,MG]	DCAE, No 1 SoTT, Cosford
	XW320	BAC Jet Provost T5A (9015M) [71]	DCAE, No 1 SoTT, Cosford
	XW321	BAC Jet Provost T5A (9154M) [62,MH]	DCAE, No 1 SoTT, Cosford
	XW323	BAC Jet Provost T5A (9166M) [86]	RAF Museum, Hendon
	XW324	BAC Jet Provost T5 (G-BWSG) [K]	Privately owned, East Midlands
	XW325	BAC Jet Provost T5B (G-BWGF) [E]	Privately owned, Woodvale
	XW327	BAC Jet Provost T5A (9130M) [62]	DCAE, No 1 SoTT, Cosford
	XW328	BAC Jet Provost T5A (9177M) [75,MI]	DCAE, No 1 SoTT, Cosford
	XW330	BAC Jet Provost T5A (9195M) [82,MJ]	DCAE, No 1 SoTT, Cosford
	XW333	BAC Jet Provost T5A (G-BVTC)	Global Aviation, Humberside
	XW353	BAC Jet Provost T5A (9090M) [3]	RAF Cranwell, on display
	XW354	BAC Jet Provost T5A (XW355/G-JPTV)	Privately owned, Church Fenton
	XW358	BAC Jet Provost T5A (9181M) [59,MK]	*Currently not known*
	XW360	BAC Jet Provost T5A (9153M) [61,ML]	DCAE, No 1 SoTT, Cosford
	XW361	BAC Jet Provost T5A (9192M) [81,MM]	DCAE, No 1 SoTT, Cosford
	XW363	BAC Jet Provost T5A [36]	Privately owned, Millom
	XW364	BAC Jet Provost T5A (9188M) [35,MN]	DCAE, No 1 SoTT, Cosford
	XW367	BAC Jet Provost T5A (9193M) [64,MO]	DCAE, No 1 SoTT, Cosford
	XW370	BAC Jet Provost T5A (9196M) [72,MP]	DCAE, No 1 SoTT, Cosford
	XW375	BAC Jet Provost T5A (9149M) [52]	DCAE, No 1 SoTT, Cosford
	XW404	BAC Jet Provost T5A (9049M)	Privately owned, Exeter
	XW405	BAC Jet Provost T5A (9187M) [J,MQ]	Privately owned, Ashclyst Farm, Exeter
	XW409	BAC Jet Provost T5A (9047M)	Privately owned, Hawarden
	XW410	BAC Jet Provost T5A (9125M) [80,MR]	DCAE, No 1 SoTT, Cosford
	XW416	BAC Jet Provost T5A (9191M) [84,MS]	DCAE, No 1 SoTT, Cosford
	XW418	BAC Jet Provost T5A (9173M) [MT]	DCAE, No 1 SoTT, Cosford
	XW419	BAC Jet Provost T5A (9120M) [125]	Privately owned, Bournemouth
	XW420	BAC Jet Provost T5A (9194M) [83,MU]	DCAE, No 1 SoTT, Cosford

Serial	Type (code/other identity)	Owner/operator, location or fate	Notes
XW422	BAC Jet Provost T5A (G-BWEB) [3]	Privately owned, Kemble	
XW423	BAC Jet Provost T5A (G-BWUW) [14]	Deeside College, Connah's Quay, Clwyd	
XW425	BAC Jet Provost T5A (9200M) [H,MV]	DCAE, No 1 SoTT, Cosford	
XW430	BAC Jet Provost T5A (9176M) [77,MW]	DCAE, No 1 SoTT, Cosford	
XW432	BAC Jet Provost T5A (9127M) [76,MX]	DCAE, No 1 SoTT, Cosford	
XW433	BAC Jet Provost T5A (G-JPRO)	Air Atlantique Classic Flight, Coventry	
XW434	BAC Jet Provost T5A (9091M) [78,MY]	DCAE, No 1 SoTT, Cosford	
XW436	BAC Jet Provost T5A (9148M) [68]	DCAE, No 1 SoTT, Cosford	
XW530	HS Buccaneer S2B	Buccaneer Service Station, Elgin	
XW541	HS Buccaneer S2B (8858M) <ff>	Privately owned, Mold	
XW544	HS Buccaneer S2B (8857M) [Y]	Privately owned, Bruntingthorpe	
XW547	HS Buccaneer S2B (9095M/9169M) [R]	RAF Museum, Hendon	
XW550	HS Buccaneer S2B <ff>	Privately owned, West Horndon, Essex	
XW560	SEPECAT Jaguar S <ff>	Boscombe Down Aviation Collection	
XW563	SEPECAT Jaguar S (*XX822*/8563M)	County Hall, Norwich, on display	
XW566	SEPECAT Jaguar B	Farnborough Air Sciences Trust, Farnborough	
XW612	WS Scout AH1 (G-BXRR)	Privately owned, Thruxton	
XW613	WS Scout AH1 (G-BXRS)	Privately owned, New Milton, Hants	
XW616	WS Scout AH1	AAC Dishforth, instructional use	
XW630	HS Harrier GR3	RNAS Yeovilton, Fire Section	
XW635	Beagle D5/180 (G-AWSW)	Privately owned, Spanhoe	
XW664	HS Nimrod R1	RAF No 51 Sqn, Waddington	
XW665	HS Nimrod R1	RAF Waddington (wfu)	
XW666	HS Nimrod R1 <ff>	Aeroventure, Doncaster	
XW763	HS Harrier GR3 (9002M/9041M) <ff>	Privately owned, Wigston, Leics	
XW768	HS Harrier GR3 (9072M) [N]	MoD DFTDC, Manston	
XW784	Mitchell-Procter Kittiwake I (G-BBRN) [VL]	Privately owned, RNAS Yeovilton	
XW795	WS Scout AH1	Blessingbourne Museum, Fivemiletown, Co Tyrone, NI	
XW796	WS Scout AH1	Gunsmoke Paintball, Hadleigh, Suffolk	
XW838	WS Lynx (TAD 009)	DCAE SEAE, Arborfield	
XW839	WS Lynx	The Helicopter Museum, Weston-super-Mare	
XW844	WS Gazelle AH1	Vector Aerospace Fleetlands Apprentice School	
XW846	WS Gazelle AH1	AAC No 665 Sqn/5 Regt, Aldergrove	
XW847	WS Gazelle AH1	AAC GDSH, Middle Wallop	
XW848	WS Gazelle AH1 [D]	Privately owned, Colsterworth, Leics	
XW849	WS Gazelle AH1 [G]	AAC GDSH, Middle Wallop	
XW851	WS Gazelle AH1	Privately owned, Durham	
XW852	WS Gazelle HCC4 (9331M)	DCAE, No 1 SoTT, Cosford	
XW854	WS Gazelle HT2 (G-TIZZ) [46/CU]	Privately owned, Redhill	
XW855	WS Gazelle HCC4	RAF Museum, Hendon	
XW858	WS Gazelle HT3 (G-DMSS) [C]	Privately owned, Murton, York	
XW860	WS Gazelle HT2 (TAD 021)	DCAE SEAE, Arborfield	
XW862	WS Gazelle HT3 (G-CBKC) [D]	Privately owned, Fowlmere	
XW863	WS Gazelle HT2 (TAD 022)	Privately owned, Fairoaks	
XW864	WS Gazelle HT2 [54/CU]	FAA Museum, stored RNAS Yeovilton	
XW865	WS Gazelle AH1 [5C]	AAC No 29 Flt, BATUS, Suffield, Canada	
XW866	WS Gazelle HT3 (G-BXTH) [E]	Privately owned, Wigtown, D&G	
XW870	WS Gazelle HT3 (9299M) [F]	MoD DFTDC, Manston	
XW888	WS Gazelle AH1 (TAD 017)	DCAE SEAE, Arborfield	
XW889	WS Gazelle AH1 (TAD 018)	DCAE SEAE, Arborfield	
XW890	WS Gazelle HT2	RNAS Yeovilton, on display	
XW892	WS Gazelle AH1 (G-CGKX/9292M) [C]	Privately owned, Babcary, Somerset	
XW893	WS Gazelle AH1 <ff>	*Scrapped at Hurstbourne Tarrant, 2010*	
XW897	WS Gazelle AH1	DCAE, No 1 SoTT, Cosford	
XW899	WS Gazelle AH1 [Z]	DCAE, No 1 SoTT, Cosford	
XW900	WS Gazelle AH1 (TAD 900)	Army, Bramley, Hants	
XW902	WS Gazelle HT3 (G-CGJY) [H]	Privately owned, Hurstbourne Tarrant, Hants	

Notes	Serial	Type (code/other identity)	Owner/operator, location or fate
	XW904	WS Gazelle AH1 [H]	AAC GDSH, Middle Wallop
	XW906	WS Gazelle HT3 [J]	AAC, stored Middle Wallop
	XW908	WS Gazelle AH1 [A]	QinetiQ, Boscombe Down (spares use)
	XW909	WS Gazelle AH1	Privately owned, Colsterworth, Leics
	XW912	WS Gazelle AH1 (TAD 019)	DCAE SEAE, Arborfield
	XW913	WS Gazelle AH1	Privately owned, Colsterworth, Leics
	XW917	HS Harrier GR3 (8975M)	RAF Cottesmore, at main gate
	XW919	HS Harrier GR3 [W]	*Sold to Poland, June 2010*
	XW922	HS Harrier GR3 (8885M)	MoD DFTDC, Manston
	XW923	HS Harrier GR3 (8724M) <ff>	RAF Wittering, Fire Section
	XW924	HS Harrier GR3 (9073M) [G]	RAF Coningsby, preserved
	XW927	HS Harrier T4 <ff>	Privately owned, Sproughton
	XW934	HS Harrier T4 [Y]	Farnborough Air Sciences Trust, Farnborough
	XW994	Northrop Chukar D1	FAA Museum, stored RNAS Yeovilton
	XW999	Northrop Chukar D1	Davidstow Airfield & Cornwall At War Museum
	XX105	BAC 1-11/201AC (G-ASJD)	MoD Boscombe Down, for scrapping
	XX108	SEPECAT Jaguar GR1(mod)	Imperial War Museum, Duxford
	XX109	SEPECAT Jaguar GR1 (8918M) [GH]	City of Norwich Aviation Museum
	XX110	SEPECAT Jaguar GR1 (8955M) [EP]	DCAE, No 1 SoTT, Cosford
	XX110	SEPECAT Jaguar GR1 <R> (BAPC 169)	DCAE, No 1 SoTT, Cosford
	XX112	SEPECAT Jaguar GR3A [EA]	DCAE, No 1 SoTT, Cosford
	XX115	SEPECAT Jaguar GR1 (8821M) (fuselage)	DCAE, No 1 SoTT, Cosford
	XX116	SEPECAT Jaguar GR3A [EO]	MoD DFTDC, Manston
	XX117	SEPECAT Jaguar GR3A [ES]	DCAE, No 1 SoTT, Cosford
	XX119	SEPECAT Jaguar GR3A (8898M) [AI]$	DCAE, No 1 SoTT, Cosford
	XX121	SEPECAT Jaguar GR1 [EQ]	Privately owned, Charlwood, Surrey
	XX139	SEPECAT Jaguar T4 [PT]	Privately owned, Sproughton
	XX140	SEPECAT Jaguar T2 (9008M) <ff>	Privately owned, Chesterfield
	XX141	SEPECAT Jaguar T2A (9297M) [Y]	DCAE, TCF, RAFC Cranwell
	XX144	SEPECAT Jaguar T2A [U]	Privately owned, Sproughton
	XX145	SEPECAT Jaguar T2A	RAFC Cranwell Fire Section
	XX146	SEPECAT Jaguar T4 [GT]	Privately owned, Wellbeck, Lincs
	XX150	SEPECAT Jaguar T4 [FY]	Privately owned, Bentwaters
	XX153	WS Lynx AH1 (9320M)	Museum of Army Flying, Middle Wallop
	XX154	HS Hawk T1	MoD/ETPS, Boscombe Down
	XX156	HS Hawk T1	RAF No 4 FTS/*208(R) Sqn*, Valley
	XX157	HS Hawk T1A	RN FRADU, Culdrose
	XX158	HS Hawk T1A	RN FRADU, Culdrose
	XX159	HS Hawk T1A $	RN FRADU, Culdrose
	XX160	HS Hawk T1	RN, stored Shawbury
	XX161	HS Hawk T1W	RAF, stored Shawbury
	XX162	HS Hawk T1	RAF Centre of Aviation Medicine, Boscombe Down
	XX165	HS Hawk T1	RAF No 4 FTS/*208(R) Sqn*, Valley
	XX167	HS Hawk T1W	RAF No 4 FTS/*208(R) Sqn*, Valley
	XX168	HS Hawk T1	RN, stored Shawbury
	XX169	HS Hawk T1	RN FRADU, Culdrose
	XX170	HS Hawk T1	RN, Culdrose (damaged)
	XX171	HS Hawk T1	RAF No 4 FTS/*208(R) Sqn*, Valley
	XX172	HS Hawk T1	RN, stored Shawbury
	XX173	HS Hawk T1	RN, stored Shawbury
	XX174	HS Hawk T1	RAF No 4 FTS/*208(R) Sqn*, Valley
	XX175	HS Hawk T1	RAF, stored Shawbury
	XX176	HS Hawk T1W	RAF No 4 FTS/*19(R) Sqn*, Valley
	XX177	HS Hawk T1	RAF *Red Arrows*, Scampton
	XX178	HS Hawk T1W	RAF No 4 FTS/*19(R) Sqn*, Valley
	XX179	HS Hawk T1W	RAF *Red Arrows*, Scampton
	XX181	HS Hawk T1W	RAF No 4 FTS/*208(R) Sqn*, Valley
	XX184	HS Hawk T1 [CQ]	RAF No 100 Sqn, Leeming
	XX185	HS Hawk T1	RAF No 4 FTS/*208(R) Sqn*, Valley
	XX187	HS Hawk T1A	RAF No 4 FTS/*208(R) Sqn*, Valley
	XX188	HS Hawk T1A	RAF No 4 FTS/*19(R) Sqn*, Valley
	XX189	HS Hawk T1A	RAF No 4 FTS/*19(R) Sqn*, Valley
	XX190	HS Hawk T1A [CN]	RAF, stored Shawbury

Serial	Type (code/other identity)	Owner/operator, location or fate	Notes
XX191	HS Hawk T1A	RAF, stored Shawbury	
XX194	HS Hawk T1A	RAF No 4 FTS/*208(R) Sqn*, Valley	
XX195	HS Hawk T1W	RAF, stored Shawbury	
XX198	HS Hawk T1A [CG]	RAF No 100 Sqn, Leeming	
XX199	HS Hawk T1A	RAF No 4 FTS/*19(R) Sqn*, Valley	
XX200	HS Hawk T1A [CG]	RAF, stored Shawbury	
XX201	HS Hawk T1A	RAF No 4 FTS/*208(R) Sqn*, Valley	
XX202	HS Hawk T1A [CF]	RAF No 100 Sqn, Leeming	
XX203	HS Hawk T1A [CC]	RAF No 100 Sqn, Leeming	
XX204	HS Hawk T1A	RAF No 4 FTS/*19(R) Sqn*, Valley	
XX205	HS Hawk T1A $	RN FRADU, Culdrose	
XX217	HS Hawk T1A	RN FRADU, Culdrose	
XX218	HS Hawk T1A	RAF No 4 FTS/*208(R) Sqn*, Valley	
XX219	HS Hawk T1A	RAF, stored Shawbury	
XX220	HS Hawk T1A	RAF No 4 FTS/*208(R) Sqn*, Valley	
XX221	HS Hawk T1A	RN FRADU, Culdrose	
XX222	HS Hawk T1A [CI]	RAF No 100 Sqn, Leeming	
XX223	HS Hawk T1 <ff>	Privately owned, Charlwood, Surrey	
XX224	HS Hawk T1W	RAF No 4 FTS/*208(R) Sqn*, Valley	
XX225	HS Hawk T1	RN, stored Shawbury	
XX226	HS Hawk T1	RN, stored Shawbury	
XX227	HS Hawk T1 <R> (*XX226*/BAPC 152)	RAF M&RU, Bottesford	
XX227	HS Hawk T1A	RAF *Red Arrows*, Scampton	
XX228	HS Hawk T1A [CG]	RAF, stored Shawbury	
XX230	HS Hawk T1A	RN FRADU, Culdrose (on repair)	
XX231	HS Hawk T1W	RAF No 4 FTS/*208(R) Sqn*, Valley	
XX232	HS Hawk T1	RAF, stored Shawbury	
XX233	HS Hawk T1	*Crashed 23 March 2010, Kasteli, Crete*	
XX234	HS Hawk T1	RAF No 4 FTS/*208(R) Sqn*, Valley	
XX235	HS Hawk T1W	RAF, stored Shawbury	
XX236	HS Hawk T1W	RAF No 4 FTS/*19(R) Sqn*, Valley	
XX237	HS Hawk T1	RAF *Red Arrows*, Scampton	
XX238	HS Hawk T1	RAF, stored Shawbury	
XX239	HS Hawk T1W	RAF, stored Shawbury	
XX240	HS Hawk T1	RAF, stored Shawbury	
XX242	HS Hawk T1	RAF *Red Arrows*, Scampton	
XX244	HS Hawk T1	RAF No 4 FTS/*19(R) Sqn*, Valley	
XX245	HS Hawk T1 $	RAF No 4 FTS/*208(R) Sqn*, Valley	
XX246	HS Hawk T1A [CA]	RAF No 100 Sqn, Leeming	
XX246	HS Hawk T1A <rf>	RAF CTTS, St Athan	
XX247	HS Hawk T1A	RAF No 4 FTS/*19(R) Sqn*, Valley	
XX248	HS Hawk T1A [CJ]	RAF, stored Shawbury	
XX250	HS Hawk T1	MoD/BAE Systems, Brough	
XX253	HS Hawk T1A	RAF *Red Arrows*, Scampton (damaged)	
XX254	HS Hawk T1A <ff>	MoD/DSG, St Athan	
XX254	HS Hawk T1A	MoD/BAE Systems, stored Scampton	
XX254	HS Hawk T1A <R>	Privately owned, Marlow, Bucks	
XX255	HS Hawk T1A [CL]	RAF No 100 Sqn, Leeming	
XX256	HS Hawk T1A	RAF Valley (wfu)	
XX257	HS Hawk T1A (fuselage)	Privately owned, Charlwood, Surrey	
XX258	HS Hawk T1A [CE]	RAF No 100 Sqn, Leeming	
XX260	HS Hawk T1A	RAF *Red Arrows*, Scampton	
XX261	HS Hawk T1A $	RN FRADU, Culdrose	
XX263	HS Hawk T1A $	RAF No 4 FTS/*208(R) Sqn*, Valley	
XX264	HS Hawk T1A	RAF *Red Arrows*, Scampton	
XX265	HS Hawk T1A	RAF, stored Shawbury	
XX266	HS Hawk T1A	RAF *Red Arrows*, Scampton	
XX278	HS Hawk T1A	MoD/BAE Systems, Brough	
XX280	HS Hawk T1A [CM]	RAF No 100 Sqn, Leeming	
XX281	HS Hawk T1A	RN FRADU, Culdrose	
XX283	HS Hawk T1W	RAF No 4 FTS/*19(R) Sqn*, Valley	
XX284	HS Hawk T1A [CA]	RAF, stored Shawbury	
XX285	HS Hawk T1A $	RAF No 100 Sqn, Leeming	
XX286	HS Hawk T1A	RAF No 4 FTS/*19(R) Sqn*, Valley	
XX287	HS Hawk T1A	RAF No 4 FTS/*19(R) Sqn*, Valley	
XX289	HS Hawk T1A [CO]	RAF No 100 Sqn, Leeming	
XX290	HS Hawk T1W [CU]	RAF, stored Shawbury	
XX292	HS Hawk T1	RAF, stored Shawbury	
XX294	HS Hawk T1	RAF *Red Arrows*, Scampton	
XX295	HS Hawk T1W	RAF, stored Shawbury	
XX296	HS Hawk T1	RAF, stored Shawbury	

Notes	Serial	Type (code/other identity)	Owner/operator, location or fate
	XX299	HS Hawk T1W	RAF, stored Shawbury
	XX301	HS Hawk T1A $	RN FRADU, Culdrose
	XX303	HS Hawk T1A	RN FRADU, Culdrose
	XX304	HS Hawk T1A <rf>	Cardiff International Airport Fire Section
	XX306	HS Hawk T1A	RAF *Red Arrows*, Scampton
	XX307	HS Hawk T1 $	RAF No 4 FTS/208(R) Sqn, Valley
	XX308	HS Hawk T1	RAF *Red Arrows*, Scampton
	XX308	HS Hawk T1 <R> (*XX263*/BAPC 171)	RAF M&RU, Bottesford
	XX309	HS Hawk T1	RAF, stored Shawbury
	XX310	HS Hawk T1W	RAF, stored Shawbury
	XX311	HS Hawk T1	RAF, stored Shawbury
	XX312	HS Hawk T1W	RAF No 4 FTS/*19(R) Sqn*, Valley
	XX313	HS Hawk T1W	RAF No 4 FTS/*19(R) Sqn*, Valley
	XX314	HS Hawk T1W	RAF No 4 FTS/*19(R) Sqn*, Valley
	XX315	HS Hawk T1A	RAF No 4 FTS/*19(R) Sqn*, Valley
	XX316	HS Hawk T1A	RN FRADU, Culdrose
	XX317	HS Hawk T1A	RAF No 4 FTS/*19(R) Sqn*, Valley
	XX318	HS Hawk T1A [CN]	RAF No 100 Sqn, Leeming
	XX319	HS Hawk T1A	RAF Centre of Aviation Medicine, Boscombe Down
	XX320	HS Hawk T1A <ff>	Privately owned, Scampton
	XX321	HS Hawk T1A	MoD/BAE Systems, Warton
	XX322	HS Hawk T1A	RAF *Red Arrows*, Cranwell
	XX323	HS Hawk T1A	RAF, stored Shawbury
	XX324	HS Hawk T1A	RAF No 4 FTS/*19(R) Sqn*, Valley
	XX325	HS Hawk T1A $	RAF, stored Shawbury
	XX326	HS Hawk T1A <ff>	MoD/DSG, St Athan
	XX326	HS Hawk T1A	MoD/BAE Systems, Brough (on rebuild)
	XX327	HS Hawk T1	RAF Centre of Aviation Medicine, Boscombe Down
	XX329	HS Hawk T1A [CJ]	RAF No 100 Sqn, Leeming
	XX330	HS Hawk T1A	RN FRADU, Culdrose
	XX331	HS Hawk T1A	RN FRADU, Culdrose
	XX332	HS Hawk T1A [CD]	RAF No 100 Sqn, Leeming
	XX335	HS Hawk T1A	RAF No 4 FTS/*208(R) Sqn*, Valley
	XX337	HS Hawk T1A	RN FRADU, Culdrose
	XX338	HS Hawk T1	RAF No 4 FTS/*19(R) Sqn*, Valley
	XX339	HS Hawk T1A [CK]	RAF No 100 Sqn, Leeming
	XX341	HS Hawk T1 ASTRA	MoD/ETPS, Boscombe Down
	XX342	HS Hawk T1 [2]	MoD/ETPS, Boscombe Down
	XX343	HS Hawk T1 [3] (wreck)	Boscombe Down Aviation Collection
	XX345	HS Hawk T1A [CE]	RAF, stored Shawbury
	XX346	HS Hawk T1A [CH]	RAF No 100 Sqn, Leeming
	XX348	HS Hawk T1A	RAF Leeming (on rebuild)
	XX349	HS Hawk T1W	RAF No 4 FTS/*19(R) Sqn*, Valley
	XX350	HS Hawk T1A	RAF, stored Shawbury
	XX351	HS Hawk T1A	RAF, stored Shawbury
	XX371	WS Gazelle AH1	Privately owned, Colsterworth, Leics
	XX372	WS Gazelle AH1	MoD/QinetiQ, Boscombe Down
	XX375	WS Gazelle AH1	Privately owned, Shepherds Bush
	XX378	WS Gazelle AH1 [Q]	AAC, stored Shawbury
	XX379	WS Gazelle AH1 [Y]	AAC, stored Shawbury
	XX380	WS Gazelle AH1 [A]	Wattisham Airfield Museum
	XX381	WS Gazelle AH1 [C]	AAC GDSH, Middle Wallop
	XX383	WS Gazelle AH1 [D]	Privately owned, Colsterworth, Leics
	XX384	WS Gazelle AH1	AAC, Dishforth
	XX386	WS Gazelle AH1	Privately owned, Colsterworth, Leics
	XX387	WS Gazelle AH1 (TAD 014)	Privately owned, stored Cranfield
	XX388	WS Gazelle AH1 <ff>	*Scrapped at Hurstbourne Tarrant, 2010*
	XX392	WS Gazelle AH1	Army, Middle Wallop, preserved
	XX393	WS Gazelle AH1 <ff>	*Scrapped at Hurstbourne Tarrant, 2010*
	XX394	WS Gazelle AH1 [X]	Privately owned, Colsterworth, Leics
	XX396	WS Gazelle HT3 (8718M) [N]	DCAE, TCF, RAFC Cranwell
	XX398	WS Gazelle AH1	Privately owned, Colsterworth, Leics
	XX399	WS Gazelle AH1 [B]	AAC, stored Shawbury
	XX403	WS Gazelle AH1 [U]	AAC, stored Shawbury
	XX405	WS Gazelle AH1	AAC No 665 Sqn/5 Regt, Aldergrove
	XX406	WS Gazelle HT3 (G-CBSH) [P]	Privately owned, Rochester
	XX409	WS Gazelle AH1	Privately owned, Colsterworth, Leics
	XX410	WS Gazelle AH1 [X]	Aeroventure, Doncaster
	XX411	WS Gazelle AH1 <rf>	FAA Museum, RNAS Yeovilton

Serial	Type (code/other identity)	Owner/operator, location or fate	Notes
XX412	WS Gazelle AH1 [B]	DCAE, No 1 SoTT, Cosford	
XX413	WS Gazelle AH1 <ff>	*Scrapped at Hurstbourne Tarrant, 2010*	
XX414	WS Gazelle AH1 [V]	Privately owned, Hurstbourne Tarrant, Hants	
XX416	WS Gazelle AH1	Privately owned, Colsterworth, Leics	
XX418	WS Gazelle AH1	Privately owned, Hurstbourne Tarrant, Hants	
XX419	WS Gazelle AH1	AAC GDSH, Middle Wallop	
XX431	WS Gazelle HT2 (9300M) [43/CU]	RAF Shawbury, for display	
XX433	WS Gazelle AH1 <ff>	Privately owned, Hurstbourne Tarrant, Hants	
XX435	WS Gazelle AH1 (fuselage)	QinetiQ, Boscombe Down (spares use)	
XX437	WS Gazelle AH1	Privately owned, Colsterworth, Leics	
XX438	WS Gazelle AH1 [F]	Privately owned, Colsterworth, Leics	
XX439	WS Gazelle AH1	Privately owned, Colsterworth, Leics	
XX440	WS Gazelle AH1 (G-BCHN)	Vector Aerospace Fleetlands Apprentice School	
XX442	WS Gazelle AH1 [E]	AAC, stored Shawbury	
XX443	WS Gazelle AH1 [Y]	DCAE, stored HMS Sultan, Gosport	
XX444	WS Gazelle AH1	Wattisham Airfield Museum	
XX445	WS Gazelle AH1 [T]	Privately owned, Colsterworth, Leics	
XX447	WS Gazelle AH1 [D1]	AAC, stored Shawbury	
XX449	WS Gazelle AH1	MoD/QinetiQ, Boscombe Down	
XX450	WS Gazelle AH1 [D]	*Scrapped at St Mary Bourne, Hants, 2010*	
XX453	WS Gazelle AH1	MoD/QinetiQ, Boscombe Down	
XX454	WS Gazelle AH1 (TAD 023) (fuselage)	DCAE SEAE, Arborfield	
XX455	WS Gazelle AH1	Privately owned, Colsterworth, Leics	
XX456	WS Gazelle AH1	Privately owned, Colsterworth, Leics	
XX457	WS Gazelle AH1 <ff>	East Midlands Airport Aeropark	
XX460	WS Gazelle AH1	AAC, stored Shawbury	
XX462	WS Gazelle AH1 [W]	Privately owned, Colsterworth, Leics	
XX466	HS Hunter T66B/T7	Guernsey Airport Fire Section	
XX467	HS Hunter T66B/T7 (XL605/G-TVII) [86]	Hunter Flying Ltd, Exeter	
XX476	HP137 Jetstream T2 (N1037S) [561/CU]	RN No 750 NAS, Culdrose	
XX477	HP137 Jetstream T1 (G-AXXS/8462M) <ff>	Aeroventure, Doncaster	
XX478	HP137 Jetstream T2 (G-AXXT) [564/CU]	RN No 750 NAS, Culdrose	
XX479	HP137 Jetstream T2 (G-AXUR)	RN, Predannack Fire School	
XX481	HP137 Jetstream T2 (G-AXUP) [560/CU]	RN No 750 NAS, Culdrose	
XX482	SA Jetstream T1 [J]	Privately owned, Hixon, Staffs	
XX483	SA Jetstream T2 [562] <ff>	Dumfries & Galloway Avn Mus, Dumfries	
XX484	SA Jetstream T2 [566/CU]	RN No 750 NAS, Culdrose	
XX486	SA Jetstream T2 [567/CU]	RN No 750 NAS, Culdrose	
XX487	SA Jetstream T2 [568/CU]	RN No 750 NAS, Culdrose	
XX488	SA Jetstream T2 [562/CU]	*Scrapped at Culdrose, 24 January 2011*	
XX491	SA Jetstream T1 [K]	Northbrook College, Shoreham, instructional use	
XX492	SA Jetstream T1 [A]	Newark Air Museum, Winthorpe	
XX494	SA Jetstream T1 [B]	Privately owned, Gamston	
XX495	SA Jetstream T1 [C]	Bedford College, instructional use	
XX496	SA Jetstream T1 [D]	RAF Museum, Cosford	
XX499	SA Jetstream T1 [G]	Brooklands Museum, Weybridge	
XX500	SA Jetstream T1 [H]	Privately owned, Sproughton	
XX510	WS Lynx HAS2 [69/DD]	SFDO, RNAS Culdrose	
XX513	SA Bulldog T1 (G-CCMI) [10]	Privately owned, Meppershall	
XX515	SA Bulldog T1 (G-CBBC) [4]	Privately owned, Blackbushe	
XX518	SA Bulldog T1 (G-UDOG) [S]	Privately owned, North Weald	
XX520	SA Bulldog T1 (9288M) [A]	No 172 Sqn ATC, Haywards Heath	
XX521	SA Bulldog T1 (G-CBEH) [H]	Privately owned, East Dereham, Norfolk	
XX522	SA Bulldog T1 (G-DAWG) [06]	Privately owned, Barton	
XX524	SA Bulldog T1 (G-DDOG) [04]	Privately owned, Malaga, Spain	
XX525	SA Bulldog T1 (G-CBJJ) [03]	Privately owned, Kortrijk, Belgium	
XX528	SA Bulldog T1 (G-BZON) [D]	Privately owned, Earls Colne	
XX530	SA Bulldog T1 (XX637/9197M) [F]	No 2175 Sqn ATC, RAF Kinloss	
XX534	SA Bulldog T1 (G-EDAV) [B]	Privately owned, Tollerton	
XX537	SA Bulldog T1 (G-CBCB) [C]	Privately owned, RAF Halton	
XX538	SA Bulldog T1 (G-TDOG) [O]	Privately owned, Shobdon	
XX539	SA Bulldog T1 [L]	Privately owned, Derbyshire	
XX543	SA Bulldog T1 (G-CBAB) [F]	Privately owned, Duxford	
XX546	SA Bulldog T1 (G-WINI) [03]	Privately owned, Blackbushe	

Notes	Serial	Type (code/other identity)	Owner/operator, location or fate
	XX549	SA Bulldog T1 (G-CBID) [6]	Privately owned, White Waltham
	XX550	SA Bulldog T1 (G-CBBL) [Z]	Privately owned, Fenland
	XX551	SA Bulldog T1 (G-BZDP) [E]	Privately owned, RAF Cranwell
	XX554	SA Bulldog T1 (G-BZMD) [09]	Privately owned, Wellesbourne Mountford
	XX557	SA Bulldog T1	Privately owned, stored Fort Paull, Yorks
	XX561	SA Bulldog T1 (G-BZEP) [7]	Privately owned, Biggin Hill
	XX611	SA Bulldog T1 (G-CBDK) [7]	Privately owned, Coventry
	XX612	SA Bulldog T1 (G-BZXC) [A,03]	Privately owned, Carnegie College, Dunfermline
	XX614	SA Bulldog T1 (G-GGRR) [V]	Privately owned, White Waltham
	XX619	SA Bulldog T1 (G-CBBW) [T]	Privately owned, Coventry
	XX621	SA Bulldog T1 (G-CBEF) [H]	Privately owned, Leicester
	XX622	SA Bulldog T1 (G-CBGX) [B]	Privately owned, Shoreham
	XX623	SA Bulldog T1 [M]	Privately owned, Hurstbourne Tarrant, Hants
	XX624	SA Bulldog T1 (G-KDOG) [E]	Privately owned, North Weald
	XX626	SA Bulldog T1 (9290M/G-CDVV) [W,02]	Privately owned, Wellesbourne Mountford
	XX628	SA Bulldog T1 (G-CBFU) [9]	Privately owned, Faversham
	XX629	SA Bulldog T1 (G-BZXZ) [V]	Privately owned, Wellesbourne Mountford
	XX630	SA Bulldog T1 (G-SIJW) [5]	Privately owned, Cranfield
	XX631	SA Bulldog T1 (G-BZXS) [W]	Privately owned, Sligo, Eire
	XX633	SA Bulldog T1 [X]	Privately owned, Diseworth, Leics
	XX634	SA Bulldog T1 [T]	Newark Air Museum, Winthorpe
	XX636	SA Bulldog T1 (G-CBFP) [Y]	Privately owned, Cranfield
	XX638	SA Bulldog T1 (G-DOGG)	Privately owned, Hurstbourne Tarrant, Hants
	XX653	SA Bulldog T1 [E]	Parkway College, Stoke Gifford, Glos
	XX654	SA Bulldog T1 [3]	RAF Museum, Cosford
	XX655	SA Bulldog T1 (9294M) [V] <ff>	Aeroventure, Doncaster
	XX656	SA Bulldog T1 [C]	Privately owned, Derbyshire
	XX658	SA Bulldog T1 (G-BZPS) [07]	Privately owned, Wellesbourne Mountford
	XX659	SA Bulldog T1 [E]	Privately owned, Derbyshire
	XX664	SA Bulldog T1 (F-AZTV) [04]	Privately owned, Pontoise, France
	XX665	SA Bulldog T1 (9289M)	No 2409 Sqn ATC, Halton
	XX667	SA Bulldog T1 (G-BZFN) [16]	Privately owned, Ronaldsway, IoM
	XX668	SA Bulldog T1 (G-CBAN) [1]	Privately owned, Egginton
	XX671	SA Bulldog T1 [D]	Privately owned, Diseworth, Leics
	XX687	SA Bulldog T1 [F]	Barry Technical College, Cardiff Airport
	XX690	SA Bulldog T1 [A]	James Watt College, Greenock
	XX692	SA Bulldog T1 (G-BZMH) [A]	Privately owned, Wellesbourne Mountford
	XX693	SA Bulldog T1 (G-BZML) [07]	Privately owned, Elmsett
	XX694	SA Bulldog T1 (G-CBBS) [E]	Privately owned, stored Sturgate
	XX695	SA Bulldog T1 (G-CBBT) [3]	Privately owned, Sherburn-in-Elmet
	XX698	SA Bulldog T1 (G-BZME) [9]	Privately owned, Breighton
	XX699	SA Bulldog T1 (G-CBCV) [F]	Privately owned, North Coates
	XX700	SA Bulldog T1 (G-CBEK) [17]	Privately owned, Blackbushe
	XX702	SA Bulldog T1 (G-CBCR) [π]	Privately owned, Egginton
	XX704	SA122 Bulldog (G-BCUV/G-112)	Privately owned, Bournemouth
	XX705	SA Bulldog T1 [5]	QinetiQ Boscombe Down, Apprentice School
	XX707	SA Bulldog T1 (G-CBDS) [4]	Privately owned, Caernarfon
	XX711	SA Bulldog T1 (G-CBBU) [X]	Privately owned, Egginton
	XX720	SEPECAT Jaguar GR3A [FL]	Privately owned, Sproughton
	XX722	SEPECAT Jaguar GR1 (9252M) <ff>	RAF St Athan, instructional use
	XX723	SEPECAT Jaguar GR3A [EU]	DCAE, No 1 SoTT, Cosford
	XX724	SEPECAT Jaguar GR3A [EC]	DCAE, No 1 SoTT, Cosford
	XX725	SEPECAT Jaguar GR3A [T]	DCAE, No 1 SoTT, Cosford
	XX726	SEPECAT Jaguar GR1 (8947M) [EB]	DCAE, No 1 SoTT, Cosford
	XX727	SEPECAT Jaguar GR1 (8951M) [ER]	DCAE, No 1 SoTT, Cosford
	XX729	SEPECAT Jaguar GR3A [EL]	DCAE, No 1 SoTT, Cosford
	XX730	SEPECAT Jaguar GR1 (8952M) [EC]	*To Poland, 2010*
	XX733	SEPECAT Jaguar GR1B [EB] (wreck)	Privately owned, Faygate
	XX734	SEPECAT Jaguar GR1 (8816M)	Gatwick Aviation Museum, Charlwood
	XX736	SEPECAT Jaguar GR1 (9110M) <ff>	Aeroventure, Doncaster
	XX738	SEPECAT Jaguar GR3A [ED]	DCAE, No 1 SoTT, Cosford
	XX739	SEPECAT Jaguar GR1 (8902M) [I]	RAF Syerston, instructional use
	XX741	SEPECAT Jaguar GR1A [04]	Bentwaters Cold War Museum

Serial	Type (code/other identity)	Owner/operator, location or fate	Notes
XX743	SEPECAT Jaguar GR1 (8949M) [EG]	DCAE, No 1 SoTT, Cosford	
XX744	SEPECAT Jaguar GR1 (9251M)	Mayhem Paintball, Abridge, Essex	
XX745	SEPECAT Jaguar GR1A [GV]	MoD/QinetiQ, Boscombe Down	
XX746	SEPECAT Jaguar GR1 (8895M) [S]	DCAE, No 1 SoTT, Cosford	
XX747	SEPECAT Jaguar GR1 (8903M)	DCAE, TCF, RAFC Cranwell	
XX748	SEPECAT Jaguar GR3A [EG]	DCAE, No 1 SoTT, Cosford	
XX751	SEPECAT Jaguar GR1 (8937M) [10]	RAF Syerston, instructional use	
XX752	SEPECAT Jaguar GR3A [EK]	DCAE, No 1 SoTT, Cosford	
XX753	SEPECAT Jaguar GR1 (9087M) <ff>	Newark Air Museum, Winthorpe	
XX756	SEPECAT Jaguar GR1 (8899M) [W]	DCAE, No 1 SoTT, Cosford	
XX757	SEPECAT Jaguar GR1 (8948M) [CU]	DCAE, No 1 SoTT, Cosford	
XX761	SEPECAT Jaguar GR1 (8600M) <ff>	Boscombe Down Aviation Collection	
XX763	SEPECAT Jaguar GR1 (9009M)	Bournemouth Aviation Museum	
XX764	SEPECAT Jaguar GR1 (9010M)	Privately owned, Woodmancote, W Sussex	
XX765	SEPECAT Jaguar ACT	RAF Museum, Cosford	
XX766	SEPECAT Jaguar GR3A [EF]	DCAE, No 1 SoTT, Cosford	
XX767	SEPECAT Jaguar GR3A [FK]	DCAE, No 1 SoTT, Cosford	
XX818	SEPECAT Jaguar GR1 (8945M) [DE]	DCAE, No 1 SoTT, Cosford	
XX819	SEPECAT Jaguar GR1 (8923M) [CE]	DCAE, No 1 SoTT, Cosford	
XX821	SEPECAT Jaguar GR1 (8896M) [P]	DCAE, TCF, RAFC Cranwell	
XX824	SEPECAT Jaguar GR1 (9019M) [AD]	DCAE, No 1 SoTT, Cosford	
XX825	SEPECAT Jaguar GR1 (9020M) [BN]	DCAE, No 1 SoTT, Cosford	
XX826	SEPECAT Jaguar GR1 (9021M) [34,JH]	Privately owned, Sproughton	
XX829	SEPECAT Jaguar T2A [GZ]	Privately owned, Sproughton	
XX830	SEPECAT Jaguar T2 <ff>	City of Norwich Aviation Museum	
XX832	SEPECAT Jaguar T2A [EZ]	Privately owned, Bentwaters	
XX833	SEPECAT Jaguar T2B	DCAE, No 1 SoTT, Cosford	
XX835	SEPECAT Jaguar T4 [EX]	DCAE, No 1 SoTT, Cosford	
XX836	SEPECAT Jaguar T2A [X]	Privately owned, Sproughton	
XX837	SEPECAT Jaguar T2 (8978M) [Z]	DCAE, TCF, RAFC Cranwell	
XX838	SEPECAT Jaguar T4 [FZ]	Privately owned, Bentwaters	
XX840	SEPECAT Jaguar T4 [EY]	DCAE, No 1 SoTT, Cosford	
XX841	SEPECAT Jaguar T4	Privately owned, Tunbridge Wells	
XX842	SEPECAT Jaguar T2A [FX]	Privately owned, Bentwaters	
XX845	SEPECAT Jaguar T4 [EV]	RN, Predannack Fire School	
XX847	SEPECAT Jaguar T4 [EZ]	DCAE, No 1 SoTT, Cosford	
XX885	HS Buccaneer S2B (9225M/G-HHAA)	Hawker Hunter Aviation, Scampton	
XX888	HS Buccaneer S2B <ff>	Privately owned, Barnstaple	
XX889	HS Buccaneer S2B [T]	Blackburn Buccaneer Society, Kemble	
XX892	HS Buccaneer S2B <ff>	Privately owned, Perthshire	
XX893	HS Buccaneer S2B <ff>	Privately owned, Ashford, Kent	
XX894	HS Buccaneer S2B [020/R]	Buccaneer Supporters Club, Bruntingthorpe	
XX897	HS Buccaneer S2B(mod)	Privately owned, Bournemouth	
XX899	HS Buccaneer S2B <ff>	Midland Air Museum, Coventry	
XX900	HS Buccaneer S2B	Cold War Jets Collection, Bruntingthorpe	
XX901	HS Buccaneer S2B	Yorkshire Air Museum, Elvington	
XX907	WS Lynx AH1	AgustaWestland, Yeovil, Fire Section	
XX910	WS Lynx HAS2	The Helicopter Museum, Weston-super-Mare	
XX914	BAC VC10/1103 (8777M) <rf>	RAF Defence Movements School, Brize Norton	
XX919	BAC 1-11/402AP (PI-C1121) <ff>	Boscombe Down Aviation Collection	
XX946	Panavia Tornado (P02) (8883M) [WT]	RAF Museum, Cosford	
XX947	Panavia Tornado (P03) (8797M)	Shoreham Airport, on display	
XX958	SEPECAT Jaguar GR1 (9022M) [BK]	DCAE, No 1 SoTT, Cosford	
XX959	SEPECAT Jaguar GR1 (8953M) [CJ]	DCAE, No 1 SoTT, Cosford	
XX965	SEPECAT Jaguar GR1A (9254M) [C]	DCAE, TCF, RAFC Cranwell	

Notes	Serial	Type (code/other identity)	Owner/operator, location or fate
	XX967	SEPECAT Jaguar GR1 (9006M) [AC]	DCAE, No 1 SoTT, Cosford
	XX968	SEPECAT Jaguar GR1 (9007M) [AJ]	DCAE, No 1 SoTT, Cosford
	XX969	SEPECAT Jaguar GR1 (8897M) [01]	DCAE, No 1 SoTT, Cosford
	XX970	SEPECAT Jaguar GR3A [EH]	DCAE, No 1 SoTT, Cosford
	XX974	SEPECAT Jaguar GR3 [FE]	Privately owned, Sproughton
	XX975	SEPECAT Jaguar GR1 (8905M) [07]	DCAE, No 1 SoTT, Cosford
	XX976	SEPECAT Jaguar GR1 (8906M) [BD]	DCAE, No 1 SoTT, Cosford
	XX977	SEPECAT Jaguar GR1 (9132M) [DL,05] <rf>	Privately owned, Sproughton
	XX979	SEPECAT Jaguar GR1A (9306M) <ff>	Air Defence Radar Museum, Neatishead
	XZ103	SEPECAT Jaguar GR3A [EF]	DCAE, No 1 SoTT, Cosford
	XZ104	SEPECAT Jaguar GR3A [FM]	DCAE, No 1 SoTT, Cosford
	XZ106	SEPECAT Jaguar GR3A [FD,FW]	RAF Manston History Museum
	XZ107	SEPECAT Jaguar GR3A [FH]	Privately owned, Bentwaters
	XZ109	SEPECAT Jaguar GR3A [EN]	DCAE, No 1 SoTT, Cosford
	XZ112	SEPECAT Jaguar GR3A [GW]	DCAE, No 1 SoTT, Cosford
	XZ113	SEPECAT Jaguar GR3 [FD]	Privately owned, Bentwaters
	XZ114	SEPECAT Jaguar GR3 [EO]	DCAE, No 1 SoTT, Cosford
	XZ115	SEPECAT Jaguar GR3 [ER]	DCAE, No 1 SoTT, Cosford
	XZ117	SEPECAT Jaguar GR3 [ES]	DCAE, No 1 SoTT, Cosford
	XZ118	SEPECAT Jaguar GR3	Tate Modern, North Southwark
	XZ119	SEPECAT Jaguar GR1A (9266M) [FG]	Royal Scottish Mus'm of Flight, E Fortune
	XZ130	HS Harrier GR3 (9079M) [A]	No 1034 Sqn ATC, Tolworth, Surrey
	XZ131	HS Harrier GR3 (9174M) <ff>	No 2156 Sqn ATC, Brierley Hill, W Midlands
	XZ132	HS Harrier GR3 (9168M) [C]	DCAE, TCF, RAFC Cranwell
	XZ133	HS Harrier GR3 [10]	Imperial War Museum, Duxford
	XZ135	HS Harrier GR3 (8848M) <ff>	RAF M&RU, Bottesford (wfu)
	XZ138	HS Harrier GR3 (9040M) <ff>	RAFC Cranwell, Trenchard Hall
	XZ145	HS Harrier T4 [45]	RN, Predannack Fire School
	XZ146	HS Harrier T4 (9281M) [S]	RAF Wittering, on display
	XZ166	WS Lynx HAS2 <ff>	Farnborough Air Sciences Trust, Farnborough
	XZ170	WS Lynx AH9	DCAE SEAE, Arborfield
	XZ171	WS Lynx AH7	Army, Salisbury Plain
	XZ172	WS Lynx AH7	DCAE SEAE, Arborfield
	XZ173	WS Lynx AH7 <ff>	Privately owned, Hixon, Staffs
	XZ174	WS Lynx AH7 <ff>	MoD Police, Gosport, instructional use
	XZ175	WS Lynx AH7	Warfighters R6 Centre, Barby, Northants
	XZ176	WS Lynx AH7 [X]	AAC No 671 Sqn/7 Regt, Middle Wallop
	XZ177	WS Lynx AH7	RM No 847 NAS, Yeovilton
	XZ178	WS Lynx AH7 <ff>	Privately owned,
	XZ179	WS Lynx AH7	AAC No 1 Regt, Gütersloh
	XZ180	WS Lynx AH7	MoD/Vector Aerospace, Fleetlands
	XZ181	WS Lynx AH1	AAC Middle Wallop Fire Section
	XZ182	WS Lynx AH7	MoD/Vector Aerospace, stored Fleetlands
	XZ183	WS Lynx AH7 <ff>	MoD/Vector Aerospace, stored Fleetlands
	XZ184	WS Lynx AH7	AAC No 9 Regt, Dishforth
	XZ185	WS Lynx AH7	AAC No 9 Regt, Dishforth
	XZ187	WS Lynx AH7	DCAE SEAE, Arborfield
	XZ188	WS Lynx AH7	DCAE SEAE, Arborfield
	XZ190	WS Lynx AH7 [F]	RM No 847 NAS, Yeovilton
	XZ191	WS Lynx AH7	AAC No 9 Regt, Dishforth
	XZ192	WS Lynx AH7	MoD/Vector Aerospace, Fleetlands
	XZ193	WS Lynx AH7 <ff>	Privately owned,
	XZ194	WS Lynx AH7 [L]	MoD/Vector Aerospace, Fleetlands
	XZ195	WS Lynx AH7 <ff>	Privately owned, Hixon, Staffs
	XZ196	WS Lynx AH7 [T]	AAC No 671 Sqn/7 Regt, Middle Wallop
	XZ197	WS Lynx AH7 <ff>	MoD/Vector Aerospace, stored Fleetlands
	XZ198	WS Lynx AH7 <ff>	MoD/Vector Aerospace, stored Fleetlands
	XZ203	WS Lynx AH7 [F]	AAC No 671 Sqn/7 Regt, Middle Wallop
	XZ205	WS Lynx AH7 <ff>	AAC GDSH, Middle Wallop
	XZ206	WS Lynx AH7 <ff>	Privately owned, Hixon, Staffs
	XZ207	WS Lynx AH7	DCAE SEAE, Arborfield
	XZ208	WS Lynx AH7	AAC No 1 Regt, Gütersloh

Serial	Type (code/other identity)	Owner/operator, location or fate	Notes
XZ209	WS Lynx AH7 <ff>	MoD, Boscombe Down	
XZ210	WS Lynx AH7	AAC No 1 Regt, Gütersloh	
XZ211	WS Lynx AH7	AAC No 1 Regt, Gütersloh	
XZ212	WS Lynx AH7 [X]	MoD/Vector Aerospace, Fleetlands	
XZ213	WS Lynx AH1 (TAD 213)	Vector Aerospace Fleetlands Apprentice School	
XZ214	WS Lynx AH7	AAC No 657 Sqn, Odiham	
XZ215	WS Lynx AH7	AAC No 9 Regt, Dishforth	
XZ216	WS Lynx AH7	AAC No 1 Regt, Gütersloh	
XZ217	WS Lynx AH7	Privately owned,	
XZ218	WS Lynx AH7	Warfighters R6 Centre, Barby, Northants	
XZ219	WS Lynx AH7	AAC No 9 Regt, Dishforth	
XZ220	WS Lynx AH7 [U]	AAC GDSH, Middle Wallop	
XZ221	WS Lynx AH7 [Z]	AAC No 671 Sqn/7 Regt, Middle Wallop	
XZ222	WS Lynx AH7	AAC No 657 Sqn, Odiham	
XZ228	WS Lynx HAS3GMS [313]	RN No 815 NAS, HQ Flt, Yeovilton	
XZ229	WS Lynx HAS3GMS [360/MC]	AAC GDSH, Middle Wallop	
XZ230	WS Lynx HAS3GMS <ff>	Privately owned,	
XZ232	WS Lynx HAS3GMS	MoD/Vector Aerospace, stored Fleetlands	
XZ233	WS Lynx HAS3S [306]	RN No 815 NAS, HQ Flt, Yeovilton	
XZ234	WS Lynx HAS3S [630]	AAC GDSH, Middle Wallop	
XZ235	WS Lynx HAS3S(ICE) [435]	MoD/Vector Aerospace, stored Fleetlands	
XZ236	WS Lynx HMA8 [LST-1]	RN ETS, Yeovilton, GI use	
XZ237	WS Lynx HAS3S [631]	RN No 702 NAS, Yeovilton	
XZ238	WS Lynx HAS3S(ICE) [434/EE]	MoD/Vector Aerospace, stored Fleetlands	
XZ239	WS Lynx HAS3GMS [633]	AAC GDSH, Middle Wallop	
XZ245	WS Lynx HAS3GMS	MoD/Vector Aerospace, stored Fleetlands	
XZ246	WS Lynx HAS3S(ICE) [434/EE]	MoD/Vector Aerospace, stored Fleetlands	
XZ248	WS Lynx HAS3S [666]	SFDO, RNAS Culdrose	
XZ250	WS Lynx HAS3S [631]$	AAC GDSH, Middle Wallop	
XZ252	WS Lynx HAS3S	Privately owned, Hixon, Staffs	
XZ254	WS Lynx HAS3S [632]	RN No 702 NAS, Yeovilton	
XZ255	WS Lynx HMA8SRU [314]	RN No 815 NAS, HQ Flt, Yeovilton	
XZ257	WS Lynx HAS3S <ff>	Privately owned, Hixon, Staffs	
XZ287	BAe Nimrod AEW3 (9140M) (fuselage)	RAF TSW, Stafford	
XZ290	WS Gazelle AH1	AAC GDSH, Middle Wallop	
XZ291	WS Gazelle AH1	Privately owned, Colsterworth, Leics	
XZ292	WS Gazelle AH1	Privately owned, Colsterworth, Leics	
XZ294	WS Gazelle AH1 [X]	AAC, stored Shawbury	
XZ295	WS Gazelle AH1	AAC, stored Shawbury	
XZ296	WS Gazelle AH1 [V]	Privately owned, Colsterworth, Leics	
XZ298	WS Gazelle AH1 <ff>	AAC, Middle Wallop	
XZ299	WS Gazelle AH1 (G-CDXE)	*Sold to Russia, August 2010*	
XZ303	WS Gazelle AH1	AAC, stored Shawbury	
XZ304	WS Gazelle AH1	Privately owned, Colsterworth, Leics	
XZ305	WS Gazelle AH1 (TAD 020)	DCAE AESS *HMS Sultan*, Gosport	
XZ307	WS Gazelle AH1	Vector Aerospace Fleetlands Apprentice School	
XZ308	WS Gazelle AH1	QinetiQ, Boscombe Down (spares use)	
XZ309	WS Gazelle AH1	*Scrapped*	
XZ311	WS Gazelle AH1 [U]	AAC, stored Shawbury	
XZ312	WS Gazelle AH1	RAF Henlow, instructional use	
XZ313	WS Gazelle AH1 <ff>	AAC GDSH, Middle Wallop	
XZ314	WS Gazelle AH1 [A]	Privately owned, Colsterworth, Leics	
XZ315	WS Gazelle AH1 <ff>	Privately owned, Babcary, Somerset	
XZ316	WS Gazelle AH1 [B]	DCAE, No 1 SoTT, Cosford	
XZ318	WS Gazelle AH1 (fuselage)	Tong Paintball Park, Shropshire	
XZ320	WS Gazelle AH1	AAC No 667 Sqn/7 Regt, Middle Wallop	
XZ321	WS Gazelle AH1 (G-CDNS)	*Repainted as G-CDNS*	
XZ322	WS Gazelle AH1 (9283M) [N]	DCAE, No 1 SoTT, Cosford	
XZ323	WS Gazelle AH1 [J]	AAC, stored Shawbury	
XZ324	WS Gazelle AH1	Privately owned, Colsterworth, Leics	
XZ325	WS Gazelle AH1 [T]	DCAE SEAE, Arborfield	
XZ326	WS Gazelle AH1	AAC No 665 Sqn/5 Regt, Aldergrove	
XZ327	WS Gazelle AH1	AAC Middle Wallop (recruiting aid)	
XZ328	WS Gazelle AH1 [C]	AAC, stored Shawbury	
XZ329	WS Gazelle AH1 (G-BZYD) [J]	Privately owned, East Harston, Bucks	
XZ330	WS Gazelle AH1 [Y]	AAC Wattisham, instructional use	
XZ331	WS Gazelle AH1 [D]	AAC, stored Shawbury	
XZ332	WS Gazelle AH1 [O]	DCAE SEAE, Arborfield	
XZ333	WS Gazelle AH1 [A]	REME Museum, Arborfield	

Notes	Serial	Type (code/other identity)	Owner/operator, location or fate
	XZ334	WS Gazelle AH1	AAC No 665 Sqn/5 Regt, Aldergrove
	XZ335	WS Gazelle AH1	North-East Aircraft Museum, Usworth
	XZ337	WS Gazelle AH1 [Z]	AAC, stored Shawbury
	XZ338	WS Gazelle AH1 [Y]	Privately owned, Colsterworth, Leics
	XZ340	WS Gazelle AH1	AAC No 29 Flt, BATUS, Suffield, Canada
	XZ341	WS Gazelle AH1	AAC, stored Shawbury
	XZ342	WS Gazelle AH1	AAC No 8 Flt, Credenhill
	XZ343	WS Gazelle AH1	AAC, stored Shawbury
	XZ344	WS Gazelle AH1 [Y]	Privately owned, Colsterworth, Leics
	XZ345	WS Gazelle AH1 [M]	AAC No 671 Sqn/7 Regt, Middle Wallop
	XZ346	WS Gazelle AH1	AAC Netheravon, at main gate
	XZ347	WS Gazelle AH1	Privately owned, Hurstbourne Tarrant, Hants
	XZ349	WS Gazelle AH1 [G]	AAC, stored Shawbury
	XZ356	SEPECAT Jaguar GR3A [FU]	Privately owned, Bentwaters
	XZ358	SEPECAT Jaguar GR1A (9262M) [L]	DCAE, TCF, RAFC Cranwell
	XZ360	SEPECAT Jaguar GR3 [FN]	Privately owned, Bentwaters
	XZ361	SEPECAT Jaguar GR3 [FT]	*To Greece, 2010*
	XZ363	SEPECAT Jaguar GR1A <R> (*XX824*/BAPC 151) [A]	RAF M&RU, Bottesford
	XZ364	SEPECAT Jaguar GR3A <ff>	Privately owned, Tunbridge Wells
	XZ366	SEPECAT Jaguar GR3A [FC]	Privately owned, Bentwaters
	XZ367	SEPECAT Jaguar GR3 [GP]	DCAE, No 1 SoTT, Cosford
	XZ368	SEPECAT Jaguar GR1 [8900M] [E]	DCAE, No 1 SoTT, Cosford
	XZ369	SEPECAT Jaguar GR3A [EU]	Privately owned, Bentwaters
	XZ370	SEPECAT Jaguar GR1 (9004M) [JB]	DCAE, No 1 SoTT, Cosford
	XZ371	SEPECAT Jaguar GR1 (8907M) [AP]	DCAE, No 1 SoTT, Cosford
	XZ372	SEPECAT Jaguar GR3 [FV]	Privately owned, Bentwaters
	XZ374	SEPECAT Jaguar GR1 (9005M) [JC]	DCAE, No 1 SoTT, Cosford
	XZ375	SEPECAT Jaguar GR1A (9255M) <ff>	City of Norwich Aviation Museum
	XZ377	SEPECAT Jaguar GR3A [EP]	DCAE, No 1 SoTT, Cosford
	XZ378	SEPECAT Jaguar GR1A [EP]	Privately owned, Topsham, Devon
	XZ382	SEPECAT Jaguar GR1 (8908M)	Cold War Jets Collection, Bruntingthorpe
	XZ383	SEPECAT Jaguar GR1 (8901M) [AF]	DCAE, No 1 SoTT, Cosford
	XZ384	SEPECAT Jaguar GR1 (8954M) [BC]	DCAE, No 1 SoTT, Cosford
	XZ385	SEPECAT Jaguar GR3A [FT]	Privately owned, Bentwaters
	XZ389	SEPECAT Jaguar GR1 (8946M) [BL]	DCAE, No 1 SoTT, Cosford
	XZ390	SEPECAT Jaguar GR1 (9003M) [DM]	DCAE, No 1 SoTT, Cosford
	XZ391	SEPECAT Jaguar GR3A [ET]	DCAE, No 1 SoTT, Cosford
	XZ392	SEPECAT Jaguar GR3A [EM]	DCAE, No 1 SoTT, Cosford
	XZ394	SEPECAT Jaguar GR3 [FG]	Privately owned, Bentwaters
	XZ396	SEPECAT Jaguar GR3A [EQ]	Privately owned, Bentwaters
	XZ398	SEPECAT Jaguar GR3A [EQ]	DCAE, No 1 SoTT, Cosford
	XZ399	SEPECAT Jaguar GR3A [EJ]	DCAE, No 1 SoTT, Cosford
	XZ400	SEPECAT Jaguar GR3A [FQ]	Privately owned, Bentwaters
	XZ431	HS Buccaneer S2B (9233M) <ff>	Privately owned, Market Drayton, Shropshire
	XZ440	BAe Sea Harrier FA2 [40/DD]	SFDO, RNAS Culdrose
	XZ455	BAe Sea Harrier FA2 [001] (wreck)	Privately owned, Queensbury, W Yorks
	XZ457	BAe Sea Harrier FA2 [104/VL]	Boscombe Down Aviation Collection
	XZ459	BAe Sea Harrier FA2 [126]	Privately owned, Sussex
	XZ492	BAe Sea Harrier FA2 (wreck)	Privately owned, Faygate
	XZ493	BAe Sea Harrier FRS1 (comp XV760) [001/N]	FAA Museum, RNAS Yeovilton
	XZ493	BAe Sea Harrier FRS1 <ff>	RN Yeovilton, Fire Section
	XZ494	BAe Sea Harrier FA2 [128]	Privately owned, Wedmore, Somerset
	XZ497	BAe Sea Harrier FA2 [126]	Privately owned, Charlwood
	XZ499	BAe Sea Harrier FA2 [003]	FAA Museum, RNAS Yeovilton
	XZ559	Slingsby T61F Venture T2 (G-BUEK)	Privately owned, Tibenham
	XZ570	WS61 Sea King HAS5(mod)	RN, Predannack Fire School
	XZ574	WS61 Sea King HAS6	FAA Museum, RNAS Yeovilton
	XZ575	WS61 Sea King HU5	MoD/AFD/QinetiQ, Boscombe Down

Serial	Type (code/other identity)	Owner/operator, location or fate	Notes
XZ576	WS61 Sea King HAS6	DCAE AESS, *HMS Sultan*, Gosport	
XZ578	WS61 Sea King HU5	RN No 771 NAS, Prestwick	
XZ579	WS61 Sea King HAS6 [707/PW]	DCAE AESS, *HMS Sultan*, Gosport	
XZ580	WS61 Sea King HC6 [ZB]	MoD/Vector Aerospace, stored Fleetlands	
XZ581	WS61 Sea King HAS6 [69/CU]	DCAE AESS, *HMS Sultan*, Gosport	
XZ585	WS61 Sea King HAR3 [A]	MoD/Vector Aerospace, Fleetlands	
XZ586	WS61 Sea King HAR3 [B]	RAF No 202 Sqn, E Flt, Leconfield	
XZ587	WS61 Sea King HAR3 [C]	MoD/Vector Aerospace, Fleetlands	
XZ588	WS61 Sea King HAR3 [D]	RAF No 202 Sqn, D Flt, Lossiemouth	
XZ589	WS61 Sea King HAR3 [E]	RAF No 202 Sqn, D Flt, Lossiemouth	
XZ590	WS61 Sea King HAR3 [F]	RAF SKAMG, RNAS Yeovilton	
XZ591	WS61 Sea King HAR3 [G]	RAF SKAMG, RNAS Yeovilton	
XZ592	WS61 Sea King HAR3	RAF SKAMG, RNAS Yeovilton	
XZ593	WS61 Sea King HAR3 [I]	RAF No 202 Sqn, A Flt, Boulmer	
XZ594	WS61 Sea King HAR3	RAF No 22 Sqn, C Flt/No 203(R) Sqn, Valley	
XZ595	WS61 Sea King HAR3 [K]	RAF No 22 Sqn, C Flt/No 203(R) Sqn, Valley	
XZ596	WS61 Sea King HAR3 [L]	RAF No 22 Sqn, C Flt/No 203(R) Sqn, Valley	
XZ597	WS61 Sea King HAR3 [M]	MoD/Vector Aerospace, FleetlandsXZ598	
XZ598	WS61 Sea King HAR3	RAF No 202 Sqn, A Flt, Boulmer	
XZ599	WS61 Sea King HAR3 [P]	RAF No 1564 Flt, Mount Pleasant, FI	
XZ605	WS Lynx AH7 [L]	AAC No 671 Sqn/7 Regt, Middle Wallop	
XZ606	WS Lynx AH7	AAC No 1 Regt, Gütersloh	
XZ607	WS Lynx AH7	MoD/Vector Aerospace, Fleetlands	
XZ608	WS Lynx AH7	AAC No 657 Sqn, Odiham	
XZ609	WS Lynx AH7	AAC No 657 Sqn, Odiham	
XZ611	WS Lynx AH7 <ff>	Privately owned, Hixon, Staffs	
XZ612	WS Lynx AH7	RM No 847 NAS, Yeovilton	
XZ613	WS Lynx AH7 [F]	AAC Stockwell Hall, Middle Wallop	
XZ615	WS Lynx AH7 <ff>	Privately owned,	
XZ616	WS Lynx AH7	AAC No 657 Sqn, Odiham	
XZ617	WS Lynx AH7	AAC No 667 Sqn/7 Regt, Middle Wallop	
XZ630	Panavia Tornado GR1 (8976M)	RAF Halton, on display	
XZ631	Panavia Tornado GR1	Yorkshire Air Museum, Elvington	
XZ641	WS Lynx AH7	AAC No 657 Sqn, Odiham	
XZ642	WS Lynx AH7	MoD/Vector Aerospace, Fleetlands	
XZ643	WS Lynx AH7	AAC No 1 Regt, Gütersloh	
XZ645	WS Lynx AH7	AAC No 657 Sqn, Odiham	
XZ646	WS Lynx AH7 (really XZ649)	Bristol University, instructional use	
XZ647	WS Lynx AH7 <ff>	*Currently not known*	
XZ648	WS Lynx AH7 <ff>	Privately owned,	
XZ651	WS Lynx AH7	AAC No 657 Sqn, Odiham	
XZ652	WS Lynx AH7	AAC No 9 Regt, Dishforth	
XZ653	WS Lynx AH7	RM No 847 NAS, Yeovilton	
XZ654	WS Lynx AH7	AAC No 1 Regt, Gütersloh	
XZ655	WS Lynx AH7 <ff>	Privately owned,	
XZ661	WS Lynx AH7 [V]	AAC No 671 Sqn/7 Regt, Middle Wallop	
XZ663	WS Lynx AH7 <ff>	Privately owned, Hixon, Staffs	
XZ664	WS Lynx AH7	Warfighters R6 Centre, Barby, Northants	
XZ665	WS Lynx AH7	Warfighters R6 Centre, Barby, Northants	
XZ666	WS Lynx AH7	DCAE SEAE, Arborfield	
XZ669	WS Lynx AH7 [I]	AAC No 657 Sqn, Odiham	
XZ670	WS Lynx AH7	AAC No 1 Regt, Gütersloh	
XZ671	WS Lynx AH7 <ff>	AgustaWestland, Yeovil, instructional use	
XZ672	WS Lynx AH7 [H]	*Currently not known*	
XZ673	WS Lynx AH7	MoD/Vector Aerospace, stored Fleetlands	
XZ674	WS Lynx AH7	AAC No 1 Regt, Gütersloh	
XZ675	WS Lynx AH7 [H]	AAC GDSH, Middle Wallop	
XZ676	WS Lynx AH7 [N]	AAC GDSH, Middle Wallop	
XZ677	WS Lynx AH7	AAC No 9 Regt, Dishforth	
XZ678	WS Lynx AH7	RM No 847 NAS, Yeovilton	
XZ679	WS Lynx AH7	AAC No 9 Regt, Dishforth	
XZ680	WS Lynx AH7 [E]	AAC No 671 Sqn/7 Regt, Middle Wallop	
XZ689	WS Lynx HMA8SRU [316]	RN No 815 NAS, HQ Flt, Yeovilton	
XZ690	WS Lynx HMA8SRU [301]	RN No 815 NAS, HQ Flt, Yeovilton	
XZ691	WS Lynx HMA8SRU [365]	RN No 815 NAS, *Argyll* Flt, Yeovilton	
XZ692	WS Lynx HMA8SRU [642]	MoD/Vector Aerospace, Fleetlands	
XZ693	WS Lynx HAS3S [311]	RN No 815 NAS, HQ Flt, Yeovilton	
XZ694	WS Lynx HAS3GMS [434]	AAC GDSH, Middle Wallop	

Notes	Serial	Type (code/other identity)	Owner/operator, location or fate
	XZ696	WS Lynx HAS3GMS [633]	RN No 702 NAS, Yeovilton
	XZ697	WS Lynx HMA8SRU [641]	RN No 702 NAS, Yeovilton
	XZ698	WS Lynx HMA8SRU [348/CM]	RN No 815 NAS, *Chatham* Flt, Yeovilton
	XZ699	WS Lynx HAS2	FAA Museum, RNAS Yeovilton
	XZ719	WS Lynx HMA8SRU [315]	MoD/Vector Aerospace, Fleetlands
	XZ720	WS Lynx HAS3GMS [312]	RN No 815 NAS, HQ Flt, Yeovilton
	XZ721	WS Lynx HAS3GMS [309]	MoD/Vector Aerospace, Fleetlands
	XZ722	WS Lynx HMA8SRU [645]$	RN No 702 NAS, Yeovilton
	XZ723	WS Lynx HMA8SRU [444]	RN No 815 NAS, *Montrose* Flt, Yeovilton
	XZ725	WS Lynx HMA8SRU [415]	RN No 815 NAS, *Monmouth* Flt, Yeovilton
	XZ726	WS Lynx HMA8SRU [411]	RN No 815 NAS, *Edinburgh* Flt, Yeovilton
	XZ727	WS Lynx HAS3S [307]	RN No 815 NAS, HQ Flt, Yeovilton
	XZ728	WS Lynx HMA8 [326/AW]	RNAS Yeovilton, on display
	XZ729	WS Lynx HMA8SRU [350]	RN No 815 NAS, *Cumberland* Flt, Yeovilton
	XZ730	WS Lynx HAS3S [634]	RN No 702 NAS, Yeovilton
	XZ731	WS Lynx HMA8SRU [332/LP]	RN No 815 NAS, *Liverpool* Flt, Yeovilton
	XZ732	WS Lynx HMA8SRU [452]	RN No 815 NAS, Yeovilton
	XZ733	WS Lynx HAS3GMS [305]	RN No 815 NAS, HQ Flt, Yeovilton
	XZ735	WS Lynx HAS3GMS [404]	MoD/Vector Aerospace, stored Fleetlands
	XZ736	WS Lynx HMA8SRU [451/DA]	RN No 815 NAS, *Daring* Flt, Yeovilton
	XZ791	Northrop Shelduck D1	Davidstow Airfield & Cornwall At War Museum
	XZ795	Northrop Shelduck D1	Museum of Army Flying, Middle Wallop
	XZ920	WS61 Sea King HU5 [707/PW]	RN No 771 NAS, Prestwick
	XZ921	WS61 Sea King HAS6 [269/N]	DCAE, stored *HMS Sultan*, Gosport
	XZ922	WS61 Sea King HC6 [ZA]	DCAE, stored *HMS Sultan*, Gosport
	XZ930	WS Gazelle HT3 (A2713) [Q]	DCAE AESS, *HMS Sultan*, Gosport
	XZ934	WS Gazelle HT3 (G-CBSI) [U]	Privately owned, Babcary, Somerset
	XZ935	WS Gazelle HCC4	DCAE, No 1 SoTT, Cosford
	XZ936	WS Gazelle HT2 [6]	MoD/ETPS, Boscombe Down
	XZ936	WS Gazelle HT3 (XZ933/G-CGJZ)	Privately owned, Hurstbourne Tarrant, Hants
	XZ937	WS Gazelle HT2 (G-CBKA) [Y]	*Repainted as G-CBKA*
	XZ939	WS Gazelle HT2 [9]	MoD/ETPS, Boscombe Down
	XZ941	WS Gazelle HT2 (9301M) [B]	DCAE, No 1 SoTT, Cosford
	XZ942	WS Gazelle HT2 (9305M) [42/CU]	AAC, Middle Wallop, instructional use
	XZ964	BAe Harrier GR3 [D]	Royal Engineers Museum, Chatham
	XZ966	BAe Harrier GR3 (9221M) [G]	MoD DFTDC, Manston
	XZ968	BAe Harrier GR3 (9222M) [3G]	Muckleborough Collection, Weybourne
	XZ969	BAe Harrier GR3 [69]	RN, Predannack Fire School
	XZ971	BAe Harrier GR3 (9219M)	HQ DSDA, Donnington, Shropshire, on display
	XZ987	BAe Harrier GR3 (9185M) [C]	RAF Stafford, at main gate
	XZ990	BAe Harrier GR3 <ff>	*Currently not known*
	XZ990	BAe Harrier GR3 <rf>	RAF Wittering, derelict
	XZ991	BAe Harrier GR3 (9162M) [3A]	DCAE, No 1 SoTT, Cosford
	XZ993	BAe Harrier GR3 (9240M) <ff>	Privately owned, Welshpool
	XZ994	BAe Harrier GR3 (9170M) [U]	RAF Defence Movements School, Brize Norton
	XZ995	BAe Harrier GR3 (9220M/G-CBGK) [3G]	Privately owned, Dunboyne, Eire
	XZ996	BAe Harrier GR3 [96]	RN, Predannack Fire School
	XZ997	BAe Harrier GR3 (9122M) [V]	RAF Museum, Hendon
	ZA101	BAe Hawk 100 (G-HAWK)	BAE Systems Warton, Overseas Customer Training Centre
	ZA105	WS61 Sea King HAR3 [Q]	RAF No 22 Sqn, C Flt/No 203(R) Sqn, Valley
	ZA110	BAe Jetstream T2 (F-BTMI) [563/CU]	RN No 750 NAS, Culdrose
	ZA111	BAe Jetstream T2 (9Q-CTC) [565/CU]	RN No 750 NAS, Culdrose
	ZA126	WS61 Sea King ASaC7 [191]	RN No 857 NAS, Culdrose
	ZA127	WS61 Sea King HAS6 [509/CU]	DCAE, stored *HMS Sultan*, Gosport
	ZA128	WS61 Sea King HAS6 [010]	DCAE, stored *HMS Sultan*, Gosport
	ZA129	WS61 Sea King HAS6 <ff>	*Scrapped*
	ZA130	WS61 Sea King HU5 [19]	MoD/Vector Aerospace, Fleetlands
	ZA131	WS61 Sea King HAS6 [271/N]	DCAE, No 1 SoTT, Cosford
	ZA133	WS61 Sea King HAS6 [831/CU]	DCAE, stored HMS Sultan, Gosport
	ZA134	WS61 Sea King HU5	RN No 771 NAS, Culdrose
	ZA135	WS61 Sea King HAS6 [05]	DCAE, stored *HMS Sultan*, Gosport
	ZA136	WS61 Sea King HAS6 [018]	DCAE, AESS, *HMS Sultan*, Gosport (wreck)
	ZA137	WS61 Sea King HU5 [20]	MoD/Vector Aerospace, Fleetlands

Serial	Type (code/other identity)	Owner/operator, location or fate	Notes
ZA144	BAe VC10 K2 (G-ARVC) <ff>	RAF JARTS, St Athan	
ZA147	BAe VC10 K3 (5H-MMT) [F]	RAF No 101 Sqn, Brize Norton	
ZA148	BAe VC10 K3 (5Y-ADA) [G]	RAF No 101 Sqn, Brize Norton	
ZA149	BAe VC10 K3 (5X-UVJ) [H]	RAF No 101 Sqn, Brize Norton	
ZA150	BAe VC10 K3 (5H-MOG) [J]	RAF No 101 Sqn, Brize Norton	
ZA166	WS61 Sea King HU5 [16]	RN No 771 NAS, Culdrose	
ZA167	WS61 Sea King HU5 [22/CU]	RN No 771 NAS, Culdrose	
ZA168	WS61 Sea King HAS6 [830/CU]	DCAE, AESS, *HMS Sultan*, Gosport	
ZA169	WS61 Sea King HAS6 [515/CW]	DCAE, No 1 SoTT, Cosford	
ZA170	WS61 Sea King HAS5	DCAE, stored *HMS Sultan*, Gosport	
ZA175	BAe Sea Harrier FA2	Norfolk & Suffolk Avn Museum, Flixton	
ZA176	BAe Sea Harrier FA2 [126/R]	Newark Air Museum, Winthorpe	
ZA195	BAe Sea Harrier FA2	Tangmere Military Aviation Museum	
ZA209	Short MATS-B	Museum of Army Flying, Middle Wallop	
ZA220	Short MATS-B	Privately owned, Awbridge, Hants	
ZA250	BAe Harrier T52 (G-VTOL)	Brooklands Museum, Weybridge	
ZA254	Panavia Tornado F2 (9253M) (fuselage)	RAF Marham, instructional use	
ZA267	Panavia Tornado F2 (9284M)	RAF Marham, instructional use	
ZA291	WS61 Sea King HC4 [N]	RN No 848 NAS, Yeovilton	
ZA292	WS61 Sea King HC4 [WU]	MoD/Vector Aerospace, Fleetlands	
ZA293	WS61 Sea King HC4+ [A]	RN SKAMG, Yeovilton	
ZA295	WS61 Sea King HC4+ [U]	RN No 846 NAS, Yeovilton	
ZA296	WS61 Sea King HC4+ [Q]	RN SKAMG, Yeovilton	
ZA297	WS61 Sea King HC4+ [W]	RN No 846 NAS, Yeovilton	
ZA298	WS61 Sea King HC4+ [Y]	MoD/Vector Aerospace, Fleetlands (damaged)	
ZA299	WS61 Sea King HC4+ [D]	RN No 845 NAS, Yeovilton	
ZA310	WS61 Sea King HC4 [B]	RN No 845 NAS, Yeovilton	
ZA312	WS61 Sea King HC4	MoD/AugustaWestland, Yeovil	
ZA313	WS61 Sea King HC4+ [M]	RN No 845 NAS, Yeovilton	
ZA314	WS61 Sea King HC4 [WT]	MoD/Vector Aerospace, Fleetlands	
ZA319	Panavia Tornado GR1 (9315M)	DSDA, Bicester, on display	
ZA320	Panavia Tornado GR1 (9314M) [TAW]	DCAE, No 1 SoTT, Cosford	
ZA322	Panavia Tornado GR1 (9334M) [TAC]	*Scrapped at RAF Marham*	
ZA323	Panavia Tornado GR1 [TAZ]	DCAE, No 1 SoTT, Cosford	
ZA325	Pavavia Tornado GR1 <ff>	RAF Manston History Museum	
ZA325	Panavia Tornado GR1 [TAX] <rf>	RAF, stored Shawbury	
ZA326	Panavia Tornado GR1P	MoD, Boscombe Down (wfu)	
ZA327	Panavia Tornado GR1 <ff>	BAE Systems, Warton	
ZA328	Panavia Tornado GR1	Marsh Lane Technical School, Preston	
ZA353	Panavia Tornado GR1 [B-53]	Privately owned, Queensbury, W Yorks	
ZA354	Panavia Tornado GR1	Yorkshire Air Museum, Elvington	
ZA355	Panavia Tornado GR1 (9310M) [TAA]	RA, stored Lossiemouth	
ZA356	Panavia Tornado GR1 <ff>	RAF Marham, instructional use	
ZA357	Panavia Tornado GR1 [TTV]	DCAE, No 1 SoTT, Cosford	
ZA359	Panavia Tornado GR1	BAE Systems Warton, Overseas Customer Training Centre	
ZA360	Panavia Tornado GR1 (9318M) <ff>	RAF Marham, instructional use	
ZA361	Panavia Tornado GR1 [TD]	Privately owned, New York, Lincs	
ZA362	Panavia Tornado GR1 [AJ-F]	Highland Aviation Museum, Inverness	
ZA365	Panavia Tornado GR4 [001]	RAF No 15(R) Sqn, Lossiemouth	
ZA367	Panavia Tornado GR4 [002,KC-N]	RAF No 12 Sqn, Lossiemouth	
ZA369	Panavia Tornado GR4A [003] $	RAF No 13 Sqn, Marham	
ZA370	Panavia Tornado GR4A [004]	RAF No 617 Sqn, Lossiemouth	
ZA371	Panavia Tornado GR4A [005]	RAF No 13 Sqn, Marham	
ZA372	Panavia Tornado GR4A [006]	RAF, Lossiemouth	
ZA373	Panavia Tornado GR4A [007,H]	RAF No 15(R) Sqn, Lossiemouth	
ZA375	Panavia Tornado GR1 (9335M) [AJ-W]	RAF Marham, Fire Section	
ZA393	Panavia Tornado GR4 [008]	RAF No 14 Sqn, Lossiemouth	
ZA395	Panavia Tornado GR4A [009]	RAF No 31 Sqn, Marham	
ZA398	Panavia Tornado GR4A [010,AJ-N]	RAF No 617 Sqn, Lossiemouth	
ZA399	Panavia Tornado GR1 (9316M) [AJ-C]	DCAE, No 1 SoTT, Cosford	
ZA400	Panavia Tornado GR4A [011]	RAF No 9 Sqn, Marham	
ZA401	Panavia Tornado GR4A [012]	RAF No 13 Sqn, Marham	
ZA402	Panavia Tornado GR4A	MoD/BAE Systems, Warton	
ZA404	Panavia Tornado GR4A [013]	RAF No 2 Sqn, Marham	

Notes	Serial	Type (code/other identity)	Owner/operator, location or fate
	ZA405	Panavia Tornado GR4A [014]	RAF No 15(R) Sqn, Lossiemouth
	ZA406	Panavia Tornado GR4 [015]	RAF No 14 Sqn, Lossiemouth
	ZA407	Panavia Tornado GR1 (9336M) [AJ-N]	RAF Marham, on display
	ZA409	Panavia Tornado GR1 [VII]	RAF Lossiemouth (wfu)
	ZA410	Panavia Tornado GR4 [016]	RAF No 15(R) Sqn, Lossiemouth
	ZA411	Panavia Tornado GR1 [TT]	MoD/BAE Systems, Warton
	ZA412	Panavia Tornado GR4 [017]	RAF No 9 Sqn, Marham
	ZA446	Panavia Tornado GR4 [018]	RAF, stored Shawbury
	ZA447	Panavia Tornado GR4 [EB-R]	RAF AWC/FJWOEU/No 41(R) Sqn, Coningsby
	ZA449	Panavia Tornado GR4 [020]	RAF No 15(R) Sqn, Lossiemouth
	ZA450	Panavia Tornado GR1 (9317M) [TH]	DCAE, No 1 SoTT, Cosford
	ZA452	Panavia Tornado GR4 [021]	RAF No 31 Sqn, Marham
	ZA453	Panavia Tornado GR4 [022]	RAF No 12 Sqn, Lossiemouth
	ZA456	Panavia Tornado GR4 [023]	RAF No 135 Sqn, Marham
	ZA457	Panavia Tornado GR1 [AJ-J]	RAF Museum, Hendon
	ZA458	Panavia Tornado GR4 [024]	RAF No 15(R) Sqn, Lossiemouth
	ZA459	Panavia Tornado GR4 [F] $	RAF No 14 Sqn, Lossiemouth
	ZA461	Panavia Tornado GR4 [026]	RAF No 31 Sqn, Marham
	ZA462	Panavia Tornado GR4 [027]	RAF No 14 Sqn, Lossiemouth
	ZA463	Panavia Tornado GR4 [028]	RAF No 12 Sqn, Lossiemouth
	ZA465	Panavia Tornado GR1 [FF]	Imperial War Museum, Duxford
	ZA469	Panavia Tornado GR4 [029] $	RAF No 31 Sqn, Marham
	ZA470	Panavia Tornado GR4	RAF, stored Shawbury
	ZA472	Panavia Tornado GR4 [031]	RAF No 31 Sqn, Marham
	ZA473	Panavia Tornado GR4 [032]	RAF No 12 Sqn, Lossiemouth
	ZA474	Panavia Tornado GR1 (9312M)	RAF, stored Lossiemouth
	ZA475	Panavia Tornado GR1 (9311M)	RAF Lossiemouth, on display
	ZA492	Panavia Tornado GR4 [033]	RAF No 15(R) Sqn, Lossiemouth
	ZA541	Panavia Tornado GR4 [034]	RAF No 15(R) Sqn, Lossiemouth
	ZA542	Panavia Tornado GR4 [035]	RAF No 14 Sqn, Lossiemouth
	ZA543	Panavia Tornado GR4 [036]	RAF No 12 Sqn, Lossiemouth
	ZA544	Panavia Tornado GR4 [037]	RAF No 15(R) Sqn, Lossiemouth
	ZA546	Panavia Tornado GR4 [AG]	RAF No 617 Sqn, Lossiemouth
	ZA547	Panavia Tornado GR4 [039]	RAF No 2 Sqn, Marham
	ZA548	Panavia Tornado GR4 [040]	RAF No 15(R) Sqn, Lossiemouth
	ZA549	Panavia Tornado GR4 [041]	RAF No 15(R) Sqn, Lossiemouth
	ZA550	Panavia Tornado GR4 [042]	RAF No 617 Sqn, Lossiemouth
	ZA551	Panavia Tornado GR4 [043]	RAF No 13 Sqn, Marham
	ZA552	Panavia Tornado GR4 [044]	RAF No 15(R) Sqn, Lossiemouth
	ZA553	Panavia Tornado GR4 [045]	RAF No 9 Sqn, Marham
	ZA554	Panavia Tornado GR4 [046]	RAF No 617 Sqn, Lossiemouth
	ZA556	Panavia Tornado GR4 [047]	RAF No 14 Sqn, Lossiemouth
	ZA556	Panavia Tornado GR1 <R> (*ZA368*/BAPC 155) [Z]	RAF M&RU, Bottesford
	ZA557	Panavia Tornado GR4 [048]	RAF No 31 Sqn, Marham
	ZA559	Panavia Tornado GR4 [049]	RAF No 12 Sqn, Lossiemouth
	ZA560	Panavia Tornado GR4 [050]	RAF, Lossiemouth
	ZA562	Panavia Tornado GR4 [051]	RAF No 9 Sqn, Marham
	ZA563	Panavia Tornado GR4	RAF, stored Shawbury
	ZA564	Panavia Tornado GR4 $	RAF No 31 Sqn, Marham
	ZA585	Panavia Tornado GR4 [054]	RAF No 13 Sqn, Marham
	ZA587	Panavia Tornado GR4 [055]	RAF No 13 Sqn, Marham
	ZA588	Panavia Tornado GR4 [056]	RAF, Marham
	ZA589	Panavia Tornado GR4 [057]	RAF No 12 Sqn, Lossiemouth
	ZA591	Panavia Tornado GR4 [058]	RAF No 13 Sqn, Marham
	ZA592	Panavia Tornado GR4 [059]	RAF No 9 Sqn, Marham
	ZA594	Panavia Tornado GR4 [060]	RAF No 13 Sqn, Marham
	ZA595	Panavia Tornado GR4 [061]	RAF No 617 Sqn, Lossiemouth
	ZA597	Panavia Tornado GR4 [063]	RAF No 12 Sqn, Lossiemouth
	ZA598	Panavia Tornado GR4 [064]	RAF No 15(R) Sqn, Lossiemouth
	ZA600	Panavia Tornado GR4 [EB-G]	RAF AWC/FJWOEU/No 41(R) Sqn, Coningsby
	ZA601	Panavia Tornado GR4 [AJ-G,066]	MoD/BAE Systems, Warton
	ZA602	Panavia Tornado GR4 [067]	RAF No 2 Sqn, Marham
	ZA604	Panavia Tornado GR4 [068]	RAF No 12 Sqn, Lossiemouth
	ZA606	Panavia Tornado GR4 [069]	RAF No 31 Sqn, Marham
	ZA607	Panavia Tornado GR4 [070]	RAF No 12 Sqn, Lossiemouth
	ZA608	Panavia Tornado GR4	RAF, stored Shawbury
	ZA609	Panavia Tornado GR4 [072]	MoD/AFD/QinetiQ, Boscombe Down

Serial	Type (code/other identity)	Owner/operator, location or fate	Notes
ZA611	Panavia Tornado GR4 [EB-L]	RAF AWC/FJWOEU/No 41(R) Sqn, Coningsby	
ZA612	Panavia Tornado GR4 [IV]	MoD/BAE Systems, Warton	
ZA613	Panavia Tornado GR4 [075]	RAF No 2 Sqn, Marham	
ZA614	Panavia Tornado GR4 [076]	RAF No 13 Sqn, Marham	
ZA630	Slingsby T61F Venture T2 (G-BUGL)	Privately owned, Tibenham	
ZA634	Slingsby T61F Venture T2 (G-BUHA) [C]	Privately owned, Saltby, Leics	
ZA652	Slingsby T61F Venture T2 (G-BUDC)	Privately owned, Enstone	
ZA670	B-V Chinook HC2 (N37010) [AA]	RAF Odiham Wing	
ZA671	B-V Chinook HC2 (N37011) [AB]	RAF No 1310 Flt, Kandahar, Afghanistan	
ZA674	B-V Chinook HC2 (N37019)	RAF Odiham Wing	
ZA675	B-V Chinook HC2 (N37020) [AE]	RAF No 1310 Flt, Kandahar, Afghanistan	
ZA676	B-V Chinook HC1 (N37021/9230M) [FG] (wreck)	*Currently not known*	
ZA677	B-V Chinook HC2 (N37022) [AF]	MoD/Vector Aerospace, Fleetlands	
ZA678	B-V Chinook HC1 (N37023/9229M) [EZ] (wreck)	RAF Odiham, BDRT	
ZA679	B-V Chinook HC2 (N37025) [AG]	RAF Odiham Wing	
ZA680	B-V Chinook HC2 (N37026) [AH]	RAF Odiham Wing	
ZA681	B-V Chinook HC2 (N37027) [AI]	MoD/Vector Aerospace, Fleetlands	
ZA682	B-V Chinook HC2 (N37029) [AJ]	RAF Odiham Wing	
ZA683	B-V Chinook HC2 (N37030) [AK]	MoD/Vector Aerospace, Fleetlands	
ZA684	B-V Chinook HC2 (N37031) [AL]	RAF No 1310 Flt, Kandahar, Afghanistan	
ZA704	B-V Chinook HC2 (N37033) [AM]	RAF Odiham Wing	
ZA705	B-V Chinook HC2 (N37035) [AN]	RAF Odiham Wing	
ZA707	B-V Chinook HC2 (N37040) [AO]	RAF Odiham Wing	
ZA708	B-V Chinook HC2 (N37042) [AP]	MoD/Vector Aerospace, Fleetlands	
ZA710	B-V Chinook HC2 (N37044) [AR]	MoD/Vector Aerospace, Fleetlands	
ZA711	B-V Chinook HC2 (N37046)	MoD/Vector Aerospace, Fleetlands	
ZA712	B-V Chinook HC2 (N37047) [AT]	RAF Odiham Wing	
ZA713	B-V Chinook HC2 (N37048) [AU]	MoD/Vector Aerospace, Fleetlands	
ZA714	B-V Chinook HC2 (N37051) [AV]	MoD/Vector Aerospace, Fleetlands	
ZA717	B-V Chinook HC1 (N37056/9238M) (wreck)	*Scrapped*	
ZA718	B-V Chinook HC2 (N37058) [BN]	MoD/Vector Aerospace, Fleetlands	
ZA720	B-V Chinook HC2 (N37060)	MoD/Vector Aerospace, Fleetlands	
ZA726	WS Gazelle AH1 [F1]	Privately owned, Colsterworth, Leics	
ZA728	WS Gazelle AH1 [E]	Privately owned, Colsterworth, Leics	
ZA729	WS Gazelle AH1	AAC Wattisham, BDRT	
ZA731	WS Gazelle AH1	AAC No 29 Flt, BATUS, Suffield, Canada	
ZA733	WS Gazelle AH1	Vector Aerospace Fleetlands Apprentice School	
ZA734	WS Gazelle AH1	*Scrapped*	
ZA735	WS Gazelle AH1	DCAE SEAE, Arborfield	
ZA736	WS Gazelle AH1	AAC No 29 Flt, BATUS, Suffield, Canada	
ZA737	WS Gazelle AH1	Museum of Army Flying, Middle Wallop	
ZA766	WS Gazelle AH1	AAC GDSH, Middle Wallop	
ZA768	WS Gazelle AH1 [F] (wreck)	MoD/Vector Aerospace, stored Fleetlands	
ZA769	WS Gazelle AH1 [K]	DCAE SEAE, Arborfield	
ZA771	WS Gazelle AH1	DCAE, No 1 SoTT, Cosford	
ZA772	WS Gazelle AH1	AAC GDSH, Middle Wallop	
ZA773	WS Gazelle AH1 [F]	AAC, stored Shawbury	
ZA774	WS Gazelle AH1	Privately owned, Babcary, Somerset	
ZA775	WS Gazelle AH1	AAC, stored Shawbury	
ZA776	WS Gazelle AH1 [F]	Privately owned, Colsterworth, Leics	
ZA804	WS Gazelle HT3	Privately owned, Solstice Park, Amesbury, Wilts	
ZA935	WS Puma HC1	RAF No 33 Sqn/No 230 Sqn, Benson	
ZA936	WS Puma HC1	RAF No 33 Sqn/No 230 Sqn, Benson	
ZA937	WS Puma HC1	RAF No 33 Sqn/No 230 Sqn, Benson	
ZA939	WS Puma HC1	RAF No 33 Sqn/No 230 Sqn, Benson	
ZA940	WS Puma HC1	RAF No 33 Sqn/No 230 Sqn, Benson	
ZA947	Douglas Dakota C3 [AI]	RAF BBMF, Coningsby	
ZB500	WS Lynx 800 (G-LYNX/ZA500)	The Helicopter Museum, Weston-super-Mare	
ZB506	WS61 Sea King Mk 4X	MoD/AFD/QinetiQ, Boscombe Down	
ZB507	WS61 Sea King HC4 [F]	MoD/Vector Aerospace, Fleetlands	
ZB601	BAe Harrier T4 (fuselage)	RNAS Yeovilton, Fire Section	

Notes	Serial	Type (code/other identity)	Owner/operator, location or fate
	ZB603	BAe Harrier T8 [T03/DD]	SFDO, RNAS Culdrose
	ZB604	BAe Harrier T8 [722]	RAF Wittering
	ZB615	SEPECAT Jaguar T2A	DCAE, TCF, RAFC Cranwell
	ZB625	WS Gazelle HT3 [N]	MoD/AFD/QinetiQ, Boscombe Down
	ZB627	WS Gazelle HT3 (G-CBSK) [A]	Privately owned, Hurstbourne Tarrant, Hants
	ZB646	WS Gazelle HT2 (G-CBGZ) [59/CU]	Privately owned, Knebworth
	ZB647	WS Gazelle HT2 (G-CBSF) [40]	Privately owned, Redhill
	ZB665	WS Gazelle AH1	AAC, stored Shawbury
	ZB667	WS Gazelle AH1	AAC GDSH, Middle Wallop
	ZB668	WS Gazelle AH1 (TAD 015)	DCAE SEAE, Arborfield
	ZB669	WS Gazelle AH1	AAC No 665 Sqn/5 Regt, Aldergrove
	ZB670	WS Gazelle AH1	AAC Dishforth, on display
	ZB671	WS Gazelle AH1	AAC No 29 Flt, BATUS, Suffield, Canada
	ZB672	WS Gazelle AH1	Army Training Regiment, Winchester
	ZB673	WS Gazelle AH1 [P]	Privately owned, Colsterworth, Leics
	ZB674	WS Gazelle AH1	AAC, stored Shawbury
	ZB677	WS Gazelle AH1 [5B]	AAC No 29 Flt, BATUS, Suffield, Canada
	ZB678	WS Gazelle AH1	AAC No 665 Sqn/5 Regt, Aldergrove
	ZB679	WS Gazelle AH1	AAC, stored Shawbury
	ZB682	WS Gazelle AH1	No 93 Sqn ATC, Colerne
	ZB683	WS Gazelle AH1	AAC No 665 Sqn/5 Regt, Aldergrove
	ZB684	WS Gazelle AH1	RAF Defence Movements School, Brize Norton
	ZB686	WS Gazelle AH1 <ff>	The Helicopter Museum, Weston-super-Mare
	ZB688	WS Gazelle AH1	Privately owned, Colsterworth, Leics
	ZB689	WS Gazelle AH1	AAC No 665 Sqn/5 Regt, Aldergrove
	ZB690	WS Gazelle AH1	MoD, stored Shawbury
	ZB691	WS Gazelle AH1 [S]	AAC No 671 Sqn/7 Regt, Middle Wallop
	ZB692	WS Gazelle AH1 [C,Y]	AAC No 671 Sqn/7 Regt, Middle Wallop
	ZB693	WS Gazelle AH1	AAC No 665 Sqn/5 Regt, Aldergrove
	ZB697	Mil Mi-17 Mk.IV (103M02)	*Donated to the Afghan Air Force, March 2010*
	ZB698	Mil Mi-17 Mk.IV (103M03)	*Donated to the Afghan Air Force, March 2010*
	ZD230	BAC Super VC10 K4 (G-ASGA) <ff>	Privately owned, Crondall, Hants
	ZD240	BAC Super VC10 K4 (G-ASGL) <ff>	Privately owned, Crondall, Hants
	ZD241	BAC Super VC10 K4 (G-ASGM) [N]	RAF No 1312 Flt, Mount Pleasant, FI
	ZD242	BAC Super VC10 K4 (G-ASGP) [P]	MoD VISSAGE Project, Boscombe Down
	ZD249	WS Lynx HAS3S [307]	MoD/Vector Aerospace, Fleetlands
	ZD250	WS Lynx HAS3S [635]	RN No 702 NAS, Yeovilton
	ZD251	WS Lynx HAS3S	RN, stored Yeovilton
	ZD252	WS Lynx HMA8SRU [338/CT]	RN No 815 NAS, *Campbeltown* Flt, Yeovilton
	ZD254	WS Lynx HAS3S [306]	DCAE AESS, *HMS Sultan*, Gosport
	ZD255	WS Lynx HAS3GMS [316]	MoD/Vector Aerospace, stored Fleetlands
	ZD257	WS Lynx HMA8SRU [642]	RN No 702 NAS, Yeovilton
	ZD258	WS Lynx HMA8SRU [646]	MoD/Vector Aerospace, Fleetlands
	ZD259	WS Lynx HMA8SRU [404/IR]	RN No 815 NAS, *Iron Duke* Flt, Yeovilton
	ZD260	WS Lynx HMA8SRU [303]	RN No 815 NAS, HQ Flt, Yeovilton
	ZD261	WS Lynx HMA8SRU [301]	MoD/Vector Aerospace, stored Fleetlands
	ZD262	WS Lynx HMA8SRU [301]	RN No 815 NAS, HQ Flt, Yeovilton
	ZD263	WS Lynx HAS3S [306]	MoD/Vector Aerospace, Fleetlands
	ZD264	WS Lynx HAS3GMS [407]	MoD/Vector Aerospace, Fleetlands
	ZD265	WS Lynx HMA8SRU [644]	RN No 702 NAS, Yeovilton
	ZD266	WS Lynx HMA8SRU [302]	RN No 815 NAS, HQ Flt, Yeovilton
	ZD267	WS Lynx HMA8 (comp XZ672) [LST-2]	RN ETS, Yeovilton, GI use
	ZD268	WS Lynx HMA8SRU [643]	RN No 702 NAS, Yeovilton
	ZD272	WS Lynx AH7 [W]	AAC GDSH, Middle Wallop
	ZD273	WS Lynx AH7 [A]	AAC No 671 Sqn/7 Regt, Middle Wallop
	ZD274	WS Lynx AH7	AAC No 9 Regt, Dishforth
	ZD276	WS Lynx AH7	Mayhem Paintball, Abridge, Essex
	ZD277	WS Lynx AH7 [U]	AAC No 671 Sqn/7 Regt, Middle Wallop
	ZD278	WS Lynx AH7	AAC No 9 Regt, Dishforth
	ZD279	WS Lynx AH7 <ff>	Privately owned,
	ZD280	WS Lynx AH7	AAC No 9 Regt, Dishforth

Serial	Type (code/other identity)	Owner/operator, location or fate	Notes
ZD281	WS Lynx AH7 [K]	MoD/Vector Aerospace, Fleetlands	
ZD282	WS Lynx AH7	RM No 847 NAS, Yeovilton	
ZD283	WS Lynx AH7	AAC No 657 Sqn, Odiham	
ZD284	WS Lynx AH7	AAC No 9 Regt, Dishforth	
ZD285	WS Lynx AH7	MoD/AFD/QinetiQ, Boscombe Down	
ZD318	BAe Harrier GR7	RAF Cottesmore, for RAF Museum, Hendon	
ZD319	BAe Harrier GR7A	RAF Cottesmore, for IWM Duxford	
ZD320	BAe Harrier GR9 [21]	RAF Cottesmore, for RAF Museum, Cosford	
ZD321	BAe Harrier GR9 [02]	RAF HM&SF, Cottesmore (wfu)	
ZD322	BAe Harrier GR9A [03A]	RAF HM&SF, Cottesmore (wfu)	
ZD323	BAe Harrier GR7 [04]	RAF HM&SF, Cottesmore (wfu)	
ZD327	BAe Harrier GR9 [08A,SH-M]	RAF HM&SF, Cottesmore (wfu)	
ZD328	BAe Harrier GR9 [09]	RAF HM&SF, Cottesmore (wfu)	
ZD329	BAe Harrier GR9A [10]	RAF HM&SF, Cottesmore (wfu)	
ZD330	BAe Harrier GR9 [$]	RAF HM&SF, Cottesmore (wfu)	
ZD346	BAe Harrier GR9 [13]	RAF HM&SF, Cottesmore (wfu)	
ZD347	BAe Harrier GR9A [14]	RAF HM&SF, Cottesmore (wfu)	
ZD348	BAe Harrier GR9A [15A]	RAF HM&SF, Cottesmore (wfu)	
ZD351	BAe Harrier GR9A [$]	RAF HM&SF, Cottesmore (wfu)	
ZD352	BAe Harrier GR9 [19]	RAF HM&SF, Cottesmore (wfu)	
ZD353	BAe Harrier GR5 (fuselage)	BAE Systems, Brough	
ZD354	BAe Harrier GR9 [21]	RAF HM&SF, Cottesmore (wfu)	
ZD375	BAe Harrier GR9 [23]	RAF HM&SF, Cottesmore (wfu)	
ZD376	BAe Harrier GR7A [24A]	RAF HM&SF, Cottesmore (wfu)	
ZD378	BAe Harrier GR9A [26A]	RAF HM&SF, Cottesmore (wfu)	
ZD379	BAe Harrier GR9 [27]	RAF HM&SF, Cottesmore (wfu)	
ZD380	BAe Harrier GR9A [28A]	RAF HM&SF, Cottesmore (wfu)	
ZD401	BAe Harrier GR9 [30]	RAF HM&SF, Cottesmore (wfu)	
ZD402	BAe Harrier GR9 [31]	RAF HM&SF, Cottesmore (wfu)	
ZD403	BAe Harrier GR9 [32,JX-B]	RAF HM&SF, Cottesmore (wfu)	
ZD404	BAe Harrier GR7A [33A]	RAF HM&SF, Cottesmore (wfu)	
ZD405	BAe Harrier GR9 [34]	RAF HM&SF, Cottesmore (wfu)	
ZD406	BAe Harrier GR9 [35] $	RAF HM&SF, Cottesmore (wfu)	
ZD407	BAe Harrier GR7 [36]	RAF HM&SF, Cottesmore (wfu)	
ZD409	BAe Harrier GR9 [38]	RAF HM&SF, Cottesmore (wfu)	
ZD410	BAe Harrier GR9 [39]$	RAF HM&SF, Cottesmore (wfu)	
ZD411	BAe Harrier GR7 [40]	RAF HM&SF, Cottesmore (wfu)	
ZD412	BAe Harrier GR5 (fuselage)	Privately owned, Charlwood	
ZD431	BAe Harrier GR7A [43A]	RAF HM&SF, Cottesmore (wfu)	
ZD433	BAe Harrier GR9A [45A]	RAF HM&SF, Cottesmore (wfu)	
ZD435	BAe Harrier GR9 [47]	RAF HM&SF, Cottesmore (wfu)	
ZD436	BAe Harrier GR9A [48A]	RAF HM&SF, Cottesmore (wfu)	
ZD437	BAe Harrier GR9 [EB-J]	RAF HM&SF, Cottesmore (wfu)	
ZD438	BAe Harrier GR9 [50]	RAF HM&SF, Cottesmore (wfu)	
ZD461	BAe Harrier GR9A [51A]	RAF HM&SF, Cottesmore (wfu)	
ZD462	BAe Harrier GR7 (9302M) [52]	Privately owned, Sproughton	
ZD463	BAe Harrier GR7 [53]	RAF HM&SF, Cottesmore (wfu)	
ZD465	BAe Harrier GR9 [55]	MoD/BAE Systems, Warton	
ZD466	BAe Harrier GR7 [56]	RAF HM&SF, Cottesmore (wfu)	
ZD467	BAe Harrier GR9A [57A]	RAF HM&SF, Cottesmore (wfu)	
ZD468	BAe Harrier GR9 [58]	RAF HM&SF, Cottesmore (wfu)	
ZD469	BAe Harrier GR7A [59A]	RAF HM&SF, Cottesmore (wfu)	
ZD470	BAe Harrier GR9 [60]	RAF HM&SF, Cottesmore (wfu)	
ZD476	WS61 Sea King HC4+ [WZ]	RN No 846 NAS, Yeovilton	
ZD477	WS61 Sea King HC4 [E]	RN SKAMG, Yeovilton	
ZD478	WS61 Sea King HC4 [J]	DCAE, stored *HMS Sultan*, Gosport	
ZD479	WS61 Sea King HC4 [WQ]	RN No 848 NAS, Yeovilton	
ZD480	WS61 Sea King HC4+ [J]	RN No 845 NAS, Yeovilton	
ZD559	WS Lynx AH7	MoD/AFD/QinetiQ, Boscombe Down	
ZD560	WS Lynx AH7	MoD/ETPS, Boscombe Down	
ZD565	WS Lynx HMA8SRU [410/GC]	RN No 815 NAS, *Gloucester* Flt, Yeovilton	
ZD566	WS Lynx HMA8SRU [407]	RN No 815 NAS, *York* Flt, Yeovilton	
ZD574	B-V Chinook HC2 (N37077) [DB]	RAF Odiham Wing	
ZD575	B-V Chinook HC2 (N37078) [DC]	RAF Odiham Wing	
ZD578	BAe Sea Harrier FA2 [000,122]	RNAS Yeovilton, at main gate	
ZD579	BAe Sea Harrier FA2 [79/DD]	SFDO, RNAS Culdrose	
ZD580	BAe Sea Harrier FA2 [710]	Privately owned, Cheshire	
ZD581	BAe Sea Harrier FA2 [124]	RN, Predannack Fire School	
ZD582	BAe Sea Harrier FA2 [002/N]	Privately owned, Banbury, Oxon	
ZD607	BAe Sea Harrier FA2	DCAE AESS, *HMS Sultan*, Gosport	
ZD608	BAe Sea Harrier FA2 [731]	*Sold to Greece, 2010*	
ZD610	BAe Sea Harrier FA2 [006/N]	Privately owned, Dunsfold	

Notes	Serial	Type (code/other identity)	Owner/operator, location or fate
	ZD611	BAe Sea Harrier FA2	RNAS Culdrose Fire Section
	ZD612	BAe Sea Harrier FA2	Privately owned, Topsham, Devon
	ZD613	BAe Sea Harrier FA2 [127/R]	Privately owned, Cross Green, Leeds
	ZD614	BAe Sea Harrier FA2 [122/R]	Privately owned, Sproughton
	ZD620	BAe 125 CC3	RAF No 32(The Royal) Sqn, Northolt
	ZD621	BAe 125 CC3	RAF No 32(The Royal) Sqn, Northolt
	ZD625	WS61 Sea King HC4+ [P]	RN No 848 NAS, Yeovilton
	ZD626	WS61 Sea King HC4+ [S]	RN No 845 NAS, Yeovilton
	ZD627	WS61 Sea King HC4 [WO]	RN No 848 NAS, Yeovilton
	ZD630	WS61 Sea King HAS6 [012/L]	DCAE, stored *HMS Sultan*, Gosport
	ZD631	WS61 Sea King HAS6 [66] (fuselage)	Privately owned, St Agnes, Cornwall
	ZD633	WS61 Sea King HAS6 [014/L]	DCAE, stored *HMS Sultan*, Gosport
	ZD634	WS61 Sea King HAS6 [503]	DCAE, stored *HMS Sultan*, Gosport
	ZD636	WS61 Sea King ASaC7 [182/CU]	RN No 854 NAS, Culdrose
	ZD637	WS61 Sea King HAS6 [700/PW]	DCAE, AESS, *HMS Sultan*, Gosport
	ZD667	BAe Harrier GR3 (9201M) [67]	RN, Predannack Fire School
	ZD703	BAe 125 CC3	RAF No 32(The Royal) Sqn, Northolt
	ZD704	BAe 125 CC3	RAF No 32(The Royal) Sqn, Northolt
	ZD707	Panavia Tornado GR4 [077]	RAF No 12 Sqn, Lossiemouth
	ZD708	Panavia Tornado GR4	RAF, stored Shawbury
	ZD709	Panavia Tornado GR4 [078]	RAF No 13 Sqn, Marham
	ZD710	Panavia Tornado GR1 <ff>	Privately owned, Ruthin, Denbighshire
	ZD711	Panavia Tornado GR4 [079]	RAF No 15(R) Sqn, Lossiemouth
	ZD712	Panavia Tornado GR4 [080] $	RAF No 15(R) Sqn, Lossiemouth
	ZD713	Panavia Tornado GR4 [081]	RAF No 31 Sqn, Marham
	ZD714	Panavia Tornado GR4 [AJ-W]	RRAF No 12 Sqn, Lossiemouth
	ZD715	Panavia Tornado GR4 [083]	RAF No 617 Sqn, Lossiemouth
	ZD716	Panavia Tornado GR4 [084]	RAF No 15(R) Sqn, Lossiemouth
	ZD719	Panavia Tornado GR4 [085]	RAF No 15(R) Sqn, Lossiemouth
	ZD720	Panavia Tornado GR4 [086]	RAF No 31 Sqn, Marham
	ZD739	Panavia Tornado GR4 [087]	RAF No 9 Sqn, Marham
	ZD740	Panavia Tornado GR4 [088]	RAF No 31 Sqn, Marham
	ZD741	Panavia Tornado GR4 [089]	RAF No 15(R) Sqn, Lossiemouth
	ZD742	Panavia Tornado GR4 [090]	RAF No 15(R) Sqn, Lossiemouth
	ZD743	Panavia Tornado GR4 [091]	RAF No 12 Sqn, Lossiemouth
	ZD744	Panavia Tornado GR4 [092]	RAF No 15(R) Sqn, Lossiemouth
	ZD745	Panavia Tornado GR4 [093]	RAF No 2 Sqn, Marham
	ZD746	Panavia Tornado GR4 [094]	RAF No 2 Sqn, Marham
	ZD747	Panavia Tornado GR4 [095]	RAF No 15(R) Sqn, Lossiemouth
	ZD748	Panavia Tornado GR4 [096]	RAF No 2 Sqn, Marham
	ZD749	Panavia Tornado GR4 [097]	RAF No 9 Sqn, Marham
	ZD788	Panavia Tornado GR4 [098]	RAF No 31 Sqn, Marham
	ZD790	Panavia Tornado GR4 [099]	RAF No 31 Sqn, Marham
	ZD792	Panavia Tornado GR4 [100]	RAF No 2 Sqn, Marham
	ZD793	Panavia Tornado GR4 [101]	RAF No 15(R) Sqn, Lossiemouth
	ZD810	Panavia Tornado GR4 [102]	RAF No 617 Sqn, Lossiemouth
	ZD811	Panavia Tornado GR4 [103]	RAF No 12 Sqn, Marham
	ZD812	Panavia Tornado GR4 [104]	RAF No 15(R) Sqn, Lossiemouth
	ZD842	Panavia Tornado GR4 [105]	RAF No 15(R) Sqn, Lossiemouth
	ZD843	Panavia Tornado GR4 [106]	RAF No 31 Sqn, Marham
	ZD844	Panavia Tornado GR4 [107]	RAF No 2 Sqn, Marham
	ZD847	Panavia Tornado GR4 [108]	RAF, Lossiemouth
	ZD848	Panavia Tornado GR4 [109]	RAF No 15(R) Sqn, Lossiemouth
	ZD849	Panavia Tornado GR4 [110]	RAF No 617 Sqn, Lossiemouth
	ZD850	Panavia Tornado GR4 [111]	RAF No 2 Sqn, Marham
	ZD851	Panavia Tornado GR4 [112]	RAF No 617 Sqn, Lossiemouth
	ZD890	Panavia Tornado GR4 [113]	RAF No 2 Sqn, Marham
	ZD892	Panavia Tornado GR4 [TG]	RAF, stored Shawbury
	ZD895	Panavia Tornado GR4 [115]	RAF No 15(R) Sqn, Lossiemouth
	ZD899	Panavia Tornado F2	MoD, Boscombe Down, spares use
	ZD902	Panavia Tornado F2A(TIARA)	MoD/AFD/QinetiQ, Boscombe Down
	ZD906	Panavia Tornado F2 (comp ZE294) <ff>	RAF Leuchars, BDRT
	ZD932	Panavia Tornado F2 (comp ZE255) (9308M) (fuselage)	ARF, RAF St Athan
	ZD934	Panavia Tornado F2 (comp ZE786) <ff>	*Currently not known*
	ZD936	Panavia Tornado F2 (comp ZE251) <ff>	Boscombe Down Aviation Collection
	ZD938	Panavia Tornado F2 (comp ZE295) <ff>	Privately owned, Chester

Serial	Type (code/other identity)	Owner/operator, location or fate	Notes
ZD939	Panavia Tornado F2 (comp ZE292) <ff>	DCAE Cosford, instructional use	
ZD948	Lockheed TriStar KC1 (G-BFCA)	RAF No 216 Sqn, Brize Norton	
ZD949	Lockheed TriStar K1 (G-BFCB)	MoD/Marshalls, stored Cambridge	
ZD950	Lockheed TriStar KC1 (G-BFCC)	RAF No 216 Sqn, Brize Norton	
ZD951	Lockheed TriStar K1 (G-BFCD)	RAF No 216 Sqn, Brize Norton	
ZD952	Lockheed TriStar KC1 (G-BFCE)	RAF No 216 Sqn, Brize Norton	
ZD953	Lockheed TriStar KC1 (G-BFCF)	RAF No 216 Sqn, Brize Norton	
ZD980	B-V Chinook HC2 (N37082) [DD]	RAF Odiham Wing	
ZD981	B-V Chinook HC2 (N37083)	RAF Odiham Wing	
ZD982	B-V Chinook HC2 (N37085) [DF]	MoD/Vector Aerospace, Fleetlands	
ZD983	B-V Chinook HC2 (N37086) [DG]	RAF No 1310 Flt, Kandahar, Afghanistan	
ZD984	B-V Chinook HC2 (N37088) [DH]	RAF Odiham Wing	
ZD990	BAe Harrier T8 [T90/DD]	SFDO, RNAS Culdrose	
ZD991	BAe Harrier T8 (9228M) [722/VL]	*Sold to Greece, 2010*	
ZD992	BAe Harrier T8 [724] (fuselage)	Privately owned, Sproughton	
ZD993	BAe Harrier T8 [723/VL]	MoD, Boscombe Down (spares use)	
ZD996	Panavia Tornado GR4A [EB-B]	RAF AWC/FJWOEU/No 41(R) Sqn, Coningsby	
ZE116	Panavia Tornado GR4A [116]	RAF No 12 Sqn, Lossiemouth	
ZE157	Panavia Tornado F3 [TY]	RAF Leeming, for scrapping	
ZE158	Panavia Tornado F3 [FF]	*Scrapped at Leeming, September 2010*	
ZE163	Panavia Tornado F3 (comp ZG753) [HY]	RAF No 111 Sqn, Leuchars	
ZE164	Panavia Tornado F3 [HO]	RAF Leuchars, WLT	
ZE165	Panavia Tornado F3 [GE]	RAF, stored Shawbury	
ZE168	Panavia Tornado F3 [HH]	RAF No 111 Sqn, Leuchars	
ZE200	Panavia Tornado F3 [HN]	RAF Leeming, for scrapping	
ZE201	Panavia Tornado F3 [HU]	RAF Leeming, for scrapping	
ZE203	Panavia Tornado F3 [GA]	MoD/AFD/QinetiQ, Boscombe Down	
ZE204	Panavia Tornado F3 [FC]	RAF, stored Shawbury	
ZE208	Panavia Tornado F3 (MM55060)	*Scrapped*	
ZE250	Panavia Tornado F3 [TR]	RAF Leeming, for scrapping	
ZE288	Panavia Tornado F3 (comp ZD940) [HA] $	RAF Leeming, for scrapping	
ZE292	Panavia Tornado F3 (comp ZD939) [FE]	RAF Leeming, for scrapping	
ZE294	Panavia Tornado F3 (comp ZD906) [DD]	*Scrapped*	
ZE338	Panavia Tornado F3 [GJ]	RAF Leeming, for scrapping	
ZE339	Panavia Tornado F3 <ff>	*Currently not known*	
ZE340	Panavia Tornado F3 (*ZE758*/9298M) [GO]	DCAE, No 1 SoTT, Cosford	
ZE341	Panavia Tornado F3 [HI]	RAF Leeming, for scapping	
ZE342	Panavia Tornado F3 [HP]	RAF No 111 Sqn, Leuchars	
ZE343	Panavia Tornado F3 (comp ZD900) [DZ]	RAF Leeming, for scrapping	
ZE350	McD F-4J(UK) Phantom (9080M) <ff>	Privately owned, Ingatestone, Essex	
ZE352	McD F-4J(UK) Phantom (9086M) <ff>	Privately owned, Hooton Park	
ZE360	McD F-4J(UK) Phantom (9059M) [O]	MoD DFTDC, Manston	
ZE368	WS61 Sea King HAR3 [R]	RAF No 1564 Flt, Mount Pleasant, FI	
ZE369	WS61 Sea King HAR3 [S]	RAF No 22 Sqn, C Flt/No 203(R) Sqn, Valley	
ZE370	WS61 Sea King HAR3 [T]	RAF No 202 Sqn, E Flt, Leconfield	
ZE375	WS Lynx AH9A	MoD/AgustaWestland, Yeovil (conversion)	
ZE376	WS Lynx AH9A	MoD/AgustaWestland, Yeovil (conversion)	
ZE378	WS Lynx AH7	AAC No 657 Sqn, Odiham	
ZE379	WS Lynx AH7	AAC Dishforth, BDRT	
ZE380	WS Lynx AH9	AAC No 9 Regt, Dishforth	
ZE381	WS Lynx AH7 [X]	DCAE SEAE, Arborfield	
ZE395	BAe 125 CC3	RAF No 32(The Royal) Sqn, Northolt	
ZE396	BAe 125 CC3	RAF No 32(The Royal) Sqn, Northolt	
ZE410	Agusta A109A (AE-334)	Museum of Army Flying, stored Middle Wallop	
ZE411	Agusta A109A (AE-331)	FAA Museum, stored RNAS Yeovilton	
ZE412	Agusta A109A	DCAE SEAE, Arborfield	
ZE413	Agusta A109A	Army Whittington Barracks, Lichfield, GI use	
ZE416	Agusta A109E Power Elite (G-ESLH)	MoD/ETPS, Boscombe Down	

Notes	Serial	Type (code/other identity)	Owner/operator, location or fate
	ZE418	WS61 Sea King ASaC7 [186]	RN No 849 NAS, Culdrose
	ZE420	WS61 Sea King ASaC7 [189]	MoD/Vector Aerospace, Fleetlands
	ZE422	WS61 Sea King ASaC7 [192]	RN No 857 NAS, Culdrose
	ZE425	WS61 Sea King HC4 [WR]	RN No 848 NAS, Yeovilton
	ZE426	WS61 Sea King HC4 [WX]	RN No 848 NAS, Yeovilton
	ZE427	WS61 Sea King HC4+ [K]	RN CHFMU, Yeovilton
	ZE428	WS61 Sea King HC4+ [H]	RN No 845 NAS, Yeovilton
	ZE432	BAC 1-11/479FU (DQ-FBV)	MoD/ETPS, Boscombe Down
	ZE433	BAC 1-11/479FU (DQ-FBQ)	MoD, Boscombe Down (wfu)
	ZE438	BAe Jetstream T3 [76]	RN, stored Cranwell
	ZE439	BAe Jetstream T3 [77]	RN, stored Cranwell
	ZE440	BAe Jetstream T3 [78]	RN, stored Shawbury
	ZE441	BAe Jetstream T3 [79]	RN, stored Cranwell
	ZE449	SA330L Puma HC1 (9017M/PA-12)	RAF PDSH, Benson (wreck)
	ZE477	WS Lynx 3	The Helicopter Museum, Weston-super-Mare
	ZE495	Grob G103 Viking T1 (BGA3000) [VA]	RAF No 625 VGS, Hullavington
	ZE496	Grob G103 Viking T1 (BGA3001) [VB]	RAF No 661 VGS, Kirknewton
	ZE498	Grob G103 Viking T1 (BGA3003) [VC]	RAF No 614 VGS, Wethersfield
	ZE499	Grob G103 Viking T1 (BGA3004) [VD]	RAF ACCGS/No 643 VGS, Syerston
	ZE502	Grob G103 Viking T1 (BGA3007) [VF]	RAF No 611 VGS, Watton
	ZE503	Grob G103 Viking T1 (BGA3008) [VG]	RAF No 615 VGS, Kenley
	ZE504	Grob G103 Viking T1 (BGA3009) [VH]	RAF No 614 VGS, Wethersfield
	ZE520	Grob G103 Viking T1 (BGA3010) [VJ]	RAF No 661 VGS, Kirknewton
	ZE521	Grob G103 Viking T1 (BGA3011) [VK]	RAF No 626 VGS, Predannack
	ZE522	Grob G103 Viking T1 (BGA3012) [VL]	RAF No 625 VGS, Hullavington
	ZE524	Grob G103 Viking T1 (BGA3014) [VM]	RAF No 611 VGS, Watton
	ZE526	Grob G103 Viking T1 (BGA3016) [VN]	RAF No 625 VGS, Hullavington
	ZE527	Grob G103 Viking T1 (BGA3017) [VP]	RAF No 626 VGS, Predannack
	ZE528	Grob G103 Viking T1 (BGA3018) [VQ]	RAF CGMF, Syerston
	ZE529	Grob G103 Viking T1 (BGA3019) (comp ZE655) [VR]	RAF No 621 VGS, Hullavington
	ZE530	Grob G103 Viking T1 (BGA3020) [VS]	RAF CGMF, Syerston
	ZE531	Grob G103 Viking T1 (BGA3021) [VT]	RAF No 622 VGS, Upavon
	ZE532	Grob G103 Viking T1 (BGA3022) [VU]	RAF ACCGS/No 643 VGS, Syerston
	ZE533	Grob G103 Viking T1 (BGA3023) [VV]	RAF No 661 VGS, Kirknewton
	ZE550	Grob G103 Viking T1 (BGA3025) [VX]	RAF CGMF, Syerston (damaged)
	ZE551	Grob G103 Viking T1 (BGA3026) [VY]	RAF No 614 VGS, Wethersfield
	ZE552	Grob G103 Viking T1 (BGA3027) [VZ]	RAF No 615 VGS, Kenley
	ZE553	Grob G103 Viking T1 (BGA3028) [WA]	RAF No 615 VGS, Kenley
	ZE554	Grob G103 Viking T1 (BGA3029) [WB]	RAF No 615 VGS, Kenley
	ZE555	Grob G103 Viking T1 (BGA3030) [WC]	RAF ACCGS/No 643 VGS, Syerston
	ZE556	Grob G103 Viking T1 (BGA3031) <ff>	No 1360 Sqn ATC, Nottingham
	ZE557	Grob G103 Viking T1 (BGA3032) [WE]	RAF No 621 VGS, Hullavington

Serial	Type (code/other identity)	Owner/operator, location or fate	Notes
ZE558	Grob G103 Viking T1 (BGA3033) [WF]	RAF CGMF, Syerston	
ZE559	Grob G103 Viking T1 (BGA3034) [WG]	RAF No 661 VGS, Kirknewton	
ZE560	Grob G103 Viking T1 (BGA3035) [WH]	RAF No 625 VGS, Hullavington	
ZE561	Grob G103 Viking T1 (BGA3036) [WJ]	RAF No 621 VGS, Hullavington	
ZE562	Grob G103 Viking T1 (BGA3037) [WK]	RAF No 626 VGS, Predannack	
ZE563	Grob G103 Viking T1 (BGA3038) [WL]	RAF CGMF, stored Syerston	
ZE564	Grob G103 Viking T1 (BGA3039) [WN]	RAF No 622 VGS, Upavon	
ZE584	Grob G103 Viking T1 (BGA3040) [WP]	RAF CGMF, stored Syerston	
ZE585	Grob G103 Viking T1 (BGA3041) [WQ]	RAF No 614 VGS, Wethersfield	
ZE586	Grob G103 Viking T1 (BGA3042) [WR]	RAF CGMF, Syerston	
ZE587	Grob G103 Viking T1 (BGA3043) [WS]	RAF CGMF, Syerston	
ZE590	Grob G103 Viking T1 (BGA3046) [WT]	RAF No 661 VGS, Kirknewton	
ZE591	Grob G103 Viking T1 (BGA3047) [WU]	RAF No 662 VGS, Arbroath	
ZE592	Grob G103 Viking T1 (BGA3048) <ff>	RAFGSA, stored Henlow	
ZE593	Grob G103 Viking T1 (BGA3049) [WW]	RAF CGMF, Syerston	
ZE594	Grob G103 Viking T1 (BGA3050) [WX]	RAF No 661 VGS, Kirknewton	
ZE595	Grob G103 Viking T1 (BGA3051) [WY]	RAF No 661 VGS, Kirknewton	
ZE600	Grob G103 Viking T1 (BGA3052) [WZ]	RAF No 622 VGS, Upavon	
ZE601	Grob G103 Viking T1 (BGA3053) [XA]	RAF CGMF, Syerston	
ZE602	Grob G103 Viking T1 (BGA3054) [XB]	RAF No 662 VGS, Arbroath	
ZE603	Grob G103 Viking T1 (BGA3055) [XC]	RAF CGMF, Syerston	
ZE604	Grob G103 Viking T1 (BGA3056) [XD]	RAF No 621 VGS, Hullavington	
ZE605	Grob G103 Viking T1 (BGA3057) [XE]	RAF No 626 VGS, Predannack	
ZE606	Grob G103 Viking T1 (BGA3058) [XF]	RAF No 622 VGS, Upavon	
ZE607	Grob G103 Viking T1 (BGA3059) [XG]	RAF No 622 VGS, Upavon	
ZE608	Grob G103 Viking T1 (BGA3060) [XH]	RAF ACCGS/No 643 VGS, Syerston	
ZE609	Grob G103 Viking T1 (BGA3061) [XJ]	RAF CGMF, stored Syerston	
ZE610	Grob G103 Viking T1 (BGA3062) [XK]	RAF No 614 VGS, Wethersfield	
ZE611	Grob G103 Viking T1 (BGA3063) [XL]	RAF No 611 VGS, Watton	
ZE613	Grob G103 Viking T1 (BGA3065) [XM]	RAF No 621 VGS, Hullavington	
ZE614	Grob G103 Viking T1 (BGA3066) [XN]	RAF No 614 VGS, Wethersfield	
ZE625	Grob G103 Viking T1 (BGA3067) [XP]	RAF No 625 VGS, Hullavington	
ZE626	Grob G103 Viking T1 (BGA3068) [XQ]	RAF No 626 VGS, Predannack	
ZE627	Grob G103 Viking T1 (BGA3069) [XR]	RAF ACCGS/No 643 VGS, Syerston	
ZE628	Grob G103 Viking T1 (BGA3070) [XS]	RAF No 622 VGS, Upavon	
ZE629	Grob G103 Viking T1 (BGA3071) [XT]	RAF No 662 VGS, Arbroath	

Notes	Serial	Type (code/other identity)	Owner/operator, location or fate
	ZE630	Grob G103 Viking T1 (BGA3072) [XU]	RAF No 662 VGS, Arbroath
	ZE631	Grob G103 Viking T1 (BGA3073) [XV]	RAF No 615 VGS, Kenley
	ZE632	Grob G103 Viking T1 (BGA3074) [XW]	RAF No 662 VGS, Arbroath
	ZE633	Grob G103 Viking T1 (BGA3075) [XX]	RAF CGMF, Syerston
	ZE636	Grob G103 Viking T1 (BGA3078) [XZ]	RAF ACCGS/No 643 VGS, Syerston
	ZE637	Grob G103 Viking T1 (BGA3079) [YA]	RAF No 615 VGS, Kenley
	ZE650	Grob G103 Viking T1 (BGA3080) [YB]	RAF No 615 VGS, Kenley
	ZE651	Grob G103 Viking T1 (BGA3081) [YC]	RAF No 615 VGS, Kenley
	ZE652	Grob G103 Viking T1 (BGA3082) [YD]	RAF No 614 VGS, Wethersfield
	ZE653	Grob G103 Viking T1 (BGA3083) [YE]	RAF No 625 VGS, Hullavington
	ZE656	Grob G103 Viking T1 (BGA3086) [YH]	RAF No 611 VGS, Watton
	ZE657	Grob G103 Viking T1 (BGA3087) [YJ]	RAF ACCGS/No 643 VGS, Syerston
	ZE658	Grob G103 Viking T1 (BGA3088) [YK]	RAF No 611 VGS, Watton
	ZE677	Grob G103 Viking T1 (BGA3090) [YM]	RAF CGMF, Syerston
	ZE678	Grob G103 Viking T1 (BGA3091) [YN]	RAF ACCGS/No 643 VGS, Syerston
	ZE679	Grob G103 Viking T1 (BGA3092) [YP]	RAF No 621 VGS, Hullavington
	ZE680	Grob G103 Viking T1 (BGA3093) [YQ]	RAF ACCGS/No 643 VGS, Syerston
	ZE681	Grob G103 Viking T1 (BGA3094) <ff>	RAF Hullavington
	ZE682	Grob G103 Viking T1 (BGA3095) [YS]	RAF No 662 VGS, Arbroath
	ZE683	Grob G103 Viking T1 (BGA3096) [YT]	RAF CGMF, Syerston
	ZE684	Grob G103 Viking T1 (BGA3097) [YU]	RAF No 611 VGS, Watton
	ZE685	Grob G103 Viking T1 (BGA3098) [YV]	RAF CGMF, stored Syerston
	ZE686	Grob G103 Viking T1 (BGA3099) <ff>	RAF Museum, Hendon
	ZE690	BAe Sea Harrier FA2 [90/DD]	SFDO, RNAS Culdrose
	ZE691	BAe Sea Harrier FA2 [710]	Classic Autos, Winsford, Cheshire
	ZE692	BAe Sea Harrier FA2 [92/DD]	SFDO, RNAS Culdrose
	ZE693	BAe Sea Harrier FA2 [717]	Privately owned, Sproughton
	ZE694	BAe Sea Harrier FA2 [004]	Midland Air Museum, Coventry
	ZE695	BAe Sea Harrier FA2	Tate Modern, North Southwark
	ZE697	BAe Sea Harrier FA2 [006]	Privately owned, Binbrook
	ZE698	BAe Sea Harrier FA2 [001]	Privately owned, Charlwood
	ZE700	BAe 146 CC2 (G-6-021)	RAF No 32(The Royal) Sqn, Northolt
	ZE701	BAe 146 CC2 (G-6-029)	RAF No 32(The Royal) Sqn, Northolt
	ZE704	Lockheed TriStar C2 (N508PA)	RAF No 216 Sqn, Brize Norton
	ZE705	Lockheed TriStar C2 (N509PA)	RAF No 216 Sqn, Brize Norton
	ZE706	Lockheed TriStar C2A (N503PA)	RAF No 216 Sqn, Brize Norton
	ZE731	Panavia Tornado F3 [GP]	*Scrapped at Leeming, 2010*
	ZE734	Panavia Tornado F3 [JU]$	RAF No 111 Sqn, Leuchars
	ZE737	Panavia Tornado F3 [GK]	RAF, stored Shawbury
	ZE757	Panavia Tornado F3 $	RAF Leeming, for scrapping
	ZE760	Panavia Tornado F3 (MM7206) [AP]	RAF Coningsby, on display
	ZE761	Panavia Tornado F3 (MM7203)	*Scrapped*
	ZE763	Panavia Tornado F3 [HD]	RAF No 111 Sqn, Leuchars
	ZE764	Panavia Tornado F3 [HK]	RAF No 111 Sqn, Leuchars
	ZE785	Panavia Tornado F3 [HS]	RAF Leeming, for scrapping
	ZE788	Panavia Tornado F3 [HV]	RAF Leeming, for scrapping
	ZE790	Panavia Tornado F3 [HC]	RAF Leeming, for scrapping
	ZE791	Panavia Tornado F3 [HF,JU-L]	RAF No 111 Sqn, Leuchars

Serial	Type (code/other identity)	Owner/operator, location or fate	Notes
ZE794	Panavia Tornado F3 [FL]	MoD/AFD/QinetiQ, Boscombe Down	
ZE808	Panavia Tornado F3 [HJ]	RAF Leeming, for scrapping	
ZE810	Panavia Tornado F3 [GG]	RAF Leeming, for scrapping	
ZE831	Panavia Tornado F3 [GN]	RAF Leeming, for scrapping	
ZE832	Panavia Tornado F3 (MM7202) [XP]	*Scrapped*	
ZE834	Panavia Tornado F3 [HA]	RAF No 111 Sqn, Leuchars	
ZE837	Panavia Tornado F3 (MM55057) [TD]	MoD/DSG, stored St Athan	
ZE838	Panavia Tornado F3 [GH]	RAF Leeming, for scrapping	
ZE887	Panavia Tornado F3 [GF] $	RAF Museum, Hendon	
ZE907	Panavia Tornado F3 [DA]	*Scrapped at Leeming, March 2010*	
ZE908	Panavia Tornado F3 [TB]	*Scrapped*	
ZE934	Panavia Tornado F3 [TA]	Royal Scottish Mus'm of Flight, E Fortune	
ZE936	Panavia Tornado F3 [HE]	RAF Leeming, for scrapping	
ZE961	Panavia Tornado F3 [HB]	RAF No 111 Sqn, Leuchars	
ZE963	Panavia Tornado F3 [YT]	RAF Leeming, for scrapping	
ZE965	Panavia Tornado F3 [HZ]	RAF Leeming, for scrapping	
ZE966	Panavia Tornado F3 [VT]	Museum of Science & Industry, stored Manchester	
ZE967	Panavia Tornado F3 [UT]	RAF Leuchars, at main gate	
ZE968	Panavia Tornado F3	*Scrapped at Leeming, April 2010*	
ZE969	Panavia Tornado F3 [FH]	*Scrapped at Leeming, April 2010*	
ZE983	Panavia Tornado F3 [HL]	RAF No 111 Sqn, Leuchars	
ZF115	WS61 Sea King HC4 [R]	RN No 846 NAS, Yeovilton	
ZF116	WS61 Sea King HC4 [WP]	RN No 845 NAS, Yeovilton	
ZF117	WS61 Sea King HC4 [X]	RN No 846 NAS, Yeovilton	
ZF118	WS61 Sea King HC4+ [O]	RN No 845 NAS, Yeovilton	
ZF119	WS61 Sea King HC4 [WY]	RN No 848 NAS, Yeovilton	
ZF120	WS61 Sea King HC4 [Z]	RN No 848 NAS, Yeovilton	
ZF121	WS61 Sea King HC4 [T]	RN No 848 NAS, Yeovilton	
ZF122	WS61 Sea King HC4+ [V]	RN No 846 NAS, Yeovilton	
ZF123	WS61 Sea King HC4 [WW]	RN No 848 NAS, Yeovilton	
ZF124	WS61 Sea King HC4+ [L]	RN No 846 NAS, Yeovilton	
ZF135	Shorts Tucano T1	RAF No 1 FTS, Linton-on-Ouse	
ZF137	Shorts Tucano T1	RAF No 1 FTS/*207(R) Sqn*, Linton-on-Ouse	
ZF139	Shorts Tucano T1	RAF, stored Linton-on-Ouse	
ZF140	Shorts Tucano T1	RAF No 1 FTS/*207(R) Sqn*, Linton-on-Ouse	
ZF142	Shorts Tucano T1	RAF No 1 FTS, Linton-on-Ouse	
ZF143	Shorts Tucano T1	RAF No 1 FTS, Linton-on-Ouse	
ZF144	Shorts Tucano T1	RAF No 1 FTS, Linton-on-Ouse	
ZF145	Shorts Tucano T1	RAF No 1 FTS, Linton-on-Ouse	
ZF160	Shorts Tucano T1	RAF, stored Shawbury	
ZF161	Shorts Tucano T1	RAF, stored Shawbury	
ZF163	Shorts Tucano T1	RAF, stored Shawbury	
ZF166	Shorts Tucano T1	RAF, stored Shawbury	
ZF167	Shorts Tucano T1 (fuselage)	Shorts, Belfast	
ZF169	Shorts Tucano T1	RAF No 1 FTS/*72(R) Sqn*, Linton-on-Ouse	
ZF170	Shorts Tucano T1 [MP-A]	RAF No 1 FTS/*76(R) Sqn*, Linton-on-Ouse	
ZF171	Shorts Tucano T1 [LZ-R] $	RAF No 1 FTS, Linton-on-Ouse	
ZF172	Shorts Tucano T1 [MP-D]	RAF No 1 FTS/*76(R) Sqn*, Linton-on-Ouse	
ZF202	Shorts Tucano T1	RAF Linton-on-Ouse, on display	
ZF203	Shorts Tucano T1	RAF, stored Shawbury	
ZF204	Shorts Tucano T1	RAF No 1 FTS/*207(R) Sqn*, Linton-on-Ouse	
ZF205	Shorts Tucano T1	RAF No 1 FTS/*72(R) Sqn*, Linton-on-Ouse	
ZF209	Shorts Tucano T1	RAF No 1 FTS/*72(R) Sqn*, Linton-on-Ouse	
ZF210	Shorts Tucano T1	RAF No 1 FTS, Linton-on-Ouse	
ZF211	Shorts Tucano T1	RAF, stored Shawbury	
ZF212	Shorts Tucano T1	RAF, stored Shawbury	
ZF239	Shorts Tucano T1 [MP-T]	RAF No 1 FTS/*76(R) Sqn*, Linton-on-Ouse	
ZF240	Shorts Tucano T1	RAF No 1 FTS/*207(R) Sqn*, Linton-on-Ouse	
ZF242	Shorts Tucano T1	RAF, stored Shawbury	
ZF243	Shorts Tucano T1	RAF No 1 FTS/*207(R) Sqn*, Linton-on-Ouse	
ZF244	Shorts Tucano T1	RAF No 1 FTS/*72(R) Sqn*, Linton-on-Ouse	
ZF263	Shorts Tucano T1	RAF, stored Shawbury	
ZF264	Shorts Tucano T1 [MP-Q]	RAF No 1 FTS/*76(R) Sqn*, Linton-on-Ouse	
ZF267	Shorts Tucano T1	Privately owned, Norwich	
ZF268	Shorts Tucano T1	RAF, stored Shawbury	
ZF269	Shorts Tucano T1 [MP-O]	RAF No 1 FTS/*76(R) Sqn*, Linton-on-Ouse	
ZF284	Shorts Tucano T1	*Sold to the USA*	
ZF286	Shorts Tucano T1	RAF, stored Shawbury	

Notes	Serial	Type (code/other identity)	Owner/operator, location or fate
	ZF287	Shorts Tucano T1	RAF No 1 FTS/*72(R) Sqn*, Linton-on-Ouse
	ZF288	Shorts Tucano T1	RAF, stored Shawbury
	ZF289	Shorts Tucano T1	RAF No 1 FTS, Linton-on-Ouse
	ZF290	Shorts Tucano T1	RAF No 1 FTS/*207(R) Sqn*, Linton-on-Ouse
	ZF291	Shorts Tucano T1	RAF No 1 FTS, Linton-on-Ouse
	ZF292	Shorts Tucano T1	RAF No 1 FTS/*207(R) Sqn*, Linton-on-Ouse
	ZF293	Shorts Tucano T1	RAF No 1 FTS/*207(R) Sqn*, Linton-on-Ouse
	ZF294	Shorts Tucano T1	RAF No 1 FTS/*207(R) Sqn*, Linton-on-Ouse
	ZF295	Shorts Tucano T1 $	RAF No 1 FTS/*72(R) Sqn*, Linton-on-Ouse
	ZF315	Shorts Tucano T1	RAF, stored Shawbury
	ZF317	Shorts Tucano T1 [QJ-F] $	RAF No 1 FTS, Linton-on-Ouse
	ZF318	Shorts Tucano T1 $	RAF, stored Shawbury
	ZF319	Shorts Tucano T1	RAF No 1 FTS, Linton-on-Ouse
	ZF338	Shorts Tucano T1 $	RAF No 1 FTS, Linton-on-Ouse
	ZF339	Shorts Tucano T1	RAF No 1 FTS/*72(R) Sqn*, Linton-on-Ouse
	ZF341	Shorts Tucano T1	RAF No 1 FTS/*207(R) Sqn*, Linton-on-Ouse
	ZF342	Shorts Tucano T1	RAF No 1 FTS, Linton-on-Ouse
	ZF343	Shorts Tucano T1	RAF No 1 FTS/*72(R) Sqn*, Linton-on-Ouse
	ZF345	Shorts Tucano T1	RAF, stored Shawbury
	ZF347	Shorts Tucano T1	RAF No 1 FTS, Linton-on-Ouse
	ZF348	Shorts Tucano T1	RAF No 1 FTS, Linton-on-Ouse
	ZF349	Shorts Tucano T1	RAF No 1 FTS/*207(R) Sqn*, Linton-on-Ouse
	ZF350	Shorts Tucano T1	RAF, stored Shawbury
	ZF372	Shorts Tucano T1	RAF, stored Shawbury
	ZF373	Shorts Tucano T1 (G-CEHJ)	*Sold to the USA, October 2010*
	ZF374	Shorts Tucano T1	RAF No 1 FTS, Linton-on-Ouse
	ZF376	Shorts Tucano T1	RAF, stored Shawbury
	ZF377	Shorts Tucano T1	RAF No 1 FTS, Linton-on-Ouse
	ZF378	Shorts Tucano T1 [MP-W]	RAF No 1 FTS/*76(R) Sqn*, Linton-on-Ouse
	ZF379	Shorts Tucano T1	RAF No 1 FTS, Linton-on-Ouse
	ZF380	Shorts Tucano T1	RAF, stored Shawbury
	ZF405	Shorts Tucano T1	RAF, stored Shawbury
	ZF406	Shorts Tucano T1	RAF No 1 FTS, Linton-on-Ouse
	ZF407	Shorts Tucano T1	RAF No 1 FTS, Linton-on-Ouse
	ZF408	Shorts Tucano T1	RAF, stored Shawbury
	ZF409	Shorts Tucano T1	RAF No 1 FTS, Linton-on-Ouse
	ZF410	Shorts Tucano T1	RAF, stored Shawbury
	ZF412	Shorts Tucano T1	RAF, stored Shawbury
	ZF414	Shorts Tucano T1	RAF, stored Shawbury
	ZF416	Shorts Tucano T1	RAF, stored Shawbury
	ZF417	Shorts Tucano T1	RAF No 1 FTS/*207(R) Sqn*, Linton-on-Ouse
	ZF418	Shorts Tucano T1	RAF, stored Shawbury
	ZF446	Shorts Tucano T1	RAF, stored Shawbury
	ZF447	Shorts Tucano T1	RAF, stored Shawbury
	ZF448	Shorts Tucano T1 $	RAF No 1 FTS/*72(R) Sqn*, Linton-on-Ouse
	ZF449	Shorts Tucano T1	RAF, stored Shawbury
	ZF483	Shorts Tucano T1	RAF, stored Shawbury
	ZF484	Shorts Tucano T1	RAF, stored Shawbury
	ZF485	Shorts Tucano T1 (G-BULU)	RAF No 1 FTS, Linton-on-Ouse
	ZF486	Shorts Tucano T1	RAF, stored Shawbury
	ZF487	Shorts Tucano T1	RAF, stored Shawbury
	ZF488	Shorts Tucano T1	RAF, stored Shawbury
	ZF489	Shorts Tucano T1	RAF No 1 FTS/*207(R) Sqn*, Linton-on-Ouse
	ZF490	Shorts Tucano T1	RAF, stored Shawbury
	ZF491	Shorts Tucano T1	RAF No 1 FTS, Linton-on-Ouse
	ZF492	Shorts Tucano T1	RAF, stored Shawbury
	ZF510	Shorts Tucano T1	MoD/AFD/QinetiQ, Boscombe Down
	ZF511	Shorts Tucano T1	MoD/AFD/QinetiQ, Boscombe Down
	ZF512	Shorts Tucano T1	RAF No 1 FTS/*72(R) Sqn*, Linton-on-Ouse
	ZF513	Shorts Tucano T1	RAF, stored Shawbury
	ZF514	Shorts Tucano T1	RAF, stored Shawbury
	ZF515	Shorts Tucano T1	RAF No 1 FTS/*72(R) Sqn*, Linton-on-Ouse
	ZF516	Shorts Tucano T1	RAF, stored Shawbury
	ZF534	BAe EAP	Loughborough University
	ZF537	WS Lynx AH9	AAC No 9 Regt, Dishforth
	ZF538	WS Lynx AH9	AAC No 9 Regt, Dishforth
	ZF539	WS Lynx AH9A	RM No 847 NAS, Yeovilton
	ZF540	WS Lynx AH9	AAC No 9 Regt, Dishforth
	ZF557	WS Lynx HMA8SRU [375/SM]	Mod/ Vector Aerospace, Fleetlands
	ZF558	WS Lynx HMA8SRU [426/PD]	RN No 815 NAS, *Portland* Flt, Yeovilton
	ZF560	WS Lynx HMA8SRU [412]	RN No 815 NAS, *Cornwall* Flt, Yeovilton
	ZF562	WS Lynx HMA8SRU [315]	RN No 815 NAS, HQ Flt, Yeovilton

Serial	*Type (code/other identity)*	*Owner/operator, location or fate*	*Notes*
ZF563	WS Lynx HMA8SRU [348/CM]	MoD/Vector Aerospace, Fleetlands	
ZF573	PBN 2T Islander CC2 (G-SRAY)	RAF Northolt Station Flight	
ZF579	BAC Lightning F53	Gatwick Aviation Museum, Charlwood	
ZF580	BAC Lightning F53	BAE Systems Samlesbury, at main gate	
ZF581	BAC Lightning F53	BAE Systems, Rochester, on display	
ZF582	BAC Lightning F53 <ff>	Bournemouth Aviation Museum	
ZF583	BAC Lightning F53	Solway Aviation Society, Carlisle	
ZF584	BAC Lightning F53	Dumfries & Galloway Avn Mus, Dumfries	
ZF587	BAC Lightning F53 <ff>	Lashenden Air Warfare Museum, Headcorn	
ZF588	BAC Lightning F53 [L]	East Midlands Airport Aeropark	
ZF594	BAC Lightning F53	*Repainted as XS933*	
ZF595	BAC Lightning T55 (fuselage)	Privately owned, Binbrook	
ZF596	BAC Lightning T55 <ff>	RAF Millom Museum, Millom	
ZF622	Piper PA-31 Navajo Chieftain 350 (N3548Y)	RAF/AWC/No 206(R) Sqn, Boscombe Down	
ZF641	EHI-101 [PP1]	SFDO, RNAS Culdrose	
ZF649	EHI-101 Merlin (A2714) [PP5]	DCAE AESS, HMS Sultan, Gosport	
ZG101	EHI-101 (mock-up) [GB]	AgustaWestland, Yeovil	
ZG347	Northrop Chukar D2	Davidstow Airfield & Cornwall At War Museum	
ZG471	BAe Harrier GR7 [61A]	RAF HM&SF, Cottesmore (wfu)	
ZG472	BAe Harrier GR9A [62]	RAF HM&SF, Cottesmore (wfu)	
ZG474	BAe Harrier GR9 [64]	RAF HM&SF, Cottesmore (wfu)	
ZG477	BAe Harrier GR9 [$]	RAF HM&SF, Cottesmore (wfu)	
ZG479	BAe Harrier GR9A [69A]	RAF HM&SF, Cottesmore (wfu)	
ZG480	BAe Harrier GR9 [70]	RAF HM&SF, Cottesmore (wfu)	
ZG500	BAe Harrier GR9 [71]	RAF HM&SF, Cottesmore (wfu)	
ZG501	BAe Harrier GR9 [EB-Q]	RAF HM&SF, Cottesmore (wfu)	
ZG502	BAe Harrier GR9 [$]	RAF HM&SF, Cottesmore (wfu)	
ZG503	BAe Harrier GR9 [EB-Z]	RAF HM&SF, Cottesmore (wfu)	
ZG504	BAe Harrier GR9A [75A]	RAF HM&SF, Cottesmore (wfu)	
ZG505	BAe Harrier GR9 [76]	RAF HM&SF, Cottesmore (wfu)	
ZG506	BAe Harrier GR9A [$]	RAF HM&SF, Cottesmore (wfu)	
ZG507	BAe Harrier GR9 [78]	RAF HM&SF, Cottesmore (wfu)	
ZG508	BAe Harrier GR9 [79]	RAF HM&SF, Cottesmore (wfu)	
ZG509	BAe Harrier GR7 [80]	RAF HM&SF, Cottesmore (wfu)	
ZG510	BAe Harrier GR9A [EB-Y]	RAF HM&SF, Cottesmore (wfu)	
ZG511	BAe Harrier GR9A [82A]	RAF HM&SF, Cottesmore (wfu)	
ZG530	BAe Harrier GR9 [84]	RAF HM&SF, Cottesmore (wfu)	
ZG531	BAe Harrier GR9 [85]	RAF HM&SF, Cottesmore (wfu)	
ZG631	Northrop Chukar D2	Farnborough Air Sciences Trust, Farnborough	
ZG705	Panavia Tornado GR4A [118]	RAF No 15(R) Sqn, Lossiemouth	
ZG706	Panavia Tornado GR1A [E]	MoD/DSG, stored St Athan	
ZG707	Panavia Tornado GR4A [119]	MoD/AFD/QinetiQ, Boscombe Down	
ZG709	Panavia Tornado GR4A [120]	RAF No 9 Sqn, Marham	
ZG712	Panavia Tornado GR4A [122]	RAF No 13 Sqn, Marham	
ZG713	Panavia Tornado GR4A [123]	RAF No 13 Sqn, Marham	
ZG714	Panavia Tornado GR4A [124]	RAF No 31 Sqn, Marham	
ZG726	Panavia Tornado GR4A [125]	RAF No 2 Sqn, Marham	
ZG727	Panavia Tornado GR4A [126]	RAF No 9 Sqn, Marham	
ZG729	Panavia Tornado GR4A [127]	RAF No 617 Sqn, Lossiemouth	
ZG731	Panavia Tornado F3 [HV]	*Scrapped at RAF Leeming, May 2010*	
ZG732	Panavia Tornado F3 (MM7227) [WU]	*Scrapped*	
ZG750	Panavia Tornado GR4 [128]	RAF No 15(R) Sqn, Lossiemouth	
ZG751	Panavia Tornado F3 [HI]	RAF Leeming, for scrapping	
ZG752	Panavia Tornado GR4 [129]	RAF No 13 Sqn, Marham	
ZG753	Panavia Tornado F3 [H]	RAF Leeming, for scrapping	
ZG754	Panavia Tornado GR4 [130]	RAF No 15(R) Sqn, Lossiemouth	
ZG755	Panavia Tornado F3 [F]	RAF Leeming, for scrapping	
ZG756	Panavia Tornado GR4 [BX]	RAF No 12 Sqn, Lossiemouth	
ZG769	Panavia Tornado GR4	RAF, stored Shawbury (damaged)	
ZG771	Panavia Tornado GR4 [133]	RAF No 617 Sqn, Lossiemouth	
ZG773	Panavia Tornado GR4	MoD/BAE Systems, Warton	
ZG774	Panavia Tornado F3 [HM]	RAF Leeming, for scrapping	
ZG775	Panavia Tornado GR4 [134]	RAF No 12 Sqn, Lossiemouth	
ZG777	Panavia Tornado GR4 [135]	RAF AWC/FJWOEU/No 41 (R) Sqn	
ZG779	Panavia Tornado GR4 [136]	RAF No 9 Sqn, Marham	
ZG791	Panavia Tornado GR4 [137]	RAF No 2 Sqn, Marham	
ZG792	Panavia Tornado GR4 [138]	*Crashed 27 January 2011, off Gairloch*	

Notes	Serial	Type (code/other identity)	Owner/operator, location or fate
	ZG794	Panavia Tornado GR4 [TN]	RAF, stored Lossiemouth
	ZG797	Panavia Tornado F3 [D]	RAF Leeming, for scrapping
	ZG798	Panavia Tornado F3 [GQ]	RAF Leuchars, instructional use
	ZG816	WS61 Sea King HAS6 [014/L]	DCAE, stored *HMS Sultan*, Gosport
	ZG817	WS61 Sea King HAS6 [702/PW]	DCAE AESS, *HMS Sultan*, Gosport
	ZG818	WS61 Sea King HAS6 [707/PW]	DCAE, stored *HMS Sultan*, Gosport
	ZG819	WS61 Sea King HAS6 [265/N]	DCAE AESS, *HMS Sultan*, Gosport
	ZG820	WS61 Sea King HC4+ [I]	RN No 845 NAS, Yeovilton
	ZG821	WS61 Sea King HC4+ [G]	RN No 846 NAS, Yeovilton
	ZG822	WS61 Sea King HC4 [WS]	RN No 848 Sqn, Yeovilton
	ZG844	PBN 2T Islander AL1 (G-BLNE)	AAC No 651 Sqn/5 Regt, Aldergrove
	ZG845	PBN 2T Islander AL1 (G-BLNT)	AAC No 651 Sqn/5 Regt, Aldergrove
	ZG846	PBN 2T Islander AL1 (G-BLNU)	AAC No 651 Sqn/5 Regt, Aldergrove
	ZG847	PBN 2T Islander AL1 (G-BLNV)	AAC No 651 Sqn/5 Regt, Aldergrove
	ZG848	PBN 2T Islander AL1 (G-BLNY)	AAC No 651 Sqn/5 Regt, Aldergrove
	ZG857	BAe Harrier GR9 [EB-Z]	RAF HM&SF, Cottesmore (wfu)
	ZG858	BAe Harrier GR9 $	RAF HM&SF, Cottesmore (wfu)
	ZG859	BAe Harrier GR9A [91A]	RAF HM&SF, Cottesmore (wfu)
	ZG860	BAe Harrier GR9	MoD, Boscombe Down (wfu)
	ZG862	BAe Harrier GR9 [94]	RAF HM&SF, Cottesmore (wfu)
	ZG875	WS61 Sea King HAS6 [013/L]	DCAE, stored *HMS Sultan*, Gosport (damaged)
	ZG884	WS Lynx AH9A	RM No 847 NAS, Yeovilton
	ZG885	WS Lynx AH9A	MoD/Augusta Westland, Yeovil
	ZG886	WS Lynx AH9A	RM No 847 NAS, Yeovilton
	ZG887	WS Lynx AH9A	AAC No 9 Regt, Dishforth
	ZG888	WS Lynx AH9A	RM No 847 NAS, Yeovilton
	ZG889	WS Lynx AH9A	MoD/Vector Aerospace, Fleetlands
	ZG914	WS Lynx AH9A	AAC No 9 Regt, Dishforth
	ZG915	WS Lynx AH9A	MoD/Augusta Westland, Yeovil
	ZG916	WS Lynx AH9A	MoD/Vector Aerospace, Fleetlands
	ZG917	WS Lynx AH9	AAC No 9 Regt, Dishforth
	ZG918	WS Lynx AH9	AAC No 9 Regt, Dishforth
	ZG919	WS Lynx AH9A	AAC No 9 Regt, Dishforth
	ZG920	WS Lynx AH9A	MoD/AgustaWestland, Yeovil (conversion)
	ZG921	WS Lynx AH9A	MoD/AgustaWestland, Yeovil (conversion)
	ZG922	WS Lynx AH9	AgustaWestland, Yeovil, Fire Section
	ZG923	WS Lynx AH9A	MoD/AgustaWestland, Yeovil (conversion)
	ZG969	Pilatus PC-9 (HB-HQE)	BAE Systems Warton
	ZG989	PBN 2T Islander ASTOR (G-DLRA)	MoD/Britten-Norman, Bembridge
	ZG993	PBN 2T Islander AL1 (G-BOMD)	AAC, stored Shawbury
	ZG994	PBN 2T Islander AL1 (G-BPLN) (fuselage)	Britten-Norman, stored Bembridge
	ZG995	PBN 2T Defender AL1 (G-SURV)	AAC No 651 Sqn/5 Regt, Aldergrove
	ZG996	PBN 2T Defender AL2 (G-BWPR)	AAC No 651 Sqn/5 Regt, Aldergrove
	ZG997	PBN 2T Defender AL2 (G-BWPV)	AAC No 651 Sqn/5 Regt, Aldergrove
	ZG998	PBN 2T Defender AL1 (G-BWPX)	AAC No 651 Sqn/5 Regt, Aldergrove
	ZH001	PBN 2T Defender AL2 (G-CEIO)	AAC No 651 Sqn/5 Regt, Aldergrove
	ZH002	PBN 2T Defender AL2 (G-CEIP)	AAC No 651 Sqn/5 Regt, Aldergrove
	ZH003	PBN 2T Defender AL2 (G-CEIR)	AAC No 651 Sqn/5 Regt, Aldergrove
	ZH004	PBN 2T Defender T3 (G-BWPO)	AAC No 651 Sqn/5 Regt, Aldergrove
	ZH005	PBN 2T Defender AL2	DE&S/Britten-Norman, for AAC
	ZH006	PBN 2T Defender AL2	DE&S/Britten-Norman, for AAC
	ZH101	Boeing E-3D Sentry AEW1	RAF No 8 Sqn, Waddington
	ZH102	Boeing E-3D Sentry AEW1	RAF No 8 Sqn, Waddington
	ZH103	Boeing E-3D Sentry AEW1	RAF No 8 Sqn, Waddington
	ZH104	Boeing E-3D Sentry AEW1	RAF, stored Waddington
	ZH105	Boeing E-3D Sentry AEW1	RAF, stored Waddington
	ZH106	Boeing E-3D Sentry AEW1	RAF No 8 Sqn, Waddington
	ZH107	Boeing E-3D Sentry AEW1	RAF No 8 Sqn, Waddington
	ZH115	Grob G109B Vigilant T1 [TA]	RAF No 642 VGS, Linton-on-Ouse
	ZH116	Grob G109B Vigilant T1 [TB]	RAF No 618 VGS, Odiham
	ZH117	Grob G109B Vigilant T1 [TC]	RAF No 642 VGS, Linton-on-Ouse
	ZH118	Grob G109B Vigilant T1 [TD]	RAF No 664 VGS, Newtownards
	ZH119	Grob G109B Vigilant T1 [TE]	RAF No 613 VGS, Halton
	ZH120	Grob G109B Vigilant T1 [TF]	RAF No 632 VGS, Ternhill
	ZH121	Grob G109B Vigilant T1 [TG]	RAF No 612 VGS, Abingdon
	ZH122	Grob G109B Vigilant T1 [TH]	RAF No 616 VGS, Henlow
	ZH123	Grob G109B Vigilant T1 [TJ]	RAF ACCGS/No 644 VGS, Syerston
	ZH124	Grob G109B Vigilant T1 [TK]	RAF No 631 VGS, Woodvale

Serial	*Type (code/other identity)*	*Owner/operator, location or fate*	*Notes*
ZH125	Grob G109B Vigilant T1 [TL]	RAF ACCGS/No 644 VGS, Syerston	
ZH126	Grob G109B Vigilant T1 (D-KGRA) [TM]	RAF CGMF, Syerston	
ZH127	Grob G109B Vigilant T1 (D-KEEC) [TN]	RAF No 616 VGS, Henlow	
ZH128	Grob G109B Vigilant T1 [TP]	RAF No 624 VGS, Chivenor RMB	
ZH129	Grob G109B Vigilant T1 [TQ]	RAF No 632 VGS, Ternhill	
ZH139	BAe Harrier GR7 <R> (BAPC 191/*ZD472*)	RAF M&RU, Bottesford (wfu)	
ZH144	Grob G109B Vigilant T1 [TR]	RAF No 635 VGS, Topcliffe	
ZH145	Grob G109B Vigilant T1 [TS]	RAF No 633 VGS, Cosford	
ZH146	Grob G109B Vigilant T1 [TT]	RAF No 642 VGS, Linton-on-Ouse	
ZH147	Grob G109B Vigilant T1 [TU]	RAF ACCGS/No 644 VGS, Syerston	
ZH148	Grob G109B Vigilant T1 [TV]	RAF No 645 VGS, Topcliffe	
ZH184	Grob G109B Vigilant T1 [TW]	RAF No 632 VGS, Ternhill	
ZH185	Grob G109B Vigilant T1 [TX]	RAF No 636 VGS, Swansea	
ZH186	Grob G109B Vigilant T1 [TY]	RAF No 613 VGS, Halton	
ZH187	Grob G109B Vigilant T1 [TZ]	RAF No 664 VGS, Newtownards	
ZH188	Grob G109B Vigilant T1 [UA]	RAF CGMF, Syerston	
ZH189	Grob G109B Vigilant T1 [UB]	RAF No 636 VGS, Swansea	
ZH190	Grob G109B Vigilant T1 [UC]	RAF No 624 VGS, Chivenor RMB	
ZH191	Grob G109B Vigilant T1 [UD]	RAF No 613 VGS, Halton	
ZH192	Grob G109B Vigilant T1 [UE]	RAF No 633 VGS, Cosford	
ZH193	Grob G109B Vigilant T1 [UF]	RAF No 631 VGS, Woodvale	
ZH194	Grob G109B Vigilant T1 [UG]	RAF No 624 VGS, Chivenor RMB	
ZH195	Grob G109B Vigilant T1 [UH]	RAF No 642 VGS, Linton-on-Ouse	
ZH196	Grob G109B Vigilant T1 [UJ]	RAF No 663 VGS, Kinloss	
ZH197	Grob G109B Vigilant T1 [UK]	RAF No 618 VGS, Odiham	
ZH200	BAe Hawk 200	BAE Systems Warton	
ZH205	Grob G109B Vigilant T1 [UL]	RAF No 635 VGS, Topcliffe	
ZH206	Grob G109B Vigilant T1 [UM]	RAF No 631 VGS, Woodvale	
ZH207	Grob G109B Vigilant T1 [UN]	RAF ACCGS/No 644 VGS, Syerston	
ZH208	Grob G109B Vigilant T1 [UP]	RAF No 645 VGS, Topcliffe	
ZH209	Grob G109B Vigilant T1 [UQ]	RAF No 624 VGS, Chivenor RMB	
ZH211	Grob G109B Vigilant T1 [UR]	RAF No 616 VGS, Henlow	
ZH247	Grob G109B Vigilant T1 [US]	RAF No 618 VGS, Odiham	
ZH248	Grob G109B Vigilant T1 [UT]	RAF No 645 VGS, Topcliffe	
ZH249	Grob G109B Vigilant T1 [UU]	RAF No 634 VGS, St Athan	
ZH257	B-V CH-47C Chinook (9217M) (fuselage)	RAF Odiham, BDRT	
ZH263	Grob G109B Vigilant T1 [UV]	RAF No 637 VGS, Little Rissington	
ZH264	Grob G109B Vigilant T1 [UW]	RAF No 613 VGS, Halton	
ZH265	Grob G109B Vigilant T1 [UX]	RAF No 637 VGS, Little Rissington	
ZH266	Grob G109B Vigilant T1 [UY]	RAF No 633 VGS, Cosford	
ZH267	Grob G109B Vigilant T1 [UZ]	RAF No 645 VGS, Topcliffe	
ZH268	Grob G109B Vigilant T1 [SA]	RAF No 612 VGS, Abingdon	
ZH269	Grob G109B Vigilant T1 [SB]	RAF ACCGS/No 644 VGS, Syerston	
ZH270	Grob G109B Vigilant T1 [SC]	RAF No 616 VGS, Henlow	
ZH271	Grob G109B Vigilant T1 [SD]	RAF No 637 VGS, Little Rissington	
ZH278	Grob G109B Vigilant T1 (D-KAIS) [SF]	RAF No 616 VGS, Henlow	
ZH279	Grob G109B Vigilant T1 (D-KNPS) [SG]	RAF No 664 VGS, Newtownards	
ZH536	PBN 2T Islander CC2 (G-BSAH)	RAF Northolt Station Flight	
ZH537	PBN 2T Islander CC2 (G-SELX)	RAF Northolt Station Flight	
ZH540	WS61 Sea King HAR3A	RAF No 22 Sqn, B Flt, Wattisham	
ZH541	WS61 Sea King HAR3A [V]	RAF SKAMG, RNAS Yeovilton	
ZH542	WS61 Sea King HAR3A [W]	RAF No 22 Sqn, B Flt, Wattisham	
ZH543	WS61 Sea King HAR3A [X]	MoD/Vector Aerospace, Fleetlands	
ZH544	WS61 Sea King HAR3A	RAF No 22 Sqn, A Flt, Chivenor RMB	
ZH545	WS61 Sea King HAR3A [Z] $	RAF No 22 Sqn, A Flt, Chivenor RMB	
ZH552	Panavia Tornado F3 [HW]	MoD/AFD/QinetiQ, Boscombe Down	
ZH553	Panavia Tornado F3 [RT]	RAF, stored Shawbury	
ZH554	Panavia Tornado F3 [HX,JU-C]	RAF No 111 Sqn, Leuchars	
ZH555	Panavia Tornado F3 [PT]	RAF Leeming, for scrapping	
ZH557	Panavia Tornado F3 [NT]	RAF Leeming, for scrapping	
ZH588	Eurofighter Typhoon (DA2)	RAF Museum, Hendon	
ZH590	Eurofighter Typhoon (DA4)	Imperial War Museum, Duxford	
ZH653	BAe Harrier T10	MoD Boscombe Down (wfu)	
ZH654	BAe Harrier T10 <ff>	RAF, Cottesmore	
ZH655	BAe Harrier T10 (fuselage)	*Scrapped*	
ZH657	BAe Harrier T12 [105]	RAF HM&SF, Cottesmore (wfu)	

Notes	Serial	Type (code/other identity)	Owner/operator, location or fate
	ZH658	BAe Harrier T10 [106]	RAF HM&SF, Cottesmore (wfu)
	ZH659	BAe Harrier T12 [107]	RAF HM&SF, Cottesmore (wfu)
	ZH660	BAe Harrier T12 [108]	RAF HM&SF, Cottesmore (wfu)
	ZH661	BAe Harrier T12 [109]	RAF HM&SF, Cottesmore (wfu)
	ZH662	BAe Harrier T10 [110]	RAF HM&SF, Cottesmore (wfu)
	ZH663	BAe Harrier T12 [111]	RAF HM&SF, Cottesmore (wfu)
	ZH664	BAe Harrier T12 [112]	RAF HM&SF, Cottesmore (wfu)
	ZH665	BAe Harrier T12A [113]	RAF HM&SF, Cottesmore (wfu)
	ZH763	BAC 1-11/539GL (G-BGKE)	RAF/AWC/No 206(R) Sqn, Boscombe Down
	ZH775	B-V Chinook HC2 (N7424J) [HB]	RAF Odiham Wing
	ZH776	B-V Chinook HC2 (N7424L) [HC]	RAF No 1310 Flt, Kandahar, Afghanistan
	ZH777	B-V Chinook HC2 (N7424M) [HE]	RAF Odiham Wing
	ZH796	BAe Sea Harrier FA2 [001/L]	SFDO, RNAS Culdrose
	ZH797	BAe Sea Harrier FA2 [97/DD]	SFDO, RNAS Culdrose
	ZH798	BAe Sea Harrier FA2 [98/DD]	SFDO, RNAS Culdrose
	ZH799	BAe Sea Harrier FA2 [730]	Privately owned, Tunbridge Wells
	ZH800	BAe Sea Harrier FA2 (ZH801) [123]	RAF Cottesmore, preserved
	ZH801	BAe Sea Harrier FA2 (ZH800) [001]	RAF Cottesmore, preserved
	ZH802	BAe Sea Harrier FA2 [02/DD]	SFDO, RNAS Culdrose
	ZH803	BAe Sea Harrier FA2 [03/DD]	SFDO, RNAS Culdrose
	ZH804	BAe Sea Harrier FA2 [003/L]	SFDO, RNAS Culdrose
	ZH806	BAe Sea Harrier FA2 [007]	Privately owned, Bentwaters
	ZH807	BAe Sea Harrier FA2 <ff>	Privately owned, Newport, Isle of Wight
	ZH809	BAe Sea Harrier FA2 $	*Sold to Greece, August 2010*
	ZH810	BAe Sea Harrier FA2 [125]	Privately owned, Sproughton
	ZH811	BAe Sea Harrier FA2 [002/L]	SFDO, RNAS Culdrose
	ZH812	BAe Sea Harrier FA2 [005/L]	Privately owned, Sproughton
	ZH813	BAe Sea Harrier FA2 [13/DD]	SFDO, RNAS Culdrose
	ZH814	Bell 212HP AH1 (G-BGMH)	AAC No 7 Flt, Brunei
	ZH815	Bell 212HP AH1 (G-BGCZ)	AAC No 7 Flt, Brunei
	ZH816	Bell 212HP AH1 (G-BGMG)	AAC No 7 Flt, Brunei
	ZH821	EHI-101 Merlin HM1	AgustaWestland, Yeovil, Fire Section
	ZH822	EHI-101 Merlin HM1	RN, stored Shawbury
	ZH823	EHI-101 Merlin HM1	RN, stored Shawbury
	ZH824	EHI-101 Merlin HM1	RN No 820 NAS, Culdrose
	ZH825	EHI-101 Merlin HM1 [583]	RN, stored Shawbury
	ZH826	EHI-101 Merlin HM2	MoD/AgustaWestland, Yeovil (conversion)
	ZH827	EHI-101 Merlin HM1 [82]	RN No 824 NAS, Culdrose
	ZH828	EHI-101 Merlin HM1 [11]	RN No 820 NAS, Culdrose
	ZH829	EHI-101 Merlin HM2	MoD/AgustaWestland, Yeovil (conversion)
	ZH830	EHI-101 Merlin HM1	MoD/AFD/QinetiQ, Boscombe Down
	ZH831	EHI-101 Merlin HM2	MoD/AgustaWestland, Yeovil (conversion)
	ZH832	EHI-101 Merlin HM1	RN No 829 NAS, *Richmond* Flt, Culdrose
	ZH833	EHI-101 Merlin HM1 [85]	RN No 824 NAS, Culdrose
	ZH834	EHI-101 Merlin HM1 [86]	RN No 824 NAS, Culdrose
	ZH835	EHI-101 Merlin HM1 [65]	RN MDMF, Culdrose
	ZH836	EHI-101 Merlin HM1	RN No 829 NAS, Culdrose
	ZH837	EHI-101 Merlin HM1 [65]	RN No 820 NAS, Culdrose
	ZH838	EHI-101 Merlin HM1 [66]	RN No 814 NAS, Culdrose
	ZH839	EHI-101 Merlin HM1 [83]	RN MDMF, Culdrose
	ZH840	EHI-101 Merlin HM1 [81]	RN No 824 NAS, Culdrose
	ZH841	EHI-101 Merlin HM1 [82]	RN No 829 NAS, Culdrose
	ZH842	EHI-101 Merlin HM1 [88]	RN No 824 NAS, Culdrose
	ZH843	EHI-101 Merlin HM2 [12]	MoD/AgustaWestland, Yeovil (conversion)
	ZH844	EHI-101 Merlin HM1	*Scrapped*
	ZH845	EHI-101 Merlin HM1 [67]	RN No 814 NAS, Culdrose
	ZH846	EHI-101 Merlin HM1	RN No 820 NAS, Culdrose
	ZH847	EHI-101 Merlin HM1 [13]	RN MDMF, Culdrose
	ZH848	EHI-101 Merlin HM1 [503]	RN No 829 NAS, *St Albans* Flt, Culdrose
	ZH849	EHI-101 Merlin HM1	RN MDMF, Culdrose
	ZH850	EHI-101 Merlin HM1 [16]	RN No 820 NAS, Culdrose
	ZH851	EHI-101 Merlin HM1	RN No 824 NAS, Culdrose
	ZH852	EHI-101 Merlin HM1	RN MDMF, Culdrose
	ZH853	EHI-101 Merlin HM1 [13]	RN No 820 NAS, Culdrose
	ZH854	EHI-101 Merlin HM1 [84]	RN No 824 NAS, Culdrose
	ZH855	EHI-101 Merlin HM1 [70]	RN No 814 NAS, Culdrose
	ZH856	EHI-101 Merlin HM1	RN No 829 NAS, Culdrose
	ZH857	EHI-101 Merlin HM1 [10]	RN No 820 NAS, Culdrose
	ZH858	EHI-101 Merlin HM1	RN No 829 NAS, *Westminster* Flt, Culdrose
	ZH860	EHI-101 Merlin HM1 [68]	RN No 814 NAS, Culdrose

Serial	Type (code/other identity)	Owner/operator, location or fate	Notes
ZH861	EHI-101 Merlin HM1 [84]	RN MDMF, Culdrose	
ZH862	EHI-101 Merlin HM1	RN No 829 NAS, Culdrose	
ZH863	EHI-101 Merlin HM1 [11]	RN MDMF, Culdrose	
ZH864	EHI-101 Merlin HM1 [65]	RN No 814 NAS, Culdrose	
ZH865	Lockheed C-130J-30 Hercules C4 (N130JA)	RAF No 24 Sqn/No 30 Sqn, Lyneham	
ZH866	Lockheed C-130J-30 Hercules C4 (N130JE)	RAF No 24 Sqn/No 30 Sqn, Lyneham	
ZH867	Lockheed C-130J-30 Hercules C4 (N130JJ)	RAF/AWC/No 206(R) Sqn, Boscombe Down	
ZH868	Lockheed C-130J-30 Hercules C4 (N130JN)	RAF No 24 Sqn/No 30 Sqn, Lyneham	
ZH869	Lockheed C-130J-30 Hercules C4 (N130JV)	RAF No 24 Sqn/No 30 Sqn, Lyneham	
ZH870	Lockheed C-130J-30 Hercules C4 (*N73235*/N78235)	RAF No 24 Sqn/No 30 Sqn, Lyneham	
ZH871	Lockheed C-130J-30 Hercules C4 (N73238)	RAF No 24 Sqn/No 30 Sqn, Lyneham	
ZH872	Lockheed C-130J-30 Hercules C4 (N4249Y)	RAF No 24 Sqn/No 30 Sqn, Lyneham	
ZH873	Lockheed C-130J-30 Hercules C4 (N4242N)	RAF No 24 Sqn/No 30 Sqn, Lyneham	
ZH874	Lockheed C-130J-30 Hercules C4 (N41030)	RAF No 24 Sqn/No 30 Sqn, Lyneham	
ZH875	Lockheed C-130J-30 Hercules C4 (N4099R)	RAF No 24 Sqn/No 30 Sqn, Lyneham	
ZH877	Lockheed C-130J-30 Hercules C4 (N4081M)	RAF No 24 Sqn/No 30 Sqn, Lyneham	
ZH878	Lockheed C-130J-30 Hercules C4 (N73232)	RAF No 24 Sqn/No 30 Sqn, Lyneham	
ZH879	Lockheed C-130J-30 Hercules C4 (N4080M)	RAF No 24 Sqn/No 30 Sqn, Lyneham	
ZH880	Lockheed C-130J Hercules C5 (N73238)	RAF No 24 Sqn/No 30 Sqn, Lyneham	
ZH881	Lockheed C-130J Hercules C5 (N4081M)	RAF No 24 Sqn/No 30 Sqn, Lyneham	
ZH882	Lockheed C-130J Hercules C5 (N4099R)	RAF No 24 Sqn/No 30 Sqn, Lyneham	
ZH883	Lockheed C-130J Hercules C5 (N4242N)	RAF No 24 Sqn/No 30 Sqn, Lyneham	
ZH884	Lockheed C-130J Hercules C5 (N4249Y)	RAF No 24 Sqn/No 30 Sqn, Lyneham	
ZH885	Lockheed C-130J Hercules C5 (N41030)	RAF No 1312 Flt, Mount Pleasant, FI	
ZH886	Lockheed C-130J Hercules C5 (N73235)	RAF No 24 Sqn/No 30 Sqn, Lyneham	
ZH887	Lockheed C-130J Hercules C5 (N4187W)	RAF No 24 Sqn/No 30 Sqn, Lyneham	
ZH888	Lockheed C-130J Hercules C5 (N4187)	RAF No 24 Sqn/No 30 Sqn, Lyneham	
ZH889	Lockheed C-130J Hercules C5 (N4099R)	RAF No 24 Sqn/No 30 Sqn, Lyneham	
ZH890	Grob G109B Vigilant T1 [SE]	RAF No 612 VGS, Abingdon	
ZH891	B-V Chinook HC2A (N20075) [HF]	RAF Odiham Wing	
ZH892	B-V Chinook HC2A (N2019V) [HG]	RAF Odiham Wing	
ZH893	B-V Chinook HC2A (N2025L) [HH]	RAF No 1310 Flt, Kandahar, Afghanistan	
ZH894	B-V Chinook HC2A (N2026E) [HI]	RAF Odiham Wing	
ZH895	B-V Chinook HC2A (N2034K) [HJ]	RAF Odiham Wing	
ZH896	B-V Chinook HC2A (N2038G) [HK]	MoD/Vector Aerospace, Fleetlands	
ZH897	B-V Chinook HC3R (N2045G)	RAF Odiham Wing	
ZH898	B-V Chinook HC3R (N2057Q)	RAF Odiham Wing	
ZH899	B-V Chinook HC3R (N2057R)	RAF Odiham Wing	
ZH900	B-V Chinook HC3R (N2060H)	RAF Odiham Wing	
ZH901	B-V Chinook HC3R (N2060M)	RAF Odiham Wing	
ZH902	B-V Chinook HC3R (N2064W)	RAF Odiham Wing	
ZH903	B-V Chinook HC3R (N20671)	RAF Odiham Wing	
ZH904	B-V Chinook HC3R (N2083K)	RAF Odiham Wing	
ZH917	Panavia Tornado IDS (RSAF 6631)	MoD/BAE Systems, Warton	
ZJ100	BAe Hawk 102D	MoD/BAE Systems, stored Brough	
ZJ117	EHI-101 Merlin HC3	MoD/AgustaWestland, Yeovil	
ZJ118	EHI-101 Merlin HC3 [B]	RAF No 28 Sqn/No 78 Sqn, Benson	

Notes	Serial	Type (code/other identity)	Owner/operator, location or fate
	ZJ119	EHI-101 Merlin HC3 [C]	RAF No 1419 Flt, Kandahar, Afghanistan
	ZJ120	EHI-101 Merlin HC3 [D]	RAF MDMF, RNAS Culdrose
	ZJ121	EHI-101 Merlin HC3 [E]	RAF No 28 Sqn/No 78 Sqn, Benson
	ZJ122	EHI-101 Merlin HC3 [F]	RAF No 28 Sqn/No 78 Sqn, Benson
	ZJ123	EHI-101 Merlin HC3 [G]	RAF No 28 Sqn/No 78 Sqn, Benson
	ZJ124	EHI-101 Merlin HC3 [H]	RAF No 28 Sqn/No 78 Sqn, Benson
	ZJ125	EHI-101 Merlin HC3 [J]	RAF MDMF, RNAS Culdrose
	ZJ126	EHI-101 Merlin HC3 [K]	RAF No 28 Sqn/No 78 Sqn, Benson
	ZJ127	EHI-101 Merlin HC3 [L]	RAF No 28 Sqn/No 78 Sqn, Benson
	ZJ128	EHI-101 Merlin HC3 [M]	RAF No 1419 Flt, Kandahar, Afghanistan
	ZJ129	EHI-101 Merlin HC3 [N]	RAF No 1419 Flt, Kandahar, Afghanistan
	ZJ130	EHI-101 Merlin HC3 [O]	RAF MDMF, RNAS Culdrose
	ZJ131	EHI-101 Merlin HC3 [P]	RAF No 1419 Flt, Kandahar, Afghanistan
	ZJ132	EHI-101 Merlin HC3 [Q]	RAF MDMF, RNAS Culdrose
	ZJ133	EHI-101 Merlin HC3 [R]	MoD/AgustaWestland, Yeovil (on repair)
	ZJ134	EHI-101 Merlin HC3 [S]	RAF No 28 Sqn/No 78 Sqn, Benson
	ZJ135	EHI-101 Merlin HC3 [T]	RAF No 1419 Flt, Kandahar, Afghanistan
	ZJ136	EHI-101 Merlin HC3 [U]	RAF MDMF, RNAS Culdrose
	ZJ137	EHI-101 Merlin HC3 [W]	RAF No 28 Sqn/No 78 Sqn, Benson
	ZJ138	EHI-101 Merlin HC3 [X]	*Crashed 23 June 2010, Afghanistan*
	ZJ164	AS365N-2 Dauphin 2 (G-BTLC)	RN/Bond Helicopters, Plymouth
	ZJ165	AS365N-2 Dauphin 2 (G-NTOO)	RN/Bond Helicopters, Plymouth
	ZJ166	WAH-64 Apache AH1 (N9219G)	AAC No 673 Sqn/7 Regt, Middle Wallop
	ZJ167	WAH-64 Apache AH1 (N3266B)	AAC No 4 Regt, Wattisham
	ZJ168	WAH-64 Apache AH1 (N3123T)	AAC No 673 Sqn/7 Regt, Middle Wallop
	ZJ169	WAH-64 Apache AH1 (N3114H)	AAC No 4 Regt, Wattisham
	ZJ170	WAH-64 Apache AH1 (N3065U)	AAC No 673 Sqn/7 Regt, Middle Wallop
	ZJ171	WAH-64 Apache AH1 (N3266T)	AAC No 4 Regt, Wattisham
	ZJ172	WAH-64 Apache AH1	AAC No 4 Regt, Wattisham
	ZJ173	WAH-64 Apache AH1 (N3266W)	AAC No 673 Sqn/7 Regt, Middle Wallop
	ZJ174	WAH-64 Apache AH1	AAC No 4 Regt, Wattisham
	ZJ175	WAH-64 Apache AH1 (N3218V)	AAC No 4 Regt, Wattisham
	ZJ176	WAH-64 Apache AH1	AAC No 3 Regt, Wattisham
	ZJ177	WAH-64 Apache AH1	AAC, stored Wattisham (damaged)
	ZJ178	WAH-64 Apache AH1	AAC No 4 Regt, Wattisham
	ZJ179	WAH-64 Apache AH1	AAC No 4 Regt, Wattisham
	ZJ180	WAH-64 Apache AH1	AAC No 673 Sqn/7 Regt, Middle Wallop
	ZJ181	WAH-64 Apache AH1	AAC No 3 Regt, Wattisham
	ZJ182	WAH-64 Apache AH1	AAC No 3 Regt, Wattisham
	ZJ183	WAH-64 Apache AH1	AAC No 4 Regt, Wattisham
	ZJ184	WAH-64 Apache AH1	AAC No 4 Regt, Wattisham
	ZJ185	WAH-64 Apache AH1	AAC No 3 Regt, Wattisham
	ZJ186	WAH-64 Apache AH1	AAC No 3 Regt, Wattisham
	ZJ187	WAH-64 Apache AH1	AAC No 3 Regt, Wattisham
	ZJ188	WAH-64 Apache AH1	AAC No 3 Regt, Wattisham
	ZJ189	WAH-64 Apache AH1	AAC No 3 Regt/No 4 Regt, Wattisham
	ZJ190	WAH-64 Apache AH1	AAC No 3 Regt, Wattisham
	ZJ191	WAH-64 Apache AH1	AAC No 4 Regt, Wattisham
	ZJ192	WAH-64 Apache AH1	AAC No 673 Sqn/7 Regt, Middle Wallop
	ZJ193	WAH-64 Apache AH1	AAC No 3 Regt, Wattisham
	ZJ194	WAH-64 Apache AH1	AAC No 673 Sqn/7 Regt, Middle Wallop
	ZJ195	WAH-64 Apache AH1	AAC No 4 Regt, Wattisham
	ZJ196	WAH-64 Apache AH1	AAC No 3 Regt, Wattisham
	ZJ197	WAH-64 Apache AH1	AAC, stored Wattisham
	ZJ198	WAH-64 Apache AH1	AAC No 4 Regt, Wattisham
	ZJ199	WAH-64 Apache AH1	AAC No 3 Regt, Wattisham
	ZJ200	WAH-64 Apache AH1	AAC No 3 Regt, Wattisham
	ZJ202	WAH-64 Apache AH1	AAC No 3 Regt, Wattisham
	ZJ203	WAH-64 Apache AH1	AAC No 3 Regt, Wattisham
	ZJ204	WAH-64 Apache AH1	AAC No 3 Regt, Wattisham
	ZJ205	WAH-64 Apache AH1	AAC No 4 Regt, Wattisham
	ZJ206	WAH-64 Apache AH1	AAC No 673 Sqn/7 Regt, Middle Wallop
	ZJ207	WAH-64 Apache AH1	AAC No 4 Regt, Wattisham
	ZJ208	WAH-64 Apache AH1	AAC No 3 Regt, Wattisham
	ZJ209	WAH-64 Apache AH1	AAC No 3 Regt, Wattisham
	ZJ210	WAH-64 Apache AH1	AAC No 673 Sqn/7 Regt, Middle Wallop
	ZJ211	WAH-64 Apache AH1	AAC No 673 Sqn/7 Regt, Middle Wallop
	ZJ212	WAH-64 Apache AH1	AAC No 673 Sqn/7 Regt, Middle Wallop
	ZJ213	WAH-64 Apache AH1	AAC No 673 Sqn/7 Regt, Middle Wallop
	ZJ214	WAH-64 Apache AH1	AAC, stored Wattisham
	ZJ215	WAH-64 Apache AH1	AAC No 673 Sqn/7 Regt, Middle Wallop
	ZJ216	WAH-64 Apache AH1	AAC No 3 Regt, Wattisham

Serial	Type (code/other identity)	Owner/operator, location or fate	Notes
ZJ217	WAH-64 Apache AH1	AAC No 4 Regt, Wattisham	
ZJ218	WAH-64 Apache AH1	AAC No 4 Regt, Wattisham	
ZJ219	WAH-64 Apache AH1	AAC No 673 Sqn/7 Regt, Middle Wallop	
ZJ220	WAH-64 Apache AH1	AAC No 4 Regt, Wattisham	
ZJ221	WAH-64 Apache AH1	AAC No 673 Sqn/7 Regt, Middle Wallop	
ZJ222	WAH-64 Apache AH1	AAC No 4 Regt, Wattisham	
ZJ223	WAH-64 Apache AH1	AAC No 673 Sqn/7 Regt, Middle Wallop	
ZJ224	WAH-64 Apache AH1	AAC No 3 Regt, Wattisham	
ZJ225	WAH-64 Apache AH1	AAC No 3 Regt, Wattisham	
ZJ226	WAH-64 Apache AH1	AAC No 4 Regt, Wattisham	
ZJ227	WAH-64 Apache AH1	AAC, stored Wattisham	
ZJ228	WAH-64 Apache AH1	AAC No 3 Regt, Wattisham	
ZJ229	WAH-64 Apache AH1	AAC No 3 Regt, Wattisham	
ZJ230	WAH-64 Apache AH1	AAC No 4 Regt, Wattisham	
ZJ231	WAH-64 Apache AH1	AAC No 3 Regt, Wattisham	
ZJ232	WAH-64 Apache AH1	AAC No 4 Regt, Wattisham	
ZJ233	WAH-64 Apache AH1	AAC No 4 Regt, Wattisham	
ZJ234	Bell 412EP Griffin HT1 (G-BWZR) [S]	DHFS No 60(R) Sqn, RAF Shawbury	
ZJ235	Bell 412EP Griffin HT1 (G-BXBF) [I]	DHFS No 60(R) Sqn, RAF Shawbury	
ZJ236	Bell 412EP Griffin HT1 (G-BXBE) [X]	DHFS No 60(R) Sqn, RAF Shawbury	
ZJ237	Bell 412EP Griffin HT1 (G-BXFF) [T]	DHFS No 60(R) Sqn, RAF Shawbury	
ZJ238	Bell 412EP Griffin HT1 (G-BXHC) [Y]	DHFS No 60(R) Sqn, RAF Shawbury	
ZJ239	Bell 412EP Griffin HT1 (G-BXFH) [R]	DHFS No 60(R) Sqn, RAF Shawbury	
ZJ240	Bell 412EP Griffin HT1 (G-BXIR) [U]	DHFS No 60(R) Sqn, RAF Shawbury	
ZJ241	Bell 412EP Griffin HT1 (G-BXIS) [L]	DHFS No 60(R) Sqn/SARTU, RAF Valley	
ZJ242	Bell 412EP Griffin HT1 (G-BXDK) [E]	DHFS No 60(R) Sqn/SARTU, RAF Valley	
ZJ243	AS350BA Squirrel HT2 (G-BWZS)	School of Army Aviation/No 670 Sqn, Middle Wallop	
ZJ244	AS350BA Squirrel HT2 (G-BXMD)	School of Army Aviation/No 670 Sqn, Middle Wallop	
ZJ245	AS350BA Squirrel HT2 (G-BXME)	School of Army Aviation/No 670 Sqn, Middle Wallop	
ZJ246	AS350BA Squirrel HT2 (G-BXMJ)	School of Army Aviation/No 670 Sqn, Middle Wallop	
ZJ248	AS350BA Squirrel HT2 (G-BXNE)	School of Army Aviation/No 670 Sqn, Middle Wallop	
ZJ249	AS350BA Squirrel HT2 (G-BXNJ)	School of Army Aviation/No 670 Sqn, Middle Wallop	
ZJ250	AS350BA Squirrel HT2 (G-BXNY)	School of Army Aviation/No 670 Sqn, Middle Wallop	
ZJ251	AS350BA Squirrel HT2 (G-BXOG)	School of Army Aviation/No 670 Sqn, Middle Wallop	
ZJ252	AS350BA Squirrel HT2 (G-BXOK)	School of Army Aviation/No 670 Sqn, Middle Wallop	
ZJ253	AS350BA Squirrel HT2 (G-BXPG)	School of Army Aviation/No 670 Sqn, Middle Wallop	
ZJ254	AS350BA Squirrel HT2 (G-BXPJ)	School of Army Aviation/No 670 Sqn, Middle Wallop	
ZJ255	AS350BB Squirrel HT1 (G-BXAG)	DHFS, RAF Shawbury	
ZJ256	AS350BB Squirrel HT1 (G-BXCE)	DHFS, RAF Shawbury	
ZJ257	AS350BB Squirrel HT1 (G-BXDJ)	DHFS, RAF Shawbury	
ZJ258	AS350BB Squirrel HT1 (G-BXEO)	RAF Shawbury (wreck)	
ZJ260	AS350BB Squirrel HT1 (G-BXGB)	DHFS, RAF Shawbury	
ZJ261	AS350BB Squirrel HT1 (G-BXGJ)	DHFS, RAF Shawbury	
ZJ262	AS350BB Squirrel HT1 (G-BXHB)	DHFS, RAF Shawbury	
ZJ264	AS350BB Squirrel HT1 (G-BXHW)	DHFS, RAF Shawbury	
ZJ265	AS350BB Squirrel HT1 (G-BXHX)	DHFS, RAF Shawbury	
ZJ266	AS350BB Squirrel HT1 (G-BXIL)	DHFS, RAF Shawbury	
ZJ267	AS350BB Squirrel HT1 (G-BXIP)	DHFS, RAF Shawbury	
ZJ268	AS350BB Squirrel HT1 (G-BXJE)	DHFS, RAF Shawbury	
ZJ269	AS350BB Squirrel HT1 (G-BXJN)	DHFS, RAF Shawbury	
ZJ270	AS350BB Squirrel HT1 (G-BXJR)	DHFS, RAF Shawbury	
ZJ271	AS350BB Squirrel HT1 (G-BXKE)	DHFS, RAF Shawbury	
ZJ272	AS350BB Squirrel HT1 (G-BXKN)	DHFS, RAF Shawbury	
ZJ273	AS350BB Squirrel HT1 (G-BXKP)	DHFS, RAF Shawbury	
ZJ274	AS350BB Squirrel HT1 (G-BXKR)	DHFS, RAF Shawbury	
ZJ275	AS350BB Squirrel HT1 (G-BXLB)	DHFS, RAF Shawbury	

Notes	Serial	Type (code/other identity)	Owner/operator, location or fate
	ZJ276	AS350BB Squirrel HT1 (G-BXLE)	DHFS, RAF Shawbury
	ZJ277	AS350BB Squirrel HT1 (G-BXLH)	DHFS, RAF Shawbury
	ZJ278	AS350BB Squirrel HT1 (G-BXMB)	DHFS, RAF Shawbury
	ZJ279	AS350BB Squirrel HT1 (G-BXMC)	DHFS, RAF Shawbury
	ZJ280	AS350BB Squirrel HT1 (G-BXMI)	DHFS, RAF Shawbury
	ZJ369	GEC Phoenix UAV	Defence Academy of the UK, Shrivenham
	ZJ449	GEC Phoenix UAV	REME Museum, Arborfield
	ZJ452	GEC Phoenix UAV	Science Museum, Wroughton
	ZJ488	GAF Jindivik 800 (A92-808)	Caernarfon Air World
	ZJ493	GAF Jindivik 800 (A92-814)	RAF Stafford
	ZJ496	GAF Jindivik 900 (A92-901)	Farnborough Air Sciences Trust, Farnborough
	ZJ514	BAE Systems Nimrod MRA4 (XV251) [PA-4] [A]	MoD/BAE Systems, Warton
	ZJ515	BAE Systems Nimrod MRA4 (XV258) [PA-5] [B]	MoD/BAE Systems, Woodford
	ZJ516	BAE Systems Nimrod MRA4 (XV247) [PA-1]	MoD/BAE Systems, stored Woodford
	ZJ517	BAE Systems Nimrod MRA4 (XV242) [PA-3/PA-13]	*Scrapped at Woodford, January 2011*
	ZJ518	BAE Systems Nimrod MRA4 (XV234) [PA-2]	MoD/BAE Systems, stored Woodford
	ZJ519	BAE Systems Nimrod MRA4 (XZ284) [PA-6]	*Cancelled*
	ZJ520	BAE Systems Nimrod MRA4 (XV233) [PA-7]	*Cancelled*
	ZJ521	BAE Systems Nimrod MRA4 (XV227) [PA-8]	*Cancelled*
	ZJ522	BAE Systems Nimrod MRA4 (XV245) [PA-9]	*Scrapped at Woodford, January 2011*
	ZJ523	BAE Systems Nimrod MRA4 (XV228) [PA-10]	*Cancelled*
	ZJ524	BAE Systems Nimrod MRA4 (XV243) [PA-11]	*Scrapped at Woodford, January 2011*
	ZJ525	BAE Systems Nimrod MRA4 (XV246) [PA-12]	*Scrapped at Woodford, January 2011*
	ZJ645	D-BD Alpha Jet (98+62)	MoD/AFD/QinetiQ, Boscombe Down
	ZJ646	D-BD Alpha Jet (98+55)	MoD/AFD/QinetiQ, Boscombe Down
	ZJ647	D-BD Alpha Jet (98+71)	MoD/AFD/QinetiQ, Boscombe Down
	ZJ648	D-BD Alpha Jet (98+09)	MoD/AFD/QinetiQ, Boscombe Down
	ZJ649	D-BD Alpha Jet (98+73)	MoD/ETPS, Boscombe Down
	ZJ650	D-BD Alpha Jet (98+35)	MoD/QinetiQ, stored Boscombe Down
	ZJ651	D-BD Alpha Jet (41+42)	MoD/ETPS, Boscombe Down
	ZJ652	D-BD Alpha Jet (41+09)	MoD/QinetiQ Boscombe Down, spares use
	ZJ653	D-BD Alpha Jet (40+22)	MoD/QinetiQ Boscombe Down, spares use
	ZJ654	D-BD Alpha Jet (41+02)	MoD/QinetiQ Boscombe Down, spares use
	ZJ655	D-BD Alpha Jet (41+19)	MoD/QinetiQ Boscombe Down, spares use
	ZJ656	D-BD Alpha Jet (41+40)	MoD/QinetiQ Boscombe Down, spares use
	ZJ690	Bombardier Sentinel R1 (C-GJRG)	RAF No 5 Sqn, Waddington
	ZJ691	Bombardier Sentinel R1 (C-FZVM)	RAF No 5 Sqn, Waddington
	ZJ692	Bombardier Sentinel R1 (C-FZWW)	RAF No 5 Sqn, Waddington
	ZJ693	Bombardier Sentinel R1 (C-FZXC)	RAF No 5 Sqn, Waddington
	ZJ694	Bombardier Sentinel R1 (C-FZYL)	RAF No 5 Sqn, Waddington
	ZJ699	Eurofighter Typhoon (PT001)	MoD/BAE Systems, Warton
	ZJ700	Eurofighter Typhoon (PS002)	MoD/BAE Systems, Warton
	ZJ703	Bell 412EP Griffin HAR2 (G-CBST) [*Spades*,3]	DHFS No 60(R) Sqn/SARTH, RAF Valley
	ZJ704	Bell 412EP Griffin HAR2 (G-CBWT) [*Clubs*,4]	RAF No 84 Sqn, Akrotiri
	ZJ705	Bell 412EP Griffin HAR2 (G-CBXL) [*Hearts*, 5]	RAF No 84 Sqn, Akrotiri
	ZJ706	Bell 412EP Griffin HAR2 (G-CBYR) [*Diamonds*, 6]	RAF No 84 Sqn, Akrotiri
	ZJ707	Bell 412EP Griffin HT1 (G-CBUB) [O]	DHFS No 60(R) Sqn, RAF Shawbury
	ZJ708	Bell 412EP Griffin HT1 (G-CBVP) [K]	DHFS No 60(R) Sqn, RAF Shawbury
	ZJ780	AS365N-3 Dauphin II (G-CEXT)	AAC No 8 Flt, Credenhill
	ZJ781	AS365N-3 Dauphin II (G-CEXU)	AAC No 8 Flt, Credenhill
	ZJ782	AS365N-3 Dauphin II (G-CEXV)	AAC No 8 Flt, Credenhill
	ZJ783	AS365N-3 Dauphin II (G-CEXW)	AAC No 8 Flt, Credenhill
	ZJ800	Eurofighter Typhoon T3 [BC]	MoD/BAE Systems, Warton (conversion)

Serial	Type (code/other identity)	Owner/operator, location or fate	Notes
ZJ801	Eurofighter Typhoon T3 [BJ]	RAF No 29(R) Sqn, Coningsby	
ZJ802	Eurofighter Typhoon T3 [BB]	RAF No 29(R) Sqn, Coningsby	
ZJ803	Eurofighter Typhoon T3 [BA]	MoD/BAE Systems, Warton (conversion)	
ZJ804	Eurofighter Typhoon T3	RAF TMF, Coningsby	
ZJ805	Eurofighter Typhoon T1A [BD,S-RO]	RAF No 29(R) Sqn, Coningsby	
ZJ806	Eurofighter Typhoon T3 [BE]	MoD/BAE Systems, Warton (conversion)	
ZJ807	Eurofighter Typhoon T1 [BF]	MoD/BAE Systems, Warton (conversion)	
ZJ808	Eurofighter Typhoon T3 [DW]	RAF No 11) Sqn, Coningsby	
ZJ809	Eurofighter Typhoon T3 [BH]	RAF No 29(R) Sqn, Coningsby	
ZJ810	Eurofighter Typhoon T1 [BI]	RAF No 29(R) Sqn, Coningsby	
ZJ811	Eurofighter Typhoon T3 [DZ]	RAF No 29(R) Sqn, Coningsby	
ZJ812	Eurofighter Typhoon T3 [BK]	MoD/BAE Systems, Warton (conversion)	
ZJ813	Eurofighter Typhoon T3 [BL]	MoD/BAE Systems, Warton (conversion)	
ZJ814	Eurofighter Typhoon T1A [QO-Z]	RAF No 3 Sqn, Coningsby	
ZJ815	Eurofighter Typhoon T3 [DY]	RAF No 11 Sqn, Coningsby	
ZJ910	Eurofighter Typhoon FGR4 [BV]	RAF No 29(R) Sqn, Coningsby	
ZJ911	Eurofighter Typhoon FGR4 [BZ]	RAF No 29(R) Sqn, Coningsby	
ZJ912	Eurofighter Typhoon FGR4 [AB,YB-F]	RAF No 17(R) Sqn, Coningsby	
ZJ913	Eurofighter Typhoon FGR4 [AC]	RAF No 17(R) Sqn, Coningsby	
ZJ914	Eurofighter Typhoon FGR4 [AF]	RAF No 17(R) Sqn, Coningsby	
ZJ915	Eurofighter Typhoon FGR4 [BY]	MoD/BAE Systems, Warton (conversion)	
ZJ916	Eurofighter Typhoon FGR4 [QO-U]	RAF No 3 Sqn, Coningsby	
ZJ917	Eurofighter Typhoon FGR4 [QO-G]	RAF No 3 Sqn, Coningsby	
ZJ918	Eurofighter Typhoon FGR4 [QO-L]	RAF No 3 Sqn, Coningsby	
ZJ919	Eurofighter Typhoon FGR4 [DC]	RAF No 11 Sqn, Coningsby	
ZJ920	Eurofighter Typhoon FGR4 [QO-A]	RAF No 3 Sqn, Coningsby	
ZJ921	Eurofighter Typhoon FGR4 [QO-H]	RAF No 3 Sqn, Coningsby	
ZJ922	Eurofighter Typhoon FGR4 [QO-C]	RAF No 3 Sqn, Coningsby	
ZJ923	Eurofighter Typhoon FGR4 [DM]	RAF No 29(R) Sqn, Coningsby	
ZJ924	Eurofighter Typhoon FGR4 [DD]	RAF No 11 Sqn, Coningsby	
ZJ925	Eurofighter Typhoon FGR4 [QO-R]	RAF No 3 Sqn, Coningsby	
ZJ926	Eurofighter Typhoon FGR4 [QO-Y]	RAF No 3 Sqn, Coningsby	
ZJ927	Eurofighter Typhoon FGR4 [QO-M]	MoD/BAE Systems, Warton (conversion)	
ZJ928	Eurofighter Typhoon FGR4 [QO-N]	RAF No 3 Sqn, Coningsby	
ZJ929	Eurofighter Typhoon F2 [DL]	RAF No 11 Sqn, Coningsby	
ZJ930	Eurofighter Typhoon FGR4 [AA]	RAF No 17(R) Sqn, Coningsby	
ZJ931	Eurofighter Typhoon F2 [DA]	RAF No 11 Sqn, Coningsby	
ZJ932	Eurofighter Typhoon F2 [DB]	RAF No 3 Sqn, Coningsby	
ZJ933	Eurofighter Typhoon FGR4 [DF]	RAF No 11 Sqn, Coningsby	
ZJ934	Eurofighter Typhoon F2 [QO-T]	RAF No 3 Sqn, Coningsby	
ZJ935	Eurofighter Typhoon FGR4 [DJ]	RAF No 11 Sqn, Coningsby	
ZJ936	Eurofighter Typhoon F2 [QO-S]	RAF No 3 Sqn, Coningsby	
ZJ937	Eurofighter Typhoon F2 [QO-W]	RAF No 3 Sqn, Coningsby	
ZJ938	Eurofighter Typhoon FGR4	MoD/BAE Systems, Warton	
ZJ939	Eurofighter Typhoon FGR4 [DXI]	RAF No 11 Sqn, Coningsby	
ZJ940	Eurofighter Typhoon FGR4	RAF, stored Coningsby	
ZJ941	Eurofighter Typhoon FGR4 [QO-J]	RAF No 3 Sqn, Coningsby	
ZJ942	Eurofighter Typhoon FGR4 [DH]	RAF No 11 Sqn, Coningsby	
ZJ943	Eurofighter Typhoon FGR4 [DK]	RAF, stored Coningsby (wreck)	
ZJ944	Eurofighter Typhoon FGR4 [F]	RAF No 1435 Flt, Mount Pleasant, FI	
ZJ945	Eurofighter Typhoon FGR4	RAF, stored Coningsby	
ZJ946	Eurofighter Typhoon FGR4 [EH]	RAF No 6 Sqn, Leuchars	
ZJ947	Eurofighter Typhoon FGR4 [DN]	RAF No 6 Sqn, Leuchars	
ZJ948	Eurofighter Typhoon FGR4	RAF, stored Coningsby	
ZJ949	Eurofighter Typhoon FGR4 [H]	RAF No 1435 Flt, Mount Pleasant, FI	
ZJ950	Eurofighter Typhoon FGR4 [C]	RAF No 1435 Flt, Mount Pleasant, FI	
ZJ951	BAE Systems Hawk 120D	MoD/BAE Systems, stored Brough	
ZJ954	SA330H Puma HC1 (SAAF 144)	RAF No 33 Sqn/No 230 Sqn, Benson	
ZJ955	SA330H Puma HC1 (SAAF 148)	RAF No 33 Sqn/No 230 Sqn, Benson	
ZJ956	SA330H Puma HC1 (SAAF 172)	MoD/Eurocopter, Oxford (conversion)	
ZJ957	SA330H Puma HC1 (SAAF 169)	RAF No 33 Sqn/No 230 Sqn, Benson	
ZJ958	SA330H Puma (SAAF 173)	DE&S, stored Bicester	
ZJ959	SA330H Puma (SAAF 184)	DE&S, stored Bicester	
ZJ960	Grob G109B Vigilant T1 (D-KSMU) [SH]	RAF No 642 VGS, Linton-on-Ouse	
ZJ961	Grob G109B Vigilant T1 (D-KLCW) [SJ]	RAF ACCGS/No 644 VGS, Syerston	
ZJ962	Grob G109B Vigilant T1 (D-KBEU) [SK]	RAF No 634 VGS, St Athan	

Notes	Serial	Type (code/other identity)	Owner/operator, location or fate
	ZJ963	Grob G109B Vigilant T1 (D-KMSN) [SL]	RAF No 635 VGS, Topcliffe
	ZJ964	Bell 212HP AH2 (G-BJGV) [A]	AAC No 25 Flt, Belize
	ZJ966	Bell 212HP AH2 (G-BJJO) [C]	AAC No 25 Flt, Belize
	ZJ967	Grob G109B Vigilant T1 (G-DEWS) [SM]	RAF No 612 VGS, Abingdon
	ZJ968	Grob G109B Vigilant T1 (N109BT) [SN]	RAF No 631 VGS, Woodvale
	ZJ969	Bell 212HP AH1 (G-BGLJ) [D]	AAC No 25 Flt, Belize
	ZJ990	EHI-101 Merlin HC3A (M-501) [AA]	RAF No 28 Sqn/No 78 Sqn, Benson
	ZJ992	EHI-101 Merlin HC3A (M-503) [AB]	RAF No 28 Sqn/No 78 Sqn, Benson
	ZJ994	EHI-101 Merlin HC3A (M-505) [AC]	RAF MDMF, RNAS Culdrose
	ZJ995	EHI-101 Merlin HC3A (M-506) [AD]	RAF No 28 Sqn/No 78 Sqn, Benson
	ZJ998	EHI-101 Merlin HC3A (M-509) [AE]	RAF No 28 Sqn/No 78 Sqn, Benson
	ZK001	EHI-101 Merlin HC3A (M-511) [AF]	RAF No 28 Sqn/No 78 Sqn, Benson
	ZK005	Grob G109B Vigilant T1 (OH-797) [SP]	RAF No 663 VGS, Kinloss
	ZK010	BAE Systems Hawk T2	MoD/BAE Systems, Warton
	ZK011	BAE Systems Hawk T2	RAF No 4 FTS/*19(R) Sqn*, Valley
	ZK012	BAE Systems Hawk T2	RAF No 4 FTS/*19(R) Sqn*, Valley
	ZK013	BAE Systems Hawk T2	RAF No 4 FTS/*19(R) Sqn*, Valley
	ZK014	BAE Systems Hawk T2	MoD/BAE Systems, Warton
	ZK015	BAE Systems Hawk T2	RAF No 4 FTS/*19(R) Sqn*, Valley
	ZK016	BAE Systems Hawk T2	RAF No 4 FTS/*19(R) Sqn*, Valley
	ZK017	BAE Systems Hawk T2	RAF No 4 FTS/*19(R) Sqn*, Valley
	ZK018	BAE Systems Hawk T2	RAF No 4 FTS/*19(R) Sqn*, Valley
	ZK019	BAE Systems Hawk T2	MoD/BAE Systems, Warton
	ZK020	BAE Systems Hawk T2	MoD/BAE Systems, Warton
	ZK021	BAE Systems Hawk T2	RAF No 4 FTS/*19(R) Sqn*, Valley
	ZK022	BAE Systems Hawk T2	MoD/BAE Systems, Warton
	ZK023	BAE Systems Hawk T2	MoD/BAE Systems, Brough
	ZK024	BAE Systems Hawk T2	RAF No 4 FTS/*19(R) Sqn*, Valley
	ZK025	BAE Systems Hawk T2	MoD/BAE Systems, Brough
	ZK026	BAE Systems Hawk T2	MoD/BAE Systems, Brough
	ZK027	BAE Systems Hawk T2	RAF No 4 FTS/*19(R) Sqn*, Valley
	ZK028	BAE Systems Hawk T2	MoD/BAE Systems, Brough
	ZK029	BAE Systems Hawk T2	MoD/BAE Systems, Brough
	ZK030	BAE Systems Hawk T2	MoD/BAE Systems, Brough
	ZK031	BAE Systems Hawk T2	MoD/BAE Systems, Brough
	ZK032	BAE Systems Hawk T2	RAF No 4 FTS/*19(R) Sqn*, Valley
	ZK033	BAE Systems Hawk T2	RAF No 4 FTS/*19(R) Sqn*, Valley
	ZK034	BAE Systems Hawk T2	RAF No 4 FTS/*19(R) Sqn*, Valley
	ZK035	BAE Systems Hawk T2	RAF No 4 FTS/*19(R) Sqn*, Valley
	ZK036	BAE Systems Hawk T2	MoD/BAE Systems, Warton
	ZK037	BAE Systems Hawk T2	MoD/BAE Systems, Warton
	ZK045	BAE Systems Hawk T2	Reservation for RAF
	ZK046	BAE Systems Hawk T2	Reservation for RAF
	ZK047	BAE Systems Hawk T2	Reservation for RAF
	ZK048	BAE Systems Hawk T2	Reservation for RAF
	ZK049	BAE Systems Hawk T2	Reservation for RAF
	ZK050	BAE Systems Hawk T2	Reservation for RAF
	ZK051	BAE Systems Hawk T2	Reservation for RAF
	ZK052	BAE Systems Hawk T2	Reservation for RAF
	ZK053	BAE Systems Hawk T2	Reservation for RAF
	ZK054	BAE Systems Hawk T2	Reservation for RAF
	ZK055	BAE Systems Hawk T2	Reservation for RAF
	ZK056	BAE Systems Hawk T2	Reservation for RAF
	ZK057	BAE Systems Hawk T2	Reservation for RAF
	ZK058	BAE Systems Hawk T2	Reservation for RAF
	ZK059	BAE Systems Hawk T2	Reservation for RAF
	ZK067	Bell 212HP AH3 (G-BFER)	RAF Shawbury, AAC/D HFS
	ZK069	Eurofighter Typhoon T	*To R Saudi AF as 301, 25 March 2010*
	ZK070	Eurofighter Typhoon T	*To R Saudi AF as 302, 25 March 2010*
	ZK071	Eurofighter Typhoon T	*To R Saudi AF as 303, 10 June 2010*
	ZK072	Eurofighter Typhoon T	*To R Saudi AF as 304, 10 June 2010*
	ZK073	Eurofighter Typhoon T	*To R Saudi AF as 305, 7 October 2010*
	ZK074	Eurofighter Typhoon T	*To R Saudi AF as 306, 7 October 2010*
	ZK075	Eurofighter Typhoon	*To R Saudi AF as 307, 25 November 2010*
	ZK076	Eurofighter Typhoon	*To R Saudi AF as 308, 25 November 2010*
	ZK077	Eurofighter Typhoon	*To R Saudi AF as 309, 9 December 2010*
	ZK078	Eurofighter Typhoon	*To R Saudi AF as 310, 9 December 2010*

Serial	Type (code/other identity)	Owner/operator, location or fate	Notes
ZK079	Eurofighter Typhoon	BAE Systems, for R Saudi AF as 311	
ZK080	Eurofighter Typhoon	BAE Systems, for R Saudi AF as 312	
ZK081	Eurofighter Typhoon	BAE Systems, for R Saudi AF as 313	
ZK082	Eurofighter Typhoon	BAE Systems, for R Saudi AF as 314	
ZK083	Eurofighter Typhoon	BAE Systems, for R Saudi AF as 315	
ZK084	Eurofighter Typhoon	BAE Systems, for R Saudi AF as 316	
ZK113	Panavia Tornado IDS (RSAF 6606)	MoD/BAE Systems, Warton	
ZK114	M2370 UAV	QinetiQ	
ZK119	Pilatus PC-9 (HB-HQU/RSAF 2204)	MoD/BAE Systems, Warton	
ZK120*	Lockheed Martin Desert Hawk DH1+ UAV	Army	
ZK150	Lockheed Martin Desert Hawk UAV	Army	
ZK155*	Honeywell T-Hawk UAV	Army	
ZK181	AgustaWestland Super Lynx Mk.130	*To Algeria as AN07, 20 September 2010*	
ZK182	AgustaWestland Super Lynx Mk.130	AgustaWestland, for Algeria as AN08	
ZK183	AgustaWestland Super Lynx Mk.130	*To Algeria as AN09, 20 September 2010*	
ZK184	AgustaWestland Super Lynx Mk.130	AgustaWestland, for Algeria as AN10	
ZK199	AS350BB Squirrel HT1 (G-DOIT)	DHFS, RAF Shawbury	
ZK200	AS350BB Squirrel HT1 (EC-EVM/G-CEYO)	DHFS, RAF Shawbury	
ZK205	Grob G109B Vigilant T1 (D-KBRU) [SS]	RAF ACCGS/No 644 VGS, Syerston	
ZK206	Bell 212EP AH2 (G-CFXE) [A]	AAC JHC/No 7 Regt, Middle Wallop	
ZK210	BAE Systems Mantis UAV	MoD/BAE Systems, Warton	
ZK300	Eurofighter Typhoon FGR4 [EJ]	RAF No 6 Sqn, Leuchars	
ZK301	Eurofighter Typhoon FGR4 [D]	RAF No 1435 Flt, Mount Pleasant, FI	
ZK302	Eurofighter Typhoon FGR4 [EA]	RAF No 6 Sqn, Leuchars	
ZK303	Eurofighter Typhoon T3	MoD TMF, Coningsby	
ZK304	Eurofighter Typhoon FGR4 [EB]	RAF No 6 Sqn, Leuchars	
ZK305	Eurofighter Typhoon FGR4 [EC]	RAF No 6 Sqn, Leuchars	
ZK306	Eurofighter Typhoon FGR4 [ED]	RAF No 6 Sqn, Leuchars	
ZK307	Eurofighter Typhoon FGR4 [EE]	RAF No 6 Sqn, Leuchars	
ZK308	Eurofighter Typhoon FGR4 [EF]	SERCO/RAF No 3 FTS/45(R) Sqn, Cranwell	
ZK309	Eurofighter Typhoon FGR4 [EG]	RAF No 6 Sqn, Leuchars	
ZK310	Eurofighter Typhoon FGR4 [EL]	RAF No 6 Sqn, Leuchars	
ZK311	Eurofighter Typhoon FGR4 [EK]	RAF No 6 Sqn, Leuchars	
ZK312	Eurofighter Typhoon FGR4 [EM]	MoD/BAE Systems, Warton	
ZK313	Eurofighter Typhoon FGR4	MoD/BAE Systems, Warton	
ZK314	Eurofighter Typhoon FGR4	MoD/BAE Systems, Warton	
ZK315	Eurofighter Typhoon FGR4	DE&S/BAE Systems, for RAF	
ZK316	Eurofighter Typhoon FGR4	DE&S/BAE Systems, for RAF	
ZK317	Eurofighter Typhoon FGR4	DE&S/BAE Systems, for RAF	
ZK318	Eurofighter Typhoon FGR4	DE&S/BAE Systems, for RAF	
ZK319	Eurofighter Typhoon FGR4	DE&S/BAE Systems, for RAF	
ZK320	Eurofighter Typhoon FGR4	DE&S/BAE Systems, for RAF	
ZK321	Eurofighter Typhoon FGR4	DE&S/BAE Systems, for RAF	
ZK379	Eurofighter Typhoon T3 [EX]	SERCO/RAF No 3 FTS/45(R) Sqn, Cranwell	
ZK380	Eurofighter Typhoon T3 [EY]	BAE Systems, for Royal Air Force of Oman	
ZK381	Eurofighter Typhoon T3	DE&S/BAE Systems, for RAF	
ZK450	Beech King Air B200 (G-RAFJ) [J]	SERCO/RAF No 3 FTS/45(R) Sqn, Cranwell	
ZK451	Beech King Air B200 (G-RAFK) [K]	SERCO/RAF No 3 FTS/45(R) Sqn, Cranwell	
ZK452	Beech King Air B200 (G-RAFL) [L]	SERCO/RAF No 3 FTS/45(R) Sqn, Cranwell	
ZK453	Beech King Air B200 (G-RAFM) [M]	SERCO/RAF No 3 FTS/45(R) Sqn, Cranwell	
ZK454	Beech King Air B200 (G-RAFN) [N]	SERCO/RAF No 3 FTS/45(R) Sqn, Cranwell	
ZK455	Beech King Air B200 (G-RAFO) [O]	SERCO/RAF No 3 FTS/45(R) Sqn, Cranwell	
ZK456	Beech King Air B200 (G-RAFP) [P]	SERCO/RAF No 3 FTS/45(R) Sqn, Cranwell	
ZK457	Beech King Air B200 (G-ROWN)	MoD/Foreign & Commonwealth Office, Iraq	
ZK458	Hawker Beechcraft King Air B200GT (G-RAFD) [D]	SERCO/RAF No 3 FTS/45(R) Sqn, Cranwell	
ZK459	Hawker Beechcraft King Air B200GT (G-RAFX) [X]	SERCO/RAF No 3 FTS/45(R) Sqn, Cranwell	
ZK460	Hawker Beechcraft King Air B200GT (G-RAFU) [U]	SERCO/RAF No 3 FTS/45(R) Sqn, Cranwell	
ZK501	Elbit Hermes 450 UAV	Army 32 Regt Royal Artillery, Larkhill	
ZK502	Elbit Hermes 450 UAV	Army 32 Regt Royal Artillery, Larkhill	
ZK503	Elbit Hermes 450 UAV	Army 32 Regt Royal Artillery, Larkhill	
ZK504	Elbit Hermes 450 UAV	Army 32 Regt Royal Artillery, Larkhill	
ZK505	Elbit Hermes 450 UAV	Army 32 Regt Royal Artillery, Larkhill	
ZK506	Elbit Hermes 450 UAV	Army 32 Regt Royal Artillery, Larkhill	
ZK507	Elbit Hermes 450 UAV	Army 32 Regt Royal Artillery, Larkhill	
ZK508	Elbit Hermes 450 UAV	Army 32 Regt Royal Artillery, Larkhill	
ZK509	Elbit Hermes 450 UAV	Army 32 Regt Royal Artillery, Larkhill	

Notes	Serial	Type (code/other identity)	Owner/operator, location or fate
	ZK510	Elbit Hermes 450 UAV	Army 32 Regt Royal Artillery, Larkhill
	ZK511	Elbit Hermes 450 UAV	Army 32 Regt Royal Artillery, Larkhill
	ZK512	Elbit Hermes 450 UAV	Army 32 Regt Royal Artillery, Larkhill
	ZK513	Elbit Hermes 450 UAV	Army 32 Regt Royal Artillery, Larkhill
	ZK514	Elbit Hermes 450 UAV	Army 32 Regt Royal Artillery, Larkhill
	ZK515	Elbit Hermes 450 UAV	Army 32 Regt Royal Artillery, Larkhill
	ZK516	Elbit Hermes 450 UAV	Army 32 Regt Royal Artillery, Larkhill
	ZK517	Elbit Hermes 450 UAV	Army 32 Regt Royal Artillery, Larkhill
	ZK518	Elbit Hermes 450 UAV	Army 32 Regt Royal Artillery, Larkhill
	ZK519	Elbit Hermes 450 UAV	Army 32 Regt Royal Artillery, Larkhill
	ZK520	Elbit Hermes 450 UAV	Army 32 Regt Royal Artillery, Larkhill
	ZK531	BAe Hawk T53 (LL-5306)	MoD/BAE Systems, stored Brough
	ZK532	BAe Hawk T53 (LL-5315)	MoD/BAE Systems, stored Brough
	ZK533	BAe Hawk T53 (LL-5317)	Aircraft Maintenance Training Academy, Doncaster
	ZK534	BAe Hawk T53 (LL-5319)	BAE Systems, Brough, systems rig
	ZK535	BAe Hawk T53 (LL-5320)	Aircraft Maintenance Training Academy, Doncaster
	ZM135	Lockheed Martin F-35C Lightning II	Reservation for RAF/RN
	ZM136	Lockheed Martin F-35C Lightning II	Reservation for RAF/RN
	ZM137	Lockheed Martin F-35C Lightning II	Reservation for RAF/RN
	ZM138	Lockheed Martin F-35C Lightning II	Reservation for RAF/RN
	ZM139	Lockheed Martin F-35C Lightning II	Reservation for RAF/RN
	ZM140	Lockheed Martin F-35C Lightning II	Reservation for RAF/RN
	ZM141	Lockheed Martin F-35C Lightning II	Reservation for RAF/RN
	ZM142	Lockheed Martin F-35C Lightning II	Reservation for RAF/RN
	ZM143	Lockheed Martin F-35C Lightning II	Reservation for RAF/RN
	ZM144	Lockheed Martin F-35C Lightning II	Reservation for RAF/RN
	ZM145	Lockheed Martin F-35C Lightning II	Reservation for RAF/RN
	ZM146	Lockheed Martin F-35C Lightning II	Reservation for RAF/RN
	ZM147	Lockheed Martin F-35C Lightning II	Reservation for RAF/RN
	ZM148	Lockheed Martin F-35C Lightning II	Reservation for RAF/RN
	ZM149	Lockheed Martin F-35C Lightning II	Reservation for RAF/RN
	ZM150	Lockheed Martin F-35C Lightning II	Reservation for RAF/RN
	ZM151	Lockheed Martin F-35C Lightning II	Reservation for RAF/RN
	ZM152	Lockheed Martin F-35C Lightning II	Reservation for RAF/RN
	ZM153	Lockheed Martin F-35C Lightning II	Reservation for RAF/RN
	ZM154	Lockheed Martin F-35C Lightning II	Reservation for RAF/RN
	ZM155	Lockheed Martin F-35C Lightning II	Reservation for RAF/RN
	ZM156	Lockheed Martin F-35C Lightning II	Reservation for RAF/RN
	ZM157	Lockheed Martin F-35C Lightning II	Reservation for RAF/RN
	ZM158	Lockheed Martin F-35C Lightning II	Reservation for RAF/RN
	ZM159	Lockheed Martin F-35C Lightning II	Reservation for RAF/RN
	ZM160	Lockheed Martin F-35C Lightning II	Reservation for RAF/RN
	ZM161	Lockheed Martin F-35C Lightning II	Reservation for RAF/RN
	ZM162	Lockheed Martin F-35C Lightning II	Reservation for RAF/RN
	ZM163	Lockheed Martin F-35C Lightning II	Reservation for RAF/RN
	ZM164	Lockheed Martin F-35C Lightning II	Reservation for RAF/RN
	ZM165	Lockheed Martin F-35C Lightning II	Reservation for RAF/RN
	ZM166	Lockheed Martin F-35C Lightning II	Reservation for RAF/RN
	ZM167	Lockheed Martin F-35C Lightning II	Reservation for RAF/RN
	ZM168	Lockheed Martin F-35C Lightning II	Reservation for RAF/RN
	ZM169	Lockheed Martin F-35C Lightning II	Reservation for RAF/RN
	ZM170	Lockheed Martin F-35C Lightning II	Reservation for RAF/RN
	ZM171	Lockheed Martin F-35C Lightning II	Reservation for RAF/RN
	ZM172	Lockheed Martin F-35C Lightning II	Reservation for RAF/RN
	ZM173	Lockheed Martin F-35C Lightning II	Reservation for RAF/RN
	ZM174	Lockheed Martin F-35C Lightning II	Reservation for RAF/RN
	ZM175	Lockheed Martin F-35C Lightning II	Reservation for RAF/RN
	ZM176	Lockheed Martin F-35C Lightning II	Reservation for RAF/RN
	ZM177	Lockheed Martin F-35C Lightning II	Reservation for RAF/RN
	ZM178	Lockheed Martin F-35C Lightning II	Reservation for RAF/RN
	ZM179	Lockheed Martin F-35C Lightning II	Reservation for RAF/RN
	ZM180	Lockheed Martin F-35C Lightning II	Reservation for RAF/RN
	ZM181	Lockheed Martin F-35C Lightning II	Reservation for RAF/RN
	ZM182	Lockheed Martin F-35C Lightning II	Reservation for RAF/RN
	ZM183	Lockheed Martin F-35C Lightning II	Reservation for RAF/RN
	ZM184	Lockheed Martin F-35C Lightning II	Reservation for RAF/RN
	ZM185	Lockheed Martin F-35C Lightning II	Reservation for RAF/RN
	ZM186	Lockheed Martin F-35C Lightning II	Reservation for RAF/RN
	ZM187	Lockheed Martin F-35C Lightning II	Reservation for RAF/RN

Serial	Type (code/other identity)	Owner/operator, location or fate	Notes
ZM188	Lockheed Martin F-35C Lightning II	Reservation for RAF/RN	
ZM189	Lockheed Martin F-35C Lightning II	Reservation for RAF/RN	
ZM190	Lockheed Martin F-35C Lightning II	Reservation for RAF/RN	
ZM191	Lockheed Martin F-35C Lightning II	Reservation for RAF/RN	
ZM192	Lockheed Martin F-35C Lightning II	Reservation for RAF/RN	
ZM193	Lockheed Martin F-35C Lightning II	Reservation for RAF/RN	
ZM194	Lockheed Martin F-35C Lightning II	Reservation for RAF/RN	
ZM195	Lockheed Martin F-35C Lightning II	Reservation for RAF/RN	
ZM196	Lockheed Martin F-35C Lightning II	Reservation for RAF/RN	
ZM197	Lockheed Martin F-35C Lightning II	Reservation for RAF/RN	
ZM198	Lockheed Martin F-35C Lightning II	Reservation for RAF/RN	
ZM199	Lockheed Martin F-35C Lightning II	Reservation for RAF/RN	
ZM200	Lockheed Martin F-35C Lightning II	Reservation for RAF/RN	
ZM400	Airbus A400M	Reservation for RAF	
ZM401	Airbus A400M	Reservation for RAF	
ZM402	Airbus A400M	Reservation for RAF	
ZM403	Airbus A400M	Reservation for RAF	
ZM404	Airbus A400M	Reservation for RAF	
ZM405	Airbus A400M	Reservation for RAF	
ZM406	Airbus A400M	Reservation for RAF	
ZM407	Airbus A400M	Reservation for RAF	
ZM408	Airbus A400M	Reservation for RAF	
ZM409	Airbus A400M	Reservation for RAF	
ZM410	Airbus A400M	Reservation for RAF	
ZM411	Airbus A400M	Reservation for RAF	
ZM412	Airbus A400M	Reservation for RAF	
ZM413	Airbus A400M	Reservation for RAF	
ZM414	Airbus A400M	Reservation for RAF	
ZM415	Airbus A400M	Reservation for RAF	
ZM416	Airbus A400M	Reservation for RAF	
ZM417	Airbus A400M	Reservation for RAF	
ZM418	Airbus A400M	Reservation for RAF	
ZM419	Airbus A400M	Reservation for RAF	
ZM420	Airbus A400M	Reservation for RAF	
ZM421	Airbus A400M	Reservation for RAF	
ZM422	Airbus A400M	*Cancelled*	
ZM423	Airbus A400M	*Cancelled*	
ZM424	Airbus A400M	*Cancelled*	
ZR283	AgustaWestland AW139 (N209YS)	For RAF	
ZR321	Agusta A109E Power Elite (G-CDVB)	RAF No 32(The Royal) Sqn, Northolt	
ZR322	Agusta A109E Power Elite (G-CDVC)	RAF No 32(The Royal) Sqn, Northolt	
ZR323	Agusta A109E Power Elite (G-CDVE)	RAF No 32(The Royal) Sqn, Northolt	
ZR324	Agusta A109E Power (G-EMHB)	DHFS, RAF Shawbury	
ZR325	Agusta A109E Power (G-BZEI)	DHFS, RAF Shawbury	
ZR326	AgustaWestland AW139 (G-CFUO) [F]	FBS Helicopters/RAF DHFS, Valley	
ZR327	AgustaWestland AW139 (G-CFVD) [B]	FBS Helicopters/RAF DHFS, Valley	
ZR328	AgustaWestland AW101 Mk.610	AgustaWestland, for Algeria	
ZR329	AgustaWestland AW101 Mk.610	AgustaWestland, for Algeria	
ZR330	AgustaWestland AW101 Mk.610	AgustaWestland, for Algeria	
ZR331	AgustaWestland AW101 Mk.610	AgustaWestland, for Algeria	
ZR332	AgustaWestland AW101 Mk.610	AgustaWestland, for Algeria	
ZR333	AgustaWestland AW101 Mk.610	AgustaWestland, for Algeria	
ZR334	AgustaWestland AW101 Mk.610	AgustaWestland, for Saudi Arabia	
ZR335	AgustaWestland AW101 Mk.610	AgustaWestland, for Saudi Arabia	
ZT800	WS Super Lynx Mk 300	MoD/AgustaWestland, Yeovil	
ZZ171	Boeing C-17A Globemaster III (00-201/N171UK)	RAF No 99 Sqn, Brize Norton	
ZZ172	Boeing C-17A Globemaster III (00-202/N172UK)	RAF No 99 Sqn, Brize Norton	
ZZ173	Boeing C-17A Globemaster III (00-203/N173UK)	RAF No 99 Sqn, Brize Norton	
ZZ174	Boeing C-17A Globemaster III (00-204/N174UK)	RAF No 99 Sqn, Brize Norton	

Notes	Serial	Type (code/other identity)	Owner/operator, location or fate
	ZZ175	Boeing C-17A Globemaster III (06-0205/N9500Z)	RAF No 99 Sqn, Brize Norton
	ZZ176	Boeing C-17A Globemaster III (08-0206/N9500B)	RAF No 99 Sqn, Brize Norton
	ZZ177	Boeing C-17A Globemaster III (09-8207/N9500B)	RAF No 99 Sqn, Brize Norton
	ZZ190	Hawker Hunter F58 (J-4066/G-HHAE)	Hawker Hunter Aviation, RNAS Yeovilton
	ZZ191	Hawker Hunter F58 (J-4058/G-HHAD)	Hawker Hunter Aviation, RNAS Yeovilton
	ZZ192	Grob G109B Vigilant T1 (D-KLVI) [SQ]	RAF No 618 VGS, Odiham
	ZZ193	Grob G109B Vigilant T1 (D-KBLO) [SR]	RAF No 613 VGS, Halton
	ZZ201	General Atomics Reaper UAV (07-111)	RAF No 39 Sqn, Creech AFB, Nevada, USA
	ZZ202	General Atomics Reaper UAV	General Atomics, USA (on repair)
	ZZ203	General Atomics Reaper UAV (08-133)	RAF No 39 Sqn, Creech AFB, Nevada, USA
	ZZ204	General Atomics Reaper UAV	RAF No 39 Sqn, Creech AFB, Nevada, USA
	ZZ205	General Atomics Reaper UAV	General Atomics, for RAF
	ZZ206	General Atomics Reaper UAV	General Atomics, for RAF
	ZZ207	General Atomics Reaper UAV	General Atomics, for RAF
	ZZ208	General Atomics Reaper UAV	General Atomics, for RAF
	ZZ209	General Atomics Reaper UAV	General Atomics, for RAF
	ZZ210	General Atomics Reaper UAV	General Atomics, for RAF
	ZZ250	BAE Systems Taranis UAV	BAE Systems, Warton
	ZZ251	BAE Systems Herti UAV	BAE Systems, Warton
	ZZ252	BAE Systems Herti UAV	BAE Systems, Warton
	ZZ253	BAE Systems Herti UAV	BAE Systems, Warton
	ZZ254	BAE Systems Herti UAV	BAE Systems, Warton
	ZZ330	Airbus A330 FSTA (EC-335)	DE&S/Airbus, for RAF
	ZZ331	Airbus A330 FSTA (EC-337)	DE&S/Airbus, for RAF
	ZZ332	Airbus A330 FSTA	Reservation for RAF
	ZZ333	Airbus A330 FSTA	Reservation for RAF
	ZZ334	Airbus A330 FSTA	Reservation for RAF
	ZZ335	Airbus A330 FSTA	Reservation for RAF
	ZZ336	Airbus A330 FSTA	Reservation for RAF
	ZZ337	Airbus A330 FSTA	Reservation for RAF
	ZZ338	Airbus A330 FSTA	Reservation for RAF
	ZZ339	Airbus A330 FSTA	Reservation for RAF
	ZZ340	Airbus A330 FSTA	Reservation for RAF
	ZZ341	Airbus A330 FSTA	Reservation for RAF
	ZZ342	Airbus A330 FSTA	Reservation for RAF
	ZZ343	Airbus A330 FSTA	Reservation for RAF
	ZZ349	AgustaWestland AW159 Lynx Wildcat	For RN/AAC
	ZZ350	AgustaWestland AW159 Lynx Wildcat	For RN/AAC
	ZZ351	AgustaWestland AW159 Lynx Wildcat	For RN/AAC
	ZZ352	AgustaWestland AW159 Lynx Wildcat	For RN/AAC
	ZZ353	AgustaWestland AW159 Lynx Wildcat	For RN/AAC
	ZZ354	AgustaWestland AW159 Lynx Wildcat	For RN/AAC
	ZZ355	AgustaWestland AW159 Lynx Wildcat	For RN/AAC
	ZZ356	AgustaWestland AW159 Lynx Wildcat	For RN/AAC
	ZZ357	AgustaWestland AW159 Lynx Wildcat	For RN/AAC
	ZZ358	AgustaWestland AW159 Lynx Wildcat	For RN/AAC
	ZZ359	AgustaWestland AW159 Lynx Wildcat	For RN/AAC
	ZZ360	AgustaWestland AW159 Lynx Wildcat	For RN/AAC
	ZZ361	AgustaWestland AW159 Lynx Wildcat	For RN/AAC

Serial	Type (code/other identity)	Owner/operator, location or fate	Notes
ZZ362	AgustaWestland AW159 Lynx Wildcat	For RN/AAC	
ZZ363	AgustaWestland AW159 Lynx Wildcat	For RN/AAC	
ZZ364	AgustaWestland AW159 Lynx Wildcat	For RN/AAC	
ZZ365	AgustaWestland AW159 Lynx Wildcat	For RN/AAC	
ZZ366	AgustaWestland AW159 Lynx Wildcat	For RN/AAC	
ZZ367	AgustaWestland AW159 Lynx Wildcat	For RN/AAC	
ZZ368	AgustaWestland AW159 Lynx Wildcat	For RN/AAC	
ZZ369	AgustaWestland AW159 Lynx Wildcat	For RN/AAC	
ZZ370	AgustaWestland AW159 Lynx Wildcat	For RN/AAC	
ZZ371	AgustaWestland AW159 Lynx Wildcat	For RN/AAC	
ZZ372	AgustaWestland AW159 Lynx Wildcat	For RN/AAC	
ZZ373	AgustaWestland AW159 Lynx Wildcat	For RN/AAC	
ZZ374	AgustaWestland AW159 Lynx Wildcat	For RN/AAC	
ZZ375	AgustaWestland AW159 Lynx Wildcat	For RN/AAC	
ZZ376	AgustaWestland AW159 Lynx Wildcat	For RN/AAC	
ZZ377	AgustaWestland AW159 Lynx Wildcat	For RN/AAC	
ZZ378	AgustaWestland AW159 Lynx Wildcat	For RN/AAC	
ZZ379	AgustaWestland AW159 Lynx Wildcat	For RN/AAC	
ZZ380	AgustaWestland AW159 Lynx Wildcat	For RN/AAC	
ZZ381	AgustaWestland AW159 Lynx Wildcat	For RN/AAC	
ZZ382	AgustaWestland AW159 Lynx Wildcat	For RN/AAC	
ZZ383	AgustaWestland AW159 Lynx Wildcat	For RN/AAC	
ZZ384	AgustaWestland AW159 Lynx Wildcat	For RN/AAC	
ZZ385	AgustaWestland AW159 Lynx Wildcat	For RN/AAC	
ZZ386	AgustaWestland AW159 Lynx Wildcat	For RN/AAC	
ZZ387	AgustaWestland AW159 Lynx Wildcat	For RN/AAC	
ZZ388	AgustaWestland AW159 Lynx Wildcat	For RN/AAC	
ZZ389	AgustaWestland AW159 Lynx Wildcat	For RN/AAC	
ZZ390	AgustaWestland AW159 Lynx Wildcat	For RN/AAC	
ZZ391	AgustaWestland AW159 Lynx Wildcat	For RN/AAC	
ZZ392	AgustaWestland AW159 Lynx Wildcat	For RN/AAC	
ZZ393	AgustaWestland AW159 Lynx Wildcat	For RN/AAC	
ZZ394	AgustaWestland AW159 Lynx Wildcat	For RN/AAC	
ZZ395	AgustaWestland AW159 Lynx Wildcat	For RN/AAC	
ZZ396	AgustaWestland AW159 Lynx Wildcat HMA1	For RN	
ZZ397	AgustaWestland AW159 Lynx Wildcat HMA1	For RN	

Notes	Serial	Type (code/other identity)	Owner/operator, location or fate
	ZZ398	AgustaWestland AW159 Lynx Wildcat AH1	For AAC
	ZZ399	AgustaWestland AW159 Lynx Wildcat AH1	For AAC
	ZZ400	AgustaWestland AW159 Lynx Wildcat	MoD/AgustaWestland, Yeovil
	ZZ401	AgustaWestland AW159 Lynx Wildcat	MoD/AgustaWestland, Yeovil
	ZZ402	AgustaWestland AW159 Lynx Wildcat	MoD/AgustaWestland, Yeovil
	ZZ403	AgustaWestland AW159 Lynx Wildcat AH1	For AAC
	ZZ404	AgustaWestland AW159 Lynx Wildcat AH1	For AAC
	ZZ405	AgustaWestland AW159 Lynx Wildcat AH1	For AAC
	ZZ406	AgustaWestland AW159 Lynx Wildcat AH1	For AAC
	ZZ407	AgustaWestland AW159 Lynx Wildcat AH1	For AAC
	ZZ408	AgustaWestland AW159 Lynx Wildcat AH1	For AAC
	ZZ409	AgustaWestland AW159 Lynx Wildcat AH1	For AAC
	ZZ410	AgustaWestland AW159 Lynx Wildcat AH1	For AAC
	ZZ411	AgustaWestland AW159 Lynx Wildcat	For RN/AAC
	ZZ412	AgustaWestland AW159 Lynx Wildcat	For RN/AAC
	ZZ413	AgustaWestland AW159 Lynx Wildcat HMA1	For RN
	ZZ414	AgustaWestland AW159 Lynx Wildcat HMA1	For RN
	ZZ415	AgustaWestland AW159 Lynx Wildcat HMA1	For RN
	ZZ416	Hawker Beechcraft Shadow R1 (G-JENC)	RAF No 5 Sqn, Waddington
	ZZ417	Hawker Beechcraft Shadow R1 G-NICY)	RAF No 5 Sqn, Waddington
	ZZ418	Hawker Beechcraft Shadow R1 (G-JIMG)	RAF No 5 Sqn, Waddington
	ZZ419	Hawker Beechcraft Shadow R1 (G-OTCS)	RAF No 5 Sqn, Waddington
	ZZ500	Hawker Beechcraft Avenger T1 (N3197D)	Cobham Leasing Ltd, Bournemouth, for RN
	ZZ501	Hawker Beechcraft Avenger T1 (N618HB)	Cobham Leasing Ltd, Bournemouth, for RN
	ZZ502	Hawker Beechcraft Avenger T1 (N63699)	Cobham Leasing Ltd, Bournemouth, for RN
	ZZ503	Hawker Beechcraft Avenger T1 (N6433F)	Cobham Leasing Ltd, Bournemouth, for RN
	ZZ504	Hawker Beechcraft Shadow R1 (N80948)	Hawker Beechcraft, for RAF
	ZZ664	Boeing RC-135W (64-14833)	Boeing, for RAF
	ZZ665	Boeing RC-135W (64-14838)	Boeing, for RAF
	ZZ666	Boeing RC-135W (64-14830)	Boeing, for RAF

MK356 is a Spitfire LF IXC operated by the Battle of Britain Memorial Flight from Coningsby.

Sedburgh TX1 WB922 (BGA4366) is caught in flight from its home base at Hullavington.
Credit: Peter R March.

Beaver XP822 is posed outside the Museum of Army Flying at Middle Wallop. Although painted over, the serial is emerging on the tail!

With four Avenger T1s on the horizon, the days of the Jetstream T2 with 750 NAS are definitely numbered. XX486 is seen here at RIAT, Fairford.

Sea King HAR3 XZ585/A was the first of these helicopters for the RAF, taking to the air for the first time in September 1977, more than 33 years ago; it still looks as good as new.

Lynx HAS3S XZ730 wears the code 634 and is operated by 702 NAS at Yeovilton.

41(R) Squadron parted company with its Harriers in late 2010 following the Strategic Defence and Security Review. ZD437 was a Harrier GR9 coded EB-J with the unit.

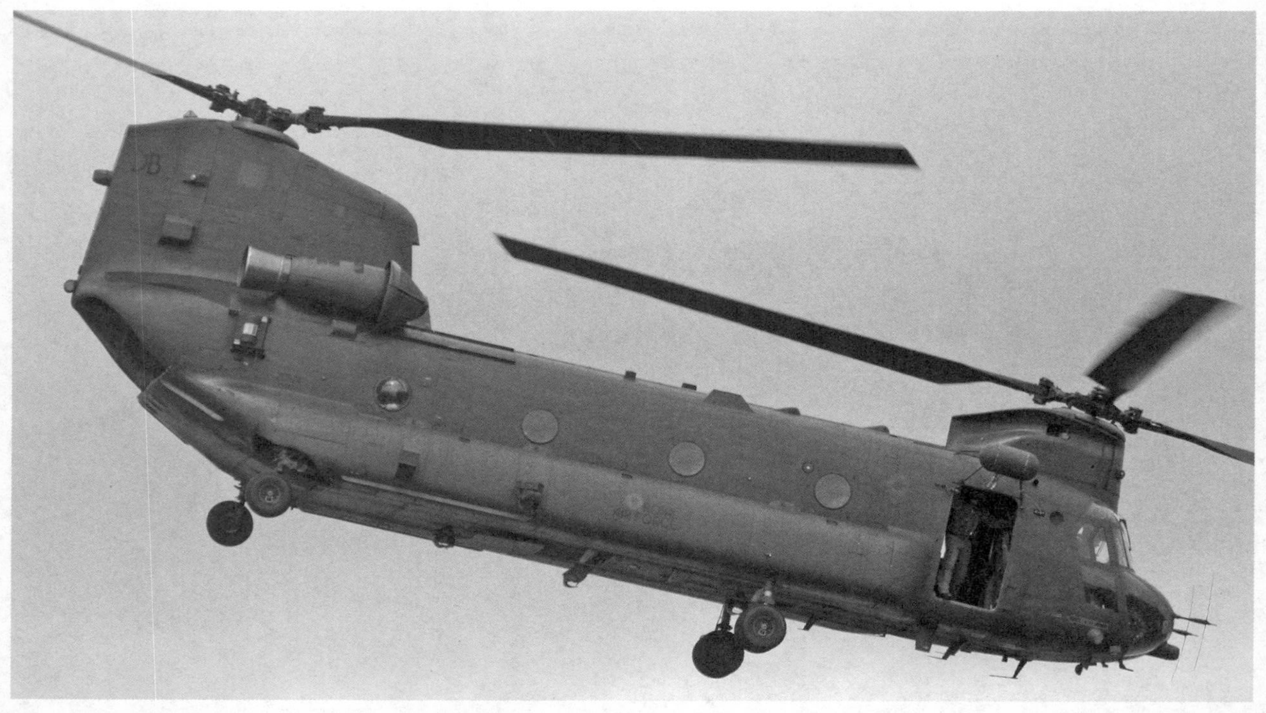

Coded DB, Chinook HC2 ZD574 was one of a handful kept in the UK for training while many of her sisters provided welcome support to UK forces deployed in Afghanistan.

2010 marked the 70th Anniversary of the Battle of Britain and Typhoon ZJ941 wore special markings on the port side of the tail to commemorate this with its QO-J code in the style worn by the squadron's Hurricanes.

Aircraft in UK Military Service with Civil Registrations

Serial	Type (code/other identity)	Owner/operator, location or fate	Notes
G-BYUA	Grob G.115E Tutor	VT Aerospace/Yorkshire Universities AS/ No 85(R) Sqn, Church Fenton	
G-BYUB	Grob G.115E Tutor	VT Aerospace/East Midlands Universities AS/No 16(R) Sqn/No 115(R) Sqn, Cranwell	
G-BYUC	Grob G.115E Tutor	VT Aerospace/East Midlands Universities AS/No 16(R) Sqn/No 115(R) Sqn, Cranwell	
G-BYUD	Grob G.115E Tutor	VT Aerospace/No 1 EFTS, Barkston Heath	
G-BYUE	Grob G.115E Tutor	VT Aerospace/East Midlands Universities AS/No 16(R) Sqn/No 115(R) Sqn, Cranwell	
G-BYUF	Grob G.115E Tutor	VT Aerospace/Northumbrian Universities AS, Leeming	
G-BYUG	Grob G.115E Tutor	VT Aerospace/Cambridge UAS/University of London AS/No 57(R) Sqn, Wyton	
G-BYUH	Grob G.115E Tutor	VT Aerospace/Southampton UAS, Boscombe Down	
G-BYUI	Grob G.115E Tutor	VT Aerospace/East Midlands Universities AS/No 16(R) Sqn/No 115(R) Sqn, Cranwell	
G-BYUJ	Grob G.115E Tutor	VT Aerospace/Yorkshire Universities AS/ No 85(R) Sqn, Church Fenton	
G-BYUK	Grob G.115E Tutor	VT Aerospace/East Midlands Universities AS/No 16(R) Sqn/No 115(R) Sqn, Cranwell	
G-BYUL	Grob G.115E Tutor	VT Aerospace/No 1 EFTS, Middle Wallop	
G-BYUM	Grob G.115E Tutor	VT Aerospace/No 1 EFTS, Barkston Heath	
G-BYUN	Grob G.115E Tutor	VT Aerospace/No 1 EFTS, Barkston Heath	
G-BYUO	Grob G.115E Tutor	VT Aerospace/Cambridge UAS/University of London AS/No 57(R) Sqn, Wyton	
G-BYUP	Grob G.115E Tutor	VT Aerospace/East Midlands Universities AS/No 16(R) Sqn/No 115(R) Sqn, Cranwell	
G-BYUR	Grob G.115E Tutor	VT Aerospace/No 1 EFTS, Barkston Heath	
G-BYUS	Grob G.115E Tutor	VT Aerospace/Yorkshire Universities AS/ No 85(R) Sqn, Church Fenton	
G-BYUU	Grob G.115E Tutor	VT Aerospace/Cambridge UAS/University of London AS/No 57(R) Sqn, Wyton	
G-BYUV	Grob G.115E Tutor	VT Aerospace/Bristol UAS, Colerne	
G-BYUW	Grob G.115E Tutor	VT Aerospace/Cambridge UAS/University of London AS/No 57(R) Sqn, Wyton	
G-BYUX	Grob G.115E Tutor	VT Aerospace/No 1 EFTS, Barkston Heath	
G-BYUY	Grob G.115E Tutor	VT Aerospace/East Midlands Universities AS/ No 16(R) Sqn/No 115(R) Sqn, Cranwell	
G-BYUZ	Grob G.115E Tutor	VT Aerospace/No 1 EFTS, Barkston Heath	
G-BYVA	Grob G.115E Tutor	VT Aerospace/No 1 EFTS, Middle Wallop	
G-BYVB	Grob G.115E Tutor	VT Aerospace/Oxford UAS, Benson	
G-BYVC	Grob G.115E Tutor	VT Aerospace/Cambridge UAS/University of London AS/No 57(R) Sqn, Wyton	
G-BYVD	Grob G.115E Tutor	VT Aerospace/No 1 EFTS, Barkston Heath	
G-BYVE	Grob G.115E Tutor	VT Aerospace/Cambridge UAS/University of London AS/No 57(R) Sqn, Wyton	
G-BYVF	Grob G.115E Tutor	VT Aerospace/RN No 727 NAS, Yeovilton	
G-BYVG	Grob G.115E Tutor	VT Aerospace/Yorkshire Universities AS/ No 85(R) Sqn, Church Fenton	
G-BYVH	Grob G.115E Tutor	VT Aerospace/No 1 EFTS, Barkston Heath	
G-BYVI	Grob G.115E Tutor	VT Aerospace/Cambridge UAS/University of London AS/No 57(R) Sqn, Wyton	
G-BYVJ	Grob G.115E Tutor	VT Aerospace/Yorkshire Universities AS/ No 85(R) Sqn, Church Fenton	
G-BYVK	Grob G.115E Tutor	VT Aerospace/RN No 727 NAS, Yeovilton	
G-BYVL	Grob G.115E Tutor	VT Aerospace/Oxford UAS, Benson	
G-BYVM	Grob G.115E Tutor	VT Aerospace/No 1 EFTS, Barkston Heath	
G-BYVO	Grob G.115E Tutor	VT Aerospace/No 1 EFTS, Barkston Heath	
G-BYVP	Grob G.115E Tutor	VT Aerospace/Cambridge UAS/University of London AS/No 57(R) Sqn, Wyton	

Notes	Serial	Type (code/other identity)	Owner/operator, location or fate
	G-BYVR	Grob G.115E Tutor	VT Aerospace/East Midlands Universities AS/No 16(R) Sqn/No 115(R) Sqn, Cranwell
	G-BYVS	Grob G.115E Tutor	VT Aerospace/East Midlands Universities AS/ No 16(R) Sqn/No 115(R) Sqn, Cranwell
	G-BYVT	Grob G.115E Tutor	VT Aerospace/Cambridge UAS/University of London AS/No 57(R) Sqn, Wyton
	G-BYVU	Grob G.115E Tutor	VT Aerospace/No 1 EFTS, Middle Wallop
	G-BYVV	Grob G.115E Tutor	VT Aerospace/Northumbrian Universities AS, Leeming
	G-BYVW	Grob G.115E Tutor	VT Aerospace/University of Wales AS, St Athan
	G-BYVX	Grob G.115E Tutor	VT Aerospace/Yorkshire Universities AS/ No 85(R) Sqn, Church Fenton
	G-BYVY	Grob G.115E Tutor	VT Aerospace/No 1 EFTS, Middle Wallop
	G-BYVZ	Grob G.115E Tutor	VT Aerospace/No 1 EFTS, Barkston Heath
	G-BYWA	Grob G.115E Tutor	VT Aerospace/University of Wales AS, St Athan
	G-BYWB	Grob G.115E Tutor	VT Aerospace/East Midlands Universities AS/No 16(R) Sqn/No 115(R) Sqn, Cranwell
	G-BYWC	Grob G.115E Tutor	VT Aerospace/Bristol UAS, Colerne
	G-BYWD	Grob G.115E Tutor	VT Aerospace/University of Wales AS, St Athan
	G-BYWE	Grob G.115E Tutor	VT Aerospace/Bristol UAS, Colerne
	G-BYWF	Grob G.115E Tutor	VT Aerospace/East Midlands Universities AS/No 16(R) Sqn/No 115(R) Sqn, Cranwell
	G-BYWG	Grob G.115E Tutor	VT Aerospace/East Midlands Universities AS/ No 16(R) Sqn/No 115(R) Sqn, Cranwell
	G-BYWH	Grob G.115E Tutor	VT Aerospace/Cambridge UAS/University of London AS/No 57(R) Sqn, Wyton
	G-BYWI	Grob G.115E Tutor	VT Aerospace/No 1 EFTS, Barkston Heath
	G-BYWJ	Grob G.115E Tutor	VT Aerospace/No 1 EFTS, Barkston Heath
	G-BYWK	Grob G.115E Tutor	VT Aerospace/Bristol UAS, Colerne
	G-BYWL	Grob G.115E Tutor	VT Aerospace/East Midlands Universities AS/No 16(R) Sqn/No 115(R) Sqn, Cranwell
	G-BYWM	Grob G.115E Tutor	VT Aerospace/RN No 727 NAS, Yeovilton
	G-BYWN	Grob G.115E Tutor	VT Aerospace/No 1 EFTS, Barkston Heath
	G-BYWO	Grob G.115E Tutor	VT Aerospace/Cambridge UAS/University of London AS/No 57(R) Sqn, Wyton
	G-BYWP	Grob G.115E Tutor	VT Aerospace/Yorkshire Universities AS/ No 85(R) Sqn, Church Fenton
	G-BYWR	Grob G.115E Tutor	VT Aerospace/Cambridge UAS/University of London AS/No 57(R) Sqn, Wyton
	G-BYWS	Grob G.115E Tutor	VT Aerospace/Cambridge UAS/University of London AS/No 57(R) Sqn, Wyton
	G-BYWT	Grob G.115E Tutor	VT Aerospace/Northumbrian Universities AS, Leeming
	G-BYWU	Grob G.115E Tutor	VT Aerospace/Oxford UAS, Benson
	G-BYWV	Grob G.115E Tutor	VT Aerospace/Yorkshire Universities AS/ No 85(R) Sqn, Church Fenton
	G-BYWW	Grob G.115E Tutor	VT Aerospace/Southampton UAS, Boscombe Down
	G-BYWX	Grob G.115E Tutor	VT Aerospace/Cambridge UAS/University of London AS/No 57(R) Sqn, Wyton
	G-BYWY	Grob G.115E Tutor	VT Aerospace/East Midlands Universities AS/No 16(R) Sqn/No 115(R) Sqn, Cranwell
	G-BYWZ	Grob G.115E Tutor	VT Aerospace/East Midlands Universities AS/ No 16(R) Sqn/No 115(R) Sqn, Cranwell
	G-BYXA	Grob G.115E Tutor	VT Aerospace/Oxford UAS, Benson
	G-BYXB	Grob G.115E Tutor	VT Aerospace/Bristol UAS, Colerne
	G-BYXC	Grob G.115E Tutor	VT Aerospace/Oxford UAS, Benson
	G-BYXD	Grob G.115E Tutor	VT Aerospace/Southampton UAS, Boscombe Down
	G-BYXE	Grob G.115E Tutor	VT Aerospace/Yorkshire Universities AS/ No 85(R) Sqn, Church Fenton
	G-BYXF	Grob G.115E Tutor	VT Aerospace/No 1 EFTS, Middle Wallop

Serial	Type (code/other identity)	Owner/operator, location or fate	Notes
G-BYXG	Grob G.115E Tutor	VT Aerospace/Yorkshire Universities AS/ No 85(R) Sqn, Church Fenton	
G-BYXH	Grob G.115E Tutor	VT Aerospace/Bristol UAS, Colerne	
G-BYXI	Grob G.115E Tutor	VT Aerospace/Southampton UAS, Boscombe Down	
G-BYXJ	Grob G.115E Tutor	VT Aerospace/Southampton UAS, Boscombe Down	
G-BYXK	Grob G.115E Tutor	VT Aerospace/RN No 727 NAS, Yeovilton	
G-BYXL	Grob G.115E Tutor	VT Aerospace/Oxford UAS, Benson	
G-BYXM	Grob G.115E Tutor	VT Aerospace/East Midlands Universities AS/No 16(R) Sqn/No 115(R) Sqn, Cranwell	
G-BYXN	Grob G.115E Tutor	VT Aerospace/East Midlands Universities AS/ No 16(R) Sqn/No 115(R) Sqn, Cranwell	
G-BYXO	Grob G.115E Tutor	VT Aerospace/Grob, Tussenhausen, Germany	
G-BYXP	Grob G.115E Tutor	VT Aerospace/Cambridge UAS/University of London AS/No 57(R) Sqn, Wyton	
G-BYXS	Grob G.115E Tutor	VT Aerospace/RN No 727 NAS, Yeovilton	
G-BYXT	Grob G.115E Tutor	VT Aerospace/Yorkshire Universities AS/ No 85(R) Sqn, Church Fenton	
G-BYXX	Grob G.115E Tutor	VT Aerospace/No 1 EFTS, Barkston Heath	
G-BYXY	Grob G.115E Tutor	VT Aerospace/Cambridge UAS/University of London AS/No 57(R) Sqn, Wyton	
G-BYXZ	Grob G.115E Tutor	VT Aerospace/East Midlands Universities AS/No 16(R) Sqn/No 115(R) Sqn, Cranwell	
G-BYYA	Grob G.115E Tutor	VT Aerospace/Northumbrian Universities AS, Leeming	
G-BYYB	Grob G.115E Tutor	VT Aerospace/No 1 EFTS, Barkston Heath	
G-CGKA	Grob G.115E Tutor	VT Aerospace/East Midlands Universities AS/No 16(R) Sqn/No 115(R) Sqn, Cranwell	
G-CGKB	Grob G.115E Tutor	VT Aerospace/East Midlands Universities AS/No 16(R) Sqn/No 115(R) Sqn, Cranwell	
G-CGKC	Grob G.115E Tutor	VT Aerospace/East Midlands Universities AS/No 16(R) Sqn/No 115(R) Sqn, Cranwell	
G-CGKD	Grob G.115E Tutor	VT Aerospace/University of Birmingham AS, Cosford	
G-CGKE	Grob G.115E Tutor	VT Aerospace/University of Birmingham AS, Cosford	
G-CGKF	Grob G.115E Tutor	VT Aerospace/University of Birmingham AS, Cosford	
G-CGKG	Grob G.115E Tutor	VT Aerospace/University of Birmingham AS, Cosford	
G-CGKH	Grob G.115E Tutor	VT Aerospace/University of Birmingham AS, Cosford	
G-CGKI	Grob G.115E Tutor	VT Aerospace/East of Scotland UAS, Leuchars	
G-CGKJ	Grob G.115E Tutor	VT Aerospace/East of Scotland UAS, Leuchars	
G-CGKK	Grob G.115E Tutor	VT Aerospace/East of Scotland UAS, Leuchars	
G-CGKL	Grob G.115E Tutor	VT Aerospace/East of Scotland UAS, Leuchars	
G-CGKM	Grob G.115E Tutor	VT Aerospace/East of Scotland UAS, Leuchars	
G-CGKN	Grob G.115E Tutor	VT Aerospace/Universities of Glasgow & Strathclyde AS, Glasgow	
G-CGKO	Grob G.115E Tutor	VT Aerospace/Universities of Glasgow & Strathclyde AS, Glasgow	
G-CGKP	Grob G.115E Tutor	VT Aerospace/Liverpool UAS/Manchester and Salford Universities AS, Woodvale	
G-CGKR	Grob G.115E Tutor	VT Aerospace/Liverpool UAS/Manchester and Salford Universities AS, Woodvale	
G-CGKS	Grob G.115E Tutor	VT Aerospace/Liverpool UAS/Manchester and Salford Universities AS, Woodvale	
G-CGKT	Grob G.115E Tutor	VT Aerospace/Liverpool UAS/Manchester and Salford Universities AS, Woodvale	

Notes	Serial	Type (code/other identity)	Owner/operator, location or fate
	G-CGKU	Grob G.115E Tutor	VT Aerospace/Liverpool UAS/Manchester and Salford Universities AS, Woodvale
	G-CGKV	Grob G.115E Tutor	VT Aerospace/Liverpool UAS/Manchester and Salford Universities AS, Woodvale
	G-CGKW	Grob G.115E Tutor	VT Aerospace/Liverpool UAS/Manchester and Salford Universities AS, Woodvale
	G-CGKX	Grob G.115E Tutor	VT Aerospace/Liverpool UAS/Manchester and Salford Universities AS, Woodvale
	G-FFRA	Dassault Falcon 20DC (N902FR)	Cobham Leasing Ltd, Bournemouth
	G-FRAD	Dassault Falcon 20E	Cobham Leasing Ltd, Bournemouth
	G-FRAF	Dassault Falcon 20E (N911FR)	Cobham Leasing Ltd, Bournemouth
	G-FRAH	Dassault Falcon 20DC (N900FR)	Cobham Leasing Ltd, Durham/Tees Valley
	G-FRAI	Dassault Falcon 20E (N901FR)	Cobham Leasing Ltd, Bournemouth
	G-FRAJ	Dassault Falcon 20E (N903FR)	Cobham Leasing Ltd, Bournemouth
	G-FRAK	Dassault Falcon 20DC (N905FR)	Cobham Leasing Ltd, Durham/Tees Valley
	G-FRAL	Dassault Falcon 20DC (N904FR)	Cobham Leasing Ltd, Bournemouth
	G-FRAO	Dassault Falcon 20DC (N906FR)	Cobham Leasing Ltd, Durham/Tees Valley
	G-FRAP	Dassault Falcon 20DC (N908FR)	Cobham Leasing Ltd, Durham/Tees Valley
	G-FRAR	Dassault Falcon 20DC (N909FR)	Cobham Leasing Ltd, Durham/Tees Valley
	G-FRAS	Dassault Falcon 20C (117501)	Cobham Leasing Ltd, Durham/Tees Valley
	G-FRAT	Dassault Falcon 20C (117502)	Cobham Leasing Ltd, Bournemouth
	G-FRAU	Dassault Falcon 20C (117504)	Cobham Leasing Ltd, Durham/Tees Valley
	G-FRAW	Dassault Falcon 20ECM (117507)	Cobham Leasing Ltd, Durham/Tees Valley
	G-FRBA	Dassault Falcon 20C	Cobham Leasing Ltd, Bournemouth
	G-RAFD	Hawker Beechcraft King Air B200GT	*To ZK458, June 2010*
	G-RAFO	Beech Super King Air B200	*To ZK455, November 2010*
	G-RAFP	Beech Super King Air B200	*To ZK456, November 2010*
	G-RAFU	Hawker Beechcraft King Air B200GT	*To ZK460, July 2010*
	G-RAFX	Hawker Beechcraft King Air B200GT	*To ZK459, June 2010*

Tutor G-BYXN was operated as the Tutor display aircraft for 2010. It is normally based at Cranwell.

RAF Maintenance Command/Support Command/ Logistics Command 'M' number cross-reference

1764M/K4972
2015M/K5600
2292M/K8203
2361M/K6035
3118M/H5199/(BK892)
3858M/X7688
4354M/BL614
4552M/T5298
5377M/EP120
5405M/LF738
5466M/*BN230*/(LF751)
5690M/MK356
5718M/BM597
5758M/DG202
6457M/ML427
6490M/LA255
6640M/RM694
6850M/TE184
6946M/RW388
6948M/DE673
6960M/MT847
7008M/EE549
7014M/N6720
7015M/NL985
7035M/*K2567*/(DE306)
7060M/VF301
7090M/EE531
7118M/LA198
7119M/LA226
7150M/PK683
7154M/WB188
7174M/VX272
7175M/VV106
7200M/VT812
7241M/TE311/*(MK178)*
7243M/TE462
7245M/RW382
7246M/TD248
7256M/TB752
7257M/TB252
7279M/TB752
7281M/TB252
7288M/PK724
7293M/*TB675*/(RW393)
7323M/VV217
7325M/R5868
7326M/VN485
7362M/475081/(VP546)
7416M/WN907
7421M/WT660
7422M/WT684
7428M/WK198
7432M/WZ724
7438M/*18671*/(WP905)
7443M/WX853
7458M/WX905
7464M/XA564
7470M/XA553
7473M/XE946
7491M/WT569
7496M/WT612
7499M/WT555
7510M/WT694
7525M/WT619
7530M/WT648
7532M/WT651
7533M/WT680
7544M/WN904
7548M/PS915
7556M/WK584
7564M/XE982
7570M/XD674
7582M/WP190
7583M/WP185
7602M/WE600
7605M/WS692
7606M/WV562
7607M/TJ138
7615M/WV679
7616M/WW388
7618M/WW442
7622M/WV606
7631M/VX185
7641M/XA634
7645M/WD293
7648M/XF785
7673M/WV332
7689M/*WW421*/(WW450)
7694M/WV486
7696M/WV493
7698M/WV499
7704M/TW536
7705M/WL505
7706M/WB584
7709M/WT933
7711M/PS915
7712M/WK281
7715M/XK724
7716M/WS776
7718M/WA577
7719M/WK277
7726M/XM373
7737M/XD602
7741M/VZ477
7750M/WK864/(WL168)
7751M/WL131
7755M/WG760
7758M/PM651
7759M/PK664
7761M/XH318
7762M/XE670
7764M/XH318
7770M/XF506/(WT746)
7793M/XG523
7796M/WJ676
7798M/XH783
7806M/TA639
7809M/XA699
7816M/WG763
7817M/TX214
7825M/WK991
7827M/XA917
7829M/XH992
7839M/WV781
7841M/WV783
7851M/WZ706
7854M/XM191
7855M/XK416
7859M/XP283
7860M/XL738
7862M/XR246
7863M/XP248
7864M/XP244
7865M/TX226
7866M/XH278
7868M/WZ736
7869M/WK935
7872M/*WZ826*/(XD826)
7881M/WD413
7883M/XT150
7887M/XD375
7891M/XM693
7894M/XD818
7895M/WF784
7898M/XP854
7900M/WA576
7906M/WH132
7917M/WA591
7928M/XE849
7930M/WH301
7931M/RD253
7932M/WZ744
7933M/XR220
7937M/WS843
7938M/XH903
7939M/XD596
7940M/XL764
7955M/XH767
7957M/XF545
7960M/WS726
7961M/WS739
7964M/WS760
7965M/WS792
7967M/WS788
7971M/XK699
7973M/WS807
7979M/XM529
7980M/XM561
7982M/XH892
7983M/XD506
7984M/XN597
7986M/WG777
7988M/XL149
7990M/XD452
7997M/XG452
7998M/*XM515*/(XD515)
8005M/WG768
8009M/XG518
8010M/XG547
8012M/VS562
8017M/XL762
8018M/XN344
8019M/WZ869
8021M/XL824
8022M/XN341
8027M/XM555
8032M/XH837
8034M/XL703
8041M/XF690
8043M/XF836
8046M/XL770
8049M/WE168
8050M/XG329
8052M/WH166
8054AM/XM410
8054BM/XM417
8055AM/XM402
8055BM/XM404
8056M/XG337
8057M/XR243
8063M/WT536
8070M/EP120
8072M/PK624
8073M/TB252
8075M/RW382
8078M/XM351
8080M/XM480
8081M/XM468
8082M/XM409
8084M/XM369
8086M/TB752
8092M/WK654
8094M/WT520
8097M/XN492
8101M/WH984
8102M/WT486
8103M/WR985
8106M/WR982
8114M/WL798
8117M/WR974
8118M/WZ549
8119M/WR971
8121M/XM474
8124M/WZ572
8128M/WH775
8130M/WH798
8131M/WT507
8140M/XJ571
8142M/XJ560
8147M/XR526
8151M/WV795
8153M/WV903
8154M/WV908
8155M/WV797
8156M/XE339
8158M/XE369
8160M/XD622
8161M/XE993
8162M/WM913
8164M/*WN105*/(WF299)
8165M/WH791
8169M/WH364
8173M/XN685
8176M/WH791
8177M/WM224
8179M/XN928
8183M/*XN972*/(XN962)
8184M/WT520
8186M/WR977
8187M/WH791
8189M/*WD615* (WD646)
8190M/XJ918
8192M/XR658
8198M/WT339
8203M/XD377
8205M/XN819
8206M/WG419
8208M/WG303
8209M/WG418
8210M/WG471
8211M/WK570
8213M/WK626
8215M/WP869
8216M/WP927
8229M/XM355
8230M/XM362
8234M/XN458
8235M/XN549

RAF Maintenance Cross-reference

8236M/XP573
8237M/XS179
8238M/XS180
8344M/WH960
8350M/WH840
8352M/XN632
8355M/KN645
8357M/WK576
8359M/WF825
8361M/WB670
8362M/WG477
8364M/WG464
8365M/XK421
8366M/XG454
8367M/XG474
8368M/XF926
8369M/WE139
8370M/N1671
8371M/XA847
8372M/K8042
8373M/P2617
8375M/NX611
8376M/RF398
8377M/R9125
8378M/T9707
8379M/DG590
8380M/Z7197
8382M/VR930
8383M/K9942
8384M/X4590
8385M/N5912
8386M/NV778
8387M/T6296
8388M/XL993
8389M/VX573
8392M/SL674
8394M/WG422
8395M/WF408
8396M/XK740
8399M/WR539
8401M/XP686
8406M/XP831
8407M/XP585
8408M/XS186
8409M/XS209
8410M/XR662
8413M/XM192
8414M/XM173
8417M/XM144
8422M/XM169
8427M/XM172
8429M/XH592
8434M/XM411
8436M/XN554
8437M/WG362
8439M/WZ846
8440M/WD935
8442M/XP411
8452M/XK885
8453M/XP745
8458M/XP672
8459M/XR650
8460M/XP680
8462M/XX477
8463M/XP355
8464M/XJ758
8465M/W1048
8466M/L-866
8467M/WP912
8468M/MM5701/(BT474)
8469M/100503
8470M/584219
8471M/701152
8472M/120227/(VN679)
8473M/WP190
8474M/494083
8475M/360043/(PJ876)
8476M/24
8477M/4101/(DG200)
8478M/10639
8479M/730301
8481M/191614
8482M/112372/(VK893)
8483M/420430
8484M/5439
8485M/997
8486M/BAPC 99
8487M/J-1172
8488M/WL627
8491M/WJ880
8493M/XR571
8494M/XP557
8501M/XP640
8502M/XP686
8508M/XS218
8509M/XT141
8514M/XS176
8535M/XN776
8538M/XN781
8545M/XN726
8546M/XN728
8548M/WT507
8549M/WT534
8554M/TG511
8561M/XS100
8563M/*XX822*/(XW563)
8565M/*WT720*/(E-408)
8566M/XV279
8573M/XM708
8575M/XP542
8576M/XP502
8578M/XR534
8581M/WJ775
8582M/XE874
8583M/BAPC 94
8585M/XE670
8586M/XE643
8588M/XR681
8589M/XR700
8590M/XM191
8591M/XA813
8595M/XH278
8598M/WP270
8600M/XX761
8602M/PF179/(XR541)
8604M/XS104
8606M/XP530
8608M/XP540
8610M/XL502
8611M/WF128
8618M/XS111/(XP504)
8620M/XP534
8621M/XR538
8624M/XR991/(XS102)
8627M/XP558
8628M/XJ380
8630M/WG362
8631M/XR574
8633M/3W-17/MK732
8634M/WP314
8640M/XR977
8642M/XR537
8645M/XD163
8648M/XK526
8653M/XS120
8655M/XN126
8656M/XP405
8657M/VZ634
8661M/XJ727
8662M/XR458
8666M/XE793
8668M/WJ821
8671M/XJ435
8672M/XP351
8673M/XD165
8676M/XL577
8679M/XF526
8680M/XF527
8681M/XG164
8682M/XP404
8693M/WH863
8696M/WH773
8702M/XG196
8703M/VW453
8706M/XF383
8708M/XF509
8709M/XG209
8710M/XG274
8711M/XG290
8713M/XG225
8718M/XX396
8719M/XT257
8724M/XW923
8726M/XP299
8727M/XR486
8728M/WT532
8729M/WJ815
8733M/XL318
8736M/XF375
8739M/XH170
8740M/WE173
8741M/XW329
8743M/WD790
8746M/XH171
8749M/XH537
8751M/XT255
8753M/WL795
8762M/WH740
8764M/XP344
8768M/A-522
8769M/A-528
8770M/XL623
8771M/XM602
8772M/WR960
8777M/XX914
8778M/XM598
8779M/XM607
8780M/WK102
8781M/WE982
8782M/XH136
8783M/XW272
8785M/XS642
8789M/XK970
8792M/XP345
8793M/XP346
8794M/XP398
8796M/XK943
8797M/XX947
8799M/WV787
8800M/XG226
8807M/XL587
8810M/XJ825
8816M/XX734
8818M/XK527
8820M/VP952
8821M/XX115
8822M/VP957
8828M/XS587
8830M/N-294/(XF515)
8831M/XG160
8832M/XG168/(XG172)
8833M/XL569
8834M/XL571
8836M/XL592
8838M/34037/(429356)
8839M/69/(XG194)
8840M/XG252
8841M/XE606
8848M/XZ135
8853M/XT277
8855M/XT284
8857M/XW544
8858M/XW541
8863M/XG154
8867M/XK532
8868M/WH775
8869M/WH957
8870M/WH964
8871M/WJ565
8873M/XR453
8874M/XE597
8875M/XE624
8876M/VM791/(XA312)
8880M/XF435
8881M/XG254
8883M/XX946
8884M/VX275
8885M/XW922
8886M/XA243
8888M/XA231
8889M/XN239
8890M/WT532
8892M/XL618
8895M/XX746
8896M/XX821
8897M/XX969
8898M/XX119
8899M/XX756
8900M/XZ368
8901M/XZ383
8902M/XX739
8903M/XX747
8905M/XX975
8906M/XX976
8907M/XZ371
8908M/XZ382
8909M/XV784
8910M/XL160
8911M/XH673
8918M/XX109
8919M/XT486
8920M/XT469
8921M/XT466
8922M/XT467
8923M/XX819
8924M/XP701
8925M/XP706
8931M/XV779
8932M/XR718
8934M/XR749
8935M/XR713
8937M/XX751
8938M/WV746
8941M/XT456
8942M/XN185
8943M/XE799
8944M/WZ791
8945M/XX818
8946M/XZ389
8947M/XX726
8948M/XX757
8949M/XX743

8951M/XX727
8953M/XX959
8954M/XZ384
8955M/XX110
8957M/XN582
8961M/XS925
8967M/XV263
8969M/XR753
8972M/XR754
8973M/XS922
8974M/XM473
8975M/XW917
8976M/XZ630
8978M/XX837
8984M/XN551
8985M/WK127
8986M/XV261
8987M/XM358
8990M/XM419
8995M/XM425
8996M/XM414
8998M/XT864
9002M/XW763
9003M/XZ390
9004M/XZ370
9005M/XZ374
9006M/XX967
9007M/XX968
9008M/XX140
9009M/XX763
9010M/XX764
9011M/XM412
9012M/XN494
9014M/XN584
9015M/XW320
9017M/ZE449
9019M/XX824
9020M/XX825
9021M/XX826
9022M/XX958
9026M/XP629
9027M/XP556
9028M/XP563
9032M/XR673
9033M/XS181
9036M/XM350
9038M/XV810
9039M/XN586
9040M/XZ138
9041M/XW763
9042M/XL954
9044M/XS177
9047M/XW409
9048M/XM403
9049M/XW404
9052M/WJ717
9056M/XS488
9059M/ZE360
9066M/XV582
9067M/XV586
9070M/XV581
9072M/XW768
9073M/XW924
9075M/XV752
9076M/XV808
9078M/XV753
9079M/XZ130
9080M/ZE350
9086M/ZE352
9087M/XX753
9090M/XW353
9091M/XW434
9092M/XH669
9093M/WK124
9095M/XW547
9096M/WV322
9098M/XV406
9103M/XV411
9110M/XX736
9111M/XW421
9115M/XV863
9117M/XV161
9118M/XV253
9119M/XW303
9120M/XW419
9122M/XZ997
9123M/XT773
9125M/XW410
9127M/XW432
9130M/XW327
9131M/DD931
9132M/XX977
9133M/413573
9134M/XT288
9136M/XT891
9137M/XN579
9139M/XV863
9140M/XZ287
9141M/XV118
9143M/XN589
9145M/XV863
9146M/XW299
9147M/XW301
9148M/XW436
9149M/XW375
9150M/FX760
9151M/XT907
9152M/XV424
9153M/XW360
9154M/XW321
9155M/WL679
9162M/XZ991
9163M/XV415
9166M/XW323
9167M/XV744
9168M/XZ132
9169M/XW547
9170M/XZ994
9172M/XW304
9173M/XW418
9174M/XZ131
9175M/P1344
9176M/XW430
9177M/XW328
9179M/XW309
9180M/XW311
9181M/XW358
9185M/XZ987
9187M/XW405
9188M/XW364
9190M/XW318
9191M/XW416
9192M/XW361
9193M/XW367
9194M/XW420
9195M/XW330
9196M/XW370
9197M/XX530/
(XX637)
9199M/XW290
9200M/XW425
9201M/ZD667
9203M/3066
9205M/E449
9206M/F6314
9207M/8417/18
9208M/F938
9210M/MF628
9211M/733682
9212M/KL216/
(45-49295)
9213M/N5182
9215M/XL164
9216M/XL190
9217M/ZH257
9218M/XL563
9219M/XZ971
9221M/XZ966
9222M/XZ968
9224M/XL568
9225M/XX885
9226M/XV865
9227M/XB812
9229M/ZA678
9230M/ZA676
9233M/XZ431
9234M/XV864
9236M/WV318
9237M/XF445
9239M/7198/18
9241M/XS639
9242M/XH672
9246M/XS714
9248M/WB627
9249M/WV396
9251M/XX744
9252M/XX722
9253M/ZA254
9254M/XX965
9255M/XZ375
9257M/XX962
9258M/XW265
9259M/XS710
9260M/XS734
9261M/W2068
9262M/XZ358
9263M/XW267
9264M/XS735
9265M/WK585
9266M/XZ119
9267M/XW269
9268M/XR529
9269M/XT914
9270M/XZ145
9272M/XS486
9273M/XS726
9274M/XS738
9275M/XS729
9276M/XS733
9277M/XT601
9278M/XS643
9279M/XT681
9280M/XV804
9281M/XZ146
9283M/XZ322
9284M/ZA267
9285M/XR806
9286M/XT905
9287M/WP962
9288M/XX520
9289M/XX665
9290M/XX626
9292M/XW892
9293M/XX830
9294M/XX655
9295M/XV497
9298M/ZE340
9299M/XW870
9300M/XX431
9301M/XZ941
9302M/ZD462
9303M/XV709
9305M/XZ942
9306M/XX979
9308M/ZD932
9310M/ZA355
9311M/ZA475
9312M/ZA474
9314M/ZA320
9315M/ZA319
9316M/ZA399
9317M/ZA450
9318M/ZA360
9319M/XR516
9320M/XX153
9321M/XZ367
9322M/ZB686
9323M/XV643
9324M/XV659
9326M/XV653
9328M/ZD607
9329M/ZD578
9330M/ZB684
9331M/XW852
9332M/XZ935
9335M/ZA375
9336M/ZA407
9337M/ZA774
9338M/ZA325
9339M/ZA323
9340M/XX745
9341M/ZA357
9342M/XR498
9343M/XR506
9344M/XV706

Ships' Numeric Code — Deck Letters Analysis

	0	1	2	3	4	5	6	7	8	9
33			LP						CT	
34									CM	
35	CL	CL								
36	MC					AY	LB			
37			NL			SM				
38										
40					IR			YK		
41	GC	EB	CW	CW		MM		NM		
42	EX	SU			KT	PD	SB			
43					EE	EE				
44					MR					
45		DA							LA	
46			WM							
47					RM					

RN Code – Squadron – Base – Aircraft Cross-check

Deck/Base Code Numbers	*Letters*	*Unit*	*Location*	*Aircraft Type(s)*
010 — 020	CU	820 NAS	Culdrose	Merlin HM1
180 — 190	CU	849 NAS	Culdrose	Sea King ASaC7
180 — 190	CU	854 NAS	Culdrose	Sea King ASaC7
180 — 190	CU	857 NAS	Culdrose	Sea King ASaC7
264 — 274	CU	814 NAS	Culdrose	Merlin HM1
300 — 308	VL	815 NAS	Yeovilton	Lynx HAS3/HMA8
311 — 316	VL	815 NAS, B Section	Yeovilton	Lynx HAS3/HMA8
321 — 474	*	815 NAS	Yeovilton	Lynx HAS3/HMA8
500 — 515	CU	829 NAS	Culdrose	Merlin HM1
560 — 568	CU	750 NAS	Culdrose	Jetstream T2
580 — 588	CU	824 NAS	Culdrose	Merlin HM1
630 — 645	VL	702 NAS	Yeovilton	Lynx HAS3
817 — 831	CU	771 NAS	Culdrose	Sea King HU5/HAS6

*See foregoing separate ships' Deck Letters Analysis
Note that only the 'last two' digits of the Code are worn by some aircraft types, especially helicopters.

RN Landing Platform and Shore Station Code-letters

Code	Deck Letters	Vessel Name & Pennant No	Vessel Type & Unit
—	AB	HMS *Albion* (L14)	Assault
—	AS	RFA *Argus* (A135)	Aviation Training ship
365	AY	HMS *Argyll* (F231)	Type 23 (815 NAS)
—	BV	RFA *Black Rover* (A273)	Fleet tanker
—	CB	RFA *Cardigan Bay* (L3009)	Landing ship
350/1	CL	HMS *Cumberland* (F85)	Type 22 (815 NAS)
348	CM	HMS *Chatham* (F87)	Type 22 (815 NAS)
338	CT	HMS *Campbeltown* (F86)	Type 22 (815 NAS)
—	CU	RNAS Culdrose (HMS *Seahawk*)	
412/3	CW	HMS *Cornwall* (F99)	Type 22 (815 NAS)
451	DA	HMS *Daring* (D32)	Type 45 (815 NAS)
—	DC	HMS *Dumbarton Castle* (P265)	Fishery protection
—	DG	RFA *Diligence* (A132)	Maintenance
411	EB	HMS *Edinburgh* (D97)	Type 42 (815 NAS)
434/5	EE	HMS *Endurance* (A171)	Ice Patrol (815 NAS)
420	EX	HMS *Exeter* (D89)	Type 42 (815 NAS)
—	FA	RFA *Fort Austin* (A386)	Support ship
—	FE	RFA *Fort Rosalie* (A385)	Support ship
410	GC	HMS *Gloucester* (D96)	Type 42 (815 NAS)
—	GV	RFA *Gold Rover* (A271)	Fleet tanker
404	IR	HMS *Iron Duke* (F234)	Type 23 (815 NAS)
425	KT	HMS *Kent* (F78)	Type 23 (815 NAS)
—	L	HMS *Illustrious* (R06)	Carrier
457	LA	HMS *Lancaster* (F229)	Type 23 (829 NAS)
366	LB	RFA *Largs Bay* (L3006)	Landing ship
—	LC	HMS *Leeds Castle* (P258)	Fishery protection
332	LP	HMS *Liverpool* (D92)	Type 42 (815 NAS)
—	MB	RFA *Mounts Bay* (L3008)	Landing ship
360	MC	HMS *Manchester* (D95)	Type 42 (815 NAS)
415	MM	HMS *Monmouth* (F235)	Type 23 (829 NAS)
444	MR	HMS *Montrose* (F236)	Type 23 (815 NAS)
372	NL	HMS *Northumberland* (F238)	Type 23 (829 NAS)
417	NM	HMS *Nottingham* (D91)	Type 42 (815 NAS)
—	O	HMS *Ocean* (L12)	Helicopter carrier
426	PD	HMS *Portland* (F79)	Type 23 (815 NAS)
474	RM	HMS *Richmond* (F239)	Type 23 (815 NAS)
427	SB	HMS *St Albans* (F83)	Type 23 (815 NAS)
375	SM	HMS *Somerset* (F82)	Type 23 (815 NAS)
422	SU	HMS *Sutherland* (F81)	Type 23 (815 NAS)
—	VL	RNAS Yeovilton (HMS *Heron*)	
462	WM	HMS *Westminster* (F237)	Type 23 (829 NAS)
407	YK	HMS *York* (D98)	Type 42 (815 NAS)
—	—	HMS *Bulwark* (L15)	Assault
—	—	HMS *Dauntless* (D33)	Type 45
—	—	HMS *Defender* (D36)	Type 45
—	—	HMS *Diamond* (D34)	Type 45
—	DR	HMS *Dragon* (D35)	Type 45
—	—	HMS *Duncan* (D37)	Type 45
—	—	RFA *Fort Victoria* (A387)	Auxiliary Oiler
—	—	RFA *Fort George* (A388)	Auxiliary Oiler
—	—	RFA *Lyme Bay* (L3007)	Landing ship
—	—	RFA *Wave Knight* (A389)	Fleet tanker
—	—	RFA *Wave Ruler* (A390)	Fleet tanker

Royal Air Force Squadron Markings

This table gives brief details of the markings worn by aircraft of RAF squadrons at the beginning of 2011. While this may help to identify the operator of a particular machine, it may not always give the true picture. For example, from time to time aircraft are loaned to other units while others wear squadron marks but are actually operated on a pool basis. Squadron badges are usually located on the front fuselage.

Squadron	*Type(s) operated*	*Base(s)*	*Distinguishing marks & other comments*
No 2 Sqn	Tornado GR4/GR4A	RAF Marham	Badge: A wake knot on a white circular background flanked on either side by black and white triangles. Tail fin has a black stripe with white triangles and the badge repeated on it.
No 3 Sqn	Typhoon T1A/F2/FGR4	RAF Coningsby	Badge: A blue cockatrice on a white circular background flanked by two green bars edged with yellow. Tail fin as a green stripe edged with yellow. Aircraft are coded QO-*
No 5 Sqn	Sentinel R1/ Shadow R1	RAF Waddington	Badge (on tail): A green maple leaf on a white circle over a red horizontal band.
No 6 Sqn	Typhoon T3/FGR4	RAF Leuchars	Badge (on tail): A red, winged can opener on a blue shield, edged in red. The roundel is flanked by a red zigzag on a blue background. Aircraft are coded E*.
No 7 Sqn	Chinook HC2/HC2A/ HC3R	RAF Odiham	Badge (on tail): A blue badge containing the seven stars of Ursa Major ('The Plough') in yellow. Aircraft pooled with No 18 Sqn and No 27 Sqn.
No 8 Sqn	Sentry AEW1	RAF Waddington	Badge (on tail): A grey, sheathed, Arabian dagger. Aircraft pooled with No 54(R) Sqn.
No 9 Sqn	Tornado GR4/GR4A	RAF Marham	Badge: A green bat on a black circular background, flanked by yellow and green horizontal stripes. The green bat also appears on the tail, edged in yellow.
No 11 Sqn	Typhoon T3/F2/FGR4	RAF Coningsby	Badge (on tail): Two eagles in flight on a white shield. The roundel is flanked by yellow and black triangles. Aircraft are coded D*
No 12 Sqn	Tornado GR4/GR4A	RAF Lossiemouth	Roundel is superimposed on a green chevron. Tail fin has a black & white horizontal stripe with the squadron badge, a fox's head on a white circle, in the middle.
No 13 Sqn	Tornado GR4/GR4A	RAF Marham	A yellow lightning flash on a green and blue background on the nose. Badge (on tail): A lynx's head over a dagger on a white shield.
No 14 Sqn	Tornado GR4/GR4A	RAF Lossiemouth	Badge: A red cross on a white circle, with wings either side, flanked by blue diamonds on a white background. The blue diamonds are repeated horizontally across the tail.
No 15(R) Sqn [NTOCU]	Tornado GR4/GR4A	RAF Lossiemouth the tail.	Roman numerals XV appear in white on
No 16(R) Sqn	Tutor	RAF Cranwell	No markings carried. Aircraft pooled with East Midlands UAS and No 115(R) Sqn.

Squadron	*Type(s) operated*	*Base(s)*	*Distinguishing marks & other comments*
No 17(R) Sqn	Typhoon T3/FGR4	RAF Coningsby	Badge (on tail): A gauntlet on a black and white shield. Roundel is flanked by two white bars which have a pair of jagged black lines running along them horizontally. Aircraft are coded A*.
No 18 Sqn	Chinook HC2/HC2A/ HC3R	RAF Odiham	Badge (on tail): A red winged horse on a black circle. Aircraft pooled with No 7 Sqn and No 27 Sqn.
No 19(R) Sqn	Hawk T1/T1A/T1W/T2	RAF Valley	Badge (on tail): A fish flanked by two wings on a yellow circle. Aircraft also carry blue and white checks either side of the roundel on the fuselage. Aircraft pooled with No 208(R) Sqn; part of No 4 FTS.
No 22 Sqn	Sea King HAR3/HAR3A	A Flt: RMB Chivenor B Flt: Wattisham C Flt: RAF Valley	Badge: A black pi symbol in front of a white Maltese cross on a red circle.
No 24 Sqn	Hercules C4/C5	RAF Lyneham	No squadron markings carried. Aircraft pooled with No 30 Sqn.
No 27 Sqn	Chinook HC2/HC2A/ HC3R	RAF Odiham	Badge (on tail): A dark green elephant on a green circle, flanked by green and dark green stripes. Aircraft pooled with No 7 Sqn and No 18 Sqn.
No 28 Sqn	Merlin HC3/HC3A	RAF Benson	Badge: A winged horse above two white crosses on a red shield. Aircraft pooled with No 78 Sqn.
No 29(R) Sqn [TOCU]	Typhoon T1/T1A/F2/T3/ FGR4	RAF Coningsby	Badge (on tail): An eagle in flight, preying on a buzzard, with three red Xs across the top. The roundel is flanked by two white bars outlined by a red line, each containing three red Xs. Aircraft are coded B*.
No 30 Sqn	Hercules C4/C5	RAF Lyneham	No squadron markings carried. Aircraft pooled with No 24 Sqn.
No 31 Sqn	Tornado GR4/GR4A	RAF Marham	Badge: A gold, five-pointed star on a yellow circle flanked by yellow and green checks. The star is repeated on the tail.
No 32(The Royal) Sqn	BAe 125 CC3/146 CC2/ Agusta 109	RAF Northolt	No squadron markings carried but aircraft carry a distinctive livery with a red stripe, edged in blue v along the middle of the fuselage and a red tail.
No 33 Sqn	Puma HC1	RAF Benson	Badge: A stag's head.
No 39 Sqn	Predator/ Reaper	Nellis AFB Creech AFB	No markings worn
No 41(R) Sqn [FJWOEU]	Tornado GR4	RAF Coningsby	Badge: A red, double armed cross, flanked by red and white horizontal stripes. Stripes repeated on tail.
No 45(R) Sqn	Raytheon Beech Super King Air 200/200GT	RAF Cranwell	Aircraft carry a dark blue stripe on the tail superimposed with red diamonds. Part of No 3 FTS.
No 47 Sqn	Hercules C1/C3/C3A	RAF Lyneham	No squadron markings usually carried.
No 51 Sqn	Nimrod R1	RAF Waddington	Badge (on tail): A red goose in flight.
No 54(R) Sqn [ISTAR OCU]	Sentry AEW1/Nimrod R1	RAF Waddington	Based aircraft as required.

RAF Squadron Markings

Squadron	*Type(s) operated*	*Base(s)*	*Distinguishing marks & other comments*
No 56(R) Sqn [ISTAR Test & Evaluation Sqn]	Nimrod R1/Shadow R1/ Sentry AEW1/ Sentinel R1	RAF Waddington	Based aircraft as required.
No 57(R) Sqn	Tutor	RAF Wyton	No markings carried. Aircraft pooled with Cambridge UAS and University of London AS.
No 60(R) Sqn	Griffin HT1	RAF Shawbury [DHFS] & RAF Valley [SARTU]	No squadron markings usually carried.
No 72(R) Sqn	Tucano T1	RAF Linton-on-Ouse	Badge: A black swift in flight on a red disk, flanked by blue bars edged with red. The blue bars edged with red also flank the roundel on the fuselage; part of No 1 FTS
No 76(R) Sqn	Tucano T1	RAF Linton-on-Ouse	Badge (on tail): A black lion on a white square. Aircraft are coded MP-*; part of No 1 FTS
No 78 Sqn	Merlin HC3/HC3A	RAF Benson	Badge: A yellow, heraldic tiger with two tails, on a black circle. Aircraft pooled with No 28 Sqn.
No 84 Sqn	Griffin HAR2	RAF Akrotiri	Badge (on tail): A scorpion on a playing card symbol (diamonds, clubs etc). Aircraft carry a vertical light blue stripe through the roundel on the fuselage.
No 85(R) Sqn	Tutor	RAF Church Fenton	No markings carried. Aircraft pooled with Yorkshire Universities AS.
No 99 Sqn	Globemaster III	RAF Brize Norton	Badge (on tail): A black puma leaping.
No 100 Sqn	Hawk T1A	RAF Leeming	Badge (on tail): A skull in front of two bones crossed. Aircraft are usually coded C*. Incorporates the Joint Forward Air Control Training and Standards Unit (JFACTSU)
No 101 Sqn	VC10 C1K/K3	RAF Brize Norton	Badge (on tail): A lion behind a castle turret.
No 111 Sqn	Tornado F3	RAF Leuchars	Badge (on tail): A cross in front of crossed swords on a light grey circle, flanked by a stripe of darker grey.
No 115(R) Sqn	Tutor	RAF Cranwell	No markings carried. Aircraft pooled with East Midlands UAS and No 16(R) Sqn.
No 202 Sqn	Sea King HAR3	A Flt: RAF Boulmer D Flt: RAF Lossiemouth E Flt: RAF Leconfield	Badge: A mallard alighting on a white circle.
No 203(R) Sqn	Sea King HAR3	RAF Valley	Badge: A green sea horse on a white circle.
No 206(R) Sqn [HAT&ES]	Hercules C1/C3/C3A/C4 C5	RAF Lyneham/ Boscombe Down	No squadron markings usually carried.
No 207(R) Sqn	Tucano T1	RAF Linton-on-Ouse	Badge: A red winged lion on a white disk. The roundel on the fuselage is by red bars edged with yellow; part of No 1 FTS

Squadron	*Type(s) operated*	*Base(s)*	*Distinguishing marks & other comments*
No 208(R) Sqn	Hawk T1/T1A/T1W	RAF Valley	Badge (on tail): A Sphinx inside a white circle, flanked by flashes of yellow. Aircraft also carry blue and yellow bars either side of the roundel on the fuselage and a blue and yellow chevron on the nose. Aircraft pooled with No 19(R) Sqn; part of No 4 FTS.
No 216 Sqn	TriStar K1/KC1/C2/C2A	RAF Brize Norton	Badge (on tail): An eagle in flight with a bomb in its claws.
No 230 Sqn	Puma HC1	RAF Benson	Badge: A tiger in front of a palm tree on a black pentagon.
No 617 Sqn	Tornado GR4/GR4A	RAF Lossiemouth	Badge: Dam breached, flanked on either side by red lightning flashes on a black background. Tail fin is black with a red lightning flash.
No 1312 Flt	VC10 K3/K4 (101 Sqn) Hercules	Mount Pleasant, FI	Badge (on tail): A red Maltese cross on a white circle, flanked by red and white horizontal bars.
No 1419 Flt	Merlin HC3	Afghanistan	No markings carried.
No 1435 Flt	Typhoon FGR4	Mount Pleasant, FI	Badge (on tail): A red Maltese cross on a white circle, flanked by red and white horizontal bars.
No 1564 Flt	Chinook HC2/ Sea King HAR3	Mount Pleasant, FI	No markings known.

2010 saw the end of the Harrier in UK service, with its withdrawal announced in the Strategic Defence and Security Review in October. GR9 ZG858 wore special markings and belonged to 4(R) Squadron, which moved from Wittering to Cottesmore as the Harrier force began to be retired.

University Air Squadrons/Air Experience Flights*

Some UAS aircraft carry squadron badges and markings, usually on the tail. Squadron crests all consist of a white circle surrounded by a blue circle, topped with a red crown and having a yellow scroll beneath. Each differs by the motto on the scroll, the UAS name running around the blue circle & by the contents at the centre and it is the latter which are described below. All AEFs come under the administration of local UASs and these are listed here.

UAS	*Base*	*Marks*
Bristol UAS/ No 3 AEF	Colerne	A sailing ship on water.
Cambridge UAS/ No 5 AEF	RAF Wyton	A heraldic lion in front of a red badge. Aircraft pooled with University of London AS
East Midlands Universities AS/ No 7 AEF	RAF Cranwell	A yellow quiver, full of arrows.
East of Scotland UAS/ No 12 AEF	RAF Leuchars	An open book in front of a white diagonal cross edged in blue.
Liverpool UAS	RAF Woodvale	A bird atop an open book, holding a branch in its beak. Aircraft pooled with Manchester and Salford Universities AS
Manchester and Salford Universities AS/ No 10 AEF	RAF Woodvale	A bird of prey with a green snake in its beak. Aircraft pooled with Liverpool UAS
Northumbrian Universities AS/ No 11 AEF	RAF Leeming	A white cross on a blue background.
Oxford UAS/ No 6 AEF	RAF Benson	An open book in front of crossed swords.
Southampton UAS/ No 2 AEF	Boscombe Down	A red stag in front of a stone pillar.
Universities of Glasgow and Strathclyde AS/ No 4 AEF	Glasgow	A bird of prey in flight, holding a branch in its beak, in front of an upright sword.
University of Birmingham AS/ No 8 AEF	DCAE Cosford	A blue griffon with two heads.
University of London AS	RAF Wyton	A globe superimposed over an open book. Aircraft pooled with Cambridge UAS
University of Wales AS/ No 1 AEF	MoD St Athan	A red Welsh dragon in front of an open book, clasping a sword. Some aircraft have the dragon in front of white and green squares.
Yorkshire Universities AS/ No 9 AEF	RAF Church Fenton	An open book in front of a Yorkshire rose with leaves.

Fleet Air Arm Squadron Markings

This table gives brief details of the markings worn by aircraft of FAA squadrons. Squadron badges, when worn, are usually located on the front fuselage. All FAA squadron badges (other than 800 NAS) comprise a crown atop a circle edged in gold braid and so the badge details below list only what appears in the circular part.

Squadron	*Type(s) operated*	*Base(s)*	*Distinguishing marks & other comments*
No 702 NAS	Lynx HAS3/HMA8	RNAS Yeovilton	Badge: A Lynx rearing up in front of a circle comprising alternate dark blue and white sectors.
No 727 NAS	Tutor	RNAS Yeovilton	Badge: The head of Britannia wearing a gold helmet on a background of blue and white waves.
No 750 NAS	Jetstream T2	RNAS Culdrose	Badge: A Greek runner bearing a torch & sword on a background of blue and white waves.
No 771 NAS	Sea King HU5/HAS6	RNAS Culdrose & Prestwick	Badge: Three bees on a background of blue and white waves.
No 814 NAS	Merlin HM1	RNAS Culdrose	Badge: A winged tiger mask on a background of dark blue and white waves.
No 815 NAS	Lynx HAS3/HMA8	RNAS Yeovilton	Badge: A winged, gold harpoon on a background of blue and white waves.
No 820 NAS	Merlin HM1	RNAS Culdrose	Badge: A flying fish on a background of blue and white waves.
No 824 NAS	Merlin HM1	RNAS Culdrose	Badge: A heron on a background of blue and white waves.
No 829 NAS	Merlin HM1	RNAS Culdrose	Badge: A kingfisher hovering on a background of blue and white waves.
No 845 NAS	Sea King HC4	RNAS Yeovilton	Badge: A dragonfly on a background of blue and white waves.
No 846 NAS	Sea King HC4	RNAS Yeovilton	Badge: A swordsman riding a winged horse whilst attacking a serpent on a background of blue and white waves. Aircraft are usually coded V*.
No 847 NAS	Lynx AH7/AH9A	RNAS Yeovilton	Badge: A gold sea lion on a blue background.
No 848 NAS	Sea King HC4	RNAS Yeovilton	Badge: Inside a red circle, a hawk in flight with a torpedo in its claws above white and blue waves. Aircraft are usually coded W*.
No 849 NAS	Sea King ASaC7	RNAS Culdrose	Badge: A winged streak of lightning with an eye in front on a background of blue and white waves.
No 854 NAS	Sea King ASaC7	RNAS Culdrose	Badge: A winged lion in front of a sword.
No 857 NAS	Sea King ASaC7	RNAS Culdrose	Badge: A hand emerging from the waves, clutching a sword aloft.

UK Military Aircraft Code Decode

This section lists the codes worn by some UK military aircraft and, alongside, the serial of the aircraft currently wearing this code. It should be pointed out that in some cases more than one aircraft wears the same code but the aircraft listed is the one believed to be in service with the unit concerned at the time of going to press. This list will be updated regularly and those with Internet access can download the latest version via the 'AirNet' Web Site, www.aviation-links.co.uk.

ROYAL AIR FORCE

AgustaWestland AW.139

B	ZR327
F	ZR326

BAC VC10

Code	*Serial*
F	ZA147
G	ZA148
H	ZA149
J	ZA150
N	ZD241
R	XR808
S	XV101
T	XV102
U	XV104
V	XV105
W	XV106
X	XV107
Y	XV108

Beech King Air 200

Code	*Serial*
D	ZK458
J	ZK450
K	ZK451
L	ZK452
M	ZK453
N	ZK454
O	ZK455
P	ZK456
U	ZK460
X	ZK459

Bell 412EP Griffin HT1

Code	*Serial*
E	ZJ242
I	ZJ235
K	ZJ708
L	ZJ241
O	ZJ707
R	ZJ239
S	ZJ234
T	ZJ237
U	ZJ240
X	ZJ236
Y	ZJ238

B-V Chinook

Code	*Serial*
AA	ZA670
AB	ZA671
AE	ZA675
AF	ZA677
AG	ZA679
AH	ZA680
AI	ZA681
AJ	ZA682
AK	ZA683
AL	ZA684
AM	ZA704
AN	ZA705
AO	ZA707
AP	ZA708
AR	ZA710
AT	ZA712
AU	ZA713
AV	ZA714
BN	ZA718
DB	ZD574
DC	ZD575
DD	ZD980
DF	ZD982
DG	ZD983
DH	ZD984
HB	ZH775
HC	ZH776
HE	ZH777
HF	ZH891
HG	ZH892
HH	ZH893
HI	ZH894
HJ	ZH895
HK	ZH896

EHI-101 Merlin

Code	*Serial*
B	ZJ118
C	ZJ119
D	ZJ120
E	ZJ121
F	ZJ122
G	ZJ123
H	ZJ124
J	ZJ125
K	ZJ126
L	ZJ127
M	ZJ128
N	ZJ129
O	ZJ130
P	ZJ131
Q	ZJ132
R	ZJ133
S	ZJ134
T	ZJ135
U	ZJ136
W	ZJ137
X	ZJ138
AA	ZJ990
AB	ZJ992
AC	ZJ994
AD	ZJ995
AE	ZJ998
AF	ZK001

Eurofighter Typhoon

Code	*Serial*
C	ZJ950
D	ZK301
F	ZJ944
H	ZJ949
AA	ZJ930
AB	ZJ912
AC	ZJ913
AF	ZJ914
BA	ZJ803
BB	ZJ802
BD	ZJ805
BE	ZJ806
BH	ZJ809
BI	ZJ810
BJ	ZJ801
BK	ZJ812
BL	ZJ813
BV	ZJ910
BY	ZJ915
BZ	ZJ911
DA	ZJ931
DB	ZJ932
DC	ZJ919
DD	ZJ924
DF	ZJ933
DH	ZJ942
DJ	ZJ935
DL	ZJ929
DM	ZJ923
DN	ZJ947
DW	ZJ808
DY	ZJ815
DZ	ZJ811
DXI	ZJ939
EA	ZK302
EB	ZK304
EC	ZK305
ED	ZK306
EE	ZK307
EF	ZK308
EG	ZK309
EH	ZJ946
EJ	ZK300
EK	ZK311
EL	ZK310
EM	ZK312
EX	ZK379
EY	ZK380
QO-A	ZJ920
QO-C	ZJ922
QO-G	ZJ917
QO-H	ZJ921
QO-J	ZJ941
QO-L	ZJ918
QO-M	ZJ927
QO-N	ZJ928
QO-R	ZJ925
QO-S	ZJ936
QO-T	ZJ934
QO-U	ZJ916
QO-W	ZJ937
QO-Y	ZJ926
QO-Z	ZJ814
S-RO	ZJ805
YB-F	ZJ912

HS Hawk T1

Code	*Serial*
CA	XX246
CC	XX203
CD	XX332
CE	XX258

CF	XX202
CG	XX198
CH	XX346
CI	XX222
CJ	XX329
CK	XX339
CL	XX255
CM	XX280
CN	XX318
CO	XX289
CQ	XX184

Panavia Tornado F3

Code	*Serial*
HA	ZE834
HB	ZE961
HD	ZE763
HF	ZE791
HH	ZE168
HI	ZE341
HK	ZE764
HL	ZE983
HP	ZE342
HW	ZH552
HX	ZH554
HY	ZE163
JU	ZE734
JU-C	ZH554
JU-L	ZE791

Panavia Tornado GR4

Code	*Serial*
001	ZA365
002	ZA367
003	ZA369
004	ZA370
005	ZA371
006	ZA372
007	ZA373
008	ZA393
009	ZA395
010	ZA398
011	ZA400
012	ZA401
013	ZA404
014	ZA405
015	ZA406
016	ZA410
017	ZA412
018	ZA446
020	ZA449
021	ZA452
022	ZA453
023	ZA456
024	ZA458
026	ZA461
027	ZA462
028	ZA463
029	ZA469
031	ZA472
032	ZA473
033	ZA492
034	ZA541
035	ZA542
036	ZA543
037	ZA544
039	ZA547
040	ZA548
041	ZA549
042	ZA550
043	ZA551
044	ZA552
045	ZA553
046	ZA554
047	ZA556
048	ZA557
049	ZA559
050	ZA560
051	ZA562
054	ZA585
055	ZA587
056	ZA588
057	ZA589
058	ZA591
059	ZA592
060	ZA594
061	ZA595
062	ZA596
063	ZA597
064	ZA598
066	ZA601
067	ZA602
068	ZA604
069	ZA606
070	ZA607
075	ZA613
076	ZA614
077	ZD707
078	ZD709
079	ZD711
080	ZD712
081	ZD713
083	ZD715
084	ZD716
085	ZD719
086	ZD720
087	ZD739
088	ZD740
089	ZD741
090	ZD742
091	ZD743
092	ZD744
093	ZD745
094	ZD746
095	ZD747
096	ZD748
097	ZD749
098	ZD788
099	ZD790
100	ZD792
101	ZD793
102	ZD810
103	ZD811
104	ZD812
105	ZD842
106	ZD843
107	ZD844
108	ZD847
109	ZD848
110	ZD849
111	ZD850
112	ZD851
113	ZD890
115	ZD895
116	ZE116
118	ZG705
119	ZG707
120	ZG709
122	ZG712
123	ZG713
124	ZG714
125	ZG726
126	ZG727
128	ZG750
129	ZG752
130	ZG754
131	ZG756
133	ZG771
134	ZG775
135	ZG777
136	ZG779
137	ZG791
C	ZA371
F	ZA459
H	ZA373
M	ZG729
AG	ZA546
IV	ZA612
TN	ZG794
AJ-G	ZA601
AJ-N	ZA398
AJ-W	ZD714
EB-B	ZD996
EB-G	ZA600
EB-L	ZA611
EB-R	ZA447
KC-N	ZA367

Shorts Tucano T1

Code	*Serial*
LZ-R	ZF171
MP-A	ZF170
MP-D	ZF172
MP-O	ZF269
MP-Q	ZF264
MP-T	ZF239
MP-W	ZF378
QJ-F	ZF317

WS61 Sea King

Code	*Serial*
A	XZ585
B	XZ586
C	XZ587
D	XZ588
E	XZ589
F	XZ590
G	XZ591
I	XZ593
K	XZ595
L	XZ596
M	XZ597
P	XZ599
Q	ZA105
R	ZE368
S	ZE369
T	ZE370
V	ZH541
W	ZH542
X	ZH543
Z	ZH545

ROYAL NAVY

BAe/SA Jetstream

Code	*Serial*
562	XX488
563	ZA110
565	ZA111
566	XX484
567	XX486
568	XX487

EHI-101 Merlin

Code	*Serial*
10	ZH857
11	ZH828
13	ZH853
65	ZH837
66	ZH838

67	ZH845
68	ZH860
70	ZH855
81	ZH840
82	ZH841
84	ZH854
85	ZH833
86	ZH834
88	ZH842

WS Lynx

Code	*Serial*
301	ZD262
302	ZD266
303	ZD260
305	XZ733
306	XZ233
307	XZ727
311	XZ693
312	XZ720
313	XZ228
314	XZ255
315	ZF562
316	XZ689
332	XZ731
338	ZD252
348	XZ698
350	XZ729
365	XZ691
375	ZF557
404	ZD259
407	ZD566
410	ZD565
411	XZ726
412	ZF560
415	XZ725
426	ZF558
435	XZ696
444	XZ723
451	XZ736
452	XZ732
631	XZ237
632	XZ254
633	XZ696
634	XZ730
635	ZD250
636	ZD249
641	XZ697
642	ZD257
643	ZD268
644	ZD265
645	XZ722

WS61 Sea King

Code	*Serial*
16	ZA166
19	ZA130
20	ZA137
21	XV666
22	ZA167
26	XV661
27	XV673
28	XV647
29	XV705
180	XV649
181	XV697
182	ZD636
183	XV671
184	XV707
185	XV656
186	ZE418
187	XV672
188	XV714
189	ZE420
190	XV664
191	ZA126
192	ZE422
707	XZ920
818	XV648
823	XV699
A	ZA293
B	ZA310
D	ZA299
E	ZD477
F	ZB507
G	ZG821
H	ZE428
I	ZG820
J	ZD480
K	ZE427
L	ZF124
M	ZA313
N	ZA291
O	ZF118
P	ZD625
Q	ZA296
R	ZF115
S	ZD626
T	ZF121
U	ZA295
V	ZF122
W	ZA297
X	ZF117
Y	ZA298
Z	ZF120
WO	ZD627
WP	ZF116
WQ	ZD479
WR	ZE425
WS	ZG822
WT	ZA314
WU	ZA292
WW	ZF123
WX	ZE426
WY	ZF119
WZ	ZD476
ZB	XZ580

ARMY AIR CORPS

WS Gazelle AH1

Code	*Serial*
C	ZB692
M	XZ345
S	ZB691

WS Lynx AH7

Code	*Serial*
A	ZD273
E	XZ680
F	XZ203
H	XZ675
K	ZD281
L	XZ605
T	XZ196
U	ZD277
V	XZ661
W	ZD272
X	XZ176
Z	XZ221

Tornado F3 ZE163 wearing the code HY and the colours of No 111 Squadron depicts another type soon to be seen no more in UK skies.

Wearing a striking blue, silver and white colour scheme, Agusta 109 ZE416 is operated by the Empire Test Pilots' School at Boscombe Down.

The King Air is one type where the UK military fleet is actually growing and this one, ZK452, belongs to 45(R) Sqn based with 3 FTS at Cranwell.

ZR322 is one of three Agusta 109s operated by 32 (The Royal) Sqn from RAF Northolt.

Historic Aircraft in Overseas Markings

Some *historic, classic* and *warbird* aircraft carry the markings of overseas air arms and can be seen in the UK, mainly preserved in museums and collections or taking part in air shows.

Notes	Serial	Type (code/other identity)	Owner/operator, location or fate
	AFGHANISTAN		
	-	Hawker Afghan Hind (BAPC 82)	RAF Museum, Cosford
	ARGENTINA		
	-	Bell UH-1H Iroquois (AE-406/*998-8888*) [Z]	RAF Valley, instructional use
	0729	Beech T-34C Turbo Mentor	FAA Museum, stored RNAS Yeovilton
	0767	Aermacchi MB339AA	Rolls-Royce Heritage Trust, stored Derby
	A-515	FMA IA58 Pucara (ZD485)	RAF Museum, Cosford
	A-517	FMA IA58 Pucara (G-BLRP)	Privately owned, Channel Islands
	A-522	FMA IA58 Pucara (8768M)	FAA Museum, at NE Aircraft Museum, Usworth
	A-528	FMA IA58 Pucara (8769M)	Norfolk & Suffolk Avn Museum, Flixton
	A-533	FMA IA58 Pucara (ZD486) <ff>	Privately owned, Cheltenham
	A-549	FMA IA58 Pucara (ZD487)	Imperial War Museum, Duxford
	AE-409	Bell UH-1H Iroquois [656]	Museum of Army Flying, Middle Wallop
	AE-422	Bell UH-1H Iroquois	FAA Museum, stored RNAS Yeovilton
	AUSTRALIA		
	369	Hawker Fury ISS (F-AZXL) [D]	Privately owned, Avignon, France
	A2-4	Supermarine Seagull V (VH-ALB)	RAF Museum, Hendon
	A16-199	Lockheed Hudson IIIA (G-BEOX) [SF-R]	RAF Museum, Hendon
	A17-48	DH82A Tiger Moth (G-BPHR)	Privately owned, Wanborough, Wilts
	A19-144	Bristol 156 Beaufighter XIc (JM135/A8-324)	The Fighter Collection, Duxford
	A92-255	GAF Jindivik 102	DPA/QinetiQ, Boscombe Down, apprentice use
	A92-664	GAF Jindivik 4A	Boscombe Down Aviation Collection
	A92-708	GAF Jindivik 4A	Bristol Aero Collection, stored Kemble
	A92-908	GAF Jindivik 900 (ZJ503)	No 2445 Sqn ATC, Llanbedr
	N6-766	DH115 Sea Vampire T22 (XG766/G-VYPO) [808]	Privately owned, Bournemouth
	BELGIUM		
	A-41	SA318C Alouette II	The Helicopter Museum, Weston-super-Mare
	FT-36	Lockheed T-33A Shooting Star	Dumfries & Galloway Avn Mus, Dumfries
	H-50	Noorduyn AT-16 Harvard IIB (OO-DAF)	Privately owned, Brasschaat, Belgium
	HD-75	Hanriot HD1 (G-AFDX)	RAF Museum, Hendon
	IF-68	Hawker Hunter F6 <ff>	Privately owned,
	L-44	Piper L-18C Super Cub (OO-SPQ)	Royal Aéro Para Club de Spa, Belgium
	L-47	Piper L-18C Super Cub (OO-SPG)	Aeroclub Brasschaat VZW, Brasschaat, Belgium
	L-156	Piper L-18C Super Cub (OO-LGB)	Aeroclub Brasschaat VZW, Brasschaat, Belgium
	MT-23	Fouga CM170 Magister	Privately owned, Market Drayton
	V-4	SNCAN Stampe SV-4B (OO-EIR)	Antwerp Stampe Centre, Antwerp-Deurne, Belgium
	V-18	SNCAN Stampe SV-4B (OO-GWD)	Antwerp Stampe Centre, Antwerp-Deurne, Belgium
	V-29	SNCAN Stampe SV-4B (OO-GWB)	Antwerp Stampe Centre, Antwerp-Deurne, Belgium
	V-66	SNCAN Stampe SV-4C (OO-GWA)	Antwerp Stampe Centre, Antwerp-Deurne, Belgium
	BOLIVIA		
	FAB184	SIAI-Marchetti SF.260W (G-SIAI)	Privately owned, Booker
	BRAZIL		
	1317	Embraer T-27 Tucano	Shorts, Belfast (engine test bed)

Notes	*Serial*	*Type (code/other identity)*	*Owner/operator, location or fate*
	BURKINA FASO		
	BF8431	SIAI-Marchetti SF.260 (G-NRRA) [31]	Privately owned, Oaksey Park
	CANADA		
	-	Lockheed T-33A Shooting Star (17473)	Midland Air Museum, Coventry
	622	Piasecki HUP-3 Retriever (51-16622/N6699D)	The Helicopter Museum, Weston-super-Mare
	920	VS Stranraer (CF-BXO) [Q-N]	RAF Museum, Hendon
	3349	NA64 Yale (G-BYNF)	Privately owned, Duxford
	5450	Hawker Hurricane XII (G-TDTW)	Hawker Restorations Ltd, Milden
	5487	Hawker Hurricane II (G-CBOE)	Privately owned, Thruxton
	9041	Bristol 149 Bolingbroke IV <ff>	Manx Aviation Museum, Ronaldsway
	9048	Bristol 149 Bolingbroke IV <ff>	Bristol Aero Collection, Kemble
	9048	Bristol 149 Bolingbroke IV <rf>	Bristol Aero Collection, stored Filton
	9754	Consolidated PBY-5A Catalina (VP-BPS) [P]	Privately owned, Lee-on-Solent
	9893	Bristol 149 Bolingbroke IVT	Imperial War Museum store, Duxford
	9940	Bristol 149 Bolingbroke IVT	Royal Scottish Mus'm of Flight, E Fortune
	15195	Fairchild PT-19A Cornell	RAF Museum Reserve Collection, Stafford
	16693	Auster J/1N Alpha (G-BLPG) [693]	Privately owned, Clacton
	18393	Avro Canada CF-100 Canuck 4B (G-BCYK)	Imperial War Museum, Duxford
	18671	DHC1 Chipmunk 22 (WP905/7438M/G-BNZC) [671]	The Shuttleworth Collection, Old Warden
	20249	Noorduyn AT-16 Harvard IIB (PH-KLU) [XS-249]	Privately owned, Texel, The Netherlands
	20310	CCF T-6J Texan (G-BSBG) [310]	Privately owned, Tatenhill
	21417	Canadair CT-133 Silver Star	Yorkshire Air Museum, Elvington
	23140	Canadair CL-13 Sabre [AX] <rf>	Midland Air Museum, Coventry
	23380	Canadair CL-13 Sabre <rf>	Privately owned, Haverigg
	FH153	Noorduyn AT-16 Harvard IIB (G-BBHK) [58]	Privately owned, Hullavington
	FJ777	Boeing-Stearman PT-17D Kaydet (41-8689/G-BIXN)	Privately owned, Rendcomb
	KN448	Douglas Dakota IV <ff>	Science Museum, South Kensington
	CHINA		
	61762	Nanchang CJ-6A Chujiao (G-CGFS) [72]	Privately owned, Seething
	2632016	Nanchang CJ-6A Chujiao (G-BXZB) (also wears *2632019*)	Privately owned, Hibaldstow
	2751219	Nanchang CJ-6A Chujiao (G-BVVG) [68]	Privately owned, Fishburn
	CZECH REPUBLIC		
	0219	Mil Mi-24D (340219)	*Sold to The Netherlands, 2010*
	3677	Letov S-103 (MiG-15bisSB) (613677)	Royal Scottish Mus'm of Flight, E Fortune
	3794	Letov S-102 (MiG-15) (623794) (starboard side only, painted in Polish marks as 1972 on port side)	Norfolk & Suffolk Avn Museum, Flixton
	9147	Mil Mi-4	The Helicopter Museum, Weston-super-Mare
	JT-10	VS361 Spitfire FR IXE (SL633/G-CZAF)	*Sold as N633VS, August 2010*
	DENMARK		
	A-011	SAAB A-35XD Draken	Privately owned, Westhoughton, Lancs
	AR-107	SAAB S-35XD Draken	Newark Air Museum, Winthorpe
	E-419	Hawker Hunter F51 (G-9-441)	North-East Aircraft Museum, Usworth
	E-420	Hawker Hunter F51 (G-9-442)	Privately owned, Walton-on-Thames
	E-421	Hawker Hunter F51 (G-9-443)	Brooklands Museum, Weybridge
	E-423	Hawker Hunter F51 (G-9-444)	Privately owned, Enstone
	E-424	Hawker Hunter F51 (G-9-445)	Aeroventure, Doncaster
	ET-272	Hawker Hunter T7 <ff>	Boulton Paul Association, Wolverhampton
	ET-273	Hawker Hunter T7 <ff>	*Repainted in Dutch marks as N-302*
	K-682	Douglas C-47A Skytrain (OY-BPB)	Foreningen For Flyvende Mus, Vaerlose, Denmark

Serial	Type (code/other identity)	Owner/operator, location or fate	Notes
L-866	Consolidated PBY-6A Catalina (8466M)	RAF Museum, Cosford	
P-129	DHC-1 Chipmunk 22 (OY-ATO)	Privately owned, Roskilde, Denmark	
R-756	Lockheed F-104G Starfighter	Midland Air Museum, Coventry	
S-881	Sikorsky S-55C	The Helicopter Museum, Weston-super-Mare	
S-882	Sikorsky S-55C	Paintball Adventure West, Lulsgate	
S-886	Sikorsky S-55C	Hamburger Hill Paintball, Marksbury, Somerset	
S-887	Sikorsky S-55C	The Helicopter Museum, Weston-super-Mare	
ECUADOR			
FAE 259	BAC Strikemaster 80A (G-UPPI) [T59]	Privately owned, Exeter	
EGYPT			
158	Heliopolis Gomhouria Mk 6	Privately owned, Breighton	
356	Heliopolis Gomhouria Mk 6	Privately owned, Breighton	
764	Mikoyan MiG-21SPS <ff>	Privately owned, Northampton	
773	WS61 Sea King 47 (WA.823)	RNAS Yeovilton Fire Section	
774	WS61 Sea King 47 (WA.822)	DCAE AESS, *HMS Sultan*, Gosport	
775	WS61 Sea King 47 (WA.824)	DCAE AESS, *HMS Sultan*, Gosport	
776	WS61 Sea King 47 (WA.825)	DCAE AESS, *HMS Sultan*, Gosport	
0446	Mikoyan MiG-21UM <ff>	Thameside Aviation Museum, Tilbury	
7907	Sukhoi Su-7 <ff>	Robertsbridge Aviation Society, Mayfield	
FINLAND			
GN-101	Folland Gnat F1 (XK741)	Midland Air Museum, Coventry	
VI-3	Valtion Viima 2 (OO-EBL)	Privately owned, Brasschaat, Belgium	
FRANCE			
1/4513	Spad XIII <R> (G-BFYO/*S3398*)	American Air Museum, Duxford	
37	Nord 3400 (G-ZARA) [MAB]	Privately owned, Swanton Morley	
67	SNCAN 1101 Noralpha (F-GMCY) [CY]	Privately owned, la Ferté-Alais, France	
70	Dassault Mystère IVA	Midland Air Museum, Coventry	
78	Nord 3202B-1 (G-BIZK)	Privately owned, Little Snoring	
79	Dassault Mystère IVA [2-EG]	Norfolk & Suffolk Avn Museum, Flixton	
82	Curtiss Hawk 75 (G-CCVH)	The Fighter Collection, Duxford	
82	NA T-28D Fennec (F-AZKG)	Privately owned, Strasbourg, France	
83	Dassault Mystère IVA [8-MS]	Newark Air Museum, Winthorpe	
83	Morane-Saulnier MS.733 Alcyon (F-AZKS)	Privately owned, Montlucon, France	
84	Dassault Mystère IVA [8-NF]	Lashenden Air Warfare Museum, Headcorn	
85	Dassault Mystère IVA [8-MV]	Cold War Jets Collection, Bruntingthorpe	
104	MH1521M Broussard (F-GHFG) [307-FG]	Privately owned, Montceau-les-Mines, France	
105	Nord N2501F Noratlas (F-AZVM) [62-SI]	Le Noratlas de Provence, Marseilles, France	
106	MH1521M Broussard (F-GKJT) [33-JT]	Privately owned, Montceau-les-Mines, France	
108	MH1521M Broussard (F-BNEX) [50S9]	Privately owned, Lelystad, The Netherlands	
108	SO1221 Djinn (FR108) [CDL]	The Helicopter Museum, Weston-super-Mare	
121	Dassault Mystère IVA [8-MY]	City of Norwich Aviation Museum	
128	Morane-Saulnier MS.733 Alcyon (F-BMMY)	Privately owned, St Cyr, France	
143	Morane-Saulnier MS.733 Alcyon (G-MSAL)	Privately owned, Spanhoe	
146	Dassault Mystère IVA [8-MC]	North-East Aircraft Museum, Usworth	
156	SNCAN Stampe SV-4B (G-NIFE)	Privately owned, Gloucester	
157	Morane-Saulnier MS.230 Et2 (G-AVEB) [M-573,01]	Privately owned, Didcot	
208	MH1521C1 Broussard (G-YYYY) [IR]	Privately owned, Eggesford	
261	MH1521M Broussard (F-GIBN) [30-QA]	Privately owned, Rotterdam, The Netherlands	
282	Dassault MD311 Flamant (F-AZFX) [316-KY]	Memorial Flt Association, la Ferté-Alais, France	
290	Dewoitine D27 (F-AZJD)	Les Casques de Cuir, la Ferté-Alais, France	
316	MH1521M Broussard (F-GGKR) [315-SN]	Privately owned, Lognes, France	
318	Dassault Mystère IVA [8-NY]	Dumfries & Galloway Avn Mus, Dumfries	

Notes	*Serial*	*Type (code/other identity)*	*Owner/operator, location or fate*
	319	Dassault Mystère IVA [8-ND]	Rebel Air Museum, Andrewsfield
	319	Grumman TBM-3E Avenger (HB-RDG) [4F.6]	Privately owned, Lausanne, Switzerland
	354	Morane-Saulnier MS315E-D2 (G-BZNK)	Privately owned, Hemswell
	394	SNCAN Stampe SV-4C (G-BIMO)	Privately owned, White Waltham
	538	Dassault Mirage IIIE [3-QH]	Yorkshire Air Museum, Elvington
	17473	Lockheed T-33A Shooting Star	*Repainted in Canadian marks*
	42157	NA F-100D Super Sabre [11-ML]	North-East Aircraft Museum, Usworth
	54439	Lockheed T-33A Shooting Star (55-4439) [WI]	North-East Aircraft Museum, Usworth
	63938	NA F-100F Super Sabre [11-EZ]	Lashenden Air Warfare Museum, Headcorn
	121748	Grumman F8F-2P Bearcat (F-AZRJ) [5834/P]	Privately owned, Anemasse, France
	125716	Douglas AD-4N Skyraider (F-AZFN) [22-DG]	Privately owned, Mélun, France
	127002	Douglas AD-4NA Skyraider (F-AZHK) [20-LN]	Privately owned, Avignon, France
	133704	CV F4U-5NL Corsair (124541/F-AZYS) [14.F.6]	Meier Motors, Bremgarten, Germany
	517692	NA T-28S Fennec (G-TROY) [142]	Privately owned, Duxford
	18-5395	Piper L-18C Super Cub (52-2436/G-CUBJ) [CDG]	Privately owned, Old Warden
	51-7545	NA T-28S Fennec (N14113)	Privately owned, Duxford
	C850	Salmson 2A2 <R>	Barton Aviation Heritage Society, Barton
	MS824	Morane-Saulnier Type N <R> (G-AWBU)	Privately owned, Booker
	N1977	Nieuport Scout 17/23 <R> (N1723/G-BWMJ) [8]	Privately owned, Popham
	GERMANY		
	-	Fieseler Fi103R-IV (V-1) (BAPC 91)	Lashenden Air Warfare Museum, Headcorn
	-	Fokker Dr1 Dreidekker <R> (BAPC 88)	FAA Museum stored, RNAS Yeovilton
	-	Messerschmitt Bf109 <R> (6357/BAPC 74) [6]	Kent Battle of Britain Museum, Hawkinge
	1	Flug Werk FW190A-8/N (990013/F-AZZJ)	*Crashed 12 June 2010, Hyères, France*
	1	Hispano HA 1.112M1L Buchón (G-AWHE)	Privately owned, Duxford
	1	Messerschmitt Bf109G <R> (BAPC 240)	Yorkshire Air Museum, Elvington
	2	Messerschmitt Bf109G-10 (151591/D-FDME)	*Repainted as 3, 2010*
	3	Messerschmitt Bf109G-10 (D-FDME)	Messerschmitt Stiftung, Manching, Germany
	3	SNCAN 1101 Noralpha (G-BAYV)	Barton Aviation Heritage Society, Barton
	6	Messerschmitt Bf109G-2/Trop (10639/8478M/G-USTV)	RAF Museum, Hendon
	7	Messerschmitt Bf109G-4 (D-FWME)	Messerschmitt Stiftung, Manching, Germany
	8	Focke-Wulf Fw190 <R> (G-WULF)	Privately owned, Halfpenny Green
	9	Focke-Wulf Fw190 <R> (G-CCFW)	Privately owned, Little Rissington
	10	Hispano HA 1.112M1L Buchón (C4K-102/G-BWUE)	Historic Flying Ltd, Duxford
	14	Hispano HA 1.112M1L Buchón (G-AWHE)	*Repainted as 1, 2010*
	14	Messerschmitt Bf109 <R> (BAPC 67)	Kent Battle of Britain Museum, Hawkinge
	14	Nord 1002 (G-ETME)	Privately owned, White Waltham
	14	SNCAN 1101 Noralpha (G-BSMD)	Privately owned, Prestwick
	87	Heinkel He111 <R> <ff>	Privately owned, East Kirkby
	152/17	Fokker Dr1 Dreidekker <R> (F-AZPQ)	Les Casques de Cuir, la Ferté-Alais, France
	152/17	Fokker Dr1 Dreidekker <R> (G-BVGZ)	Privately owned, Breighton

Serial	Type (code/other identity)	Owner/operator, location or fate	Notes
157/18	Fokker D.VIII <R> (BAPC 239)	Norfolk & Suffolk Air Museum, Flixton	
210/16	Fokker EIII (BAPC 56)	Science Museum, South Kensington	
403/17	Fokker Dr1 Dreidekker <R> (G-CDXR)	Privately owned, Popham	
416/15	Fokker EIII <R> (G-GSAL)	Privately owned, Aston Down	
422/15	Fokker EIII <R> (G-AVJO)	Privately owned, Booker	
422/15	Fokker EIII <R> (G-FOKR)	Privately owned, Damyn's Hall, Essex	
425/17	Fokker Dr1 Dreidekker <R> (BAPC 133)	Kent Battle of Britain Museum, Hawkinge	
477/17	Fokker Dr1 Dreidekker <R> (G-FOKK)	Privately owned, Sywell	
556/17	Fokker Dr1 Dreidekker <R> (G-CFHY)	Privately owned, Tibenham	
626/8	Fokker DVII <R> (N6268)	Privately owned, Booker	
764	Mikoyan MiG-21SPS <ff>	Privately owned, Booker	
959	Mikoyan MiG-21SPS	Midland Air Museum, Coventry	
1190	Messerschmitt Bf109E-3 [4]	Imperial War Museum, Duxford	
1480	Messerschmitt Bf109 <R> (BAPC 66) [6]	Kent Battle of Britain Museum, Hawkinge	
1801/18	Bowers Fly Baby 1A (G-BNPV)	Privately owned, Chessington	
1803/18	Bowers Fly Baby 1A (G-BUYU)	Privately owned, Chessington	
1983	Messerschmitt Bf109E-3 (G-EMIL)	Privately owned, Colchester	
2100	Focke-Wulf Fw189A-1 (G-BZKY) [V7+1H]	Privately owned, Sandown	
3523	Messerschmitt Bf109E-7	*Sold to the US*	
4034	Messerschmitt Bf109E (G-CDTI)	*Currently not known*	
4101	Messerschmitt Bf109E-3 (DG200/8477M) [12]	RAF Museum, Hendon	
4477	CASA 1.131E Jungmann (G-RETA) [GD+EG]	The Shuttleworth Collection, Old Warden	
6234	Junkers Ju87R-4 (G-STUK)	*Currently not known*	
7198/18	LVG CVI (G-AANJ/9239M)	RAF Museum Restoration Centre, Cosford	
8417/18	Fokker DVII (9207M)	RAF Museum, Hendon	
12802	Antonov An-2T (D-FOFM)	Historische Flugzeuge, Grossenhain, Germany	
100143	Focke-Achgelis Fa330A-1	Imperial War Museum, Duxford	
100502	Focke-Achgelis Fa330A-1	Privately owned, Millom	
100503	Focke-Achgelis Fa330A-1 (8469M)	RAF Museum, Cosford	
100509	Focke-Achgelis Fa330A-1	Science Museum, stored Wroughton	
100545	Focke-Achgelis Fa330A-1	FAA Museum, stored RNAS Yeovilton	
100549	Focke-Achgelis Fa330A-1	Lashenden Air Warfare Museum, Headcorn	
110451	Fieseler Fi156D Storch (G-STOR)	Privately owned, Surrey	
112372	Messerschmitt Me262A-2a (AM.51/VK893/8482M) [4]	RAF Museum, Hendon	
120076	Heinkel He162A-2 Salamander (VH523/AM.59) [4]	Aero Vintage, Westfield, Sussex	
120227	Heinkel He162A-2 Salamander (VN679/AM.65/8472M) [2]	RAF Museum, Hendon	
120235	Heinkel He162A-1 Salamander (AM.68)	Imperial War Museum, Lambeth	
191316	Messerschmitt Me163B Komet	Science Museum, South Kensington	
191454	Messerschmitt Me163B Komet <R> (BAPC 271)	The Shuttleworth Collection, Old Warden	
191461	Messerschmitt Me163B Komet (191614/8481M) [14]	RAF Museum, Cosford	
191659	Messerschmitt Me163B Komet (8480M) [15]	Royal Scottish Mus'm of Flight, E Fortune	
211028	Focke-Wulf Fw190D-9 (G-DORA)	*Sold to the US, May 2010*	
280020	Flettner Fl282/B-V20 Kolibri (frame only)	Midland Air Museum, Coventry	
360043	Junkers Ju88R-1 (PJ876/8475M) [D5+EV]	RAF Museum, Hendon	
420430	Messerschmitt Me410A-1/U2 (AM.72/8483M) [3U+CC]	RAF Museum, Cosford	
475081	Fieseler Fi156C-7 Storch (VP546/AM.101/7362M) [GM+AK]	RAF Museum, Cosford	

Historic Aircraft in Overseas Markings

Notes	*Serial*	*Type (code/other identity)*	*Owner/operator, location or fate*
	494083	Junkers Ju87D-3 (8474M) [RI+JK]	RAF Museum, Hendon
	500453	Messerschmitt Me262A-1a (N94503)	*To the US, 2008*
	584219	Focke-Wulf Fw190F-8/U1 (AM.29/8470M) [38]	RAF Museum, Hendon
	701152	Heinkel He111H-23 (8471M) [NT+SL]	RAF Museum, Hendon
	730301	Messerschmitt Bf110G-4 (AM.34/8479M) [D5+RL]	RAF Museum, Hendon
	733682	Focke-Wulf Fw190A-8/R7 (AM.75/9211M)	Imperial War Museum, Lambeth
	980554	Flug Werk FW190A-8/N (G-FWAB)	Meier Motors, Bremgarten, Germany
	2+1	Focke-Wulf Fw190 <R> (G-SYFW) [7334]	Privately owned, Wickenby
	17+TF	CASA 1.133C Jungmeister (G-BZTJ)	Privately owned, Turweston
	22+35	Lockheed F-104G Starfighter	Privately owned, Bruntingthorpe
	22+57	Lockheed F-104G Starfighter	Privately owned, Spanhoe
	23.02	Albatros B.II <R> (D-EKGH)	Historischer Flugzeugbau, Fürstenwalde, Germany
	28+08	Aero L-39ZO Albatros (142/28+04)	Pinewood Studios, Bucks
	2E+RA	Fieseler Fi-156C-3 Storch (F-AZRA)	Amicale J-B Salis, la Ferté-Alais, France
	4+1	Focke-Wulf Fw190 <R> (G-BSLX)	Privately owned, Norwich
	4V+GH	Amiot AAC1/Ju52 (Port.AF 6316) [9]	Imperial War Museum, Duxford
	6G+ED	Slepcev Storch (G-BZOB) [5447]	Privately owned, Croydon, Cambs
	58+89	Dornier Do28D-2 Skyservant (D-ICDY)	Privately owned, Uetersen, Germany
	80+39	MBB Bo.105M	Privately owned, Coney Park, Leeds
	80+40	MBB Bo.105M	Privately owned, Coney Park, Leeds
	80+55	MBB Bo.105M	Lufthansa Resource Technical Training, Kemble
	80+77	MBB Bo.105M	Luftwaffe Resource Technical Training, Kemble
	81+00	MBB Bo.105M (D-HZYR)	The Helicopter Museum, Weston-super-Mare
	96+21	Mil Mi-24D (406)	Imperial War Museum, Duxford
	96+26	Mil Mi-24D (421)	The Helicopter Museum, Weston-super-Mare
	97+04	Putzer Elster B (G-APVF)	Privately owned, Wickenby
	98+14	Sukhoi Su-22M-4	Hawker Hunter Aviation Ltd, stored Scampton
	99+24	NA OV-10B Bronco (F-AZKM)	Privately owned, Montelimar, France
	99+32	NA OV-10B Bronco (G-BZGK)	Privately owned, Rotterdam, The Netherlands
	AZ+JU	CASA 3.52L (F-AZJU)	Amicale J-B Salis, la Ferté-Alais, France
	BU+CC	CASA 1.131E Jungmann (G-BUCC)	Privately owned, Sandown
	CF+HF	Morane-Saulnier MS502 (EI-AUY)	Imperial War Museum, Duxford
	D5397/17	Albatros DVA <R> (G-BFXL)	FAA Museum, stored RNAS Yeovilton
	DM+BK	Morane-Saulnier MS505 (G-BPHZ)	Historic Aircraft Collection, Duxford
	ES+BH	Messerschmitt Bf108B-2 (D-ESBH)	Messerschmitt Stiftung, Manching, Germany
	FI+S	Morane-Saulnier MS505 (G-BIRW)	Royal Scottish Mus'm of Flight, E Fortune
	FM+BB	Messerschmitt Bf109G-6 (D-FMBB)	Messerschmitt Stiftung, Manching, Germany
	FW+WC	Flug Werk Fw190A-8/N (D-FWWC)	Flug Werk, Manching, Germany
	GL+SU	Bücker Bü1181B-1 Bestmann (D-EQXE)	Quax Flieger, Hamm, Germany
	GM+AI	Fieseler Fi156A Storch (2088/G-STCH)	Privately owned, Old Warden
	LG+03	Bücker Bü133C Jungmeister (G-AEZX)	Privately owned, Milden

Serial	*Type (code/other identity)*	*Owner/operator, location or fate*	*Notes*
NJ+C11	Nord 1002 (G-ATBG)	Privately owned, Audley End	
NQ+NR	Klemm Kl35D (D-EQXD)	Quax Flieger, Hamm, Germany	
NV+KG	Focke-Wulf Fw44J Stieglitz (D-ENAY)	Quax Flieger, Hamm, Germany	
S4+A07	CASA 1.131E Jungmann (G-BWHP)	Privately owned, Yarcombe, Devon	
S5+B06	CASA 1.131E Jungmann 2000 (G-BSFB)	Privately owned, Old Buckenham	
GHANA			
G-102	SA122 Bulldog	Privately owned, stored Salisbury	
G-108	SA122 Bulldog (G-BCUP)	Privately owned, stored Salisbury	
GREECE			
52-6541	Republic F-84F Thunderflash [541]	North-East Aircraft Museum, Usworth	
63-8418	Northrop F-5A	Martin-Baker Ltd, Chalgrove, Fire Section	
HONG KONG			
HKG-5	SA128 Bulldog (G-BULL)	Privately owned, Old Sarum	
HKG-6	SA128 Bulldog (G-BPCL)	Privately owned, North Weald	
HKG-11	Slingsby T.67M Firefly 200 (G-BYRY)	Privately owned, Oxford	
HKG-13	Slingsby T.67M Firefly 200 (G-BXKW)	Privately owned, Spanhoe	
HUNGARY			
501	Mikoyan MiG-21PF	Imperial War Museum, Duxford	
503	Mikoyan MiG-21SMT (G-BRAM)	RAF Museum, Cosford	
INDIA			
Q497	EE Canberra T4 (WE191) (fuselage)	Dumfries & Galloway Avn Mus, Dumfries	
HA561	Hawker Tempest II (MW743)	Privately owned, stored Wickenby	
IN609	BAe Sea Harrier FRS51	*Returned to India, 3 February 2009*	
INDONESIA			
LL-5313	BAe Hawk T53	BAE Systems, Brough, on display	
IRAQ			
333	DH115 Vampire T55 <ff>	Aeroventure, Doncaster	
ITALY			
MM5701	Fiat CR42 (BT474/8468M) [13-95]	RAF Museum, Hendon	
MM52801	Fiat G46-3B (G-BBII) [4-97]	Privately owned, Sandown	
MM53692	CCF T-6G Texan	RAeS Medway Branch, Rochester	
MM53774	Fiat G59-4B (I-MRSV) [181]	Privately owned, Parma, Italy	
MM54099	NA T-6G Texan (G-BRBC) [RR-56]	Privately owned, Chigwell	
MM54532	SIAI-Marchetti SF.260AM (G-ITAF) [70-42]	Privately owned, Leicester	
MM57247	SIAI-Marchetti SM.1019 (G-SIMA)	*Sold to the US, May 2010*	
MM81205	Agusta A109A-2 SEM [GF-128]	The Helicopter Museum, Weston-super-Mare	
MM54-2372	Piper L-21B Super Cub	Privately owned, Kesgrave, Suffolk	
JAPAN			
-	Yokosuka MXY 7 Ohka II (BAPC 159)	Defence School, Chattenden	
24	Kawasaki Ki100-1B (8476M/BAPC 83)	RAF Museum, Hendon	
997	Yokosuka MXY 7 Ohka II (8485M/BAPC 98)	Museum of Science & Industry, Manchester	
5439	Mitsubishi Ki46-III (8484M/BAPC 84)	RAF Museum, Cosford	
15-1585	Yokosuka MXY 7 Ohka II (BAPC 58)	Science Museum, at FAA Museum, RNAS Yeovilton	
I-13	Yokosuka MXY 7 Ohka II (8486M/BAPC 99)	RAF Museum, Cosford	
Y2-176	Mitsubishi A6M3-2 Zero (3685) [76]	Imperial War Museum, Duxford	

Historic Aircraft in Overseas Markings

Notes	*Serial*	*Type (code/other identity)*	*Owner/operator, location or fate*
	JORDAN		
	408	SA125 Bulldog (G-BDIN)	Privately owned, Lasham
	KUWAIT		
	113	BAC Strikemaster 80A (G-CFBK) [D]	Privately owned, North Weald
	MYANMAR		
	UB441	VS361 Spitfire IX (ML119/G-SDNI)	Privately owned, Sandown
	THE NETHERLANDS		
	16-218	Consolidated PBY-5A Catalina (2459/PH-PBY)	Neptune Association, Lelystad, The Netherlands
	174	Fokker S-11 Instructor (E-31/G-BEPV) [K]	Privately owned, Spanhoe
	179	Fokker S-11 Instructor (PH-ACG) [K]	Privately owned, Lelystad, The Netherlands
	197	Fokker S-11 Instructor (PH-GRY) [K]	KLu Historic Flt, Gilze-Rijen, The Netherlands
	204	Lockheed SP-2H Neptune [V]	RAF Museum, Cosford
	A-12	DH82A Tiger Moth (PH-TYG)	Privately owned, Gilze-Rijen, The Netherlands
	B-64	Noorduyn AT-16 Harvard IIB (PH-LSK)	KLu Historic Flt, Gilze-Rijen, The Netherlands
	B-71	Noorduyn AT-16 Harvard IIB (PH-MLM)	KLu Historic Flt, Gilze-Rijen, The Netherlands
	B-118	Noorduyn AT-16 Harvard IIB (PH-IIB)	KLu Historic Flt, Gilze-Rijen, The Netherlands
	B-182	Noorduyn AT-16 Harvard IIB (PH-TBR)	KLu Historic Flt, Gilze-Rijen, The Netherlands
	E-14	Fokker S-11 Instructor (PH-AFS)	Privately owned, Lelystad, The Netherlands
	E-15	Fokker S-11 Instructor (G-BIYU)	Privately owned, Bagby
	E-20	Fokker S-11 Instructor (PH-GRB)	Privately owned, Gilze-Rijen, The Netherlands
	E-27	Fokker S-11 Instructor (PH-HOL)	Privately owned, Lelystad, The Netherlands
	E-32	Fokker S-11 Instructor (PH-HOI)	Privately owned, Gilze-Rijen, The Netherlands
	E-36	Fokker S-11 Instructor (PH-ACG)	*Repainted as 179, 2008*
	E-39	Fokker S-11 Instructor (PH-HOG)	Privately owned, Lelystad, The Netherlands
	G-29	Beech D18S (PH-KHV)	KLu Historic Flt, Gilze-Rijen, The Netherlands
	H-98	VS509 Spitfire T9 (G-CCCA)	*Repainted in British marks as QV-I, May 2010*
	H-99	VS509 Spitfire T9 (G-ILDA)	*Repainted as SM520, June 2010*
	MH424	VS361 Spitfire LFIXC (MJ271/H-53)	Privately owned, Duxford
	MK732	VS361 Spitfire LFIXC (8633M/PH-OUQ) [3W-17]	KLu Historic Flt, Gilze-Rijen, The Netherlands
	N-202	Hawker Hunter F6 [10] <ff>	Privately owned, Stockport
	N-250	Hawker Hunter F6 (G-9-185) <ff>	Imperial War Museum, Duxford
	N-268	Hawker Hunter FGA78 (Qatar QA-10)	Yorkshire Air Museum, Elvington
	N-294	Hawker Hunter F6A (XF515/G-KAXF)	Stichting Hawker Hunter Foundation, Leeuwarden, The Netherlands
	N-302	Hawker Hunter T7 (ET-273/G-9-431) <ff>	Aeroventure, Doncaster
	N-315	Hawker Hunter T7 (comp XM121)	Privately owned, Netherley, Aberdeenshire
	N-321	Hawker Hunter T8C (G-BWGL)	Stichting Hawker Hunter Foundation, Leeuwarden, The Netherlands
	N5-149	NA B-25J Mitchell (44-29507/ *HD346*/PH-XXV) [232511]	KLu Historic Flt, Gilze-Rijen, The Netherlands
	R-18	Auster III (PH-NGK)	KLu Historic Flt, Gilze-Rijen, The Netherlands
	R-55	Piper L-18C Super Cub (52-2466/G-BLMI)	Privately owned, White Waltham
	R-109	Piper L-21B Super Cub (54-2337/PH-GAZ)	KLu Historic Flt, Gilze-Rijen, The Netherlands
	R-122	Piper L-21B Super Cub (54-2412/PH-PPW)	KLu Historic Flt, Gilze-Rijen, The Netherlands

Serial	Type (code/other identity)	Owner/operator, location or fate	Notes
R-124	Piper L-21B Super Cub (54-2414/PH-APA)	Privately owned, Eindhoven, The Netherlands	
R-137	Piper L-21B Super Cub (54-2427/PH-PSC)	Privately owned, Gilze-Rijen, The Netherlands	
R-151	Piper L-21B Super Cub (54-2441/G-BIYR)	Privately owned, Yarcombe, Devon	
R-156	Piper L-21B Super Cub (54-2446/G-ROVE)	Privately owned, Headcorn	
R-163	Piper L-21B Super Cub (54-2453/G-BIRH)	Privately owned, Hinton-in-the-Hedges	
R-167	Piper L-21B Super Cub (54-2457/G-LION)	Privately owned, Turweston, Bucks	
R-170	Piper L-21B Super Cub (52-6222/PH-ENJ)	Privately owned, Midden Zealand, The Netherlands	
R-177	Piper L-21B Super Cub (54-2467/PH-KNR)	KLu Historic Flt, Gilze-Rijen, The Netherlands	
R-181	Piper L-21B Super Cub (54-2471/PH-GAU)	Privately owned, Gilze-Rijen, The Netherlands	
R-345	Piper J-3C Cub (PH-UCS)	Privately owned, Hilversum, The Netherlands	
S-9	DHC2 L-20A Beaver (55-4585/PH-DHC)	KLu Historic Flt, Gilze-Rijen, The Netherlands	
NEW ZEALAND			
NZ3909	WS Wasp HAS1 (XT782/G-KANZ)	Kennet Aviation, stored North Weald	
NZ6361	BAC Strikemaster 87 (OJ5/G-BXFP)	Privately owned, Chalgrove	
NORTH KOREA			
-	WSK Lim-2 (MiG-15) (01420/G-BMZF)	FAA Museum, RNAS Yeovilton	
NORTH VIETNAM			
1211	WSK Lim-5 (MiG-17F) (G-MIGG)	Privately owned, North Weald	
NORWAY			
848	Piper L-18C Super Cub (LN-ACL) [FA-N]	Privately owned, Norway	
56321	SAAB S91B Safir (G-BKPY)	Newark Air Museum, Winthorpe	
PX-M	DH115 Vampire T55 (LN-DHZ)	Privately owned, Rygge, Norway	
OMAN			
425	BAC Strikemaster 82A (G-SOAF)	Privately owned, Hawarden	
801	Hawker Hunter T66B <ff>	Privately owned, Exeter	
801	Hawker Hunter T66B <rf>	Privately owned, Hawarden	
853	Hawker Hunter FR10 (XF426)	RAF Museum, Hendon	
POLAND			
05	WSK SM-2 (Mi-2) (S2-03006)	The Helicopter Museum, Weston-super-Mare	
309	WSK SBLim-2A (MiG-15UTI) <ff>	R Scottish Mus'm of Flight, stored Granton	
408	WSK-PZL Mielec TS-11 Iskra (1H-0408)	*Repainted as 1706, 2010*	
458	Mikoyan MiG-23ML (04 red/024003607)	Newark Air Museum, Winthorpe	
618	Mil Mi-8P (10618)	The Helicopter Museum, Weston-super-Mare	
1018	WSK-PZL Mielec TS-11 Iskra (1H-1018/G-ISKA)	Cold War Jets Collection, Bruntingthorpe	
1120	WSK Lim-2 (MiG-15bis)	RAF Museum, Cosford	
1706	WSK-PZL Mielec TS-11 Iskra (1H-0408)	Midland Air Museum, Coventry	
1972	Letov S-102 (MiG-15) (623794) (port side only, painted in Czech marks as 3794 on starboard side)	Norfolk & Suffolk Avn Museum, Flixton	
PORTUGAL			
85	Isaacs Fury II (G-BTPZ)	Privately owned, Ormskirk	
1350	OGMA/DHC1 Chipmunk T20 (G-CGAO)	Privately owned, Spanhoe	

Notes	Serial	Type (code/other identity)	Owner/operator, location or fate
	1360	OGMA/DHC1 Chipmunk T20 (G-BYYU) (fuselage)	Privately owned, Little Stoughton
	1365	OGMA/DHC1 Chipmunk T20 (G-DHPM)	Privately owned, Sywell
	1367	OGMA/DHC1 Chipmunk T20 (G-UANO)	Privately owned, Spanhoe
	1372	OGMA/DHC1 Chipmunk T20 (HB-TUM)	Privately owned, Switzerland
	1373	OGMA/DHC1 Chipmunk T20 (G-CBJG)	Privately owned, Winwick, Cambs
	1375	OGMA/DHC1 Chipmunk T20 (F-AZJV)	Privately owned, Valenciennes, France
	1377	DHC1 Chipmunk 22 (G-BARS)	Privately owned, Yeovilton
	1741	CCF T-6J Texan (G-HRVD)	Privately owned, Bruntingthorpe
	1747	CCF T-6J Texan (20385/G-BGPB)	The Aircraft Restoration Co, Duxford
	3303	MH1521M Broussard (G-CBGL)	Privately owned, Bruntingthorpe
	QATAR		
	QA12	Hawker Hunter FGA78 <ff>	Privately owned, Cwmbran
	QP30	WS Lynx Mk 28 (G-BFDV/TD 013)	DCAE SEAE, Arborfield
	QP31	WS Lynx Mk 28	Vector Aerospace Fleetlands Apprentice School
	QP32	WS Lynx Mk 28 (TAD 016)	DCAE SEAE, Arborfield
	ROMANIA		
	29	LET L-29 Delfin <ff>	Privately owned, Shropshire
	42	LET L-29 Delfin	Privately owned, Catshill, Worcs
	47	LET L-29 Delfin	Privately owned, Ashton-under-Lyne
	53	LET L-29 Delfin (99954)	Privately owned, Bruntingthorpe
	RUSSIA (& FORMER SOVIET UNION)		
	-	LET L-29S Delfin (491273/YL-PAG)	Privately owned, Breighton
	-	Mil Mi-24D (3532461715415)	Privately owned, Dunsfold
	-	Mil Mi-24D (3532464505029)	Midland Air Museum, Coventry
	-	Yakovlev Yak-52 (811202/YL-CBI)	Privately owned, Hawarden
	1 w	SPP Yak C-11 (G-BZMY)	Privately owned, Little Gransden
	01 y	Yakovlev Yak-52 (9311709/G-YKSZ)	Privately owned, White Waltham
	03 bl	Yakovlev Yak-55M (910103/RA-01274)	Privately owned, Halfpenny Green
	03 w	Yakovlev Yak-18A (1160403/G-CEIB)	Privately owned, Wickenby
	03 w	Yakovlev Yak-52 (899803/G-YAKR)	Privately owned, North Weald
	05 r	Yakovlev Yak-50 (832507/YL-CBH)	Privately owned, Hawarden
	5 w	Yakovlev Yak-3UA (0470204/D-FYGJ)	Privately owned, Sleap
	07 y	WSK SM-1 (Mi-1) (Polish AF 2007)	The Helicopter Museum, Weston-super-Mare
	07 y	Yakovlev Yak-18M (G-BMJY)	Privately owned, East Garston, Bucks
	07 r	Yakovlev Yak-52 (9011107/G-HYAK)	Privately owned, Exeter
	09 y	Yakovlev Yak-52 (9411809/G-BVMU)	Privately owned, Shipdham
	9 w	SPP Yak C-11 (1701139/G-OYAK)	Privately owned, Little Gransden
	9 y	Polikarpov Po-2 (0094/G-BSSY)	The Shuttleworth Collection, Old Warden
	10 si	Yakovlev Yak-52 (9111205/G-YAKF)	Privately owned, White Waltham
	10 y	Yakovlev Yak-50 (801810/G-BTZB)	Privately owned, Lee-on-Solent
	10 y	Yakovlev Yak-52 (822710/G-CBMD)	Privately owned, Headcorn
	11 y	SPP Yak C-11 (G-YCII)	Privately owned, Woodchurch, Kent
	12 r	LET L-29 Delfin (194555/ES-YLM/G-DELF)	Privately owned, Manston
	15 w	SPP Yak C-11 (170103/D-FYAK)	Classic Aviation Company, Hannover, Germany

Serial	*Type (code/other identity)*	*Owner/operator, location or fate*	*Notes*
18 r	LET L-29S Delfin (591771/YL-PAF)	Privately owned, Hawarden	
20 w	Lavochkin La-11	The Fighter Collection, Duxford	
20 bl	Yakovlev Yak-52 (790404/YL-CBJ)	Privately owned, Hawarden	
21 w	Yakovlev Yak-3UA (0470203/G-CDBJ)	Privately owned, Headcorn	
21 w	Yakovlev Yak-9UM (0470403/D-FENK)	Privately owned, Magdeburg, Germany	
23 y	Bell P-39Q Airacobra (44-2911)	Privately owned, Sussex	
23 w	Mikoyan MiG-27D (83712515040)	Privately owned, Hawarden	
26 bl	Yakovlev Yak-52 (9111306/G-BVXK)	Privately owned, White Waltham	
27 w	Yakovlev Yak-3UTI-PW (9/04623/F-AZIM)	Privately owned, la Ferté-Alais, France	
27 r	Yakovlev Yak-52 (9111307/G-YAKX)	Privately owned, Popham	
31 bl	Yakovlev Yak-52 (9111311/G-YAKV)	Privately owned, Rendcomb	
33 r	Yakovlev Yak-50 (853206/G-YAKZ)	Privately owned, White Waltham	
33 w	Yakovlev Yak-52 (899915/G-YAKH)	Privately owned, White Waltham	
35 r	Sukhoi Su-17M-3 (25102)	Privately owned, Hawarden	
36 w	LET/Yak C-11 (171101/G-KYAK)	Privately owned, North Weald	
36 r	Yakovlev Yak-52 (9111604/G-IUII)	Privately owned, North Weald	
42 w	Yakovlev Yak-52 (888911/G-CBRU)	Privately owned, Enstone	
43 bl	Yakovlev Yak-52 (877601/G-BWSV)	Privately owned, North Weald	
48 bl	Yakovlev Yak-52 (9111413/G-CBSN)	Privately owned, Manston	
49 r	Yakovlev Yak-50 (822305/G-YAKU)	Privately owned, Henstridge	
50 bk	Yakovlev Yak-50 (812101/G-CBPM)	Privately owned, High Cross	
50 gy	Yakovlev Yak-52 (9111415/G-CBRW)	Meier Motors, Bremgarten, Germany	
51 r	LET L-29 Delfin (893019/G-BZNT)	Privately owned, Caernarfon	
51 y	Yakovlev Yak-50 (812004/G-BWYK)	Privately owned, West Meon, Hants	
52 w	Yakovlev Yak-52 (9612001/G-CCJK)	Privately owned, White Waltham	
52 y	Yakovlev Yak-52 (878202/G-BWVR)	Privately owned, Barton	
54 r	Sukhoi Su-17M (69004)	Privately owned, Hawarden	
55 y	Yakovlev Yak-52 (9111505/G-BVOK)	Privately owned, Shoreham	
56 r	Yakovlev Yak-52 (811504)	Privately owned, Hawarden	
61 r	Yakovlev Yak-50 (842710/G-YAKM)	Privately owned, Henstridge	
66 r	Yakovlev Yak-52 (855905/G-YAKN)	Privately owned, Henstridge	
67 r	Yakovlev Yak-52 (822013/G-CBSL)	Privately owned, Church Fenton	
69 r	Hawker Hunter FGA9 (8839M/XG194)	Wattisham Airfield Museum	
69 bl	Yakovlev Yak-52 (899413/G-XYAK)	Privately owned, Old Buckenham	
69 y	Yakovlev Yak-52 (888712/G-CCSU)	Privately owned, Germany	
71 r	Mikoyan MiG-27K (61912507006)	Newark Air Museum, Winthorpe	
74 w	Yakovlev Yak-52 (877404/ G-LAOK) [JA-74, IV-62]	Privately owned, Tollerton	
93 w	Yakovlev Yak-50 (853001/G-JYAK) [R]	Privately owned, North Weald	
100 bl	Yakovlev Yak-52 (866904/G-YAKI)	Privately owned, Popham	

Notes	Serial	Type (code/other identity)	Owner/operator, location or fate
	100 w	Yakovlev Yak-3M (0470107/D-FJAK)	Meier Motors, Bremgarten, Germany
	139 y	Yakovlev Yak-52 (833810/G-BWOD)	Privately owned, Sywell
	526 bk	Mikoyan MiG-29 (2960725887) <ff>	Fenland & West Norfolk Aviation Museum, Wisbech
	1342	Yakovlev Yak-1 (G-BTZD)	Privately owned, Westfield, Sussex
	1870710	Ilyushin Il-2 (G-BZVW)	Privately owned, Wickenby
	1878576	Ilyushin Il-2 (G-BZVX)	Privately owned, Wickenby
	1-12	Yakovlev Yak-52 (9011013/RA-02293)	Privately owned, Halfpenny Green
	(RK858)	VS361 Spitfire LFIX (G-CGJE)	The Fighter Collection, Duxford
	(SM639)	VS361 Spitfire LFIX	Privately owned, Catfield
	SAUDI ARABIA		
	1104	BAC Strikemaster 80 (G-SMAS)	Privately owned, Hawarden
	1112	BAC Strikemaster 80 (G-FLYY)	Privately owned, Hawarden
	1120	BAC Strikemaster 80A (G-RSAF)	Privately owned, Hawarden
	1130	BAC Strikemaster 80A (G-VPER)	Privately owned, Exeter
	1133	BAC Strikemaster 80A (G-BESY)	Imperial War Museum, Duxford
	53-686	BAC Lightning F53 (G-AWON/ZF592)	City of Norwich Aviation Museum
	55-713	BAC Lightning T55 (ZF598) [C]	Midland Air Museum, Coventry
	SINGAPORE		
	311	BAC Strikemaster 84 (G-MXPH)	Privately owned, North Weald
	323	BAC Strikemaster 81 (N21419)	Privately owned, stored Hawarden
	SOUTH AFRICA		
	91	Westland Wasp HAS1 (pod)	Privately owned, Oaksey Park
	92	Westland Wasp HAS1 (G-BYCX)	Privately owned, Chiseldon
	221	DH115 Vampire T55 <ff>	Privately owned, Hemel Hempstead
	6130	Lockheed Ventura II (AJ469)	RAF Museum, stored Cosford
	7429	NA AT-6D Harvard III (D-FASS)	Privately owned, Aachen, Germany
	SOUTH VIETNAM		
	24550	Cessna L-19E Bird Dog (G-PDOG) [GP]	Privately owned, Lincs
	SPAIN		
	B.2I-27	CASA 2.111B (He111H-16) (B.2I-103)	Imperial War Museum, stored Duxford
	C.4E-88	Messerschmitt Bf109E	Privately owned, East Garston, Bucks
	E.3B-143	CASA 1.131E Jungmann (G-JUNG)	Privately owned, White Waltham
	E.3B-153	CASA 1.131E Jungmann (G-BPTS) [781-75]	Privately owned, Duxford
	E.3B-350	CASA 1.131E Jungmann (G-BHPL) [05-97]	Privately owned, Henstridge
	(E.3B-369)	CASA 1.131E Jungmann (G-BPDM) [781-32]	Privately owned, Heighington
	E.3B-494	CASA 1.131E Jungmann (G-CDLC) [81-47]	Privately owned, Chiseldon
	E.3B-521	CASA 1.131E Jungmann [781-3]	RAF Museum, Hendon
	E.18-2	Piper PA-31P Navajo 425 [42-71]	Bentwaters Cold War Museum
	EM-01	DH60G Moth (G-AAOR)	Privately owned, Rendcomb
	ES.1-4	Bücker Bü133C Jungmeister (G-BUTX)	Privately owned, Breighton
	ES.1-16	CASA 1.133L Jungmeister	Privately owned, Stretton, Cheshire
	SWEDEN		
	-	Thulin A/Bleriot XI (SE-XMC)	Privately owned, Loberod, Sweden
	081	CFM 01 Tummelisa <R> (SE-XIL)	Privately owned, Loberod, Sweden
	2542	Fiat CR42 (G-CBLS)	The Fighter Collection, Duxford
	5033	Klemm Kl35D (SE-BPT) [78]	Privately owned, Barkaby, Sweden
	5060	Klemm Kl35D (SE-BPU) [174]	Privately owned, Barkaby, Sweden
	05108	DH60 Moth	Privately owned, Langham
	17239	SAAB B-17A (SE-BYH) [7-J]	Flygvapenmuseum, Linköping, Sweden
	28693	DH100 Vampire FB6 (J-1184/SE-DXY) [9-G]	Scandinavian Historic Flight, Oslo, Norway
	29640	SAAB J-29F [20-08]	Midland Air Museum, Coventry

Serial	*Type (code/other identity)*	*Owner/operator, location or fate*	*Notes*
29670	SAAB J-29F (SE-DXB) [10-R]	Flygvapenmuseum/F10 Wing, Angelholm, Sweden	
32028	SAAB 32A Lansen (G-BMSG)	Privately owned, Cranfield	
34066	Hawker Hunter F58 (J-4089/LN-HNT) [9-G]	Scandinavian Historic Flight, Halmstad, Scandinavian Historic Flight, Halmstad,	
35075	SAAB J-35A Draken [40]	Dumfries & Galloway Aviation Museum	
35515	SAAB J-35F Draken [49]	Irvin-GQ, Llangeinor	
37918	SAAB AJSH-37 Viggen [57]	Newark Air Museum, Winthorpe	
60140	SAAB 105 (SE-DXG) [140-5]	Flygvapenmuseum/F10 Wing, Angelholm, Sweden	
91130	SAAB S91A Safir (SE-BNN) [10-30]	Privately owned, Barkaby, Sweden	
SWITZERLAND			
-	DH112 Venom FB54 (J-1758/N203DM)	Grove Technology Park, Wantage, Oxon	
A-10	CASA 1.131E Jungmann (G-BECW)	Privately owned, Rochester	
A-12	Bücker Bu131B Jungmann (G-CCHY)	Privately owned, Booker	
A-57	CASA 1.131E Jungmann (G-BECT)	Privately owned, Goodwood	
A-701	Junkers Ju52/3m (HB-HOS)	Ju-Air, Dubendorf, Switzerland	
A-702	Junkers Ju52/3m (HB-HOT)	Ju-Air, Dubendorf, Switzerland	
A-703	Junkers Ju52/3m (HB-HOP)	Ju-Air, Dubendorf, Switzerland	
A-806	Pilatus P3-03 (G-BTLL)	Privately owned, stored Headcorn	
C-552	EKW C-3605 (G-DORN)	Privately owned, Bournemouth	
C-558	EKW C-3605 (G-CCYZ)	Privately owned, Wickenby	
J-1008	DH100 Vampire FB6	Mosquito Aircraft Museum, London Colney	
J-1169	DH100 Vampire FB6	Privately owned, Henley-on-Thames	
J-1172	DH100 Vampire FB6 (8487M)	RAF Museum Reserve Collection, Stafford	
J-1573	DH112 Venom FB50 (G-VICI)	Privately owned, Bournemouth	
J-1605	DH112 Venom FB50 (G-BLID)	Gatwick Aviation Museum, Charlwood, Surrey	
J-1629	DH112 Venom FB50	Air Atlantique Classic Flight, stored Compton Verney	
J-1649	DH112 Venom FB50	Privately owned, Shropshire	
J-1704	DH112 Venom FB54	RAF Museum, Cosford	
J-1712	DH112 Venom FB54 <ff>	Privately owned, Connah's Quay, Flintshire	
J-1790	DH112 Venom FB50 (J-1632/G-VNOM)	Mosquito Aircraft Museum, London Colney	
J-4015	Hawker Hunter F58 (J-4040/HB-RVS)	Privately owned, St Stephan, Switzerland	
J-4021	Hawker Hunter F58 (G-HHAC)	Hawker Hunter Aviation Ltd, Scampton	
J-4064	Hawker Hunter F58 (HB-RVQ)	Fliegermuseum Altenrhein, Switzerland	
J-4083	Hawker Hunter F58 (G-EGHH)	Privately owned, Exeter	
J-4086	Hawker Hunter F58 (HB-RVU)	Privately owned, Altenrhein, Switzerland	
J-4091	Hawker Hunter F58	*Sold as N335AX, September 2010*	
J-4201	Hawker Hunter T68 (HB-RVR)	Amici dell'Hunter, Sion, Switzerland	
J-4205	Hawker Hunter T68 (HB-RVP)	Fliegermuseum Altenrhein, Switzerland	
U-80	Bücker Bü133D Jungmeister (G-BUKK)	Privately owned, Kirdford, W Sussex	
U-95	Bücker Bü133C Jungmeister (G-BVGP)	Privately owned, Booker	
U-99	Bücker Bü133C Jungmeister (G-AXMT)	Privately owned, Breighton	
U-110	Pilatus P-2 (G-PTWO)	Privately owned, Earls Colne	
V-54	SE3130 Alouette II (G-BVSD)	Privately owned, Glos	
USA			
-	Noorduyn AT-16 Harvard IIB (KLu B-168)	American Air Museum, Duxford	
001	Ryan ST-3KR Recruit (G-BYPY)	Privately owned, Old Warden	
14	Boeing-Stearman A75N-1 Kaydet (G-ISDN)	Privately owned, Kemble	
23	Fairchild PT-23 (N49272)	Privately owned, Sleap	
26	Boeing-Stearman A75N-1 Kaydet (G-BAVO)	Privately owned, Tibenham	
27	NA SNJ-7 Texan (90678/G-BRVG)	Privately owned, Goodwood	
43	Noorduyn AT-16 Harvard IIB (43-13064/G-AZSC) [SC]	Privately owned, North Weald	

Historic Aircraft in Overseas Markings

Notes	Serial	Type (code/other identity)	Owner/operator, location or fate
	44	Boeing-Stearman D75N-1 Kaydet (42-15852/G-RJAH)	Privately owned, Duxford
	85	WAR P-47 Thunderbolt <R> (G-BTBI)	Privately owned, Perth
	104	Boeing-Stearman PT-13D Kaydet (42-16931/N4712V) [W]	Privately owned, Hardwick, Norfolk
	112	Boeing-Stearman PT-13D Kaydet (42-17397/G-BSWC)	Privately owned, Staverton
	164	Boeing-Stearman PT-13B Kaydet (N60320)	Privately owned, Baldock, Herts
	284	Curtiss P-40B Warhawk (41-13297/G-CDWH) [18P]	The Fighter Collection, Duxford
	379	Boeing-Stearman PT-13D Kaydet (42-14865/G-ILLE)	Privately owned, Tibenham
	399	Boeing-Stearman N2S-5 Kaydet (38495/N67193)	Privately owned, Gelnhausen, Germany
	441	Boeing-Stearman N2S-4 Kaydet (30010/G-BTFG)	Privately owned, Manston
	466	Boeing-Stearman PT-13A Kaydet (37-0089/N731)	Privately owned, Audley End
	540	Piper L-4H Grasshopper (43-29877/G-BCNX)	Privately owned, Monewden
	560	Bell UH-1H Iroquois (73-22077/G-HUEY)	Privately owned, North Weald
	578	Boeing-Stearman N2S-5 Kaydet (N1364V)	Privately owned, North Weald
	586	Boeing-Stearman N2S-3 Kaydet (07874/N74650)	Privately owned, Popham
	628	Beech D17S (44-67761/N18V)	Privately owned, stored East Garston, Bucks
	669	Boeing-Stearman A75N-1 Kaydet (37869/G-CCXA)	Privately owned, Old Buckenham
	699	Boeing-Stearman N2S-3 Kaydet (38233/G-CCXB)	Privately owned, Old Buckenham
	716	Boeing-Stearman PT-13D Kaydet (42-17553/N1731B)	Privately owned, Compton Abbas
	718	Boeing-Stearman PT-13D Kaydet (42-17555/N5345N)	Privately owned, Tibenham
	744	Boeing-Stearman A75N-1 Kaydet (42-16532/OO-USN)	Privately owned, Wevelgem, Belgium
	854	Ryan PT-22 Recruit (42-17378/G-BTBH)	Privately owned, Old Warden
	855	Ryan PT-22 Recruit (41-15510/N56421)	Privately owned, Sleap
	897	Aeronca 11AC Chief (G-BJEV) [E]	Privately owned, English Bicknor, Glos
	985	Boeing-Stearman PT-13D Kaydet (42-16930/OO-OPS)	Privately owned, Antwerp, Belgium
	1102	Boeing-Stearman N2S-5 Kaydet (G-AZLE) [102]	Privately owned, Tongham
	1164	Beech D18S (G-BKGL)	The Aircraft Restoration Co, Duxford
	1180	Boeing-Stearman N2S-3 Kaydet (3403/G-BRSK)	Privately owned, Morley
	3072	NA T-6G Texan (49-3072/G-TEXN) [72]	Privately owned, Shoreham
	3397	Boeing-Stearman N2S-3 Kaydet (G-OBEE) [174]	Privately owned, Old Buckenham
	3403	Boeing-Stearman N2S-3 Kaydet (N75TQ) [180]	Privately owned, Tibenham
	3583	Piper L-4B Grasshopper (45-0583/G-FINT) [44-D]	Privately owned, Redhill
	4406	Naval Aircraft Factory N3N-3 (G-ONAF) [12]	Privately owned, Sandown
	6136	Boeing-Stearman A75N-1 Kaydet (42-16136/G-BRUJ) [205]	Privately owned, Liverpool
	6171	NA F-86D Sabre (51-6171)	North-East Aircraft Museum, Usworth
	6771	Republic F-84F Thunderstreak (BAF FU-6)	RAF Museum, stored Cosford
	7797	Aeronca L-16A Grasshopper (47-0797/G-BFAF)	Privately owned, Finmere
	8084	NA AT-6D Texan (42-85068/LN-AMY)	The Old Flying Machine Company, Duxfords

Serial	*Type (code/other identity)*	*Owner/operator, location or fate*	*Notes*
8178	NA F-86A Sabre (48-0178/G-SABR) [FU-178]	Golden Apple Operations/ARC, Duxford	
8242	NA F-86A Sabre (48-0242) [FU-242]	Midland Air Museum, Coventry	
01532	Northrop F-5E Tiger II <R>	RAF Alconbury on display	
02538	Fairchild PT-19B (N33870)	Privately owned, Mendlesham, Suffolk	
07539	Boeing-Stearman N2S-3 Kaydet (N63590) [143]	Privately owned, Billericay	
14286	Lockheed T-33A Shooting Star (51-4286)	American Air Museum, Duxford	
O-14419	Lockheed T-33A Shooting Star (51-4419)	Midland Air Museum, Coventry	
14863	NA AT-6D Harvard III (41-33908/G-BGOR)	Privately owned, Rednal	
15154	Bell OH-58A Kiowa (70-15154)	Defence Academy of the UK, Shrivenham	
15372	Piper L-18C Super Cub (51-15372/N123SA) [372-A]	Privately owned, Anwick, Lincs	
15990	Bell AH-1F Hueycobra (70-15990)	Museum of Army Flying, Middle Wallop	
16011	Hughes OH-6A Cayuse (69-16011/G-OHGA)	Privately owned, Wesham, Lancs	
16037	Piper J-3C Cub 65 (G-BSFD)	Privately owned, Sleap	
16445	Bell AH-1F Hueycobra (69-16445)	Defence Academy of the UK, Shrivenham	
16506	Hughes OH-6A Cayuse (67-16506)	The Helicopter Museum, Weston-super-Mare	
16544	NA AT-6A Texan (41-16544/N13FY) [FY]	Privately owned, Hilversum, The Netherlands	
16579	Bell UH-1H Iroquois (66-16579)	The Helicopter Museum, Weston-super-Mare	
16718	Lockheed T-33A Shooting Star (51-6718)	City of Norwich Aviation Museum	
17962	Lockheed SR-71A Blackbird (61-7962)	American Air Museum, Duxford	
18263	Boeing-Stearman PT-17 Kaydet (41-8263/N38940) [822]	Privately owned, Tibenham	
19252	Lockheed T-33A Shooting Star (51-9252)	Tangmere Military Aviation Museum	
21509	Bell UH-1H Iroquois (72-21509/G-UHIH)	Privately owned, Blackpool	
21605	Bell UH-1H Iroquois (72-21605)	American Air Museum, Duxford	
24538	Kaman HH-43F Huskie (62-4535)	Midland Air Museum, stored Coventry	
24541	Cessna L-19E Bird Dog (N134TT)	Privately owned, Yarcombe, Devon	
24568	Cessna L-19E Bird Dog (LN-WNO)	Army Aviation Norway, Kjeller, Norway	
28521	CCF T-6J Texan(G-TVIJ) [TA-521]	Privately owned, Woodchurch, Kent	
30274	Piper AE-1 Cub Cruiser (N203SA)	Privately owned, Coldridge, Devon	
30861	NA TB-25J Mitchell (44-30861/N9089Z)	Privately owned, Booker	
31145	Piper L-4B Grasshopper (43-1145/G-BBLH) [26-G]	Privately owned, Biggin Hill	
31171	NA B-25J Mitchell (44-31171/N7614C)	American Air Museum, Duxford	
31430	Piper L-4B Grasshopper (43-1430/G-BHVV)	Privately owned, Perranporth	
31952	Aeronca O-58B Defender (G-BRPR)	Privately owned, Belchamp Water	
34037	NA TB-25N Mitchell (44-29366/N9115Z/8838M)	RAF Museum, Hendon	
37414	McD F-4C Phantom II (63-7414)	Midland Air Museum, stored Coventry	
39624	Wag Aero Sport Trainer (G-BVMH) [39-D]	Privately owned, Temple Bruer	
40467	Grumman F6F-5K Hellcat (80141/G-BTCC) [19]	The Fighter Collection, Duxford	
41386	Thomas-Morse S4 Scout <R> (G-MJTD)	Privately owned, Lutterworth	

Notes	*Serial*	*Type (code/other identity)*	*Owner/operator, location or fate*
	42165	NA F-100D Super Sabre (54-2165) [VM]	American Air Museum, Duxford
	42196	NA F-100D Super Sabre (54-2196)	Norfolk & Suffolk Avn Museum, Flixton
	43517	Boeing-Stearman N2S-5 Kaydet (42-109578/G-NZSS)	Privately owned, Tibenham
	46214	Grumman TBM-3E Avenger (69327/CF-KCG) [X-3]	American Air Museum, Duxford
	48846	Boeing B-17G Flying Fortress (44-8846/F-AZDX) [DS-M]	*Withdrawn from use, March 2010*
	53319	Grumman TBM-3R Avenger (HB-RDG) [319-RB]	*Repainted in French marks, 2010*
	54433	Lockheed T-33A Shooting Star (55-4433)	Norfolk & Suffolk Avn Museum, Flixton
	54884	Piper L-4J Grasshopper (45-4884/N61787) [57-D]	Privately owned, Sywell
	56498	Douglas C-54Q Skymaster (N44914)	Privately owned, stored North Weald
	60312	McD F-101F Voodoo (56-0312)	Midland Air Museum, Coventry
	60689	Boeing B-52D Stratofortress (56-0689)	American Air Museum, Duxford
	63000	NA F-100D Super Sabre (54-2212) [FW-000]	USAF Croughton, Oxon, at gate
	63319	NA F-100D Super Sabre (54-2269) [FW-319]	RAF Lakenheath, on display
	63428	Republic F-105G Thunderchief (62-4428) [WW]	*Repainted as 62-428*
	66692	Lockheed U-2CT (56-6692)	American Air Museum, Duxford
	70270	McD F-101B Voodoo (57-270) (fuselage)	Midland Air Museum, Coventry
	80105	Replica SE5a <R> (PH-WWI/G-CCBN) [19]	Privately owned, Thruxton
	80995	Cessna 337D Super Skymaster (F-BRPQ)	Privately owned, Strasbourg, France
	82062	DHC U-6A Beaver (58-2062)	Midland Air Museum, Coventry
	91822	Republic F-105D Thunderchief (59-1822)	*To Poland, June 2010*
	93542	CCF T-6J Harvard IV (G-BRLV) [LTA-542]	Privately owned, North Weald
	96995	CV F4U-4 Corsair (OE-EAS) [BR-37]	Flying Bulls, Salzburg, Austria
	111836	NA AT-6C Harvard IIA (41-33262/G-TSIX) [JZ-6]	Privately owned, Church Fenton
	111989	Cessna L-19A Bird Dog (51-11989/N33600)	Museum of Army Flying, Middle Wallop
	114700	NA T-6G Texan (51-14700/G-TOMC)	Privately owned, Netherthorpe
	115042	NA T-6G Texan (51-15042/G-BGHU) [TA-042]	Privately owned, Headcorn
	115227	NA T-6G Texan (51-15227/G-BKRA)	Privately owned, Staverton
	115302	Piper L-18C Super Cub (51-15302/G-BJTP) [TP]	Privately owned, Defford
	115373	Piper L-18C Super Cub (51-15373/G-AYPM) [A-373]	Privately owned, Coldridge, Devon
	115684	Piper L-21A Super Cub (51-15684/G-BKVM) [DC]	Privately owned, Strubby
	121714	Grumman F8F-2P Bearcat (G-RUMM) [201-B]	The Fighter Collection, Duxford
	124143	Douglas AD-4NA Skyraider (F-AZDP) [205-RM]	Amicale J-B Salis, la Ferté-Alais, France
	124485	Boeing B-17G Flying Fortress (44-85784/G-BEDF)[DF-A]	B-17 Preservation Ltd, Duxford
	124724	CV F4U-5NL Corsair (F-AZEG) [22]	Les Casques de Cuir, la Ferté-Alais, France
	126922	Douglas AD-4NA Skyraider (G-RADR) [402-AK]	Kennet Aviation, North Weald
	134076	NA AT-6D Texan (41-34671/F-AZSC) [TA076]	Privately owned, Yvetot, France
	138179	NA T-28A Trojan (OE-ESA) [BA]	The Flying Bulls, Salzburg, Austria
	138266	NA T-28B Trojan (HB-RCT) [266-CT]	Jet Alpine Fighter, Sion, Switzerland

Serial	*Type (code/other identity)*	*Owner/operator, location or fate*	*Notes*
140547	NA T-28C Trojan (F-AZHN) [IF-28]	Privately owned, Toussus le Noble, France	
140566	NA T-28C Trojan (N556EB) [252]	Privately owned, la Ferté-Alais, France	
146289	NA T-28C Trojan (N99153) [2W]	Norfolk & Suffolk Avn Museum, Flixton	
150225	WS58 Wessex 60 (G-AWOX) [123]	Privately owned, Lulsgate	
155529	McD F-4J(UK) Phantom II (ZE359) [AJ-114]	American Air Museum, Duxford	
155848	McD F-4S Phantom II [WT-11]	Royal Scottish Mus'm of Flight, E Fortune	
159233	HS AV-8A Harrier [CG-33]	Imperial War Museum North, Salford Quays	
162068	McD AV-8B Harrier II <ff>	Privately owned, Queensbury, W Yorks	
162071	McD AV-8B Harrier II (fuselage)	Rolls-Royce, Filton	
162074	McD AV-8B Harrier II <ff>	Privately owned, South Molton, Devon	
162730	McD AV-8B Harrier II <ff>	Privately owned, Liverpool	
162737	McD AV-8B Harrier II (fuselage)	MoD, Boscombe Down	
162958	McD AV-8B Harrier II <ff>	QinetiQ, Farnborough	
162964	McD AV-8B Harrier II <ff>	Tri Sim Ltd, Peterborough	
162964	McD AV-8B Harrier II <rf>	Privately owned, Charlwood, Surrey	
163205	McD AV-8B Harrier II (fuselage)	Privately owned, Queensbury, W Yorks	
163423	McD AV-8B Harrier II <ff>	QinetiQ, Boscombe Down	
163423	McD AV-8B Harrier II <rf>	Privately owned, Sproughton	
210855	Curtiss P-40M Kittyhawk (43-5802/G-KITT)	Hangar 11 Collection, North Weald	
217786	Boeing-Stearman PT-17 Kaydet (41-8169/CF-EQS) [25]	American Air Museum, Duxford	
224319	Douglas C-47B Skytrain (44-77047/G-AMSN) <ff>	Privately owned, Sussex	
226413	Republic P-47D Thunderbolt (45-49192/N47DD) [ZU-N]	American Air Museum, Duxford	
231983	Boeing B-17G Flying Fortress (44-83735/F-BDRS)[IY-G]	American Air Museum, Duxford	
234539	Fairchild PT-19B Cornell (42-34539/N50429) [63]	Privately owned, Dunkeswell	
236657	Piper L-4A Grasshopper (42-36657/G-BGSJ) [72-D]	Privately owned, Langport	
238410	Piper L-4A Grasshopper (42-38410/G-BHPK) [44-A]	Privately owned, Tibenham	
241079	Waco CG-4A Hadrian <R>	Assault Glider Association, Shawbury	
243809	Waco CG-4A Hadrian (BAPC 185)	Museum of Army Flying, Middle Wallop	
252983	Schweizer TG-3A (42-52983/N66630)	Imperial War Museum, stored Duxford	
298177	Stinson L-5A Sentinel (42-98177/N6438C) [8-R]	Privately owned, Tibenham	
314887	Fairchild Argus III (43-14887/G-AJPI)	Privately owned, Eelde, The Netherlands	
315211	Douglas C-47A Skytrain (43-15211/N1944A) [J8-B]	Privately owned, Little Rissington	
315509	Douglas C-47A Skytrain (43-15509/G-BHUB) [W7-S]	American Air Museum, Duxford	
317964	Waco CG-4A Hadrian (*237123*/BAPC 157) (fuselage)	Yorkshire Air Museum, Elvington	
329282	Piper J-3C Cub 65 (N46779)	Privately owned, Abbots Bromley	
329405	Piper L-4H Grasshopper (43-29405/G-BCOB) [23-A]	Privately owned, South Walsham, Norfolk	
329417	Piper L-4A Grasshopper (42-38400/G-BDHK)	Privately owned, English Bicknor, Glos	
329471	Piper L-4H Grasshopper (43-29471/G-BGXA) [44-F]	Privately owned, Martley, Worcs	
329601	Piper L-4H Grasshopper (43-29601/G-AXHR) [44-D]	Privately owned, Nayland	
329854	Piper L-4H Grasshopper (43-29854/G-BMKC) [44-R]	Privately owned, Newtownards	
329934	Piper L-4H Grasshopper (43-29934/G-BCPH) [72-B]	Privately owned, Thatcham	
330238	Piper L-4H Grasshopper (43-30238/G-LIVH) [24-A]	Privately owned, Eaglescott	
330372	Piper L-4H Grasshopper (43-30372/G-AISX)	Privately owned, Booker	
330485	Piper L-4H Grasshopper (43-30485/G-AJES) [44-C]	Privately owned, Shifnal	

Historic Aircraft in Overseas Markings

Notes	Serial	Type (code/other identity)	Owner/operator, location or fate
	411622	NA P-51D Mustang (44-74427/F-AZSB) [G4-C]	Amicale J-B Salis, la Ferté-Alais, France
	413317	NA P-51D Mustang (44-74409/N51RT) [VF-B]	RAF Museum, Hendon
	413521	NA P-51D Mustang (44-13521/G-MRLL) [5Q-B]	Privately owned, Hardwick, Norfolk
	413573	NA P-51D Mustang (44-73415/9133M/N6526D) [B6-V]	RAF Museum, Cosford
	413704	NA P-51D Mustang (44-73149/G-BTCD) [B7-H]	The Old Flying Machine Company, Duxford
	414151	NA P-51D Mustang (44-73140/NL314BG) [HO-M]	Privately owned, Greenham Common
	414419	NA P-51D Mustang (45-15118/G-MSTG) [LH-F]	Privately owned, Hardwick, Norfolk
	414450	NA P-51D Mustang (44-73877/N167F) [B6-S]	Scandinavian Historic Flight, Antwerp, Belgium
	433915	Consolidated PBV-1A Canso A (RCAF 11005/G-PBYA)	Privately owned, Duxford
	434602	Douglas A-26B Invader (44-34602/LN-IVA) [B]	Scandinavian Historic Flight, Rygge, Norway
	436021	Piper J/3C Cub 65 (G-BWEZ)	Privately owned, Strathaven, Strathclyde
	442268	Noorduyn AT-16 Harvard IIB (KF568/LN-TEX) [TA-268]	Scandinavian Historic Flight, Oslo, Norway
	454467	Piper L-4J Grasshopper (45-4467/G-BILI) [44-J]	Privately owned, White Waltham
	454537	Piper L-4J Grasshopper (45-4537/G-BFDL) [04-J]	Privately owned, Shempston Farm, Lossiemouth
	458811	NA B-25J Mitchell (45-8811/F-AZZU) [SB]	Privately owned, la Ferté-Alais, France
	461748	Boeing B-29A Superfortress (44-61748/G-BHDK) [Y]	American Air Museum, Duxford
	463209	NA P-51D Mustang <R> (BAPC 255) [WZ-S]	American Air Museum, Duxford
	472035	NA P-51D Mustang (44-72035/G-SIJJ)	Hangar 11 Collection, North Weald
	472216	NA P-51D Mustang (44-72216/G-BIXL) [HO-M]	Privately owned, East Garston, Bucks
	472218	CAC-18 Mustang 22 (A68-192/G-HAEC) [WZ-I]	Privately owned, Woodchurch, Kent
	472218	NA P-51D Mustang (44-73979) [WZ-I]	Imperial War Museum, Lambeth
	472218	Titan T-51 Mustang (G-MUZY) [WZ-I]	Privately owned, Damyns Hall, Essex
	472773	NA P-51D Mustang (44-72773/D-FPSI) [QP-M]	Meier Motors, Bremgarten, Germany
	473871	NA TF-51D Mustang (44-73871/D-FTSI) [TF-871]	Meier Motors, Bremgarten, Germany
	474008	Jurca MJ77 Gnatsum (G-PSIR) [VF-R]	Privately owned, Lewes
	474425	NA P-51D Mustang (44-74425/PH-PSI) [OC-G]	Privately owned, Lelystad, The Netherlands
	474923	NA P-51D Mustang (44-74923/N6395)	Privately owned, Lelystad, The Netherlands
	479744	Piper L-4H Grasshopper (44-79744/G-BGPD) [49-M]	Privately owned, Marsh, Bucks
	479766	Piper L-4H Grasshopper (44-79766/G-BKHG) [63-D]	Privately owned, Frogland Cross
	479897	Piper L-4H Grasshopper (44-79897/G-BOXJ) [JD]	Privately owned, Rochester
	480015	Piper L-4H Grasshopper (44-80015/G-AKIB) [44-M]	Privately owned, Perranporth
	480133	Piper L-4J Grasshopper (44-80133/G-BDCD) [44-B]	Privately owned, Slinfold
	480173	Piper L-4J Grasshopper (44-80609/G-RRSR) [57-H]	Privately owned, Wellesbourne Mountford
	480321	Piper L-4J Grasshopper (44-80321/G-FRAN) [44-H]	Privately owned, Rayne, Essex
	480480	Piper L-4J Grasshopper (44-80480/G-BECN) [44-E]	Privately owned, Rayne, Essex
	480551	Piper L-4J Grasshopper (44-80551/LN-KLT) [43-S]	Scandinavian Historic Flight, Oslo, Norway

Serial	*Type (code/other identity)*	*Owner/operator, location or fate*	*Notes*
480636	Piper L-4J Grasshopper (44-80636/G-AXHP) [58-A]	Privately owned, Spanhoe	
480723	Piper L-4J Grasshopper (44-80723/G-BFZB) [E5-J]	Privately owned, Egginton	
480752	Piper L-4J Grasshopper (44-80752/G-BCXJ) [39-E]	Privately owned, Old Sarum	
483868	Boeing B-17G Flying Fortress (44-83868/N5237V) [A-N]	RAF Museum, Hendon	
493209	NA T-6G Texan (49-3209/G-DDMV/41)	Privately owned, Rochester	
511701A	Beech C-45H (51-11701/G-BSZC) [AF258]	Privately owned, Bryngwyn Bach	
779465	Hiller UH-12C (N5315V)	Privately owned, Lower Upham, Hants	
2100882	Douglas C-47A Skytrain (42-100882/N473DC) [3X-P]	Privately owned, Liverpool	
2100884	Douglas C-47A Skytrain (42-100884/N147DC) [L4-D]	Privately owned, Dunsfold	
2105915	Curtiss P-40N Kittyhawk (42-105915/F-AZKU) [12]	Privately owned, la Ferté-Alais, France	
00195700	Cessna F.150G (G-USAA)	Privately owned, Halfpenny Green	
3-1923	Aeronca O-58B Defender (43-1923/G-BRHP)	Privately owned, Chiseldon	
18-2001	Piper L-18C Super Cub (52-2401/G-BIZV)	Privately owned, Croydon, Cambs	
39-139	Beech YC-43 Traveler (N295BS)	Duke of Brabant AF, Eindhoven, The Netherlands	
40-2538	Fairchild PT-19A Cornell (N33870)	Privately owned, Mendelsham, Suffolk	
41-19393	Douglas A-20C Havoc (wreck)	WWII Remembrance Museum, Handcross, W Sussex	
41-33275	NA AT-6C Texan (G-BICE) [CE]	Privately owned, Great Oakley, Essex	
42-12417	Noorduyn AT-16 Harvard IIB (KLu. B-163)	Newark Air Museum, Winthorpe	
42-35870	Taylorcraft DCO-65 (G-BWLJ) [129]	Privately owned, Nayland	
42-58678	Taylorcraft DF-65 (G-BRIY) [IY]	Privately owned, Carlisle	
42-78044	Aeronca 11AC Chief (G-BRXL)	Privately owned, Andrewsfield	
42-84555	NA AT-6D Harvard III (FAP.1662/G-ELMH) [EP-H]	Privately owned, Hardwick, Norfolk	
42-93510	Douglas C-47A Skytrain [CM] <ff>	Privately owned, Kew	
43-9628	Douglas A-20G Havoc <ff>	Privately owned, Hinckley, Leics	
43-11137	Bell P-63C Kingcobra (wreck)	WWII Remembrance Museum, Handcross, W Sussex	
43-21664	Douglas A-20G Havoc (wreck)	WWII Remembrance Museum, Handcross, W Sussex	
43-36140	NA B-25J Mitchell <ff>	WWII Remembrance Museum, Handcross, W Sussex	
44-4315	Bell P-63C Kingcobra	WWII Remembrance Museum, Handcross, W Sussex	
44-4368	Bell P-63C Kingcobra	Privately owned, Surrey	
44-13954	NA P-51D Mustang (G-UAKE)	Mustang Restoration Co Ltd, Coventry	
44-14574	NA P-51D Mustang (fuselage)	East Essex Aviation Museum, Clacton	
44-42914	Douglas DC-4 (N31356)	Privately owned, stored North Weald	
44-51228	Consolidated B-24M Liberator [EC]	American Air Museum, Duxford	
44-79609	Piper L-4H Grasshopper (G-BHXY) [PR]	Privately owned, Bealbury, Cornwall	
44-80594	Piper L-4J Grasshopper (G-BEDJ)	Privately owned, White Waltham	
44-80647	Piper L-4J Grasshopper (D-EGAF)	The Vintage Aircraft Co, Fürstenwalde, Germany	
44-83184	Fairchild UC-61K Argus III (G-RGUS)	Privately owned, Snitterby	
51-9036	Lockheed T-33A Shooting Star	Newark Air Museum, Winthorpe	
51-15319	Piper L-18C Super Cub (G-FUZZ) [A-319]	Privately owned, Elvington	
51-15555	Piper L-18C Super Cub (G-OSPS)	Privately owned, Weston, Eire	
52-8543	CCF T-6J Texan (G-BUKY) [66]	Privately owned, Breighton	
54-005	NA F-100D Super Sabre (54-2163)	Dumfries & Galloway Avn Mus, Dumfries	

Notes	Serial	Type (code/other identity)	Owner/operator, location or fate
	54-174	NA F-100D Super Sabre (54-2174) [SM]	Midland Air Museum, Coventry
	54-2223	NA F-100D Super Sabre	Newark Air Museum, Winthorpe
	54-2445	Piper L-21B Super Cub (G-OTAN) [A-445]	Privately owned, Andrewsfield
	54-2447	Piper L-21B Super Cub (G-SCUB)	Privately owned, Anwick
	62-428	Republic F-105G Thunderchief (62-4428) [WW]	USAF Croughton, Oxon, at gate
	63-699	McD F-4C Phantom II (63-7699) [CG]	Midland Air Museum, Coventry
	64-17657	Douglas B-26K Counter Invader (N99218) <ff>	WWII Remembrance Museum, Handcross, W Sussex
	65-777	McD F-4C Phantom II (63-7419) [LN]	RAF Lakenheath, on display
	67-120	GD F-111E Aardvark (67-0120) [UH]	American Air Museum, Duxford
	68-0060	GD F-111E Aardvark <ff>	Dumfries & Galloway Avn Mus, Dumfries
	68-8284	Sikorsky MH-53M Pave Low IV	RAF Museum, Cosford
	72-1447	GD F-111F Aardvark <ff>	American Air Museum, Duxford
	72-448	GD F-111E Aardvark (68-0011) [LN]	RAF Lakenheath, on display
	74-0177	GD F-111F Aardvark [FN]	RAF Museum, Cosford
	76-020	McD F-15A Eagle (76-0020)	American Air Museum, Duxford
	76-124	McD F-15B Eagle (76-0124) [LN]	RAF Lakenheath, instructional use
	77-259	Fairchild A-10A Thunderbolt (77-0259) [AR]	American Air Museum, Duxford
	80-219	Fairchild GA-10A Thunderbolt (80-0219) [AR]	RAF Alconbury, on display
	82-23762	B-V CH-47D Chinook <ff>	RAF Odiham, instructional use
	83-24104	B-V CH-47D Chinook [BN] <ff>	RAF Museum, Hendon
	92-048	McD F-15A Eagle (74-0131) [LN]	RAF Lakenheath, on display
	146-11042	Wolf WII Boredom Fighter (G-BMZX) [7]	Privately owned, Tibenham
	146-11083	Wolf WII Boredom Fighter (G-BNAI) [5]	Privately owned, Haverfordwest
	G-57	Piper L-4A Grasshopper (42-36375/G-AKAZ)	Privately owned, Duxford
	YEMEN		
	104	BAC Jet Provost T.52A (G-PROV)	Privately owned, North Weald
	YUGOSLAVIA		
	30139	Soko P-2 Kraguj [139]	Privately owned, Biggin Hill
	30140	Soko P-2 Kraguj (G-RADA) [140]	Privately owned, Biggin Hill
	30146	Soko P-2 Kraguj (G-BSXD) [146]	Privately owned, Linton-on-Ouse
	30149	Soko P-2 Kraguj (G-SOKO) [149]	Privately owned, Fenland
	30151	Soko P-2 Kraguj [151]	Privately owned, Sopley, Hants

Wearing Chinese markings, this Nanchang CJ-6A Chujiao, G-BVVG, carries the serial 2751219

MiG-23ML 458 is on display at the superb Newark Air Museum in Polish markings.

Irish Military Aircraft Markings

Notes	Serial	Type (code/other identity)	Owner/operator, location
	C7	Avro 631 Cadet (EI-AGO)	IAC, Baldonnel
	34	Miles M14A Magister I (N5392)	National Museum of Ireland, Dublin
	141	Avro 652A Anson C19	IAC Museum, Baldonnel
	164	DHC1 Chipmunk T20	IAC Museum, Baldonnel
	168	DHC1 Chipmunk T20	IAC Museum, Baldonnel
	172	DHC1 Chipmunk T20	IAC, stored Baldonnel
	173	DHC1 Chipmunk T20	South East Aviation Enthusiasts, Dromod
	176	DH104 Dove 4 (VP-YKF)	South East Aviation Enthusiasts, Waterford
	181	Percival P56 Provost T51	*Scrapped at Thatcham, 2010*
	183	Percival P56 Provost T51	IAC Museum, Baldonnel
	184	Percival P56 Provost T51	South East Aviation Enthusiasts, Dromod
	187	DH115 Vampire T55	South East Aviation Enthusiasts, Dromod
	191	DH115 Vampire T55	IAC Museum, Baldonnel
	192	DH115 Vampire T55	South East Aviation Enthusiasts, Dromod
	195	Sud SA316 Alouette III (F-WJDH)	IAC Museum, Baldonnel
	198	DH115 Vampire T11 (XE977)	National Museum of Ireland, Dublin
	199	DHC1 Chipmunk T22	IAC, stored Baldonnel
	202	Sud SA316 Alouette III	Ulster Aviation Society, Long Kesh
	203	Reims-Cessna FR172H	IAC No 104 Sqn/1 Operations Wing, Baldonnel
	205	Reims-Cessna FR172H	IAC No 104 Sqn/1 Operations Wing, Baldonnel
	206	Reims-Cessna FR172H	IAC No 104 Sqn/1 Operations Wing, Baldonnel
	207	Reims-Cessna FR172H	IAC, stored Waterford
	208	Reims-Cessna FR172H	IAC No 104 Sqn/1 Operations Wing, Baldonnel
	210	Reims-Cessna FR172H	IAC No 104 Sqn/1 Operations Wing, Baldonnel
	215	Fouga CM170 Super Magister	Dublin Institute of Technology
	216	Fouga CM170 Super Magister	National Museum of Ireland, Dublin
	218	Fouga CM170 Super Magister	Shannon Aerospace, Shannon Airport
	219	Fouga CM170 Super Magister	IAC Museum, Baldonnel
	220	Fouga CM170 Super Magister	Cork University, instructional use
	231	SIAI SF-260WE Warrior	IAC Museum, stored Baldonnel
	240	Beech Super King Air 200MR	IAC No 102 Sqn/1 Operations Wing, Baldonnel
	251	Grumman G1159C Gulfstream IV (N17584)	IAC No 102 Sqn/1 Operations Wing, Baldonnel
	252	Airtech CN.235 MPA Persuader	IAC No 101 Sqn/1 Operations Wing, Baldonnel
	253	Airtech CN.235 MPA Persuader	IAC No 101 Sqn/1 Operations Wing, Baldonnel
	254	PBN-2T Defender 4000 (G-BWPN)	IAC No 106 Sqn/1 Operations Wing, Baldonnel
	255	AS355N Twin Squirrel (G-BXEV)	*Sold as F-GRTM, October 2010*
	256	Eurocopter EC135T-1 (G-BZRM)	IAC No 106 Sqn/1 Operations Wing, Baldonnel
	258	Gates Learjet 45 (N5009T)	IAC No 102 Sqn/1 Operations Wing, Baldonnel
	260	Pilatus PC-9M (HB-HQS)	IAC Flying Training School, Baldonnel
	261	Pilatus PC-9M (HB-HQT)	IAC Flying Training School, Baldonnel
	262	Pilatus PC-9M (HB-HQU)	IAC Flying Training School, Baldonnel
	263	Pilatus PC-9M (HB-HQV)	IAC Flying Training School, Baldonnel
	264	Pilatus PC-9M (HB-HQW)	IAC Flying Training School, Baldonnel
	266	Pilatus PC-9M (HB-HQY)	IAC Flying Training School, Baldonnel
	267	Pilatus PC-9M (HB-HQZ)	IAC Flying Training School, Baldonnel
	268	Pilatus PC-9M	IAC (option)
	269	Pilatus PC-9M	IAC (option)
	270	Eurocopter EC135P-2	IAC No 302 Sqn/3 Operations Wing, Baldonnel
	271	Eurocopter EC135P-2	IAC No 302 Sqn/3 Operations Wing, Baldonnel
	272	Eurocopter EC135T-2 (G-CECT)	IAC No 106 Sqn/1 Operations Wing, Baldonnel
	273	Eurocopter EC135P-2	IAC, on order

Serial	Type (code/other identity)	Owner/operator, location	Notes
274	AgustaWestland AW139	IAC No 301 Sqn/3 Operations Wing, Baldonnel	
275	AgustaWestland AW139	IAC No 301 Sqn/3 Operations Wing, Baldonnel	
276	AgustaWestland AW139	IAC No 301 Sqn/3 Operations Wing, Baldonnel	
277	AgustaWestland AW139	IAC No 301 Sqn/3 Operations Wing, Baldonnel	
278	AgustaWestland AW139	IAC No 301 Sqn/3 Operations Wing, Baldonnel	
279	AgustaWestland AW139	IAC No 301 Sqn/3 Operations Wing, Baldonnel	

001 is a Ryan ST-3KR Recruit, G-BYPY and is based at Old Warden. It has no military history.

This is a rare Piper AE-1, N203SA. It has a hatch on the upper rear fuselage for loading stretchers.

Overseas Military Aircraft Markings

Aircraft included in this section include those likely to be seen visiting UK civil and military airfields on transport flights, exchange visits, exercises and for air shows. It is not a comprehensive list of all aircraft operated by the air arms concerned.

ALGERIA
Force Aérienne Algérienne/ Al Quwwat al Jawwiya al Jaza'eriya

Airbus A.340-541
Ministry of Defence, Boufarik
7T-VPP

Lockheed C-130H Hercules
2 Escadre de Transport Tactique et Logistique, Boufarik
7T-WHE (4935)
7T-WHF (4934)
7T-WHI (4930)
7T-WHJ (4928)
7T-WHQ (4926)
7T-WHR (4924)
7T-WHS (4912)
7T-WHT (4911)
7T-WHY (4913)
7T-WHZ (4914)

Lockheed C-130H-30 Hercules
2 Escadre de Transport Tactique et Logistique, Boufarik
7T-WHA (4997)
7T-WHB (5224)
7T-WHD (4987)
7T-WHL (4989)
7T-WHM (4919)
7T-WHN (4894)
7T-WHO (4897)
7T-WHP (4921)

Grumman G.1159C Gulfstream IVSP
Ministry of Defence, Boufarik
7T-VPC (1418)
7T-VPM (1421)
7T-VPR (1288)
7T-VPS (1291)

Gulfstream Aerospace Gulfstream V
Ministry of Defence, Boufarik
7T-VPG (617)

ARMENIA
Armenian Government

Airbus A.319CJ-132
Armenian Government, Yerevan
EK-RA01

AUSTRALIA
Royal Australian Air Force

Airbus A.330-203 MRTT
33 Sqn, Amberley
A39-001 (on order)
A39-002 (on order)
A39-003
A39-004 (on order)
A39-005 (on order)

Boeing 737-7DF/-7DT/-7ES AEW&C
34 Sqn, Canberra
A30-001 737-7ES
A30-002 737-7ES
A30-003 737-7ES
A30-004 737-7ES
A30-005 737-7ES
A30-006 737-7ES
A36-001 737-7DT
A36-002 737-7DF

Boeing C-17A Globemaster III
36 Sqn, Amberley
A41-206
A41-207
A41-208
A41-209

Canadair CL.604 Challenger
34 Sqn, Canberra
A37-001
A37-002
A37-003

Lockheed C-130H Hercules/ C-130J-30 Hercules II
37 Sqn, Richmond, NSW
C-130H
A97-001
A97-002
A97-003
A97-004
A97-005
A97-006
A97-007
A97-008$
A97-009
A97-011
C-130J-30
A97-440
A97-441
A97-442
A97-447
A97-448
A97-449
A97-450
A97-464
A97-465
A97-466
A97-467
A97-468

Lockheed AP-3C Orion
10/11 Sqns, 92 Wing, Edinburgh, NSW
A9-656 10 Sqn
A9-657 11 Sqn
A9-658 10 Sqn
A9-659 11 Sqn
A9-660 11 Sqn
A9-661 10 Sqn
A9-662 11 Sqn
A9-663 11 Sqn
A9-664 11 Sqn
A9-665 10 Sqn
A9-751 11 Sqn
A9-752 10 Sqn
A9-753 10 Sqn
A9-755 10 Sqn
A9-756 11 Sqn
A9-757 10 Sqn
A9-758 10 Sqn
A9-759 10 Sqn
A9-760 10 Sqn

AUSTRIA
Öesterreichische Luftstreitkräfte

Agusta-Bell AB.212/Bell 212*
1. & 2. leichte Transporthubschrauberstaffel, Linz
5D-HB
5D-HC
5D-HD
5D-HF
5D-HG
5D-HH
5D-HI
5D-HJ
5D-HK
5D-HL
5D-HN
5D-HO
5D-HP
5D-HQ
5D-HR
5D-HS
5D-HT
5D-HU
5D-HV
5D-HW
5D-HX
5D-HY*
5D-HZ

Bell OH-58B Kiowa
Mehrzweckhubschrauberstaffel, Tulln
3C-OA
3C-OB
3C-OC
3C-OD
3C-OE
3C-OG
3C-OH
3C-OI
3C-OJ
3C-OK $
3C-OL

Eurofighter
EF.2000
Überwachungsgeschwader:
1.Staffel & 2.Staffel, Zeltweg
7L-WA
7L-WB
7L-WC
7L-WD
7L-WE
7L-WF
7L-WG
7L-WH
7L-WI
7L-WJ
7L-WK
7L-WL
7L-WM
7L-WN
7L-WO

Lockheed
C-130K Hercules
Lufttransportstaffel, Linz
8T-CA
8T-CB
8T-CC

Pilatus
PC-6B/B2-H2 Turbo Porter/
PC-6B/B2-H4 Turbo Porter*
leichte Lufttransportstaffel,
Tulln
3G-EA
3G-EB
3G-EC
3G-ED
3G-EE
3G-EF
3G-EG
3G-EH
3G-EJ
3G-EK
3G-EL
3G-EM
3G-EN*

Pilatus
PC-7 Turbo Trainer
Lehrabteilung Fläche, Zeltweg
3H-FA
3H-FB
3H-FC
3H-FD
3H-FE
3H-FF
3H-FG
3H-FH
3H-FI
3H-FJ
3H-FK
3H-FL
3H-FM
3H-FN
3H-FO
3H-FP

SAAB 105ÖE
Überwachungsgeschwader:
Düsentrainerstaffel, Linz
(yellow)
B (105402)
D (105404)
E (105405)
G (105407)
I (105409)
J (105410)
(green)
B (105412)
D (105414)
GF-16 (105416)$
GG-17 (105417)
(red)
B (105422)
C (105423)
D (105424)
E (105425)
RF-26 (105426)$
G (105427)
H (105428)
I (105429)
J (105430)
(blue)
A (105431)
B (105432)
C (105433)
D (105434)
E (105435)
F (105436)
G (105437)
J (105440)

Sikorsky S-70A
mittlere
Transporthubschrauberstaffel,
Tulln
6M-BA
6M-BB
6M-BC
6M-BD
6M-BE
6M-BF
6M-BG
6M-BH
6M-BI

BAHRAIN
BAE RJ.85/RJ.100*
Bahrain Defence Force
A9C-AWL*
A9C-BDF*
A9C-HWR

Boeing 747SP-Z5
Bahrain Amiri Flt
A9C-HAK

Boeing 747-4P8
Bahrain Amiri Flt
A9C-HMK

Boeing 767-4SFER
Bahrain Amiri Flt
A9C-HMH

Grumman
G.1159 Gulfstream IITT/
G.1159C Gulfstream IV-SP
Govt of Bahrain
A9C-BAH Gulfstream IV-SP
A9C-BG Gulfstream IITT

Gulfstream Aerospace
G.450
Govt of Bahrain
A9C-BHR

Gulfstream Aerospace
G.550
Govt of Bahrain
A9C-BRN

BELGIUM
Composante Aérienne Belge/
Belgische Luchtcomponent
D-BD Alpha Jet E
11 Smaldeel (1 Wg),
Cazaux, France (ET 02.008)
AT-01
AT-02
AT-03
AT-05
AT-06
AT-08
AT-10
AT-11
AT-12
AT-13
AT-14
AT-15
AT-17
AT-18
AT-19
AT-20
AT-21
AT-22
AT-23
AT-24
AT-25
AT-26
AT-27
AT-28
AT-29
AT-30
AT-31
AT-32$
AT-33

Airbus A.330-321
21 Smaldeel (15 Wg),
Melsbroek
CS-TMT

Dassault
Falcon 900B
21 Smaldeel (15 Wg),
Melsbroek
CD-01

Embraer
ERJ.135LR/ERJ.145LR*
21 Smaldeel (15 Wg),
Melsbroek
CE-01
CE-02
CE-03* $
CE-04*

Lockheed
C-130H Hercules
20 Smaldeel (15 Wg),
Melsbroek
CH-01
CH-03
CH-04
CH-05
CH-07$
CH-08
CH-09
CH-10

CH-11
CH-12
CH-13

Dassault
Falcon 20-5
21 Smaldeel (15 Wg),
Melsbroek
CM-01 $
CM-02

General Dynamics
F-16 MLU
1,350 Smaldeel (2 Wg),
Florennes [FS];
31,349 Smaldeel, OCU (10 Wg),
Kleine-Brogel [BL]

FA-56	F-16A	2 Wg
FA-57	F-16A	2 Wg
FA-67	F-16A	2 Wg
FA-68	F-16A	2 Wg
FA-69	F-16A	10 Wg
FA-70	F-16A	10 Wg
FA-71	F-16A	2 Wg
FA-72	F-16A	2 Wg$
FA-77	F-16A	2 Wg
FA-81	F-16A	10 Wg
FA-82	F-16A	10 Wg
FA-83	F-16A	2 Wg
FA-84	F-16A	2 Wg
FA-86	F-16A	10 Wg
FA-87	F-16A	10 Wg$
FA-89	F-16A	2 Wg
FA-91	F-16A	2 Wg
FA-92	F-16A	2 Wg
FA-94	F-16A	2 Wg$
FA-95	F-16A	2 Wg
FA-97	F-16A	10 Wg
FA-98	F-16A	2 Wg
FA-99	F-16A	10 Wg
FA-100	F-16A	2 Wg$
FA-101	F-16A	10 Wg
FA-102	F-16A	10 Wg
FA-103	F-16A	10 Wg
FA-104	F-16A	10 Wg
FA-106	F-16A	2 Wg
FA-107	F-16A	10 Wg
FA-108	F-16A	2 Wg
FA-109	F-16A	2 Wg
FA-110	F-16A	10 Wg$
FA-111	F-16A	10 Wg
FA-114	F-16A	10 Wg
FA-115	F-16A	2 Wg
FA-116	F-16A	10 Wg
FA-117	F-16A	2 Wg
FA-118	F-16A	10 Wg
FA-119	F-16A	10 Wg
FA-120	F-16A	10 Wg
FA-121	F-16A	2 Wg
FA-123	F-16A	10 Wg
FA-124	F-16A	10 Wg
FA-125	F-16A	10 Wg
FA-126	F-16A	2 Wg
FA-127	F-16A	10 Wg
FA-128	F-16A	10 Wg
FA-129	F-16A	10 Wg
FA-130	F-16A	2 Wg
FA-131	F-16A	10 Wg$
FA-132	F-16A	10 Wg
FA-133	F-16A	10 Wg
FA-134	F-16A	10 Wg$
FA-135	F-16A	10 Wg
FA-136	F-16A	2 Wg
FB-05	F-16B	10 Wg
FB-09	F-16B	2 Wg
FB-10	F-16B	10 Wg
FB-12	F-16B	10 Wg
FB-14	F-16B	10 Wg
FB-15	F-16B	10 Wg
FB-17	F-16B	10 Wg
FB-18	F-16B	2 Wg$
FB-20	F-16B	10 Wg
FB-21	F-16B	2 Wg
FB-22	F-16B	2 Wg
FB-23	F-16B	10 Wg
FB-24	F-16B	10 Wg

Piper L-21B Super Cub
Centre Militaire de Vol à Voile
Bases: Florennes,
Goetsenhoeven
& Zoersel
LB-01
LB-02
LB-03
LB-05

Westland Sea
King Mk48/48A*
40 Smaldeel, Koksijde
RS-02
RS-03*
RS-04
RS-05$

SIAI Marchetti
SF260D*/SF260M/SF260M+
Ecole de Pilotage
Elementaire (5 Sm/1 Wg),
Bevekom
ST-02+
ST-03+
ST-04+
ST-06+
ST-12
ST-15+
ST-16+
ST-17+
ST-18+
ST-19+
ST-20+
ST-22+
ST-23+
ST-24+
ST-25+
ST-26+
ST-27+$
ST-30+$
ST-31+
ST-32+
ST-34+
ST-35+
ST-36+
ST-40*$
ST-41*
ST-42*
ST-43*
ST-44*
ST-45*
ST-46*
ST-47*
ST-48*$

Sud Aviation
SA.316B Alouette III
40 Smaldeel, Koksijde;

M-2	[OT-ZPB]
M-3	[OT-ZPC]

Composante Terrestre Belge/
Belgische Landcomponent
Agusta A109HA/HO*
17 Smaldeel MRH, Beauvechain;
18 Smaldeel MRH, Beauvechain;
SLV, Beauvechain

H-01*	SLV
H-02*	18 Sm MRH
H-05*	18 Sm MRH
H-07*	17 Sm MRH
H-20	17 Sm MRH
H-21	18 Sm MRH
H-22	17 Sm MRH
H-23	17 Sm MRH
H-24	17 Sm MRH
H-25	18 Sm MRH
H-26	18 Sm MRH
H-27	18 Sm MRH
H-28	17 Sm MRH
H-29	18 Sm MRH
H-31	18 Sm MRH
H-33	18 Sm MRH
H-35	18 Sm MRH
H-36	17 Sm MRH
H-38	17 Sm MRH
H-40	18 Sm MRH
H-41	17 Sm MRH
H-42	SLV
H-44	17 Sm MRH
H-45	17 Sm MRH
H-46	17 Sm MRH

Police Fédérale/Federal Politie
Cessna 182 Skylane
Luchsteundetachment,
Melsbroek

G-01	C.182Q
G-04	C.182R

MDH
MD.520N
Luchsteundetachment,
Melsbroek
G-14
G-15

MDH
MD.900/MD.902* Explorer
Luchsteundetachment,
Melsbroek
G-10
G-11
G-12
G-16*

BOTSWANA
Botswana Defence Force
Bombardier Global Express
VIP Sqn, Sir Seretse Kharma IAP,
Gaborone
OK-1

Lockheed
C-130B Hercules
Z10 Sqn, Thebephatshwa
OM-1

OM-2
OM-3

BRAZIL
Força Aérea Brasileira
Boeing KC-137
2° GT, 2° Esq, Galeão
2401
2402
2403
2404

Embraer
EMB.190-190IGW (VC-2)
1° Grupo de Transport Especial,
1° Esq, Brasilia
2590
2591

Lockheed
C-130 Hercules
1° GT, 1° Esq, Galeão;
1° GTT, 1° Esq, Afonsos

2451	C-130E	1° GTT
2453	C-130E	1° GTT
2454	C-130E	1° GTT
2456	C-130E	1° GTT
2458	SC-130E	1° GT
2459	C-130E	1° GTT
2461	KC-130H	1° GT
2462	KC-130H	1° GT
2463	C-130H	1° GT
2464	C-130H	1° GT
2465	C-130H	1° GT
2466	C-130H	1° GT
2467	C-130H	1° GT
2470	C-130M	1° GT
2471	C-130H	1° GT
2472	C-130H	1° GT
2473	C-130H	1° GT
2474	C-130H	1° GT
2475	C-130H	1° GT
2476	C-130H	1° GT
2477	C-130H	1° GT
2478	C-130H	1° GT
2479	C-130H	1° GT

BRUNEI
Airbus A.340
Brunei Govt, Bandar Seri Bergawan
V8-BKH A.340-212

Boeing 747-430
Brunei Govt, Bandar Seri Bergawan
V8-ALI

Boeing 767-27GER
Brunei Govt, Bandar Seri Bergawan
V8-MHB

BULGARIA
Bulgarsky Voenno-Vazdushni Sily
Aeritalia C-27J Spartan
16 TAB, Sofia/Vrazhdebna
071
072
073

Antonov An-30
16 TAP, Sofia/Dobroslavtzi
055

Pilatus PC.XII/45
16 TAP, Sofia/Dobroslavtzi
020

Bulgarian Govt
Airbus A.319-112
Bulgarian Govt/BH Air, Sofia
LZ-AOA
LZ-AOB

Dassault Falcon 2000
Bulgarian Govt, Sofia
LZ-OOI

Tupolev Tu-154M
Bulgarian Govt, Sofia
LZ-BTZ

BURKINA FASO
Boeing 727-14/727-282*
Govt of Burkina Faso, Ouagadougou
XT-BBE
XT-BFA*

CAMEROON
Grumman
G.1159A Gulfstream III
Govt of Cameroon, Yaounde
TJ-AAW

CANADA
Canadian Forces
Lockheed
CC-130 Hercules
CC-130E/CC-130E(SAR)*
413 Sqn, Greenwood (SAR) (14 Wing);
424 Sqn, Trenton (SAR) (8 Wing);
426 Sqn, Trenton (8 Wing);
435 Sqn, Winnipeg (17 Wing);
436 Sqn, Trenton (8 Wing)

130305*	8 Wing
130307	14 Wing
130308*	8 Wing
130313	8 Wing
130319	8 Wing
130320	14 Wing
130323	8 Wing
130327	8 Wing
130328	8 Wing

CC-130H/CC-130H(T)*

130332	8 Wing
130333	17 Wing
130334	8 Wing
130335	8 Wing
130336	8 Wing
130337	8 Wing
130338*	17 Wing
130339*	17 Wing
130340*	17 Wing
130341*	17 Wing
130342*	17 Wing

CC-130H-30

130343	8 Wing
130344	8 Wing

CC-130J Hercules II

130601	8 Wing
130602	8 Wing
130603	8 Wing
130604	8 Wing
130605	8 Wing
130606	(on order)
130607	14 Wing
130608	(on order)
130609	(on order)
130610	(on order)
130611	(on order)
130612	(on order)
130613	(on order)
130614	(on order)
130615	(on order)
130616	(on order)
130617	(on order)

Lockheed
CP-140 Aurora
404 Sqn, Greenwood (14 Wing);
405 Sqn, Greenwood (14 Wing);
407 Sqn, Comox (19 Wing)

140101	407 Sqn
140102	407 Sqn
140103	407 Sqn
140104	14 Wing
140105	14 Wing
140106	14 Wing
140107	407 Sqn
140108	14 Wing
140109	14 Wing
140110	14 Wing
140111	14 Wing
140112	407 Sqn
140113	14 Wing
140114	14 Wing
140115	407 Sqn
140116	14 Wing
140117	407 Sqn
140118	407 Sqn

De Havilland Canada
CT-142
402 Sqn, Winnipeg (17 Wing)

142803	CT-142
142804	CT-142
142805	CT-142
142806	CT-142

Canadair
CC-144 Challenger
412 Sqn, Ottawa (8 Wing)

144601	CC-144A
144614	CC-144B
144615	CC-144B
144616	CC-144B
144617	CC-144C
144618	CC-144C

Airbus
CC-150 Polaris
(A310-304/A310-304F*)
437 Sqn, Trenton (8 Wing)

15001	[991]
15002*	[992]
15003*	[993]
15004*	[994]
15005*	[995]

Boeing CC-177 (C-17A Globemaster III)
429 Sqn, Trenton (8 Wing)
177701
177702
177703
177704

CHAD
Boeing 737-74Q
Chad Government, N'djamena
TT-ABD

CHILE
Fuerza Aérea de Chile
Boeing 707
Grupo 10, Santiago
902 707-351C
903 707-330B
904 707-358C

Boeing 737
Grupo 10, Santiago
921 737-58N
922 737-330

Boeing 767-3Y0ER
Grupo 10, Santiago
985

Boeing KC-135E Stratotanker
Grupo 10, Santiago
981

Extra EA-300L
Los Halcones
145 [2]
146 [5]
147 [6]
149 [1]
1268 [3]

Grumman G.1159C Gulfstream IV
Grupo 10, Santiago
911

Lockheed C-130H Hercules
Grupo 10, Santiago
995
996

CROATIA
Hrvatske Zračne Snage
Pilatus PC-9*/PC-9M
92 ZB, Pula;
93 ZB, Zadar
051* 93 ZB
052* 93 ZB
053* 93 ZB
054 93 ZB
055 93 ZB
056 93 ZB
057 93 ZB
058 93 ZB
059 93 ZB
060 93 ZB
061 93 ZB
062 93 ZB
063 93 ZB
064 93 ZB
065 93 ZB
066 93 ZB
067 92 ZB
068 93 ZB
069 93 ZB
070 93 ZB

Canadair CL.601 Challenger
Croatian Govt, Zagreb
9A-CRO
9A-CRT

CZECH REPUBLIC
Ceske Vojenske Letectvo
Aero L-39/L-59 Albatros
222.TL/22.zL, Náměšt;
CLV, Pardubice
0103 L-39C CLV
0106 L-39C CLV
0107 L-39C CLV
0108 L-39C CLV
0113 L-39C CLV
0115 L-39C CLV
0441 L-39C CLV
0444 L-39C CLV
0445 L-39C CLV
2341 L-39ZA 222.TL/22.zL
2344 L-39ZA 222.TL/22.zL
2347 L-39ZA 222.TL/22.zL
2350 L-39ZA 222.TL/22.zL
2415 L-39ZA 222.TL/22.zL
2418 L-39ZA 222.TL/22.zL
2421 L-39ZA 222.TL/22.zL
2424 L-39ZA 222.TL/22.zL
2427 L-39ZA 222.TL/22.zL
2430 L-39ZA 222.TL/22.zL
2433 L-39ZA 222.TL/22.zL $
2436 L-39ZA 222.TL/22.zL
3903 L-39ZA 222.TL/22.zL
5015 L-39ZA 222.TL/22.zL
5017 L-39ZA 222.TL/22.zL
5019 L-39ZA 222.TL/22.zL

Aero L-159A ALCA/L-159B/ L-159T-1
212.TL/21.zTL, Cáslav;
LZO, Praha/Kbely
L-159A
6048 212.TL/21.zTL
6049 212.TL/21.zTL
6050 212.TL/21.zTL
6051 212.TL/21.zTL
6052 212.TL/21.zTL
6053 212.TL/21.zTL
6054 212.TL/21.zTL
6055 212.TL/21.zTL
6057 212.TL/21.zTL
6058 212.TL/21.zTL
6059 212.TL/21.zTL
6060 212.TL/21.zTL
6061 212.TL/21.zTL
6062 212.TL/21.zTL
6063 212.TL/21.zTL
6064 212.TL/21.zTL
6065 212.TL/21.zTL
6066 212.TL/21.zTL$
6068 212.TL/21.zTL
6070 212.TL/21.zTL
L-159B
5831 LZO
5832 LZO
6069 212.TL/21.zTL
6073
L-159T-1
6067 212.TL/21.zTL$
6071 212.TL/21.zTL
6072 212.TL/21.zTL
6075 212.TL/21.zTL

Airbus A.319CJ-115X
241.dlt/24.zDL, Praha/Kbely
2801
3085

Antonov An-26/An-26Z-1M*
242.dl/24.zDL, Praha/Kbely
2408
2409
2507$
3209*
4201

Canadair CL.601-3A Challenger
241.dlt/24.zDL, Praha/Kbely
5105

CASA C-295M
242.dl/24.zDL, Praha/Kbely
0452
0453
0454 (on order)
0455 (on order)

LET 410 Turbolet
242.dl/24.zDL, Praha/Kbely;
CLV, Pardubice
0731 L-410UVP-E CLV
0928 L-410UVP-T CLV
1132 L-410UVP-T 242.dl
1134 L-410UVP-T 242.dl
1504 L-410UVP 242.dl
1525 L-410FG 242.dl
1526 L-410FG 242.dl
2312 L-410UVP-E 242.dl
2601 L-410UVP-E 242.dl
2602 L-410UVP-E 242.dl
2710 L-410UVP-E 242.dl

Mil Mi-17/ Mi-171Sh*
231.vrl/23.zVrL, Přerov;
CLV, Pardubice
0803 231.vrl/23.zVrL
0811 231.vrl/23.zVrL
0828 231.vrl/23.zVrL
0832 231.vrl/23.zVrL
0834 231.vrl/23.zVrL
0835 231.vrl/23.zVrL
0836 CLV
0837 CLV
0839 231.vrl/23.zVrL
0840 231.vrl/23.zVrL
0848 231.vrl/23.zVrL
0849 231.vrl/23.zVrL
0850 231.vrl/23.zVrL
9767* 231.vrl/23.zVrL
9774* 231.vrl/23.zVrL
9781* 231.vrl/23.zVrL
9799* 231.vrl/23.zVrL
9806* 231.vrl/23.zVrL
9813* 231.vrl/23.zVrL
9825* 231.vrl/23.zVrL

9837* 231.vrl/23.zVrL
9844* 231.vrl/23.zVrL
9868* 231.vrl/23.zVrL
9873* 231.vrl/23.zVrL
9887* 231.vrl/23.zVrL
9892* 231.vrl/23.zVrL
9904* 231.vrl/23.zVrL
9915* 231.vrl/23.zVrL
9926* 231.vrl/23.zVrL

Mil Mi-24/Mi-35
221.lbvr/22.zL, Náměšt
0702 Mi-24V1
0788 Mi-24V1
0790 Mi-24V1
0815 Mi-24V1
0835 Mi-24V2
0981 Mi-24V2
3361 Mi-35
3362 Mi-35
3365 Mi-35
3366 Mi-35
3367 Mi-35
3368 Mi-35
3369 Mi-35
3370 Mi-35
3371 Mi-35
6050 Mi-24V
7353 Mi-24V$
7354 Mi-24V
7355 Mi-24V
7356 Mi-24V
7357 Mi-24V
7358 Mi-24V
7360 Mi-24V

SAAB Gripen
211.TL/21.zTL, Cáslav
JAS 39C
9234
9235
9236
9237
9238
9239
9240
9241
9242
9243
9244
9245
JAS 39D
9819 $
9820 $

Yakovlev Yak-40
241.dlt/24.zDL, Praha/Kbely
0260 Yak-40
1257 Yak-40K

DENMARK
Flyvevåbnet
Lockheed
C-130J-30 Hercules II
Eskadrille 721, Aalborg
B-536
B-537
B-538
B-583

Canadair
CL.604 Challenger
Eskadrille 721, Aalborg
C-080
C-168 $
C-172

General Dynamics
F-16 MLU
Eskadrille 727, Skrydstrup;
Eskadrille 730, Skrydstrup;
416th FTS/412th TW, Edwards AFB, USA
E-004 F-16A Esk 730
E-005 F-16A
E-006 F-16A Esk 727
E-007 F-16A Esk 730
E-008 F-16A Esk 727
E-011 F-16A Esk 727
E-016 F-16A Esk 727
E-017 F-16A Esk 730
E-018 F-16A Esk 730
E-024 F-16A Esk 730
E-070 F-16A Esk 730
E-074 F-16A Esk 730
E-075 F-16A Esk 727
E-107 F-16A Esk 727
E-180 F-16A Esk 727
E-182 F-16A Esk 727
E-184 F-16A Esk 727
E-187 F-16A Esk 730
E-188 F-16A Esk 727
E-189 F-16A Esk 730
E-190 F-16A Esk 730
E-191 F-16A Esk 730
E-192 F-16A Esk 727
E-193 F-16A Esk 727
E-194 F-16A Esk 727$
E-195 F-16A Esk 727
E-196 F-16A Esk 730
E-197 F-16A Esk 730
E-198 F-16A Esk 727
E-199 F-16A Esk 730
E-200 F-16A Esk 727
E-202 F-16A Esk 730
E-203 F-16A Esk 730
E-596 F-16A Esk 730
E-597 F-16A Esk 730
E-598 F-16A Esk 727
E-599 F-16A Esk 727
E-600 F-16A Esk 727
E-601 F-16A Esk 730
E-602 F-16A Esk 727
E-603 F-16A Esk 727
E-604 F-16A Esk 730
E-605 F-16A Esk 727
E-606 F-16A Esk 730
E-607 F-16A Esk 727
E-608 F-16A Esk 727
E-609 F-16A Esk 730
E-610 F-16A Esk 730
E-611 F-16A Esk 727
ET-022 F-16B Esk 727
ET-197 F-16B Esk 727
ET-198 F-16B Esk 730
ET-199 F-16B Esk 727
ET-204 F-16B Esk 730$
ET-206 F-16B Esk 730
ET-207 F-16B Esk 727
ET-208 F-16B Esk 730
ET-210 F-16B 412th TW
ET-612 F-16B Esk 727
ET-613 F-16B Esk 727
ET-614 F-16B Esk 727
ET-615 F-16B Esk 730

AgustaWestland
EH.101 Mk.512
Eskadrille 722, Karup
Detachments at:
Aalborg, Roskilde, Ronne, Skrydstrup
M-502
M-504
M-507
M-508
M-510
M-512
M-513
M-514
M-515
M-516
M-517
M-518
M-519
M-520

Aérospatiale
AS.550C-2 Fennec
Eskadrille 724, Karup
P-090
P-234
P-254
P-275
P-276
P-287
P-288
P-319
P-320
P-339
P-352
P-369

SAAB
T-17 Supporter
Eskadrille 721, Aalborg;
Flyveskolen, Karup (FLSK)
T-401 FLSK
T-402 Esk 721
T-403 FLSK
T-404 FLSK
T-405 FLSK
T-407 Esk 721
T-408 FLSK
T-409 FLSK
T-410 FLSK
T-411 FLSK
T-412 FLSK
T-413 FLSK
T-414 Esk 721
T-415 FLSK
T-417 FLSK
T-418 Esk 721
T-419 FLSK
T-420 FLSK
T-421 FLSK
T-423 FLSK
T-425 FLSK
T-426 FLSK
T-427 FLSK
T-428 FLSK
T-429 FLSK
T-430 FLSK
T-431 Esk 721
T-432 FLSK

Sœvaernets Flyvetjaeneste (Navy)
Westland Lynx Mk 90B
Eskadrille 728, Karup
S-134
S-142
S-170
S-175
S-181
S-191
S-249
S-256

ECUADOR
Fuerza Aérea Ecuatoriana
Embraer ERJ.135 Legacy 600
Escuadrón de Transporte 1114, Quito
FAE-051

EGYPT
Al Quwwat al-Jawwiya il Misriya
Lockheed C-130H/C-130H-30* Hercules
16 Sqn, Cairo West
1271/SU-BAB
1273/SU-BAD
1274/SU-BAE
1275/SU-BAF
1277/SU-BAI
1278/SU-BAJ
1279/SU-BAK
1280/SU-BAL
1281/SU-BAM
1282/SU-BAN
1283/SU-BAP
1284/SU-BAQ
1285/SU-BAR
1286/SU-BAS
1287/SU-BAT
1288/SU-BAU
1289/SU-BAV
1290/SU-BEW
1291/SU-BEX
1292/SU-BEY
1293/SU-BKS*
1294/SU-BKT*
1295/SU-BKU*
1296
1297
1298

Egyptian Govt
Airbus A.340-211
Egyptian Govt, Cairo
SU-GGG

Cessna 680 Citation Sovereign
Egyptian Govt, Cairo
SU-BRF
SU-BRG

Grumman G.1159A Gulfstream III/ G.1159C Gulfstream IV/ G.1159C Gulfstream IV-SP/ Gulfstream 400
Egyptian Air Force/Govt, Cairo
SU-BGM Gulfstream IV
SU-BGU Gulfstream III
SU-BGV Gulfstream III
SU-BNC Gulfstream IV
SU-BND Gulfstream IV
SU-BNO Gulfstream IV-SP
SU-BNP Gulfstream IV-SP
SU-BPE Gulfstream 400
SU-BPF Gulfstream 400

FINLAND
Suomen Ilmavoimat
CASA C-295M
Tukilentolaivue, Jyväskylä/Tikkakoski
CC-1
CC-2

Fokker F.27 Friendship
Tukilentolaivue, Jyväskylä/Tikkakoski
FF-1 F.27-100
FF-3 F.27-400M

McDonnell Douglas F-18 Hornet
Hävittäjälentolaivue 11, Roveniemi;
Hävittäjälentolaivue 21, Tampere/Pirkkala;
Hävittäjälentolaivue 31, Kuopio/Rissala;
Koelentokeskus, Halli
F-18C Hornet
HN-401 HavLLv 21
HN-402 HavLLv 11
HN-403 HavLLv 21
HN-404 HavLLv 21
HN-405 HavLLv 21
HN-406 HavLLv 11
HN-407 HavLLv 11
HN-408 HavLLv 21
HN-409 HavLLv 21
HN-410 HavLLv 21
HN-411 HavLLv 11
HN-412 HavLLv 31
HN-413 HavLLv 21
HN-414 KoelntK
HN-415 HavLLv 21
HN-416 HavLLv 11
HN-417 HavLLv 21
HN-418 HavLLv 31
HN-419 HavLLv 31
HN-420 HavLLv 31
HN-421 HavLLv 21
HN-422 HavLLv 31
HN-423 HavLLv 11
HN-424 HavLLv 31
HN-425 HavLLv 31
HN-426 HavLLv 31
HN-427 HavLLv 31
HN-428 HavLLv 21
HN-429 HavLLv 31
HN-431 HavLLv 31
HN-432 HavLLv 11
HN-433 HavLLv 31
HN-434 HavLLv 11
HN-435 HavLLv 31
HN-436 HavLLv 31
HN-437 HavLLv 31
HN-438 HavLLv 31
HN-439 HavLLv 31
HN-440 HavLLv 21
HN-441 HavLLv 11
HN-442 HavLLv 21
HN-443 HavLLv 21
HN-444 HavLLv 31
HN-445 HavLLv 31
HN-446 HavLLv 31
HN-447 HavLLv 11
HN-448 HavLLv 21
HN-449 HavLLv 11
HN-450 HavLLv 21
HN-451 HavLLv 31
HN-452 HavLLv 11
HN-453 HavLLv 31
HN-454 HavLLv 21
HN-455 HavLLv 21
HN-456 HavLLv 11
HN-457 HavLLv 31
F-18D Hornet
HN-461 HavLLv 21
HN-462 KoelntK
HN-463 HavLLv 21
HN-464 HavLLv 21
HN-465 HavLLv 31
HN-466 HavLLv 11
HN-467 HavLLv 21

BAe Hawk 51/51A*
Hävittäjälentolaivue 41, Kauhava;
Koelentokeskus, Halli
Hawk 51
HW-301 HavLLv 41
HW-303 HavLLv 41
HW-304 HavLLv 41
HW-306 HavLLv 41
HW-307 HavLLv 41
HW-308 HavLLv 41
HW-309 HavLLv 41
HW-310 HavLLv 41
HW-311 HavLLv 41
HW-312 HavLLv 41
HW-314 HavLLv 41
HW-315 HavLLv 41
HW-316 HavLLv 41
HW-318 HavLLv 41
HW-319 HavLLv 41
HW-320 HavLLv 41
HW-321 KoelntK
HW-322 HavLLv 41
HW-326 HavLLv 41
HW-327 HavLLv 41
HW-328 HavLLv 41
HW-329 HavLLv 41
HW-330 HavLLv 41
HW-331 HavLLv 41
HW-332 HavLLv 41
HW-333 HavLLv 41
HW-334 HavLLv 41
HW-337 HavLLv 41
HW-338 HavLLv 41
HW-339 HavLLv 41
HW-340 HavLLv 41
HW-341 HavLLv 41
HW-342 HavLLv 41
HW-343 HavLLv 41
HW-344 HavLLv 41
HW-345 HavLLv 41
HW-346 HavLLv 41
HW-347 HavLLv 41

HW-348 HavLLv 41
HW-349 HavLLv 41
HW-350 HavLLv 41

Hawk 51A

HW-351 HavLLv 41
HW-352 HavLLv 41
HW-353 HavLLv 41
HW-354 HavLLv 41
HW-355 HavLLv 41
HW-356 HavLLv 41
HW-357 HavLLv 41

Hawk 66

HW-360
HW-361
HW-362
HW-363
HW-364
HW-365
HW-366
HW-367
HW-368
HW-369
HW-370
HW-371
HW-372
HW-373
HW-374
HW-375
HW-376
HW-377

Gates Learjet 35A

Tukilentolaivue, Jyväskylä/Tikkakoski;
Tukilentolaivue (Det.), Kuopio/Rissala*

LJ-1*
LJ-2
LJ-3

FRANCE

Armée de l'Air

Airbus A.310-304

ET 03.060 *Esterel*, Paris/Charles de Gaulle

418 F-RADC
421 F-RADA
422 F-RADB

Airbus A.319CJ-115

ETEC 00.065, Villacoublay

1485 F-RBFA
1556 F-RBFB

Airbus A.330-223

ETEC 00.065, Villacoublay

240 (F-RARF)

Airbus A.340-212

ET 03.060 *Esterel*, Paris/Charles de Gaulle

075 F-RAJA
081 F-RAJB

Airtech CN-235M-200

ETL 01.062 *Vercours*, Creil;
ET 03.062 *Ventoux*, Mont-de-Marsan;
ETOM 00.052 *La Tontouta*, Noumea;
ETOM 00.058 *Antilles*, Fort de France;
ETOM 00.082 *Maine*, Faaa-Tahiti

045	62-IB	03.062
065	82-IC	00.082
066	52-ID	00.052
071	62-IE	03.062
072	82-IF	00.082
105	52-IG	00.052
107	52-IH	00.052
111	62-II	01.062
114	62-IJ	01.062
123	62-IM	01.062
128	62-IK	03.062
129	62-IL	01.062
137	62-IN	01.058
141	62-IO	00.058
152	62-IP	01.062
156	62-IQ	01.062
158	62-IR	01.062
160	62-IS	01.062
165	62-IT	01.062

Boeing C-135 Stratotanker

GRV 02.093 *Bretagne*, Istres

470	C-135FR	93-CA
471	C-135FR	93-CB
472	C-135FR	93-CC
474	C-135FR	93-CE
475	C-135FR	93-CF
497	KC-135R	93-CM$
525	KC-135R	93-CN
574	KC-135R	93-CP
735	C-135FR	93-CG
736	C-135FR	93-CH
737	C-135FR	93-CI
738	C-135FR	93-CJ
739	C-135FR	93-CK
740	C-135FR	93-CL

Boeing E-3F Sentry

EDCA 00.036, Avord

201 36-CA
202 36-CB
203 702-CC
204 36-CD

CASA 212-300 Aviocar

CEV, Cazaux & Istres

378 MP
386 MQ

Cessna 310

CEV, Cazaux & Istres

190	310N	BL
193	310N	BG
194	310N	BH
513	310N	BE
569	310R	CS
820	310Q	CL
981	310Q	BF

D-BD Alpha Jet

AMD-BA, Istres;
CEAM (EC 02.330), Mont-de-Marsan (BA 118);
CEV, Cazaux (BA 120) & Istres (BA 125);
EAC 00.314, Tours (BA 705);
EE 02.002 *Côte d'Or* & EC 03.002 Alsace Dijon (BA 102);
EPNER, Istres (BA 125);
ETO 01.008 *Saintonge* & ETO 02.008 *Nice*, Cazaux (BA 120);
GE 00.312, Salon de Provence (BA 701);
Patrouille de France (PDF) (EPAA 20.300), Salon de Provence (BA 701)

01	F-ZJTS	CEV
E1		CEV
E3		
E4		CEV
E5	314-LV	00.314
E7	705-TU	00.314
E8		CEV
E9	102-LF	03.002
E10	*314-UL*	00.314
E11	102-UB	02.002
E12		CEV
E13		
E14	2-FG	02.002
E15		CEV
E17	314-AA	00.314
E18	705-AK	00.314
E19		
E20	705-MS	00.314
E21		
E22	705-LS	00.314
E23	314-UG	00.314
E24	8-MP	01.008
E25	705-TJ	00.314
E26	102-ND	02.008
E28	314-AB	00.314
E29	102-NB	02.008
E30	8-MD	01.008
E31	F-TERK	*PDF* [5]
E32	102-FI	02.002
E33	102-FJ	02.002
E34		*PDF*
E35	120-MA	01.008
E36	314-UF	00.314
E37	120-NL	02.008
E38	314-LH	00.314
E41	F-TERA	*PDF* [4]
E42	705-TA	00.314
E43		
E44	120-RE	01.008
E45	705-TF	00.314
E46	F-TERN	*PDF* [7]
E47	705-AC	00.314
E48	8-MH	01.008
E49	705-LB	00.314
E51	705-AD	00.314
E52		
E53	120-LI	02.008
E55		
E58	314-TK	00.314
E59	705-LY	00.314
E60		EPNER
E61	102-LQ	02.002
E63		
E64	314-TL	00.314
E65		
E66	8-ME	01.008
E67	314-TD$	00.314
E68	8-MO	01.008
E69		
E72	705-LA	00.314
E73	120-NE	02.008
E74	8-MI	01.008
E75	705-AE	00.314
E76	102-RJ	02.002
E79	102-NA	02.008
E80		CEV

E81	2-FO	02.002
E82	705-LW	00.314
E83	705-TZ	00.314
E84	314-UK	00.314
E85	F-UGFF	*PDF* [9]
E86	102-FB	02.002
E87	102-LC	03.002
E88	314-LL	00.314
E89	118-LX	CEAM
E90	705-TH	00.314
E91	102-ML	02.002
E92	314-FL	00.314
E93	705-TX	00.314
E94	F-TERH	*PDF* [6]
E95	F-TERQ	*PDF* [8]
E96	314-TC	00.314
E97	102-MB	02.002
E98	118-MF	CEAM
E99	102-AH	02.002
E100		
E101	314-TT	00.314
E102	120-LM	01.008
E103	314-UA	00.314
E104	705-TG	00.314
E105	102-FM	02.002
E106		
E107	314-UD	00.314
E108	120-AF	01.008
E109	705-AG	00.314
E110	705-AH	00.314
E112	118-AO	CEAM
E113	314-TD	00.314
E114	F-TERR	*PDF* [2]
E115	120-MR	01.008
E116	120-FN	01.008
E117	F-TERI	*PDF*
E118	314-LN	00.314
E119	314-FE	00.314
E120	314-LG	00.314
E121	705-LE	00.314
E123	314-RM	00.314
E124	120-RN	01.008
E125	314-LK	00.314
E126		
E127	102-FK	02.002
E128	314-TM	00.314
E129	314-LP	00.314
E130	F-TERP	*PDF* [1]
E131		
E132	314-LZ	00.314
E133		
E134	F-TERM	*PDF* [0]
E135	F-TERX	*PDF*
E136	120-RP	01.008
E137	314-LJ	00.314
E138	314-RQ	00.314
E139	314-FC	00.314
E140	102-FA	02.002
E141	120-NF	02.008
E142	314-LO	00.314
E143	8-MQ	01.008
E144	120-AK	01.008
E145		
E146	314-RR	00.314
E147	314-LT	00.314
E148	705-LU	00.314
E149		
E150		
E151	2-FD	02.002
E152	705-RT	00.314
E153		
E154	120-AL	01.008
E155	8-NP	02.008
E156	314-TI	00.314
E157	314-UC	00.314
E158	F-TERF	*PDF*
E159		
E160	314-UH	00.314
E161		
E162	F-TERJ	*PDF*
E163	F-TERB	*PDF*
E164		
E165	F-TERE	*PDF* [3]
E166	705-RW	00.314
E167	120-MN	01.008
E168		
E169		
E170	314-UN	00.314
E171	314-LR	00.314
E173		
E176		

Dassault
Falcon 7X
ETEC 00.065, Villacoublay
68 (F-RAFA)
86 (F-RAFB)

Dassault
Falcon 20
CEV, Cazaux & Istres
Falcon 20C

79	CT
86	CG
96	CB
104	CW
131	CD
138	CR
188	CX

Falcon 20E

252	CA
263	CY
288	CV

Falcon 20F

342	CU
375	CZ

Dassault
Falcon 50
ETEC 00.065, Villacoublay

5	F-RAFI
27	(F-RAFK)
34	(F-RAFL)
78	F-RAFJ

Dassault
Falcon 900
ETEC 00.065, Villacoublay

02	(F-RAFP)
004	(F-RAFQ)

Dassault
Mirage F.1
CEAM (EC 05.330),
Mont-de-Marsan (BA 118);
CEV, Cazaux (BA 120) & Istres (BA 125);
ER 02.033 Savoie,
Reims (BA 112)
Mirage F.1CT

226	112-QS	02.033
227	330-AP	CEAM
229	112-QW	02.033
236	112-QR	02.033
242	112-QA	02.033
253	112-QU	02.033
256	112-SH	02.033
267	112-QC	02.033
271	112-QQ	02.033
273	112-QF	02.033
274	112-QJ	02.033
278	112-SG	02.033
281		AMD-BA

Mirage F.1B

502	112-SW	02.033
507	112-SE	02.033
510	112-SL	02.033
514	112-SA	02.033
516	112-SI	02.033
517	112-SC	02.033
518	112-SR $	02.033

Mirage F.1CR

602	CEV	
603	112-NU	02.033
604	112-CF	
605	33-CO	
606	112-CU	02.033
607	112-ND	02.033
608		
610	112-CI	02.033
611	112-NM	02.033
612	112-MZ	02.033
613	112-CC	
614	112-NR	02.033
615	118-MZ	CEAM
616	112-NX	02.033
617	33-NE	02.033
620	112-CT	
622	112-FA	02.033
623	112-AW	
624	112-NY	02.033
627	112-NA	02.033
630	33-CN	
631	112-AA	02.033
632	112-CQ	02.033
634	112-CK	02.033
635	112-NP	02.033
636	112-NL	02.033
637	112-CP	02.033
638	112-CD	02.033
640	112-NV	02.033
641	112-NI	02.033
642	112-CG	
643	112-CE	
645	112-CH	
646	112-NW	02.033
647	112-CB	
648		
649	112-CR	02.033
650	112-NZ	02.033
651		
653	112-CV	02.033
654	118-NC	CEAM
655	112-NG	02.033
656	112-CS	
657	112-CL	02.033
658	112-NQ	02.033
659	112-NT	02.033
660	112-CY	
661	112-NK	02.033
662	112-NF	

Dassault
Mirage 2000B
AMD-BA, Istres;
CEAM *Cote d'Argent*,
Mont-de-Marsan (BA 118);
CEV, Cazaux (BA 120) & Istres (BA 125);

EC 02.005 *Ile de France*, Orange (BA 115);
EC 01.012 *Cambrésis*, Cambrai (BA 103)

501	(BX1)	CEV
506	115-OD	02.005
509	115-OK	02.005
510	115-OQ	02.005
523	115-KJ	02.005
524	115-OA	02.005
525	118-AM	CEAM
526	115-YP	02.005
527	115-OR	02.005
528	115-KS	02.005
529	115-OC	02.005
530	115-OL	02.005

Dassault
Mirage 2000C/2000-5F*

CEAM *Cote d'Argent*, Mont-de-Marsan (BA 118);
CEV, Istres (BA 125);
GC 01.002 *Cigognes*, Dijon (BA 102);
EC 02.005 *Ile de France*, Orange (BA 115);
EC 03.011 *Corse*, Djibouti (BA 188);
EC 01.012 *Cambrésis*, Cambrai (BA 103)
EC.03.030 *Lorraine*, Al Dhafra

01*		CEV
1	5-OJ	02.005
2		CEV
3	115-OG	02.005
5	115-OT	02.005
8	115-OO	02.005
11	5-OF	02.005
12	115-OH	02.005
16	115-OX	02.005
17	115-OZ	02.005
20	115-OB	02.005
38*	102-EI	01.002
40*	102-EX	01.002
41*	102-FZ	01.002
42*	102-EY	01.002
43*	102-EJ	01.002
44*	102-EQ	01.002
45*	102-EF	01.002
46*	102-EN	01.002
47*	102-EP	01.002
48*	102-EW	01.002
49*	102-EA	01.002
51*	330-AS	CEAM
52*	102-EH	01.002
53*		
54*	102-EZ	01.002
55*	102-EU	02.005
56*	102-EG	01.002
57*	102-ET	01.002
58*	102-EL	01.002
59*	102-EV	01.002
61*	102-ME	01.002
62*	102-ED	01.002
63*	102-EM	01.002
64	330-AQ	CEAM
65*	2-EK	01.002
66*	102-EO	01.002
67*	104-MH	03.030
68*	102-ER	01.002
70*	102-AD	01.002
71*	102-EE	01.002
73*	102-ES	02.005
74*	102-EK	01.002
77*	118-AX	CEAM
78*	102-EC	01.002
79	115-LE	02.005
80	103-LI	01.012
81	33-LB	04.033
82	103-YL	01.012
83	188-YC	03.011
85	103-LK	01.012
86	12-LL	01.012
87	103-LA	01.012
88	103-KV	01.012
89	115-KA	02.005
90	115-YS	02.005
91	103-YR$	01.012
92	330-AW	CEAM
93	115-YA	02.005
94	115-KB	02.005
95	103-KM	
96	103-KI	
97	115-YK	02.005
98	103-YU	01.012
99	115-YB	02.005
100	188-YF	03.011
101	103-KE	01.012
102	103-KR	
103	188-YN	03.011
104		01.012
105	103-LJ	01.012
106	103-KL	
107	103-YD	01.012
108	103-LC	01.012
109	103-YH	01.012
111	188-KF	03.011
112	103-KQ	
113	115-YO	02.005
114	103-KU	01.012
115	115-YM	02.005
117	115-LD	02.005
118	103-YG	01.012
119		
120	103-KC	
121	103-KN	01.012
122	103-YE	01.012
123	103-KD	01.012
124	103-YT	01.012

Dassault
Mirage 2000D

AMD-BA, Istres;
CEAM (ECE 05.330), Mont-de-Marsan (BA 118);
CEV, Istres (BA 125);
EC 01.003 *Navarre*, EC 02.003 *Champagne* & EC 03.003 *Ardennes*, ETD 02.007, *Argonne* Nancy (BA 133);
EC 03.011 *Corse*, Djibouti (BA 188)

601	133-JG	02.003
602	133-XJ	03.003
603	3-XL	03.003
604	133-IP	01.003
605	133-LF	02.003
606	133-JC	02.003
607		CEV
609	3-IF	01.003
610	133-XX	03.003
611	133-JP	02.003
612	3-JK	02.003
613	133-MO	02.003
614	133-JU	02.003
615	133-JY	02.003
616	118-XH	CEAM
617	133-IS	01.003
618	3-XC	03.003
619	3-IM	01.003
620	133-IU	01.003
622	3-IL	01.003
623	133-MP	02.003
624	133-IT	01.003
625	133-XG	03.003
626	133-IC	01.003
627	133-JO	02.003
628	133-JL	02.003
629	3-XO	03.003
630	188-XD	03.011
631	133-IH	02.007
632	133-XE	03.003
634	133-JE	01.003
635	118-AS	CEAM
636	133-JV	02.003
637	133-XQ	03.003
638	133-IJ	01.003
639	3-JJ	02.003
640	133-IN	01.003
641	133-JW	02.003
642	133-IE	01.003
643	133-JD	02.003
644		CEV
645		
646	133-MQ	03.003
647	133-IO	01.003
648	133-XT	03.003
649	133-XY	03.003
650	133-IA	02.003
651	133-LG	02.003
652	133-XN	03.003
653	133-LH	02.003
654	133-ID	01.003
655		
657	133-JM	03.003
658	133-JN	02.003
659	133-XR	03.003
660	118-JF	CEAM
661	133-XI	03.003
662	133-XA	03.003
664	133-IW	01.003
665	133-AF	01.003
666	133-IQ	01.003
667	133-JZ	02.003
668	118-IG$	CEAM
669	133-AL	02.007
670	133-XF	03.003
671	133-XK	03.003
672	133-XV	03.003
673		CEV
674	133-IR	01.003
675	133-JI	02.003
676		CEV
677	133-JT	01.003
678	3-JA	02.003
679	133-JX	01.003
680	133-XM	03.003
681	133-AG	01.003
682	133-JR	02.003
683	133-IV	01.003
684	3-IW	01.003
685	133-XZ	03.003
686	133-JH	02.003
D02		CEV

Dassault Mirage 2000N

CEAM (ECE 05.330), *Côte d'Argent,* Mont-de-Marsan (BA 118);
CEV, Istres (BA 125);
EC 02.004 *Lafayette,* & EC 03.004 *Limousin,* Istres (BA 125)

301	CEV	
304	4-CA	03.004
305	116-CS	02.004
306	116-BL	02.004
307	116-CH	02.004
309	4-AO	
310	116-BE	02.004
311	116-AF	
312	116-CN	03.004
313	116-BG	02.004
316	4-AU	02.004
317	4-BP	02.004
319	4-AC	
320	125-CD	03.004
322	116-CP	02.004
323	116-AN	02.004
324	116-CX	03.004
325	4-CC	03.004
326	4-AS	
327	4-CJ	03.004
329	4-BH	02.004
330	116-AT	
331	4-BO	02.004
332	116-BN	02.004
333	4-AB	02.004
334		CEV
335	125-CI	03.004
336	116-BI	02.004
337	116-BF	
338	4-CG	03.004
339	116-AD	02.004
340	125-AA	03.004
341	116-BT	02.004
342	125-BA	02.004
343	116-AH	02.004
344	116-BV	02.004
345	116-BU	02.004
348	4-AL	
349	116-BM	02.004
350	125-AJ	03.004
351	125-AQ	03.004
353	125-AM	03.004
354	125-BJ	02.004
355	4-AE	
356	125-BX	02.004
357	125-CO	03.004
358	116-BQ	02.004
359	4-AK	
360	125-CB	03.004
361	125-CK	03.004
362	125-CU	03.004
364	116-BB	02.004
365	4-AI	
366	125-BC	02.004
367	116-AW	
368	116-AR	
369	4-AG	
370	125-CQ	03.004
371	125-BD	02.004
372	125-CM	03.004
373	125-CF	03.004
374	116-BS	02.004
375	125-CL	03.004

Dassault Rafale-B

AMD-BA, Istres;
CEAM (ECE 02.330), Mont-de-Marsan (BA 118);
CEV, Istres (BA 125);
EC 01.007 *Provence,* EC 01.091 *Gascogne* & ETR 02.092 *Aquitaine,* St Dizier (BA 113)

301		CEV
302		CEV
303	118-EA	CEAM
304	118-EB$	CEAM
305	118-EC$	CEAM
306	113-IB	01.091
307	113-IA	01.091
308	113-HA	01.007
309	113-HB	01.007
310	113-HC	02.092
311	113-HD	01.007
312	113-HF	01.007
313	113-HI	01.007
314	113-HP	01.007
315	113-HK	01.091
317	113-HO	01.007
318	113-HM	01.007
319	113-HN	01.007
320	113-HV	01.007
321	113-HQ	01.007
322	113-HU	01.091
323	113-HT	01.007
324	113-HW	01.007
325	113-HX	01.007
326	113-HY	01.007
327	113-HZ	01.007
328	113-IC	01.091
329	113-ID	01.091
330	113-IE	01.091
331	IF	CEAM
332	IG	CEAM
333	113-IH	01.091
334	113-II	01.091
335	113-IJ	01.091
336	113-IK	01.091
337	113-IL	01.091
338	113-IO	01.091
339		
340		
B01		CEV

Dassault Rafale-C

AMD-BA, Istres;
CEAM (ECE 02.330), *Côte d'Argent* Mont-de-Marsan (BA 118);
CEV, Istres (BA 125);
EC 01.007 *Provence,* EC 01.091 *Gascogne,* ETR 02.092 *Aquitaine,* St Dizier (BA 113)

101	113-EF	CEV
102	113-EF	01.007
103	113-HR	01.007
104	113-HH	01.007
105	113-HE	01.007
106	104-HG	03.030
107	113-HJ	01.007
108	113-HS	01.007
109	113-IM	01.091
110	113-IN	01.091
111	113-IP	01.091
112	113-IQ	01.091
113	113-	01.091
114	113-IS	01.091
115	113-IT	01.091
116	113-IU	01.091
117	113-IV	01.091
118	113-IW	01.091
119	113-IX	01.091
120	113-IY	01.091
121	113-IZ	01.091
122	113-GA	
123	113-GB	
124	113-GC	
125		
126		
127		
128		
129		
130		
C01		CEV

DHC-6 Twin Otter 200/300*

GAM 00.056 *Vaucluse,* Evreux;
ETOM 00.058 *Guadeloupe,* Pointe-à-Pitre

292	CC	00.056
298	F-RACD	00.056
300	F-RACE	00.056
730*	CA	00.058
745*	CV	00.056

Embraer EMB.121AA/AN* Xingu

EAT 00.319, Avord

054	YX
055*	YZ
064	YY
066*	ZA
070*	ZC
072	YA
073	YB
075	YC
076	YD
078	YE
080	YF
082	YG
083*	ZE
084	YH
086	YI
089	YJ
090*	ZF
091	YK
092	YL
095	YM
096	YN
098	YO
099	YP
101	YR
102	YS
103	YT
105	YU
107	YV
108	YW
111	YQ

Eurocopter AS.332 Super Puma/ AS.532 Cougar/ EC.725AP Cougar

EH 01.044 *Solenzara,* Solenzara;
EH 01.067 *Pyrénées,*

Cazaux;
EH 03.067 *Parisis*, Villacoublay;
EH 05.067 *Alpilles*, Aix-en-Provence;
GAM 00.056 *Vaucluse*, Evreux;
CEAM, Mont-de-Marsan

2014	AS.332C	PN	05.067
2057	AS.332C	PO	00.082
2093	AS.332L	PP	05.067
2233	AS.332L-1	FY	00.056
2235	AS.332L-1	67-FZ	03.067
2244	AS.332C	PM	01.044
2342	AS.532UL	FX	00.056
2369	AS.532UL	FW	00.056
2375	AS.532UL	FV	00.056
2377	AS.332L-1	FU	03.067
2461	EC.725AP	SA	01.067
2549	EC.725AP	SB	01.067
2552	EC.725AP	SE	01.067
2555	EC.725AP	SF	01.067
2619	EC.725AP	SC	05.067
2626	EC.725AP	SD	01.067

Eurocopter AS.555AN Fennec

ETM 01.040 *Moselle*, Metz;
ETM 02.040 *Médoc*, Bordeaux;
ETOM 00.050 *Réunion*, St Denis;
ETOM 00.052 *La Tontouta*, Noumea;
ETOM 00.055 *Ouessant*, Dakar
ETOM 00.058 *Antilles*, Fort de France;
EH 03.067 *Parisis*, Villacoublay;
EH 05.067 *Alpilles*, Aix-en-Provence;
EH 06.067 *Solenzara*, Solenzara;
ETOM 00.082 *Maine*, Faaa-Tahiti

5361	UT	01.040
5368	UU	02.040
5382	UV	05.067
5386	UX	05.067
5387	UY	03.067
5390	UZ	02.040
5391	VA	00.055
5392	VB	05.067
5393	VC	00.082
5396	VD	01.040
5397	VE	03.067
5398	VF	02.040
5399	VG$	00.050
5400	VH	01.040
5412	VI	01.040
5427	VJ	03.067
5430	VL	06.067
5431	VM	01.040
5440	VN	03.067
5441	VO	05.067
5444	VP	00.055
5445	VQ	01.040
5448	VR	03.067
5452	VS	01.040
5455	VT	00.058
5458	VV	05.067
5466	VW	01.040
5468	VX	01.040
5490	VY	05.067
5506	WA	06.067
5509	WB	05.067
5511	WC	05.067
5516	WD	03.067
5520	WE	03.067
5523	WF	03.067
5526	WG	05.067
5530	WH	05.067
5532	WI	05.067
5534	WJ	05.067
5536	WK	05.067
5559	WL	05.067

Extra EA-330LC*/EA-330SC

EVAA, Salon de Provence

03*	F-TGCH
04	F-TGCI
05	F-TGCJ

Lockheed C-130H/C-130H-30* Hercules

ET 02.061 *Franche-Comté*, Orléans

4588	61-PM
4589	61-PN
5114	61-PA
5116	61-PB
5119	61-PC
5140	61-PD
5142*	61-PE
5144*	61-PF$
5150*	61-PG
5151*	61-PH
5152*	61-PI
5153*	61-PJ
5226*	61-PK
5227*	61-PL

SOCATA TB-30 Epsilon

**Cartouche Dorée*, (EPAA 00.315) Cognac (BA 709);
EPAA 00.315, Cognac (BA 709);
SOCATA, Tarbes
Please note: A large number of these machines are kept in temporary storage at Chateaudun

1	315-UA
4	315-UC
5	315-UD
6	315-UE
7	315-UF
8	315-UG
9	315-UH
10	315-UI
12	315-UK
13	315-UL
14	315-UM
16	315-UO
21	315-UT
26	315-UY
27	315-UZ
28	315-VA
30	315-VC
32	315-VE
34	315-VG
36	315-VI
39	315-VL
40	315-VM
41	315-VN
43	315-VP
44	315-VQ
46	315-VS
47	315-VT
50	315-VW
56	315-WA
57	F-ZVLB
61	315-WD
62	315-WE
63	315-WF
64	315-WG
65	315-WH
66	315-WI
67	315-WJ
68	315-WK
69	315-WL
70	315-WM
73	315-WP
74	315-WQ
77	315-WT
78	315-WU
79	315-WV
80	315-WW
82	315-WY
83	315-WZ
84	315-XA
85	315-XB
87	315-XD
89	315-XF
90	F-SEXG [0]*
91	315-XH
92	315-XI
93	315-XJ
95	315-XL
96	315-XM
97	315-XN
99	315-XP
100	315-XQ
101	F-SEXR [1]*
102	F-SEXS [2]*
103	315-XT
104	F-SEXU [3]*
105	315-XV
106	315-XW
108	315-XY
110	315-YA
111	315-YB
112	315-YC
113	315-YD
114	315-YE
115	315-YF
116	315-YG
117	315-YH
118	315-YI
120	315-YK
121	315-YL
122	315-YM
125	315-YP
127	315-YR
129	315-YT
130	315-YU
131	315-YV
132	315-YW
133	315-YX
134	315-YY
136	315-ZA
138	315-ZC
139	315-ZD
140	315-ZE
141	F-SEZF [4]*
142	315-ZG
143	315-ZH

144	315-ZI
146	315-ZK
149	315-ZM
150	315-ZN
152	315-ZO
153	315-ZP
154	315-ZQ
155	315-ZR
159	315-ZT

SOCATA TBM 700A
CEAM (EC 02.330), Mont-de-Marsan;
CEV, Cazaux & Istres;
ETM 01.040 *Moselle*, Metz;
ET 00.043 *Médoc*, Bordeaux;
ETEC 00.065, Villacoublay;
EdC 00.070, Chateaudun

33	XA	00.043
77	XD	01.040
78	XE	CEAM
93	XL	00.065
95	XH	CEAM
103	XI	00.065
104	XJ	00.070
105	XK	00.065
106	MN	CEV
110	XP	01.040
111	XM	01.040
117	XN	01.040
125	XO	00.065
131	XQ	00.065
146	XR	00.065
147	XS	00.065

Transall C-160NG GABRIEL*/ C-160R
CEAM (EET 06.330), Mont-de-Marsan;
CEV, Cazaux & Istres;
EEA 00.054 *Dunkerque*, Metz;
ET 01.061 *Touraine* &
ET 03.061 *Poitou*, Orléans;
ET 01.064 *Bearn* &
ET 02.064 Anjou, Evreux;
ETOM 00.050 *Réunion*, St Denis;
ETOM 00.055 *Ouessant*, Dakar;
ETOM 00.058 Guadeloupe, Pointe-à-Pitre;
ETOM 00.088 *Larzac*, Djibouti

RA02	C-160R	61-MI	01.061
R1	C-160R	61-MA	01.061
R2	C-160R	61-MB	00.050
R3	C-160R	61-MC	00.058
R4	C-160R	61-MD	01.061
R11	C-160R	61-MF	01.061
R15	C-160R	61-MJ	01.061
R18	C-160R	61-MM	01.061
R42	C-160R	61-MN	01.061
R51	C-160R	61-MW$	01.061
R54	C-160R	61-MZ	01.061
R55	C-160R	61-ZC	03.061
R86	C-160R	61-ZD	03.061
R87	C-160R	61-ZE	00.050
R89	C-160R	61-ZG	03.061
R90	C-160R	61-ZH	03.061
R91	C-160R	61-ZI	03.061
R92	C-160R	61-ZJ	03.061
R93	C-160R	61-ZK	03.061
R94	C-160R	61-ZL	03.061
R95	C-160R	61-ZM	03.061
R96	C-160R	61-ZN	03.061
R97	C-160R	61-ZA	03.061
R98	C-160R	61-ZP	00.050
R99	C-160R	61-ZQ	03.061
R153	C-160R	61-ZS	03.061
R154	C-160R	61-ZT	03.061
R157	C-160R	61-ZW	03.061
R158	C-160R	61-ZX	03.061
R159	C-160R	61-ZY	03.061
R160	C-160R	61-ZZ	03.061
R201	C-160R	64-GA	01.064
R202	C-160R	64-GB	02.064
R203	C-160R	64-GC	01.064
R204	C-160R	64-GD	02.064
R205	C-160R	64-GE	01.064
R206	C-160R	64-GF	02.064
R207	C-160R	64-GG	01.064
R208	C-160R	64-GH$	02.064
R210	C-160R	64-GJ	02.064
R211	C-160R	64-GK	01.064
R212	C-160R	64-GL	02.064
R213	C-160R	64-GM	01.064
R214	C-160R	64-GN	02.064
R215	C-160R	64-GO	01.064
F216	C-160NG*	54-GT	00.054
R217	C-160R	64-GQ	01.064
R218	C-160R	64-GR$	02.064
F221	C-160NG*	GS	00.054
R223	C-160R	64-GW	01.064
R224	C-160R	64-GX	02.064
R225	C-160R	64-GY	01.064
R226	C-160R	64-GZ	02.064

Aéronavale/Marine
Dassault-Breguet Atlantique 2
21 Flottille, Nimes/Garons;
23 Flottille, Lorient/Lann Bihoué

1	21F
2	21F
3	21F
4	23F
6	23F
9	21F$
10	21F
11	21F
12	23F
13	21F
14	23F
15	21F
16	21F
17	21F$
18	21F
19	23F
20	23F
21	21F
25	21F
26	21F
27	23F
28	21F

Dassault Falcon 10(MER)
ES 57, Landivisiau

32
101
129
133
143
185

Dassault Falcon 20G Guardian
25 Flottille, Papeete & Tontouta

48
65
72
77
80

Dassault Falcon 50 SURMAR
24 Flottille, Lorient/Lann Bihoué

7
30
36
132

Dassault Rafale-M
12 Flottille, Landivisiau;
AMD-BA, Istres;
CEPA, Istres;
CEV, Istres
ETR, 02.092 *Aquitaine*, St Dizier

M01	CEV
M02	CEV
1	CEV
11	12F
12	12F
13	12F
14	12F
15	12F
16	12F
17	12F
18	12F
19	12F
20	12F
21	12F
23	12F
24	12F
26	12F
27	CEPA
28	12F
29	12F
30	
31	

Dassault Super Etendard
11 Flottille, Landivisiau;
17 Flottille, Landivisiau;
CEV, Cazaux & Istres

1	17F
2	11F
4	17F
6	11F
8	17F
10	17F
11	17F
12	11F
13	11F
14	CEV
15	17F$

16 11F
17 17F
18 17F
19 17F
24 17F
28 11F
30 11F
31 17F
32 17F
33 17F
35 11F
37 17F
39 17F
41 11F
43 11F
44 17F
45 17F
46 17F
47 11F
48 17F
50 11F
51 17F
52 17F
55 17F
57 17F
59 17F
61 11F
62 17F
65 17F
68 CEV
69 11F
71 17F

Embraer
EMB.121AN Xingu
24 Flottille, Lorient/Lann Bihoué;
28 Flottille, Nimes/Garons
30 24F
47 24F
65 28F
67 28F$
68 24F
69 24F
71 28F
74 24F$
77 28F
79 28F
81 24F
85 24F
87 24F

Eurocopter
AS.365/AS.565 Panther
35 Flottille, Hyères,
(with detachments at Cherbourg, Lanvéoc/ Poulmic, La Rochelle & Le Touquet)
36 Flottille, Hyères
17 AS.365N 35F
19 AS.365N 35F
24 AS.365N 35F
57 AS.365N 35F
81 AS.365N 35F
91 AS.365N 35F
157 AS.365N 35F
313 AS.365F1 35F
318 AS.365F1 35F
322 AS.365F1 35F
355 AS.565MA 36F
362 AS.565MA 35F
403 AS.565UA 36F
436 AS.565MA 36F
452 AS.565MA 36F
453 AS.565MA 35F
466 AS.565MA 36F
482 AS.565MA 36F
486 AS.565MA 36F
488 AS.565MA 36F
503 AS.565MA 35F
505 AS.565MA 36F
506 AS.565MA 35F
507 AS.565MA 36F
510 AS.365N3 35F
511 AS.565MA 36F
519 AS.565MA 36F
522 AS.565MA 36F$
524 AS.565MA 36F
542 AS.565MA 36F

Eurocopter
EC.225LP Super Puma 2+
32 Flottille,
Lanvéoc/Poulmic
2741
2752

NH Industries
NH.90-NFH/NH.90-NHC*
Caiman
31 Flottille, Hyères;
CEPA, Hyàres
F-ZWTO (1018)
2 CEPA
3*

Northrop Grumman
E-2C Hawkeye
4 Flottille,
Lorient/Lann Bihoué
1 (165455)
2 (165456)
3 (166417)

Sud
SA.316B/SA.319B/SE.3160
Alouette III
35 Flottille, Hyères;
ES 22/ESHE, Lanvéoc/Poulmic
13 SE.3160 35F
14 SE.3160 22S
18 SE.3160 22S
41 SE.3160 22S
100 SA.319B 22S
114 SA.319B 22S
161 SA.319B 22S
237 SA.319B 22S
244 SE.3160 35F
245 SE.3160 22S
268 SA.319B 22S
279 SE.3160 22S
302 SA.319B 22S
303 SA.319B 22S
309 SA.319B 22S
314 SA.319B 22S
347 SA.319B 22S
358 SA.319B 22S
731 SA.316B 22S
806 SA.316B 22S
809 SA.316B 22S
997 SA.319B 22S

Westland
Lynx HAS2(FN)/HAS4(FN)*
34 Flottille, Lanvéoc/Poulmic
(with a detachment at Hyères)
CEPA, Hyères
260
263
264
267
269
270
271
272$
273
276
621
623
624
625
627
801*
802*
804*
806*
807*
808*
810*
811*
812*
813*
814*

Aviation Legére de l'Armée de Terre (ALAT)
Aérospatiale
SA.330Ba Puma
1 RHC, Phalsbourg;
3 RHC, Etain;
5 RHC, Pau;
4 RHFS, Pau;
EALAT, Dax & Le Luc;
ESAM, Bourges;
GAM/STAT, Valence;
GIH, Cazaux
1005 DCA ESAM
1006 DAA
1020 DAB 5 RHC
1036 DAC 1 RHC
1037 DAD 5 RHC
1049 DAE 5 RHC
1052 DCB EALAT
1055 DAF GIH
1056 DCC GAM/STAT
1057 DCD EALAT
1069 DAG 1 RHC
1071 DCE EALAT
1073 DCF
1078 DAH GIH
1093 DCG 3 RHC
1100 DAJ 3 RHC
1102 DAK
1107 DAL
1109 DAM 3 RHC
1114 DCH
1122 DCI
1123 DCJ 5 RHC
1128 DAN 1 RHC
1130 DCK 5 RHC
1135 DCL 1 RHC
1136 DCM 1 RHC
1142 DCN
1143 DAO 1 RHC
1145 DCO 3 RHC
1149 DAP EALAT
1150 DCP 3 RHC
1155 DCQ 4 RHFS
1156 DAQ 1 RHC

1163 DCR EALAT
1164 DCS 1 RHC
1165 DCT 1 RHC
1171 DCU 1 RHC
1172 DCV 1 RHC
1173 DAR
1176 DAS 3 RHC
1177 DCW 3 RHC
1179 DCX 5 RHC
1182 DCY 1 RHC
1186 DCZ 5 RHC
1189 DAT 3 RHC
1190 DDA 1 RHC
1192 DDB 1 RHC
1196 DDC EALAT
1197 DAU 5 RHC
1198 DDD 1 RHC
1204 DAV 1 RHC
1206 DDE 3 RHC
1211 DAW
1213 DDF 1 RHC
1214 DAX 3 RHC
1217 DAY
1219 DAZ 1 RHC
1222 DDG 1 RHC
1223 DDH EALAT
1228 DDI
1231 DDK 5 RHC
1232 DBA 1 RHC
1235 DDL
1236 DDM EALAT
1239 DDN EALAT
1243 DBB 5 RHC
1244 DDO 5 RHC
1248 DBC 3 RHC
1252 DDP EALAT
1255 DDQ 5 RHC
1256 DDR GAM/STAT
1260 DDS EALAT
1262 DBD 5 RHC
1269 DDT 5 RHC
1277 DBE 1 RHC
1411 DDU 1 RHC
1417 DBF
1419 DDV 1 RHC
1438 DBG GAM/STAT
1447 DDW 1 RHC
1451 DBH 1 RHC
1507 DBI 3 RHC
1510 DBJ
1512 DBK
1519 DBL 1 RHC
1617 DBM 1 RHC
1632 DBN
1634 DBO 3 RHC
1654 DBP 5 RHC
1662 DDX EALAT
1663 DBQ 4 RHFS
5682 DBR 4 RHFS

Aérospatiale
SA.341/342 Gazelle

1 RHC, Phalsbourg;
3 RHC, Etain;
5 RHC, Pau;
4 RHFS, Pau;
COMALAT, Villacoublay;
EALAT, Dax & Le Luc;
EFA, Le Luc;
EHADT, Etain;
ESAM, Bourges;
GAM/STAT, Valence

SA.341F Gazelle

1119 GHA EALAT
1129 GHB EALAT
1131 GQG
1149 GQH 1 RHC
1171 GQI 1 RHC
1175 GHC
1194 GQJ 5 RHC
1198 GHD EALAT
1267 GHE EALAT
1285 GQK 4 RHFS
1291 GQA EALAT
1353 GHF EALAT
1369 GQL 1 RHC
1372 GQM 3 RHC
1383 GQN 5 RHC
1399 GQB EALAT
1416 GQO 5 RHC
1419 GHG EALAT
1420 GQP 3 RHC
1447 GQC
1451 GQQ 1 RHC
1463 GQR 4 RHFS
1467 GHH EALAT
1483 GQS 3 RHC
1487 GQT 4 RHFS
1501 GHI EALAT
1504 GQD EALAT
1508 GQW 1 RHC
1518 GQX 1 RHC
1519 GHJ EALAT
1522 GQU
1523 GQE EALAT
1536 GHK
1540 GHL EALAT
1541 GHM EALAT
1544 GQF EALAT
1562 GQV 1 RHC
1565 GHN EALAT
1593 GQY 3 RHC
1594 GHO EALAT
1597 GHP EALAT
1598 GHQ EALAT
1607 GHR EALAT
1608 GHS EALAT
1611 GHT EALAT
1612 GHU EALAT
1619 GHV EALAT
1657 GHX EALAT
1659 GHY EALAT
1672 GHZ EALAT
1678 GIA EALAT
1690 GIB EALAT
1693 GIC EALAT
1718 GQZ 5 RHC

SA.342L1 Gazelle

4205 GEA EALAT
4206 GEB EALAT
4207 GEC 3 RHC
4208 GED GAM/STAT
4209 GEE EALAT
4210 GEF 1 RHC
4211 GEG EALAT
4212 GEH ESAM
4214 GEI EALAT
4215 GEJ EALAT
4216 GEK GAM/STAT
4217 GEL 1 RHC
4218 GEM 1 RHC
4219 GEN 4 RHFS
4220 GEO 1 RHC
4221 GEP EALAT
4222 GEQ
4223 GER 3 RHC
4224 GES 1 RHC
4225 GET GAM/STAT
4226 GEU GAM/STAT
4227 GEV 1 RHC
4228 GEW 1 RHC
4229 GEX 4 RHFS
4230 GEY
4231 GEZ 1 RHC
4232 GFA
4233 GFB 3 RHC
4234 GFC

SA.342M Gazelle

1732 GJA EALAT
3458 GNA EALAT
3459 GAA 1 RHC
3476 GAB 4 RHFS
3477 GJB EALAT
3511 GJC EALAT
3512 GAC 1 RHC
3513 GNB COMALAT
3529 GJD EALAT
3530 GAD 4 RHFS
3531 GJE EALAT
3546 GJF EALAT
3547 GJG EFA
3548 GAE
3549 GNC EALAT
3564 GAF 3 RHC
3567 GMA EALAT
3615 GJH EALAT
3617 GND COMALAT
3848 GAG 5 RHC
3849 GAH 5 RHC
3850 GAI 1 RHC
3851 GJI EALAT
3852 GNE EALAT
3853 GNF EALAT
3855 GJJ EALAT
3856 GAJ 5 RHC
3857 GJK EALAT
3858 GNG EHADT
3859 GAK 4 RHFS
3862 GAL 1 RHC
3863 GAM 3 RHC
3864 GJL ESAM
3865 GAN 3 RHC
3867 GJM EALAT
3868 GAO 1 RHC
3870 GME
3896 GNJ
3911 GAP 1 RHC
3921 GAQ 5 RHC
3929 GJN EALAT
3930 GMF
3938 GAR EALAT
3939 GMG
3947 GAS 5 RHC
3948 GAT 1 RHC
3956 GNK
3957 GAU
3964 GAV 3 RHC
3965 GJO EALAT
3973 GNL
3992 GNM EALAT
3996 GAW 5 RHC
4008 GNN
4014 GJP GAM/STAT
4018 GAX
4019 GAY 3 RHC
4020 GAZ 1 RHC
4022 GJQ EALAT
4023 GMH ESAM
4026 GBA 1 RHC

4032	GNO	EALAT
4034	GBB	1 RHC
4038	GJR	EALAT
4039	GBC	1 RHC
4042	GMB	EALAT
4047	GJS	EALAT
4048	GBD	EALAT
4049	GNP	EALAT
4053	GBE	1 RHC
4055	GJT	
4059	GBF	1 RHC
4060	GNQ	EALAT
4061	GBG	GAM/STAT
4065	GNR	EALAT
4066	GBH	3 RHC
4067	GJU	EALAT
4071	GNS	EHADT
4072	GBI	1 RHC
4078	GJV	EALAT
4079	GMC	5 RHC
4083	GNT	EALAT
4084	GBJ	3 RHC
4091	GBK	1 RHC
4095	GBL	3 RHC
4096	GNU	EALAT
4102	GJW	EALAT
4103	GJX	EALAT
4108	GBM	
4109	GBN	5 RHC
4114	GBO	EALAT
4115	GBP	3 RHC
4118	GNV	EALAT
4119	GBQ	1 RHC
4120	GBR	EALAT
4123	GJY	EALAT
4124	GBS	4 RHFS
4135	GNW	
4136	GBT	1 RHC
4140	GBU	1 RHC
4141	GBV	
4142	GBW	5 RHC
4143	GNX	EALAT
4144	GBX	1 RHC
4145	GBY	1 RHC
4146	GNY	EALAT
4151	GBZ	3 RHC
4155	GCA	3 RHC
4158	GCB	5 RHC
4159	GNZ	EALAT
4160	GCC	3 RHC
4161	GCD	1 RHC
4162	GCE	5 RHC
4164	GCF	4 RHFS
4166	GJZ	EALAT
4168	GCG	5 RHC
4171	GMI	EALAT
4172	GCH	
4175	GCI	4 RHFS
4176	GKA	EALAT
4177	GKB	EALAT
4178	GOA	
4179	GCJ	1 RHC
4180	GCK	GAM/STAT
4181	GCL	3 RHC
4182	GKC	EALAT
4183	GOB	
4184	GOC	EHADT
4185	GKD	EALAT
4186	GCM	1 RHC
4187	GKE	EALAT
4189	GCN	
4190	GMJ	EALAT
4191	GCO	4 RHFS
4192	GOD	
4194	GMD	1 RHC
4195	GCP	3 RHC
4198	GCQ	3 RHC
4201	GMK	EALAT

Aérospatiale
AS.532UL Cougar
1 RHC, Phalsbourg;
4 RHFS, Pau;
GAM/STAT, Valence

2252	CGA	GAM/STAT
2267	CGC	4 RHFS
2272	CGE	1 RHC
2273	CGF	1 RHC
2282	CGG	
2285	CGH	
2290	CGI	1 RHC
2293	CGJ	4 RHFS
2299	CGK	4 RHFS
2300	CGL	1 RHC
2301	CGM	1 RHC
2303	CGN	1 RHC
2316	CGO	
2323	CGQ	4 RHFS
2324	CGR	4 RHFS
2325	CGS	
2327	CGT	
2331	CGU	
2336	CGV	4 RHFS
2443	CGW	
2446	CGX	1 RHC

Eurocopter
(EC.665 Tigre)
5 RHC, Pau;
EFA, Le Luc;
GAM/STAT, Valence

2001	BHH	EFA
2002	BHI	EFA
2003	BHJ	EFA
2004	BHK	EFA
2006	BHL	EFA
2009	BHB	EFA
2010	BHA	5 RHC
2011	BHM	5 RHC
2012	BHT	GAM/STAT
2013	BHC	5 RHC
2015	BHD	5 RHC
2018	BHE	5 RHC
2019	BHF	5 RHC
2021	BHN	EFA
2022	BHG	5 RHC
2023	BHP	5 RHC
2024	BHO	5 RHC
2025	BHQ	5 RHC
2026	BHR	GAM/STAT
2027	BHS	5 RHC
2028	BHU	5 RHC
2029	BHV	5 RHC
2030	BHW	5 RHC
2031	BHX	5 RHC
2034		
2035		
2037		

Eurocopter
EC.725AP Cougar
GIH, Cazaux

2611	CAA
2628	CAB
2630	CAC
2631	CAD
2633	CAE
2638	CAF
2640	CAG
2642	CAH

Pilatus
PC-6B/B2-H4 Turbo Porter
1 GSALAT, Montauban

887	MCA
888	MCB
889	MCC
890	MCD
891	MCE

SOCATA
TBM 700A/TBM 700B*
EAAT, Rennes

35	ABW
70	ABX
80	ABY
94	ABZ
99	ABO
100	ABP
115	ABQ
136	ABR
139	ABS
156*	ABT
159*	ABU
160*	ABV

French Govt
Aérospatiale
AS.350B Ecureuil
Gendarmerie;
Sécurité Civile*

F-MCSF	(2225)	AS.350B-1
F-MJCA	(1028)	AS.350BA
F-MJCB	(1574)	AS.350B
F-MJCC	(1916)	AS.350B-1
F-MJCD	(1576)	AS.350B
F-MJCE	(1812)	AS.350B
F-MJCF	(1691)	AS.350BA
F-MJCG	(1753)	AS.350B
F-MJCH	(1756)	AS.350B
F-MJCI	(2222)	AS.350B-1
F-MJCJ	(1809)	AS.350B
F-MJCL	(1811)	AS.350B
F-MJCM	(1952)	AS.350B
F-MJCN	(2044)	AS.350BA
F-MJCO	(1917)	AS.350B-1
F-MJCP	(2045)	AS.350B
F-MJCQ	(2057)	AS.350BA
F-MJCR	(2088)	AS.350B
F-MJCS	(1575)	AS.350B
F-MJCT	(2104)	AS.350B
F-MJCU	(2117)	AS.350B
F-MJCV	(2118)	AS.350B
F-MJCW	(2218)	AS.350BA
F-MJCX	(2219)	AS.350B
F-MJCZ	(1467)	AS.350BA
F-MJEB	(1692)	AS.350B
F-MJEC	(1810)	AS.350B
F-ZBBN		AS.350B*
F-ZBEA		AS.350B
F-ZBFC		AS.350B-1*
F-ZBFD		AS.350B-1*

Aérospatiale
AS.355 Twin Ecureuil
Douanes Francaises

F-ZBAD	AS.355F-2
F-ZBEF	AS.355F-1
F-ZBEK	AS.355F-1

F-ZBEL AS.355F-1

Beech
Super King Air B200
Sécurité Civile
F-ZBFJ 98
F-ZBFK 96
F-ZBMB 97

Canadair CL-415
Sécurité Civile
F-ZBEG 39
F-ZBEU 42
F-ZBFN 33
F-ZBFP 31
F-ZBFS 32
F-ZBFV 37
F-ZBFW 38
F-ZBFX 34
F-ZBFY 35
F-ZBME 44
F-ZBMF 45
F-ZBMG 48

Cessna F.406 Caravan II
Douanes Francaises
F-ZBAB (0025)
F-ZBBB (0039)
F-ZBCE (0042)
F-ZBCF (0077)
F-ZBCG (0066)
F-ZBCH (0075)
F-ZBCI (0070)
F-ZBCJ (0074)
F-ZBEP (0006)
F-ZBES (0017)
F-ZBFA (0001)
F-ZBGA (0086)
F-ZBGD (0090)
F-ZBGE (0061)

Conair
Turbo Firecat
Sécurité Civile
F-ZBAA 22
F-ZBAP 12
F-ZBAZ 01
F-ZBCZ 23
F-ZBEH 20
F-ZBET 15
F-ZBEW 11
F-ZBEY 07
F-ZBMA 24

De Havilland Canada
DHC-8Q-402MR
Sécurité Civile
F-ZBMC 73
F-ZBMD 74

Eurocopter
EC.135T-2
Douanes Francaises*;
Gendarmerie
F-MJDA (0642)
F-MJDB (0654)
F-MJDC (0717)
F-MJDD (0727)
F-MJDE (0747)
F-MJDF (0757)
F-MJDG (0772)
F-MJDH (0787)
F-MJDI (0797)
F-MJDJ (0806)
F-MJDK (0857)
F-MJDL (0867)
F-ZBGF*
F-ZBGG*
F-ZBGH*
F-ZBGI*
F-ZBGJ*

Eurocopter
EC.145
Gendarmerie;
Sécurité Civile*
F-MJBA (9008) EC.145C-1
F-MJBB (9014) EC.145C-1
F-MJBC (9018) EC.145C-1
F-MJBD (9019) EC.145C-1
F-MJBE (9025) EC.145C-1
F-MJBF (9035) EC.145C-2
F-MJBG (9036) EC.145C-2
F-MJBH (9037) EC.145C-2
F-MJBI (9127) EC.145C-2
F-MJBJ (9140) EC.145C-2
F-MJBK (9162) EC.145C-2
F-MJBM (9113) EC.145C-2
F-MJBN (9173) EC.145C-2
F-MJBO (9124) EC.145C-2
F-MJBR (9169) EC.145C-2
F-MJBT (9173) EC.145C-2
F-ZBPA EC.145C-1*
F-ZBPD EC.145C-1*
F-ZBPE EC.145C-1*
F-ZBPF EC.145C-1*
F-ZBPG EC.145C-1*
F-ZBPH EC.145C-1*
F-ZBPI EC.145C-1*
F-ZBPJ EC.145C-1*
F-ZBPK EC.145C-1*
F-ZBPL EC.145C-1*
F-ZBPM EC.145C-1*
F-ZBPN EC.145C-1*
F-ZBPO EC.145C-1*
F-ZBPP EC.145C-2*
F-ZBPQ EC.145C-2*
F-ZBPS EC.145C-2*
F-ZBPT EC.145C-2*
F-ZBPU EC.145C-2*
F-ZBPV EC.145C-2*
F-ZBPW EC.145C-2*
F-ZBPX EC.145C-2*
F-ZBPY EC.145C-2*
F-ZBPZ EC.145C-2*
F-ZBQA EC.145C-2*
F-ZBQB EC.145C-2*
F-ZBQC EC.145C-2*
F-ZBQD EC.145C-2*
F-ZBQE EC.145C-2*
F-ZBQF EC.145C-2*
F-ZBQG EC.145C-2*
F-ZBQH EC.145C-2*
F-ZBQI EC.145C-2*
F-ZBQJ EC.145C-2*
F-ZBQK EC.145C-2*

Civil operated aircraft in military use
BAE Jetstream 41
AVDEF, Nimes/Garons
F-HAVD
F-HAVF

Dassault Falcon 20
AVDEF, Nimes/Garons
F-GPAA Falcon 20ECM
F-GPAB Falcon 20E
F-GPAD Falcon 20E

Grob G120A-F
ECATS, Cognac
F-GUKA
F-GUKB
F-GUKC
F-GUKD
F-GUKE
F-GUKF
F-GUKG
F-GUKH
F-GUKI
F-GUKJ
F-GUKK
F-GUKL
F-GUKM
F-GUKN
F-GUKO
F-GUKP
F-GUKR
F-GUKS
F-GUKV
F-GUKX

GABON
Grumman
G.1159C Gulfstream IVSP
Gabonese Government,
Libreville
TR-KSP

GERMANY
Please note that German serials do not officially include the '+' part in them but aircraft wearing German markings are often painted with a cross in the middle, which is why it is included here.
Luftwaffe, Marineflieger
Airbus A.310-304/MRTT*
1/FBS, Köln-Bonn
10+21
10+22 (wfu)
10+23
10+24*
10+25*
10+26*
10+27*

Canadair
CL601-1A Challenger
3/FBS, Köln-Bonn
12+04
12+05
12+06
12+07

Airbus A.319CJ-115X
3/FBS, Köln-Bonn
15+01
15+02

Airbus A.340-313X
3/FBS, Köln-Bonn
16+01 (on order)
16+02 (on order)

Eurofighter
EF.2000GS/EF.2000GT*

EADS, Manching;
JbG-31 *Boelcke*, Nörvenich;
JG-73 *Steinhoff*, Laage;
JG-74 *Molders*, Neuburg/Donau;
TsLw-1, Kaufbeuren;
WTD-61, Ingolstadt

30+02*	JG-73
30+03*	JG-73
30+04*	JG-73
30+05*	JG-73
30+06	JG-74
30+07	TsLw-1
30+09	JG-74
30+10*	JG-73
30+11	JG-73
30+12	JG-73
30+14*	JG-73
30+15	JG-73
30+17*	JG-73
30+20*	JG-73 $
30+22	EADS
30+23	JbG-31
30+24*	JG-73
30+25	JG-74
30+26	TsLw-1
30+27*	JG-73
30+28	JG-73
30+29	JG-74
30+30	JG-74
30+31*	JG-74
30+32	JG-74
30+33	JG-74
30+35*	JG-74
30+38*	JG-73
30+39	JG-74
30+40	JbG-31
30+42*	JG-73
30+45	JG-73
30+46	JG-73
30+47	JG-73
30+48	JG-74
30+49	JG-73
30+50	JG-73
30+51	JG-73
30+52	JG-73
30+53	JG-73
30+54*	JbG-31
30+55	JG-73
30+56	JG-73
30+57	JG-73
30+58	JG-74
30+59	EADS
30+60	JG-73
30+61	JG-74
30+62	JG-73
30+63	JG-74
30+64	JG-74
30+65	JG-74
30+66	JbG-31
30+67	
30+68	
30+69	
30+70	
31+14	JbG-31
31+15	TsLw-1
31+16	JG-73
31+17	JG-73
31+18	JG-73
31+19	JG-73
31+20	JG-73
31+21	JG-73
31+22	JG-73
98+03*	EADS
98+04	EADS
98+07	EADS
98+31*	EADS

McD F-4F Phantom

JG-71 *Richthofen*, Wittmundhaven;
TsLw-1, Kaufbeuren;
WTD-61, Ingolstadt

37+01	JG-71$
37+04	TsLw-1
37+14	TsLw-1$
37+15	WTD-61
37+22	JG-71
37+26	JG-71
37+48	JG-71$
37+63	JG-71
37+65	JG-71
37+77	JG-71
37+79	JG-71
37+81	JG-71
37+84	JG-71
37+85	JG-71
37+89	JG-71
37+92	JG-71
37+96	JG-71
38+00	JG-71
38+01	JG-71
38+02	JG-71
38+10	JG-71
38+13	WTD-61
38+16	JG-71
38+26	JG-71
38+28	JG-71
38+29	JG-71
38+33	JG-71
38+37	JG-71
38+39	$
38+42	JG-71
38+43	JG-71
38+44	JG-71
38+45	JG-71
38+46	JG-71
38+48	JG-71
38+50	JG-71
38+53	JG-71
38+57	JG-71
38+58	JG-71
38+60	JG-71
38+61	TsLw-1
38+62	JG-71
38+66	JG-71
38+67	JG-71
38+68	JG-71
38+70	JG-71
38+73	JG-71
38+74	JG-71
38+75	JG-71
99+91	WTD-61

Panavia Tornado Strike/ Trainer[1]/ECR[2]

AkG-51 *Immelmann*, Schleswig/Jagel;
EADS, Manching;
GAFFTC, Holloman AFB, USA;
JbG-32, Lechfeld;
JbG-33, Büchel;
TsLw-1, Kaufbeuren;
WTD-61, Ingolstadt

43+01[1]	JbG-33
43+02[1]	JbG-33
43+07[1]	AkG-51
43+08[1]	JbG-32
43+10[1]	JbG-33
43+18	JbG-33
43+20	
43+23[1]	JbG-33
43+25	JbG-33
43+29[1]	
43+31[1]	GAFFTC
43+32	
43+34	TsLw-1
43+35[1]	AkG-51
43+37[1]	JbG-32
43+38	JbG-32
43+42[1]	GAFFTC
43+43[1]	JbG-32
43+45[1]	JbG-32
43+46	AkG-51
43+48	AkG-51
43+50	AkG-51
43+52	JbG-33
43+54	TsLw-1
43+58	JbG-33
43+59	TsLw-1
43+71	JbG-32
43+72	JbG-33
43+73	AkG-51
43+75	GAFFTC
43+87	JbG-33
43+92[1]	AkG-51
43+94[1]	GAFFTC
43+97[1]	AkG-51
43+98	AkG-51
44+00	JbG-33
44+02	JbG-32
44+06	JbG-32
44+13	TsLw-1
44+16[1]	JbG-33
44+17	AkG-51
44+21	
44+23	JbG-33
44+26	JbG-33
44+29	JbG-33
44+30	JbG-32
44+33	JbG-33
44+34	AkG-51
44+38[1]	GAFFTC
44+46	AkG-51
44+58	JbG-32
44+61	AkG-51
44+64	AkG-51
44+65	AkG-51
44+69	AkG-51
44+70	
44+72[1]	GAFFTC
44+73[1]	
44+75[1]	AkG-51
44+78	AkG-51
44+79	JbG-33
44+80	AkG-51
44+90	AkG-51
44+92	JbG-33
44+96	AkG-51
45+00	JbG-33
45+04	JbG-33
45+06	AkG-51$
45+07	JbG-33
45+08	AkG-51
45+09	JbG-33
45+10	JbG-32
45+12[1]	JbG-32

45+13[1] AkG-51
45+14[1] GAFFTC
45+15[1] GAFFTC
45+16[1] JbG-33
45+17 GAFFTC
45+19 AkG-51
45+20 AkG-51
45+21 JbG-33
45+22 AkG-51
45+23
45+25 WTD-61
45+28 JbG-33
45+31 JbG-33
45+33 JbG-33
45+34 JbG-33
45+35 AkG-51
45+36
45+38 JbG-32$
45+39 JbG-32
45+40 JbG-33
45+41 JbG-32
45+43 JbG-33
45+45 JbG-33
45+47 TsLw-1
45+49 JbG-33
45+50 AkG-51
45+51 AkG-51
45+52 JbG-33
45+53 TsLw-1
45+54 GAFFTC
45+56 $
45+57 AkG-51
45+59 JbG-33
45+60[1] AkG-51
45+61[1] AkG-51
45+64 AkG-51
45+66 JbG-33
45+67 AkG-51
45+68 JbG-33
45+69 JbG-33
45+70[1] JbG-33
45+71 JbG-32
45+72 JbG-32
45+73[1] GAFFTC
45+74 TsLw-1
45+76 JbG-33
45+77[1] JbG-33
45+78 JbG-33
45+79 JbG-33
45+81
45+82
45+83 JbG-33
45+84
45+85 AkG-51
45+86 JbG-33
45+87 JbG-33
45+88
45+90 JbG-33
45+91 JbG-33
45+92 JbG-33
45+93 JbG-33
45+94 JbG-33
45+96 JbG-33
45+98 GAFFTC
45+99[1] GAFFTC$
46+00[1] GAFFTC
46+01 JbG-33
46+02 JbG-33
46+04[1] GAFFTC
46+05[1] GAFFTC
46+07[1] GAFFTC
46+08[1] JbG-32
46+09[1] GAFFTC
46+10 AkG-51
46+11 JbG-33
46+12 GAFFTC
46+13 AkG-51
46+14 AkG-51
46+15 AkG-51
46+18 JbG-33
46+19 JbG-33
46+20 AkG-51
46+21 JbG-33
46+22 AkG-51
46+23[2] JbG-32$
46+24[2] JbG-32
46+25[2] JbG-32
46+26[2] JbG-32
46+27[2] JbG-32
46+28[2] JbG-32
46+29[2] JbG-32$
46+30[2] JbG-32
46+31[2] JbG-32
46+32[2] JbG-32
46+33[2] JbG-32
46+34[2] JbG-32
46+35[2] JbG-32
46+36[2] JbG-32
46+37[2] JbG-32
46+38[2] JbG-32
46+39[2] JbG-32
46+40[2] WTD-61
46+41[2] JbG-32
46+43[2] JbG-32
46+44[2] JbG-32
46+45[2] JbG-32
46+46[2] JbG-32
46+48[2] JbG-32
46+49[2] JbG-32
46+50[2] JbG-32
46+51[2] JbG-32
46+52[2] JbG-32
46+53[2] JbG-32
46+54[2] JbG-32
46+55[2] JbG-32
46+56[2] JbG-32
46+57[2] JbG-32
98+59 WTD-61
98+60 WTD-61
98+77 WTD-61
98+79[2] WTD-61

Transall C-160D
LTG-61 (1.LwDiv), Landsberg;
LTG-62 (1.LwDiv), Wunstorf;
LTG-63 (4.LwDiv), Hohn;
WTD-61, Ingolstadt
50+06 LTG-63
50+07 LTG-61
50+08 LTG-61
50+09 LTG-61
50+10 LTG-62
50+17 LTG-62
50+29 LTG-62
50+33 LTG-62
50+34 LTG-63
50+36 LTG-62
50+37 LTG-62
50+38 LTG-61
50+40 LTG-63
50+41 LTG-62
50+42 LTG-63
50+44 LTG-61
50+45 LTG-63
50+46 LTG-62
50+47 LTG-61
50+48 LTG-61$
50+49 LTG-61
50+51 LTG-61
50+53 LTG-61
50+54 LTG-63
50+55 LTG-62
50+56 LTG-63
50+57 LTG-62
50+58 LTG-63
50+59 LTG-62
50+60 LTG-62
50+61 LTG-62
50+62 LTG-62
50+64 LTG-61
50+65 LTG-62
50+66 LTG-61
50+67 LTG-61
50+68 LTG-61
50+69 LTG-63
50+70 LTG-62
50+71 LTG-63
50+72 LTG-61
50+73 LTG-62
50+74 LTG-61
50+75 LTG-61
50+76 LTG-63
50+77 LTG-62
50+78 LTG-62
50+79 LTG-63
50+81 LTG-62
50+82 LTG-63
50+83 LTG-62
50+84 LTG-61
50+85 LTG-63
50+86 LTG-61
50+87 LTG-63
50+88 LTG-61
50+89 LTG-62
50+90 LTG-62
50+91 LTG-62
50+92 LTG-61
50+93 LTG-63
50+94 LTG-63
50+95 LTG-63
50+96 LTG-61
50+97 LTG-61
50+98 LTG-61
50+99 LTG-62
51+00 LTG-62
51+01 LTG-62
51+02 LTG-63
51+03 LTG-62
51+04 LTG-61
51+05 LTG-62
51+06 LTG-63
51+07 LTG-62
51+08 WTD-61
51+09 LTG-63
51+10 LTG-62
51+12 LTG-63
51+13 LTG-61
51+14 LTG-62

Dornier Do.228LM
MFG-3, Nordholz
57+01
57+04

Lockheed
P-3C Orion
MFG-3, Nordholz
60+01
60+02
60+03
60+04
60+05
60+06
60+07
60+08

Eurocopter
AS.532U-2 Cougar
3/FBS, Berlin-Tegel
82+01
82+02
82+03

Westland
Super Lynx Mk88A
MFG-3, Nordholz
83+02
83+03
83+04
83+05
83+06
83+07
83+09
83+10
83+11$
83+12
83+13
83+15
83+17
83+18
83+19
83+20
83+21
83+22
83+23
83+24
83+25

Westland
Sea King HAS41
MFG-5, Kiel-Holtenau
89+50
89+51
89+52
89+53
89+54
89+55
89+56
89+57
89+58$
89+60
89+61
89+62
89+63
89+64$
89+65
89+66
89+67
89+68
89+69
89+70
89+71

Northrop Grumman
RQ-4E Euro Hawk
WTD-61, Palmdale, USA
99+01 WTD-61
..+.. (on order)
..+.. (on order)
..+.. (on order)
..+.. (on order)

Heeresfliegertruppe
Eurocopter
EC.665 Tiger
Ecole Franco-Allemande, Le Luc, France;
KHR-36, Fritzlar;
WTD-61, Ingolstadt
74+03 WTD-61
74+05 EFA
74+06 EFA
74+07 EFA
74+08 EFA
74+09 EFA
74+10
74+11 KHR-36
74+19
74+20
74+21
74+22
74+23
74+24
74+26
74+27
74+28
74+29
74+30
74+31
74+32
74+34
74+36
74+37
98+12 WTD-61
98+14
98+15
98+16
98+17 WTD-61
98+18 Eurocopter
98+19 Eurocopter
98+20
98+21
98+23
98+25
98+26 Eurocopter
98+27

NH Industries
NH.90-TTH
HFWS, Bückeburg;
HSG-64, Holzdorf
WTD-61, Ingolstadt
78+01 HFWS
78+02 HFWS
78+03 HFWS
78+04 HFWS
78+05
78+06 HFWS
78+07 HFWS
78+08 HFWS
78+09 HFWS
78+10
78+11 HFWS
78+13
78+14
78+16
78+17
78+18
78+19
78+20
78+21
78+22
78+23
78+24
78+25
78+26
78+27
79+01
79+02 HSG-64
79+03
79+10
79+25
98+90
98+93
98+97

Eurocopter EC.135P-1
HFWS, Bückeburg
82+51
82+52
82+53
82+54
82+55
82+56
82+57
82+59
82+60
82+61
82+62
82+63
82+64
82+65

Sikorsky/VFW
CH-53G/CH-53GA/
CH-53GE/CH-53GS
HFWS, Bückeburg;
MTHR-15, Rheine-Bentlage;
MTHR-25, Laupheim;
TsLw-3, Fassberg;
WTD-61, Ingolstadt
84+01 CH-53GS WTD-61
84+05 CH-53G HFWS
84+06 CH-53G MTHR-15
84+09 CH-53G TsLw-3
84+10 CH-53G HFWS
84+11 CH-53G HFWS
84+12 CH-53G MTHR-15
84+13 CH-53G HFWS
84+14 CH-53GE HFWS
84+15 CH-53GS MTHR-15
84+16 CH-53G HFWS
84+17 CH-53G MTHR-25
84+18 CH-53G HFWS
84+19 CH-53G TsLw-3
84+24 CH-53G MTHR-15
84+25 CH-53GS MTHR-15
84+26 CH-53GE MTHR-15
84+27 CH-53G HFWS
84+28 CH-53G MTHR-25
84+29 CH-53G MTHR-15
84+30 CH-53GS MTHR-15
84+31 CH-53G MTHR-25
84+32 CH-53G MTHR-25
84+34 CH-53G MTHR-15
84+35 CH-53G MTHR-25
84+37 CH-53G HFWS
84+38 CH-53G MTHR-25
84+39 CH-53G MTHR-15
84+40 CH-53G MTHR-25
84+41 CH-53G HFWS
84+42 CH-53GS HFWS
84+43 CH-53G MTHR-25

84+44	CH-53G	MTHR-25
84+45	CH-53GS	MTHR-25
84+46	CH-53G	MTHR-15
84+47	CH-53G	MTHR-25
84+48	CH-53G	HFWS
84+49	CH-53G	HFWS
84+50	CH-53G	HFWS
84+51	CH-53GS	MTHR-25
84+52	CH-53GS	MTHR-25
84+53	CH-53GE	MTHR-25
84+54	CH-53G	MTHR-25
84+55	CH-53G	WTD-61
84+57	CH-53G	HFWS
84+58	CH-53G	MTHR-25
84+59	CH-53G	MTHR-25
84+60	CH-53G	MTHR-25
84+62	CH-53GS	MTHR-25
84+63	CH-53G	MTHR-25
84+64	CH-53GS	MTHR-25
84+65	CH-53G	HFWS
84+66	CH-53GS	MTHR-25
84+67	CH-53GS	MTHR-15
84+68	CH-53G	MTHR-25
84+69	CH-53G	HFWS
84+70	CH-53G	MTHR-15
84+71	CH-53G	MTHR-15
84+72	CH-53G	MTHR-15
84+73	CH-53GS	MTHR-15
84+74	CH-53G	MTHR-15
84+75	CH-53G	MTHR-15
84+76	CH-53G	HFWS
84+77	CH-53G	MTHR-15
84+78	CH-53GS	MTHR-15
84+79	CH-53GS	MTHR-15
84+80	CH-53G	HFWS
84+82	CH-53GE	MTHR-15
84+83	CH-53G	HFWS
84+84	CH-53G	MTHR-15
84+85	CH-53GS	MTHR-15
84+86	CH-53GA	Eurocopter
84+87	CH-53G	MTHR-15
84+88	CH-53G	HFWS
84+89	CH-53G	MTHR-15
84+90	CH-53G	MTHR-15
84+91	CH-53GS	MTHR-15
84+92	CH-53GE	MTHR-15
84+94	CH-53G	
84+95	CH-53G	MTHR-25
84+96	CH-53GE	MTHR-25
84+97	CH-53G	MTHR-25
84+98	CH-53GS	MTHR-15
84+99	CH-53G	HFWS
85+00	CH-53GS	MTHR-25
85+01	CH-53GS	MTHR-25
85+02	CH-53G	MTHR-15
85+03	CH-53G	MTHR-15
85+04	CH-53GA	MTHR-15
85+05	CH-53GS	MTHR-15
85+06	CH-53G	MTHR-25
85+07	CH-53GS	HFWS
85+08	CH-53G	MTHR-15
85+10	CH-53GS	MTHR-25
85+11	CH-53G	MTHR-25
85+12	CH-53GS	MTHR-15

MBB Bo.105P

Ecole Franco-Allemande,
  Le Luc, France;
HFUS-1, Holzdorf;
HFUS-7, Mendig;
HFVAS-100, Celle;
HFVAS-300, Mendig;
HFWS, Bückeburg;
KHR-26, Roth;
KHR-36, Fritzlar;
MTHR-15, Rheine-Bentlage;
MTHR-25, Laupheim;
THR-30, Niederstetten;
TsLw-3, Fassberg;
WTD-61, Ingolstadt

86+02	KHR-36
86+03	HFWS
86+04	HFWS
86+05	KHR-36
86+06	KHR-36
86+07	HFWS
86+08	HFWS
86+09	HFWS
86+10	HFVAS-100
86+11	MTHR-15
86+12	HFWS
86+13	THR-30
86+14	KHR-36
86+15	MTHR-25
86+16	KHR-36
86+17	HFWS
86+18	HFWS
86+19	HFWS
86+20	HFWS
86+21	HFVAS-100
86+23	TsLw-3
86+24	HFWS
86+25	HFVAS-100
86+26	HFWS
86+27	KHR-26
86+28	HFWS
86+29	HFWS
86+30	KHR-26
86+31	HFUS-1
86+32	HFWS
86+33	MTHR-25
86+34	HFVAS-100
86+35	KHR-26
86+36	HFVAS-100
86+38	KHR-36
86+39	HFWS
86+40	HFWS
86+41	HFVAS-100
86+42	KHR-26
86+44	HFWS
86+45	KHR-36
86+46	HFWS
86+47	HFVAS-100
86+48	HFVAS-100
86+49	KHR-36
86+50	KHR-36
86+51	HFWS
86+52	HFUS-1
86+53	HFVAS-100
86+54	EFA
86+55	KHR-36
86+56	HFWS
86+57	KHR-26
86+58	KHR-36
86+59	HFVAS-100
86+60	HFWS
86+61	KHR-26
86+62	HFWS
86+63	KHR-26
86+64	KHR-26
86+66	KHR-26
86+67	HFVAS-100
86+68	KHR-36
86+69	KHR-26
86+70	HFVAS-100
86+71	KHR-36
86+72	TsLw-3
86+73	HFWS
86+74	KHR-36
86+76	KHR-26
86+77	HFWS
86+78	HFVAS-300
86+79	KHR-26
86+80	HFVAS-100
86+83	TsLw-3
86+84	KHR-26
86+85	HFUS-1
86+86	HFVAS-100
86+87	
86+88	KHR-26
86+89	HFUS-1
86+90	KHR-36
86+92	KHR-36
86+93	HFWS
86+95	HFUS-1
86+96	HFWS
86+97	KHR-36
86+98	MTHR-25
86+99	HFWS
87+01	KHR-26
87+02	KHR-26
87+03	TsLw-3
87+04	KHR-26
87+06	MTHR-25
87+09	KHR-26
87+10	KHR-26
87+11	KHR-36
87+12	HFWS
87+13	KHR-36
87+15	KHR-36
87+16	HFVAS-100
87+17	KHR-36
87+18	KHR-36
87+19	KHR-36
87+20	KHR-26
87+22	
87+23	HFVAS-100
87+24	HFUS-7
87+25	KHR-26
87+26	HFUS-1
87+27	HFWS
87+28	HFVAS-100
87+29	HFWS
87+30	KHR-36
87+31	HFWS
87+34	KHR-26
87+35	KHR-26
87+37	HFWS
87+39	KHR-36
87+41	HFWS
87+43	KHR-36
87+44	HFUS-1
87+45	HFUS-1
87+46	KHR-36
87+47	HFWS
87+48	HFVAS-100
87+49	HFWS
87+50	KHR-36
87+51	HFVAS-100
87+52	HFUS-1
87+53	KHR-26
87+55	KHR-36
87+56	TsLw-3
87+58	HFWS
87+59	HFWS
87+60	KHR-36
87+61	HFWS
87+62	HFWS
87+63	HFWS

87+64 HFWS
87+65 KHR-36
87+66 KHR-36
87+67 HFWS
87+68 KHR-36
87+70 KHR-26
87+71 HFWS
87+72 THR-30
87+73 WTD-61
87+75 KHR-26
87+76 KHR-36
87+77
87+78 HFUS-1
87+79
87+80 HFUS-1
87+82 HFVAS-300
87+83 MTHR-25
87+85 HFWS
87+87 HFVAS-100
87+88 KHR-26
87+89 MTHR-25
87+90 HFWS
87+92 KHR-26
87+97 HFVAS-100
87+98 HFWS
87+99 KHR-36
88+01 KHR-36
88+02 KHR-36
88+04 KHR-36
88+05 HFWS
88+06 KHR-36
88+07 HFWS
88+08 HFWS
88+09
88+10 HFVS-910
88+11 MTHR-25
88+12 HFVAS-100

GHANA
Ghana Air Force
Dassault
Falcon 900EASy
VIP Flight, Accra
9G-EXE

GREECE
Ellinikí Polemiki Aeroporía
Aeritalia C-27J Spartan
354 Mira, Elefsís
4117
4118
4120
4121
4122
4123
4124
4125
4128
4142
4146 (on order)

Dassault Mirage 2000
331 MAPK/114 PM, Tanagra;
332 MAPK/114 PM, Tanagra
Mirage 2000BG
201 332 MAPK
202 332 MAPK
204 332 MAPK
Mirage 2000EG
210 332 MAPK
212 332 MAPK
213 332 MAPK
215 332 MAPK
216 332 MAPK
217 332 MAPK
218 332 MAPK
219 332 MAPK
220 332 MAPK
221 332 MAPK
228 332 MAPK
231 332 MAPK
232 332 MAPK
233 332 MAPK
237 332 MAPK
239 332 MAPK
241 332 MAPK
242 332 MAPK
Mirage 2000-5BG
505 331 MAPK
506 331 MAPK
507 331 MAPK
508 331 MAPK
509 331 MAPK
Mirage 2000-5EG
511 331 MAPK
514 331 MAPK
527 331 MAPK
530 331 MAPK
534 331 MAPK
535 331 MAPK
536 331 MAPK
540 331 MAPK
543 331 MAPK
545 331 MAPK
546 331 MAPK
547 331 MAPK
548 331 MAPK
549 331 MAPK
550 331 MAPK
551 331 MAPK
552 331 MAPK
553 331 MAPK
554 331 MAPK
555 331 MAPK

Embraer
ERJ-135BJ
Legacy/ERJ.145H/ERJ.135LR
352 MMYP/112 PM, Elefsís;
380 Mira/112 PM, Elefsís
135L-484 ERJ-135BJ 352 MMYP
145-209 ERJ-135LR 352 MMYP
145-374 ERJ-145H 380 Mira
145-671 ERJ-145H 380 Mira
145-729 ERJ-145H 380 Mira
145-757 ERJ-145H 380 Mira

Gulfstream Aerospace
Gulfstream V
352 MMYP/112 PM, Elefsís
678

Lockheed
C-130H Hercules
356 MTM/112 PM, Elefsís
*ECM
741*
742
743
744
745
746
747*
749
751
752$

Lockheed
F-16C/F-16D*
Fighting Falcon
330 Mira/111 PM, Nea Ankhialos;
335 Mira/116 PM, Áraxos;
336 Mira/116 PM, Áraxos;
337 Mira/110 PM, Larissa;
340 Mira/115PM, Souda;
341 Mira/111 PM, Nea Ankhialos;
343 Mira/115PM, Souda;
346 MAPK/110 PM, Larissa;
347 Mira/111 PM, Nea Ankhialos
001 335 Mira
002 335 Mira
003 335 Mira
004 335 Mira
005 335 Mira
006 335 Mira
007 335 Mira
008 335 Mira
009 335 Mira
010 335 Mira
011 335 Mira
012 335 Mira
013 335 Mira
014 335 Mira
015 335 Mira
016
017
018
019 335 Mira
020 335 Mira
021* 335 Mira
022* 335 Mira
023* 335 Mira
024* 335 Mira
025* 335 Mira
026* 335 Mira
027* 335 Mira
028* 335 Mira
029* 335 Mira
030* 335 Mira
046 341 Mira
047 347 Mira
048 341 Mira
049 347 Mira
050 341 Mira
051 347 Mira
052 341 Mira
053 347 Mira
054 341 Mira
055 347 Mira
056 341 Mira
057 347 Mira
058 341 Mira
060 341 Mira
061 347 Mira
062 341 Mira
063 347 Mira
064 341 Mira
065 347 Mira
066 341 Mira
067 347 Mira
068 341 Mira
069 347 Mira
070 341 Mira
071 347 Mira

072	341 Mira
073	347 Mira
074	341 Mira
075	347 Mira
076	341 Mira
077*	341 Mira
078*	347 Mira
079*	347 Mira
080*	341 Mira
081*	347 Mira
082*	341 Mira
083*	347 Mira
084*	341 Mira
110	330 Mira
111	330 Mira
112	346 MAPK
113	330 Mira
114	346 MAPK
115	330 Mira
116	330 Mira
117	330 Mira
118	346 MAPK
119	330 Mira
120	346 MAPK
121	330 Mira
122	346 MAPK$
124	346 MAPK
125	330 Mira
126	330 Mira
127	330 Mira
128	346 MAPK
129	330 Mira
130	346 MAPK
132	346 MAPK
133	330 Mira
134	346 MAPK
136	346 MAPK
138	346 MAPK
139	330 Mira
140	346 MAPK
141	330 Mira
143	330 Mira
144*	330 Mira
145*	330 Mira
146*	346 MAPK
147*	330 Mira
148*	346 MAPK
149*	346 MAPK
500	343 Mira
501	337 Mira
502	337 Mira
503	343 Mira
504	343 Mira
505	343 Mira
506	340 Mira
507	337 Mira
508	337 Mira
509	343 Mira
510	340/343 Mira
511	343 Mira
512	343 Mira
513	343 Mira
515	337 Mira
517	347 Mira
518	340 Mira
519	340 Mira
520	343 Mira
521	340 Mira
523	340 Mira
524	337 Mira
525	343 Mira
526	343 Mira
527	343 Mira
528	337 Mira
529	340 Mira
530	337 Mira
531	340/343 Mira
532	337 Mira
533	340 Mira
534	340 Mira
535	340 Mira
536	340 Mira
537	340 Mira
538	340 Mira
539	337 Mira
600*	343 Mira
601*	340 Mira
602*	340 Mira
603*	340 Mira
605*	340 Mira
606*	337 Mira
607*	343 Mira
608*	340 Mira
609*	337 Mira
610*	340 Mira
611*	337 Mira
612*	337 Mira
613*	343 Mira
614*	340/343 Mira
615*	343 Mira
616*	340/343 Mira
617*	343 Mira
618*	343 Mira
619*	337 Mira

LTV A-7 Corsair II
336 Mira/116 PM, Áraxos

154404	TA-7C	
155424	TA-7C	
154477	TA-7C	
155489	TA-7C	
155507	TA-7C	
155774	TA-7C	(156774)
156738	TA-7C	
156747	TA-7C	
156750	TA-7C	
156753	TA-7C	
156767	TA-7C	
156768	TA-7C	
156790	TA-7C	
156795	TA-7C	
158021	A-7E	
158824	A-7E	
158825	A-7E$	
159263	A-7E	
159274	A-7E	
159639	A-7E	
159645	A-7E	
159648	A-7E	
159967	A-7E	
159975	A-7E	
160537	A-7E	
160543	A-7E	
160552	A-7E	
160560	A-7E	
160566	A-7E	
160616	A-7E$	
160617	A-7E	
160710	A-7E	
160717	A-7E	
160728	A-7E	
160736	A-7E	
160857	A-7E	
160862	A-7E	
160865	A-7E	
160866	A-7E	

HUNGARY

Hungarian Defence Forces

Antonov An-26
59 Sz.D.REB, Kecskemét
110
405
406
407
603

Boeing
C-17A Globemaster III
Strategic Airlift Capability (SAC), Pápa, Hungary
01 (08-0001)
02 (08-0002)
03 (08-0003)

SAAB 39C/39D* Gripen
59 Sz.D.REB, Kecskemét
30
31
32
33
34
35
36
37
38
39
40
41
42*
43*

ISRAEL

Heyl ha'Avir

Boeing 707
120 Sqn, Nevatim

120	RC-707
128	RC-707
137	RC-707
140	KC-707
248	KC-707
250	KC-707
255	EC-707
260	KC-707
264	KC-707
272	VC-707
275	KC-707
290	KC-707

Lockheed
C-130 Karnaf
103 Sqn & 131 Sqn, Nevatim

102	C-130H
208	C-130E
305	C-130E
309	C-130E
310	C-130E
314	C-130E
316	C-130E
318	C-130E
420	KC-130H
427	C-130H
428	C-130H
435	C-130H
436	C-130H
522	KC-130H
545	KC-130H

ITALY

Aeronautica Militare Italiana

Aeritalia G222/C-27J Spartan

9ª Brigata Aerea,
Pratica di Mare:
14° Stormo/8° Gruppo;
46ª Brigata Aerea, Pisa:
98° Gruppo;
RSV, Pratica di Mare

G222RM

MM62139	14-20	8

G222TCM

MM62124	RS-46	RSV
MM62146	14-11	8

C-27J Spartan

CSX62127		Alenia
MM62214	46-84	98
MM62215	46-80	98
MM62217	46-81	98
MM62218	46-82	98
CSX62219	RS-50	RSV
MM62220	46-83	98
MM62221	46-85	98
MM62222	46-86	98
MM62223	46-88	98
MM62224	46-89	98
MM62225	46-90	98
MM62250	46-91	98

Aeritalia-EMB AMX/AMX-T*

32° Stormo, Amendola:
13° Gruppo & 101° Gruppo;
51° Stormo, Istrana:
103° Gruppo & 132° Gruppo;
RSV, Pratica di Mare

MM7101		
MM7114		
MM7115		
MM7125		
MM7126	$	
MM7129	32-15	13
MM7131	51-11	103
MM7132	51-01	103
MM7133	51-32	132
MM7141		
MM7143	51-21	103
MM7144	$	103
MM7146	51-25	103
MM7147	32-01$	13
MM7148	51-61	132
MM7149		
MM7151	51-51	132
MM7152		
MM7155		
MM7156		
MM7157	$	
CSX7158	RS-12	RSV
MM7159	51-10$	103
MM7160		
MM7161	51-37	132
MM7162		
MM7163		
MM7164	51-40	132
MM7165	32-16	13
MM7166	32-13	13
MM7167	51-56	132
MM7168	51-55	132
MM7169	51-66	132
MM7170	51-53	132
MM7171	51-52	132
MM7172	51-67	132
MM7173	51-63	132
MM7174	51-60	132
CSX7175		Alenia
MM7177	RS-14	RSV
MM7176		
MM7178	51-43	132
MM7179	51-64	132
MM7180	32-20	13
MM7182	51-62	132
MM7183	51-41	132
MM7184	51-65	132
MM7185	51-35	132
MM7186	51-50	132
MM7189		
MM7190	51-57	132
MM7191	51-45	132
MM7192	32-02	13
MM7193	51-54	132
MM7194	32-21	13
CSX7195		Alenia
MM7196	32-16	13
MM7197	51-46	132
MM7198	51-44$	132
MM55029*	32-50$	101
MM55030*	32-41	101
MM55031*	32-40	101
CSX55034*	RS-18	RSV
MM55035*		
MM55036*	32-51	101
MM55037*	32-64	101
MM55038*	32-53	101
MM55039*	32-54	101
MM55040*	32-52	01
MM55041*	32-55	101
MM55042*	32-56	101
MM55043*	32-65	101
MM55044*	32-57	101
MM55046*	32-47	101
MM55047*	32-53	101
MM55049*	32-66	101
MM55051*	32-42	101

Aermacchi MB339A/MB339CD*

36° Stormo, Gioia del Colle:
12° Gruppo;
51° Stormo, Istrana: 651ª SC;
61° Stormo, Lecce:
212° Gruppo &
213° Gruppo;
Aermacchi, Venegono;
Frecce Tricolori [FT]
(313° Gruppo), Rivolto
(MB339A/PAN);
RSV, Pratica di Mare

MM54442	61-112	
MM54443	61-50	
MM54446	61-01	
MM54452		
CSX54453	RS-11	RSV
MM54457	61-11	
MM54458	61-12	
MM54459	25$	
MM54463	61-17	
MM54465	61-21	
MM54467	61-23	
MM54468	61-24	
MM54473	3	[FT]
MM54475	5	[FT]
MM54477		[FT]
MM54479	50	[FT]
MM54480	2	[FT]
MM54482	4	[FT]
MM54485	0	[FT]
MM54487	8	[FT]
MM54488	61-32	
MM54492	61-36	
MM54493	51-71	
MM54496	61-42	
MM54499	61-45	
MM54500		[FT]
MM54504	61-52	
MM54505	9	[FT]
MM54507	61-55	
MM54509	61-57	
MM54510	61-60	
MM54511	61-61	
MM54512	61-62	
MM54514	61-64	
MM54515	61-65	
MM54516	61-66	
MM54517		[FT]
MM54518	61-70	
MM54532		
MM54533	61-72	
MM54534		[FT]
MM54535	61-74	
MM54536	51-	
MM54537		
MM54538	10	[FT]
MM54539	7	[FT]
MM54542		[FT]
CSX54544*	RS-30	
MM54546	51-75	
MM54547		[FT]
MM54548	61-106	
MM54549	61-107	
MM54551	1	[FT]
MM55052	6	[FT]
MM55053	61-114	
MM55054	61-15	
MM55055	61-20	
MM55058	61-41	
MM55059	61-26	
MM55062*	61-126	
MM55063*	61-127	
MM55064*	36-10	
MM55065*	36-02	
MM55066*		
MM55067*	36-07	
MM55068*	RS-33	RSV
MM55069*	61-135	
MM55070*	61-136	
MM55072*	61-140	
MM55073*	61-141	
MM55074*	36-06	
MM55075*	61-143	
MM55076*	36-04	
MM55077*	61-145	
MM55078*	61-146	
MM55079*	61-147	
MM55080*	61-150	
MM55081*	61-151	
MM55082*	61-152	
MM55084*	61-154	
MM55085*	61-155	
MM55086*	61-156	
MM55087*	61-167	
MM55088*	61-160	
MM55089*	61-161	
MM55090*	61-162	
MM55091*	RS-32	RSV

Aermacchi M311

Aermacchi, Venegono

CSX619

Aermacchi M346/T346 Master
Aermacchi, Venegono
CMX615 M346
CMX616 M346
CMX617 M346
MM55.. T346
MM55.. T346

Agusta-Sikorsky HH-3F Pelican
15° Stormo:
82° Centro SAR, Trapani/Birgi;
83° Gruppo SAR, Cervia;
84° Centro SAR, Brindisi/Casale;
85° Centro SAR, Pratica di Mare

MM80974	15-01	85
MM80975	15-02$	85
MM80977	15-04	83
MM80978	15-05	83
MM80979	15-06	85
MM80984	15-13	85
MM80985	15-14	85
MM80986	15-15	82
MM80988	15-19	85
MM80989	15-20	85
MM80990	15-21	85
MM80992	15-23	85
MM81337	15-25	83
MM81339	15-27	85
MM81341	15-29	83
MM81342	15-30	85
MM81343	15-31	85
MM81344	15-32	82
MM81345	15-33	84
MM81346	15-34	85
MM81347	15-35	84
MM81348	15-36	85
MM81349	15-37	85
MM81350	15-38	85

Airbus A.319CJ-115X
31° Stormo, Roma-Ciampino:
306° Gruppo
MM62174
MM62209
MM62243

Boeing 767T/T (767-2EYER)
9ª Brigata Aerea, Pratica di Mare:
8° Gruppo
MM62226 14-01
MM62227 14-02
MM62228 14-03
MM62229 14-04

Breguet Br.1150 Atlantic
41° Stormo, Catania:
88° Gruppo
MM40114 41-76
MM40115 41-77
MM40116 41-01
MM40117 41-02
MM40118 41-03
MM40121 41-06

Dassault Falcon 50
31° Stormo, Roma-Ciampino:
93° Gruppo
MM62026
MM62029

Dassault Falcon 900EX/900EX EASy*
31° Stormo, Roma-Ciampino:
93° Gruppo
MM62171 $
MM62172
MM62210
MM62244*
MM62245*

Eurofighter F-2000A/F-2000B* Typhoon
4° Stormo, Grosseto:
9° Gruppo & 20° Gruppo;
36° Stormo, Gioia del Colle:
12° Gruppo & 12° Gruppo;
Alenia, Torino/Caselle;
RSV, Pratica di Mare

MMX602	RS-01	Alenia
MMX603	RMV-01	Alenia
MMX614*		RSV
MM7235	36-04	12
MM7270	4-1	0
MM7271	36-03	12
MM7272	36-14	12
MM7273		
MM7274	4-10	9
CSX7275	36-11	12
MM7276	4-21	9
MM7277		
MM7278	36-05	12
MM7279	36-21	12
MM7280	4-13	9
MM7281	4-14	9
MM7282		
MM7284	36-10	12
MM7285	4-16	9
MM7286	36-02	12
MM7287	4-3	9
MM7288	4-4	9
MM7289	4-5	9
MM7290	4-7	9
MM7291	4-11	9
MM7292	4-12	9
MM7293	4-15	9
MM7294	36-26	12
MM7295	4-6$	9
MM7296	36-22	12
MM7297	36-23	12
MM7298	36-24	12
MM7299	4-20	9
MM7300	36-12	12
MM7301	4-22	9
MM7302		
MM7303	4-2	9
MM7304		
MM7305		
MM7306		
MM7307		
CSX7308		
CSX7309		
MM7310		
MM7311		
MM7312		
MM7313		
MM7314		
MM7315		
MM55092*	4-25	20
MM55093*	4-31	20
MM55094*	4-27	20
MM55095*	4-23	20
MM55096*	4-30	20
MM55097*	4-24	20
MM55128*	4-26	20
MM55129*	4-32	20
MM55130*	4-33	20
MM55131*	4-34	20
MM55132*		
MM55133*		

Lockheed C-130J/C-130J-30/KC-130J* Hercules II
46a Brigata Aerea, Pisa:
2° Gruppo & 50° Gruppo

C-130J
MM62175 46-40
MM62177 46-42
MM62178 46-43
MM62179 46-44
MM62180 46-45
MM62181 46-46
MM62182 46-47
MM62183* 46-48
MM62184 46-49
MM62185 46-50
MM62186 46-51

C-130J-30
MM62187 46-53
MM62188 46-54
MM62189 46-55
MM62190 46-56
MM62191 46-57
MM62192 46-58
MM62193 46-59
MM62194 46-60
MM62195 46-61
MM62196 46-62

Lockheed (GD) F-16A-ADF/F-16B*
37° Stormo, Trapani:
18° Gruppo
MM7236 $
MM7239
MM7240 $
MM7242
MM7244
MM7249
MM7251 $
MM7254
MM7257
MM7259
MM7262
MM7268*
MM7269*

Panavia Tornado Strike/ Trainer¹/ECR²
6° Stormo, Ghedi:
102° Gruppo &
154° Gruppo &
156° Gruppo;
50° Stormo, Piacenza:
155° Gruppo;
RSV, Pratica di Mare

MM7003	6-43	102
MM7004	6-53	102
MM7005	$	156

MM7006	6-31$	102
MM7007	6-01	154
CSX7009		Alenia
MM7011	6-13	154
MM7013	36-156	156
MM7014	RS-01	RSV
MM7015	6-32$	102
MM7016	6-20	154
MM7018	6-46	102
MM7019[2]	50-05	155
MM7020[2]	50-41	155
MM7021[2]	50-01	155
MM7022	6-23	154
MM7023	36-31	156
MM7024	36-41	156
MM7025	6-05	154
MM7026	6-35	102
MM7027[2]		
MM7028	6-67	102
MM7029		
MM7030[2]	50-04$	155
MM7031	6-61	102
MM7034[2]		
MM7035	6-27	154
MM7036[2]		
MM7038	6-37	102
MM7039	6-02	154
CSX7041[1]	RS-06	RSV
MM7042	50-57	155
MM7043	6-25	154
MM7044	50-53	155
MM7046[2]	6-06	154
CSX7047[2]	50-43	155
MM7048		
MM7049	6-64	102
MM7051[2]	50-45	155
MM7052[2]	50-02	155
MM7053[2]	50-07	155
MM7054[2]	50-40$	155
MM7055	50-42	155
MM7056	6-66	102
MM7057	6-04	154
MM7058	6-11	154
MM7059	50-47	155
MM7061	6-14	154
MM7062[2]	50-44	155
MM7063	6-26	154
MM7065	6-65	102
MM7066	50-03	155
MM7067	6-71	102
MM7068[2]	50-46	155
MM7070[2]	50-06	155
MM7071	6-12	154
MM7073[2]	6-34	102
MM7075	6-07	154
MM7078		
CMX7079[2]		Alenia
MM7080	6-33$	102
MM7081	50-52	155
MM7082[2]	50-54	155
MM7083	6-62	102
MM7084	6-03	154
CMX7085	36-50	Alenia
MM7086	6-60	102
MM7087	6-36	102
MM7088	6-10	154
MM55000[1]	6-51$	102
MM55002[1]	6-52$	102
MM55003[1]		
MM55006[1]	6-15	154
MM55007[1]	6-56	102
MM55008[1]	6-45	102
MM55009[1]	6-44	102

Piaggio
P-180AM Avanti
9ª Brigata Aerea,
Pratica di Mare:
71° Gruppo;
36° Stormo, Gioia del Colle:
636ª SC;
RSV, Pratica di Mare

MM62159	71
MM62160	71
MM62161	71
MM62162	71
MM62163	71
MM62164	RSV
MM62199	636
MM62201	71
MM62202	71
MM62203	71
MM62204	71
MM62205	71
MM62206	71
MM62207	71

Aviazione dell'Esercito
Dornier Do.228-212
28° Gruppo Squadrone
Cavalleria dell'Aria,
Viterbo

MM62156	E.I.101
MM62157	E.I.102
MM62158	E.I.103

Piaggio
P-180AM Avanti
28° Gruppo Squadrone Det,
Cavalleria dell'Aria,
Roma/Ciampino
MM62167
MM62168
MM62169

Guardia Costiera
Aérospatiale
ATR.42-400MP/-500*
2° Nucleo, Catania
3° Nucleo, Pescara

MM62170	10-01	3
MM62208*	10-02	2
MM62270	10-03	3

Guardia di Finanza
Aérospatiale
ATR.42-400MP
Gruppo Esplorazione
Aeromarittima,
Pratica di Mare

MM62165	GF-13
MM62166	GF-14
MM62230	GF-15
MM62251	GF-16

Piaggio
P-180AM Avanti
Gruppo Esplorazione
Aeromarittima,
Pratica di Mare

MM62248	GF-18
MM62249	GF-19

Marina Militare Italiana
AgustaWestland
EH.101
1° Grupelicot, La Spezia/Luni;
3° Grupelicot, Catania
Mk110 ASW

MM81480	2-01	3
MM81481	2-02	3
MM81482	2-03	3
MM81483	2-04	3
MM81484	2-05	3
MM81485	2-06	3
MM81486	2-07	3
MM81487	2-08	3
CSX81719	2-22	1
MM81726	2-23	1

Mk112 ASW

MM81488	2-09	1
MM81489	2-10	1
MM81490	2-11	1
MM81491	2-12	1

Mk410 UTY

MM81492	2-13	1
MM81493	2-14	1
MM81494	2-15	1
CSX81495	2-16	1
MM81633	2-18	1
MM81634	2-19	1
MM81635	2-20	1
MM81636	2-21	1

McDonnell Douglas
AV-8B/TAV-8B Harrier II+
Gruppo Aerei Imbarcarti,
Taranto/Grottaglie
AV-8B

MM7199	1-03
MM7200	1-04
MM7201	1-05
MM7212	1-06
MM7213	1-07
MM7214	1-08
MM7215	1-09
MM7217	1-11
MM7218	1-12
MM7219	1-13
MM7220	1-14
MM7222	1-16
MM7223	1-18
MM7224	1-19

TAV-8B

MM55032	1-01
MM55033	1-02

Piaggio
P-180AM Avanti
9ª Brigata Aerea, AMI,
Pratica di Mare:
71° Gruppo

MM62200	9-01
MM62211	9-02
MM62212	9-03

Italian Govt
Dassault Falcon 900
Italian Govt/Soc. CAI,
Roma/Ciampino
I-CAEX
I-DIES
I-NUMI

IVORY COAST
Fokker 100
Ivory Coast Govt, Abidjan
TU-VAA

Grumman
G.1159C Gulfstream IV
Ivory Coast Govt, Abidjan
TU-VAD

JAPAN
Japan Air Self Defence Force
Boeing 747-47C
701st Flight Sqn, Chitose
20-1101
20-1102

JORDAN
Al Quwwat al Jawwiya al Malakiya al Urduniya
Extra EA-300LP
Royal Jordanian Falcons, Amman
JY-RFA
JY-RFB
JY-RFC
JY-RFD
JY-RFE

Lockheed C-130H Hercules
3 Sqn, Amman/Marka
344
345
346
347

Jordanian Govt
Airbus A.318-112
Jordanian Govt, Amman
VQ-BDD

Airbus A.340-642
Jordanian Govt, Amman
JY-... (on order)

Gulfstream Aerospace G.450
Jordanian Govt, Amman
VQ-BCE

KAZAKHSTAN
Boeing 757-2M6
Govt of Kazakhstan, Almaty
UP-B5701

Boeing 767-2DKER
Govt of Kazakhstan, Almaty
UP-B6701

KENYA
Kenyan Air Force
Fokker 70ER
Kenyan Govt, Nairobi
308

KUWAIT
Al Quwwat al Jawwiya al Kuwaitiya
Lockheed
L100-30 Hercules
41 Sqn, Kuwait International
KAF 323
KAF 324
KAF 325

Kuwaiti Govt
Airbus A.300C4-620
Kuwaiti Govt, Safat
9K-AHI

Airbus A.310-308
Kuwaiti Govt, Safat
9K-ALD

Airbus A.319CJ-115X
Kuwaiti Govt, Safat
9K-GEA

Airbus A.320-212
Kuwaiti Govt, Safat
9K-AKD

Airbus A.340-542
Kuwaiti Govt, Safat
9K-GBA
9K-GBB

Boeing 747-469
Kuwaiti Govt, Safat
9K-ADE

Gulfstream Aerospace G.550
Kuwaiti Govt, Safat
9K-GFA

Gulfstream Aerospace Gulfstream V
Kuwaiti Govt/Kuwait Airways, Safat
9K-AJD
9K-AJE
9K-AJF

KYRGYZSTAN
Tupolev Tu-154M
Govt of Kyrgyzstan, Bishkek
EX-85718

LITHUANIA
Karines Oro Pajegos
Aeritalia C-27J Spartan
Transporto Eskadrile, Siauliai-Zokniai
06
07
08

Antonov An-26RV
Transporto Eskadrile, Siauliai-Zokniai
03
04
05

LET 410UVP Turbolet
Transporto Eskadrile, Siauliai-Zokniai
01
02

Mil Mi-8
Sraigtasparniu Eskadrile, Panevezys/Pajuostis
02 Mi-8T
09 Mi-8T
10 Mi-8T
11 Mi-8PS
21 Mi-8MTV-1
22 Mi-8MTV-1
28 Mi-8T

LUXEMBOURG
NATO
Boeing 707TCA (CT-49A)
NAEW&CF, Geilenkirchen, Germany
LX-N20000
LX-N20199

Boeing E-3A
NAEW&CF, Geilenkirchen, Germany
LX-N90442
LX-N90443$
LX-N90444
LX-N90445
LX-N90446
LX-N90447
LX-N90448
LX-N90449
LX-N90450
LX-N90451
LX-N90452
LX-N90453
LX-N90454
LX-N90455
LX-N90456
LX-N90458
LX-N90459

MACEDONIA
Macedonian Govt
Bombardier Lear 60
Macedonian Govt, Skopje
Z3-MKD

MALAYSIA
Royal Malaysian Air Force/ Tentera Udara Diraja Malaysia
Boeing 737-7H6
2 Sqn, Simpang
M53–01

Bombardier
BD.700-1A10 Global Express
2 Sqn, Simpang
M48-02

Dassault Falcon 900
2 Sqn, Simpang
M37-01

Lockheed
C-130 Hercules
14 Sqn, Labuan;
20 Sqn, Subang

M30-01	C-130T	20 Sqn
M30-02	C-130H	20 Sqn
M30-03	C-130H	14 Sqn
M30-04	C-130H-30	20 Sqn
M30-05	C-130H-30	14 Sqn
M30-06	C-130H-30	14 Sqn
M30-07	C-130T	20 Sqn
M30-08	C-130H(MP)	20 Sqn
M30-09	C-130H(MP)	20 Sqn
M30-10	C-130H-30	20 Sqn
M30-11	C-130H-30	20 Sqn
M30-12	C-130H-30	20 Sqn
M30-14	C-130H-30	20 Sqn
M30-15	C-130H-30	20 Sqn
M30-16	C-130H-30	20 Sqn

Malaysian Govt
Airbus A.319CJ-115X
9M-NAA

MALTA
Bombardier
Learjet 60
Govt of Malta, Luqa
9H-AFK

MEXICO
Fuerza Aérea Mexicana
Boeing 757-225
8° Grupo Aéreo, Mexico City
TP-01 (XC-UJM)

Armada de Mexico
Gulfstream Aerospace G.450
PRIMESCTRANS, Mexico City
AMT-205

MOROCCO
Force Aérienne Royaume Marocaine/ Al Quwwat al Jawwiya al Malakiya Marakishiya
Aeritalia
C-27J Spartan
Escadrille de Transport 3, Kenitra
CN-AMN
CN-AMO (on order)
CN-AMP (on order)
CN-AMQ (on order)

Airtech
CN.235M-100
Escadrille de Transport 3, Kenitra

023	CNA-MA
024	CNA-MB
025	CNA-MC
026	CNA-MD
027	CN-AME
028	CNA-MF
031	CNA-MG

CAP-232
Marche Verte

28	CN-ABP [2]
29	CN-ABQ [6]
31	CN-ABR [5]
36	CN-ABS [4]
37	CN-ABT [3]
41	CN-ABU [7]
42	CN-ABV [1]
43	CN-ABW
44	CN-ABX [8]

Lockheed
C-130H Hercules
Escadrille de Transport 3, Kenitra

4535	CNA-OA	C-130H
4551	CNA-OC	C-130H
4575	CNA-OD	C-130H
4581	CNA-OE	C-130H
4583	CNA-OF	C-130H
4713	CNA-OG	C-130H
4733	CNA-OI	C-130H
4738	CNA-OJ	C-130H
4739	CNA-OK	C-130H
4742	CNA-OL	C-130H
4875	CN-AOM	C-130H
4876	CNA-ON	C-130H
4877	CNA-OO	C-130H
4888	CNA-OP	C-130H
4892	CNA-OQ	C-130H
4907	CNA-OR	KC-130H
4909	CNA-OS	KC-130H

Govt of Morocco
Boeing 737-8KB
Govt of Morocco, Rabat
CN-MVI

Cessna 560 Citation V
Govt of Morocco, Rabat
CNA-NV
CNA-NW

Cessna
560XLS Citation Excel
Govt of Morocco, Rabat
CN-AMJ
CN-AMK

Dassault Falcon 50
Govt of Morocco, Rabat
CN-ANO

Grumman
G.1159 Gulfstream IITT/
G.1159A Gulfstream III
Govt of Morocco, Rabat
CNA-NL Gulfstream IITT
CNA-NU Gulfstream III

Gulfstream Aerospace G.550
Govt of Morocco, Rabat
CN-AMS

NAMIBIA
Dassault Falcon 900B
Namibian Govt, Windhoek
V5-NAM

NETHERLANDS
Koninklijke Luchtmacht
Agusta-Bell AB.412SP
303 Sqn, Leeuwarden
R-01
R-02
R-03

Boeing-Vertol
CH-47 Chinook
298 Sqn, Defence Helicopter Command, Gilze-Rijen
CH-47D Chinook
D-101
D-102
D-103
D-106
D-661
D-662
D-663
D-664
D-665
D-666
D-667
CH-47F Chinook
D-890 (on order)
D-891 (on order)
D-892 (on order)
D-893 (on order)
D-894 (on order)
D-895 (on order)

Eurocopter
AS.532U-2 Cougar
300 Sqn, Defence Helicopter Command, Gilze-Rijen
S-400
S-419
S-433
S-438
S-440
S-441
S-442
S-444
S-445
S-447
S-450
S-453
S-454
S-456
S-457
S-458
S-459

Fokker 50
334 Sqn, Eindhoven
U-05
U-06

General Dynamics
F-16
Now operated on a pool basis. Squadron markings carried do not necessarily reflect the squadron operating.
311/312/313 Sqns, Volkel;
322/323 Sqns, Leeuwarden;
306 Sqn/162nd FW, Tucson, Arizona, USA

J-001	F-16AM	312 Sqn
J-002	F-16AM	312 Sqn
J-003	F-16AM	162nd FW
J-004	F-16AM	162nd FW
J-005	F-16AM	311 Sqn
J-006	F-16AM	311 Sqn
J-008	F-16AM	313 Sqn$
J-009	F-16AM	313 Sqn
J-010	F-16AM	162nd FW
J-011	F-16AM	312 Sqn
J-013	F-16AM	312 Sqn
J-014	F-16AM	313 Sqn
J-015	F-16AM	323 Sqn$
J-016	F-16AM	312 Sqn
J-017	F-16AM	311 Sqn
J-018	F-16AM	313 Sqn
J-019	F-16AM	162nd FW
J-020	F-16AM	322 Sqn
J-021	F-16AM	312 Sqn
J-055	F-16AM	313 Sqn$
J-057	F-16AM	311 Sqn
J-060	F-16AM	322 Sqn
J-061	F-16AM	311 Sqn
J-062	F-16AM	313 Sqn
J-063	F-16AM	313 Sqn
J-064	F-16BM	322 Sqn
J-065	F-16BM	162nd FW
J-066	F-16BM	323 Sqn
J-067	F-16BM	162nd FW
J-135	F-16AM	322 Sqn
J-136	F-16AM	311 Sqn
J-142	F-16AM	323 Sqn
J-144	F-16AM	323 Sqn

J-145	F-16AM	162nd FW
J-146	F-16AM	323 Sqn
J-193	F-16AM	323 Sqn
J-196	F-16AM	313 Sqn
J-197	F-16AM	311 Sqn
J-199	F-16AM	311 Sqn
J-201	F-16AM	322 Sqn
J-202	F-16AM	323 Sqn
J-203	F-16AM	323 Sqn
J-208	F-16BM	162nd FW
J-209	F-16BM	306 Sqn
J-210	F-16BM	323 Sqn
J-254	F-16AM	311 Sqn
J-362	F-16AM	323 Sqn
J-366	F-16AM	162nd FW
J-367	F-16AM	162nd FW
J-368	F-16BM	312 Sqn
J-369	F-16BM	311 Sqn
J-508	F-16AM	313 Sqn
J-509	F-16AM	322 Sqn
J-510	F-16AM	162nd FW
J-511	F-16AM	313 Sqn
J-512	F-16AM	323 Sqn
J-513	F-16AM	323 Sqn
J-514	F-16AM	313 Sqn
J-515	F-16AM	311 Sqn
J-516	F-16AM	322 Sqn
J-616	F-16AM	323 Sqn
J-623	F-16AM	162nd FW
J-624	F-16AM	322 Sqn
J-628	F-16AM	322 Sqn
J-630	F-16AM	311 Sqn
J-631	F-16AM	323 Sqn
J-632	F-16AM	322 Sqn
J-635	F-16AM	312 Sqn
J-637	F-16AM	312 Sqn
J-638	F-16AM	311 Sqn
J-641	F-16AM	312 Sqn
J-642	F-16AM	311 Sqn
J-643	F-16AM	313 Sqn
J-644	F-16AM	313 Sqn
J-646	F-16AM	312 Sqn
J-647	F-16AM	162nd FW
J-866	F-16AM	311 Sqn
J-868	F-16AM	323 Sqn
J-869	F-16AM	322 Sqn
J-870	F-16AM	162nd FW
J-871	F-16AM	323 Sqn
J-872	F-16AM	323 Sqn
J-873	F-16AM	323 Sqn
J-876	F-16AM	322 Sqn
J-877	F-16AM	323 Sqn
J-879	F-16AM	322 Sqn
J-881	F-16AM	323 Sqn
J-882	F-16BM	162nd FW
J-884	F-16BM	162nd FW

Grumman
G.1159C Gulfstream IV
334 Sqn, Eindhoven
V-11

Lockheed
C-130H/C-130H-30* Hercules
336 Sqn, Eindhoven
G-273*
G-275*
G-781
G-988

MDH
AH-64D Apache Longbow
301 Sqn, Defence Helicopter Command, Gilze-Rijen
Q-01
Q-02
Q-03
Q-04
Q-05
Q-06
Q-07
Q-08
Q-09
Q-10
Q-11
Q-12
Q-13
Q-14
Q-15
Q-16
Q-17
Q-18
Q-19$
Q-21
Q-22
Q-23
Q-24
Q-25
Q-26
Q-27
Q-28
Q-29
Q-30

NH Industries
NH.90-NFH
7 & 860 Sqn, De Kooij
N-088 (on order)
N-102 (on order)
N-110
N-147 (on order)
N-164
N-175 (on order)

McDonnell Douglas
DC-10*/KDC-10
334 Sqn, Eindhoven
T-235
T-255*
T-264

Pilatus
PC-7 Turbo Trainer
131 EMVO Sqn, Woensdrecht
L-01
L-02
L-03
L-04
L-05
L-06
L-07
L-08
L-09
L-10
L-11
L-12
L-13

Sud Alouette III
300 Sqn, Defence Helicopter Command, Gilze-Rijen
A-247
A-275
A-292
A-301

Westland SH-14D Lynx
Defence Helicopter Command (7 Sqn & 860 Sqn), De Kooij (7 Sqn operates 860 Sqn aircraft on loan)
260
261
262
265
266
267
272
273
274
277
278
279
280
281
283

Kustwacht
Dornier Do.228-212
Base: Schiphol
PH-CGC
PH-CGN

Netherlands Govt
Fokker 70
Dutch Royal Flight, Schiphol
PH-KBX

NEW ZEALAND
Royal New Zealand Air Force
Boeing 757-2K2
40 Sqn, Whenuapai
NZ7571
NZ7572

Lockheed
C-130H Hercules
40 Sqn, Whenuapai
NZ7001
NZ7002
NZ7003
NZ7004
NZ7005

Lockheed
P-3K Orion
5 Sqn, Whenuapai
NZ4201
NZ4202
NZ4203
NZ4204
NZ4205
NZ4206

NIGER
Government of Niger
Boeing 737-2N9C
Government of Niger, Niamey
5U-BAG

NIGERIA
Federal Nigerian Air Force
Lockheed
C-130H/C-130H-30* Hercules
88 MAG, Lagos
NAF-910
NAF-912
NAF-913
NAF-917*

NAF-918*

Nigerian Govt
BAe HS.125-800B
Federal Govt of Nigeria, Lagos
5N-AGZ

Boeing 737-7N6
Federal Govt of Nigeria, Lagos
5N-FGT [001]

Dassault Falcon 900
Federal Govt of Nigeria, Lagos
5N-FGE
5N-FGO

Grumman
G.1159C Gulfstream IV
Federal Govt of Nigeria, Lagos
5N-FGP

Gulfstream Aerospace
Gulfstream V
Federal Govt of Nigeria, Lagos
5N-FGS

NORWAY
Luftforsvaret

Bell 412HP*/412SP
339 Skv, Bardufoss;
720 Skv, Rygge

139	339 Skv
140	720 Skv
141	720 Skv
142	720 Skv
143	339 Skv
144	339 Skv
145*	720 Skv
146	339 Skv
147	720 Skv
148	339 Skv
149	720 Skv
161	339 Skv
162	339 Skv
163	720 Skv
164*	720 Skv
165	720 Skv
166*	720 Skv
167	720 Skv
194	720 Skv

Dassault
Falcon 20 ECM
717 Skv, Rygge
041
053
0125

General Dynamics
F-16 MLU
331 Skv, Bodø;
332 Skv, Bodø;
338 Skv, Ørland
[All operate from a pool and belong to the FLO]

272	F-16A
273	F-16A
275	F-16A
276	F-16A
277	F-16A
279	F-16A
281	F-16A
282	F-16A
284	F-16A
285	F-16A
286	F-16A
288	F-16A
289	F-16A
291	F-16A
292	F-16A
293	F-16A
295	F-16A
297	F-16A
298	F-16A $
299	F-16A
302	F-16B
304	F-16B
305	F-16B
306	F-16B
658	F-16A
659	F-16A
660	F-16A
661	F-16A
662	F-16A
663	F-16A
664	F-16A
665	F-16A
666	F-16A
667	F-16A
668	F-16A
669	F-16A
670	F-16A
671	F-16A $
672	F-16A
673	F-16A
674	F-16A
675	F-16A
677	F-16A
678	F-16A
680	F-16A
681	F-16A
682	F-16A
683	F-16A
686	F-16A
687	F-16A
688	F-16A
689	F-16B
690	F-16B
691	F-16B
692	F-16B $
693	F-16B
711	F-16B

Lockheed
C-130J-30 Hercules II
335 Skv, Gardermoen
5601
5607
5629
5630

Lockheed P-3C Orion
333 Skv, Andøya
3296
3297
3298
3299

Lockheed P-3N Orion
333 Skv, Andøya
4576
6603

NH Industries
NH.90-NFH
334 Skv, Sola
013

Westland
Sea King Mk 43/ Mk 43A/Mk 43B
330 Skv:
A Flt, Bodø;
B Flt, Banak;
C Flt, Ørland;
D Flt, Sola

060	Mk 43
062	Mk 43
066	Mk 43
069	Mk 43
070	Mk 43
071	Mk 43B
072	Mk 43
073	Mk 43
074	Mk 43
189	Mk 43A
322	Mk 43B
329	Mk 43B
330	Mk 43B

Kystvakt (Coast Guard)
Westland Lynx Mk86
337 Skv, Bardufoss
207
216
228
232
235

OMAN
Royal Air Force of Oman

Airbus A.320-214X
4 Sqn, Seeb
554
555
556 (on order)

Lockheed
C-130H Hercules
16 Sqn, Seeb
501
502
503

Omani Govt
Airbus A.320-233
Govt of Oman, Seeb
A4O-AA

Boeing 747-430
Govt of Oman, Seeb
A4O-OMN

Boeing 747SP-27
Govt of Oman, Seeb
A4O-SO

Grumman
G.1159C Gulfstream IV
Govt of Oman, Seeb
A4O-AB
A4O-AC

PAKISTAN
Pakistan Fiza'ya

Boeing 707-340C
12 Sqn, Islamabad
68-19866

Pakistani Govt
Airbus A.310-304
Govt of Pakistan, Karachi
AP-OOI

Boeing 737-33A
Govt of Pakistan, Karachi
AP-BEH

Cessna 560 Citation VI
Govt of Pakistan, Karachi
J-754

Gulfstream Aerospace G.1159C Gulfstream IV-SP
Govt of Pakistan, Karachi
J-755

Gulfstream Aerospace G.450
Govt of Pakistan, Karachi
J-756

POLAND
Sily Powietrzne RP

CASA C-295M
13 ELTR, Powidz
011
012ø
013
014
015
016
017
018
020
021
022

Embraer EMB.175-200LR
36 SPLT, Warszawa
SP-LIG
SP-LIH

Lockheed C-130E Hercules
14 ELTR, Powidz
1501
1502
1503
1504 (on order)
1505 (on order)
1506
1507

Lockheed Martin (GD) F-16C/F-16D* Fighting Falcon
3 ELT, Poznan/Krzesiny;
6 ELT, Poznan/Krzesiny;
10 ELT, Lask;
412th TW, Edwards AFB, USA

4040	412th TW
4041	6 ELT
4042	3 ELT
4043	3 ELT
4044	3 ELT
4045	3 ELT
4046	3 ELT
4047	3 ELT
4048	3 ELT
4049	3 ELT
4050	3 ELT
4051	3 ELT
4052	6 ELT
4053	6 ELT
4054	6 ELT
4055	6 ELT
4056	6 ELT
4057	6 ELT
4058	6 ELT
4059	6 ELT
4060	6 ELT
4061	6 ELT
4062	6 ELT
4063	10 ELT
4064	10 ELT
4065	10 ELT
4066	10 ELT
4067	10 ELT
4068	10 ELT
4069	10 ELT
4070	10 ELT
4071	10 ELT
4072	10 ELT
4073	10 ELT
4074	10 ELT
4075	10 ELT
4076*	3 ELT
4077*	3 ELT
4078*	3 ELT
4079*	3 ELT
4080*	3 ELT
4081*	3 ELT
4082*	6 ELT
4083*	6 ELT
4084*	6 ELT
4085*	10 ELT
4086*	10 ELT
4087*	10 ELT

Mikoyan MiG-29A/UB
1 ELT, Minsk/Mazowiecki;
41 ELT, Malbork

15*	1 ELT $
28*	1 ELT
38	1 ELT
40	1 ELT
42*	1 ELT
54	1 ELT
56	1 ELT
59	1 ELT
65	41 ELT
66	41 ELT
67	41 ELT
70	41 ELT
77	41 ELT
83	1 ELT
89	1 ELT
92	41 ELT
105	1 ELT
108	1 ELT
111	1 ELT
114	1 ELT
115	1 ELT
4101	41 ELT
4103	41 ELT
4104	41 ELT
4105	1 ELT
4110*	41 ELT
4113	41 ELT
4116	41 ELT
4120	41 ELT
4121	41 ELT
4122	41 ELT
4123*	41 ELT

PZL 130TC-1/TC-II* Orlik
2 OSL, Radom
012
014
015
016
017
018
019
020
022
023
024
025
026
027
029
030
031
032
033
035
036
037
038
040
041
042
043
044
045
046
047*
048
049
050
051
052

PZL M28 Bryza
2 ELTL, Bydgoszcz;
13 ELTR, Powidz;
14 ELTR, Powidz;
11 OSL, Deblin;
36 SPLT, Warszawa

0203	M28TD	1 OSL
0204	M28TD	1 OSL
0205	M28TD	1 OSL
0206	M28TD	36 SPLT
0207	M28TD	1 OSL
0208	M28TD	36 SPLT
0209	M28TD	13 ELTR
0210	M28TD	13 ELTR
0211	M28TD	13 ELTR
0212	M28TD	13 ELTR
0213	M28PT	13 ELTR
0214	M28PT	13 ELTR
0215	M28PT	13 ELTR
0216	M28PT	36 SPLT
0217	M28PT	1 OSL
0218	M28PT	(on order)
0219	M28PT	(on order)
0723	M28TD	14 ELTL
1003	M28TD	2 ELTL

Sukhoi Su-22UM-3K*/Su-22M-4
7 ELT, Swidwin;
40 ELT, Swidwin
001*
308* 40 ELT
310* 7 ELT
508* 40 ELT
509* 40 ELT
605*
706* 40 ELT
707* 7 ELT
3203
3215
3304
3306
3508
3509 40 ELT
3612 40 ELT
3710 40 ELT
3713 40 ELT$
3715 40 ELT
3816 40 ELT
3817 40 ELT
3819
3920 40 ELT
4604
7308 7 ELT
7309 7 ELT
7410 7 ELT
7411 7 ELT
7412 7 ELT
8101 40 ELT
8102
8103
8205 7 ELT
8308
8309 40 ELT
8310 40 ELT
8715 40 ELT
8816 40 ELT
8818
8919
9102 40 ELT$
9204 40 ELT
9306
9409 40 ELT
9615 40 ELT
9616 7 ELT

Yakovlev Yak-40
36 SPLT, Warszawa
044
045
047
048

Lotnictwo Marynarki Wojennej
PZL M28 Bryza
28 EL, Gdynia/Babie Doly;
30 EL, Cewice/Siemirowice
0404 M28B-E 28 EL
0405 M28B-E 28 EL
0810 M28B-1R 30 EL
1006 M28B-1R 30 EL
1008 M28B-1R 30 EL
1017 M28B-1R 30 EL
1022 M28B-1R 30 EL
1114 M28B-1R 28 EL
1115 M28B-1R 30 EL
1116 M28B-1R 28 EL
1117 M28B-1 28 EL
1118 M28B-1 28 EL

Straz Graniczna (Polish Border Guard)
PZL M28 05 Skytruck
Base: Gdansk/Rebiechowo
SN-50YG
SN-60YG

PORTUGAL
Força Aérea Portuguesa
Aérospatiale SA.330S-1 Puma
Esq 751, Beja
19502
19503
19504 $

Aérospatiale TB-30 Epsilon
Esq 101, Beja
11401
11402
11403
11404
11405 $
11406
11407
11409
11410
11411
11413
11414
11415
11416
11417
11418

CASA 212A/212-MP Aviocar
CASA 212A
Esq 401, Lisbon/Montijo
16504
16505
16510
16512
16513
16517
CASA 212-300MP
17201
17202

CASA C-295M/CASA C-295MPA*
Esq 502, Lisbon/Montijo
(with a detachment at Lajes)
16701
16702
16703
16704
16705
16706
16707
16708* (on order)
16709*
16710*
16711* (on order)
16712* (on order)

D-BD Alpha Jet
Esq 103, Beja;
Asas de Portugal, Beja*
15202*
15206*
15208*
15211$
15214
15220*
15225*
15226
15227*
15229
15230
15231
15232*
15235
15236
15237*
15244
15246
15247
15250*

Dassault Falcon 50
Esq 504, Lisbon/Montijo
17401
17402
17403

EHI EH-101 Mk514/Mk515/Mk516
Esq 751, Lisbon/Montijo
Mk514
19601
19602
19603
19604
19605*
19606*
Mk515
19607
19608
Mk516
19609
19610
19611
19612

Lockheed C-130H/C-130H-30* Hercules
Esq 501, Lisbon/Montijo
16801*
16802*
16803$
16804
16805
16806*

Lockheed Martin (GD) F-16 Fighting Falcon
(MLU aircraft are marked with a *)
Esq 201, Monte Real;
Esq 301, Monte Real
15101 F-16A* Esq 201/301
15102 F-16A* Esq 201/301
15103 F-16A Esq 201/301
15104 F-16A* Esq 201/301
15105 F-16A* Esq 201
15106 F-16A Esq 201
15107 F-16A* Esq 201/301
15108 F-16A* Esq 201
15109 F-16A Esq 201
15110 F-16A Esq 201
15112 F-16A* Esq 201/301

15113	F-16A	Esq 201
15114	F-16A	Esq 201
15115	F-16A*	Esq 201/301
15116	F-16A*	Esq 201/301
15117	F-16A	Esq 201
15118	F-16B*	Esq 201/301
15119	F-16B*	Esq 201/301
15120	F-16B	Esq 201
15121	F-16A*	Esq 201/301
15122	F-16A*	Esq 201/301
15123	F-16A	Esq 301
15124	F-16A*	Esq 201/301
15125	F-16A*	Esq 201/301
15126	F-16A*	Esq 201/301
15127	F-16A*	Esq 201/301
15128	F-16A*	Esq 201/301
15129	F-16A*	Esq 201/301
15130	F-16A*	Esq 201/301
15131	F-16A	Esq 301
15132	F-16A	
15133	F-16A*	Esq 201/301
15134	F-16A*	Esq 201/301
15135	F-16A*	
15136	F-16A	
15137	F-16B*	Esq 201/301
15138	F-16A*	Esq 201/301
15139	F-16B*	Esq 201/301
15141	F-16A	

Lockheed
P-3C/P-3P Orion
Esq 601, Beja
14805 P-3P
14807 P-3C
14808 P-3C
14809 P-3C
14810 P-3C
14811 P-3C

Marinha
Westland
Super Lynx Mk 95
Esq de Helicopteros,
Lisbon/Montijo
19201
19202
19203
19204
19205

QATAR
Airbus A.319CJ-133
Qatari Govt, Doha
A7-HHJ
A7-MED

Airbus A.320-232
Qatari Govt, Doha
A7-AAG

Airbus A.330-202/-203*
Qatari Govt, Doha
A7-HHM*
A7-HJJ

Airbus A.340-211/-541*
Qatari Govt, Doha
A7-HHH*
A7-HHK

Boeing
C-17A Globemaster III
Qatar Emiri Air Force, Doha
MAA (08-0201)
MAB (08-0202)
MAC (on order)
MAD (on order)

Bombardier
Global Express
Qatari Govt/Qatar Airways,
Doha
A7-AAM

ROMANIA
Fortele Aeriene Romania
Alenia C-27J Spartan
Escadrilla 902,
Bucharest/Otopeni
2701
2702
2703 (on order)
2704 (on order)
2705 (on order)
2706 (on order)
2707 (on order)

Antonov An-26
Escadrilla 902,
Bucharest/Otopeni
801
808
809
810

Lockheed
C-130B/C-130H* Hercules
Escadrilla 901,
Bucharest/Otopeni
5927
5930
6150
6166*
6191*

Romanian Govt
Boeing 707-3K1C
Romanian Govt,
Bucharest/Otopeni
YR-ABB

RUSSIA
Voenno-Vozdushniye Sily Rossioki Federatsii (Russian Air Force)
Antonov An-30B
(Open Skies)
Base: Chalovskiy
01 black

Sukhoi Su-27
TsAGI, Gromov Flight
Institute, Zhukhovsky
595 Su-27P
597 Su-30
598 Su-27P

Russian Govt
Ilyushin Il-62M
Russian Govt, Moscow
RA-86466
RA-86467
RA-86468
RA-86539
RA-86540
RA-86559
RA-86561
RA-86712

Ilyushin Il-96-300
Russian Govt, Moscow
RA-96012
RA-96016
RA-96018
RA-96019

Tupolev Tu-134A
Russian Govt, Moscow
RA-65904

Tupolev Tu-154M
Russian Govt, Moscow;
Open Skies*
RA-85155
RA-85631
RA-85655*
RA-85666

Tupolev Tu-214SR
Russian Govt, Moscow
RA-64515
RA-64516

SAUDI ARABIA
Al Quwwat al Jawwiya as Sa'udiya
Airbus A.380-203MRTT
.... (on order)
.... (on order)

BAe 125-800/-800B*
1 Sqn, Riyadh
HZ-105
HZ-109*
HZ-110*
HZ-130*

Boeing 737-7DP/-8DP*
1 Sqn, Riyadh
HZ-101
HZ-102*

Boeing
E-3A/KE-3A/RE-3A/RE-3B
Sentry
18 Sqn, Riyadh;
19 Sqn, Riyadh

1801	E-3A	18 Sqn
1802	E-3A	18 Sqn
1803	E-3A	18 Sqn
1804	E-3A	18 Sqn
1805	E-3A	18 Sqn
1811	KE-3A	18 Sqn
1812	KE-3A	18 Sqn
1813	KE-3A	18 Sqn
1814	KE-3A	18 Sqn
1815	KE-3A	18 Sqn
1816	KE-3A	18 Sqn
1818	KE-3A	18 Sqn
1901	RE-3A	19 Sqn
1902	RE-3B	19 Sqn

Cessna 550 Citation II
1 Sqn, Riyadh
HZ-133
HZ-134
HZ-135
HZ-136

Grumman
G.1159C Gulfstream IV
1 Sqn, Riyadh
HZ-103

Lockheed
C-130/L.100 Hercules
1 Sqn, Prince Sultan AB;
4 Sqn, Jeddah;
16 Sqn, Prince Sultan AB;
32 Sqn, Prince Sultan AB

111	VC-130H	1 Sqn
112	VC-130H	1 Sqn
451	C-130E	4 Sqn
452	C-130E	4 Sqn
455	C-130E	4 Sqn
461	C-130H	4 Sqn
462	C-130H	4 Sqn
463	C-130H	4 Sqn
464	C-130H	4 Sqn
465	C-130H	4 Sqn
466	C-130H	4 Sqn
467	C-130H	4 Sqn
468	C-130H	4 Sqn
472	C-130H	4 Sqn
473	C-130H	4 Sqn
474	C-130H	4 Sqn
475	C-130H	4 Sqn
483	C-130E	4 Sqn
1601	C-130H	16 Sqn
1602	C-130H	16 Sqn
1603	C-130H	16 Sqn
1604	C-130H	16 Sqn
1605	C-130H	16 Sqn
1606	C-130E	16 Sqn
1607	C-130E	16 Sqn
1608	C-130E	16 Sqn
1609	C-130E	16 Sqn
1611	C-130E	16 Sqn
1614	C-130H	16 Sqn
1615	C-130H	16 Sqn
1618	C-130H	16 Sqn
1619	C-130H	16 Sqn
1622	C-130H-30	16 Sqn
1623	C-130H	16 Sqn
1624	C-130H	16 Sqn
1625	C-130H	16 Sqn
1626	C-130H	16 Sqn
1630	C-130H-30	16 Sqn
1631	L.100-30	16 Sqn
1632	L.100-30	16 Sqn
3201	KC-130H	32 Sqn
3202	KC-130H	32 Sqn
3203	KC-130H	32 Sqn
3204	KC-130H	32 Sqn
3205	KC-130H	32 Sqn
3206	KC-130H	32 Sqn
3207	KC-130H	32 Sqn
HZ-114	VC-130H	1 Sqn
HZ-115	VC-130H	1 Sqn
HZ-116	VC-130H	1 Sqn
HZ-117	L.100-30	1 Sqn
HZ-128	L.100-30	1 Sqn
HZ-129	L.100-30	1 Sqn
HZ-132	L.100-30	1 Sqn

Saudi Govt
Boeing 747-3G1/468*
Saudi Royal Flight, Jeddah
HZ-HM1A
HZ-HM1*

Boeing 747SP-68
Saudi Govt, Jeddah;
Saudi Royal Flight, Jeddah

HZ-AIF	Govt
HZ-AIJ	Royal Flight
HZ-HM1B	Royal Flight

Boeing 757-23A
Saudi Govt, Jeddah
HZ-HMED

Boeing MD-11
Saudi Royal Flight, Jeddah
HZ-AFAS
HZ-HM7

Dassault Falcon 900
Saudi Govt, Jeddah
HZ-AFT
HZ-AFZ

Grumman
G.1159A Gulfstream III
Armed Forces Medical Services, Riyadh;
Saudi Govt, Jeddah

HZ-AFN	Govt
HZ-AFR	Govt
HZ-MS3	AFMS

Grumman
G.1159C Gulfstream IV/ Gulfstream IV-SP*
Armed Forces Medical Services, Riyadh;
Saudi Govt, Jeddah

HZ-AFU	Govt
HZ-AFV	Govt
HZ-AFW	Govt
HZ-AFX	Govt
HZ-AFY	Govt
HZ-MFL	Govt
HZ-MS4*	AFMS

Gulfstream Aerospace
Gulfstream V
Armed Forces Medical Services, Riyadh
HZ-MS5A
HZ-MS5B

Lockheed
C-130H/L.100 Hercules
Armed Forces Medical Services, Riyadh

HZ-MS06	L.100-30
HZ-MS07	C-130H
HZ-MS09	L.100-30

SINGAPORE

Republic of Singapore Air Force

Boeing
KC-135R Stratotanker
112 Sqn, Changi
750
751
752
753

Lockheed
C-130 Hercules
122 Sqn, Paya Lebar

720	KC-130B
721	KC-130B
724	KC-130B
725	KC-130B
730	C-130H
731	C-130H
732	C-130H
733	C-130H
734	KC-130H
735	C-130H

SLOVAKIA

Slovenské Vojenske Letectvo

Aero L-39 Albatros
Zmiešané Letecké Kridlo 'Otta Smika', Sliač:
2 Stíhacia Letka [SL]

1701	L-39ZAM
1730	L-39ZAM
4703	L-39ZAM
4707	L-39ZA
5251	L-39CM
5252	L-39CM
5253	L-39CM
5254	L-39CM
5301	L-39CM
5302	L-39CM

Antonov An-26
Dopravniho Kridlo 'Generála Milana Ratislava Štefánika', Malacky:
1 Dopravná Roj
2506
3208

LET 410 Turbolet
Dopravniho Kridlo 'Generála Milana Ratislava Štefánika', Malacky:
2 Dopravná Roj

1133	L-410T
1521	L-410FG
2311	L-410UVP
2421	L-410UVP
2718	L-401UVP-E
2721	L-401UVP-E

Mikoyan MiG-29AS/UBS
Zmiešané Letecké Kridlo *'Otta Smika', Sliač:*
1 Stíhacia Letka [SL]

0619	MiG-29AS
0921	MiG-29AS
1303	MiG-29UBS $
2123	MiG-29AS
3709	MiG-29AS
3911	MiG-29AS
5304	MiG-29UBS
6124	MiG-29AS
6425	MiG-29AS
6526	MiG-29AS
6627	MiG-29AS
6728	MiG-29AS

Mil M-17/M-17M*
Vrtulnikové Letcecké Kridlo 'Generálplukovníka Jána Ambrusa', Prešov:
2 Bitevná Vrtul'nikova Letka
0807
0808
0812

0820
0821
0823*
0824
0826
0827
0841
0842
0844
0845
0846
0847

Mil Mi-24
Vrtulnikové Letcecké Kridlo 'Generálplukovníka Jána Ambrusa', Prešov:
1 Bitevná Vrtul'nikova Letka

0100	Mi-24D
0149	Mi-24D
0150	Mi-24D
0215	Mi-24D
0222	Mi-24D
0223	Mi-24D
0704	Mi-24V
0707	Mi-24V
0708	Mi-24V
0786	Mi-24V
0787	Mi-24V
0813	Mi-24V
0814	Mi-24V
0832	Mi-24V
0833	Mi-24V
0927	Mi-24V
4009	Mi-24D
6040	Mi-24DU

Slovak Govt
Yakovlev Yak-40
Slovak Govt, Bratislava/Ivanka
OM-BYE
OM-BYL

SLOVENIA
Slovene Army
LET 410UVP-E
LTO, Brnik
L4-01

Pilatus PC-9M
1/2/3 OSBL, Cerklje
L9-51
L9-53
L9-61
L9-62
L9-63
L9-64
L9-65
L9-66
L9-67
L9-68
L9-69

SOUTH AFRICA
South African Air Force/
Suid Afrikaanse Lugmag
Boeing 737-7ED
21 Sqn, Waterkloof
ZS-RSA

Dassault Falcon 900
21 Sqn, Waterkloof
ZS-NAN

Lockheed
C-130B/C-130BZ* Hercules
28 Sqn, Waterkloof
401
402*
403
404
405*
406*
407*

SPAIN
Ejército del Aire
Airbus A.310-304
Grupo 45, Torrejón

T.22-1	45-50
T.22-2	45-51

Airtech
CN.235M-10 (T.19A)/
CN.235M-100 (T.19B)/
CN.235M-100(MPA) (D.4)/
CN.235M VIGMA (T.19B)*
Grupo Esc, Matacán (74);
801 Esc, Palma/ Son San Juan;
Guardia Civil (09)

D.4-01	(801 Esc)
D.4-02	(801 Esc)
D.4-03	(801 Esc)
D.4-04	(801 Esc)
D.4-05	(801 Esc)
TR.19A-01	403-01
TR.19A-02	403-02
T.19B-03	35-21
T.19B-04	35-22
T.19B-05	35-23
T.19B-07	74-25
T.19B-11	35-29
T.19B-13	74-31
T.19B-14	74-32
T.19B-15	74-33
T.19B-16	74-34
T.19B-17	74-35
T.19B-18	74-36
T.19B-19	74-19
T.19B-20	74-38
T.19B-21*	09-501
T.19B-22*	09-502

Boeing 707
47 Grupo Mixto, Torrejón

TK.17-1	331B	47-01
T.17-2	331B	47-02
T.17-3	368C	47-03
TM.17-4	351C	47-04

CASA 101EB Aviojet
Grupo 54, Torrejón;
Grupo de Escuelas de Matacán (74);
AGA, San Javier (79);
Patrulla Aguila, San Javier*

E.25-01	79-01
E.25-05	79-05
E.25-06	79-06
E.25-07	79-07
E.25-08	79-08
E.25-09	79-09
E.25-10	79-10
E.25-11	79-11
E.25-12	79-12
E.25-13	79-13
E.25-14	79-14
E.25-15	79-15
E.25-16	79-16
E.25-17	74-40
E.25-18	74-42
E.25-19	79-19
E.25-20	79-20
E.25-21	79-21
E.25-22	79-22 [1]*
E.25-23	79-23 [3]*
E.25-24	79-24
E.25-25	79-25 [9]*
E.25-26	79-26
E.25-27	79-27
E.25-28	79-28 [2]*
E.25-29	74-45
E.25-31	79-31
E.25-33	74-02
E.25-34	74-44
E.25-35	54-20
E.25-37	79-37
E.25-38	79-38
E.25-40	79-40 [4]*
E.25-41	74-41
E.25-43	74-43
E.25-44	79-44
E.25-45	79-45
E.25-46	79-46
E.25-47	79-47
E.25-48	79-48
E.25-49	79-49
E.25-50	79-33
E.25-51	74-07
E.25-52	79-34 [5]*
E.25-53	74-09
E.25-54	79-35
E.25-55	54-21
E.25-56	74-11
E.25-57	74-12
E.25-59	74-13
E.25-61	54-22
E.25-62	79-17
E.25-63	74-17
E.25-65	79-95
E.25-66	74-20
E.25-67	74-21
E.25-68	74-22
E.25-69	79-97 [7]*
E.25-71	74-25
E.25-72	74-26
E.25-73	79-98
E.25-74	74-28
E.25-75	74-29
E.25-76	74-30
E.25-78	79-02 [6]*
E.25-79	79-39
E.25-80	79-03
E.25-81	74-34
E.25-83	74-35
E.25-84	79-04
E.25-86	79-32
E.25-87	79-29$
E.25-88	74-39

CASA 212 Aviocar
212A (T.12B)/
212DE (TM.12D)/
212S (D.3A)/
212S1 (D.3B)/
212-200 (T.12D)/
212-200 (TR.12D)
47 Grupo Mixto, Torrejón;
CLAEX, Torrejón (54);
Ala 72, Alcantarilla;
Grupo Esc, Matacán (74);
403 Esc, Getafe;
801 Esc, Palma/
Son San Juan;
803 Esc, Cuatro Vientos;
INTA, Torrejón

D.3A-2	(803 Esc)
D.3B-3	(803 Esc)
D.3B-7	(801 Esc)
T.12B-13	72-01
T.12B-21	72-03
T.12B-22	72-02
T.12B-37	72-05
T.12B-49	72-07
T.12B-55	72-08
T.12B-61	47-11
T.12B-63	72-14
T.12B-65	72-11
T.12B-66	72-09
T.12B-67	74-81
T.12B-69	72-15
T.12B-70	72-17
TM.12D-72	47-12
T.12D-75	47-14
TR.12D-76	37-60
TR.12D-77	37-61
TR.12D-78	37-62
TR.12D-80	37-64
TR.12D-81	37-65

CASA C-295M
Ala 35, Getafe

T.21-01	35-39
T.21-02	35-40
T.21-03	35-41
T.21-04	35-42
T.21-05	35-43
T.21-06	35-44
T.21-07	35-45
T.21-08	35-46
T.21-09	35-47
T.21-10	35-48
T.21-11	35-49
T.21-12	35-50
T.21-13	35-51

Cessna 560 Citation VI
403 Esc, Getafe

TR.20-01	403-11
TR.20-02	403-12
TR.20-03	403-21

Dassault Falcon 20D/E
47 Grupo Mixto, Torrejón

TM.11-1	20E	47-21
TM.11-2	20D	47-22
TM.11-3	20D	47-23
TM.11-4	20E	47-24

Dassault Falcon 900/900B*
Grupo 45, Torrejón

T.18-1	45-40
T.18-2	45-41
T.18-3*	45-42
T.18-4*	45-43
T.18-5*	45-44

Dassault
Mirage F.1BM*/F.1M
Ala 14, Albacete

C.14-13	14-07
C.14-15	14-09
C.14-17	14-11
C.14-22	14-15
CE.14-27*	14-76
CE.14-30*	14-71
C.14-36	14-18
C.14-37	14-19
C.14-38	14-20
C.14-41	14-22$
C.14-42	14-23
C.14-43	14-24
C.14-44	14-25
C.14-45	14-26
C.14-54	14-30
C.14-56	14-31
C.14-57	14-32
C.14-60	14-34
C.14-63	14-36
C.14-64	14-37$
C.14-66	14-38
C.14-67	14-39
C.14-68	14-40
C.14-69	14-41
C.14-70	14-42
C.14-72	14-44
C.14-73	14-45
CE.14-87*	14-73
C.14-91	14-49
C.16-41	11-21
C.16-42	11-21
C.16-43	11-21
C.16-44	
C.16-45	
C.16-46	
C.16-47	
C.16-48	

Eurofighter
EF.2000/EF.2000(T)* Tifón
Ala 11, Morón;
CASA, Getafe

CE.16-01*	11-70
CE.16-02*	11-71
CE.16-03*	11-72
CE.16-04*	11-73
CE.16-05*	11-74
CE.16-06*	11-75
CE.16-07*	11-76
CE.16-09*	11-78
CE.16-10*	
CE.16-11*	
CE.16-12*	
C.16-20	11-91
C.16-21	11-01
C.16-22	11-02
C.16-23	11-03
C.16-24	11-04
C.16-25	11-05
C.16-26	11-06
C.16-27	11-07
C.16-28	11-08
C.16-29	11-09
C.16-30	11-10
C.16-31	11-11
C.16-32	11-12
C.16-33	11-13
C.16-34	11-14
C.16-35	11-15
C.16-36	11-16
C.16-37	11-17
C.16-38	11-18
C.16-39	11-19
C.16-40	11-20

Fokker
F.27M Friendship 400MPA
802 Esc, Gando, Las Palmas

D.2-01	
D.2-02	802-11
D.2-03	

Lockheed
C-130H/C-130H-30/
KC-130H Hercules
311 Esc/312 Esc (Ala 31),
Zaragoza

TL.10-01	C-130H-30	31-01
T.10-02	C-130H	31-02
T.10-03	C-130H	31-03
T.10-04	C-130H	31-04
TK.10-5	KC-130H	31-50
TK.10-6	KC-130H	31-51
TK.10-07	KC-130H	31-52
T.10-8	C-130H	31-05
T.10-9	C-130H	31-06
T.10-10	C-130H	31-07
TK.10-11	KC-130H	31-53
TK.10-12	KC-130H	31-54

Lockheed
P-3A/P-3M Orion
Grupo 22, Morón

P.3-01	P-3A	22-21
P.3B-08	P-3M	22-31
P.3B-09	P-3M	22-32
P.3B-10	P-3M	22-33
P.3B-11	P-3M	22-34
P.3B-12	P-3M	22-35

McDonnell Douglas
F-18 Hornet
Ala 12, Torrejón;
Ala 15, Zaragoza;
Esc 462, Gran Canaria

EF-18B+/EF-18BM Hornet

CE.15-1*	15-70$
CE.15-2*	15-71
CE.15-3	15-72
CE.15-4*	15-73
CE.15-5	15-74
CE.15-6	15-75
CE.15-7*	15-76
CE.15-8*	12-71
CE.15-9	15-77
CE.15-10	12-73
CE.15-11	12-74
CE.15-12*	12-75

EF-18A+/EF-18AM* Hornet

C.15-13*	12-01
C.15-14	15-01
C.15-15	15-02$
C.15-16*	15-03
C.15-18*	15-05
C.15-20	15-07
C.15-21	15-08
C.15-22*	15-09
C.15-23	15-10
C.15-24	15-11

C.15-25 15-12
C.15-26 15-13$
C.15-27 15-14
C.15-28 15-15
C.15-29 15-16
C.15-30 15-17
C.15-31 15-18
C.15-32 15-19
C.15-33 15-20
C.15-34* 12-50$
C.15-35 15-22
C.15-36 15-23
C.15-37 15-24
C.15-38 15-25
C.15-39 15-26
C.15-40 15-27
C.15-41 15-28
C.15-43* 15-30
C.15-44* 12-02
C.15-45* 12-03
C.15-46* 12-04
C.15-47 15-31
C.15-48* 12-06
C.15-49* 12-07
C.15-50* 12-08
C.15-51* 12-09
C.15-52* 12-10
C.15-53* 12-11
C.15-54* 12-12
C.15-55 12-13
C.15-56 12-14
C.15-57* 12-15
C.15-59* 12-17
C.15-60 12-18
C.15-61 12-19
C.15-62 12-20
C.15-64 15-34
C.15-65* 12-23
C.15-66 12-24
C.15-67 15-33
C.15-68* 12-26
C.15-69* 12-27
C.15-70* 12-28
C.15-72* 12-30

F/A-18A/EF-18AM* Hornet
C.15-73 46-01
C.15-75 46-03
C.15-77 46-05
C.15-79 46-07
C.15-80 21-08
C.15-81 46-09
C.15-82 46-10
C.15-83 46-11
C.15-84 46-12
C.15-85 46-13
C.15-86* 46-14
C.15-87 46-15
C.15-88 46-16
C.15-89* 46-17
C.15-90 46-18
C.15-92 46-20
C.15-93* 46-21
C.15-94 46-22
C.15-95 46-23
C.15-96 46-24

Arma Aérea de l'Armada Española
BAe/McDonnell Douglas EAV-8B/EAV-8B+/ TAV-8B Harrier II
Esc 009, Rota
EAV-8B
VA.1A-19 01-907
VA.1A-22 01-911
EAV-8B+
VA.1B-24 01-914
VA.1B-25 01-915
VA.1B-26 01-916
VA.1B-27 01-917
VA.1B-28 01-918
VA.1B-29 01-919
VA.1B-30 01-920
VA.1B-35 01-923
VA.1B-36 01-924
VA.1B-37 01-925
VA.1B-38 01-926
VA.1B-39 01-927
TAV-8B
VAE.1A-33 01-922

Cessna 550 Citation II
Esc 004, Rota
U.20-1 01-405
U.20-2 01-406
U.20-3 01-407

Cessna 650 Citation VII
Esc 004, Rota
U.21-01 01-408

SUDAN
Dassault Falcon 50
Sudanese Govt, Khartoum
ST-PSR

Dassault Falcon 900B
Sudanese Govt, Khartoum
ST-PSA

SWEDEN
Svenska Flygvapnet
Grumman G.1159C Gulfstream 4 (Tp.102A/S.102B Korpen/ Tp.102C)
Flottiljer 17M, Stockholm/Bromma & Malmslätt
Tp.102A
102001 021
S.102B Korpen
102002 022
102003 023
Tp.102C
102004 024

Lockheed C-130H Hercules (Tp.84)
Flottiljer 7, Såtenäs
84001 841
84002 842
84003 843
84004 844
84005 845
84006 846
84007 847
84008 848

Rockwell Sabreliner-40 (Tp.86)
FMV, Malmslätt
86001 861

SAAB JAS 39 Gripen
Flottiljer 4, Östersund/ Frösön;
Flottiljer 7, Såtenäs [G];
Flottiljer 17, Ronneby/ Kallinge;
Flottiljer 21, Luleå/ Kallax
FMV, Malmslätt
JAS 39
39-5 55 FMV
JAS 39A
39101 51 FMV
39131 131 F7
39132 132 F7
39133 133 FMV
39134 134 FMV
39135 135 F21
39136 136 F7
39138 138 F7
39143 143 F7
39144 44 SAAB
39146 146 F7
39150 150 F7
39151 151 F7
39154 154 F7
39159 159 F7
39167 167 F7
39168 168 F7
39170 170 F17
39171 171 F17
39172 172 F7
39174 174 F7
39176 176 F17
39178 178 F17
39179 179 F17
39180 180 F17
39181 181 F7
39182 182 F7
39183 183 F17
39185 185 F7
39188 188 F17
39189 189 F17
39190 190 F17
39191 191 F17
39192 192 F7
39193 193 F7
39194 194 F21
39195 195 F7
39196 196 F7
39198 198 F7
39199 199 F7
39200 200 F7
39201 201 F7
39202 202 F7
39203 203 F7
39204 204 F7
39205 205 F7
39206 206 F7
JAS 39B
39800 58 FMV
39801 801 F7
39802 802 SAAB
39804 804 F7
39805 805 F7
39806 806 F7
39807 807 F7
39808 808 F7
39809 809 F7
39810 810 F7
39811 811 F7
39812 812 F7
39813 813 F7

39814	814	F7

JAS 39C

39-6	6	SAAB
39208	208	F21
39209	209	F17
39210	210	F17
39211	211	F21
39212	212	F17
39213	213	F7
39214	214	F21
39215	215	F21
39216	216	F21
39217	217	F7
39218	218	F21
39219	219	F21
39220	220	F17
39221	221	F17
39222	222	F21
39223	223	F17
39224	224	F17
39225	225	F21
39226	226	F21
39227	227	F7
39228	228	F21
39229	229	F17
39230	230	F17
39231	231	F21
39232	232	F21
39233	233	F17
39246	246	F21
39247	247	SAAB
39248	248	F21
39249	249	F21
39250	250	F21
39251	251	FMV
39252	252	F21
39253	253	F21
39254	254	FMV
39255	255	F21
39256	256	F17
39257	257	F21
39258	258	F21
39260	260	F17
39261	261	F21
39262	262	F17
39263	263	F21
39264	264	FMV
39265	265	F21
39266		
39267	267	F21
39268	268	F7
39269	269	F17
39270	270	F21
39271	271	F17
39272	272	F21
39273	273	F21
39274	274	F21
39275	275	F21
39276	276	F17
39277	277	F21
39278	278	F17
39279	279	F21
39280	280	F21
39281	281	F17
39282	282	
39283		
39284		
39285		
39286		
39287		
39288		
39289		
39290		
39291		
39292		
39293		
39294		

JAS 39D

39815	815	F21
39816	816	F21
39817	817	FMV
39818		
39821	821	F7
39822	822	F17
39823	823	F7
39824	824	F7
39825	825	F21
39826	826	F21
39827	827	FMV
39829	829	FMV
39830		
39831		
39832		
39833		
39834		
39835		
39836		
39837		
39838		
39839		
39840		
39841		
39842		

JAS 39NG

39-7	SAAB

SAAB
SF.340 (OS.100 & Tp.100C)/ SF.340AEW&C (S.100B & S.100D) Argus

Flottiljer 17, Ronneby/ Kallinge;
Flottiljer 17M, Malmslätt;
Flottiljer 21, Luleå/ Kallax;
TSFE, Malmslätt

OS.100

100001	001	F17M

S.100B

100002	002	F17M
100005	005	F17M

Tp.100C

100008	008	F17

S.100D

100003	003	F17M
100004	004	TSFE

Förvarsmaktens Helikopterflottilj
Aérospatiale
AS.332M-1 Super Puma (Hkp.10/Hkp.10B[1]/Hkp.10D[2])

1.HkpSkv, Luleå/Kallax;
3.HkpSkv, Berga, Goteborg/Säve, & Ronneby/Kallinge

10401	91	3.HkpSkv
10402[2]	92	3.HkpSkv
10403[1]	93	1.HkpSkv
10405	95	3.HkpSkv
10406[1]	96	1.HkpSkv
10407[2]	97	3.HkpSkv
10408[1]	98	1.HkpSkv
10410[1]	90	3.HkpSkv
10411	88	3.HkpSkv
10412	89	3.HkpSkv

Agusta
A109LUH Power (Hkp.15)

2.HkpSkv, Linkoping/Malmen;
3.HkpSkv, Berga, Ronneby/Kallinge

Hkp.15A

15021	21	2.HkpSkv
15022	22	2.HkpSkv
15023	23	2.HkpSkv
15024	24	2.HkpSkv
15025	25	2.HkpSkv
15026	26	2.HkpSkv
15027	27	2.HkpSkv
15028	28	2.HkpSkv
15029	29	2.HkpSkv
15030	30	2.HkpSkv
15031	31	2.HkpSkv
15032	32	2.HkpSkv
15034	34	2.HkpSkv

Hkp.15B

15033	33	2.HkpSkv
15035	35	2.HkpSkv
15036	36	2.HkpSkv
15037	37	2.HkpSkv
15038	38	2.HkpSkv
15039	39	2.HkpSkv
15040	40	2.HkpSkv

MBB Bo.105CBS (Hkp.9A)

2.HkpSkv, Linkoping/Malmen;
3.HkpSkv, Berga, Ronneby/Kallinge

09201	01	2.HkpSkv
09202	02	2.HkpSkv
09203	03	2.HkpSkv
09206	06	2.HkpSkv
09207	07	2.HkpSkv
09208	08	3.HkpSkv
09211	11	2.HkpSkv
09212	12	2.HkpSkv
09215	15	2.HkpSkv
09216	16	3.HkpSkv
09217	17	2.HkpSkv
09218	18	2.HkpSkv
09219	19	2.HkpSkv
09220	20	2.HkpSkv

NH Industries
NH.90

2.HkpSkv, Linkoping/Malmen;
FMV, Malmslätt

NH.90-HCV (Hkp.14A)

141042	42	2.HkpSkv
141043	43	2.HkpSkv
141044	44	2.HkpSkv
141045	45	FMV
141046	46	FMV
141047	47	FMV
141054	54	

NH.90-ASW (Hkp.14B)

142055	55	(on order)
142056	56	(on order)

Swedish Coast Guard
Bombardier DHC-8Q-311

Base: Nykoping

SE-MAA	[501]
SE-MAB	[502]
SE-MAC	[503]

SWITZERLAND
Schweizerische Flugwaffe
(Most aircraft are pooled centrally. Some carry unit badges but these rarely indicate actual operators.)

Aérospatiale AS.332M-1/AS.532UL Super Puma
Lufttransport Staffel 3 (LtSt 3), Dübendorf;
Lufttransport Staffel 5 (LtSt 5), Payerne;
Lufttransport Staffel 6 (LtSt 6), Alpnach;
Lufttransport Staffel 8 (LtSt 8), Alpnach
Detachments at Emmen, Meiringen & Sion

AS.332M-1
T-311
T-312
T-313
T-314
T-315
T-316
T-317
T-318
T-319
T-320
T-321
T-322
T-323
T-324
T-325

AS.532UL
T-331
T-332
T-333
T-334
T-335
T-336
T-337
T-338
T-339
T-340
T-341
T-342

Beech 1900D
Lufttransportdienst des Bundes, Dübendorf
T-729

Beech King Air 350C
Lufttransportdienst des Bundes, Dübendorf
T-721

Cessna 560XL Citation Excel
Lufttransportdienst des Bundes, Dübendorf
T-784

Dassault Falcon 50
Lufttransportdienst des Bundes, Dübendorf
T-783

Eurocopter EC.135P-2*/EC.635P-2
Lufttransportdienst des Bundes, Dübendorf (LTDB);
Lufttransport Geschwader 2 (LTG 2), Alpnach;
Lufttransport Staffel 3 (LtSt 3), Dübendorf;
Lufttransport Staffel 5 (LtSt 5), Payerne;
Lufttransport Staffel 6 (LtSt 6), Alpnach;
Lufttransport Staffel 8 (LtSt 8), Alpnach
Detachments at Emmen, Meiringen & Sion

T-351* LTDB
T-352* LTDB
T-353 LTG 2
T-354 LTG 2
T-355 LTG 2
T-356 LTG 2
T-357 LTG 2
T-358 LTG 2
T-359 LTG 2
T-360 LTG 2
T-361 LTG 2
T-362 LTG 2
T-363 LTG 2
T-364 LTG 2
T-365 LTG 2
T-366 LTG 2
T-367 LTG 2
T-368 LTG 2
T-369 LTG 2
T-370 LTG 2

McDonnell Douglas F/A-18 Hornet
Flieger Staffel 11 (FlSt 11), Meiringen;
Escadrille d'Aviation 17 (EdAv 17), Payerne;
Flieger Staffel 18 (FlSt 18), Payerne

F/A-18C
J-5001
J-5002
J-5003
J-5004
J-5005
J-5006
J-5007
J-5008
J-5009
J-5010
J-5011$
J-5012
J-5013
J-5014
J-5015
J-5016
J-5017$
J-5018$
J-5019
J-5020
J-5021
J-5022
J-5023
J-5024
J-5025
J-5026

F/A-18D
J-5232
J-5233
J-5234
J-5235
J-5236
J-5237
J-5238

Northrop F-5 Tiger II
Armasuisse, Emmen;
Escadrille d'Aviation 6 (EdAv 6), Sion;
Flieger Staffel 8 (FlSt 8), Meiringen;
Flieger Staffel 19 (FlSt 19), Sion;
Patrouille Suisse, Emmen (*P. Suisse*)

F-5E
J-3004
J-3005
J-3014
J-3015
J-3030
J-3033
J-3036
J-3038
J-3041
J-3043
J-3044
J-3052
J-3053
J-3055
J-3057
J-3062
J-3063
J-3065
J-3067
J-3068
J-3069
J-3070
J-3072
J-3073
J-3074
J-3076
J-3077
J-3079
J-3080 *P. Suisse*
J-3081 *P. Suisse*
J-3082 *P. Suisse*
J-3083 *P. Suisse*
J-3084 *P. Suisse*
J-3085 *P. Suisse*
J-3086 *P. Suisse*
J-3087 *P. Suisse*
J-3088 *P. Suisse*
J-3089 *P. Suisse*
J-3090 *P. Suisse*
J-3091 *P. Suisse*
J-3092
J-3093
J-3094
J-3095
J-3097
J-3098

F-5F
J-3201
J-3202
J-3203
J-3204
J-3205
J-3206
J-3207
J-3208
J-3209
J-3210

J-3211
J-3212

Pilatus
PC.6B/B2-H2 Turbo Porter
Lufttransport Staffel 7
(LtSt 7), Emmen
V-612
V-613
V-614
V-616
V-617
V-618
V-619
V-620
V-622$
V-623
V-631
V-632
V-633
V-634
V-635

Pilatus PC-7/NCPC-7*
Turbo Trainer
Instrumentation Flieger
Staffel 14 (InstruFlSt 14),
Dübendorf;
Pilotenschule, Emmen
A-904
A-909
A-910
A-912*
A-913*
A-914*
A-915*
A-916*
A-917*
A-918*
A-919*
A-922*
A-923*
A-924*
A-925*
A-926*
A-927*
A-928*
A-929*
A-930*
A-931*
A-932*
A-933*
A-934*
A-935*
A-936*
A-937*
A-938*
A-939*
A-940*
A-941*

Pilatus PC-9
Zielfliegerstaffel 12,
Sion
C-401
C-402
C-403
C-405
C-406
C-407
C-408
C-409
C-410
C-411
C-412

Pilatus PC-21
Pilotenschule, Emmen
A-101
A-102
A-103
A-104
A-105
A-106
A-107 (on order)
A108 (on order)

Swiss Govt
Pilatus PC-12/45
Swiss Govt, Emmen
HB-FOG

SYRIA
Dassault Falcon 900
Govt of Syria, Damascus
YK-ASC

TANZANIA
Airbus A.340-542
Tanzanian Govt, Dar-es-Salaam
5H-... (on order)

Gulfstream Aerospace G.550
Tanzanian Govt, Dar-es-Salaam
5H-ONE

THAILAND
Airbus A.310-324
Royal Flight, Bangkok
L.13-1/34 (HS-TYQ) [60202]

Boeing 737-448/-4Z6/-8Z6
Royal Flight, Bangkok
HS-CMV 4Z6 [11-111, 90401]
HS-HRH 448 [99-999, 90409]
HS-TYS 8Z6 [55-555]

TUNISIA
Airbus A.340-541
Govt of Tunisia, Tunis
TS-KRT

Boeing 737-7HJ
Govt of Tunisia, Tunis
TS-IOO

TURKEY
Türk Hava Kuvvetleri
Boeing 737-7FS AEW&C
131 Filo, Konya
06-001 (on order)
06-002 (on order)
06-003 (on order)
06-004 (on order)

Boeing
KC-135R Stratotanker
101 Filo, Incirlik
57-2609
58-0110
60-0325
60-0326
62-3539
62-3563
62-3567

Cessna 650 Citation VII
212 Filo, Ankara/Etimesğut
004
005

Gulfstream Aerospace G.550
212 Filo, Ankara/Etimesğut
09-001
10-002

Grumman
G.1159C Gulfstream IV
211 Filo, Ankara/Etimesğut
91-003
TC-ATA
TC-GAP/001

Lockheed
C-130E Hercules
222 Filo, Erkilet
63-3186
63-3187
63-3188
63-3189
70-1947
71-1468
73-0991

Transall C-160D
221 Filo, Erkilet
68-020
68-023
69-019
69-021
69-024
69-026
69-027
69-028
69-029
69-031
69-032
69-033 $
69-034
69-035
69-036
69-038
69-040

TUSAS-GD F-16C/F-16D*
Fighting Falcon
3 AJEÜ, Konya:
132 Filo;
4 AJÜ, Akinci:
141 Filo, 142 Filo
& 143/Öncel Filo;
5 AJÜ, Merzifon:
151 Filo & 152 Filo;
6 AJÜ, Bandirma:
161 Filo & 162 Filo;
8 AJÜ, Diyarbakir:
181 Filo & 182 Filo;
9 AJÜ, Balikesir:
191 Filo & 192 Filo
86-0066 Öncel Filo
86-0068 Öncel Filo
86-0069 Öncel Filo
86-0070 Öncel Filo$
86-0071 Öncel Filo
86-0072 Öncel Filo
86-0192* Öncel Filo
86-0193* Öncel Filo
86-0194* Öncel Filo
86-0195* Öncel Filo

86-0196* Öncel Filo
87-0002* Öncel Filo
87-0003* Öncel Filo
87-0009 Öncel Filo
87-0010 Öncel Filo
87-0011 Öncel Filo
87-0013 Öncel Filo$
87-0014 Öncel Filo
87-0015 Öncel Filo
87-0016 Öncel Filo
87-0017 Öncel Filo
87-0018 Öncel Filo
87-0019 Öncel Filo
87-0020 Öncel Filo
87-0021 Öncel Filo
88-0013* Öncel Filo
88-0014* 141 Filo
88-0015* 141 Filo
88-0019 Öncel Filo
88-0020 Öncel Filo
88-0021 142 Filo
88-0024 142 Filo
88-0025 142 Filo
88-0026 142 Filo
88-0027 142 Filo
88-0028 191 Filo
88-0029 142 Filo
88-0030 142 Filo
88-0031 142 Filo
88-0032 142 Filo
88-0033 141 Filo
88-0034 141 Filo
88-0035 141 Filo
88-0036 141 Filo
88-0037 141 Filo
89-0022 141 Filo
89-0023 141 Filo
89-0024 141 Filo
89-0025 141 Filo
89-0026 141 Filo
89-0027 141 Filo
89-0028 141 Filo
89-0030 141 Filo
89-0031 141 Filo
89-0034 162 Filo
89-0035 162 Filo
89-0036 141 Filo
89-0037 162 Filo
89-0038 162 Filo
89-0040 162 Filo
89-0041 162 Filo
89-0042* 142 Filo
89-0043* 162 Filo
89-0044* 162 Filo
89-0045* 182 Filo
90-0004 162 Filo
90-0005 162 Filo
90-0006 162 Filo
90-0007 162 Filo
90-0008 162 Filo
90-0009 162 Filo
90-0010 162 Filo
90-0011 162 Filo
90-0012 161 Filo
90-0013 161 Filo
90-0014 162 Filo
90-0016 161 Filo
90-0017 161 Filo
90-0018 161 Filo
90-0019 161 Filo
90-0020 162 Filo
90-0021 161 Filo
90-0022* 161 Filo
90-0023* 161 Filo
90-0024* 161 Filo
91-0001 161 Filo
91-0002 161 Filo
91-0003 161 Filo
91-0004 161 Filo
91-0005 161 Filo
91-0006 161 Filo
91-0007 161 Filo
91-0008 141 Filo
91-0010 141 Filo
91-0011 141 Filo
91-0012 141 Filo
91-0013 192 Filo
91-0014 141 Filo
91-0015 182 Filo
91-0016 182 Filo
91-0017 182 Filo
91-0018 182 Filo
91-0020 182 Filo
91-0022* 141 Filo
91-0024* 141 Filo
92-0001 182 Filo
92-0002 182 Filo
92-0003 162 Filo
92-0004 182 Filo
92-0005 191 Filo
92-0006 182 Filo
92-0007 182 Filo
92-0008 191 Filo
92-0009 191 Filo
92-0010 182 Filo
92-0011 182 Filo
92-0012 182 Filo
92-0013 182 Filo
92-0014 182 Filo
92-0015 182 Filo
92-0016 182 Filo
92-0017 182 Filo
92-0018 182 Filo
92-0019 181 Filo
92-0020 181 Filo
92-0021 181 Filo
92-0022* 181 Filo
92-0023* 181 Filo
92-0024* 182 Filo
93-0001 181 Filo
93-0003 181 Filo
93-0004 181 Filo
93-0005 181 Filo
93-0006 181 Filo
93-0007 181 Filo
93-0008 181 Filo
93-0009 181 Filo
93-0010 132 Filo
93-0011 181 Filo
93-0012 181 Filo
93-0013 181 Filo
93-0658 151 Filo
93-0659 151 Filo
93-0660 152 Filo
93-0661 151 Filo
93-0663 151 Filo
93-0664 151 Filo
93-0665 152 Filo
93-0667 151 Filo
93-0668 151 Filo
93-0669 151 Filo
93-0670 151 Filo
93-0671 151 Filo
93-0672 152 Filo
93-0673 152 Filo
93-0674 152 Filo
93-0675 152 Filo
93-0676 192 Filo
93-0677 192 Filo$
93-0678 192 Filo
93-0679 192 Filo
93-0680 192 Filo$
93-0681 192 Filo
93-0682 192 Filo
93-0683 192 Filo
93-0684 192 Filo
93-0685 192 Filo
93-0686 192 Filo
93-0687 192 Filo
93-0688 192 Filo
93-0689 192 Filo
93-0690 192 Filo
93-0691* 151 Filo
93-0692* 151 Filo$
93-0693* 152 Filo
93-0694* 192 Filo
93-0695* 192 Filo
93-0696* 192 Filo$
94-0071 192 Filo
94-0072 191 Filo
94-0073 191 Filo
94-0074 191 Filo
94-0075 191 Filo
94-0076 191 Filo
94-0077 191 Filo
94-0078 191 Filo
94-0079 191 Filo
94-0080 191 Filo
94-0082 191 Filo
94-0083 191 Filo
94-0084 191 Filo
94-0085 191 Filo
94-0086 191 Filo
94-0088 152 Filo
94-0089 152 Filo
94-0090 152 Filo
94-0091 152 Filo
94-0092 152 Filo
94-0093 152 Filo
94-0094 152 Filo
94-0095 152 Filo
94-0096 152 Filo
94-0105* 151 Filo
94-0106* 191 Filo
94-0108* 152 Filo
94-0109* 151 Filo
94-0110* 152 Filo
94-1557* 152 Filo
94-1558* Öncel Filo
94-1559* 152 Filo
94-1560* 151 Filo
94-1561* 191 Filo
94-1562* 192 Filo
94-1563* 192 Filo
94-1564* 191 Filo

Turkish Govt
Airbus A.319CJ-115X
Turkish Govt, Ankara
TC-ANA

Gulfstream Aerospace G.550
Turkish Govt, Ankara
TC-DAP

TURKMENISTAN
BAe 1000B
Govt of Turkmenistan, Ashkhabad
EZ-B021

Boeing 757-23A
Govt of Turkmenistan, Ashkhabad
EZ-A010

UGANDA
Gulfstream Aerospace G.550
Govt of Uganda, Entebbe
5X-UGF

UKRAINE
Ukrainian Air Force
Ilyushin Il-76MD
321 TAP, Uzin
76413
76531
76536
76537
76559
76564
76565
76566
76580
76585
76596
76598
76601
76633
76637
76645
76647
76657
76661
76665
76677
76683
76697
76698
76699
76767
86915
86922
86923

Airbus A.319CJ-115X
Govt of Ukraine, Kiev
P4-ARL

Ilyushin Il-62M
Govt of Ukraine, Kiev
UR-86527
UR-86528

UNITED ARAB EMIRATES
United Arab Emirates Air Force
AgustaWestland AW.139
Dubai Air Wing
DU-139
DU-140
DU-141
DU-142
DU-143

Airbus A.330-243MRTT
... (on order)
... (on order)

Lockheed C-130H/L.100-30* Hercules
Abu Dhabi
1211
1213
1214
1217*
Dubai
312*

UAE Govt
Airbus A.319CJ-113X
Dubai Air Wing
A6-ESH

Airbus A.320-232
Govt of Abu Dhabi;
Govt of Dubai
A6-DLM Abu Dhabi
A6-HMS Dubai

BAE RJ.85/RJ.100*
Govt of Abu Dhabi;
Govt of Dubai
A6-AAB* Abu Dhabi
A6-RJ1 Dubai

Boeing 737-7BC/7F0/8AJ/8EC/8EO/8EX
Govt of Abu Dhabi;
Govt of Dubai
A6-AUH 8EX Dubai
A6-DFR 7BC Abu Dhabi
A6-HEH 8AJ Dubai
A6-HRS 7F0 Dubai
A6-MRM 8EC Dubai
A6-MRS 8EO Dubai

Boeing 747-412F/422/433/48E/4F6
Dubai Air Wing;
Govt of Abu Dhabi
A6-COM 433 Dubai
A6-GGP 412F Dubai
A6-HRM 422 Dubai
A6-MMM 422 Dubai
A6-UAE 48E Dubai
A6-YAS 4F6 Abu Dhabi

Boeing 747SP-31
Govt of Dubai
A6-SMR

Boeing 767-341ER/35RER*
Govt of Abu Dhabi
A6-JBD
A6-SIL*

Boeing 777-2ANER
Govt of Abu Dhabi
A6-ALN

Grumman G.1159C Gulfstream IV
Dubai Air Wing
A6-HHH

VENEZUELA
Fuerza Aérea Venezolana
Airbus A.319CJ-133X
Esc 41, Caracas
0001

YEMEN
Boeing 747SP-27
Govt of Yemen, Sana'a
7O-YMN

YUGOSLAVIA
Dassault Falcon 50
Govt of Yugoslavia, Belgrade
YU-BNA

This Alpha Jet depicts the new French Air Force coding system. The 120 in the code on E154 indicates that it is based at BA.120, Cazaux.

Gazelle 4210 of the Armee de Terre depicts the recent recoding of French Army helicopters.

Futuristic looking Italian Air Force Avanti MM62202 climbs away from Fairford following the air show.

It may be painted grey, it may look like an airliner but Boeing 757-2K2 NZ7572 of the RNZAF is a real favourite for its extraordinary displays at airshows.

Su-22UM-3K 308 of the Polish Air Force is an example of a type that is becoming a rarity in European skies.

Overseas Military Aircraft Code Decode

This section lists the codes worn by some overseas air forces and, alongside, the serial of the aircraft currently wearing this code. This list will be updated occasionally and those with Internet access can download the latest version via the 'AirNet' Web Site, www.aviation-links.co.uk and via the MAM2009 Yahoo! Group.

FRANCE

D-BD Alpha Jet

0 [PDF] E134
1 [PDF] E130
2 [PDF] E114
3 [PDF] E165
4 [PDF] E41
5 [PDF] E31
6 [PDF] E94
7 [PDF] E46
8 [PDF] E95
9 [PDF] E85
2-FD E151
2-FG E14
2-FO E81
8-MD E30
8-ME E66
8-MH E48
8-MI E74
8-MN E167
8-MO E68
8-MP E24
8-MQ E143
8-NP E155
102-AH E99
102-FA E140
102-FB E86
102-FI E32
102-FJ E33
102-FK E127
102-FM E105
102-LC E87
102-LF E9
102-LQ E61
102-MB E97
102-ML E91
102-NA E79
102-NB E29
102-ND E26
102-RJ E76
118-AO E112
118-LX E89
118-MF E98
120-AF E108
120-AK E144
120-AL E154
120-FN E116
120-LI E53
120-LM E102
120-MA E35
120-MR E115
120-NE E73
120-NF E141
120-NL E37
120-RE E44
120-RN E124
120-RP E136
314-AA E17
314-AB E28
314-FC E139
314-FE E119
314-FL E92
314-LG E120
314-LH E38
314-LJ E137
314-LK E125
314-LL E88
314-LN E118
314-LO E142
314-LP E129
314-LR E171
314-LT E147
314-LV E5
314-LW E82
314-LZ E132
314-RM E123
314-RQ E138
314-RR E146
314-TB E67
314-TD E113
314-TF E45
314-TI E156
314-TK E58
314-TL E64
314-TT E101
314-TZ E83
314-UA E103
314-UC E157
314-UD E107
314-UF E36
314-UG E23
314-UH E160
314-UK E84
314-UN E170
705-AC E47
705-AD E51
705-AE E75
705-AG E109
705-AH E110
705-AK E18
705-LA E72
705-LB E49
705-LE E121
705-LS E22
705-LU E148
705-LY E59
705-MS E20
705-RT E152
705-RW E166
705-TA E42
705-TG E104
705-TH E90
705-TJ E25
705-TU E7
705-TX E93
705-UB E11
F-TERA E41
F-TERB E163
F-TERD E121
F-TERE E165
F-TERF E158
F-TERH E94
F-TERI E117
F-TERJ E162
F-TERK E31
F-TERM E134
F-TERN E46
F-TERP E130
F-TERQ E95
F-TERR E114
F-TERX E135
LM E102

Dassault Mirage F.1

33-CN 630
33-CO 605
33-CQ 632
33-NE 617
33-NJ 612
112-AA 631
112-AW 623
112-CB 647
112-CC 613
112-CD 638
112-CE 643
112-CF 604
112-CG 642
112-CH 645
112-CI 610
112-CK 634
112-CL 657
112-CP 637
112-CQ 632
112-CR 649
112-CS 656
112-CT 620
112-CU 606
112-CV 653
112-CY 660
112-FA 622
112-NA 627
112-NC 654
112-ND 607
112-NF 662
112-NG 655
112-NI 641
112-NK 661
112-NL 636
112-NM 611
112-NP 635
112-NQ 658
112-NR 614
112-NT 659
112-NU 603
112-NV 640
112-NW 646
112-NX 616
112-NY 624
112-NZ 650
112-QA 242
112-QC 267
112-QF 273
112-QJ 274
112-QK 231
112-QQ 271
112-QR 236
112-QS 226
112-QU 253
112-QW 229
112-SA 514
112-SC 517
112-SE 507
112-SG 278
112-SH 256
112-SI 516

112-SK 519
112-SL 510
112-SR 518
112-SW 502
118-MZ 615
118-NC 654
330-AP 227

Dassault Mirage 2000

2-EK 65
3-IF 609
3-IL 622
3-IM 619
3-IW 684
3-JA 678
3-JJ 639
3-JK 612
3-XC 618
3-XL 603
3-XO 629
4-AB 333
4-AC 319
4-AE 355
4-AG 369
4-AI 365
4-AK 359
4-AL 348
4-AO 309
4-AS 326
4-AU 316
4-BH 329
4-BO 331
4-BP 317
4-CA 304
4-CC 325
4-CG 338
4-CJ 327
5-OF 11
5-OJ 1
12-KB 94
12-KR 102
12-LL 86
33-LB 81
102-AD 70
102-EA 49
102-EC 78
102-ED 62
102-EE 71
102-EF 45
102-EG 56
102-EH 52
102-EI 38
102-EJ 43
102-EK 74
102-EL 58
102-EM 63
102-EN 46
102-EO 66
102-EP 47
102-EQ 44
102-ER 68
102-ES 73
102-ET 57
102-EU 55
102-EV 59
102-EW 48
102-EX 40
102-EY 42
102-EZ 54
102-FZ 41
102-ME 61
103-KC 120
103-KD 123
103-KE 101
103-KI 96
103-KL 106
103-KM 95
103-KN 121
103-KQ 112
103-KR 102
103-KU 114
103-KV 88
103-LA 87
103-LC 108
103-LI 80
103-LJ 105
103-LK 85
103-YD 107
103-YE 122
103-YG 118
103-YH 109
103-YL 82
103-YO 113
103-YR 91
103-YT 124
103-YU 98
104-MH 67
115-KA 89
115-KB 94
115-KJ 523
115-KS 528
115-LD 117
115-LE 79
115-OA 524
115-OB 20
115-OC 529
115-OD 506
115-OG 3
115-OH 12
115-OK 509
115-OL 530
115-OO 8
115-OQ 510
115-OR 527
115-OT 5
115-OX 16
115-OZ 17
115-YA 93
115-YB 99
115-YK 97
115-YM 115
115-YP 526
115-YS 90
116-AD 339
116-AF 311
116-AH 343
116-AN 323
116-AR 368
116-AT 330
116-AW 367
116-BB 364
116-BE 310
116-BF 337
116-BG 313
116-BI 336
116-BL 306
116-BM 349
116-BN 332
116-BQ 358
116-BS 374
116-BT 341
116-BU 345
116-BV 344
116-CH 307
116-CN 312
116-CP 322
116-CS 305
116-CX 324
118-AM 525
118-AS 635
118-AX 77
118-EB 76
118-IG 668
118-JF 660
118-XH 616
125-AA 340
125-AJ 350
125-AM 353
125-AQ 351
125-BA 342
125-BC 366
125-BD 371
125-BJ 354
125-BX 356
125-CB 360
125-CD 320
125-CF 373
125-CI 335
125-CK 361
125-CL 375
125-CM 372
125-CO 357
125-CQ 370
125-CU 362
133-AF 665
133-AG 681
133-AL 669
133-IA 650
133-IC 626
133-ID 654
113-IE 642
133-IH 631
133-IJ 638
133-IN 640
133-IO 647
133-IP 604
133-IQ 666
133-IR 674
133-IS 617
133-IT 624
133-IU 620
133-IV 683
133-IW 664
133-JC 606
133-JD 643
133-JE 634
133-JG 601
133-JH 686
133-JI 675
133-JL 628
133-JM 657
133-JN 658
133-JO 627
133-JP 611
133-JR 682
133-JT 677
133-JU 614
133-JV 636
133-JW 641
133-JX 679
133-JY 615
133-JZ 667
133-LF 605
133-LG 651
133-LH 653
133-MO 613
133-MP 623
133-MQ 646
133-XA 662

133-XE	632
133-XF	670
133-XG	625
133-XI	661
133-XJ	602
133-XL	671
133-XM	680
133-XN	652
133-XQ	637
133-XR	659
133-XT	648
133-XV	672
133-XX	610
133-XY	649
133-XZ	685
188-KF	111
188-XD	630
188-YC	83
188-YN	103
330-AQ	64
330-AS	51
330-AW	92

Dassault Rafale

104-HG	106
113-GA	122
113-GB	123
113-GC	124
113-HA	308
113-HB	309
113-HC	310
113-HD	311
113-HE	105
113-HF	312
113-HH	104
113-HI	313
113-HJ	107
113-HK	315
113-HM	318
113-HN	319
113-HO	317
113-HP	314
113-HQ	321
113-HR	103
113-HS	108
113-HT	323
113-HU	322
113-HV	320
113-HX	325
113-HY	326
113-HZ	327
113-IA	307
113-IB	306
113-IC	328
113-IE	330
113-IH	333
113-II	334
113-IJ	335
113-IK	336
113-IL	337
113-IM	109
113-IN	110
113-IO	338
113-IP	111
113-IQ	112
113-IR	113
113-IS	114
113-IT	115
113-IU	116
113-IV	117
113-IW	118
113-IX	119
113-IY	120
113-IZ	121
118-EA	303
118-EB	304
118-EC	305
IF	331
IG	332

ITALY

Aeritalia-EMB AMX

32-01	MM7147
32-02	MM7192
32-05	MM7170
32-07	MM7196
32-13	MM7166
32-15	MM7129
32-16	MM7165
32-20	MM7180
32-21	MM7194
32-40	MM55031
32-41	MM55030
32-42	MM55051
32-47	MM55046
32-50	MM55029
32-51	MM55036
32-52	MM55040
32-53	MM55047
32-54	MM55039
32-55	MM55041
32-56	MM55042
32-57	MM55044
32-64	MM55037
32-65	MM55043
32-66	MM55049
51-01	MM7132
51-10	MM7159
51-11	MM7131
51-21	MM7143
51-25	MM7146
51-32	MM7133
51-35	MM7185
51-37	MM7161
51-40	MM7164
51-41	MM7183
51-43	MM7178
51-44	MM7198
51-45	MM7191
51-46	MM7197
51-50	MM7186
51-51	MM7151
51-52	MM7171
51-53	MM7160
51-54	MM7193
51-55	MM7168
51-56	MM7167
51-57	MM7190
51-60	MM7174
51-61	MM7148
51-62	MM7182
51-63	MM7173
51-64	MM7179
51-65	MM7184
51-66	MM7169
51-67	MM7172
RS-12	CSX7158
RS-14	MM7177
RS-18	MM55034

Aermacchi MB339

0 [FT]	MM54485
1 [FT]	MM54551
2 [FT]	MM54480
3 [FT]	MM54473
4 [FT]	MM54482
5 [FT]	MM54475
6 [FT]	MM55052
7 [FT]	MM54539
8 [FT]	MM54487
9 [FT]	MM54505
10 [FT]	MM54538
25	MM54459
50 [FT]	MM54479
36-02	MM55065
36-04	MM55076
36-10	MM55064
36-06	MM55074
36-07	MM55067
51-71	MM54493
51-75	MM54546
51-76	MM54543
61-01	MM54446
61-11	MM54457
61-12	MM54458
61-15	MM55054
61-17	MM54463
61-20	MM55055
61-21	MM54465
61-23	MM54467
61-24	MM54468
61-26	MM55059
61-32	MM54488
61-36	MM54492
61-41	MM55058
61-42	MM54496
61-45	MM54499
61-50	MM54443
61-52	MM54504
61-55	MM54507
61-57	MM54509
61-60	MM54510
61-61	MM54511
61-62	MM54512
61-64	MM54514
61-65	MM54515
61-66	MM54516
61-70	MM54518
61-72	MM54533
61-74	MM54535
61-106	MM54548
61-107	MM54549
61-112	MM54442
61-114	MM55053
61-126	MM55062
61-127	MM55063
61-135	MM55069
61-136	MM55070
61-140	MM55072
61-141	MM55073
61-143	MM55075
61-145	MM55077
61-146	MM55078
61-147	MM55079
61-150	MM55080
61-151	MM55081
61-152	MM55082
61-154	MM55084
61-155	MM55085
61-156	MM55086
61-157	MM55087
61-160	MM55088
61-161	MM55089
61-162	MM55090
RS-11	CSX54453
RS-30	CSX54544
RS-32	MM55091
RS-33	MM55068

Eurofighter Typhoon

4-1 MM7270
4-2 MM7303
4-3 MM7287
4-4 MM7288
4-5 MM7289
4-6 MM7295
4-7 MM7290
4-11 MM7291
4-12 MM7292
4-13 MM7280
4-14 MM7281
4-15 MM7293
4-16 MM7285
4-20 MM7299
4-22 MM7301
4-23 MM55095
4-24 MM55097
4-25 MM55092
4-26 MM55128
4-27 MM55094
4-30 MM55096
4-31 MM55093
4-32 MM55129
4-33 MM55130
36-02 MM7273
36-03 MM7271
36-04 MM7235
36-05 MM7278
36-06 MM7276
36-07 MM7274
36-10 MM7284
36-11 CSX7275
36-12 MM7300
36-14 MM7272
36-21 MM7279
36-22 MM7296
36-23 MM7297
36-24 MM7298
36-26 MM7294
RMV-01 MMX603
RS-01 MMX602

Panavia Tornado

6-01 MM7007
6-02 MM7039
6-04 MM7057
6-05 MM7025
6-06 MM7046
6-07 MM7075
6-10 MM7088
6-11 MM7058
6-12 MM7071
6-13 MM7011
6-14 MM7061
6-15 MM55006
6-20 MM7016
6-23 MM7022
6-25 MM7043
6-26 MM7063
6-27 MM7035
6-31 MM7006
6-32 MM7015
6-33 MM7080
6-34 MM7073
6-35 MM7026
6-36 MM7087
6-37 MM7038
6-43 MM7003
6-44 MM55009
6-45 MM55008
6-46 MM7018
6-51 MM55000
6-52 MM55001
6-53 MM7004
6-56 MM55007
6-60 MM7086
6-61 MM7031
6-62 MM7083
6-64 MM7049
6-65 MM7065
6-66 MM7056
6-67 MM7028
6-71 MM7067
36-31 MM7023
36-41 MM7024
36-50 CSX7085
36-156 MM7013
50-01 MM7021
50-02 MM7052
50-03 MM7066
50-04 MM7030
50-05 MM7019
50-06 MM7070
50-07 MM7053
50-40 MM7054
50-41 MM7020
50-42 MM7055
50-43 CSX7047
50-44 MM7062
50-45 MM7051
50-46 MM7068
50-47 MM7059
50-52 MM7081
50-53 MM7044
50-54 MM7082
50-57 MM7042
RS-01 MM7014
RS-06 CSX7041

SPAIN

CASA 101EB Aviojet

54-20 E.25-35
54-21 E.25-55
54-22 E.25-61
74-02 E.25-33
74-07 E.25-51
74-09 E.25-53
74-11 E.25-56
74-12 E.25-57
74-13 E.25-59
74-17 E.25-63
74-20 E.25-66
74-21 E.25-67
74-22 E.25-68
74-25 E.25-71
74-26 E.25-72
74-28 E.25-74
74-29 E.25-75
74-30 E.25-76
74-34 E.25-81
74-35 E.25-83
74-39 E.25-88
74-40 E.25-17
74-41 E.25-41
74-42 E.25-18
74-43 E.25-43
74-44 E.25-34
74-45 E.25-29
79-01 E.25-01
79-02 E.25-78
79-03 E.25-80
79-04 E.25-84
79-05 E.25-05
79-06 E.25-06
79-07 E.25-07
79-08 E.25-08
79-09 E.25-09
79-10 E.25-10
79-11 E.25-11
79-12 E.25-12
79-13 E.25-13
79-14 E.25-14
79-15 E.25-15
79-16 E.25-16
79-17 E.25-62
79-20 E.25-20
79-21 E.25-21
79-22 E.25-22
79-23 E.25-23
79-24 E.25-24
79-25 E.25-25
79-26 E.25-26
79-27 E.25-27
79-28 E.25-28
79-29 E.25-87
79-31 E.25-31
79-32 E.25-86
79-33 E.25-50
79-34 E.25-52
79-35 E.25-54
79-37 E.25-37
79-38 E.25-38
79-39 E.25-79
79-40 E.25-40
79-44 E.25-44
79-45 E.25-45
79-46 E.25-46
79-47 E.25-47
79-48 E.25-48
79-49 E.25-49
79-95 E.25-65
79-97 E.25-69
79-98 E.25-73

CASA 212 Aviocar

37-60 TR.12D-76
37-61 TR.12D-77
37-62 TR.12D-78
37-63 TR.12D-79
37-64 TR.12D-80
37-65 TR.12D-81
47-11 T.12B-61
47-12 TM.12D-72
47-14 T.12D-75
54-11 TM.12D-74
72-01 T.12B-13
72-02 T.12B-22
72-03 T.12B-21
72-05 T.12B-37
72-07 T.12B-49
72-08 T.12B-55
72-09 T.12B-66
72-11 T.12B-65
72-14 T.12B-63
72-15 T.12B-69
72-17 T.12B-70
74-81 T.12B-67

US Military Aircraft Markings

All USAF and US Army aircraft have been allocated a fiscal year (FY) number since 1921. Individual aircraft are given a serial according to the fiscal year in which they are ordered. The numbers commence at 0001 and are prefixed with the year of allocation. For example F-15C Eagle 84-001 (84-0001) was the first aircraft ordered in 1984. The fiscal year (FY) serial is carried on the technical data block which is usually stencilled on the left-hand side of the aircraft just below the cockpit. The number displayed on the fin is a corruption of the FY serial. Most tactical aircraft carry the fiscal year in small figures followed by the last three or four digits of the serial in large figures. Large transport and tanker aircraft such as C-130s and KC-135s sometimes display a five-figure number commencing with the last digit of the appropriate fiscal year and four figures of the production number. An example of this is KC-135R 58-0128 which displays 80128 on its fin.

US Army serials have been allocated in a similar way to USAF serials although in recent years an additional zero has been added so that all US Army serials now have the two-figure fiscal year part followed by five digits. This means that, for example C-20E 70140 is officially 87-00140 although as yet this has not led to any alterations to serials painted on aircraft.

USN and USMC serials follow a straightforward numerical sequence which commenced, for the present series, with the allocation of 00001 to an SB2C Helldiver by the Bureau of Aeronautics in 1940. Numbers in the 168000 series are presently being issued. They are usually carried in full on the rear fuselage of the aircraft.

US Coast Guard serials began with the allocation of the serial 1 to a Loening OL-5 in 1927.

UK-based USAF Aircraft

The following aircraft are normally based in the UK. They are listed in numerical order of type with individual aircraft in serial number order, as depicted on the aircraft. The number in brackets is either the alternative presentation of the five-figure number commencing with the last digit of the fiscal year, or the fiscal year where a five-figure serial is presented on the aircraft. Where it is possible to identify the allocation of aircraft to individual squadrons by means of colours carried on fin or cockpit edge, this is also provided.

Type				Notes
McDonnell Douglas				
F-15C Eagle/F-15D Eagle/				
F-15E Strike Eagle				
LN: 48th FW, RAF Lakenheath:				
492nd FS *bl*ue/white				
493rd FS black/*y*ellow				
494th FS *r*ed/white				
00-3000	F-15E			
00-3001	F-15E	*r*		
00-3002	F-15E	*r*		
00-3003	F-15E	*r*		
00-3004	F-15E	*r*		
01-2000	F-15E	*r*		
01-2001	F-15E	*m*	[48th OG]	
01-2002	F-15E	*r*	[494th FS]	
01-2003	F-15E	*r*		
01-2004	F-15E	*m*	[48th FW]	
83-0018	F-15C	*y*		
84-0001	F-15C	*y*		
84-0010	F-15C	*y*		
84-0014	F-15C	*y*		
84-0015	F-15C	*y*		
84-0019	F-15C	*y*		
84-0027	F-15C	*y*	[493rd FS]	
84-0044	F-15D	*y*		
86-0147	F-15C	*y*		
86-0154	F-15C	*y*		
86-0156	F-15C	*y*		
86-0159	F-15C	*y*		
86-0160	F-15C	*y*		
86-0163	F-15C	*y*		
86-0164	F-15C	*y*		
86-0165	F-15C	*y*		
86-0166	F-15C			
86-0167	F-15C	*y*		
86-0171	F-15C	*y*		
86-0172	F-15C	*y*		

Type			Notes
86-0174	F-15C	*y*	
86-0175	F-15C	*y*	
86-0176	F-15C	*y*	
86-0178	F-15C	*y*	
86-0182	F-15D	*y*	
91-0301	F-15E	*bl*	
91-0302	F-15E	*bl*	
91-0303	F-15E	*bl*	
91-0304	F-15E	*bl*	
91-0306	F-15E	*r*	
91-0307	F-15E	*bl*	
91-0308	F-15E	*bl*	
91-0309	F-15E	*bl*	
91-0310	F-15E	*r*	
91-0311	F-15E	*bl*	
91-0312	F-15E	*bl*	
91-0313	F-15E	*r*	
91-0314	F-15E	*r*	
91-0315	F-15E	*r*	
91-0316	F-15E		
91-0317	F-15E	*r*	
91-0318	F-15E	*r*	
91-0320	F-15E	*r*	
91-0321	F-15E	*bl*	
91-0324	F-15E	*r*	
91-0326	F-15E	*r*	
91-0329	F-15E	*bl*	
91-0331	F-15E	*r*	
91-0332	F-15E	*bl*	
91-0334	F-15E	*r*	
91-0335	F-15E	*r*	
91-0602	F-15E	*r*	
91-0603	F-15E	*r*	
91-0604	F-15E	*r*	
91-0605	F-15E	*bl*	
92-0364	F-15E	*r*	
96-0201	F-15E	*bl*	

Type			Notes
96-0202	F-15E	*bl*	
96-0204	F-15E	*bl*	
96-0205	F-15E	*bl*	
97-0217	F-15E	*bl*	
97-0218	F-15E	*bl*	
97-0219	F-15E	*bl*	
97-0220	F-15E	*bl*	
97-0221	F-15E	*bl* [492nd FS]	
97-0222	F-15E	*r*	
98-0131	F-15E	*bl*	
98-0132	F-15E	*bl*	
98-0133	F-15E	*bl*	
98-0134	F-15E	*bl*	
98-0135	F-15E	*bl*	

Sikorsky HH-60G Pave Hawk
56th RQS/48th FW,
RAF Lakenheath [LN]

Type	Notes
26109 (FY88)	
26205 (FY89)	
26206 (FY89)	
26208 (FY89)	
26212 (FY89)	

Lockheed MC-130 Hercules
352nd SOG, RAF Mildenhall:
7th SOS* & 67th SOS,

Type		Notes
14854 (FY64)	MC-130P	
50991 (FY65)	MC-130P	
50992 (FY65)	MC-130P	
60215 (FY66)	MC-130P	
60220 (FY66)	MC-130P	
70023 (FY87)	MC-130H*	
80195 (FY88)	MC-130H*	
81803 (FY88)	MC-130H*	
90283 (FY89)	MC-130H*	
95825 (FY69)	MC-130P	

Boeing KC-135 Stratotanker
351st ARS/100th ARW,
RAF Mildenhall [D] *(r/w/bl)*

Type		Notes
00328 (FY60)	KC-135R	
10304 (FY61)	KC-135R	
10306 (FY61)	KC-135R	
23499 (FY62)	KC-135R	
23519 (FY62)	KC-135R	
23551 (FY62)	KC-135R	
23565 (FY62)	KC-135R	
37979 (FY63)	KC-135R	
38006 (FY63)	KC-135R	
38019 (FY63)	KC-135R	
71448 (FY57)	KC-135R	
71493 (FY57)	KC-135R	
80016 (FY58)	KC-135R	
80086 (FY58)	KC-135T	
80093 (FY58)	KC-135R	

89-2023 is an F-16C Fighting Falcon operated by the 555th Fighter Squadron of the 31st Fighter Wing, Aviano, Italy. These machines are still crowd pleasers at airshows.

European-based USAF Aircraft

These aircraft are normally based in Western Europe with the USAFE. They are shown in numerical order of type designation, with individual aircraft in serial number order as carried on the aircraft. Fiscal year (FY) details are also provided if necessary. The unit allocation and operating bases are given for most aircraft.

Notes	Type		
	Fairchild		
	A-10C Thunderbolt II		
	SP: 52nd FW, Spangdahlem, Germany:		
	81st FS *y*ellow		
	80-0275	*y*	
	80-0281	*y*	[81st FS]
	81-0945	*y*	
	81-0948	*y*	
	81-0952	*y*	[81st FS]
	81-0956	*y*	
	81-0960	*y*	
	81-0962	*y*	
	81-0963	*y*	
	81-0966	*y*	
	81-0976	*y*	
	81-0978	*y*	
	81-0980	*y*	
	81-0981	*y*	
	81-0983	*y*	
	81-0985	*y*	
	81-0988	*y*	
	81-0991	*y*	
	81-0992	*y*	[52nd OG]
	82-0646	*y*	
	82-0647	*y*	
	82-0649	*y*	
	82-0650	*y*	
	82-0654	*y*	
	82-0656	*y*	
	Beech		
	C-12 Super King Air		
	US Embassy Flight, Budapest, Hungary		
	FY83		
	30495	C-12D	
	FY76		
	60168	C-12C	
	Lockheed (GD)		
	F-16CJ/F-16DJ* Fighting Falcon		
	AV: 31st FW, Aviano, Italy:		
	480th FS *pur*ple/white		
	555th FS *green*/yellow		
	SP: 52nd FW, Spangdahlem, Germany:		
	480th FS *r*ed		
	87-0350	AV *gn*	
	87-0351	AV *m*	[31st OSS]
	87-0355	AV *pr*	
	87-0359	AV *gn*	
	88-0413	AV *pr*	
	88-0425	AV *gn*	
	88-0435	AV *gn*	
	88-0443	AV *pr*	
	88-0444	AV *pr*	
	88-0446	AV *gn*	
	88-0491	AV *pr*	
	88-0510	AV *pr*	[510th FS]
	88-0516	AV	
	88-0525	AV *pr*	
	88-0526	AV *gn*	

Notes	Type		
	88-0532	AV *gn*	
	88-0535	AV *gn*	
	88-0541	AV *pr*	
	89-2001	AV *m*	[31st FW]
	89-2008	AV *pr*	
	89-2009	AV *pr*	
	89-2011	AV *pr*	
	89-2016	AV *pr*	
	89-2018	AV *gn*	
	89-2023	AV *gn*	
	89-2024	AV *gn*	
	89-2026	AV *gn*	
	89-2029	AV *pr*	
	89-2030	AV *pr*	
	89-2035	AV *gn*	[555th FS]
	89-2038	AV *gn*	
	89-2039	AV *gn*	
	89-2041	AV *gn*	
	89-2044	AV *gn*	
	89-2046	AV *pr*	
	89-2047	AV *pr*	
	89-2049	AV *pr*	[USAFE]
	89-2057	AV *pr*	
	89-2068	AV *gn*	
	89-2096	AV *pr*	
	89-2102	AV *pr*	
	89-2118	AV *pr*	
	89-2137	AV *pr*	[31st OG]
	89-2152	AV	
	89-2178*	AV *gn*	
	90-0709	AV *pr*	
	90-0772	AV *gn*	
	90-0773	AV *gn*	
	90-0777*	AV *pr*	
	90-0795*	AV *gn*	
	90-0796*	AV *pr*	
	90-0800*	AV *gn*	
	90-0813	SP *r*	
	90-0818	SP *r*	
	90-0827	SP *r*	
	90-0829	SP *r*	
	90-0833	SP *r*	
	90-0843*	SP *r*	
	91-0338	SP *r*	
	91-0340	SP *r*	
	91-0342	SP *r*	
	91-0343	SP *r*	
	91-0344	SP *r*	
	91-0352	SP *m*	[52nd FW]
	91-0358	SP *r*	
	91-0360	SP *r*	
	91-0361	SP	
	91-0366	SP *r*	[480 FS]
	91-0368	SP	
	91-0396	SP *r*	
	91-0402	SP	
	91-0403	SP	
	91-0407	SP *r*	
	91-0412	SP	
	91-0416	SP	
	91-0417	SP *r*	
	91-0472*	SP	
	91-0474*	SP	

Type | Notes

92-3918 SP
96-0080 SP
96-0083 SP *r*

Grumman
C-20H Gulfstream IV
76th AS/86th AW, Ramstein, Germany
FY90
00300
FY92
20375

Gates C-21A
Learjet
76th AS/86th AW, Ramstein, Germany
FY84
40081
40082
40083
40084
40085
40087
40109
40110
40111
40112

Gulfstream Aerospace
C-37A Gulfstream V
76th AS/86th AW, Ramstein, Germany
309th AS/86th AW, Chievres, Belgium
FY01
10076 (309th AS)
FY99
90402 (76th AS)

Boeing C-40B
76th AS/86th AW, Ramstein, Germany
FY02
20042

Lockheed C-130J
Hercules II
37th AS/86th AW, Ramstein, Germany [RS] *(bl/w)*

68610	(FY06)	
68611	(FY06)	
68612	(FY06)	
78608	(FY07)	
78609	(FY07)	
78613	(FY07)	
78614	(FY07)	
88601	(FY08)	[86th AW]
88602	(FY08)	[86th OG]
88603	(FY08)	[37th AS]
88604	(FY08)	
88605	(FY08)	
88606	(FY08)	
88607	(FY08)	

European-based US Navy Aircraft

Notes | Type

Fairchild C-26D
NAF Naples, Italy;
NAF Sigonella, Italy

900528	Sigonella
900530	Sigonella
900531	Naples
910502	Naples

European-based US Army Aircraft

Notes | Type

Beech
C-12 Huron
'E' Co, 6th Btn, 52nd Avn Reg't, Stuttgart;
'F' Co, 6th Btn, 52nd Avn Reg't, Wiesbaden;
'A' Co, 2nd Btn, 228th Avn Reg't, Heidelberg;
1st Military Intelligence Btn, Wiesbaden;
SHAPE Flight Det, Chievres

FY84		
40156	C-12U	F/6-52nd Avn
40157	C-12U	E/6-52nd Avn
40158	C-12U	F/6-52nd Avn
40160	C-12U	E/6-52nd Avn
40161	C-12U	F/6-52nd Avn
40162	C-12U	F/6-52nd Avn
40163	C-12U	F/6-52nd Avn
40165	C-12U	F/6-52nd Avn
40173	C-12U	F/6-52nd Avn
40180	C-12U	E/6-52nd Avn
FY94		
40315	C-12R	A/2-228th Avn
40316	C-12R	A/2-228th Avn
40318	C-12R	A/2-228th Avn
40319	C-12R	A/2-228th Avn
FY85		
50147	RC-12K	1st MIB
50148	RC-12K	1st MIB
50149	RC-12K	1st MIB
50150	RC-12K	1st MIB
50152	RC-12K	1st MIB
50153	RC-12K	1st MIB
FY86		
60079	C-12J	SHAPE Flt Det

Grumman
C-20E Gulfstream III
HQ US Army Europe, Ramstein, *Germany*
FY87
70140

Notes	Type
	Cessna UC-35A
	Citation V
	'F' Co, 6th Btn, 52nd Avn Reg't, Wiesbaden
	FY95
	50123
	50124
	FY97
	70101
	70102
	70105
	Boeing-Vertol CH-47D Chinook
	'B' Co, 5th Btn, 158th Avn Reg't, Ansbach
	FY87
	70072
	70073
	FY88
	80099
	80100
	80101
	80102
	80103
	80104
	80106
	FY89
	90138
	90139
	90140
	90141
	90142
	90143
	90144
	90145

Sikorsky H-60 Black Hawk
'A' Co, 3rd Btn, 158th Avn Reg't, Ansbach;
'B' Co, 3rd Btn, 158th Avn Reg't, Ansbach;
'A' Co, 5th Btn, 158th Avn Reg't, Ansbach;
'C' Co, 5th Btn, 158th Avn Reg't, Ansbach;
SHAPE Flight Det, Chievres;
'G' Co, 6th Btn, 52nd Avn Reg't, Coleman Barracks;
'C' Co, 1st Btn, 214th Avn Reg't, Landstuhl;
6th Avn Co, Vicenza, Italy

Notes	Type		
	FY79		
	23330	UH-60A	C/1-214th Avn
	FY82		
	23735	UH-60A	C/1-214th Avn
	23745	UH-60A	C/1-214th Avn
	23750	UH-60A	C/1-214th Avn
	23752	UH-60A	C/1-214th Avn
	23754	UH-60A	C/1-214th Avn
	23755	UH-60A	C/1-214th Avn
	23756	UH-60A	C/1-214th Avn
	23757	UH-60A	C/1-214th Avn
	FY83		
	23855	UH-60A	C/1-214th Avn
	23868	UH-60A	C/1-214th Avn
	23869	UH-60A	C/1-214th Avn
	FY84		
	23951	UH-60A	C/1-214th Avn
	23975	UH-60A	
	FY86		
	24531	UH-60A	C/1-214th Avn
	24532	UH-60A	C/1-214th Avn
	24538	UH-60A	C/1-214th Avn
	24551	UH-60A	C/1-214th Avn
	FY87		
	24583	UH-60A	SHAPE Flt Det
	24584	UH-60A	SHAPE Flt Det
	24589	UH-60A	C/1-214th Avn
	24642	UH-60A	C/1-214th Avn
	24643	UH-60A	C/1-214th Avn
	24644	UH-60A	C/1-214th Avn
	24645	UH-60A	C/1-214th Avn
	24647	UH-60A	SHAPE Flt Det
	24656	UH-60A	C/1-214th Avn
	26001	UH-60A	C/5-158th Avn
	26003	UH-60A	G/6-52nd Avn
	26004	UH-60A	C/1-214th Avn
	FY88		
	26019	UH-60A	C/1-214th Avn
	26020	UH-60A	C/1-214th Avn
	26021	UH-60A	G/6-52nd Avn
	26023	UH-60A	C/1-214th Avn
	26026	UH-60A	G/6-52nd Avn
	26027	UH-60A	C/1-214th Avn
	26031	UH-60A	C/1-214th Avn
	26037	UH-60A	C/5-158th Avn
	26039	UH-60A	C/5-158th Avn
	26040	UH-60A	A/5-158th Avn
	26045	UH-60A	C/5-158th Avn
	26052	UH-60A	G/6-52nd Avn
	26054	UH-60A	C/1-214th Avn
	26055	UH-60A	C/1-214th Avn
	26063	UH-60A	G/6-52nd Avn
	26067	UH-60A	G/6-52nd Avn
	26071	UH-60A	G/6-52nd Avn
	26072	UH-60A	C/1-214th Avn
	26075	UH-60A	C/1-214th Avn
	26080	UH-60A	C/1-214th Avn
	26085	UH-60A	C/1-214th Avn
	26086	UH-60A	C/1-214th Avn
	FY89		
	26145	UH-60A	G/6-52nd Avn
	26153	UH-60A	C/1-214th Avn
	26165	UH-60A	C/1-214th Avn
	FY94		
	26551	UH-60L	G/6-52nd Avn
	26572	UH-60L	A/5-158th Avn
	26573	UH-60L	A/5-158th Avn
	26577	UH-60L	A/5-158th Avn
	FY95		
	26621	UH-60L	A/5-158th Avn
	26628	UH-60L	A/5-158th Avn
	26629	UH-60L	A/5-158th Avn
	26630	UH-60L	A/5-158th Avn
	26631	UH-60L	A/5-158th Avn
	26632	UH-60L	A/5-158th Avn
	26633	UH-60L	A/5-158th Avn
	26635	UH-60L	A/5-158th Avn
	26636	UH-60L	A/5-158th Avn
	26637	UH-60L	A/5-158th Avn
	26638	UH-60L	A/5-158th Avn
	26639	UH-60L	A/5-158th Avn
	26640	UH-60L	A/5-158th Avn
	26641	UH-60L	3-158th Avn
	26642	UH-60L	3-158th Avn
	26643	UH-60L	3-158th Avn
	26644	UH-60L	A/5-158th Avn
	26647	UH-60L	A/5-158th Avn
	26648	UH-60L	A/5-158th Avn
	26650	UH-60L	3-158th Avn
	26651	UH-60L	3-158th Avn

Type			Notes
26652	UH-60L	3-158th Avn	
FY96			
26674	UH-60L	3-158th Avn	
26675	UH-60L	3-158th Avn	
26676	UH-60L	3-158th Avn	
26677	UH-60L	3-158th Avn	
26678	UH-60L	3-158th Avn	
26680	UH-60L	3-158th Avn	
26683	UH-60L	3-158th Avn	
26684	UH-60L	3-158th Avn	
26687	UH-60L	3-158th Avn	
26690	UH-60L	3-158th Avn	
26691	UH-60L	3-158th Avn	
FY97			
26763	UH-60L	3-158th Avn	
26766	UH-60L	A/5-158th Avn	

MDH AH-64D Apache
2nd Btn, 159th Avn Reg't, Illesheim;
3rd Btn, 159th Avn Reg't, Illesheim

Type		Notes
FY00		
05175	2-159th Avn	
05178	2-159th Avn	
05190	3-159th Avn	
05199	2-159th Avn	
05205	2-159th Avn	
05207	2-159th Avn	
05208	2-159th Avn	
05209	2-159th Avn	
05212	2-159th Avn	
05213	2-159th Avn	
05214	2-159th Avn	
05215	2-159th Avn	
05217	2-159th Avn	
05218	2-159th Avn	
05220	2-159th Avn	
05225	2-159th Avn	
05226	2-159th Avn	
05230	3-159th Avn	
05232	2-159th Avn	
FY01		
05233	3-159th Avn	
05243	3-159th Avn	
05273	3-159th Avn	
05274	3-159th Avn	
05284	3-159th Avn	
FY04		
05462	2-159th Avn	
FY05		
07005	2-159th Avn	
07006	2-159th Avn	
07013	2-159th Avn	
FY96		
05007	3-159th Avn	
05009	3-159th Avn	
05015	3-159th Avn	
05020	3-159th Avn	
05021	3-159th Avn	
05022	3-159th Avn	
FY06		
07014	2-159th Avn	
07018	2-159th Avn	
07019	2-159th Avn	
07020	2-159th Avn	
07021	2-159th Avn	
FY07		
05516	2-159th Avn	
FY08		
05540	2-159th Avn	
05541	2-159th Avn	
05542	2-159th Avn	
05543	2-159th Avn	
05544	2-159th Avn	
05545	2-159th Avn	
05550	2-159th Avn	
05553	2-159th Avn	
05554	2-159th Avn	
05555	2-159th Avn	
05556	2-159th Avn	
FY99		
05109	3-159th Avn	
05126	3-159th Avn	
05139	3-159th Avn	
05143	3-159th Avn	

Eurocopter UH-72A Lakota
Joint Multinational Readiness
Centre, Hohenfels

Type	Notes
FY07	
72029	
FY09	
72095	
72096	
72097	
72098	
72100	
FY10	
72105	
72106	
72107	
72108	

US-based USAF Aircraft

The following aircraft are normally based in the USA but are likely to be seen visiting the UK from time to time. The presentation is in numerical order of the type, commencing with the B-**1B** and concluding with the C-**135**. The aircraft are listed in numerical progression by the serial actually carried externally. Fiscal year information is provided, together with details of mark variations and in some cases operating units. Where base-code letter information is carried on the aircrafts' tails, this is detailed with the squadron/base data; for example the 7th Wing's B-1B 60105 carries the letters DY on its tail, thus identifying the Wing's home base as Dyess AFB, Texas.

Type — *Notes*

Rockwell B-1B Lancer
7th BW, Dyess AFB, Texas [DY]:
9th BS (*bk/w*), 13th BS (*r*)
& 28th BS (*bl/w*);
28th BW, Ellsworth AFB,
South Dakota [EL]:
34th BS (*bk/r*) & 37th BS (*bk/y*);
337th TES/53rd Wg, Dyess AFB,
Texas [OT] *bk/gy*;
77th WPS/57th Wg, Dyess AFB,
Texas [WA] *y/bk*;
419th FLTS/412th TW, Edwards AFB,
California [ED]

Notes	Type		
	FY85		
	50059	7th BW	*bk/w $*
	50060	28th BW	*bk/r*
	50061	7th BW	*bl/w*
	50064	7th BW	*bl/w*
	50065	7th BW	*bl/w*
	50066	28th BW	
	50068	412th TW	
	50069	7th BW	
	50072	57th Wg	*y/bk*
	50073	7th BW	*bk/w $*
	50074	7th BW	*bk/w*
	50075	412th TW	
	50077	28th BW	*bk/r*
	50079	28th BW	*bk/r*
	50080	7th BW	*bk/w*
	50081	28th BW	*bk/r*
	50084	28th BW	*bk/r*
	50085	28th BW	*bk/y*
	50088	7th BW	*bk/w*
	50089	7th BW	*bl/w*
	50090	7th BW	*bl/w*
	50091	28th BW	*bk/r*
	FY86		
	60094	28th BW	*bk/y $*
	60095	28th BW	*bk/r*
	60097	7th BW	*bl/w*
	60098	7th BW	*bk/w*
	60099	28th BW	*bk/y $*
	60100	7th BW	*bl/w*
	60101	7th BW	*bl/w*
	60102	28th BW	*bk/y*
	60103	7th BW	*bl/w*
	60104	28th BW	*bk/y*
	60105	7th BW	*bl/w*
	60107	7th BW	
	60108	7th BW	*bl/w*
	60109	7th BW	*bk/w*
	60110	7th BW	*bk/w*
	60111	28th BW	*bk/r*
	60112	7th BW	*bl/w*
	60113	28th BW	*bk/y*
	60115	28th BW	*bk/r*
	60117	7th BW	*bk/w*
	60118	28th BW	*bk/y*
	60119	7th BW	
	60120	7th BW	*bl/w*
	60121	28th BW	*bk/y*
	60122	7th BW	*r*
	60123	7th BW	
	60124	7th BW	*bl/w $*
	60125	28th BW	*bk/r*
	60126	7th BW	*bk/w*
	60129	28th BW	*bk/r*
	60130	28th BW	*bk/y*
	60132	7th BW	*bl/w*
	60133	7th BW	*bk/w*
	60134	28th BW	*bk/r*
	60135	7th BW	*bl/w*
	60136	53rd Wg	*bk/gy*
	60137	7th BW	*bl/w*
	60138	7th BW	*y/bk*
	60139	28th BW	*bl/y $*
	60140	7th BW	*bk/w*

Northrop B-2 Spirit
419th FLTS/412th TW, Edwards AFB, California [ED];
509th BW, Whiteman AFB, Missouri [WM]:
13th BS, 393rd BS & 715th BS
(Names are given where known. Each begins *Spirit of ...*)

Notes	Type		
	FY90		
	00040	509th BW	*Alaska*
	00041	509th BW	*Hawaii*
	FY92		
	20700	509th BW	*Florida*
	FY82		
	21066	509th BW	*America*
	21067	509th BW	*Arizona*
	21068	412th TW	*New York*
	21069	509th BW	*Indiana*
	21070	509th BW	*Ohio*
	21071	509th BW	*Mississippi*
	FY93		
	31085	509th BW	*Oklahoma*
	31086	509th BW	*Kitty Hawk*
	31087	509th BW	*Pennsylvania*
	31088	509th BW	*Louisiana*
	FY88		
	80328	509th BW	*Texas*
	80329	509th BW	*Missouri*
	80330	509th BW	*California*
	80331	509th BW	*South Carolina*
	80332	509th BW	*Washington*
	FY89		
	90128	509th BW	*Nebraska*
	90129	509th BW	*Georgia*

Lockheed U-2
9th RW, Beale AFB, California [BB]:
1st RS, 5th RS
& 99th RS (*bk/r*);
Lockheed, Palmdale;
Warner Robins Air Logistics Centre [WR]

Notes	Type		
	FY68		
	68-10329	U-2S	9th RW
	68-10331	U-2S	9th RW
	68-10336	U-2S	WR ALC
	68-10337	U-2S	9th RW
	FY80		
	80-1064	TU-2S	9th RW
	80-1065	TU-2S	9th RW
	80-1066	U-2S	9th RW
	80-1067	U-2S	Lockheed
	80-1068	U-2S	9th RW
	80-1069	U-2S	9th RW
	80-1070	U-2S	9th RW
	80-1071	U-2S	9th RW
	80-1073	U-2S	9th RW
	80-1074	U-2S	9th RW
	80-1076	U-2S	9th RW
	80-1077	U-2S	9th RW
	80-1078	TU-2S	9th RW
	80-1079	U-2S	9th RW
	80-1080	U-2S	9th RW
	80-1081	U-2S	9th RW
	80-1083	U-2S	9th RW
	80-1084	U-2S	9th RW
	80-1085	U-2S	9th RW
	80-1086	U-2S	9th RW
	80-1087	U-2S	9th RW
	80-1089	U-2S	9th RW
	80-1090	U-2S	9th RW
	80-1091	TU-2S	9th RW
	80-1092	U-2S	9th RW
	80-1093	U-2S	9th RW
	80-1094	U-2S	9th RW
	80-1096	U-2S	9th RW
	80-1099	U-2S	9th RW

Type | *Notes*

Boeing E-3 Sentry
552nd ACW, Tinker AFB, Oklahoma [OK] (*w*):
960th ACS, 963rd ACS, 964th ACS, 965th ACS & 966th ACTS;
961st ACS/18th Wg, Kadena AB, Japan [ZZ] (*or*);
962nd ACS/3rd Wg, Elmendorf AFB, Alaska [AK] (*gn*)

Serial	Type	
FY80		
00137	E-3C	*w*
00138	E-3C	*r*
00139	E-3C	*gn*
FY81		
10004	E-3C	*or*
10005	E-3C	w
FY71		
11407	E-3B	*or$*
11408	E-3B	*w*
FY82		
20006	E-3C	w
20007	E-3C	w
FY83		
30008	E-3C	w
30009	E-3C	w
FY73		
31674	JE-3C	Boeing
31675	E-3B	*r*
FY75		
50556	E-3B	*w*
50557	E-3B	*r*
50558	E-3B	*gn*
50559	E-3B	*r*
50560	E-3B	*w*
FY76		
61604	E-3B	*w*
61605	E-3B	*or*
61606	E-3B	*r*
61607	E-3B	*w*
FY77		
70351	E-3B	*w*
70352	E-3B	*w*
70353	E-3B	*w*
70355	E-3B	*gn*
70356	E-3B	*or*
FY78		
80576	E-3B	*r*
80577	E-3B	*w*
80578	E-3B	*w*
FY79		
90001	E-3B	*w*
90002	E-3B	*w*
90003	E-3B	*m*

Boeing E-4B
1st ACCS/55th Wg, Offutt AFB, Nebraska [OF]

31676	(FY73)
31677	(FY73)
40787	(FY74)
50125	(FY75)

Lockheed
C-5 Galaxy/C-5M Super Galaxy
60th AMW, Travis AFB, California:
21st AS (*bk/gd*) & 22nd AS (*bk/bl*);
137th AS/105th AW, Stewart AFB, New York (*bl*);
155th AS/164th AW, Memphis, Tennessee ANG (*r*);
167th AS/167th AW, Martinsburg, West Virginia ANG [WV] (*r*);
68th AS/433rd AW AFRC, Kelly AFB, Texas;
436th AW, Dover AFB, Delaware:
9th AS (y/bl);
337th AS/439th AW AFRC, Westover ARB, Massachusetts (bl/r);
418th FLTS/412th TW, Edwards AFB, California;
445th AW AFRC, Wright-Patterson AFB, Ohio (si):
89th AS & 356th AS

Serial	Type	Unit	
FY70			
00445	C-5A	433rd AW	
00446	C-5A	445th AW	*si*
00447	C-5A	445th AW	*si*
00448	C-5A	445th AW	*si*
00449	C-5A	164th AW	*r*
00451	C-5A	445th AW	*si*
00452	C-5A	167th AW	*r*
00453	C-5A	445th AW	*si*
00454	C-5A	164th AW	*r*
00455	C-5A	105th AW	*bl*
00456	C-5A	433rd AW	
00457	C-5A	445th AW	*si*
00459	C-5A	167th AW	*r*
00460	C-5A	105th AW	*bl*
00461	C-5A	445th AW	*si*
00462	C-5A	167th AW	*r*
00463	C-5A	167th AW	*r*
00464	C-5A	105th AW	*bl*
00465	C-5A	164th AW	*r*
00466	C-5A	445th AW	*si*
00467	C-5A	167th AW	*r*
FY83			
31285	C-5M	LMTAS	
FY84			
40060	C-5B	439th AW	*bl/r*
40061	C-5B	436th AW	*y/bl*
40062	C-5B	436th AW	*y/bl*
FY85			
50001	C-5B	436th AW	*m*
50002	C-5M	LMTAS	
50003	C-5B	436th AW	*y/bl*
50004	C-5B	60th AMW	
50005	C-5M	LMTAS	
50006	C-5B	439th AW	*bl/r*
50007	C-5B	436th AW	*y/bl*
50008	C-5B	60th AMW	*bk/gd*
50009	C-5B	439th AW	*bl/r*
50010	C-5B	60th AMW	*bk/gd*
FY86			
60011	C-5B	60th AMW	
60012	C-5B	439th AW	*bl/r*
60013	C-5M	436th AW	*y/bl*
60014	C-5B	439th AW	*bl/r*
60015	C-5B	60th AMW	*w*
60016	C-5B	60th AMW	*bk/bl*
60017	C-5B	436th AW	*y/bl*
60018	C-5B	439th AW	*bl/r*
60019	C-5B	439th AW	*bl/r*
60020	C-5B	436th AW	*y/bl*
60021	C-5B	439th AW	*bl/r*
60022	C-5B	60th AMW	*bk/bl*
60023	C-5B	439th AW	*bl/r*
60024	C-5B	60th AMW	*bk/bl*
60025	C-5M	436th AW	*y/bl*
60026	C-5B	60th AMW	*bk/gd*
FY87			
70027	C-5B	436th AW	*y/bl*
70028	C-5B	60th AMW	*w*
70029	C-5B	436th AW	*y/bl*

Notes	Type			
	70030	C-5B	60th AMW	*bk/bl*
	70031	C-5B	439th AW	*bl/r*
	70032	C-5B	60th AMW	*bk/bl*
	70033	C-5B	439th AW	*bl/r*
	70034	C-5B	60th AMW	*bk/bl*
	70035	C-5B	436th AW	*y/bl*
	70036	C-5B	60th AMW	*w*
	70037	C-5B	439th AW	*bl/r*
	70038	C-5B	439th AW	*bl/r*
	70039	C-5B	439th AW	*bl/r*
	70040	C-5B	60th AMW	*bk/gd*
	70041	C-5B	439th AW	*bl/r*
	70042	C-5B	60th AMW	*bk/bl*
	70043	C-5B	439th AW	*bl/r*
	70044	C-5B	60th AMW	*bk/bl*
	70045	C-5B	436th AW	*y/bl*
	FY68			
	80211	C-5A	167th AW	*r*
	80212	C-5A	105th AW	*bl*
	80213	C-5C	60th AMW	*bk/gd*
	80214	C-5A	433rd AW	
	80215	C-5A	433rd AW	
	80216	C-5C	60th AMW	*bk/gd*
	80217	C-5A	167th AW	*r*
	80219	C-5A	433rd AW	
	80220	C-5A	433rd AW	
	80221	C-5A	433rd AW	
	80222	C-5A	167th AW	*r*
	80223	C-5A	433rd AW	
	80224	C-5A	105th AW	*bl*
	80225	C-5A	167th AW	*r*
	80226	C-5A	105th AW	*bl*
	FY69			
	90001	C-5A	105th AW	*bl*
	90002	C-5A	164th AW	*r*
	90003	C-5A	445th AW	*si*
	90005	C-5A	433rd AW	
	90006	C-5A	433rd AW	
	90007	C-5A	433rd AW	
	90008	C-5A	105th AW	*bl*
	90009	C-5A	105th AW	*bl*
	90010	C-5A	164th AW	*r*
	90011	C-5A	167th AW	*r*
	90012	C-5A	105th AW	*bl*
	90013	C-5A	445th AW	*si*
	90014	C-5A	433rd AW	
	90015	C-5A	105th AW	*bl*
	90016	C-5A	433rd AW	
	90017	C-5A	164th AW	*r*
	90018	C-5A	164th AW	*r*
	90019	C-5A	164th AW	*pr*
	90020	C-5A	433rd AW	
	90021	C-5A	105th AW	*bl*
	90022	C-5A	167th AW	*r*
	90023	C-5A	105th AW	bl
	90024	C-5M	436th AW	*y/bl*
	90025	C-5A	164th AW	*r*
	90026	C-5A	433rd AW	
	90027	C-5A	167th AW	*r*

Boeing E-8 J-STARS
116th ACW, Robins AFB,
Georgia [WR]:
12th ACCS (gn), 16th ACCS (*bk*),
128th ACS/Georgia ANG (*r*)
& 330th CTS (*y*);
Grumman, Melbourne, Florida

Notes	Type			
	FY00			
	02000	E-8C	116th ACW	
	FY90			
	00175	E-8A	Grumman	
	FY01			
	12005	E-8C	116th ACW	
	FY02			
	29111	E-8C	116th ACW	
	FY92			
	23289	E-8C	116th ACW	*m*
	23290	E-8C	116th ACW	*bk*
	FY93			
	30597	E-8C	116th ACW	*gn*
	31097	E-8C	116th ACW	*r*
	FY94			
	40284	E-8C	116th ACW	*r*
	40285	E-8C	116th ACW	*bk*
	FY95			
	50121	E-8C	116th ACW	*r*
	50122	E-8C	116th ACW	*r*
	FY96			
	60042	E-8C	116th ACW	*bk*
	60043	E-8C	116th ACW	*bl*
	FY86			
	60416	E-8A	116th ACW	*y*
	FY97			
	70100	E-8C	116th ACW	*r*
	70200	E-8C	116th ACW	*bk*
	70201	E-8C	116th ACW	*r*
	FY99			
	90006	E-8C	116th ACW	*gn*

McDonnell Douglas
KC-10A Extender
60th AMW, Travis AFB, California:
6th ARS & 9th ARS;
305th AMW, McGuire AFB,
New Jersey:
2nd ARS (bl/r) & 32nd ARS *(bl)*

Notes	Type		
	FY82		
	20191	60th AMW	
	20192	60th AMW	
	20193	60th AMW	
	FY83		
	30075	60th AMW	
	30076	60th AMW	
	30077	60th AMW	
	30078	60th AMW	
	30079	305th AMW	*bl/r*
	30080	60th AMW	
	30081	305th AMW	*bl*
	30082	305th AMW	*bl*
	FY84		
	40185	60th AMW	
	40186	305th AMW	*bl/r*
	40187	60th AMW	
	40188	305th AMW	bl/r
	40189	60th AMW	
	40190	305th AMW	*bl/r*
	40191	60th AMW	
	40192	305th AMW	*bl/y*
	FY85		
	50027	305th AMW	*bl/r*
	50028	305th AMW	*bl/r*
	50029	60th AMW	
	50030	305th AMW	*bl/r*
	50031	305th AMW	*bl/r*
	50032	305th AMW	*bl/y*
	50033	305th AMW	*bl*
	50034	305th AMW	*bl/r*
	FY86		
	60027	305th AMW	*bl*
	60028	305th AMW	*bl/r*
	60029	60th AMW	
	60030	305th AMW	*bl/r*
	60031	60th AMW	

Type			Notes
60032	60th AMW		
60033	60th AMW		
60034	60th AMW		
60035	305th AMW	*bl*	
60036	305th AMW	*bl*	
60037	60th AMW		
60038	60th AMW		
FY87			
70117	60th AMW		
70118	60th AMW		
70119	60th AMW		
70120	305th AMW	*bl*	
70121	305th AMW	*bl*	
70122	305th AMW	*bl/r*	
70123	305th AMW	*bl*	
70124	305th AMW	*bl/y*	
FY79			
90433	305th AMW	*bl*	
90434	305th AMW	*bl/r*	
91710	305th AMW	*bl/r*	
91711	305th AMW	*bl*	
91712	305th AMW	*bl/r*	
91713	305th AMW	*bl*	
91946	60th AMW		
91947	305th AMW	*bl*	
91948	60th AMW		
91949	305th AMW	*bl/r*	
91950	60th AMW		
91951	60th AMW		

Boeing
C-17 Globemaster III

3rd Wg, Elmendorf AFB, Alaska: 517th AS (w/bk);
15th Wg, Hickam AFB, Hawaii: 535th AS (r/y);
60th AMW, Travis AFB, California: 21st AS (bk/w);
62nd AW, McChord AFB, Washington (*gn*): 4th AS, 7th AS,8th AS & 10th AS;
58th AS/97th AMW, Altus AFB, Oklahoma (r/y);
172nd AW, Jackson Int'l Airport, Mississippi ANG: 183rd AS (bl/gd);
305th AMW, McGuire AFB, New Jersey (*bl*): 6th AS;
418th FLTS/412th TW, Edwards AFB, California [ED];
436th AW, Dover AFB, Delaware: 3rd AS (*y/r*);
437th AW, Charleston AFB, South Carolina (*y/bl*): 14th AS, 15th AS, 16th AS & 17th AS;
445th AW AFRC Wright-Patterson AFB, Ohio (*r/w*): 89th AS & 356th AS;
452nd AMW AFRC, March ARB, California (*or/y*): 729th AS

Type				Notes
FY00				
00171	C-17A	3rd Wg	*w/bk*	
00172	C-17A	97th AMW	*r/y*	
00174	C-17A	3rd Wg	*w/bk*	
00175	C-17A	62nd AW	*gn*	
00176	C-17A	62nd AW	*gn*	
00177	C-17A	62nd AW	*gn*	
00178	C-17A	62nd AW	*gn*	
00179	C-17A	62nd AW	*gn*	
00180	C-17A	62nd AW	*gn*	
00181	C-17A	62nd AW	*gn*	
00182	C-17A	62nd AW	*gn*	
00183	C-17A	62nd AW	*gn*	
00184	C-17A	62nd AW	*gn*	
00185	C-17A	62nd AW	*gn*	
FY90				
00532	C-17A	62nd AW	*gn*	
00533	C-17A	15th Wg	*r/y*	
00534	C-17A	445th AW	*r/w*	
00535	C-17A	62nd AW	*gn*	
FY01				
10186	C-17A	62nd AW	*gn*	
10187	C-17A	62nd AW	*gn*	
10188	C-17A	437th AW	*y/bl*	
10189	C-17A	437th AW	*y/bl*	
10190	C-17A	437th AW	*y/bl*	
10191	C-17A	437th AW	*y/bl*	
10192	C-17A	97th AMW	*r/y*	
10193	C-17A	437th AW	*y/bl*	
10194	C-17A	97th AMW	*r/y*	
10195	C-17A	437th AW	*y/bl*	
10196	C-17A	437th AW	*y/bl*	
10197	C-17A	437th AW	*y/bl*	
FY02				
21098	C-17A	437th AW	*y/bl*	
21099	C-17A	437th AW	*y/bl*	
21100	C-17A	437th AW	*y/bl*	
21101	C-17A	437th AW	*y/bl*	
21102	C-17A	62nd AW	*gn*	
21103	C-17A	62nd AW	*gn*	
21104	C-17A	62nd AW	*gn*	
21105	C-17A	62nd AW	*gn*	
21106	C-17A	62nd AW	*gn*	
21107	C-17A	62nd AW	*gn*	
21108	C-17A	62nd AW	*gn*	
21109	C-17A	62nd AW	*gn*	
21110	C-17A	62nd AW	*gn*	
21111	C-17A	62nd AW	*gn*	
21112	C-17A	172nd AW	*bl/gd*	
FY92				
23291	C-17A	62nd AW	*gn*	
23292	C-17A	437th AW	*y/bl*	
23293	C-17A	437th AW	*y/bl*	
23294	C-17A	62nd AW	*gn*	
FY93				
30599	C-17A	97th AMW	*r/y*	
30600	C-17A	62nd AW	*gn*	
30601	C-17A	62nd AW	*gn*	
30602	C-17A	437th AW	*y/bl*	
30603	C-17A	445th AW	*r/w*	
30604	C-17A	445th AW	*r/w*	
FY03				
33113	C-17A	172nd AW	*bl/gd*	
33114	C-17A	172nd AW	*bl/gd*	
33115	C-17A	172nd AW	*bl/gd*	
33116	C-17A	172nd AW	*bl/gd*	
33117	C-17A	172nd AW	*bl/gd*	
33118	C-17A	172nd AW	*bl/gd*	
33119	C-17A	172nd AW	*bl/gd*	
33120	C-17A	62nd AW	*gn*	
33121	C-17A	412th TW		
33122	C-17A	437th AW	*y/bl*	
33123	C-17A	437th AW	*y/bl*	
33124	C-17A	437th AW	*y/bl*	
33125	C-17A	305th AMW	*bl*	
33126	C-17A	305th AMW	*bl*	
33127	C-17A	305th AMW	*bl*	
FY94				
40065	C-17A	97th AMW	*r/y*	

Notes	Type			
	40066	C-17A	97th AMW	*r/y*
	40067	C-17A	437th AW	*y/bl*
	40068	C-17A	437th AW	*y/bl*
	40069	C-17A	437th AW	*y/bl*
	40070	C-17A	437th AW	*y/bl*
	FY04			
	44128	C-17A	305th AMW	*bl*
	44129	C-17A	305th AMW	*bl*
	44130	C-17A	305th AMW	*bl*
	44131	C-17A	305th AMW	*bl*
	44132	C-17A	305th AMW	*bl*
	44133	C-17A	305th AMW	*bl*
	44134	C-17A	305th AMW	*bl*
	44135	C-17A	305th AMW	*bl*
	44136	C-17A	305th AMW	*bl*
	44137	C-17A	305th AMW	*bl*
	44138	C-17A	452nd AMW	*or/y*
	FY95			
	50102	C-17A	97th AMW	*r/y*
	50103	C-17A	437th AW	*y/bl*
	50104	C-17A	437th AW	*y/bl*
	50105	C-17A	437th AW	*y/bl*
	50106	C-17A	62nd AW	*gn*
	50107	C-17A	437th AW	*y/bl*
	FY05			
	55139	C-17A	452nd AMW	*or/y*
	55140	C-17A	452nd AMW	*or/y*
	55141	C-17A	452nd AMW	*or/y*
	55142	C-17A	452nd AMW	*or/y*
	55143	C-17A	452nd AMW	*or/y*
	55144	C-17A	452nd AMW	*or/y*
	55145	C-17A	452nd AMW	*or/y*
	55146	C-17A	15th Wg	*r/y*
	55147	C-17A	15th Wg	*r/y*
	55148	C-17A	15th Wg	*r/y*
	55149	C-17A	15th Wg	*r/y*
	55150	C-17A	15th Wg	*r/y*
	55151	C-17A	5th Wg	*r/y*
	55152	C-17A	15th Wg	*r/y*
	55153	C-17A	15th Wg	*r/y*
	FY96			
	60001	C-17A	97th AMW	*r/y*
	60002	C-17A	436th AW	*y/r*
	60003	C-17A	62nd AW	*gn*
	60004	C-17A	437th AW	*y/bl*
	60005	C-17A	437th AW	*y/bl*
	60006	C-17A	437th AW	*y/bl*
	60007	C-17A	172nd AW	*bl/gd*
	60008	C-17A	62nd AW	*gn*
	FY06			
	66154	C-17A	60th AMW	*bk/w*
	66155	C-17A	60th AMW	*bk/w*
	66156	C-17A	60th AMW	*bk/w*
	66157	C-17A	60th AMW	*bk/w*
	66158	C-17A	60th AMW	*bk/w*
	66159	C-17A	60th AMW	*bk/w*
	66160	C-17A	60th AMW	*bk/w*
	66161	C-17A	60th AMW	*bk/w*
	66162	C-17A	60th AMW	*bk/w*
	66163	C-17A	60th AMW	*bk/w*
	66164	C-17A	60th AMW	*bk/w*
	66165	C-17A	436th AW	*y/r*
	66166	C-17A	436th AW	*y/r*
	66167	C-17A	436th AW	*y/r*
	66168	C-17A	436th AW	*y/r*
	FY87			
	70025	C-17A	412th TW	
	FY97			
	70041	C-17A	437th AW	*y/bl*
	70042	C-17A	62nd AW	*gn*
	70043	C-17A	452nd AMW	*or/y*
	70044	C-17A	445th AW	*r/w*

Notes	Type			
	70045	C-17A	437th AW	*y/bl*
	70046	C-17A	97th AW	*r/y $*
	70047	C-17A	437th AW	*y/bl*
	70048	C-17A	437th AW	*y/bl*
	FY07			
	77169	C-17A	436th AW	*y/r*
	77170	C-17A	436th AW	*y/r*
	77171	C-17A	436th AW	*y/r*
	77172	C-17A	60th AMW	*bk/w*
	77173	C-17A	436th AW	*y/r*
	77174	C-17A	436th AW	*y/r*
	77175	C-17A	436th AW	*y/r*
	77176	C-17A	436th AW	*y/r*
	77177	C-17A	436th AW	*y/r*
	77178	C-17A	436th AW	*y/r*
	77179	C-17A	60th AMW	*bk/w*
	77180	C-17A	437th AW	*y/bl*
	77181	C-17A	437th AW	*y/bl*
	77182	C-17A	437th AW	*y/bl*
	77183	C-17A	437th AW	*y/bl*
	77184	C-17A	437th AW	*y/bl*
	77185	C-17A	437th AW	*y/bl*
	77186	C-17A	437th AW	*y/bl*
	77187	C-17A	437th AW	*y/bl*
	77188	C-17A	437th AW	*y/bl*
	77189	C-17A	437th AW	*y/bl*
	FY98			
	80049	C-17A	62nd AW	*gn*
	80050	C-17A	62nd AW	*gn*
	80051	C-17A	3rd Wg	*w/bk*
	80052	C-17A	62nd AW	*gn*
	80053	C-17A	62nd AW	*gn*
	80054	C-17A	437th AW	*y/bl*
	80055	C-17A	97th AMW	*r/y*
	80056	C-17A	3rd Wg	*w/bk*
	80057	C-17A	97th AMW	*r/y*
	FY88			
	80265	C-17A	62nd AW	*gn*
	80266	C-17A	437th AW	*y/bl*
	FY08			
	88190	C-17A	437th AW	*y/bl*
	88191	C-17A	437th AW	*y/bl*
	88192	C-17A	62nd AW	*gn*
	88193	C-17A	62nd AW	*gn*
	88194	C-17A	62nd AW	*gn*
	88195	C-17A	62nd AW	*gn*
	88196	C-17A	62nd AW	*gn*
	88197	C-17A	62nd AW	*gn*
	88198	C-17A	305th AMW	*bl*
	88199	C-17A	305th AMW	*bl*
	88200	C-17A	305th AMW	*bl*
	88201	C-17A	62nd AW	*gn*
	88202	C-17A	305th AMW	*bl*
	88203	C-17A	62nd AW	*gn*
	88204	C-17A	437th AW	*y/bl*
	FY99			
	90058	C-17A	97th AMW	*r/y $*
	90059	C-17A	97th AMW	*r/y*
	90060	C-17A	62nd AW	*gn*
	90061	C-17A	62nd AW	*gn*
	90062	C-17A	97th AMW	*r/y*
	90063	C-17A	97th AMW	*r/y*
	90064	C-17A	62nd AW	*gn*
	90165	C-17A	62nd AW	*gn*
	90166	C-17A	97th AMW	*r/y*
	90167	C-17A	3rd Wg	*w/bk*
	90168	C-17A	3rd Wg	*w/bk*
	90169	C-17A	97th AMW	*r/y*
	90170	C-17A	3rd Wg	*w/bk*
	FY89			
	91189	C-17A	437th AW	*y/bl*
	91190	C-17A	62nd AW	*gn*

Type				Notes
91191	C-17A	3rd Wg	*w/bk*	
91192	C-17A	437th AW	*y/bl*	
FY09				
92205	C-17A	62nd AW	*gn*	
92206	C-17A	437th AW	*y/bl*	
92207	C-17A	437th AW	*y/bl*	
92208	C-17A	437th AW	*y/bl*	
92209	C-17A			
92210	C-17A			
92211	C-17A			
92212	C-17A			

Grumman
C-20 Gulfstream III/IV
89th AW, Andrews AFB, Maryland:
99th AS;
OSAC/PAT, US Army, Andrews AFB, Maryland;
Pacific Flight Detachment, Hickam AFB, Hawaii
C-20B Gulfstream III
FY86
60202 89th AW
60203 89th AW
60204 89th AW
60206 89th AW
C-20C Gulfstream III
FY85
50049 89th AW
50050 89th AW
FY86
60403 89th AW
C-20E Gulfstream III
FY87
70139 Pacific Flt Det
C-20F Gulfstream IV
FY91
10108 OSAC/PAT

Boeing VC-25A
Presidential Airlift Sqn/ 89th AW, Andrews AFB, Maryland
FY82
28000
FY92
29000

Pilatus U-28A
1st SOW, Hurlburt Field, Florida:
34th SOS & 319th SOS;
318th SOS/27th SOW, Cannon AFB, New Mexico
FY04
40597 318th SOS
FY05
50409 1st SOW
50419 1st SOW
50424 1st SOW
50447 1st SOW
50482 1st SOW
50556 1st SOW
50573 1st SOW
FY06
60692
FY07
70488
70711
70712 1st SOW
70736
70777 1st SOW
70821
70829 1st SOW
70838 1st SOW
70840
FY08
80790 1st SOW
80809 1st SOW
80822
80835

Boeing C-32
1st AS/89th AW, Andrews AFB, Maryland;
150th SOS/108th Wg, McGuire AFB, New Jersey
FY00
09001 C-32B 150th SOS
FY02
24452 C-32B 150th SOS
25001 C-32B 150th SOS
FY98
80001 C-32A 89th AW
80002 C-32A 89th AW
FY99
90003 C-32A 89th AW
90004 C-32A 89th AW
96143 C-32B 150th SOS

Gulfstream Aerospace
C-37 Gulfstream V
6th AMW, MacDill AFB, Florida:
310th AS;
15th ABW, Hickam AFB, Hawaii:
65th AS;
86th AW, Ramstein, Germany:
76th AS;
89th AW, Andrews AFB, Maryland:
99th AS;
OSAC/PAT, US Army, Andrews AFB, Maryland
C-37A Gulfstream V
FY01
10028 6th AMW
10029 6th AMW
10030 6th AMW
10065 15th ABW
FY02
21863 OSAC/PAT
FY04
41778 OSAC/PAT
FY97
71944 OSAC/PAT
70400 89th AW
70401 89th AW
FY99
90402 86th AW
90404 89th AW
C-37 Gulfstream V
FY06
60500 89th AW
FY09
90525 89th AW

IAI C-38A Astra
201st AS/113th FW, DC ANG, Andrews AFB, Maryland
FY94
41569
41570

Boeing C-40

15th ABW, Hickam AFB, Hawaii:
65th AS;
86th AW, Ramstein, Germany:
76th AS;
89th AW, Andrews AFB, Maryland:
1st AS;
201st AS/113th FW, DC ANG,
Andrews AFB, Maryland;
73rd AS/932nd AW AFRC, Scott AFB,
Illinois

Serial	Type	Unit
FY01		
10015	C-40B	15th ABW
10040	C-40B	89th AW
10041	C-40B	89th AW
FY02		
20042	C-40B	86th AW
20201	C-40C	201st AS
20202	C-40C	201st AS
20203	C-40C	201st AS
20204	C-40C	201st AS
FY05		
50730	C-40C	932nd AW
50932	C-40C	932nd AW
54613	C-40C	932nd AW

Boeing B-52H Stratofortress

2nd BW, Barksdale AFB,
Louisiana [LA]:
11th BS (gd), 20th BS (*bl*)
& 96th BS (*r*);
5th BW, Minot AFB,
North Dakota [MT]:
23rd BS (*r/y*) & 69th BS (*bk/y*);
49th TES/53rd TEG,
Barksdale AFB,
Louisiana [OT];
93rd BS/307th BW AFRC,
Barksdale AFB,
Louisiana [BD] (*y/bl*);
419th FLTS/412th TW Edwards AFB,
California [ED]

Serial	Unit	Notes
FY60		
00001	2nd BW	*r*
00002	2nd BW	*gd*
00003	93rd BS	*y/bl*
00004	5th BW	*r/y*
00005	5th BW	*r/y*
00007	5th BW	*r/y*
00008	2nd BW	*m$*
00009	5th BW	*bk/y*
00011	2nd BW	*gd*
00012	2nd BW	*r*
00013	2nd BW	*bl*
00015	93rd BS	*y/bl*
00016	2nd BW	*bl*
00017	2nd BW	*gd*
00018	5th BW	*r/y*
00021	2nd BW	*gd*
00022	2nd BW	*gd*
00023	5th BW	*r/y*
00024	2nd BW	
00025	2nd BW	*bl*
00026	5th BW	r/y
00028	2nd BW	*r*
00029	5th BW	r/y
00031	53rd TEG	
00032	2nd BW	*r*
00033	5th BW	*r/y*
00035	93rd BS	*y/bl*
00036	412th TW	
00037	2nd BW	*r*
00038	2nd BW	*r*
00041	93rd BS	*y/bl*
00042	93rd BS	*y/bl*
00044	5th BW	*bk/y*
00045	93rd BS	*y/bl*
00047	2nd BW	
00048	2nd BW	*bl*
00049	53rd TEG	
00050	412th TW	
00051	93rd BS	*y/bl*
00052	2nd BW	*r*
00054	2nd BW	*gd*
00055	5th BW	*r/y*
00056	5th BW	*r/y*
00057	2nd BW	*gd*
00058	2nd BW	*bl*
00059	2nd BW	*r*
00060	5th BW	*bk/y*
00061	93rd BS	*y/bl*
00062	2nd BW	*bl*
FY61		
10001	2nd BW	
10002	2nd BW	*r $*
10003	2nd BW	*bl*
10004	2nd BW	*bl*
10005	5th BW	*r/y*
10006	2nd BW	*bl*
10008	93rd BS	*y/bl*
10010	2nd BW	*bl*
10011	93rd BS	*y/bl*
10012	2nd BW	*r*
10013	2nd BW	*bl*
10014	5th BW	*r/y*
10015	2nd BW	*r*
10016	2nd BW	*bl*
10017	93rd BS	*y/bl*
10018	2nd BW	
10019	2nd BW	*gd*
10020	2nd BW	
10021	93rd BS	*y/bl*
10028	2nd BW	*bl*
10029	2nd BW	*bl*
10031	93rd BS	*y/bl*
10032	93rd BS	*y/bl*
10034	5th BW	*r/y*
10035	5th BW	*r/y*
10036	2nd BW	*bl*
10038	2nd BW	*gd*
10039	5th BW	*bk/y*
10040	5th BW	*r/y*

Lockheed C-130 Hercules

1st SOS/353rd SOG, Kadena AB,
Japan;
4th SOS/1st SOW, Hurlburt Field,
Florida;
7th SOS/352nd SOG,
RAF Mildenhall, UK;
8th SOS/1st SOW, Duke Field, Florida;
9th SOS/1st OG, Eglin AFB, Florida;
15th SOS/1st SOW, Hurlburt Field,
Florida;
16th SOS/27th SOW, Cannon AFB,
New Mexico;
17th SOS/353rd SOG, Kadena AB,
Japan;
19th AW Little Rock AFB,
Arkansas [LK]:
41st AS (w), 50th AS (*r*),
53rd AS (bk) & 61st AS (*gn*);
37th AS/86th AW, Ramstein AB,
Germany [RS] (bl/w);

Type	Notes	Type	Notes
39th RQS/920th RQW AFRC, Patrick AFB, Florida [FL]; 40th FTS/46th TW, Eglin AFB, Florida; 41st RQS/347th Wg, Moody AFB, Georgia [FT]; 43rd AW, Pope AFB, North Carolina [FT]: 2nd AS (*gn/bl*); 53rd WRS/403rd AW AFRC, Keesler AFB, Missouri; 55th ECG, Davis-Monthan AFB, Arizona [DM]: 41st ECS (*bl*) & 43rd ECS (*r*); 58th SOW, Kirtland AFB, New Mexico: 550th SOS; 67th SOS/352nd SOG, RAF Mildenhall, UK; 71st RQS/347th Wg, Moody AFB, Georgia [FT] (*bl*); 73rd SOS/27th SOW, Cannon AFB, New Mexico; 79th RQS/563rd RQG, Davis-Monthan AFB, Arizona [DM]; 95th AS/440th AW AFRC, Pope AFB, North Carolina (*w/r*); 96th AS/934th AW AFRC, Minneapolis/St Paul, Minnesota (*pr*); 102nd RQS/106th RQW, Suffolk Field, New York ANG [LI]; 105th AS/118th AW, Nashville, Tennessee ANG (*r*); 109th AS/133rd AW, Minneapolis/St Paul, Minnesota ANG [MN] (pr/bk); 115th AS/146th AW, Channel Island ANGS, California ANG [CI] (*gn*); 122nd FS/159th FW, NAS New Orleans, Louisiana ANG [JZ]; 130th AS/130th AW, Yeager Int'l Airport, Charleston West Virginia ANG [WV] (*pr/y*); 130th RQS/129th RQW, Moffet Field, California ANG [CA] (*bl*); 135th AS/135th AW, Martin State Airport, Maryland ANG [MD] (*bk/y*); 136th AS/107th AW, Niagara Falls, New York ANG; 139th AS/109th AW, Schenectady, New York ANG [NY]; 142nd AS/166th AW, New Castle County Airport, Delaware ANG [DE] (*bl*); 143rd AS/143rd AW, Quonset, Rhode Island ANG [RI] (*r*); 144th AS/176th CW, Elmendorf, Alaska ANG (*bk/y*); 154th TS/189th AW, Little Rock, Arkansas ANG (*r*); 156th AS/145th AW, Charlotte, North Carolina ANG [NC] (*bl*); 157th FS/169th FW, McEntire ANGS, South Carolina ANG [SC]; 158th AS/165th AW, Savannah, Georgia ANG (*r*); 159th FS/125th FW, Jacksonville, Florida ANG;		164th AS/179th AW, Mansfield, Ohio ANG [OH] (*bl*); 165th AS/123rd AW, Standiford Field, Kentucky ANG [KY]; 167th AS/167th AW, Martinsburg, West Virginia ANG [WV] (*r*); 169th AS/182nd AW, Peoria, Illinois ANG [IL] (*or*); 180th AS/139th AW, Rosencrans Memorial Airport, Missouri ANG [XP] (*y*); 181st AS/136th AW, NAS Dallas, Texas ANG (*bl/w*); 187th AS/153rd AW, Cheyenne, Wyoming ANG [WY] (*y/bk*); 192nd AS/152nd AW, Reno, Nevada ANG [NV] (*bl/y*); 193rd SOS/193rd SOW, Harrisburg, Pennsylvania ANG [PA]; 198th AS/156th AW, San Juan, Puerto Rico ANG; 204th AS/154th Wg, Hickam AFB, Hawaii ANG [HH]; 210th RQS/176th CW, Kulis ANGB, Alaska ANG [AK]; 314th AW, Little Rock AFB, Arkansas: 48th AS (*y*) & 62nd AS (*bl*); 317th AG, Dyess AFB, Texas: 39th AS (*r*) & 40th AS (*bl*); 327th AS/913th AW AFRC, NAS Willow Grove, Pennsylvania (*bk*); 328th AS/914th AW AFRC, Niagara Falls, New York [NF] (*bl*); 357th AS/908th AW AFRC, Maxwell AFB, Alabama (*bl*); 374th AW, Yokota AB, Japan [YJ]: 36th AS (*r*); 412th TW Edwards AFB, California: 452nd FLTS [ED]; 645th Materiel Sqn, Palmdale, California [D4]; 700th AS/94th AW AFRC, Dobbins ARB, Georgia [DB] (*bl*); 711th SOS/919th SOW AFRC, Duke Field, Florida; 731st AS/302nd AW AFRC, Peterson AFB, Colorado (*pr/w*); 757th AS/910th AW AFRC, Youngstown ARS, Ohio [YO] (bl); 758th AS/911th AW AFRC, Pittsburgh ARS, Pennsylvania (*bk/y*); 773rd AS/910th AW AFRC, Youngstown ARS, Ohio [YO] (*r*); 815th AS/403rd AW AFRC, Keesler AFB, Missouri [KT] (*r*); LMTAS, Marietta, Georgia	

C-130

Notes	Type			
	FY90			
	00162	MC-130H	15th SOS	
	00163	AC-130U	4th SOS	
	00164	AC-130U	4th SOS	
	00165	AC-130U	4th SOS	
	00166	AC-130U	4th SOS	
	00167	AC-130U	4th SOS	
	FY80			
	00320	C-130H	158th AS	*r*
	00321	C-130H	158th AS	*r*
	00322	C-130H	158th AS	*r*
	00323	C-130H	158th AS	*r*
	00324	C-130H	158th AS	*r*
	00325	C-130H	158th AS	*r*
	00326	C-130H	158th AS	*r*
	00332	C-130H	158th AS	*r*
	FY90			
	01057	C-130H	142nd AS	*bl*
	01058	MC-130W	73rd SOS	
	FY90			
	01791	C-130H	180th AS	*y*
	01792	C-130H	180th AS	*y*
	01793	C-130H	180th AS	*y*
	01794	C-130H	180th AS	*y*
	01795	C-130H	180th AS	*y*
	01796	C-130H	180th AS	*y*
	01797	C-130H	180th AS	*y*
	01798	C-130H	180th AS	*y*
	FY00			
	01934	EC-130J	193rd SOS	
	FY90			
	02103	HC-130N	210th RQS	
	09107	C-130H	757th AS	*bl*
	09108	C-130H	757th AS	*bl*
	FY81			
	10626	C-130H	700th AS	*bl*
	10627	C-130H	700th AS	*bl*
	10628	C-130H	700th AS	*bl*
	10629	C-130H	700th AS	*bl*
	10630	C-130H	700th AS	*bl*
	10631	C-130H	700th AS	*bl*
	FY68			
	10948	C-130E	19th AW	*gn*
	FY91			
	11231	C-130H	165th AS	
	11232	C-130H	165th AS	
	11233	C-130H	165th AS	
	11234	C-130H	165th AS	
	11235	C-130H	165th AS	
	11236	C-130H	165th AS	
	11237	C-130H	165th AS	
	11238	C-130H	165th AS	
	11239	C-130H	165th AS	
	FY01			
	11461	C-130J	115th AS	*gn*
	11462	C-130J	115th AS	*gn*
	FY91			
	11651	C-130H	180th AS	*y*
	11652	C-130H	180th AS	*y*
	11653	C-130H	187th AS	*y/bk*
	FY01			
	11935	EC-130J	193rd SOS	
	FY61			
	12358	C-130E	314th AW	
	12370	C-130E	314th AW	
	FY64			
	14852	HC-130P	71st RQS	*bl*
	14853	HC-130P	79th RQS	
	14854	MC-130P	67th SOS	
	14855	HC-130P	39th RQS	
	14858	MC-130P	58th SOW	
	14860	HC-130P	79th RQS	

Notes	Type			
	14861	C-130H	105th AS	*r*
	14862	EC-130H	55th ECG	
	14863	HC-130P	71st RQS	*bl*
	14864	HC-130P	39th RQS	
	14865	HC-130P	79th RQS	
	14866	C-130H	159th FS	
	FY91			
	19141	C-130H	328th AS	*bl*
	19142	C-130H	96th AS	*pr*
	19143	C-130H	328th AS	*bl*
	19144	C-130H	328th AS	*bl*
	FY82			
	20054	C-130H	144th AS	*bk/y*
	20055	C-130H	144th AS	*bk/y*
	20056	C-130H	144th AS	*bk/y*
	20057	C-130H	144th AS	*bk/y*
	20058	C-130H	144th AS	*bk/y*
	20059	C-130H	144th AS	*bk/y*
	20060	C-130H	144th AS	*bk/y*
	20061	C-130H	144th AS	*bk/y*
	FY02			
	20314	C-130J	314th AW	*y*
	FY92			
	20253	AC-130U	4th SOS	
	20547	C-130H	19th AW	*r*
	20548	C-130H	19th AW	*r*
	20549	C-130H	19th AW	*r*
	20550	C-130H	19th AW	*r*
	20551	C-130H	19th AW	*r*
	20552	C-130H	19th AW	*r*
	20553	C-130H	19th AW	*r*
	20554	C-130H	19th AW	*r*
	21094	LC-130H	139th AS	
	21095	LC-130H	139th AS	
	FY72			
	21289	C-130E	19th AW	*gn*
	FY02			
	21434	C-130J	143rd AS	*r*
	FY92			
	21451	C-130H	169th AS	*or*
	21452	C-130H	169th AS	*or*
	21453	C-130H	156th AS	*bl*
	21454	C-130H	156th AS	*bl*
	FY02			
	21463	C-130J	115th AS	*gn*
	21464	C-130J	115th AS	*gn*
	FY92			
	21531	C-130H	187th AS	*y/bk*
	21532	C-130H	187th AS	*y/bk*
	21533	C-130H	187th AS	*y/bk*
	21534	C-130H	187th AS	*y/bk*
	21535	C-130H	187th AS	*y/bk*
	21536	C-130H	187th AS	*y/bk*
	21537	C-130H	187th AS	*y/bk*
	21538	C-130H	187th AS	*y/bk*
	FY62			
	21784	C-130E		
	21787	C-130E		
	21791	MC-130E	17th SOS	
	21792	C-130E	19th AW	*gn*
	21799	C-130E	19th AW	*gn*
	21801	C-130E		
	21806	C-130E	19th AW	*gn*
	21811	C-130E	19th AW	
	21820	C-130E	198th AS	
	21823	C-130E	19th AW	*gn*
	21824	C-130E	19th AW	*gn*
	21842	C-130E	198th AS	
	21843	MC-130E	711th SOS	
	21846	C-130E		
	21849	C-130E	19th AW	*gn*
	21851	C-130E	19th AW	

Type				Notes
21855	C-130E	43rd AW		
21857	C-130E	16th SOS		
21858	C-130E	198th AS		
21859	C-130E	122nd FS		
21863	HC-130P	71st RQS	*bl*	
FY92				
23021	C-130H	773rd AS	*r*	
23022	C-130H	773rd AS	*r*	
23023	C-130H	773rd AS	*r*	
23024	C-130H	757th AS	*bl*	
23281	C-130H	96th AS	*pr*	
23282	C-130H	96th AS	*pr*	
23283	C-130H	96th AS	*pr*	
23284	C-130H	96th AS	*pr*	
23285	C-130H			
23286	C-130H	96th AS	*pr*	
23287	C-130H	96th AS	*pr*	
23288	C-130H	96th AS	*pr*	
FY02				
28155	C-130J	815th AS	*r*	
FY83				
30486	C-130H	139th AS		
30487	C-130H	139th AS		
30488	C-130H	139th AS		
30489	C-130H	139th AS		
30490	LC-130H	139th AS		
30491	LC-130H	139th AS		
30492	LC-130H	139th AS		
30493	LC-130H	139th AS		
FY93				
31036	C-130H	19th AW	*r*	
31037	C-130H	19th AW	*r*	
31038	C-130H	19th AW	*r*	
31039	C-130H	19th AW	*r*	
31040	C-130H	19th AW	*r*	
31041	C-130H	19th AW	*r*	
31096	LC-130H	139th AS		
FY83				
31212	MC-130H	17th SOS		
FY93				
31455	C-130H	156th AS	*bl*	
31456	C-130H	156th AS	*bl*	
31457	C-130H	156th AS	*bl*	
31458	C-130H	156th AS	*bl*	
31459	C-130H	156th AS	*bl*	
31561	C-130H	156th AS	*bl*	
31561	C-130H	156th AS	*bl*	
31563	C-130H	156th AS	*bl*	
FY73				
31580	EC-130H	55th ECG	*r*	
31581	EC-130H	55th ECG	*$*	
31582	C-130H	317th AG	*r*	
31583	EC-130H	55th ECG	*r*	
31584	EC-130H	55th ECG		
31585	EC-130H	55th ECG	*bl*	
31586	EC-130H	55th ECG	*bl*	
31587	EC-130H	55th ECG		
31588	EC-130H	55th ECG		
31590	EC-130H	55th ECG		
31592	EC-130H	55th ECG	*bl*	
31594	EC-130H	55th ECG	*bl*	
31595	EC-130H	55th ECG		
31597	C-130H	317th AG	*r*	
31598	C-130H	317th AG	*r*	
FY93				
32041	C-130H	169th AS	*or*	
32042	C-130H	169th AS	*or*	
32104	HC-130N	210th RQS		
32105	HC-130N	210th RQS		
32106	HC-130N	210th RQS		
FY73				
33300	LC-130H	139th AS		

Type				Notes
FY93				
37311	C-130H	187th AS	*y/bk*	
37312	C-130H	169th AS	*or*	
37313	C-130H	187th AS	*y/bk*	
37314	C-130H	187th AS	*y/bk*	
FY63				
37764	C-130E	19th AW	*gn*	
37786	C-130E			
37791	C-130E			
37796	C-130E			
37815	C-130E	193rd SOS		
37816	EC-130E	16th SOW		
37828	EC-130E	193rd SOS		
37829	C-130E	19th AW		
37831	C-130E	19th AW	*gn*	
37833	C-130E	19th AW	*gn*	
37845	C-130E	19th AW		
37848	C-130E	43rd AW		
37851	C-130E	198th AS		
37859	C-130E	198th AS		
37867	C-130E	19th AW	*gn*	
37868	C-130E	19th AW		
37896	C-130E	19th AW		
FY03				
38154	C-130J	815th AS	*r*	
FY63				
39810	C-130E	71st RQS	*bl*	
39815	C-130E	198th AS		
FY84				
40204	C-130H	700th AS	*bl*	
40205	C-130H	700th AS	*bl*	
40206	C-130H	142nd AS	*bl*	
40207	C-130H	142nd AS	*bl*	
40208	C-130H	142nd AS	*bl*	
40209	C-130H	142nd AS	*bl*	
40210	C-130H	142nd AS	*bl*	
40212	C-130H	142nd AS	*bl*	
40213	C-130H	142nd AS	*bl*	
40476	MC-130H	15th SOS		
FY64				
40510	C-130E	198th AS		
40515	C-130E	198th AS		
40521	C-130E	159th FS		
40523	MC-130E	711th SOS		
40526	C-130E			
40544	C-130E	198th AS		
40551	MC-130E	711th SOS		
40561	MC-130E	711th SOS		
40562	MC-130E	711th SOS		
40565	MC-130E	711th SOS		
40566	MC-130E	711th SOS		
40568	MC-130E	711th SOS		
40571	MC-130E	711th SOS		
FY74				
41658	C-130H	374th AW	*r*	
41659	C-130H	374th AW	*r*	
41660	C-130H	374th AW	*r*	
41661	C-130H	317th AG		
41663	C-130H	317th AG		
41664	C-130H	19th AW	*bk*	
41665	C-130H	317th AG	*bl*	
41666	C-130H	317th AG		
41667	C-130H	317th AG	*r*	
41668	C-130H	374th AW	*r $*	
41669	C-130H	317th AG	*r*	
41670	C-130H	317th AG		
41671	C-130H	317th AG	*bl*	
41673	C-130H	317th AG		
41674	C-130H	317th AG		
41675	C-130H	317th AG	*r*	
41676	C-130H	317th AG		
41677	C-130H	19th AW	*bk*	

Notes	Type			
	41679	C-130H	317th AG	*bl*
	41680	C-130H	317th AG	
	41682	C-130H	317th AG	*r*
	41684	C-130H	374th AW	*r*
	41685	C-130H	374th AW	*r*
	41687	C-130H	317th AG	*r*
	41688	C-130H	317th AG	*r*
	41689	C-130H	317th AG	*bl*
	41690	C-130H	374th AW	*r $*
	41691	C-130H	317th AG	
	41692	C-130H	374th AW	*r*
	42061	C-130H	317th AG	*r*
	42062	C-130H	374th AW	*r $*
	42063	C-130H	317th AG	*bl*
	42065	C-130H	317th AG	*bl*
	42066	C-130H	374th AW	*r $*
	42067	C-130H	317th AG	*r*
	42069	C-130H	317th AG	*bl*
	42070	C-130H	374th AW	*r*
	42071	C-130H	374th AW	*r*
	42072	C-130H	317th AG	*bl*
	42130	C-130H	317th AG	*r*
	42131	C-130H	374th AW	*r*
	42132	C-130H	317th AG	*r*
	42133	C-130H	374th AW	*r*
	42134	C-130H	317th AG	*r*
	FY04			
	43142	C-130J	314th AW	*y*
	43143	C-130J	19th AW	*w*
	43144	C-130J	314th AW	*y*
	FY94			
	46701	C-130H	169th AS	*or*
	46702	C-130H	167th AS	*r*
	46703	C-130H	169th AS	*or*
	46704	C-130H		
	46705	C-130H	167th AS	*r*
	46706	C-130H	167th AS	*r*
	46707	C-130H	130th AS	*pr/y*
	46708	C-130H	130th AS	*pr/y*
	47310	C-130H	731st AS	*pr/w*
	47315	C-130H	731st AS	*pr/w*
	47316	C-130H	731st AS	*pr/w*
	47317	C-130H	731st AS	*pr/w*
	47318	C-130H	731st AS	*pr/w*
	47319	C-130H	731st AS	*pr/w*
	47320	C-130H	731st AS	*pr/w*
	47321	C-130H	731st AS	*pr/w*
	FY94			
	48151	C-130J	19th AW	*w*
	48152	C-130J	19th AW	*w*
	FY04			
	48153	C-130J	815th AS	*r*
	FY85			
	50011	MC-130H	15th SOS	
	50035	C-130H	357th AS	*bl*
	50036	C-130H	357th AS	*bl*
	50037	C-130H	357th AS	*bl*
	50038	C-130H	357th AS	*bl*
	50039	C-130H	357th AS	*bl*
	50040	C-130H	357th AS	*bl*
	50041	C-130H	773rd AS	*r*
	50042	C-130H	357th AS	*bl*
	FY65			
	50962	TC-130H	55th ECG	
	50963	C-130H	105th AS	*r*
	50964	HC-130P	79th RQS	
	50966	C-130H	105th AS	*r*
	50967	HC-130H	122nd FS	
	50968	C-130H	105th AS	*r*
	50970	HC-130P	39th RQS	
	50971	MC-130P	58th SOW	
	50973	HC-130P	71st RQS	*bl*
	50974	HC-130P	102nd RQS	
	50975	MC-130P	58th SOW	
	50976	HC-130P	39th RQS	
	50977	HC-130H	39th RQS	
	50978	HC-130P	102nd RQS	
	50980	C-130H	105th AS	*r*
	50981	HC-130P	71st RQS	*bl*
	50982	HC-130P	71st RQS	*bl*
	50983	MC-130P	71st RQS	*bl*
	50984	C-130H	105th AS	*r*
	50985	C-130H	122nd FS	
	50986	HC-130P	71st RQS	*bl*
	50987	HC-130P	71st RQS	*bl*
	50988	HC-130P	71st RQS	*bl*
	50989	EC-130H	55th ECG	*r*
	50991	MC-130P	67th SOS	
	50992	MC-130P	67th SOS	
	50993	MC-130P	17th SOS	
	50994	MC-130P	9th SOS	
	FY95			
	51001	C-130H	109th AS	*pr/bk*
	51002	C-130H	109th AS	*pr/bk*
	FY85			
	51361	C-130H	181st AS	*bl/w*
	51362	C-130H	181st AS	*bl/w*
	51363	C-130H	181st AS	*bl/w*
	51364	C-130H	181st AS	*bl/w*
	51365	C-130H	181st AS	*bl/w*
	51366	C-130H	181st AS	*bl/w*
	51367	C-130H	181st AS	*bl/w*
	51368	C-130H	181st AS	*bl/w*
	FY05			
	51435	C-130J	143rd AS	*r*
	51436	C-130J	143rd AS	*r*
	51465	C-130J	115th AS	*gn*
	51466	C-130J	115th AS	*gn*
	53145	C-130J	19th AW	*w*
	53146	C-130J	314th AW	*y*
	53147	C-130J	314th AW	*y*
	FY95			
	56709	C-130H	156th AS	*bl*
	56710	C-130H	130th AS	*pr/y*
	56711	C-130H	156th AS	*bl*
	56712	C-130H	156th AS	bl
	FY05			
	58152	C-130J	815th AS	*r*
	58156	C-130J	815th AS	*r*
	58157	C-130J	815th AS	*r*
	58158	C-130J	815th AS	*r*
	FY66			
	60212	HC-130P	130th RQS	*bl*
	60215	MC-130P	67th SOS	
	60216	HC-130P	130th RQS	*bl*
	60217	MC-130P	9th SOS	
	60219	HC-130P	130th RQS	*bl*
	60220	MC-130P	67th SOS	
	60221	HC-130P	130th RQS	*bl*
	60222	HC-130P	102nd RQS	
	60223	MC-130P	9th SOS	
	60224	HC-130P	79th RQS	
	60225	MC-130P	9th SOS	
	FY86			
	60410	C-130H	95th AS	*w/r*
	60411	C-130H	95th AS	*w/r*
	60413	C-130H	357th AS	*bl*
	60414	C-130H	95th AS	*w/r*
	60415	C-130H	95th AS	*w/r*
	60418	C-130H	95th AS	*w/r*
	60419	C-130H	95th AS	*w/r*
	FY96			
	61003	C-130H	109th AS	*pr/bk*
	61004	C-130H	109th AS	*pr/bk*

Type				Notes
61005	C-130H	109th AS	pr/bk	
61006	C-130H	109th AS	pr/bk	
61007	C-130H	109th AS	pr/bk	
61008	C-130H	109th AS	pr/bk	
FY86				
61391	C-130H	154th TS	r	
61392	C-130H	154th TS	r	
61393	C-130H	154th TS	r	
61394	C-130H	154th TS	r	
61395	C-130H	154th TS	r	
61396	C-130H	154th TS	r	
61397	C-130H	154th TS	r	
61398	C-130H	154th TS	r	
FY06				
61437	C-130J	143rd AS	r	
61438	C-130J	143rd AS	r	
61467	C-130J	115th AS	gn	
FY86				
61699	MC-130H			
FY76				
63301	LC-130H	139th AS		
63302	LC-130H	139th AS		
FY06				
63171	C-130J	317th AG		
64631	C-130J	19th AW	w	
64632	C-130J	19th AW	w	
64633	C-130J	19th AW	w	
64634	C-130J	19th AW	w	
FY96				
65300	WC-130J	53rd WRS		
65301	WC-130J	53rd WRS		
65302	WC-130J	53rd WRS		
67322	C-130H	731st AS	pr/w	
67323	C-130H	731st AS	pr/w	
67324	C-130H	731st AS	pr/w	
67325	C-130H	731st AS	pr/w	
68153	EC-130J	193rd SOS		
68154	EC-130J	193rd SOS		
FY06				
68159	C-130J	815th AS	r	
68610	C-130J	37th AS	bl/w	
68611	C-130J	37th AS	bl/w	
68612	C-130J	37th AS	bl/w	
FY87				
70023	MC-130H	7th SOS		
70024	MC-130H			
70125	MC-130H	15th SOS		
70126	MC-130H	1st SOS		
70128	AC-130U	4th SOS		
FY97				
71351	C-130J	135th AS	bk/y	
71352	C-130J	314th AW	y	
71353	C-130J	135th AS	bk/y	
71354	C-130J	135th AS	bk/y	
FY07				
71468	C-130J	115th AS	gn	
FY97				
71931	EC-130J	193rd SOS		
FY07				
73170	C-130J	317th AG		
74635	C-130J	19th AW	w	
74636	C-130J	19th AW	w	
74637	C-130J	19th AW	w	
74638	C-130J	19th AW	w	
74639	C-130J	19th AW	w	
746310	C-130J	314th AW	m	
746311	C-130J	19th AW	w	
746312	C-130J	19th AW	w	
FY97				
75303	WC-130J	53rd WRS		
75304	WC-130J	53rd WRS		
75305	WC-130J	53rd WRS		

Type				Notes
75306	WC-130J	53rd WRS		
FY07				
78608	C-130J	37th AS	bl/w	
78609	C-130J	37th AS	bl/w	
78613	C-130J	37th AS	bl/w	
78614	C-130J	37th AS	bl/w	
FY87				
79281	C-130H	328th AS	bl	
79282	C-130H	95th AS	w/r	
79283	C-130H	96th AS	pr	
79284	MC-130W	73rd SOS		
79285	C-130H	328th AS	bl	
79286	MC-130W	73rd SOS		
79287	C-130H	96th AS	pr	
79288	MC-130W	73rd SOS		
FY88				
80191	MC-130H	1st SOS		
80192	MC-130H	1st SOS		
80193	MC-130H	16th SOS		
80194	MC-130H	58th SOW		
80195	MC-130H	7th SOS		
80264	MC-130H	1st SOS		
FY78				
80806	C-130H	758th AS	bk/y	
80807	C-130H	758th AS	bk/y	
80808	C-130H	758th AS	bk/y	
80809	C-130H	758th AS	bk/y	
80810	C-130H	758th AS	bk/y	
80811	C-130H	758th AS	bk/y	
80812	C-130H	758th AS	bk/y	
80813	C-130H	758th AS	bk/y	
FY88				
81301	MC-130W	73rd SOS		
81302	MC-130W	73rd SOS		
81303	MC-130W	73rd SOS		
81304	MC-130W	73rd SOS		
81305	MC-130W	73rd SOS		
81306	MC-130W	73rd SOS		
81307	MC-130W	73rd SOS		
81308	MC-130W	73rd SOS		
FY98				
81355	C-130J	19th AW	w	
81356	C-130J	135th AS	bk/y	
81357	C-130J	135th AS	bk/y	
81358	C-130J	135th AS	bk/y	
FY88				
81803	MC-130H	7th SOS		
FY98				
81932	EC-130J	193rd SOS		
FY88				
82101	HC-130N	102nd RQS		
82102	HC-130N	102nd RQS		
FY08				
83172	C-130J	317th AG		
83173	C-130J	317th AG		
83174	C-130J	314th AG		
FY88				
84401	C-130H	95th AS	w/r	
84402	C-130H	95th AS	w/r	
84403	C-130H	95th AS	w/r	
84404	C-130H	95th AS	w/r	
84405	C-130H	95th AS	w/r	
84406	C-130H	95th AS	w/r	
84407	C-130H	95th AS	w/r	
FY98				
85307	WC-130J	53rd WRS		
85308	WC-130J	53rd WRS		
FY08				
88601	C-130J	37th AS	bl/w $	
88602	C-130J	37th AS	bl/w $	
88603	C-130J	37th AS	bl/w $	
88604	C-130J	37th AS	bl/w	

Notes	Type			
	88605	C-130J	37th AS	*bl/w*
	88606	C-130J	37th AS	*bl/w*
	88607	C-130J	37th AS	*bl/w*
	FY09			
	90108	HC-130J		
	90109	HC-130J		
	FY89			
	90280	MC-130H	1st SOS	
	90281	MC-130H	15th SOS	
	90282	MC-130H	1st SOS	
	90283	MC-130H	7th SOS	
	FY79			
	90473	C-130H	192nd AS	*bl/y*
	90474	C-130H	192nd AS	*bl/y*
	90475	C-130H	192nd AS	*bl/y*
	90476	C-130H	192nd AS	*bl/y*
	90477	C-130H	192nd AS	*bl/y*
	90478	C-130H	192nd AS	*bl/y*
	90479	C-130H	192nd AS	*bl/y*
	90480	C-130H	192nd AS	*bl/y*
	FY89			
	90509	AC-130U	4th SOS	
	90510	AC-130U	4th SOS	
	90511	AC-130U	4th SOS	
	90512	AC-130U	4th SOS	
	90513	AC-130U	4th SOS	
	90514	AC-130U	4th SOS	
	91051	MC-130W	73rd SOS	
	91052	AC-130U	4th SOS	
	91053	AC-130U	4th SOS	
	91054	AC-130U		
	91055	C-130H	328th AS	*bl*
	91056	AC-130U	LMTAS	
	91181	C-130H	105th AS	*r*
	91182	C-130H	105th AS	*r*
	91183	C-130H	105th AS	*r*
	91184	C-130H	105th AS	*r*
	91185	C-130H	105th AS	*r*
	91186	C-130H	328th AS	*bl*
	91187	C-130H	328th AS	*bl*
	91188	C-130H	328th AS	*bl*
	FY99			
	91431	C-130J	143rd AS	*r*
	91432	C-130J	143rd AS	*r*
	91433	C-130J	143rd AS	*r*
	91933	EC-130J	193rd SOS	
	95309	WC-130J	53rd WRS	
	FY69			
	95819	MC-130P	9th SOS	
	95820	MC-130P	9th SOS	
	95821	MC-130P	58th SOW	
	95822	MC-130P	9th SOS	
	95823	MC-130P	9th SOS	
	95824	HC-130N	39th RQS	
	95825	MC-130P	67th SOS	
	95826	MC-130P	17th SOS	
	95827	MC-130P	9th SOS	
	95828	MC-130P	17th SOS	
	95829	HC-130N	58th SOW	
	95830	HC-130N	39th RQS	
	95831	MC-130P	17th SOS	
	95832	MC-130P	17th SOS	
	95833	HC-130N	58th SOW	
	96568	AC-130H	16th SOS	
	96569	AC-130H	16th SOS	
	96570	AC-130H	16th SOS	
	96572	AC-130H	16th SOS	
	96573	AC-130H	16th SOS	
	96574	AC-130H	16th SOS	
	96575	AC-130H	16th SOS	
	96577	AC-130H	16th SOS	

Notes	Type			
	FY89			
	99101	C-130H	357th AS	*bl*
	99102	C-130H	757th AS	*bl*
	99103	C-130H	757th AS	*bl*
	99104	C-130H	757th AS	*bl*
	99105	C-130H	757th AS	*bl*
	99106	C-130H	757th AS	*bl*

Boeing C-135

6th AMW, MacDill AFB, Florida: 91st ARS (*y/bl*);

15th ABW, Hickam AFB, Hawaii: 65th AS;

18th Wg, Kadena AB, Japan [ZZ]: 909th ARS (*or/bk*);

22nd ARW, McConnell AFB, Kansas: 344th ARS (*y/bk*), 349th ARS (*y/bl*) 350th ARS (*y/r*) & 384th ARS (*y/pr*);

55th Wg, Offutt AFB, Nebraska [OF]: 38th RS (*gn*), 45th RS (*bk*) & 343rd RS;

88th ABW, Wright-Patterson AFB, Ohio;

92nd ARW, Fairchild AFB, Washington: 92nd ARS (*bk*), 93rd ARS (*bl*), & 97th ARS (*y*);

97th AMW, Altus AFB, Oklahoma: 54th ARS (*y/r*);

100th ARW, RAF Mildenhall, UK [D]: 351st ARS (*r/w/bl*);

106th ARS/117th ARW, Birmingham, Alabama ANG (w/r);

108th ARS/126th ARW, Scott AFB, Illinois ANG (w/bl);

117th ARS/190th ARW, Forbes Field, Kansas ANG (*bl/y*);

121st ARW, Rickenbacker ANGB, Ohio ANG: 145th ARS & 166th ARS (*bl*);

126th ARS/128th ARW, Mitchell Field, Wisconsin ANG (*w/bl*);

132nd ARS/101st ARW, Bangor, Maine ANG (*w/gn*);

133rd ARS/157th ARW, Pease ANGB, New Hampshire ANG (*bl*);

141st ARS/108th Wg, McGuire AFB, New Jersey ANG (*r*);

151st ARS/134th ARW, Knoxville, Tennessee ANG (*w/or*);

153rd ARS/186th ARW, Meridian, Mississippi ANG (*bk/gd*);

168th ARS/168th ARW, Eielson AFB, Alaska ANG [AK] (*bl/y*);

171st ARS/127th Wg, Selfridge ANGB, Michigan ANG;

171st ARW, Greater Pittsburgh, Pennsylvania ANG: 146th ARS (*y/bk*) & 147th ARS (*bk/y*);

173rd ARS/155th ARW, Lincoln, Nebraska ANG (*r/w*);

174th ARS/185th ARW, Sioux City, Iowa ANG (*y/bk*);

191st ARS/151st ARW, Salt Lake City, Utah ANG (*bl/bk*);

196th ARS/163rd ARW, March ARB, California ANG (*bl/w*);

197th ARS/161st ARW, Phoenix, Arizona ANG;

Type				Notes
203rd ARS/15th Wg, Hickam AFB, Hawaii ANG [HH] (*y/bk*);				
366th Wg, Mountain Home AFB, Idaho [MO]:				
22nd ARS (*y/gn*);				
412th TW, Edwards AFB, California [ED]:				
418th FLTS (or);				
434th ARW AFRC, Grissom AFB, Indiana:				
72nd ARS (*bl*) & 74th ARS (*r/w*);				
452nd AMW AFRC, March ARB, California:				
336th ARS (*or/y*);				
459th ARW AFRC, Andrews AFB, Maryland:				
756th ARS (*y/bk*);				
507th ARW AFRC, Tinker AFB, Oklahoma:				
465th ARS (bl/y);				
645th Materiel Sqn, Greenville, Texas;				
916th ARW AFRC, Seymour Johnson AFB, North Carolina:				
77th ARS (*gn*);				
927th ARW AFRC, MacDill AFB, Florida:				
63rd ARS (*pr/w*)				
FY60				
00313	KC-135R	97th AMW	*y/r*	
00314	KC-135R	434th ARW	*r/w*	
00315	KC-135R	126th ARS	*w/bl*	
00316	KC-135R	174th ARS	*y/bk*	
00318	KC-135R	203rd ARS	*y/bk*	
00319	KC-135R	97th AMW	*y/r*	
00320	KC-135R	97th AMW	*y/r*	
00321	KC-135R	18th Wg	*or/bk*	
00322	KC-135R	434th ARW	*bl*	
00323	KC-135R	203rd ARS	*y/bk*	
00324	KC-135R	6th AMW	*y/bl*	
00328	KC-135R	100th ARW	*r/w/bl*	
00329	KC-135R	203rd ARS	*y/bk*	
00331	KC-135R			
00332	KC-135R	18th Wg	*or/bk*	
00333	KC-135R	92nd ARW	*bk*	
00334	KC-135R	168th ARS	*bl/y*	
00335	KC-135T	22nd ARW		
00336	KC-135T	18th Wg	*or/bk*	
00337	KC-135T	92nd ARW	*m*	
00339	KC-135T	92nd ARW		
00341	KC-135R	121st ARW	*bl*	
00342	KC-135T	92nd ARW		
00343	KC-135T	22nd ARW		
00344	KC-135T	6th AMW	*y/bl*	
00345	KC-135T	171st ARS		
00346	KC-135T	171st ARS		
00347	KC-135R	121st ARW	*bl*	
00348	KC-135R	22nd ARW		
00349	KC-135R	916th ARW	*gn*	
00350	KC-135R	100th ARW	*r/w/bl*	
00351	KC-135R	97th AMW	*y/r*	
00353	KC-135R	92nd ARW		
00355	KC-135R	22nd ARW	*r/w/bl*	
00356	KC-135R	22nd ARW		
00357	KC-135R	22nd ARW		
00358	KC-135R	108th ARS	*w/bl*	
00359	KC-135R	434th ARW	*r/w*	
00360	KC-135R	97th AMW	*y/r*	
00362	KC-135R	22nd ARW		
00363	KC-135R	434th ARW	*bl*	
00364	KC-135R	434th ARW	*r/w*	
00365	KC-135R	117th ARS	*bl/y*	
00366	KC-135R	141st ARS	*r*	

Type				Notes
00367	KC-135R	121st ARW	*bl*	
FY61				
10264	KC-135R	121st ARW	*bl*	
10266	KC-135R	117th ARS	*bl/y*	
10267	KC-135R	22nd ARW		
10272	KC-135R	434th ARW	*r/w*	
10275	KC-135R	191st ARS	*bl/bk*	
10276	KC-135R	173rd ARS	*r/w*	
10277	KC-135R	117th ARS	*bl/y*	
10280	KC-135R	452nd AMW	*or/y*	
10284	KC-135R	6th AMW	*y/bl*	
10288	KC-135R	92nd ARW	*bk*	
10290	KC-135R	203rd ARS	*y/bk*	
10292	KC-135R	97th AMW	*y/r*	
10293	KC-135R	22nd ARW		
10294	KC-135R	507th ARW	*bl/y*	
10295	KC-135R			
10298	KC-135R	126th ARS	*w/bl*	
10299	KC-135R	97th AMW	*y/r*	
10300	KC-135R	6th AMW	*y/bl*	
10302	KC-135R	106th ARS	*w/r*	
10304	KC-135R	100th ARW	*r/w/bl*	
10305	KC-135R	6th AMW	*y/bl*	
10306	KC-135R	100th ARW	*r/w/bl*	
10307	KC-135R	459th ARW	*y/bk*	
10308	KC-135R	97th AMW	*y/r*	
10309	KC-135R	126th ARS	*w/bl*	
10310	KC-135R	133rd ARS	*bl*	
10311	KC-135R	22nd ARW	*y*	
10312	KC-135R	97th AMW	*y/r*	
10313	KC-135R	916th ARW	*gn*	
10314	KC-135R	22nd ARW		
10315	KC-135R	97th AMW	*y/r*	
10317	KC-135R	141st ARS	*r*	
10318	KC-135R	141st ARS	*r*	
10320	KC-135R	412th TW	*or*	
10321	KC-135R	97th AMW	*y/r*	
10323	KC-135R	18th Wg	*or/bk*	
10324	KC-135R	452nd AMW	*or/y*	
12662	RC-135S	55th Wg	*bk*	
12663	RC-135S	55th Wg	*bk*	
12666	NC-135W	645th MS		
12667	WC-135W	55th Wg	*bk*	
12670	OC-135B	55th Wg		
12672	OC-135B	55th Wg		
FY64				
14828	KC-135R	191st ARS	*bl/bk*	
14829	KC-135R	117th ARS	*bl/y*	
14830	KC-135R	6th AMW	*y/bl*	
14831	KC-135R	197th ARS		
14832	KC-135R	203rd ARS	*y/bk*	
14833	KC-135R	6th AMW	*y/bl*	
14834	KC-135R	434th ARW	*r/w*	
14835	KC-135R	452nd AMW	*or/y*	
14836	KC-135R	133rd ARS	*bl*	
14837	KC-135R	6th AMW	*y/bl*	
14838	KC-135R	6th AMW	*y/bl*	
14839	KC-135R	108th ARS	*w/bl*	
14840	KC-135R	121st ARW	*bl*	
14841	RC-135V	55th Wg	*bl*	
14842	RC-135V	55th Wg	*gn*	
14843	RC-135V	55th Wg	*gn*	
14844	RC-135V	55th Wg	*gn*	
14845	RC-135V	55th Wg	*bl*	
14846	RC-135V	55th Wg	*gn*	
14847	RC-135U	55th Wg	*bk*	
14848	RC-135V	55th Wg	*gn*	
14849	RC-135U	55th Wg	*bk*	
FY62				
23498	KC-135R	22nd ARW		
23499	KC-135R	100th ARW	*r/w/bl*	
23500	KC-135R	126th ARS	*w/bl*	

Notes	Type			
	23502	KC-135R	18th Wg	*or/bk*
	23503	KC-135R	507th ARW	*bl/y*
	23504	KC-135R	191st ARS	*bl/bk*
	23505	KC-135R	97th AMW	*y/r*
	23506	KC-135R	133rd ARS	*bl*
	23507	KC-135R	6th AMW	*y/bl*
	23508	KC-135R	141st ARS	*r*
	23509	KC-135R	916th ARW	*gn*
	23510	KC-135R	434th ARW	*r/w*
	23511	KC-135R	121st ARW	*bl*
	23512	KC-135R	126th ARS	*w/bl*
	23513	KC-135R	132nd ARS	*w/gn*
	23514	KC-135R	203rd ARS	*y/bk*
	23515	KC-135R	133rd ARS	*bl*
	23516	KC-135R	197th ARS	
	23517	KC-135R	6th AMW	*y/bl*
	23518	KC-135R	434th ARW	*bl*
	23519	KC-135R	100th ARW	*r/w/bl*
	23520	KC-135R	133rd ARS	*bl*
	23521	KC-135R	434th ARW	*bl*
	23523	KC-135R	22nd ARW	
	23524	KC-135R	106th ARS	*w/r*
	23526	KC-135R	173rd ARS	*r/w*
	23528	KC-135R	916th ARW	*gn*
	23529	KC-135R	6th AMW	*y/bl*
	23530	KC-135R	434th ARW	*bl*
	23531	KC-135R	121st ARW	*bl*
	23533	KC-135R	97th AMW	*y/r*
	23534	KC-135R	22nd ARW	
	23537	KC-135R	916th ARW	*gn*
	23538	KC-135R	22nd ARW	
	23540	KC-135R	18th Wg	*or/bk*
	23541	KC-135R	22nd ARW	
	23542	KC-135R	916th ARW	*gn*
	23543	KC-135R	459th ARW	*y/bk*
	23544	KC-135R	141st ARS	*r*
	23545	KC-135R	22nd ARW	
	23546	KC-135R	108th ARS	*w/bl*
	23547	KC-135R	133rd ARS	*bl*
	23548	KC-135R	97th AMW	*y/r*
	23549	KC-135R	22nd ARW	
	23550	KC-135R	197th ARS	
	23551	KC-135R	100th ARW	*r/w/bl*
	23552	KC-135R	18th Wg	*or/bk*
	23553	KC-135R	97th AMW	*y/r*
	23554	KC-135R	22nd ARW	
	23556	KC-135R	459th ARW	*y/bk*
	23557	KC-135R	916th ARW	*gn*
	23558	KC-135R	452nd AMW	*or/y*
	23559	KC-135R	22nd ARW	*gy/si*
	23561	KC-135R	97th AMW	*y/r*
	23562	KC-135R	6th AMW	*y/bl*
	23564	KC-135R	22nd ARW	
	23565	KC-135R	100th ARW	*r/w/bl*
	23566	KC-135R	174th ARS	*y/bk*
	23568	KC-135R	97th AMW	*y/r*
	23569	KC-135R	22nd ARW	
	23571	KC-135R	168th ARS	*bl/y*
	23572	KC-135R	117th ARS	*bl/y*
	23573	KC-135R	22nd ARW	
	23575	KC-135R	18th Wg	*or/bk*
	23576	KC-135R	133rd ARS	*bl*
	23577	KC-135R	916th ARW	*gn*
	23578	KC-135R	141st ARS	*r*
	23580	KC-135R	916th ARW	*gn*
	23582	WC-135C	55th Wg	*bk*
	24125	RC-135W	55th Wg	*bk*
	24126	RC-135W	55th Wg	*bl*
	24127	TC-135W	55th Wg	
	24128	RC-135S	55th Wg	
	24129	TC-135W	55th Wg	*gn*
	24130	RC-135W	55th Wg	*gn*

Notes	Type			
	24131	RC-135W	55th Wg	*gn*
	24132	RC-135W	55th Wg	*gn*
	24133	TC-135S	55th Wg	*bk*
	24134	RC-135W	55th Wg	*bl*
	24135	RC-135W	55th Wg	*bk*
	24138	RC-135W	55th Wg	*gn*
	24139	RC-135W	55th Wg	*gn*
	FY63			
	37976	KC-135R	18th Wg	*or/bk*
	37977	KC-135R	22nd ARW	
	37978	KC-135R	22nd ARW	
	37979	KC-135R	100th ARW	*r/w/bl*
	37980	KC-135R	412th TW	*or*
	37981	KC-135R	108th ARS	*w/bl*
	37982	KC-135R	92nd ARW	
	37984	KC-135R	106th ARS	*w/r*
	37985	KC-135R	507th ARW	*bl/y*
	37987	KC-135R	22nd ARW	
	37988	KC-135R	173rd ARS	*r/w*
	37991	KC-135R	173rd ARS	*r/w*
	37992	KC-135R	121st ARW	*bl*
	37993	KC-135R	121st ARW	*m*
	37995	KC-135R	22nd ARW	*gy*
	37996	KC-135R	434th ARW	*bl*
	37997	KC-135R	6th AMW	*y/bl*
	37999	KC-135R	22nd ARW	
	38000	KC-135R	6th AMW	*y/bl*
	38002	KC-135R	22nd ARW	*gy/si*
	38003	KC-135R	141st ARS	*r*
	38004	KC-135R	117th ARS	*bl/y*
	38006	KC-135R	100th ARW	*r/w/bl*
	38007	KC-135R	106th ARS	*w/r*
	38008	KC-135R	92nd ARW	
	38011	KC-135R	6th AMW	*y/bl*
	38012	KC-135R	22nd ARW	
	38013	KC-135R	121st ARW	*bl*
	38014	KC-135R	916th ARW	*gn*
	38015	KC-135R	168th ARS	*bl/y*
	38017	KC-135R	97th AMW	*y/r*
	38018	KC-135R	173rd ARS	*r/w*
	38019	KC-135R	100th ARW	*r/w/bl*
	38020	KC-135R	97th AMW	*y/r*
	38021	KC-135R	97th AMW	*y/r*
	38022	KC-135R	22nd ARW	*m*
	38023	KC-135R	197th ARS	
	38024	KC-135R	452nd AMW	*or/y*
	38025	KC-135R	22nd ARW	
	38026	KC-135R	191st ARS	*bl/bk*
	38027	KC-135R		
	38028	KC-135R	168th ARS	*bl/y*
	38029	KC-135R	126th ARS	*w/bl*
	38030	KC-135R	203rd ARS	*y/bk*
	38031	KC-135R	97th AMW	*y/r*
	38032	KC-135R	434th ARW	*bl*
	38033	KC-135R	6th AMW	*y/bl*
	38034	KC-135R	22nd ARW	
	38035	KC-135R	106th ARS	*w/r*
	38036	KC-135R	197th ARS	
	38037	KC-135R		
	38038	KC-135R	197th ARS	
	38039	KC-135R	507th ARW	*bl/y*
	38040	KC-135R	141st ARS	*r*
	38041	KC-135R	434th ARW	*bl*
	38043	KC-135R	168th ARS	*bl/y*
	38044	KC-135R	916th ARW	*gn*
	38045	KC-135R	6th AMW	*y/bl*
	38871	KC-135R	22nd ARW	
	38872	KC-135R	132nd ARS	*w/gn*
	38873	KC-135R	132nd ARS	*w/gn*
	38874	KC-135R	97th AMW	*y/r*
	38875	KC-135R	117th ARS	*bl/y*
	38876	KC-135R	168th ARS	*bl/y*

Type				Notes
38877	KC-135R	18th Wg	or/bk	
38878	KC-135R	97th AMW	y/r	
38879	KC-135R			
38880	KC-135R	507th ARW	bl/y	
38881	KC-135R	18th Wg	or/bk	
38883	KC-135R	97th AMW	y/r	
38884	KC-135R	18th Wg	or/bk	
38885	KC-135R	92nd ARW		
38887	KC-135R	22nd ARW		
38888	KC-135R	6th AMW	y/bl	
39792	RC-135V	55th Wg	gn $	
FY57				
71419	KC-135R	117th ARS	bl/y	
71427	KC-135R	117th ARS	bl/y	
71428	KC-135R	151st ARS	w/or	
71430	KC-135R	133rd ARS	bl	
71432	KC-135R	106th ARS	w/r	
71435	KC-135R	191st ARS	bl/bk	
71436	KC-135R	151st ARS	w/or	
71437	KC-135R	106th ARS	w/r	
71438	KC-135R	452nd AMW	or/y	
71439	KC-135R	18th Wg	or/bk	
71440	KC-135R	22nd ARW		
71441	KC-135R	174th ARS	y/bk	
71451	KC-135R	151st ARS	w/or	
71453	KC-135R	106th ARS	w/r	
71454	KC-135R	22nd ARW		
71456	KC-135R	916th ARW	gn	
71459	KC-135R	452nd AMW	or/y	
71461	KC-135R	173rd ARS	r/w	
71462	KC-135R	121st ARW	bl	
71468	KC-135R	452nd AMW	or/y	
71469	KC-135R	121st ARW	bl	
71472	KC-135R	434th ARW	bl	
71473	KC-135R			
71474	KC-135R	97th AMW	y/r	
71483	KC-135R	92nd ARW		
71486	KC-135R	197th ARS		
71487	KC-135R	459th ARW	y/bk	
71488	KC-135R	100th ARW	r/w/bl	
71493	KC-135R	100th ARW	r/w/bl	
71499	KC-135R	191st ARS	bl/bk	
71502	KC-135R	92nd ARW		
71506	KC-135R	97th AMW	y/r	
71508	KC-135R	203rd ARS	y/bk	
71512	KC-135R	459th ARW	y/bk	
71514	KC-135R	126th ARS	w/bl	
72593	KC-135R	121st ARW	bl	
72597	KC-135R	153rd ARS	bk/gd	
72598	KC-135R	452nd AMW	or/y	
72599	KC-135R	916th ARW	gn	
72603	KC-135R	452nd AMW	or/y	
72605	KC-135R			
72606	KC-135R	174th ARS	y/bk	
FY58				
80001	KC-135R	92nd ARW	bk	
80004	KC-135R	153rd ARS	bk/gd	
80008	KC-135R	133rd ARS	bl	
80009	KC-135R	126th ARS	w/bl	
80010	KC-135R	153rd ARS	bk/gd	
80011	KC-135R	22nd ARW		
80015	KC-135R	507th ARW	bl/y	
80016	KC-135R	100th ARW	r/w/bl	
80018	KC-135R	22nd ARW		
80021	KC-135R	507th ARW	bl/y	
80023	KC-135R	108th ARS	w/bl	
80027	KC-135R	191st ARS	bl/bk	
80030	KC-135R	132nd ARS	w/gn	
80034	KC-135R	97th AMW	y/r	
80035	KC-135R	22nd ARW	y	
80036	KC-135R	100th ARW	r/w/bl	
80038	KC-135R	916th ARW	gn	
80042	KC-135T	22nd ARW		
80045	KC-135T	171st ARW	y/bk	
80046	KC-135T	22nd ARW		
80047	KC-135T	22nd ARW		
80049	KC-135T	171st ARS		
80050	KC-135T	92nd ARW	bk	
80051	KC-135R	507th ARW	bl/y	
80052	KC-135R	452nd AMW	or/y	
80054	KC-135T	171st ARW	y/bk	
80055	KC-135T	92nd ARW	bk	
80056	KC-135R	153rd ARS	bk/gd	
80057	KC-135R	174th ARS	y/bk	
80058	KC-135R	507th ARW	bl/y	
80059	KC-135R	153rd ARS	bk/gd	
80060	KC-135T	171st ARW	y/bk	
80061	KC-135T	22nd ARW		
80062	KC-135T	6th AMW	y/bl	
80063	KC-135R	507th ARW	bl/y	
80065	KC-135T	22nd ARW		
80066	KC-135R	507th ARW	bl/y	
80067	KC-135R	174th ARS	y/bk	
80069	KC-135T	92nd ARW		
80071	KC-135T	22nd ARW		
80072	KC-135T	171st ARW	y/bk	
80073	KC-135R	106th ARS	w/r	
80074	KC-135T	171st ARW	y/bk	
80075	KC-135R	507th ARW	bl/y	
80076	KC-135R	434th ARW	r/w	
80077	KC-135T	171st ARW	y/bk	
80079	KC-135R	507th ARW	bl/y	
80083	KC-135R	121st ARW	bl	
80084	KC-135T	171st ARW	y/bk	
80085	KC-135R	452nd AMW	or/y	
80086	KC-135T	100th ARW	r/w/bl	
80088	KC-135T	171st ARS		
80089	KC-135T	22nd ARW		
80092	KC-135R	92nd ARW		
80093	KC-135R	100th ARW	r/w/bl	
80094	KC-135T	92nd ARW	bk	
80095	KC-135T			
80098	KC-135R	133rd ARS	bl	
80099	KC-135T	126th ARS	w/bl	
80100	KC-135R			
80102	KC-135R	507th ARW	bl/y	
80103	KC-135T	92nd ARW	bk	
80104	KC-135R	108th ARS	w/bl	
80106	KC-135R	106th ARS	w/r	
80107	KC-135R	132nd ARS	w/gn	
80109	KC-135R	153rd ARS	bk/gd	
80112	KC-135T	171st ARW	y/bk	
80113	KC-135R	6th AMW	y/bl	
80114	KC-135R	191st ARS	bl/bk	
80117	KC-135T	171st ARW		
80118	KC-135R	92nd ARW	bk	
80119	KC-135R	97th AMW	y/r	
80120	KC-135R	6th AMW	y/bl	
80121	KC-135R	507th ARW	bl/y	
80122	KC-135R	117th ARS	bl/y	
80123	KC-135R	22nd ARW		
80124	KC-135R	22nd ARW		
80125	KC-135T	92nd ARW	bl	
80126	KC-135R	22nd ARW	y	
80128	KC-135R	97th AMW	y/r	
80129	KC-135T	171st ARS		
80130	KC-135R	126th ARS	w/bl	
FY59				
91444	KC-135R	121st ARW	bl	
91446	KC-135R	132nd ARS	w/gn	
91448	KC-135R	151st ARS	w/or	
91450	KC-135R	197th ARS		
91453	KC-135R	121st ARW	bl	
91455	KC-135R	153rd ARS	bk/gd	

Notes	Type			
	91458	KC-135R	121st ARW	bl
	91459	KC-135R	97th AMW	y/r
	91460	KC-135T	171st ARW	
	91461	KC-135R	168th ARS	bl/y
	91462	KC-135T		
	91463	KC-135R	173rd ARS	r/w
	91464	KC-135T	18th Wg	or/bk
	91466	KC-135R	108th ARS	w/bl
	91467	KC-135T	171st ARW	bk/y
	91468	KC-135T	171st ARW	
	91469	KC-135R	459th ARW	y/bk
	91470	KC-135T	92nd ARW	bk
	91471	KC-135T	92nd ARW	bk
	91472	KC-135R	203rd ARS	y/bk
	91474	KC-135T	171st ARS	
	91475	KC-135R	92nd ARW	
	91476	KC-135R	92nd ARW	
	91478	KC-135R	153rd ARS	bk/gd
	91480	KC-135T	92nd ARW	bk
	91482	KC-135R	97th AMW	y/r
	91483	KC-135R	121st ARW	bl
	91486	KC-135R	22nd ARW	
	91488	KC-135R	132nd ARS	w/gn
	91490	KC-135T	171st ARW	
	91492	KC-135R	92nd ARW	
	91495	KC-135R	173rd ARS	r/w
	91498	KC-135R	132nd ARS	w/gn
	91499	KC-135R	151st ARS	w/or
	91500	KC-135R	108th ARS	w/bl
	91501	KC-135R	97th AMW	y/r
	91502	KC-135R	97th AMW	y/r
	91504	KC-135T	171st ARW	y/bk
	91505	KC-135R	151st ARS	w/or
	91506	KC-135R	174th ARS	y/bk
	91507	KC-135R	117th ARS	bl/y
	91508	KC-135R	22nd ARW	
	91509	KC-135R	141st ARS	r
	91510	KC-135T	92nd ARW	
	91511	KC-135R	22nd ARW	
	91512	KC-135T	452nd AMW	or/y
	91513	KC-135T	92nd ARW	bk
	91515	KC-135R	92nd ARW	
	91516	KC-135R	151st ARS	w/or
	91517	KC-135R	151st ARS	w/or
	91519	KC-135R	174th ARS	y/bk
	91520	KC-135T		
	91521	KC-135R	168th ARS	bl/y
	91522	KC-135R	108th ARS	w/bl
	91523	KC-135T	171st ARW	y/bk

US-based USN/USMC Aircraft

Notes *Type*

Lockheed P-3 Orion

CinCLANT/VP-30, NAS Jacksonville, Florida;
CNO/VP-30, NAS Jacksonville, Florida;
NASC-FS, Point Mugu, California;
USNTPS, NAS Point Mugu, California;
VP-1, NAS Whidbey Island, Washington [YB];
VP-4, MCBH Kaneohe Bay, Hawaii [YD];
VP-5, NAS Jacksonville, Florida [LA];
VP-8, NAS Jacksonville, Florida [LC];
VP-9, MCBH Kaneohe Bay, Hawaii [PD];
VP-10, NAS Jacksonville, Florida [LD];
VP-16, NAS Jacksonville, Florida [LF];
VP-26, NAS Jacksonville, Florida [LK];
VP-30, NAS Jacksonville, Florida [LL];
VP-40, NAS Whidbey Island, Washington [QE];
VP-45, NAS Jacksonville, Florida [LN];
VP-46, NAS Whidbey Island, Washington [RC];
VP-47, MCBH Kaneohe Bay, Hawaii [RD];
VP-62, NAS Jacksonville, Florida [LT];
VP-69, NAS Whidbey Island, Washington [PJ];
VPU-1, NAS Jacksonville, Florida;
VPU-2, MCBH Kaneohe Bay, Hawaii;
VQ-1, NAS Whidbey Island, Washington [PR];
VQ-2, NAS Whidbey Island, Washington;
VX-1, NAS Patuxent River, Maryland;
VX-20, Patuxent River, Maryland;
VX-30, NAS Point Mugu, California;
VXS-1, Patuxent River, Maryland [RL]

Notes	Type			
	150521	[341]	NP-3D	VX-30
	150522	[340]	NP-3D	VX-30
	153442	[RL-442]	NP-3D	VXS-1
	153443	[302]	NP-3D	VX-30
	154587	[RL-587]	NP-3D	VXS-1
	154589	[RL-589]	NP-3D	VXS-1
	156507	[507]	EP-3E	VQ-1
	156510	[LL-510]	P-3C	VP-30
	156511	[511]	EP-3E	VQ-1
	156514	[514]	EP-3E	VQ-1
	156515	[LL-515]	P-3C	VP-30
	156517	[517]	EP-3E	VQ-1
	156519	[519]	EP-3E	VQ-2
	156521	[LL-521]	P-3C	VP-30
	156528	[528]	EP-3E	VQ-1
	156529	[24]	EP-3E	VQ-2
	157316	[316]	EP-3E	VQ-2
	157318	[PR-318]	EP-3E	VQ-1
	157319	[LL-319]	P-3C	VP-30
	157322	[LK-322]	P-3C	VP-26
	157325	[325]	EP-3E	VQ-2
	157326	[326]	EP-3E	VQ-2
	157329	[LL-329]	P-3C	VP-30
	157331	[331]	P-3C	VP-30
	158204	[204]	NP-3C	VX-20
	158206	[LL-206]	P-3C	VP-30
	158210	[210]	P-3C	VP-45
	158214	[LL-214]	P-3C	VP-30
	158215	[LL-215]	P-3C	VP-45
	158222	[LL-51222]	P-3C	VP-30
	158224	[YD-224]	P-3C	VP-4
	158225	[225]	P-3C	VP-8
	158227	[300]	NP-3D	VX-26
	158563	[YD-563]	P-3C	VP-4
	158564	[564]	P-3C	VP-26
	158567	[LA-567]	P-3C	VP-5
	158568	[301]	NP-3C	VX-30
	158570	[LL-570]	P-3C	VP-30
	158571	[LL-571]	P-3C	VP-30

Type				Notes
158573	[RD-573]	P-3C	VP-47	
158574		P-3C	NASC-FS	
158912	[912]	P-3C	VX-20	
158914	[914]	P-3C	VP-16	
158915	[915]	P-3C	VP-16	
158916	[916]	P-3C	VP-45	
158917	[LA-917]	P-3C	VP-5	
158918	[918]	P-3C	VP-140	
158919	[919]	P-3C	VP-9	
158921	[LD-921]	P-3C	VP-10	
158922	[922]	P-3C	VP-30	
158923	[RD-923]	P-3C	VP-47	
158924	[RD-924]	P-3C	VP-47	
158925	[925]	P-3C	VP-4	
158926	[RC-926]	P-3C	VP-46	
158927	[LF-927]	P-3C	VP-16	
158928		P-3C	VPU-2	
158929	[LA-929]	P-3C	VP-5	
158934	[934]	P-3C	VP-26	
158935	[LL-935]	P-3C	VP-30	
159318	[318]	P-3C	VP-8	
159320	[320]	P-3C	VP-46	
159322	[PD-322]	P-3C	VP-9	
159323	[323]	P-3C	VP-8	
159326	[326]	P-3C	VP-4	
159329	[LN-329]	P-3C	VP-45	
159503	[LD-503]	P-3C	VP-10	
159504		P-3C	VPU-2	
159507	[RD-507]	P-3C	VP-47	
159512	[LF-512]	P-3C	VP-16	
159513	[LL-513]	P-3C	VP-30	
159514	[LL-514]	P-3C	VP-30	
159885	[885]	P-3C	VP-40	
159887		EP-3E	VQ-2	
159889	[YD-889]	P-3C	VP-4	
159893	[26]	EP-3E	VQ-1	
159894	[LD-894]	P-3C	VP-10	
160283	[283]	P-3C	VP-47	
160285		P-3C	VPU-1	
160287	[LL-30]	P-3C	VP-30	
160290	[290]	P-3C	VX-20	
160291	[291]	EP-3E	VQ-1	
160292	[292]	P-3C	VPU-2	
160293		P-3C	NASC-FS	
160610	[610]	P-3C	VP-4	
160761	[761]	P-3C	VP-16	
160762		P-3C	VPU-2	
160763	[763]	P-3C	VQ-1	
160764	[764]	EP-3E	VQ-1	
160770	[PC] $	P-3C	VP-9	
160999	[999]	P-3C	VP-9	
161001	[PJ-001]	P-3C	VP-69	
161002	[LD-002]	P-3C	VP-10	
161005	[005]	P-3C	VX-1	
161006	[LK-006]	P-3C	VP-26	
161007	[007]	P-3C	VQ-2	
161010	[LL-010]	P-3C	VP-30	
161011	[011]	P-3C	VP-47	
161012	[PD-012]	P-3C	VP-9	
161014	[014]	P-3C	VP-10	
161121	[121]	P-3C	VQ-2	
161122	[226]	P-3C	VPU-1	
161124	[LA-124]	P-3C	VP-5	
161126	[126]	P-3C	VP-46	
161127	[LF-127]	P-3C	VP-16	
161129	[LT-129]	P-3C	VP-62	
161132	[132]	P-3C	VP-26	
161329	[329]	P-3C	VP-45	
161332	[LN-332]	P-3C	VP-45	
161333	[LC-333]	P-3C	VP-8	
161334	[LL-334]	P-3C	VP-30	
161336	[336]	P-3C	VP-46	

Type				Notes
161337	[337]	P-3C	VP-47	
161338	[338]	P-3C	VP-46	
161339	[339]	P-3C	VP-47	
161404	[404]	P-3C	VP-26	
161405	[405]	P-3C	VP-8	
161406	[406]	P-3C	VP-30	
161407	[407]	P-3C	VP-47	
161408	[PJ-408]	P-3C	VP-69	
161409	[LT-409]	P-3C	VP-62	
161410		EP-3E	VQ-1	
161411		P-3C	NASC-FS	
161412	[PJ-412]	P-3C	VP-69	
161413	[413]	P-3C	VX-1	
161414	[414]	P-3C	VP-46	
161415	[415]	P-3C	VP-8	
161586	[LC-586]	P-3C	VP-8	
161587	[587]	P-3C	VP-46	
161588	[588]	P-3C	VP-10	
161589	[589]	P-3C	VP-40	
161590	[590]	P-3C	VP-46	
161591	[LA-591]	P-3C	VP-5	
161593	[593]	P-3C	VP-8	
161594	[594]	P-3C	VP-47	
161595	[LT-595]	P-3C	VP-62	
161596	[596]	P-3C	VP-1	
161763	[763]	P-3C	VP-47	
161764	[764]	P-3C	VP-46	
161765	[765]	P-3C	VP-1	
161766	[YD-766]	P-3C	VP-4	
161767	[RD-767]	P-3C	VP-47	
162314	[314]	P-3C	VP-30	
162315	[315]	P-3C	VP-40	
162316	[LC-316]	P-3C	VP-8	
162317	[317]	P-3C	VP-9	
162318	[LD-318]	P-3C	VP-10	
162770	[770]	P-3C	VP-30	
162771	[771]	P-3C	VP-45	
162772	[772]	P-3C	VP-47	
162773	[773]	P-3C	VP-30	
162774	[774]	P-3C	VX-20	
162775	[775]	P-3C	VP-4	
162776	[LD-776]	P-3C	VP-10	
162777	[777]	P-3C	VP-26	
162778	[PD-778]	P-3C	VP-9	
162998	[998]	P-3C	VP-46	
162999	[999]	P-3C	VP-16	
163000	[000]	P-3C	VP-45	
163001	[001]	P-3C	VP-16	
163002	[002]	P-3C	VP-46	
163003	[LF-003]	P-3C	VP-16	
163004	[004]	P-3C	VP-69	
163006	[006]	P-3C	VP-47	
163289	[289]	P-3C	VP-40	
163290	[LD-290]	P-3C	VP-10	
163291	[291]	P-3C	VP-45	
163292	[292]	P-3C	VP-40	
163293	[LK-293]	P-3C	VP-26	
163294	[LA-294]	P-3C	VP-5	
163295	[295]	P-3C	VP-69	

Boeing E-6B Mercury

Boeing, McConnell AFB, Kansas;
VQ-3 & VQ-4, SCW-1,
Tinker AFB, Oklahoma

162782	VQ-3
162783	VQ-3
162784	VQ-4
163918	VQ-3
163919	VQ-3
163920	VQ-3
164386	VQ-4
164387	VQ-3

Notes Type

164388 VQ-4
164404 VQ-4
164405 VQ-4
164406 VQ-3
164407 VQ-4
164408 VQ-4
164409 VQ-4
164410 VQ-4

Boeing P-8A Poseidon
Boeing, Seattle;
VX-20, Patuxent River, Maryland
167951 VX-20
167952
167953 Boeing
167954 Boeing
167955 (on order)
167956 (on order)

McDonnell Douglas C-9B Skytrain II/DC-9-32*
VMR-1, Cherry Point MCAS, North Carolina;
VR-46, Atlanta, Georgia [JS];
VR-52, Willow Grove NAS, Pennsylvania [JT];
VR-61, Whidbey Island NAS, Washington [RS];
159113 VR-61
159114 VR-61
159116 VR-61
159118
160046 VMR-1
160047 VMR-1
160048 VR-52
160049 VR-52
160050 VR-52
160051 VR-52
161266 VR-46
161529 [JS] VR-46
161530 [JS] VR-46
164606* [RS] VR-61
164608* VR-61

Grumman C-20A/C-20D Gulfstream III/ C-20G Gulfstream IV*
VMR-Det, MCBH Kaneohe Bay, Hawaii;
VR-1, NAF Washington, Maryland;
VR-48, NAF Washington, Maryland [JR];
VR-51, MCBH Kaneohe Bay, Hawaii
C-20A
830500 VR-1
C-20D
163691 VR-1
163692 VR-1
C-20G
165093 [JR] VR-48
165094 VR-51
165151 [JR] VR-48
165152 VR-51
165153 VMR-Det

Cessna C-35 Citation V
MAW-4, Miramar MCAS, California;
MWHS-1, Futenma MCAS, Japan;
MWHS-4, NAS New Orleans;
VMR-1, Cheery Point MCAS, North Carolina;
VMR-2, NAF Washington, Maryland
165740 [EZ] UC-35C MWHS-4
165741 [EZ] UC-35C MWHS-4
165939 UC-35D MWHS-1
166374 UC-35D MWHS-1
166474 UC-35D MAW-4
166500 UC-35D MAW-4
166712 UC-35D MWHS-1
166713 UC-35D MWHS-1
166714 UC-35D MAW-4
166715 UC-35D VMR-1
166716 UC-35D (on order)
166717 UC-35D (on order)
166766 UC-35D VMR-2
166767 [VM] UC-35D VMR-2

Gulfstream Aerospace C-37B Gulfstream V
CFLSW Det, Hawaii;
VR-1, NAF Washington, Maryland
166375 CFLSW Det
166376 VR-1
166377 VR-1
166378 VR-1
166379 (on order)

Boeing C-40A Clipper
VR-57, NAS North Island, California [RX];
VR-58, NAS Jacksonville, Florida [JV];
VR-59, NAS Fort Worth JRB, Texas [RY]
165829 VR-58
165830 [RY] VR-59
165831 VR-59
165832 VR-58
165833 VR-59
165834 VR-58
165835 VR-57
165836 VR-57
166693 VR-57
166694
166695

Lockheed C-130 Hercules
VR-53, NAF Washington, Maryland [AX];
VR-54, NAS New Orleans, Louisiana [CW];
VR-55, NAS Point Mugu, California [RU];
VR-62, NAS Jacksonville, Florida [JW];
VR-64, NAS Willow Grove, Pennsylvania [BD];
VMGR-152, Futenma MCAS, Japan [QD];
VMGR-234, NAS Fort Worth, Texas [QH];
VMGR-252, Cherry Point MCAS, North Carolina [BH];
VMGR-352, MCAS Miramar, California [QB];
VMGR-452, Stewart Field, New York [NY];
VX-20, Patuxent River, Maryland;
VX-30, NAS Point Mugu, California
148891 [403] KC-130F VX-30
148893 [402] KC-130F VX-30
148897 [400] KC-130F VX-30
149807 [QD] KC-130F VMGR-152
149808 KC-130F VX-20
150686 [BH] KC-130F VMGR-252
160626 KC-130R VX-20
160627 KC-130R VX-20
162308 [QH] KC-130T VMGR-234
162309 [QH] KC-130T VMGR-234
162310 [QH] KC-130T VMGR-234
162311 [QH] KC-130T VMGR-234
162785 [QH] KC-130T VMGR-234
162786 [QH] KC-130T VMGR-234

Type				Notes
163022	[QH]	KC-130T	VMGR-234	
163023	[QH]	KC-130T	VMGR-234	
163310	[QH]	KC-130T	VMGR-234	
163311	[NY]	KC-130T	VMGR-452	
163591	[NY]	KC-130T	VMGR-452	
163592	[NY]	KC-130T	VMGR-452	
164105	[NY]	KC-130T	VMGR-452	
164106	[NY]	KC-130T	VMGR-452	
164180	[NY]	KC-130T	VMGR-452	
164181	[NY]	KC-130T	VMGR-452	
164441	[NY]	KC-130T	VMGR-452	
164442	[NY]	KC-130T	VMGR-452	
164597	[NY]	KC-130T-30	VMGR-452	
164598	[QH]	KC-130T-30	VMGR-234	
164762	[CW]	C-130T	VR-54	
164763		C-130T	Blue Angels	
164993	[BD]	C-130T	VR-64	
164994	[AX]	C-130T	VR-53	
164995	[AX]	C-130T	VR-53	
164996	[BD]	C-130T	VR-64	
164997	[AX]	C-130T	VR-53	
164998	[AX]	C-130T	VR-53	
164999	[QH]	KC-130T	VMGR-234	
165000	[QH]	KC-130T	VMGR-234	
165158	[CW]	C-130T	VR-54	
165159	[CW]	C-130T	VR-54	
165160	[CW]	C-130T	VR-54	
165161	[BD]	C-130T	VR-64	
165162	[QH]	KC-130T	VMGR-234	
165163	[QH]	KC-130T	VMGR-234	
165313	[JW]	C-130T	VR-62	
165314	[JW]	C-130T	VR-62	
165315	[NY]	KC-130T	VMGR-452	
165316	[NY]	KC-130T	VMGR-452	
165348	[CW]	C-130T	VR-54	
165349	[RU]	C-130T	VR-55	
165350	[RU]	C-130T	VR-55	
165351	[RU]	C-130T	VR-55	
165352	[NY]	KC-130T	VMGR-452	
165353	[NY]	KC-130T	VMGR-452	
165378	[RU]	C-130T	VR-55	
165379	[RU]	C-130T	VR-55	
165735	[QB]	KC-130J	VMGR-352	
165736	[QB]	KC-130J	VMGR-352	
165737	[BH]	KC-130J	VMGR-252	

Type				Notes
165738	[BH]	KC-130J	VMGR-252	
165739	[QB]	KC-130J	VMGR-352	
165809	[BH]	KC-130J	VMGR-252	
165810	[BH]	KC-130J	VMGR-252	
165957	[QD]	KC-130J	VMGR-152	
166380	[BH]	KC-130J	VMGR-252	
166381	[BH]	KC-130J	VMGR-252	
166382	[BH]	KC-130J	VMGR-252	
166472	[BH]	KC-130J	VMGR-252	
166473		KC-130J	VX-20	
166511	[BH]	KC-130J	VMGR-252	
166512	[QB]	KC-130J	VMGR-352	
166513	[BH]	KC-130J	VMGR-252	
166514	[QD]	KC-130J	VMGR-152	
166762	[QB]	KC-130J	VMGR-352	
166763	[QD]	KC-130J	VMGR-152	
166764	[BH]	KC-130J	VMGR-252	
166765	[QB]	KC-130J	VMGR-352	
167108	[QB]	KC-130J	VMGR-352	
167109	[QB]	KC-130J	VMGR-352	
167110	[QB]	KC-130J	VMGR-352	
167111	[QB]	KC-130J	VMGR-352	
167112	[BH]	KC-130J	VMGR-252	
167923	[QD]	KC-130J	VMGR-152	
167924	[QB]	KC-130J	VMGR-352	
167925	[QD]	KC-130J	VMGR-152	
167926	[QD]	KC-130J	VMGR-152	
167927	[QD]	KC-130J	VMGR-152	
167981	[QD]	KC-130J	VMGR-152	
167982	[QD]	KC-130J	VMGR-152	
167983	[QD]	KC-130J	VMGR-152	
167984	[QB]	KC-130J	VMGR-352	
167985	[QB]	KC-130J	VMGR-352	
168065	[QD]	KC-130J	VMGR-152	
168066	[QD]	KC-130J	VMGR-152	
168067	[QB]	KC-130J	VMGR-352	
168068	[QB]	KC-130J	VMGR-352	
168069		KC-130J		
168070		KC-130J		
168071		KC-130J		
168072		KC-130J		
168073		KC-130J		
168074	[QD]	KC-130J	VMGR-152	
168075	[QD]	KC-130J	VMGR-152	

61-0002 is a B-52H Stratofortress operated by the 2nd BW, based at Barksdale in Louisiana. In 2011 it will celebrate its 50th birthday.

US-based US Coast Guard Aircraft

Notes	Type	Notes	Type
	Canadair C-143A Challenger		1703 HC-130H Kodiak
	USCG, Washington DC		1704 HC-130H Kodiak
	02		1706 HC-130H Barbers Point
			1707 HC-130H Sacramento
	Gulfstream Aerospace		1708 HC-130H Kodiak
	C-37A Gulfstream V		1709 HC-130H Kodiak
	USCG, Washington DC		1711 HC-130H Barbers Point
	01		1712 HC-130H Sacramento
			1713 HC-130H Sacramento
	Lockheed C-130 Hercules		1714 HC-130H Sacramento
	USCGS Barbers Point, Hawaii;		1715 HC-130H Sacramento
	USCGS Clearwater, Florida;		1716 HC-130H Elizabeth City
	USCGS Elizabeth City, North Carolina;		1717 HC-130H Clearwater
	USCGS Kodiak, Alaska;		1718 HC-130H Sacramento
	USCGS Sacramento, California		1719 HC-130H Clearwater
	1500 HC-130H Clearwater		1720 HC-130H Clearwater
	1501 HC-130H Clearwater		1790 HC-130H Kodiak
	1502 HC-130H Clearwater		2001 HC-130J Elizabeth City
	1503 HC-130H Elizabeth City		2002 HC-130J Elizabeth City
	1504 HC-130H Elizabeth City $		2003 HC-130J Elizabeth City
	1700 HC-130H Clearwater		2004 HC-130J Elizabeth City
	1701 HC-130H Barbers Point		2005 HC-130J Elizabeth City
	1702 HC-130H Sacramento		2006 HC-130J Elizabeth City

Aircraft in US Government or Military Service with Civil Registrations

Notes	Type	Notes	Type
	Canadair CL.601/CL.604* Challenger		N85
	Federal Aviation Administration,		N86
	Oklahoma		N87
			N88*

Military Aviation Sites on the Internet

The list below is not intended to be a complete list of military aviation sites on the Internet. The sites listed cover Museums, Locations, Air Forces, Companies and Organisations that are mentioned elsewhere in 'Military Aircraft Markings'. Sites listed are in English or contain sufficient English to be reasonably easily understood. Each site address is believed to be correct at the time of going to press. Additions are welcome, via the usual address found at the front of the book, or via e-mail to admin@aviation-links.co.uk. An up to date copy of this list is to be found at http://www.aviation-links.co.uk/.

Name of site	*Internet dial (all prefixed 'http://')*
MILITARY SITES-UK	
No 2 Sqn	www.raf.mod.uk/organisation/2squadron.cfm
No 3 Sqn	www.raf.mod.uk/organisation/3squadron.cfm
No 5 Sqn	www.raf.mod.uk/organisation/5squadron.cfm
No 6 Sqn	www.raf.mod.uk/organisation/6squadron.cfm
No 7 Sqn	www.raf.mod.uk/organisation/7squadron.cfm
No 8 Sqn	8squadron.co.uk/
No 9 Sqn	www.raf.mod.uk/organisation/9squadron.cfm
No 11 Sqn	www.raf.mod.uk/organisation/11squadron.cfm
No 12 Sqn	www.raf.mod.uk/organisation/12squadron.cfm
No 13 Sqn	www.raf.mod.uk/organisation/13squadron.cfm
No 14 Sqn	www.raf.mod.uk/organisation/14squadron.cfm
No 15(R) Sqn	www.raf.mod.uk/organisation/15squadron.cfm
No 17(R) Sqn	www.raf.mod.uk/organisation/17squadron.cfm
No 18 Sqn	www.raf.mod.uk/organisation/18squadron.cfm
No 19(R) Sqn	www.rafvalley.org/19sqn/home.htm

Name of site	*Internet dial (all prefixed 'http://')*
No 22 Sqn	www.raf.mod.uk/organisation/22squadron.cfm
No 23 Sqn	www.raf.mod.uk/organisation/23squadron.cfm
No 24 Sqn	www.raf.mod.uk/organisation/24squadron.cfm
No 25 Sqn	www.raf.mod.uk/organisation/25squadron.cfm
No 27 Sqn	www.raf.mod.uk/organisation/27squadron.cfm
No 28 Sqn	www.raf.mod.uk/organisation/28squadron.cfm
No 29(R) Sqn	www.raf.mod.uk/organisation/29squadron.cfm
No 31 Sqn	www.raf.mod.uk/organisation/31squadron.cfm
No 32(The Royal) Sqn	www.raf.mod.uk/organisation/32squadron.cfm
No 33 Sqn	www.raf.mod.uk/organisation/33squadron.cfm
No 39 Sqn	www.raf.mod.uk/organisation/39squadron.cfm
No 41(R) Sqn	www.raf.mod.uk/organisation/41squadron.cfm
No 42(R) Sqn	www.raf.mod.uk/squadrons/h42.html
No 45(R) Sqn	www.raf.mod.uk/rafcranwell/aboutus/45sqn.cfm
No 51 Sqn	www.raf.mod.uk/organisation/51squadron.cfm
No 55(R) Sqn	www.raf.mod.uk/rafcranwell/aboutus/55sqn.cfm
No 60(R) Sqn	www.raf.mod.uk/organisation/60squadron.cfm
No 72(R) Sqn	www.raf.mod.uk/organisation/72squadron.cfm
No 76(R) Sqn	www.raf.mod.uk/raflintononouse/aboutus/76rsqn.cfm
No 78 Sqn	www.raf.mod.uk/organisation/78squadron.cfm
No 84 Sqn	www.raf.mod.uk/organisation/84squadron.cfm
No 99 Sqn	www.raf.mod.uk/organisation/99squadron.cfm
No 100 Sqn	www.raf.mod.uk/organisation/100squadron.cfm
No 101 Sqn	www.raf.mod.uk/organisation/101squadron.cfm
No 111 Sqn	www.raf.mod.uk/organisation/111squadron.cfm
No 120 Sqn	www.raf.mod.uk/organisation/120squadron.cfm
No 201 Sqn	www.raf.mod.uk/organisation/201squadron.cfm
No 202 Sqn	www.raf.mod.uk/organisation/202squadron.cfm
No 207(R) Sqn	www.raf.mod.uk/organisation/207squadron.cfm
No 208(R) Sqn	www.rafvalley.org/208sqn/index.html
No 216 Sqn	www.raf.mod.uk/organisation/216squadron.cfm
No 230 Sqn	www.raf.mod.uk/organisation/230squadron.cfm
No 617 Sqn	www.raf.mod.uk/organisation/617squadron.cfm
No 702 NAS	www.royalnavy.mod.uk/operations-and-support/fleet-air-arm/naval-air-squadrons/702
No 727 NAS	www.royalnavy.mod.uk/operations-and-support/fleet-air-arm/naval-air-squadrons/727
No 750 NAS	www.royalnavy.mod.uk/operations-and-support/fleet-air-arm/naval-air-squadrons/750
No 771 NAS	www.royalnavy.mod.uk/operations-and-support/fleet-air-arm/naval-air-squadrons/771
No 814 NAS	www.royalnavy.mod.uk/operations-and-support/fleet-air-arm/naval-air-squadrons/814
No 815 NAS	www.royalnavy.mod.uk/operations-and-support/fleet-air-arm/naval-air-squadrons/815
No 820 NAS	www.royalnavy.mod.uk/operations-and-support/fleet-air-arm/naval-air-squadrons/820
No 824 NAS	www.royalnavy.mod.uk/operations-and-support/fleet-air-arm/naval-air-squadrons/824
No 829 NAS	www.royalnavy.mod.uk/operations-and-support/fleet-air-arm/naval-air-squadrons/829
No 845 NAS	www.royalnavy.mod.uk/operations-and-support/fleet-air-arm/naval-air-squadrons/845
No 846 NAS	www.royalnavy.mod.uk/operations-and-support/fleet-air-arm/naval-air-squadrons/846
No 847 NAS	www.royalnavy.mod.uk/operations-and-support/fleet-air-arm/naval-air-squadrons/847
No 848 NAS	www.royalnavy.mod.uk/operations-and-support/fleet-air-arm/naval-air-squadrons/848
No 849 NAS	www.royalnavy.mod.uk/operations-and-support/fleet-air-arm/naval-air-squadrons/849
No 854 NAS	www.royalnavy.mod.uk/operations-and-support/fleet-air-arm/naval-air-squadrons/854
No 857 NAS	www.royalnavy.mod.uk/operations-and-support/fleet-air-arm/naval-air-squadrons/857
Aberdeen, Dundee and St Andrews UAS	dialspace.dial.pipex.com/town/way/gba87/adstauas/
The Army Air Corps	www.army.mod.uk/aviation/air.aspx
Cambridge University Air Squadron	www.raf.mod.uk/cambridgeuas/
East Midlands UAS	www.raf.mod.uk/eastmidlandsuas/

Internet sites

Name of site	*Internet dial (all prefixed 'http://')*
Fleet Air Arm	www.royal-navy.mod.uk/operations-and-support/fleet-air-arm
Liverpool University Air Squadron	www.raf.mod.uk/liverpooluas/
Manchester & Salford Universities Air Sqn	www.raf.mod.uk/manchesterandsalforduas/
Ministry of Defence	www.mod.uk/
Oxford University Air Sqn	www.raf.mod.uk/oxforduas/
QinetiQ	www.qinetiq.com/
RAF Benson	www.raf.mod.uk/rafbenson/
RAF Brize Norton	www.raf.mod.uk/rafbrizenorton/
RAF Church Fenton (unofficial)	www.rafchurchfenton.org.uk/
RAF College Cranwell	www.raf.mod.uk/rafcranwell/
RAF Coningsby	www.raf.mod.uk/rafconingsby/
RAF Cosford	www.raf.mod.uk/dcaecosford/
RAF Cottesmore	www.raf.mod.uk/rafcottesmore/
RAF Leuchars	www.raf.mod.uk/rafleuchars/
RAF Linton-on-Ouse	www.raf.mod.uk/raflintononouse/
RAF Lossiemouth	www.raf.mod.uk/raflossiemouth/
RAF Lyneham	www.raf.mod.uk/raflyneham/
RAF Marham	www.raf.mod.uk/rafmarham/
RAF Northolt	www.raf.mod.uk/rafnortholt/
RAF Odiham	www.raf.mod.uk/rafodiham/
RAF Shawbury	www.raf.mod.uk/rafshawbury/
RAF Valley	www.raf.mod.uk/rafvalley/
RAF Waddington	www.raf.mod.uk/rafwaddington/
RAF Wittering	www.raf.mod.uk/rafwittering/
Red Arrows	www.raf.mod.uk/reds/
Royal Air Force	www.raf.mod.uk/
Royal Air Force Reserves	www.raf.mod.uk/rafreserves/
University of London Air Sqn	www.ulas.org.uk/
Yorkshire UAS	www.raf.mod.uk/yorkshireuas/
MILITARY SITES-US	
Air Combat Command	www.acc.af.mil/
Air Force Reserve Command	www.afrc.af.mil/
Air National Guard	www.ang.af.mil/
Aviano Air Base	www.aviano.af.mil/
Liberty Wing Home Page (48th FW)	www.lakenheath.af.mil/
NASA	www.nasa.gov/
Mildenhall	www.mildenhall.af.mil/
Ramstein Air Base	www.ramstein.af.mil/
Spangdahlem Air Base	www.spangdahlem.af.mil/
USAF	www.af.mil/
USAF Europe	www.usafe.af.mil/
USAF World Wide Web Sites	www.af.mil/publicwebsites/index.asp
US Army	www.army.mil/
US Marine Corps	www.marines.mil/
US Navy	www.navy.mil/
US Navy Patrol Squadrons (unofficial)	www.vpnavy.com/
MILITARY SITES-ELSEWHERE	
Armée de l'Air	www.defense.gouv.fr/air/
Aeronautica Militare	www.aeronautica.difesa.it
Austrian Armed Forces (in German)	www.bmlv.gv.at/
Belgian Air Component	www.mil.be/aircomp/index.asp?LAN=E
Canadian Forces	www.forces.ca/
Finnish Defence Force	www.mil.fi/english/
Forca Aerea Portuguesa	www.emfa.pt/
Frecce Tricolori	users.iol.it/gromeo/
German Marine	www.deutschemarine.de/
Greek Air Force	www.haf.gr/en/
Irish Air Corps	www.military.ie/aircorps/
Israeli Defence Force/Air Force	dover.idf.il/IDF/English/
Luftforsvaret	www.mil.no/
Luftwaffe	www.luftwaffe.de/
NATO	www.nato.int/
Royal Australian Air Force	www.airforce.gov.au/
Royal Danish Air Force (in Danish)	forsvaret.dk/
Royal Netherlands AF	www.luchtmacht.nl/
Royal New Zealand AF	www.airforce.mil.nz/
Singapore Air Force	www.mindef.gov.sg/rsaf/

Name of site	Internet dial (all prefixed 'http://')
South African AF Site (unofficial)	www.saairforce.co.za/
Swedish Air Force	www.forsvarsmakten.se/sv/Forband-och-formagor/Flygvapnet/
Swedish Military Aviation (unofficial)	www.canit.se/%7Egriffon/aviation/
Turkish Air Force	www.hvkk.tsk.tr/homeEng.aspx
AIRCRAFT & AERO ENGINE MANUFACTURERS	
AgustaWestland	www.agustawestland.com/
BAE Systems	www.baesystems.com/
Bell Helicopter Textron	www.bellhelicopter.textron.com/
Boeing	www.boeing.com/
Bombardier	www.bombardier.com/
Britten-Norman	www.britten-norman.com/
CFM International	www.cfm56.com/
Dassault	www.dassault-aviation.com/
EADS	www.eads.com/
Embraer	www.embraer.com/
General Electric	www.ge.com/
Gulfstream Aerospace	www.gulfstream.com/
Hawker Beechcraft	www.hawkerbeechcraft.com/
Kaman Aerospace	www.kaman.com/
Lockheed Martin	www.lockheedmartin.com/
Rolls-Royce	www.rolls-royce.com/
SAAB	www.saab.se/
Sikorsky	www.sikorsky.com/
UK AVIATION MUSEUMS	
Aeroventure	www.aeroventure.org.uk/
Bournemouth Aviation Museum	www.aviation-museum.co.uk/
Brooklands Museum	www.brooklandsmuseum.com/
City of Norwich Aviation Museum	www.cnam.co.uk/
de Havilland Aircraft Heritage Centre	www.dehavillandmuseum.2ya.com/
Dumfries & Galloway Aviation Museum	www.dumfriesaviationmuseum.com/
Fleet Air Arm Museum	www.fleetairarm.com/
Gatwick Aviation Museum	www.gatwick-aviation-museum.co.uk/
Imperial War Museum, Duxford	www.iwm.org.uk/duxford/
Imperial War Museum, Duxford (unofficial)	dspace.dial.pipex.com/town/square/rcy85/
The Jet Age Museum	www.jetagemuseum.org/
Lincs Aviation Heritage Centre	www.lincsaviation.co.uk/
Midland Air Museum	www.midlandairmuseum.co.uk/
Museum of Army Flying	www.flying-museum.org.uk/
Museum of Berkshire Aviation	www.museumofberkshireaviation.co.uk/
Museum of Flight, East Fortune	www.nms.ac.uk/flight/index.asp
Museum of Science & Industry, Manchester	www.msim.org.uk/
Newark Air Museum	www.newarkairmuseum.org/
North East Aircraft Museum	www.neam.co.uk/
RAF Museum, Hendon	www.rafmuseum.org.uk/
Science Museum, South Kensington	www.sciencemuseum.org.uk/
Yorkshire Air Museum, Elvington	www.yorkshireairmuseum.co.uk
AVIATION SOCIETIES	
Air Britain	www.air-britain.com/
British Aircraft Preservation Council	www.bapc.org.uk/
Cleveland Aviation Society	homepage.ntlworld.com/phillip.charlton/cashome.html
East London Aviation Society	www.westrowops.co.uk/newsletter/elas.htm
LAAS International	www.laasdata.com/
Lowestoft Aviation Society	www.lowestoftaviationsociety.org/
Royal Aeronautical Society	www.raes.org.uk/
Scottish Air News	www.scottishairnews.co.uk/
Scramble (Dutch Aviation Society)	www.scramble.nl/
Solent Aviation Society	www.solent-aviation-society.co.uk/
Spitfire Society	www.spitfiresociety.com/
The Aviation Society Manchester	www.tasmanchester.com/
Ulster Aviation Society	www.ulsteraviationsociety.org/
Wolverhampton Aviation Group	www.wolverhamptonaviationgroup.co.uk/
OPERATORS OF HISTORIC AIRCRAFT	
The Aircraft Restoration Company	www.arc-duxford.co.uk/
Battle of Britain Memorial Flight	www.raf.mod.uk/bbmf/

Internet sites

Name of site	*Internet dial (all prefixed 'http://')*
The Catalina Society	www.catalina.org.uk/
De Havilland Aviation	www.dehavillandaviation.com/
Delta Jets	www.deltajets.com/
Hangar 11 Collection	www.hangar11.co.uk/
Hunter Flying	www.hunterflyingltd.co.uk/
Old Flying Machine Company	www.ofmc.co.uk/
Royal Navy Historic Flight	www.royalnavyhistoricflight.org.uk/
The Fighter Collection	www.fighter-collection.com/
The Real Aeroplane Company	www.realaero.com/
The Shuttleworth Collection	www.shuttleworth.org/
The Vulcan to the Sky Trust	www.tvoc.co.uk/
SITES RELATING TO SPECIFIC TYPES OF MILITARY AIRCRAFT	
The 655 Maintenance & Preservation Society	www.xm655.com/
B-24 Liberator	www.b24bestweb.com/
EE Canberra	www.bywat.co.uk/
English Electric Lightning - Vertical Reality	www.aviation-picture-hangar.co.uk/Lightning.html
The Eurofighter site	www.eurofighter.com/
The ex FRADU Canberra Site	www.fradu-canberras.co.uk/
The ex FRADU Hunter Site	www.fradu-hunters.co.uk/
F-4 Phantom II Society	www.f4phantom.com/
F-16: The Complete Reference	www.f-16.net/
F-86 Web Page	f-86.tripod.com/
The Gripen	www.gripen.com/
HerkyBirds.com	www.herkybirds.com/
Jet Provost Heaven	www.jetprovosts.com
K5083 - Home Page (Hawker Hurricane)	www.k5083.mistral.co.uk/
Lockheed SR-71 Blackbird	www.wvi.com/~lelandh/sr-71~1.htm
The MiG-21 Page	www.topedge.com/panels/aircraft/sites/kraft/mig.htm
P-3 Orion Research Group	www.p3orion.nl/
Thunder & Lightnings (Postwar British Aircraft)	www.thunder-and-lightnings.co.uk/
UK Apache Resource Centre	www.ukapache.com/
MISCELLANEOUS	
Aerodata	www.aerodata.org/
AeroResource	www.aerorescource.co.uk
The AirNet Web Site	www.aviation-links.co.uk/
British Military Aviation Lists	www.bmal.org.uk
Delta Reflex	www.deltareflex.com/forum
Demobbed - Out of Service British Military Aircraft	demobbed.org.uk/
Euro Demobbed	www.eurodemobbed.org.uk/
Fighter Control	fightercontrol.co.uk/
Joseph F. Baugher's US Military Serials Site	www.joebaugher.com/
Military Aviation	www.crakehal.demon.co.uk/aviation/aviation.htm
Military Aviation Review/MAP	www.mar.co.uk/
Pacific Aviation Database Organisation	www.gfiapac.com/
Plane Talk	forum.planetalk.net/
Polish Aviation Site	aviation.pol.pl/
Scramble on the Web - Air Show Reports	www.scramble.nl/airshows.htm
Target Lock Military Aviation E-zine	www.targetlock.org.uk/
UKAR Message Board	www.ukar.co.uk/
UK Military Aircraft Serials Resource Centre	www.ukserials.com/
UK Military Spotting	www.thunder-and-lightnings.co.uk/spotting/